THE BLUE GUIDES

Albania
Austria
Belgium and Luxembourg
China
Cy
Cz   Republics
De
Eg

FRANCE
France
Paris and Versailles
Burgundy
Loire Valley
Midi-Pyrénées
Normandy
South West France
Corsica

GERMANY
Berlin and Eastern Germany
Western Germany

GREECE
Greece
Athens and environs
Crete

HOLLAND
Holland
Amsterdam

HUNGARY
Hungary
Budapest

Ireland

ITALY
Northern Italy
Southern Italy
Florence
Rome and environs
Venice
Tuscany
Umbria
Sicily

Jerusalem
Jordan
Malta and Gozo
Mexico
Morocco
Moscow and St Petersburg
Portugal

Spain
Barcelona
Madrid

Sweden
Switzerland
Tunisia

TURKEY
Turkey
Istanbul

UK
England
Scotland
Wales
London
Museums and Galleries
   of London
Oxford and Cambridge
Country Houses of England
Gardens of England
Literary Britain and Ireland
Victorian Architecture in Britain
Churches and Chapels of
   Northern England
Churches and Chapels of
   Southern England
Channel Islands

USA
New York
Museums and Galleries of
   New York
Boston and Cambridge

The Benedictine Sanctuary of Santa Maria dell'Isola,
Tropea

BLUE GUIDE

Southern Italy
South of Rome to Calabria

Paul Blanchard

Atlas, maps and plans by John Flower

A & C Black
London

WW Norton
New York

Eighth edition 1996

Published by A & C Black (Publishers) Limited
35 Bedford Row, London WC1R 4JH

A CIP catalogue record of this book is available from the British Library.

ISBN 0–7136–4131–2

Published in the United States of America by
WW Norton and Company, Inc
500 Fifth Avenue, New York, NY 10110

Published simultaneously in Canada by
Penguin Books Canada Limited
10 Alcorn Avenue, Toronto
Ontario M4V 3B2

ISBN 0–393–31424–3 USA

The author and the publishers have done their best to ensure the accuracy of all the information in Blue Guide Southern Italy; however, they can accept no responsibility for any loss, injury or inconvenience sustained by any traveller as a result of information or advice contained in the guide.

Paul Blanchard was born in Amsterdam, New York. He studied art history in Florence and has lived in Italy since 1975. An active visual artist as well as an art scholar, he has taught Contemporary Art and Drawing at the Italian study centres of Sycacuse University and Florida State University, has shown his own artwork (which includes a large body of landscape photographs and other nature-related works) in Europe and the US, and has lectured on college campuses throughout the US. He has published widely in North America, Great Britain, France and Italy (including *Artyear* and several regional guides), and has contributed to European and American art magazines. In recent years he has expanded his educational activity to include the organisation of cultural tours for the San Francisco Museum of Modern Art, the Saint Louis Art Museum, the Art Institute of Chicago, and Country Walkers.

Maps and plans © A & C Black, by John Flower, with corrections by Map Creation Ltd.
Illustrations © Beatrix Blake 1996.

Printed and bound in Great Britain by The Bath Press, Somerset

PREFACE

Great things are happening in Naples. After a gradual but continuous demise that dates, perhaps, as far back as the Unification of Italy, the city is once again on the rise. A vast urban renovation programme has given new life (and a beautiful new aspect) to the city centre, buildings have been restored and repainted, and a considerable area of the waterfront, as well as several of the elegant shopping streets further inland, have become pedestrian islands. In the derelict industrial district flanking the railyards, work has begun on the construction of a whole new city, the Centro Direzionale, to designs by Japanese architect Kenzo Tanje. A new museum has been opened by the City in the Castel Nuovo, volunteer organisations and private sponsors have restored and reopened major monuments, guided tours have been organised through the mysterious spaces of 'underground Naples', and plans have been developed to convert the area of the abandoned steel works at Bagnoli into a park and scientific research centre.

And there is more. A project is underway to grant the world-famous Museo di Capodimonte administrative autonomy: already, the galleries have been thoroughly remodelled and, as this book goes to press, the collection is being rearranged to be more comprehensible to the visitor. A special section devoted to contemporary art will been added on the top floor, and the Farnese Collection, which Naples inherited 'by marriage' from Parma and which contains many masterpieces by Italian and foreign artists, will be installed in specially designed new quarters after its current tour of European museums.

Before the end of 1995, the works commissioned from prominent Neapolitan painters by the wealthy Carthusian community of San Martino will return to the rooms of the monastery, where they will be visible together for the first time; and the immense collection of figured vases formerly in storage at the Museo Archeologico Nazionale will go back on public display, in an arrangement respecting state-of-the-art museological standards. With all this excitement in the air, it is no surprise that Naples has become an attractive centre for cutting-edge art as well, hosting Italy's second most intense concentration (after Milan) of world-class commercial galleries.

Elsewhere in the region, a new wave of archaeological research has led to a flurry of discoveries, especially in Abruzzo, Basilicata, and Calabria. Although the sites have not been opened to the public, some of the finds are on display in the museums of Chieti, Policoro, and Metapontum. The single monuments and artworks that have been restored to their original splendour since the previous edition of the guide was published are too numerous to mention; one example is the Sassi di Matera, the medieval city of cave churches and rock dwellings now under the protection of Unesco.

Last but not least, the recent upswing in ecological consciousness has led to the establishment of several new national parks and nature reserves in Southern Italy, notably the Parco Nazionale del Pollino (1990), on the Pollino Massif which divides Basilicata from Calabria; the Parco Nazionale dell, Aspromonte (1991), in the wild, mountainous 'toe' of Italy, near Reggio Calabria; the Parco Nazionale del Cilento e Vallo di Diano and the Parco Nazionale del Vesuvio in Campania (1991), and the Parco Nazionale del Gargano, in Apulia (1991), which together with the fabulous Parco Nazionale d'Abruzzo (1923) and Parco Nazionale del Circeo (1934), make the South particularly attractive to the naturalist. Here may be seen several native species of flora and fauna rarely found outside their area of provenance—for instance, the Abruzzo brown bear, in the Parco Nazionale dell'Abruzzo, and the white pine, in the Parco Nazionale del Pollino.

This eighth edition of *Blue Guide Southern Italy* follows a new approach to the area's natural and cultural heritage. The itineraries have been reorganised into 20 routes (as opposed to 35 in the preceding edition), which have in turn been arranged in two groups of ten, representing the area's two principal bioregions, the Tyrrhenian and the Adriatic. These natural 'regions', with their watershed in the Apennines, have conditioned and continue to condition the climate, flora, and fauna of the Southern Italian mainland, its economical profile and the character of its inhabitants, in a manner far more profound than the administrative divisions of past or present.

A further innovation in the text is represented by the historical, rather than topographical, approach taken to Naples and its environs—a measure that enhances understanding of the area's complex stratification of art and architecture.

Route texts have been entirely rewritten. As always in the *Blue Guides*, the easiest way of reaching the famous towns and sites is suggested and side routes take travellers to the more remote areas. Many of the routes are based on the excellent road system, for the better guidance of the independent motorist; but the requirements of the traveller by rail have not been forgotten. Due attention has been paid to the approaches to Italy by road, rail, sea, and air; and particular care has been taken to provide practical information in the introductory section and at the beginning of the description of main towns. Also, for the first time the guide carries information on hotels and restaurants. These have been listed at the beginning of each route, to facilitate advance planning. Excursions and diversions are described within horizontal lines within the main body of the text. Historical background information and 'asides' are presented as indented text.

Acknowledgements

The author is indebted to all those people who contributed in various ways to the making of the book—especially to cartographer John Flower, who has designed a full complement of attractive maps and plans, and to editors Gemma Davies and Judy Tither, who have been most helpful in producing the guide. Acknowledgement is also due to Marco Panfilo and Enzo Longo of the Ente Nazionale Italiano di Turismo (Italian State Tourist Office) for their generous assistance, and to the regional, provincial, and local tourist boards whose co-operation was indispensable to the accurate preparation of the guide. Special thanks are owed to the many friends and readers who assisted in the gathering of information; to Alta Macadam, whose friendship and advice has been invaluable; and to Isabella Toraldo di Francia, who provided encouragement and support throughout the preparation of the guide. As with other volumes in the *Blue Guide* series, suggestions for the correction or improvement of the guide are gratefully welcomed.

CONTENTS

Preface 5
Acknowledgements 6

Historical Introduction, by Alexandra Douglas 9
Art in Southern Italy, by Paul Williamson 23
Glossary of art terms 36
The Geological Development of Southern Italy, by Werner Heinitz 41

Practical Information

Planning your trip 45
Getting to Southern Italy 47
On arrival 49
Where to stay 50

Food and drink 51
Travelling around 59
General information 63

Routes

I   **The Tyrrhenian Bioregion** 69
1   Rome to Naples 70
   A.   Via Frosinone, Cassino and Caserta 70
   B.   Via the Monti Lepini 79
   C.   Via the coast, with diversions 84
2   Ponza and its Archipelago 93
3–6 Naples and environs 94
   3   Antiquity 98
      A.   Ancient Naples 101
      B.   Pompeii 107
      C.   Mount Vesuvius 130
      D.   Herculaneum 136
      E.   The Phlegraean Fields 144
   4   The Early Christian Period and The Middle Ages 154
      A.   Early Christian Naples 158
      B.   Anjou and Aragon 160
      C.   The Sorrentine Peninsula and Salerno 169
   5   The Viceregal and Bourbon City 183
      A.   From Piazza del Municipio to Via Partenope 191
      B.   From Piazza Trieste and Trento to the Cathedral 195
      C.   The Palazzo Reale di Capodimonte 200
      D.   Castel Sant'Elmo, San Martino, and Villa Floridiana 206
      E.   Mergellina and Posillipo 210
      F.   The Royal Palace of Caserta 213
   6   Naples from the Late Nineteenth Century to Today 218
      A.   The Rettifilo and the Harbour 220
      B.   Capri 223
      C.   Procida and Ischia 229
7   Naples to Reggio Calabria 233
      A.   Via the Coast 233
      B.   Via Castrovillari and Cosenza 249

8   La Sila 258
      A. Cosenza to Crotone 258
      B. Rossano to Longobucco and Camigliatello 260
      C. Catanzaro to Camigliatello 261
9   Reggio Calabria and the Aspromonte 264
10   Taranto to Reggio Calabria 269

II   The Adriatic Bioregion 281
11   Ancona to Bari 283
12   Campobasso to L'Aquila and Ascoli Piceno 308
13   L'Aquila and the Gran Sasso d'Italia 318
14   Pescara to Rome 326
15   Termoli to Benevento 335
16   The Gargano Peninsula and the Tremiti Islands 338
17   Naples to Bari 343
      A. Via Benevento and Foggia 343
      B. Via Avellino 350
      C. Via Potenza 355
18   Naples to Brindisi 361
19   Bari to Lecce 371
      A. Via Brindisi 371
      B. Via Taranto 379
20   Lecce and the Salentine Peninsula 383

Maps and Plans

Atlas at back of book
Alba Fucens 333
Baia, Palatium Imperiale 150
Bari, Città Vecchia 305
  General 301
  San Nicola 303
Brindisi 376
Capri Atlas 13
Cassino, Abbey of Monte Cassino 75
Herculaneum 141
Fossanova, Abbey 81
Ischia Atlas 16
L'Aquila Atlas 14
Lecce, General 395
  Piazza del Duomo 399
  Santa Croce 397
Locri 278
Metapontum 271
Naples, Centre Atlas 2–3
  Certosa di San Martino 208

Naples cont.
  Convento di Santa Chiara 163
  Duomo 167
  General Atlas 4
  Gulf of Atlas 6–7
  Museo Archeologico Nazionale 104
  Palazzo Capodimonte 202
  San Domenico Maggiore 164
Paestum 235
Pompeii, Casa di Pansa 127
  General 112–113
  Villa dei Misteri 129
Pozzuoli 147
Reggio Calabria 266
Salerno 180
Sorrento 172
Taranto, General 386
  Museo Nazionale 389
Terracina 87

HISTORICAL INTRODUCTION

by Alexandra Douglas

Italy is the geographical centre of the Mediterranean Sea, or *Mare nostrum* (our sea), as the Romans called it. The Mediterranean waters have provided a means of intercourse between Italy and surrounding continents since prehistory. This natural vicinity to neighbouring lands has exposed the country to foreign exploration, emigration, and invasion. Time and time again her soil has been ravaged by hostile armies seeking to claim right to her boundaries, trade routes, and resources.

Yet the inhabitants of the land today called Italy have shown an extraordinary ability to defend their shores and to extend their influence outward. In antiquity, Rome systematically subjugated surrounding lands, proving herself to be the most indomitable of Mediterranean empires. In the late Middle Ages and Renaissance, the great power of the Italian city-states was exercised. Through the ages, Italians have varyingly reigned supreme militarily, economically, politically, and culturally over much of the Mediterranean. In the turbulence of Italy's history, her power has waxed and waned, but she has sustained the ability to emerge from adversity and destruction with remarkable resilience and strength.

PREHISTORY
Man first appeared in Italy about 200,000 years ago. Stone Age tools, particularly flint axes, have been found throughout the country. Neanderthal skulls of the Middle Palaeolithic (c 50,000 BC) have been discovered just outside Rome and Cro-Magnon skulls of the Upper Palaeolithic (c 10,000 BC) have also been excavated. Nevertheless, evidence of prehistoric man is sparse until the **Neolithic period** (c 5000 BC), when farmers emigrating from eastern lands gradually replaced the nomadic hunters and gatherers of earlier periods, bringing seeds for planting, domesticated animals, and hut-building skills to the region.

Worked metals began to appear in the Late Neolithic period (c 3500 BC), though metallurgy seems to have developed more strongly in the northern and central regions of Italy. During the **Bronze Age** (after 1700 BC) Mycenaeans, originating from the Greek mainland, and Minoans, originating from the island of Crete, are known to have landed in Southern Italy: Mycenaean influences have been found at Tarentum and there is evidence that the Mycenaeans traded throughout the heel of the peninsula, perhaps as far north as Etruria. Exploration by these Aegean cultures was a direct precursor to the Greek colonization of Italy.

During the **Iron Age** (after 800 BC) a civilisation of Danubian origin, called Villanovans after a large cemetery discovered at Villanova, near Bologna, came to the area. The Villanovans cremated their dead, unlike the native Italic peoples, who had long practised the rite of inhumation (burying the dead). Towards the end of the Iron Age the Villanovan culture was absorbed by indigenous cultures and their language subsumed into the Italic languages.

GREEKS AND ROMANS
The first **Greek colonies** in Italy were established as a result of the arrival of hostile, non-Greek peoples in the Aegean (and the consequent westward migration of indigenous Greeks) and of overpopulation and economic crises within the Greek

world. The Greek name for colony, *apoikia*, loosely translates as 'a home away from home'. The Greek colonists were well received by some indigenous tribes, but others met their arrival with distrust and resistance. Around 750 BC the Greeks first colonised the island of *Cumae*, near Naples, and c 760 BC the nearby island of Ischia, naming that colony *Pithecusae*. *Parthenope* (Naples) and *Poseidonia* (Paestum) were founded soon after. Further south, the cities of *Locri Epizephyrii, Metapontum, Sybaris, Croton, Taras* (Taranto), *Hydruntum* (Otranto) and *Rhegion* (Reggio Calabria) were established. Although Greek colonisation of the Mediterranean eventually extended as far afield as France and Spain, these colonies, together with Messina and Syracuse on Sicily, customarily marked the outer edge of the region known in antiquity as *Magna Graecia* or Greater Greece.

This string of Hellenic settlements led an active trading life, carrying bronzeware and various types of Attic (from *Attica*, the area of eastern Greece surrounding the city of Athens) vases and pottery. The Italic peoples of central and northern Italy developed a strong taste for Greek trade goods early on. The **Etruscans**, a powerful group of tribes in the northern and central regions of the peninsula, were particularly fond of Greek pottery, establishing workshops to copy vase styles and filling their large, painted tombs with vases to be used in the funeral banquets of the dead in the afterlife. The colonists also brought with them the cultivation of the olive, a plant that had previously existed only in the wild in Italy. The Greek alphabet, which had been adapted from the Phoenician alphabet, also made its way through the peninsula, facilitating the development on Italian soil of characters for a written script.

The Greeks traded with the less civilised Italic tribes, who prospered from their close contact with the colonists. The Italic peoples were excellent apprentices to their Greek masters in the study of architecture and sculpture, as well as the rudiments of warcraft. The Greeks, however, never possessed the organisational ability that the Romans would perfect and were therefore unable completely to transplant the marrow of their superb civilisation into the skeleton of Italy. Around 400 BC, a hinterland people known as the **Sabellians** (the term embraces the Sabines and the Samnites, as well as lesser tribes) began to migrate south, bringing with them a severe opposition to Greek rule. Later, the Etruscans also would prevent the Greeks from establishing new centres north of Cumae.

When Rome finally revolted against Etruria in 509 BC, ousting the last Etruscan king, Tarquinis, the Romans allied with the Greeks against the Sabellians, Etruscans, Phoenicians, and all other hostile forces that threatened the peace of the colonists. Gradually the Romans would expand their empire to encompass all of Italy, including the Greek colonies, and then Greece itself. Their long-standing admiration for Greek culture, which would eventually lead to the trend toward Hellenisation in Republican Rome, in all likelihood dates from this time.

The **Romans** learned early to set up complicated individual alliances with surrounding states, in such a way that Rome should become the diplomatic centre of her underlings. Allies were untaxed, protected, able to visit Rome when they wished and allowed to retain their local government; in return they were expected to provide troops for the Roman armies and to take an oath to preserve the majesty of the republic.

By proffering protection while encouraging home rule, Rome was able to instil a strong sense of duty and loyalty in her allies. She organised the state around war: militarism was her constitution, and fighting someone, somewhere, every year, was part of the Roman mental fabric. In 390 BC the capital was sacked by Gallic tribes from the north, inculcating a deep and abiding fear of the 'enemy' and teaching the Romans to react with a ferocity unrivalled in the ancient Mediterranean. There were no conditions of surrender: a hostile city was destroyed as an object lesson, after first being ravaged for its booty. Pacifism was unknown in the ancient world, where survival of the fittest was the rule.

In this scenario the Etruscans were the first to lose: they were unable to remain united under strong pressure from Roman armies, and as the Roman threat mounted, their large underprivileged class revolted against the aristocracy, further weakening the infrastructure of their society. Interestingly, the fall of the Roman Empire would follow a similar, though more complex pattern.

When Rome finally turned her sword on the Hellenic domain of Magna Graecia, the Greeks summoned Pyrrhus, King of Epirus, to their aid. Pyrrhus twice defeated the Romans (but at a terrible human cost: even today, the term 'pyrrhic victory' denotes a victory in which no one can take true glory), only to be defeated at Beneventum in 275 BC. By 264 the Roman dominion stretched to Rhegion (Reggio Calabria).

Rome defeats Carthage

Once the powers of Southern Italy had been subdued, Rome was in a position to challenge her Phoenician enemy across the sea, Carthage. The Romans latinised the Greek name Phoenician (derived from a word meaning purple because of a purple dye this Eastern Mediterranean people made from shellfish) to Punic; and the Latin phrase *punica fides*, which translates as 'gross dishonesty', expresses the rancour the Romans felt for their formidable enemy. The **Carthaginians** were a powerful mercantile nation which had long sought to control Sicily—an ambition that was thwarted after their defeat by the Romans in the First Punic War, 300–251 BC. The Second Punic War, also called the Hannabolic War (218–201 BC), was a relentless conflict of attrition that Rome nearly lost. After Hannibal's great victory at Cannae, the Roman allies of Capua and Taras deserted, bringing a terrible retribution upon themselves (the citizens of Capua were butchered and those of Taras sold into slavery) when the Romans finally claimed victory. Hannibal at last saw the destiny of Carthage when his brother Hasdrubal's head was delivered to him at his camp in Apulia by his enemy and he wearily sailed home, to be defeated later at Zama, in present-day Tunisia, by the great Roman general Scipio, who consequently received the cognomen *Africanus*.

Finally, in 149 BC, the Third (and final) **Punic War** ended with the destruction of Carthage and the surrender of its citizens. In an act of extreme savagery, even by Roman standards, the city was burned, levelled, and the ground ploughed and salted to prevent any future habitation.

The fate of southern Italy had been in the hands of the Romans since the expulsion of the Etruscans and the subjugation of the Greeks. During the Roman Republic, unrest grew in the south, beginning with the **Social War** in Samnite territory (today western Campania, Abruzzo and Molise). It is important to remember that the Social War was fought by peoples seeking Roman citizenship, not independence; the central and southern portions of the peninsula strengthened their ties with the capital as a consequence and Roman Italy became more a nation than a loose federation of conquered states.

Summer villas and retreats for the Romans

In the first century BC, Southern Italy became the **playground of the Roman élite**, the south-west coast of the peninsula boasting the largest number of summer villas and retreats in the republic. The islands of Capri and Cumae, and the coastal towns of Surrentum, Baiae, Puteoli and Neapolis were particular favourites. The ill-fated Pompeii and Herculaneum were al so popular getaway spots. This region was appropriately called *Campania felix* (fruitful or fortunate country) for its beauty, fertility, and wealth. Well-to-do Romans seeking to escape the stifling heat of the city fled to the country for solace; and the export of luxury goods, such as wine and oil, to surrounding provinces served as a substantial source of income for the region.

Paestum produced roses whose luxurious oils were as desired as they were expensive. The hills—and volcano—near Naples provided rich soil for the cultivation of fine wines, the forests abounded with game and the sea, as well as providing a sublimely relaxing environment for vacationing patricians, yielded a wide variety of fish and seaweeds to satisfy the most demanding tastes. Food fare for the Romans consisted of the likes of tree fungi in fish-fat sauce, jellyfish and eggs, boiled ostrich and dormouse with pine kernels—delicacies which were so popular that Cicero felt obliged to admonish his fellow Romans to 'eat to live, not live to eat'.

The eruption of Mount Vesuvius

Then as now, the Gulf of Naples was overshadowed by **Mount Vesuvius**, at once marvellous and ominous. Rivalled only by Mount Etna in Sicily as the most active volcano in Europe, it first awoke with a shudder in AD 63, during the reign of the emperor Nero, causing an earthquake that nearly destroyed the Campanian towns of Herculaneum and Pompeii. In the 16 years that preceded the major eruption of AD 79, shocks and tremors provided frequent and telling warnings of what was to come. Titus was emperor when Vesuvius reaped its terrible vengeance on the Neapolitan countryside, burying the towns of Pompeii and Herculaneum (which, according to Cicero, had been founded when Hercules drove the Bulls of Geryon along their shores).

Pliny the Younger, nephew of Pliny the Elder, who was killed during the eruption, gives us our only eyewitness account of the circumstances of the eruption (see Route 3C). His account of that fearsome event in August of AD 79 is important, because he does not mention any flow of lava. It is now believed that the crater threw up ashes and rocks along with a dense, noxious vapour, which is probably what killed most of the hapless inhabitants of the surrounding areas. Herculaneum was covered with heavy mud, which slid down in torrents from the belching mountain, whereas Pompeii was bombarded by small pumice stones and ashes. Though the eruption preserved these ancient towns for the pleasure and instruction of visitors centuries later, one cannot escape the sense of tragedy that pervades their narrow, ghostly streets.

The relative instability of the area, however, did nothing to deter prominent Romans from retiring there. They simply built their villas further south, closer to Surrentum and Capri. The mountain remained still until AD 472, but several other eruptions were recorded shortly after that date. The dreadful eruption of December 1631 was as calamitous as the eruption of 79. Streams of lava, clouds of ash and a tidal wave resulting from the accompanying quakes were responsible for the deaths of over 18,000 people. Many other eruptions have followed and the last recorded disturbance occurred in 1944.

Education in the Roman Republic

Throughout antiquity Neapolis was considered a city of learning, a tradition it preserved well into the Middle Ages. The privileged men of the Roman Republic, it should be pointed out, were exceptionally well educated. As young as seven, boys were taught the rudiments of Latin grammar, pronunciation, and enunciation; between the ages of eight and eleven, they spent time with their fathers and tutors mastering Greek and Latin literature. Competence was measured by culture. Something as trivial as the unorthodox pronunciation of a word had the power to label a man uneducated and therefore unacceptable. Adolescent boys were required to attend the law courts to become familiar with public speaking; and history, philosophy, and poetry were studied to provide a wide range of quotations to be used in future debates. Rhetoric was the focus of every young aristocrat's education, for his career would most certainly be public.

With very few exceptions, **Roman women** received little education and were excluded from public life; most were relegated to the roles of wife or prostitute. Indeed, women played so small a role in Roman society that they were virtually anonymous. Whereas men often bore cognomens that made reference to their personal achievements (such as Scipio *Africanus*), or at least to highly individual characteristics (Cicero translates as chick-pea and supposedly refers to an acute case of acne that afflicted the famous rhetorician), Roman men, sadly, had little imagination when it came to naming their daughters. If a father was Claudius, his first daughter was named Claudia Prima, his second, Claudia Seconda, and so forth.

Julius Caesar

One of the leading intellectuals of the Roman Republic, but also the first man to declare himself dictator and consul, was **Julius Caesar**. His name would become a title (from which the modern terms kaiser and czar derived), and his personage would become a symbol. He was a brilliant negotiator and a consummate opportunist. In 44 BC he arranged to be named 'dictator for life', rendering his opponents powerless and inspiring the enmity of all those in lesser power. The senate, whose cumulative power had been virtually absolute prior to that point, loathed him.

Caesar lost respect for his rivals—a fatal error—and flagrantly abused his position. He arrogantly insisted upon being called *Parens patriae* (Father of the Country), named a month of the year after himself (July), dressed in triumphal robes every day and even refused to stand when another Roman patrician entered the room. His assassination, on 15 March 44 BC, was plotted and carried through by members of the senate and the scale and success of the plot (Suetonius recorded that 'he was stabbed with three and twenty wounds') indicate the zeal with which the Roman ruling class desired to rid itself of him. Cicero, who after the murder placed himself at the head of the republican party and assailed Mark Antony in his Philippic orations, upon the formation of the triumvirate by Octavian, Antony and Lepidus (27 November 43) was condemned to death and his property forfeited to the state. The orator fled to his villa at Formiae, but was overtaken by Antony's soldiers and put to death on 7 December. A semblance of republican government was restored, though chaos ruled the land. Approximately 15 years later, with the establishment of the Roman Empire by Octavian Caesar (Augustus), lessons learned from Julius Caesar's mistakes would be applied with consummate skill—the most important being to lavish honour and prestige on the senate while surreptitiously sapping its power.

The Roman Empire and its decline

The elaborate system of political checks and balances perfected during the republic was lost under the empire. Elections thinly disguised an autocracy in which the role of the senate was minimal. The imperial prerogative became an instrument of personal power in the hands of one ambitious leader after another. Augustus ruled with discretion and intelligence, but his visions were distorted by later emperors, such as Tiberius, Caligula and Nero. Among the more judicious Roman emperors were Trajan and Hadrian, whose extensive military and building campaigns stretched to Asia Minor and North Africa. Some of the more well-preserved and beautiful examples of Roman imperial architecture can still be found in these places (in Southern Italy the accomplishments of Trajan and Hadrian are celebrated on reliefs of the triumphal arch at Benevento). Even Nero, though more often remembered for burning the city of Rome in 64, was responsible for some spectacular building projects.

The boundaries of the Roman world came to encompass North Africa, Asia Minor, Macedonia and Northern Europe (then Gallia, Hispania, and Britannia). Roman law and custom endured throughout this vast region until increasing pressures from northern 'barbarian' tribes combined with civil wars to break down the fabric of all that the empire had been at its zenith. Military crises, the rise of Christianity, diminishing faith in leadership and increased poverty and strife eroded the foundations of Rome's strength. The last emperor of the West (Romulus Augustulus, who died in exile in Naples) was forced to abdicate in 476 and the seat of the Roman Empire was moved to Byzantium (Constantinople), destroying political unity in Italy.

THE MIDDLE AGES
Though Rome vanished as a political entity in the fifth century of the Christian era, much of its personality was retained throughout the Middle Ages in various institutions, traditions and thought processes. Byzantium, where the Roman imperial tradition was kept alive until the Muslim conquest of the ninth century, remained a centre for the study of Greek literature and the preservation and study of ancient art. Though Italy's stronghold on European culture weakened, Greek continued to be spoken and studied in the south, where the Hellenic tradition had been firmly rooted. Latin was retained as the language of the clergy and the learned and Latin literature remained a subject of intense study, particularly in monastic communities. Modern scholars of the classics owe a considerable debt to the Church for salvaging many aspects of Roman culture.

In Southern Italy, as everywhere in Europe, the fall of the Roman Empire brought a prolonged succession of social, political, and cultural crises. After 476 the barbarian chieftain Odoacer, ostensibly acting in the name of the Eastern emperor, assumed power in Italy. He was subsequently overthrown by the Ostrogoth Theodoric of Byzantium, who established a capital at Ravenna and ruled from 493 until 526. At that time Sicily was taken by the Byzantine general Belisarius in the name of the emperor Justinian, and though the invasion met with resistance when it extended to the southern mainland, Naples, Rome, and Ravenna eventually capitulated.

Justinian's rule and Lombard invaders
Justinian's rule brought a first, brief respite to the area. The emperor left an indelible mark on the pages of art history by welding the Byzantine influence to the classical tradition in Italian art; he restored the divine sanctions of legitimate government to Italy (the Justinian code of law is still one of the more prominent forms of Roman law studied and taught in universities and even Dante gave the emperor a place in Paradise for purging the law of the verbose and irrelevant) and

he moved the seat of government from Ravenna to Rome. Nevertheless, Gothic power was not brought to an end in Italy until 552. In this unstable political atmosphere, the temporal power of the papacy grew steadily, preparing the future political destiny of Italy and Europe.

In 568 the Italian peninsula would once again be invaded by 'barbarians' from the north: this time the Lombards, whose name (Ital. longobardo) may have been inspired by the long barbs that distinguished their spears, against which the defensive strategies of the Byzantines proved inadequate. Gregory the Great, a Roman scholar and politician deeply respected within the Church, won his appellative by dissuading the Lombard invaders from sacking Rome. Thanks to his skill as a negotiator, a semblance of peace was restored to the peninsula, though Lombard duchies were established throughout the land—in our area at Benevento, Capua, Naples and Salerno.

The Holy Roman Empire

In 754 began the Frankish invasion, led by Charlemagne's father, Peptone. The Franks' struggle for control over Italy, though eventually successful, met with stern opposition on the southern mainland and on Sicily. Nevertheless, on Christmas Day 800 the Frankish invaders, in alliance with the pope, established the **Holy Roman Empire**, the title of emperor being given to Charlemagne. Power in Europe would thereafter be shared by the emperor and the pope, who became the spiritual custodian of the imperial mandate and the temporal sovereign of Rome.

This awkward division of power offered yet another group of foreigners fertile ground for invasion. In 827, the armies of a nomadic people of the deserts between Syria and Arabia, the **Saracens**, landed in Sicily, at Mazara. These Muslim invaders conquered Palermo and rapidly moved inland, establishing an enlightened government that restored Sicily to the grandeur of centuries before, when the Greeks had colonised there.

Though the Sicilians took kindly to Saracen rule, the majority of their neighbours did not. Naples, Amalfi, Sorrento and Gaeta allied to defend the southeastern mainland against the Muslims and were victorious at Ostia (the victory is celebrated by Raphael in the Vatican Stanze) in 846. Naples, however, eventually allied with the Saracens—an act that led to its excommunication by Pope John VIII. Over the subsequent decades alliances shifted constantly in Italy. Germanic invaders edged into the north, while the Lombards and the Saracens, the Byzantines and the pope, haggled over the south.

The Normans

The return of political unity to Southern Italy was facilitated by the **Norman conquests** of 1030–1130. As early as 1015, Norman adventurers had come to the south to seek their fortunes. The volatile atmosphere of the region provided opportunities for them to sell their services to whoever was prepared to pay them in gold, horses, or land. By intervening in local conflicts, a handful of Norman knights acquired a foothold in the southern hinterland, establishing their capital at Melfi.

The rapid expansion of Norman influence alarmed the papacy, which eventually took arms against the newcomers. But Pope Leo IX was defeated and captured by the formidable Robert Guiscard at Civita, in 1053, and released only after bestowing his blessing on the conquerors. Leo's successor, Nicholas II, subsequently made an alliance with the Normans, naming Guiscard the Duke of

Calabria and Apulia and future Duke of Sicily—an astute diplomatic move that legitimised Norman rule and gave the papacy a strong claim over Southern Italy and Sicily.

The Normans were excellent and benevolent administrators of their territories, over which they won papal recognition as kings in 1139. By wise tolerance of the region's Arabic, Jewish, Greek and Roman traditions, they established an authoritarian government, half Oriental, half Western, unequalled in Europe. Nevertheless, when Norman rule ended in 1189 (following the death of William II, who left no legitimate heir), Southern Italy again fell into chaos.

By a singular coincidence, the power vacuum that developed in the south came to coincide with a more general conflict for the succession to the imperial throne— a conflict rendered all the more bitter by the ambitious new pope, Innocent III, who by supporting first one, then another of the rival claimants weakened imperial power while increasing that of the papacy. The evident incompatibility between papal and imperial interests crystallized in the political and civic conflicts between Guelphs and Ghibellines which swept the peninsula. The Guelphs opposed intervention by the Holy Roman Empire into Italian affairs and were pro-papal, whereas the Ghibellines (whose ranks were made up largely of noble feudatories of the emperor) opposed the intervention of the Church in temporal matters.

Frederick of Hohenstaufen

Ascending the throne of Sicily in 1208, the young German prince Frederick of Hohenstaufen (undoubtedly one of the more judicious and beneficent sovereigns of medieval Europe, as well as a brilliant poet and architect) restored order to the island, dislodged a Northern Italian colony at Siracusa and suppressed a Saracen revolt, afterwards removing the Muslim population to Lucera on the mainland. Later, he gained the imperial crown while ostensibly acting for the papacy, then outwitted Innocent by promising to give the Sicilian throne to his young son and to lead a crusade.

As long as Honorius III was pope (1216–27) he did neither. Instead, he consolidated his position first in Northern Europe, then in the South. His diplomatic conduct of the crusade of 1228, by which he obtained a ten-year truce for pilgrims, his open criticisms of the Church, and his bestowal of the title of King of Sardinia on his natural son, Enzo, widened the breach with Pope Gregory IX (1227–41), who had excommunicated him before his departure and intrigued with his enemies in his absence. And not surprisingly, for Frederick's vision of empire was incompatible with a papacy wielding temporal power. His interest in rational science and love of classical sculpture foreshadow the Renaissance, and his summoning of the Third Estate to council precedes Simon de Montfort's like action in England by 25 years. Dante called him the father of Italian poetry.

After Frederick's death in 1250, imperial powers in Italy began to decline. His son Conrad arrived in Apulia in 1252 to claim the throne, but was opposed by Innocent IV. Conrad's sudden death during the campaign of 1254 put the papacy in the ascendant; but **Manfred**, Conrad's illegitimate brother, successfully roused Apulia against the pope. Having gained full control of Southern Italy, in 1258 Manfred was crowned King of Sicily. He extended his domain to include most of the peninsula, piling up victories as far north as Montaperti, where he defeated the Florentines. He was even made senator of Rome for supporting republicanism over papal autocracy.

Charles of Anjou

Urban IV, elected to the papacy in 1261, at once searched for a worthy candidate to champion the papal cause and expel Manfred. He chose **Charles of Anjou**, the ambitious and ruthless young brother of St Louis of France, who defeated Manfred at Benevento in 1266 and the young Conradin (son of Conrad) at Tagliacozzo two years later. The vanquished Conradin was unceremoniously beheaded in Naples, and Charles was made King of Sicily, restoring strength to the Guelph faction.

To Charles's immense good fortune, Rudolph of Hapsburg, the new Holy Roman Emperor, focused his efforts on Northern Europe and pursued a policy of non-intervention in Italy. Unlike his predecessors, he did not go to Italy to be crowned, nor did he care to dabble in its politics. So at the start Charles of Anjou had the support of the whole Guelph party and the tacit approval of the Ghibellines. But instead of consolidating his position in Italy, he embarked on a costly policy of empire building, underestimating both the consequent resentment of his subjects and the combined strength of his enemies.

Revolt broke out spontaneously at Palermo in the Sicilian Vespers, and within a month the French had been cleared from the island, mainly by massacre. The nobles allied themselves—with Peter of Aragon, Manfred's son-in-law, turning the former kingdom into a battlefield for the French and Spanish and also for rival factions of the Angevin family. Many years would pass before Peter's descendant, Alfonso of Aragon, would obtain complete control of the region (1435), establishing Spanish control south of Rome.

THE RENAISSANCE

Commerce in the Mediterranean found its crossroads in Italy, leading to the speedy development of an urban society of merchants and bankers. **City-states** blossomed as the demand for trade goods from the East increased in Western Europe. The northern port cities of Genoa, Pisa, and Venice dominated trade routes, but cities throughout central and southern Italy grew as well. Despite this burgeoning of wealth (or perhaps because of it) the mercantile city-states developed an acute sense of patriotism that perpetuated the separatism of Italy's medieval consciousness. Neighbouring cities were rarely on civil terms, unless they were under a specific alliance to protect themselves against a greater offensive power.

The growth of these communal states nevertheless provided the ground for the intellectual movement of the Renaissance, as economic and social ferment gave rise to an educated and ambitious middle class. The reconciliation between the active and contemplative life took on a new meaning as Renaissance thinkers took part in the redevelopment of government.

Southern Italy was and still is of a cast very different from that of the north. During the Renaissance, when northern cities such as Milan, Florence, and Venice were enjoying various levels of republicanism and independence, the south was crushed by an oppressive baronage and torn by wars of succession. And while Renaissance humanism (the philosophical movement that stressed the dignity of man—hence the importance of an individualistic and critical spirit—over the primacy of orthodox political and religious belief) established a firm foothold elsewhere in Italy, in the south the socio-political patterns of the Middle Ages remained substantially unchanged. Today scholars attribute the immense difference in the efficiency of democratic institutions in northern and southern Italy to this historical divergence, which led to the development of a strong social consciousness in the northern regions, and to a perpetuation of primitive—and in some cases, immoral—mechanisms of personal or family defence in the south.

In the 16C and 17C centuries Naples and the southern mainland were separated from the Spanish kingdom of Sicily and governed by separate viceroys, of whom Don Pedro de Toledo (1532–53) was perhaps the most constructive. At the end of the War of the Spanish Succession, the Treaty of Utrecht (1713) awarded Southern Italy and Sardinia to Austria; but the defeat of the Austrians at Bitonto in 1734, and the conquest of Naples by **Charles of Bourbon** in the same year, once again gave the south a dynasty of its own.

The Bourbons

The byword for misrule that the Bourbon name later became has obscured the dynasty's earlier virtues. Charles of Bourbon (1734–59) was a skilful diplomat as well as a judicious sovereign. He abolished many privileges of the nobility and clergy, built the San Carlo theatre and Capodimonte palace, initiated excavations at Pompeii and Herculaneum and began the palace at Caserta. When he went on to become King of Spain, his successor, **Ferdinand IV** (1759–99 and 1799–1806), continued his efforts to curb ecclesiastical power in the South. During the French Revolution Ferdinand was forced to abandon the throne temporarily; but with the restoration of Bourbon rule he re-entered Naples as Ferdinand I of the Two Sicilies and immediately set about establishing a severe absolute government.

Repression worsened under his successors, Francis I and Ferdinand II, who simply imprisoned liberal sympathisers. The kingdom, reduced by indolence to squalor and by corruption, persecution, and fear to moral decay, provoked Gladstone's famous denunciation of it as 'the negation of God erected into a system of government'. It is therefore no wonder that the conquest of the south in 1860–61 by **Victor Emmanuel II** the king of Piedmont and Sardinia (ruler of Southern Italy 1861–78), met with little resistance.

THE ACHIEVEMENT OF UNITY

The seeds of Italy's movement for political unity, the Risorgimento, had been planted in the north as early as the mid 18C. The unification would begin with a group of conspirators called the Carbonari (or charcoal burners, because they gathered at night, in secret), who worked to encourage a nationalistic state of mind. They were supported by **Giuseppe Mazzini** (1850–72), a radical republican who worked to inspire nationalism in the masses to fight the Austrian hold over northern Italy.

Count Camillo Cavour, as prime minister (1852–61) under Victor Emmanuel II, strove to retain the state under the House of Savoy. The intellectual Cavour represented a foil for the locomotive force of **Giuseppe Garibaldi** (1807–82), the flamboyant general whose volunteer army of the Thousand Red Shirts brought Sicily under the Savoy banner in 1860, preparing the way for Italian unification. When Garibaldi effected his surprise landing on the southern mainland, Reggio Calabria fell almost immediately and Villa San Giovanni soon after. Resistance dissolved as the march became a race for Naples, which the general entered with a small staff 48 hours ahead of the vanguard of his troops, in August 1860. Francis II, the last of the Bourbon kings, fled to Gaeta with his still loyal army; but two months later a successful campaign on the Volturno opened the way to Garibaldi's meeting with Victor Emmanuel, which sealed the unity of Italy.

The nation had been made by joining Piedmont/Sardinia, Lombardy/Venetia, the Duchy of Modena, the Duchy of Parma, the Grand Duchy of Tuscany, the Papal

States and the Kingdom of the Two Sicilies. Each of these seven states differed greatly from the others in its traditions, customs, government, economic life and even in its language, as much of the population was able to express itself only in local dialect. The social panorama was distressing, to say the least: terrible hygienic and nutritional conditions resulted in repeated cholera and typhoid epidemics and in an extraordinarily high infant mortality rate, and illiteracy was rampant.

But the problem that most afflicted the new nation was the Southern Question— the political and economic backwardness that distinguished the southern mainland, Sicily, and Sardinia from Central and Northern Italy. There industry was absent and commerce, reduced; roads were poor and far between; and the large estates were crowded with peasants who lived in conditions of extreme poverty, subject to the systematic exploitation of a corrupt aristocracy.

PROBLEMS OF UNIFICATION
Many of the destitute had fought bravely at the side of the Thousand in the hope that unification would improved their condition. But they were bitterly disappointed when Garibaldi retracted his promise to redistribute land and brutally repressed peasant uprisings in Sicily. The disillusionment continued under the governments of united Italy, which promised much but delivered little.

The first reaction to the errors committed by the nation's new rulers was a violent outbreak of brigandage, which ravaged the south in the 1860s. Poverty, burdensome taxation, and obligatory conscription (which took strong young men off the land) were among the motives for this movement, whose ranks were fed by discontented peasants (including large numbers of women), former Bourbon soldiers, young draft dodgers, and even criminals. Initially the outlaws were financed by Francis II, who nurtured hopes of regaining his throne, and tolerated by the pope, whose territory was often used as a base for their operations. But the brigands also found complicity in the *omertà* (conspiracy of silence) of the population, which saw them as avengers of the injustices suffered.

The solution put forth by the Piedmontese was to meet violence with violence: a full-scale military campaign conducted between 1861 and 1863 left more than 20 officers and 300 men dead in the field. Thousands of brigands were killed and thousands more imprisoned. A study of 1863 states: 'Brigandage is the savage and brutal protest of poverty against century-old injustice joined to other ills left over from the inauspicious reign of the Bourbons [namely] ignorance, superstition, and the absolute lack of faith in law and justice...To destroy brigandage we have spilled rivers of blood but have thought little of deeper remedies. We have been good surgeons and terrible doctors.'

The complete integration of the south into republican Italy has yet to be achieved.

FROM UNIFICATION TO FASCISM
Political development after unification was flawed by the imbalance that continued to exist between the 'real nation', made up largely of masses of illiterate peasants devoid of the right to vote, and the 'legal nation', whose social basis was constituted by the landed aristocracy and the wealthy middle class. Not surprisingly, half a century after the Risorgimento the Southern Question was still on the agenda. Parliament had produced several studies of the problem, but little in the way of concrete results. Protests voiced by eminent intellectuals had likewise gone unanswered. The few reforms that had been passed had failed to change the prevailing system of agrarian organisation (in large estates with primitive

agriculture and servile labour), and while agricultural methods gradually improved elsewhere in Europe, the impoverishment of the countryside in Italy forced hundreds of thousands of peasants to emigrate. Among those who remained behind, underdevelopment, poverty and ignorance reinforced the power of the Sicilian 'mafia' and its mainland counterpart, the Neapolitan 'camorra'.

At the close of the First World War the young Italian nation found itself on the verge of a severe social and economic crisis. The reconversion of an industry 'swollen' by the war effort and post-war inflation sharpened the country's endemic conflicts. Faith in the established order was shaken by socialist ferment, as well as by widespread discontent of the middle classes, whose real income was rapidly diminishing. The frustration of the Italian claims at the Versailles peace conference introduced a further destabilising element, the myth of the 'mutilated victory', which was used to advantage by the growing nationalist movement, whose numbers included intellectuals (such as poet **Gabriele D'Annunzio**), veterans unable to find a place in post-war society, and members of the privileged classes frightened by the prospect of a proletarian upheaval. The elections of 1919 marked the collapse of the traditional political parties and the advance of the socialists and the Catholic-inspired populists, who became essential to the creation of the coalition governments of the following years.

In November 1921 the 'Fasci Italiani di Combattimento', right-wing political activist groups that advocated an expansionistic foreign policy and a socialising domestic policy (universal suffrage, employee participation in industrial management, progressive taxation of capital, confiscation of war profits, etc.) were reorganised to form the Partito Nazionale Fascista. In August 1922 the leftist labour unions called a general strike to protest against the violent methods of the Fascist 'squadristi' (hit-squads made up of former soldiers, the unemployed, hooligans, and youths disoriented by the war), and party chief **Benito Mussolini** responded by launching an ultimatum: if the government did not take immediate action, the Fascists would themselves restore order, using every means at their disposal. On 24 October 1922, at the Fascist convention in Naples, Mussolini announced the **March on Rome**, which took place on 27 October. As the Black Shirts descended on the capital Prime Minister Luigi Facta prepared a decree ordering a state of siege, but Victor Emmanuel III, in response to the pressures of the military and the nationalists (who viewed the Fascists favourably), refused to sign. Facta resigned and, the following day, 28 October, the king called on Mussolini to form a new cabinet.

THE FASCIST SOCIAL ORDER
The Fascist movement, which arose as an outgrowth of resentments and as a tool of often contrasting interests, initially did not have a real ideology. 'My doctrine', Mussolini wrote in 1932, 'had been the doctrine of action. Fascism was born of a need for action and was itself action'. Only after the consolidation of the regime, Fascism sought to give itself a doctrine. The most coherent attempt was that of philosopher **Giovanni Gentile**, who contrasted liberal, democratic individualism, responsible for the disintegration of the social fabric, with the need for a collective solidarity in which the rights and aspirations of the individual are subordinated to the values and interests of the national community, for which the State is the only trustee and guarantor. On the economic front, the principle of 'class solidarity' was opposed to the Marxist conception of class struggle and was expressed in the theorisation of the corporative state, in which employers and employees, united in organisations that were made part of the structure of government, were expected

to work together in the greater interest of the nation. After the passage of special legislation, too complicated to discuss here, which allowed the transition from representative democracy to totalitarian dictatorship, many anti-Fascists fled to France; others were imprisoned or sent in 'forced residence' to remote parts of the country. All organised opposition to the regime was suppressed, and of the pre-Fascist political parties only the communists maintained a clandestine organisational structure.

The Italian economy went through a positive phase until 1929, supported by the government's deflationary policy and by American loans. After the 1929 crisis the Fascists began a process of government participation in industry which, without interfering with the capitalistic character of the economy, made it possible for industrial development to continue, thanks to the increasing concentration of capital, the compression of salaries, and the policy of economic self-sufficiency (autarchy). The regime had little effect on agriculture, to which it devoted above all propaganda.

THE SECOND WORLD WAR AND THE CONSTITUTIONAL ASSEMBLY
Until the mid 1930s the Fascist foreign policy followed a moderate course, favouring relations with France in order to offset the growing importance of Germany. Isolated diplomatically after the conquest of Ethiopia, however, Italy fell into line with its reactionary neighbour and, after observing the German military successes in Northern Europe, entered the war with the intention of conducting a 'parallel campaign' for the conquest of the Mediterranean and the Balkans. But a series of Italian defeats forced the Germans to intervene in both regions and undermined faith in Mussolini and his regime. In the summer of 1943 a 'court conspiracy' toppled the Fascists, and the new government headed by **Marshal Pietro Badoglio** obtained an armistice from the Allies, who had already landed on the peninusual (at Taranto and Salerno). Northern Italy was occupied by the Germans (Mussolini founded the Italian Social Republic, a German puppet state with capital at Salò), but the advance of the Allies and the bloody campaign of resistance launched by the Partisans made it clear that the end was near. On 25 April 1945 the Germans and the Fascists abandoned Milan. Mussolini, captured while attempting to escape, was executed together with other Fascist notables. On 29 April the German forces in Italy surrendered to the Allies at Caserta, and a Special Assembly elected on 2 June 1946 drafted a new Constitution that came into effect on 1 January 1948, marking the end of the monarchy and the rebirth of Italy as a parliamentary republic.

CONTEMPORARY ITALY
Between May 1946 and September 1947 the cost of living in Italy rose over 50 times with respect to pre-war levels, while average income remained at unacceptable levels, especially in the South, where agrarian reform remained a chimera. In Lazio, Apulia, and Calabria, clashes between police and an impoverished peasantry led to numerous deaths. In this difficult economic situation the nation returned to democracy in a state of 'limited sovereignty' conditioned by the authority of the United States. The affirmation of the Christian Democrats (DC) in the elections for the Constitutional Assembly marked the beginning of the prevalence of that party in Italian political life; soon afterwards the radicalisation of the contrasts between the US and the Soviet Union brought the exclusion of the left from government and the beginning of the 'centrist' policy of prime minister **Alcide De Gasperi**.

During the years of the first republican legislation the nation suffered considerable social tensions, to which De Gasperi's government—a coalition between the Christian Democrats and the lesser centrist parties—responded by repressing protest and reinforcing the police. A limited agrarian reform failed to satisfy the 'hunger for land' of the Southern peasantry, but led to the formation of the first of the political patronage structures (the 'Cassa del Mezzogiorno', or Fund for the South), with which the DC reinforced its electoral power.

In the 1950s, for the first time in the country's history, industry surpassed agriculture as the principal means of employment, and production, investment, and expenditure for consumer goods increased rapidly. But in 1963 the system's weaknesses became clear. Vast areas, especially in the South, had remained outside the 'boom'. An excessive expansion of credit had led to inflation, the stock market had reacted with a strong downturn, and many firms that had grown too fast and had not acquired the solidity necessary to weather a period of relative stagnation, failed. Only in 1965, thanks largely to a favourable balance of payments, the situation began to improve.

A return of insecurity in the 1970s, caused by the global economic crisis and by the failure of the centrist majority to deal with the demands of a changing society, led to a series of bloody terrorist episodes (known collectively as the 'stragegy of tension') aimed at destabilising the country's democratic order. The deterioration of the political atmosphere provided the ground for acts of violence by radical groups at both ends of the political spectrum (in our area right-wing thugs in Reggio Calabria turned a protest over an insignificant administrative matter into a lethal street brawl in 1970, and the Neapolitan cell of the communist-inspired Red Brigades kidnapped an eminent Christian Democrat politician in 1981), the ultimate causes of which have yet to be determined. In the 1980s the ineffectiveness of the State in checking the spread of organised crime and the interference of the parties in administrative and economic matters led to a general disillusionment with party politics and a widespread distrust of institutions. The intensive judicial action of the 90s, in which charges (ranging from corruption, to mafia association, to murder), have been brought against numerous 'untouchable' citizens, including two former prime ministers, is slowly restoring faith in government.

Today Italians again find themselves at a crossroads. The political parties that emerged at the end of the Second World War have been swept away by scandal (as in the case of the Christian Democrats and Socialists), or by the changing tides of international events (Communists), and there is much talk of a Second Republic. But perhaps more importantly, the 'economic miracle' of North-Eastern Italy, the country's fastest growing industrial region, is once again widening the gap between North and South. Only if precise steps are taken in the private as well as the public sphere, will the northward migration of human and financial resources be checked, and the savings and skill of Southern Italians ploughed back into their native soil. In this sense the complete integration of the South into united Italy has yet to be achieved.

ART IN SOUTHERN ITALY

By Paul Williamson

The south of Italy has, like Sicily, always been easy prey for foreign invaders, and thus its art has been susceptible to many different influences. Greek, Roman, Byzantine, Saracenic, Norman and other civilisations all played some part in forming the medieval art of the south, and later, when the Spanish ruled Naples, they too exerted a considerable influence on southern Italian painting, sculpture and architecture.

GREEK AND ROMAN ART

The major Greek monuments still remaining in the south are the magnificent temples at **Paestum**, south of Salerno: the so-called Temple of Neptune is one of the three best-preserved temples in Europe, and in the museum are displayed extremely rare wall paintings from the Tomb of the Diver. The excavations of Roman remains at **Pompeii** and **Herculaneum** are justifiably world-famous and will not be discussed here. Suffice it to say that a visit to Pompeii is still one of the very best ways of gaining an impression of a Roman town: with hundreds of villas and numerous wall paintings (many of which are now in the Archaelogical Museum in Naples) the scavi are much more than mere evocative ruins. A recently discovered addition to the known body of Roman monumental painting is at Oplontis, where the frescoes are in better condition than at Pompeii and Herculaneum. In sculpture, the Arch of Trajan at **Benevento** (built between 114–116 AD) has many finely carved reliefs illustrating scenes from the Emperor's life and various mythological subjects. The Via Appia and Via Traiana (the latter only from Benevento) took the Romans into the south as far as Brindisi and architectural remains of their presence on these routes are many: the most important are at Santa Maria Capua Vetere where there is an impressive amphitheatre and a mithraeum, and further south, at Lecce, there is another, less imposing, amphitheatre.

EARLY CHRISTIAN

Early Christian art is best represented by a series of fine 5C mosaics at Naples (in the Baptistery of San Giovanni al Fonte and in the Catacombs of San Gennaro) and in the chapel of Santa Matrona at San Prisco (near Santa Maria Capua Vetere), and by the 6C mosaics at Casaranello. The mosaics on the dome of the Baptistery at Naples are of the early 5C and although damaged show enough to give a good impression of the original scheme. The narrative scenes, the standing saints and the evangelist symbols at the base of the dome are beautifully picked out and the overall programme, in proportions and colour, is the equal of anything in Rome at the same time. The mosaics in the chapel of Santa Matrona in the church of San Prisco are a little later in date; they too are damaged but the most important parts of the decoration remain intact. These are the two lunettes under the dome, one showing a bust of Christ blessing, holding a book in one hand and flanked by the letters Alpha and Omega (signifying that He represents both the beginning and the end): the other shows an empty throne (the *hetimasia*) flanked by two of the evangelist symbols, the bull and the eagle (signifying Luke and John). The richly coloured dome is filled with a fleshy foliate design and inhabited by small birds. The most interesting mosaics in the **Catacomb of San Gennaro** at Naples have only recently been discovered, the best in quality being those found in the crypt of the bishops. Three are particularly interesting, showing half-length portraits of the bishops buried there: one portrait has even been identified as St Quodvultdeus, Bishop of Carthage, who died in 454. Also of great interest are the frescoes in the same catacomb (ranging in date throughout the early Middle Ages), the finest of which are those portraying the family of Theotecnus and the portrait of a certain Proculus, both delicately painted and recently restored. The mosaics in the church of Santa Maria della Croce at **Casaranello**, although composed entirely of decorative patterns with very little figural work, are perhaps the most impressive of the whole group. They are later than the above mentioned mosaics and the great subtlety in the use of colour, mainly pastel tones, sets them apart from the rest in both a technical and an aesthetic sense.

All these mosaics owe a clear debt to the early Christian art of Rome and are recognisably Italian. This will not be true at certain times in the Middle Ages when strong Byzantine influence manifests itself in the art of the area. The earliest example of Byzantine painting in southern Italy is in fact an illuminated manuscript: this is the 6C **Rossano Gospels** held in the cathedral treasury at Rossano in Calabria, which is the oldest illustrated Gospel book known today. This exquisitely illuminated book, finely and economically drawn with scenes from the New Testament placed against a background of purple vellum, is one of the key monuments of early Christian art in existence, illustrating the sophistication and luxury of the Byzantine court workshops in the East: however, this is an isolated work of art and it bears no relationship to the art of the region.

There is much early Christian sculpture in the south, mostly fragments from sarcophagi, but undoubtedly the most important and certainly the most impressive is the colossal bronze statue of a Byzantine emperor which stands outside the church of San Sepolcro in **Barletta**. It is over five metres high, and although both legs and both arms (the left from the edge of the mantle) have been altered, the effect is still awe-inspiring. There has been a good deal of discussion as to which emperor is portrayed, but opinion has settled on Marcian, who was Emperor between 450–457. The statue would have been made in Constantinople: it was washed up in the harbour of Barletta in 1309, probably from an Adriatic shipwreck.

Not much remains of the architecture of the early Christian period. Most of the churches with early foundations have subsequently been enlarged and rebuilt so that little of their original form can be discerned. The circular church of Santa Maria Maggiore at Nocera, originally a baptistery, can be dated to the 6C, and the extensive remains of the martyrium precinct of St Felix at Cimitile are earlier still, dating from the 4C onwards.

THE MIDDLE AGES
Painting
In the early Middle Ages, before the Normans brought political stability to the area, the opportunities for commissioning cycles of paintings must have been few and far between: south of Rome was a poverty-stricken wilderness with scarcely one city of the first importance, excluding Naples. But there are some paintings from these centuries, the frescoes in the oratory of San Lorenzo at San Vincenzo al Volturno (824–42), in Santa Sophia in Benevento (762), at Santi Martiri in Cimitile (10C), and in the Grotta dei Santi at Calvi (10C) being the most important. The frescoes at

San Vincenzo al Volturno are the best-preserved of the four, and are especially interesting as in the scene of the Crucifixion there appears the Abbot Epiphanius. He is identified by an inscription and wears a square nimbus, indicating that he was still alive when the fresco was made, and thus allowing us to date the paintings to his time. These early manifestations of a Benedictine-inspired art luckily escaped the ravages of the Saracenic invasions, although the neighbouring monastery did not. They are in surprisingly good condition, the most delicately painted scenes being the Annunciation, the Crucifixion, the Stoning of St Stephen and the Martyrdom of St Laurence.

By the second half of the 10C much of the southern mainland had been reunited with the Eastern Empire, and consequently the art of the region developed strong Byzantine traits: much of it must have been executed by Greek monks, such as the two painted niches in the crypt of Sante Marina e Cristina in Carpignano, near Otranto. The first, showing Christ enthroned, is signed by the painter Theophylactos and dated 959: the second, with the same subject, is dated 1020 and was executed by a painter called Eustathios—both were undoubtedly Basilian monks. Much later, in 1197, the practice of signing frescoes was still popular: Maestro Danieli signed and dated the works he executed in that year (also painted in a strongly Byzantine manner) in the crypt of San Biagio just outside the town of San Vito dei Normanni. Works such as those at Carpignano and San Vito dei Normanni were widespread in the far south, and are characterised by a distinctive, provincial interpretation of the art of Byzantine Greece, and thus their influence was limited to the south. The same could not be said of art from the Abbey of Monte Cassino in the second half of the 11C. Without doubt, the most important single event for the art of south-western Italy during the Middle Ages was the appointment of Desiderius as abbot of Monte Cassino and his subsequent development of the Abbey. It was from Monte Cassino that Desidenus, later to become Pope Victor III, prompted a revival of the arts in central and southern Italy, bringing Byzantine workmen from Constantinople and training his monks in their methods, so that the lessons should not be lost when the foreigners left. The artistic revolution that occurred at Monte Cassino was of great importance for the art of medieval Italy, because the high quality of artistry and craftsmanship delicately and successfully combined Italian and Byzantine stylistic elements to create a fresh artistic vision. The revolution went further than just stylistic change, as an early Christian revival was set in motion: materials were brought from Rome and early Christian narrative methods were re-used. Unfortunately, the medieval splendour of Monte Cassino had mostly disappeared from the Abbey even before the allied bombardment in 1944: the monastery suffered several earthquakes and, as a result, was rebuilt in the early 18C. There exists, however, a full contemporary account of the works of Desiderius and a description of what his church looked like in the Chronicle of Leo of Ostia. He tells us of the work carried out by the mosaicists from Constantinople, and states that the art of mosaic had been left uncultivated in the west for more than 500 years: although this statement is in fact incorrect, it shows that the level of craftsmanship must have sunk to a very low level in the centuries prior to the rebuilding of the Abbey at Monte Cassino. Not only mosaicists, but workers in silver, bronze, glass, ivory and stone, were brought from Constantinople to train local artisans.

A reflection of the decorative programme at Monte Cassino can be seen in the paintings which fill the interior of the basilica at **Sant'Angelo in Formis** with scenes from the Old and New Testaments lining the nave walls above the arcades, a Last Judgment scene on the west wall, and in the apse at the east end, a huge seated

Christ flanked by the evangelist symbols, below which are three archangels and Desidenus (holding a model of the church) and St Benedict (the founder of the order). Carried out a few years after the scheme at Monte Cassino, the frescoes at Sant'Angelo confirmed the advent of a new style which proved to be very long-lasting in the South, continuing with only slight changes until well into the 13C. From the 12C there is an impressive and charming apse decoration in the small church of Santa Maria in Foro Claudio near Ventaroli—it shows a seated Virgin and Child flanked by two archangels, below which is a row of standing apostles with the Archangel Michael. The style is very close to that at Sant'Angelo in Formis, although perhaps slightly cruder. Further removed from their stylistic source, and certainly more provincial, are the colourful and extensive 13C paintings to be found at Bominaco, Fossa, Ronzano, Minuto and Pianella, where the paintings, although lively and animated, are out of touch with contemporary developments in the major centres.

A group of mosaic pavements (mostly in Apulia) are both stylistically and compositionally very different from the art of Monte Cassino. Most impressive, the beautiful pavement of the cathedral at **Otranto** (executed by a priest called Pantaleon between 1163 and 1166), which is remarkably well-preserved, has a fascinating mixture of scenes, ranging from episodes from the book of Genesis to signs of the Zodiac. Also worthy of note are the pavements at Taranto and at the remote church of Santa Maria del Patirion, near Rossano.

Towards the end of the Middle Ages a common pattern of patronage began to emerge: this was the introduction of foreign artists (or artists from northern Italy) by foreign rulers to execute the most important commissions. Although Desiderius had done much the same thing at Monte Cassino a few centuries before by importing Byzantine artists and craftsmen, local artists had been trained by the visiting craftsmen, and so had continued to work in basically the same manner. From about 1300 artists would come from the north and elsewhere at the invitation of the Angevins or others to execute a single commission (rarely outside Naples), but would not settle in the region. It was, therefore, hardly surprising that no local school of painting emerged before the 17C.

Pietro Cavallini was called from Rome by Charles II of Anjou in 1308 to execute the frescoes in the church of Santa Maria Donnaregina in Naples, and although there is a certain amount of controversy over how much of the work is by him, it is fairly certain that he played a large part in the commission, perhaps planning the scheme but leaving the execution of it to assistants. We also know that Giotto worked in Naples, but nothing remains that can be attributed to him. Perhaps the most influential visitor to Naples at this time was Simone Martini of Siena, who appears to have stimulated a small following in the south. One of his finest paintings, St Louis of Toulouse crowning Robert of Anjou King of Naples (1317), was painted for the church of Santa Chiara and now hangs at Capodimonte.

Sculpture

Although the medieval sculptures in Campania and Apulia have many points of contact, there are also many differences. This is to be expected from two regions separated by a band of mountains and with different traditions. Campanian art always owed something to classical sources—not surprising in a land that had so many surviving Roman works—whereas the sculpture of Apulia developed more independently from the classical tradition and assumed a character very much of its own. The beautifully executed coloured glass inlay on the pulpits and paschal candelabra of Campania is rarely seen in Apulia and owes its existence ultimately to Saracenic sources in Sicily; likewise, the Apulian love of the sculpted portal has no parallel in Campania. There are of course sculptures in Campania and Apulia that are very close in style to one another, as common models were available in both regions.

One of the more significant groups of works of art are the bronze doors which appeared in southern Italy from about the middle of the 11C to the end of the twelfth century. The first of these are at Amalfi, and were commissioned in Constantinople by a wealthy Amalfitan merchant, Pantaleon, who had business interests in the Byzantine capital and must have been impressed by the bronze doors on the churches there. They were executed in 1065. Desiderius of Monte Cassino was so impressed by these doors when he visited Amalfi that he ordered a pair for the abbey soon afterwards—the fashion spread from there and similar doors, imported from Constantinople, were erected in Rome (San Paolo fuori le Mura), Monte Sant'Angelo, Atrani (San Salvatore), and the Duomo at Salerno. All these doors share a common technique: the bronze is engraved and the work finished in silver and niello. Those at Rome and Monte Sant'Angelo are most interesting as they are richly illustrated with narrative scenes: the doors at **Monte Sant Angelo** have 24 panels showing episodes concerning the deeds of the Archangel Michael, and were cast in 1076. The six doors mentioned so far are works of Byzantine manufacture and they exerted a tremendous influence on the appearance of the main portals of Southern Italian churches, inspiring local craftsmen to cast their own doors in a different style. The doors on the **Mausoleum of Bohemond at Canosa** were cast in 1111 and are markedly different in execution from the preceding Byzantine examples: the decorative rosettes owe more to Mohammedan art than to Byzantine, and the incised figures are far removed in style from the earlier doors, being much more refined, with the fall of drapery beautifully understood. A few years later, in 1119 and 1127, the doors on the façade and south side of Troia Cathedral were executed in a manner closer to the style of the Byzantine prototypes by an artist named in an inscription as Oderisius of Benevento. Another named artist, Barisanus of Trani, was responsible for the doors at **Trani** (about 1175), **Ravello** (1179), and Monreale in Sicily (about 1186): finally, in the fragmentary remains of the doors at Benevento Cathedral we see the work of an unknown artist towards the year 1200. These last works are truly Italian and should be related to doors in northern Italy and Europe rather than to Byzantium. Before moving on to monumental sculpture it is worth pointing out the existence of a thriving school of ivory carvers around Amalfi in the second half of the 11C and the beginning of the 12C. The outstanding work of this school is the so-called **Paliotto** (altar frontal) in the museum attached to the cathedral at Salerno: it consists of numerous ivory plaques carved with scenes from the Old and New Testaments, and once again testifies to the medieval mixture of Byzantine and Italian style found in the south at the end of the 11C.

One of the high points of medieval sculpture in the south is in its application to church fittings and furniture, such as episcopal thrones, pulpits, paschal candelabra and altar screens, and it is perhaps convenient to split the production of sculpture at this time into the different categories most often seen in the region. The earliest episcopal throne is in the cathedral at Canosa. Carved by the sculptor Romualdo for Archbishop Urso between 1078 and 1089, the marble throne is supported by two rather stiffly depicted elephants, leading one authority to conjecture that the throne was based on an Islamic chess-piece. Whether this is the case or not, it falls far below the quality of carving seen on the slightly later throne in

San Nicola di Bari (probably to be dated to around 1098), which is one of the most beautiful objects of medieval art in Italy. Three caryatid figures (two of them half naked) support the throne at the front with two lions at the back, and the borders of the throne, once decorated with coloured paste, are picked out with floral and figural designs. The importance of the Bari throne is that it represents the first manifestation of a genuinely Romanesque style in the south, with definite links to the sculpture of northern Italy and Aquitaine, especially the work of Maestro Wiligelmo at Modena cathedral. However, the throne is a work of an Apulian, not a northern sculptor. Another, less important throne is at Monte Sant'Angelo.

The pulpits of Campania, with the combination of a colourful ornamental inlay and classically carved figural work, are many in number and only the most interesting can be described here. An early 12C example may be seen in Ravello cathedral with very little sculpture—only a small eagle lectern—but with a charming illustration of Jonah and the Whale executed in glass inlay. Much more impressive are the two pulpits in **Salerno cathedral** (1173–81). These too have large areas of inlaid glass formed into geometric patterns, but they are distinguished chiefly for the· quality of the carving: especially fine work is seen in the capitals on the columns supporting the pulpits. Two later pulpits are worthy of note: that at Sessa Aurunca is a continuation of the type so convincingly handled at Salerno. The second, at Bitonto cathedral in Apulia, can be dated accurately to 1229 by an inscription. Its primary interest lies in the relief found on a side panel of the staircase: this shows a seated king with a lady and two young men before him, who have been plausibly identified as Emperor Frederick II, his wife Yolande (who died in 1228) and his two sons, Henry and Conrad. It should be pointed out that many of these pulpits have been reconstructed and restored at some time and that much of the glass inlay is not original: but very rarely is a false impression given. Like the pulpits, the paschal candelabra afforded the Campanian sculptor opportunities to work both in high relief and in glass inlay, and more often than not the sculpture on these different types of monuments shows marked similarities, as pulpit and candelabrum were usually carved at the same time. The paschal candelabrum (a huge marble candlestick for the Easter candle) normally stood to the right of the choir at the end of the nave and would have been lit from the pulpit. For this reason it is not surprising that the best examples of the Campanian paschal candelabrum are still found next to the most finely sculpted pulpits: the 12C candelabrum at Salerno and the later example at Sessa Aurunca echo the styles of the pulpits. They are heavily inlaid with glass, and the sculpture on the capital of the candelabrum at Salerno is even finer and more delicately carved than the pulpit next to it. Two other candelabra, later in date (13C), and in different styles, can be seen in the cathedrals of Gaeta and Anagni. The example at Anagni is signed by the sculptor Vassallettus and owes more to the contemporary Roman school than to the south; that at Gaeta falls between the art of the south and that of Rome and has no parallels in either place. Forty-eight panels carved round its body illustrate the life of Christ and the story of St Erasmus.

The development of the Romanesque sculpted portal in southern Italy centred on Apulia, although beautiful examples may be seen elsewhere, at **San Clemente a Casauria** in Abruzzo for instance. Ultimately influenced by French portal design transmitted through the Norman rulers, the typical Apulian portal was not just a slavish copy of its northern prototypes. The decorative tympanum, although originating in France, was transformed to carry locally-inspired scenes and specifically southern Italian imagery. To select just the most important and best preserved portals of Apulia is all that space permits, but many examples omitted are undoubtedly worth visiting: the portals of **Troia cathedral** (north portal), **Trani cathedral, San Leonardo a Siponto, San Nicola di Bari** and **Ruvo cathedral** are however, the primary monuments of the 12C, while the marvellous portal of the cathedral at Bitonto is a slightly later demonstration of Apulian Romanesque, executed around 1200.

A few decades later, Frederick II Hohenstaufen was to commission a totally different type of sculpture, which represented a complete break with the Romanesque and which was to influence the great Gothic sculpture of northern Italy. For the decoration of his **Porta Romana** outside Capua, Frederick wished to revive the classical ideal and to present himself as the equal of the Roman emperors. Accordingly, he instructed his sculptors to carve a statue of himself and various other figures (including two very fine busts) in the Roman manner, and he had these works placed in niches on the arch. Unfortunately, the gateway was destroyed in 1557, but most of the sculpture survived (if damaged) and is now displayed in the Museo Campano in Capua. These classicising sculptures were very important for the development of Italian Gothic sculpture because they appear to have strongly influenced the young Nicola Pisano before he left the south and went to work in Pisa. It is often forgotten that Nicola came from Apulia, yet his remarkable and important pulpit at Pisa (1260) owes a clear debt to the classicising school of sculptors active in the south a few years earlier: he may even have been employed in his early days in that same workshop.

The most outstanding Gothic sculpture in the south was actually carried out by a Northern Italian, **Tino di Camaino** (c 1285–1337), who was called to Naples by King Robert of Anjou in 1323 to execute the tomb monument of Catherine of Austria in San Lorenzo Maggiore. Tino stayed in Naples for the rest of his life, working both as a sculptor and as an architect for the Angevins, and he held what amounted to a monopoly on the production of the royal tomb monuments. He was responsible for seven fine tombs, three of which are in Santa Chiara—those of Mary of Anjou (1329), Charles of Calabria (1332–33), and Mary of Valois. He naturally built up a workshop, but the work produced by his followers never approached his own. The best sculpture of the next generation was again the work of northerners: Giovanni and Pacio da Firenze filled the gap left by Tino's death and were commissioned to carry out the tomb monuments of Robert of Anjou in 1343 and of Louis of Durazzo in 1344, both for the church of Santa Chiara.

Architecture

The medieval architecture of the south may, for convenience, be divided into three distinct periods: the Eastern (predominantly Byzantine) influenced period of the 10C and 11C, the Romanesque period of the 12C and early 13C, and the Gothic (14C). There will be buildings that fall outside the above-mentioned groups in matters of detail, decoration and so on, but the most important buildings in the area will be covered by these categories. The churches of the earliest period are mainly to be found in the lands that were controlled by the Byzantine Empire in the 10C and 11C, Calabria, Basilicata and Apulia. They survive because they are mostly modest in size and appearance and because they are often situated in very remote areas. These churches, usually made in local stone, are not of the first importance: they reflect the influence of Byzantine ground-plans (most are quincunx structures) and are similar to provincial Greek churches. The most handsome example is to be seen at **Stilo** (La Cattolica) in Calabria, which can probably be dated to the end of the 10C and is built of brick. Two other churches of similar appearance worth noting are at Otranto (San Pietro) and Rossano (San Marco): they are of the 11C. A slightly later church of completely different form, although with a Western ground-plan, has strong Byzantine overtones—this is the so-called Roccelletta of Squillace. Now ruined, it is still possible to pick out the clearly Constantinopolitan details on the extant walls, such as the blind arches along the nave and the niches in the apse.

By the end of the 11C the Norman occupation of Apulia had brought French architectural forms to the south-east, just as it had in the allied art of sculpture. The chief monument in this new style is the church of **San Nicola di Bari**, where the façade in particular reflects specifically Norman building types, as seen in St Etienne at Caen. San Nicola was to be the most influential building of the 12C in Apulia, as it was the prototype for many other churches being built in this rapidly prospering region. The cathedrals of Trani, Bari, and Barletta all assumed a similar form, and so popular was this particular building type that even at the very end of the century at **Bitonto cathedral** (1200) it remained virtually unchanged. At the same time buildings appeared that are not so easy to fit in with the main stylistic developments: the unfinished monastery church at Venosa, although French-inspired, would have looked very different from the group of churches above, the cathedral of **Troia** owes its origins to Pisan architecture, and a small group of churches (the masterpieces of which are the cathedrals of **Canosa** and **Molfetta**) have been influenced by eastern Mediterranean building. On the other side of the peninsula, in Campania, the diversity of building types being experimented with was ignored: the basilica was still preferred above all else. Nothing architecturally important happened in the south during the 13C: it was rather a case of isolated instances, such as the building of the Cistercian church at **Fossanova** (consecrated 1208) and Frederick II's imposing **Castel del Monte** a beautifully constructed fortress built in about 1240.

In the 14C the artistic impetus came through the Angevin dynasty in Naples, and was French-orientated. Although French architects were used at first, Neapolitan architects were working for the court by around 1300. Obviously influenced by French methods, the local architects nevertheless developed a style quite their own, as is witnessed in the churches of San Pietro a Maiella, Santa Chiara and Santa Maria Donnaregina (all built in the early 14C). The most distinguished Neapolitan architect of the day was Gagliardo Primario, who also collaborated with Tino di Camaino on the tomb monument of Catherine of Austria in San Lorenzo Maggiore: he is the architect of Santa Chiara. Outside Naples, the outstanding products of the 14C stand at the beginning and the end of the century. The Duomo at Lucera (founded by Charles II in 1300 and completed in 1317) should be grouped with the Neapolitan churches: the church of Santa Caterina d'Alessandria at Galatina (from 1391), although later, is conservative in style and owes more to the Romanesque than to the Gothic.

THE RENAISSANCE
Painting
The story of Southern Italian painting during the 15C and 16C is a sorry one. Whereas the painters of Florence, Rome, and Venice produced works of art that are known the world over, it is difficult to call to mind a single painting in Naples of the same time that could honestly be termed a masterpiece. This may be due to the nature of the patronage—although in the second half of the 15C the Aragonese rulers commissioned many works, their chief interests lay in architecture and sculpture: the painting of note that has come down to us can be described quickly.

By all accounts the major painter in Naples in the 15C was **Colantonio**, whose style shows its debt to Flemish painting in the same way as that of Antonello da Messina. His best works are at Capodimonte (a charming St Jerome and the lion) and in the church of San Pietro Martire (the polyptych of San Vincenzo Ferrer), the latter strongly reflecting the northern style. Antonello himself may have worked in Naples, but there is little evidence that he did so—only a portrait in Capodimonte. At the end of the 15C Antonio Solario, a Venetian, worked in Naples: his most important work is in the cloister at Santi Severino e Sossio, showing the Life of St Benedict. The most productive pupil of Solano's was the southern Italian Andrea da Salerno, who has left work throughout Campania. In the 16C there is nothing of note, but two painters stand above the others, Fabrizio Santafede and Corenzio, both working at the end of the century. As with many Neapolitan painters, their output was huge but the standard of painting mediocre.

Sculpture

The best sculpture of the 15C in Naples was actually executed by artists from northern Italy; some of them travelling to the south to carry out the works, some sending completed sculptures from their workshops, as **Donatello** and **Michelozzo** did in 1427, when they sent the Brancacci tomb to the church of Sant'Angelo a Nilo in Naples. In the same manner, **Antonio Rossellino** (1427–79) sent an altar of the Nativity to the church of Sant'Anna dei Lombardi (Monteoliveto) around 1475, after it had been carved in Florence. He also partly executed the tomb monument of Mary of Aragon, destined for the Piccolomini chapel of the same church, which was finished by **Benedetto da Maiano** (1442–97): Benedetto is also responsible for the relief of the Annunciation (1489) in the Mastrogiudice chapel at Monteoliveto. **Franceso Laurana** (1430–1502) and **Domenico Gagini** both worked and lived in Naples, and undertook many commissions. Gagini's contribution is not now entirely clear, but there are a number of marble Madonnas by him in Naples (one of the most beautiful is in the Chapel of Santa Barbara in the Castel Nuovo), and he was employed on the reliefs of the Triumphal Arch on the Castel Nuovo (1453–65) together with Laurana and others. Laurana, on the other hand, had a more distinctive style and many of the portrait busts carved by him survive. At the end of the 15C, Guido Mazzoni from Modena executed one of his imposing and moving groups of the Lamentation in terracotta for Monteoliveto (1492). Despite these fine sculpted works in the major churches of Naples, there was still no local school of any merit. The Aragonese court, when they needed tomb monuments or decorative sculpture, simply turned to the famous names of the north: this was only to be expected, as they could afford the best works and considered themselves to be on a level with the great families of the northern cities.

With the emergence of **Giovanni da Nola** (c 1488–1558) we see for the first time since the Middle Ages a local sculptor of the first rank. Giovanni worked all his life in Naples and was favoured with many of the most important commissions in the city. His best works are the tombs of Jacopo, Sigismondo and Ascanio Sanseverino in Santi Severino e Sossio (1539–46) and the monument of Don Pedro da Toledo in San Giacomo degli Spagnuoli (about 1545): he also worked extensively at Monteoliveto. Alongside Giovanni da Nola worked **Girolamo Santacroce** (c 1502–37), whose most original contributions are the Del Pezzo Altar at Monteoliveto (1524) and the Sinicalco Altar (1528–36) in Santa Maria delle Grazie a Caponapoli: he was probably a pupil of Giovanni Tommaso Malvito, who is known for his work as an architect. Slightly earlier than Giovanni da Nola and

Girolamo Santacroce, and also responsible to some extent for their style, came the two Spaniards **Bartolomeo Ordoñez** and **Diego de Siloe**. Ordoñez sculpted the tomb of Andrea Bonifacio in Santi Sevenno e Sossio and collaborated with Siloe on the altar in the Cappella Caracciolo di Vico in San Giovanni a Carbonara, and Siloe was responsible for a beautful relief of the Virgin and Child amongst angels in the Cappella Tocca in the cathedral. The works of these men introduced a Spanish sweetness into the Neapolitan style, transforming it from being simply a pale reflection of Tuscan sculpture and making it ever more eclectic. The work of non-Neapolitan sculptors was, however still popular, and Northern Italian sculptors were still sent for: for instance, Francesco da Sangallo (1494–1576) executed the monument of Antonio Fiodi at Monteoliveto in 1540 and around 1546 was working at Santi Severino e Sossio. In 1536, **Giovanni Angelo Montorsoli** and **Bartolomeo Ammanati** had received the commission for the Sannazaro monument, which now stands in Santa Maria del Parto: it was carved in Tuscany and sent to Naples and its style is rather idiosyncratic in Naples, strongly reflecting the influence of Michelangelo.

Architecture
Like the Gateway built by Frederick II in 1240, the **Triumphal Arch** erected on the **Castel Nuovo** under the aegis of Alfonso I (begun in 1451) was an attempt to emulate the Romans and to illustrate how enlightened the patron was in both thought and action. The sculpture has already been discussed, but even without it, the arch stands as a Renaissance monument *par excellence*, as much a summation of 15C ideals as any monument to be found in Florence or Rome. As before, many Central and Northern Italian artists were brought in to carry out the work, and this continued to be the case during the rest of the Renaissance, although a local school did emerge in the 16C. In 1485 Giuliano da Maiano was brought from Florence by Alfonso II and was asked to design the Porta Capuana. It was not completed until after his death in 1490, but it embodies a specifically Florentine Renaissance style, contrasting with the classical monumentality of the Triumphal Arch of Alfonso I. Giuliano also designed two villas for Alfonso, but unfortunately they no longer exist. As in the field of sculpture, in the early 16C local artists came to the fore and started to receive important commissions: the most successful were **Tommaso** and **Giovanni Tommaso Malvito** (Tommaso' s son) and **Donadio** and **Giovanni Francesco Mormanno** (Donadio's son-in-law). **Tommaso** is celebrated for his richly decorated crypt of San Gennaro underneath the cathedral (1497–1508) and his son is known for the equally sumptuous Cappella De Cuncto in Santa Maria delle Grazie a Caponapoli of 1517. While Donadio Mormanno's contribution is marginal, that of Giovanni Francesco is both more significant and better preserved and is best seen in the churches of Santa Maria Donnaromita (1535) and Santi Severino e Sossio.

BAROQUE
Painting
If the 16C was the nadir of Neapolitan painting, the 17C was its apotheosis, with many local painters working successfully in a refined and distinctive manner and rivalling the schools of Rome and Florence. In the time-honoured fashion, foreign artists were brought in from other cities, but rather than discouraging the native painters, they inspired them to form their own style, particularly suited to the decoration of ceilings, domes and large scale projects. **Caravaggio** (who arrived in

Naples in 1607) and the Spaniard **Ribera** could be said to have laid the foundations for the local school, which would come to be known for its dark, dramatic and intensely religious paintings. Caravaggio is represented by three paintings of great importance, the Flagellation of San Domenico Maggiore (now at Capodimonte) the Seven Acts of Mercy in the Monte della Misericordia, and a St John the Baptist (also at Capodimonte). Ribera's best work is to be seen at San Martino (a Deposition and a series of prophets). Although modifying the painting styles of Caravaggio and Ribera, the Neapolitan school clearly owes a great debt to both painters: at times it can be difficult to tell the works of members of this school apart. The most notable exponents of this 'Neapolitan style' are Giovanni Battista Caracciolo (1570–1637), Massimo Stanzione (1585–1656), Andrea Vaccaro (1598–1670), Francesco Fracanzano (1612–56) and Bernardo Cavallino (1622–54): most of these artists are represented in the Carthusian monastery of San Martino, a veritable picture gallery of the Naples school of painting. Together, they formed a very tightly-knit community and were actively hostile to foreign artists working in the city: the Roman painters **Domenichino** and **Lanfranco** were openly intimidated but stayed to paint some significant and beautiful works (their painting styles can be studied in the dome of the Cappella di San Gennaro in the cathedral).

Mattia Preti (1613–99) is of more importance and was more talented than the artists of the preceding generation. He only came to Naples from his native Calabria when he was 43, but he is well represented in the churches of the city, perhaps his best works being the paintings in the vault at San Pietro a Maiella. There are also many of his paintings, mostly from his earlier period, in the far south: 11 are in one church, San Domenico in Taverna, near Catanzaro. Undoubtedly the most influential painters at the end of the century were **Salvator Rosa** and **Luca Giordano** (1632–1705). Rosa has left little in Naples but Giordano, famous for his speed of painting, is represented everywhere. Inevitably the standard varies (some work was certainly done by assistants) but his best work is expressive and subtle: most impressive of his huge oeuvre, and conveniently grouped together, are the paintings in San Martino. **Francesco Solimena** (1657–47) took over the mantle from Giordano and was without equal in Naples in the first half of the 18C, setting up his own academy and training many painters in his manner.

Sculpture

The major sculptor of the late 16C and early 17C was **Pietro Bernini** (1562–1629), who moved to Naples in 1584 in the hope of establishing himself outside the intense competition of Rome. In this he succeeded, but although there are examples of his sculpture in Naples, it is difficult to establish the extent of his work: certainly by him is a series of six statues on the Ruffo Altar in the Girolamini. Just before he left for Rome he worked with the sculptor Naccherino on the Fontana Medina, now in Piazza Bovio (c 1600), and his son Gian Lorenzo Bernini, the greatest Baroque sculptor of all, was born in Naples in 1598.

In the 17C the most important sculptor and architect in Naples was the brilliantly versatile **Cosimo Fanzago** (1591–1678), a Lombard by birth who settled in Naples in 1608. He was responsible for many innovations in style and played a crucial part in establishing the use of coloured marbles as decorative inlay for monuments and buildings—a good illustration of this is his altar of 1635 in Santi Severino e Sossio.

The 18C saw little sculpture of international note produced in Naples. One eye-catching extravaganza, the huge fountain in the grounds of the palace at Caserta, deserves to be mentioned for its dramatic juxtaposition of sculpted and natural materials. The whole scheme was planned by Luigi Vanvitelli (1700–73) from 1752 onwards but was realised by his son Carlo between 1776–79.

Architecture

Two Florentines, **Giovan Antonio Dosio** (died 1609) and **Domenico Fontana** (died 1607), were the dominant figures at the end of the Neapolitan Renaissance. They had the seal of royal approval and worked on most of the prestigious commissions being offered at the time. Fontana was the architect of the Palazzo Reale (1600–02).

With the dawn of the 17C a thriving local school of architects began to challenge the foreign ascendancy and to provide evidence of great and original talent, especially in the sphere of surface decoration. **Fra Francesco Grimaldi** (1543–1613), a monk from Calabria, was influential, and not just in Naples. His masterpiece is San Paolo Maggiore (1583–1603). Giovan Giacomo de Conforto (died 1631) was a pupil of Dosio and after his master's death carried on with the building of San Martino until 1623. But of this small group the most mercurial and boldly talented was the Dominican, **Fra Nuvolo**, who pioneered the use of coloured decoration by facing the dome of Santa Mana di Costantinopoli (late 16C) with majolica. Apart from this experimentation with surface texture he produced daring ground-plans for San Sebastiano and San Carlo all'Arena (1631), both elliptical in shape and ahead of their time in design.

Unquestionably the two greatest names of Neapolitan Baroque architecture are **Cosimo Fanzago** and **Ferdinando Sanfelice** (1675–1748). Fanzago has already been mentioned as an outstanding sculptor, but he was also a distinguished architect, painter and planner of decorative programmes. His earlier works, such as the cloister of the Certosa di San Martino (1623–31) show his roots to be in the architecture of the previous century, with their classical lines and harmonious proportions. But in his mature works he displayed keen knowledge of the latest artistic developments in Rome and is hardly inferior to the great names of that city, Bernini and Borromini. Consider his design for Santa Maria Egiziaca a Pizzofalcone (1651–1717), a Greek cross church of marvellous subtlety, where he makes ingenious use of space. Equally ingenious is his application of decorative elements to the façades of his buildings, breaking up the solid masses into smaller units while retaining an overall unity (see San Giuseppe degli Scalzi of 1660). Sanfelice stood on an equal footing with Fanzago: he was remarkably productive, designing churches all over the city, the most notable remaining example perhaps being his Chiesa della Nunziatella (finished in the mid 1730s) with its effective polychrome façade. He also designed many important palaces, including the Palazzo Serra a Cassano (1725-26), but possibly his most original contribution was to staircase design, in that he managed to fit beautiful and seemingly spacious staircases into the most cramped environments. Another architect, **Domenico Antonio Vaccaro** (1678–1745) dominated church building with Sanfelice in the first half of the 18C and established the style of Neapolitan Rococo in his inspired treatment of church interiors, asserting complete control over plan and decoration (see for instance the church of the Concezione a Montecalvario). He was a talented sculptor, and, coming from a family of artists, he inherited a deep understanding of pictorial decoration as applied to architecture.

The outstanding achievement at the end of the 18C was the Royal palace at Caserta, planned by Luigi Vanvitelli as an Italian variation of the Versailles ideal palace-type, with extensive landscaped gardens and impressive fountain arrangements.

Outside the south-west of Italy, Baroque and Rococo styles also flourished in a number of cities in Apulia, of which Lecce is the most important, with a building history stretching without break from the 16C to the end of the 18C. It has a number of very interesting churches preserved in excellent condition, the main features being their extravagantly worked façades. A good example is the church of Santa Croce.

THE MODERN

There is very little of distinction in the South from the 19C and 20C. At the end of the 18C Raphael Mengs and Angelica Kauffmann were patronised by the Bourbon rulers and painted a number of portraits for them. Painting of international stature then disappears from the south. In sculpture there is not one single master worthy of mention. The Palace of Capodimonte, finished in 1839, is impressive more for its setting above Naples than for its architecture, and the neo-classical modernisation of the rest of the city was generally uninspired and oppressive. However, even this dullness is to be preferred to the shoddy building projects initiated in the present century. The modern movements in art can best be studied further North, in Rome and Milan especially: they seem to have passed Naples by and to have had no impact. Today as so often before, the artistic life of the city is determined by foreign contributions.

GLOSSARY OF ART TERMS

Note: explanations of further terms used in classical architecture will be found in the description of the Pompeian house, page 110.

ABACUS, flat stone in the upper part of a capital

ACROTERION, an ornamental feature on the corner or vertex of a pediment

AEDICULE, a small edifice or room

AGORA, public square or marketplace

ALA, (pl. *alae*), literally, 'wing', the lateral part of a building

AMBO (pl. *ambones*) pulpit in a Christian basilica; two pulpits on opposite sides of a church from which the gospel and epistle were read

AMBRY, a niche for church vestments and vessels

AMPHIPROSTYLE, temple with colonnades at both ends

AMPHORA, antique vase, usually of large dimensions, for oil and other liquids

ANTEFIX, ornament placed at the lower corner of the tiled roof of a temple to conceal the space between the tiles and the cornice

ANTIS, *in antis* describes the portico of a temple when the side-walls are prolonged to end in a pilaster flush with the columns of the portico

ARCHITRAVE, lowest part of the entablature

ARCHIVOLT, moulded architrave carried round an arch

ARCOSOLIO (pl. *arcosolia*), a tomb, characteristic of but not limited to catacombs, consisting of a sarcophagus set in the wall and surmounted by a niche

ATHENAION, a sanctuary dedicated to Athena

ATLANTES (or *Telamones*), male figures used as supporting columns

ATRIUM, forecourt, usually of a Byzantine church or a classical Roman house

BADIA, *abbazia*, abbey

BASILICA, originally a Roman building used for public administration; in Christian architecture, an aisled church with a clerestory and apse, and no transepts

BENEDIZARIO, a prayer book

BICLINIUM, a Roman dining bed for two; also, the room where it is located

BIFORA, a window divided externally into two equal lights by a column

BORGO, a suburb; street leading away from the centre of a town

BOTTEGA, the studio of an artist: the pupils who worked under his direction

BUCCHERO, Etruscan black terracotta ware

BUCRANIA, a common form of metope decoration—heads of oxen garlanded with flowers

CALDARIUM, or Calidarium. Room for hot or vapour baths in a Roman bath

CAMPANILE, bell-tower, often detached from the building to which it belongs

CAMPOSANTO, cemetery

CAPITAL, the top of a column

CAPITOLIUM, a temple of Jupiter, Juno, and Minerva

CARDO, the main street of a Roman town, at right angles to the decumanus

CARYATID, female figure used as a supporting column

CAVEA, the part of a theatre or amphitheatre occupied by the row of seats

CELLA, sanctuary of a temple, usually in the centre of the building

CHIAROSCURO, distribution of light

and shade, apart from colour in a painting; rarely used as a synonym for grisaille

CIBORIUM, casket or tabernacle containing the Host

CIPOLLINO, onion-marble; a greyish marble with streaks of white or green

CIPPUS, sepulchral monument in the form of an altar; a stone marking a grave or boundary

COEMETERIUM, a cemetery

COSMATESQUE, inlay work, usually dating from the 12C–16C of the famous marbleworkers of Lazio conventionally called 'Cosmati' from the name 'Casma' frequent in their families

CRYPTOPORTICUS, a semi-underground covered portico used in Roman architecture for the construction of terraces or as a covered market

CUNEUS, wedge-shaped block of seats in an antique theatre

CYCLOPEAN, the term applied to walls of unmortared masonry, older than the Etruscan civilization, and attributed by the ancients to the giant Cyclopes

DAUNII, ancient inhabitants of Apulia, a fraction of the Iapigi (the others being the Mesapii and Peucitii), who came from the Illrian (east) shore of the Adriatic

DECUMANUS, the main street of a Roman town running parallel to its longer axis

DIPTERAL, temple surrounded by a double peristyle

DIPTYCH, painting or ivory tablet in two sections

DOLIUM (pl. *dolia*), a very large ceramic jar, like the Greek pithos, used for storage of wine, water, grain, etc. The Villanovans and Etruscans often used dolia for cremation burials. The width of the mouth of the jar ranges from 40cm to 80cm; the overall height anywhere from 1m to 1.5m.

DOLMEN, a prehistoric monument (possibly a tomb) made up of two or more upright stones supporting a horizontal stone slab

DUOMO, cathedral

ENTABLATURE, the continuous horizontal element above the capital (consisting of architrave, frieze, and cornice) of a classical building

ENNEASTYLE, temple with a portico of nine columns at the end

EPHEBOS, Greek youth under training (military or university)

ETRUSCAN, of, relating to, or characteristic of Etruria, an ancient country in central Italy, its inhabitants, or their language

EXEDRA, semicircular recess in a Byzantine church

EXULTET, an illuminated scroll

EX-VOTO, tablet or small painting expressing gratitude to a saint; a votive offering (from the Latin, 'according to a vow')

FAUCES, the entrance passage of a Roman house (well seen at Herculaneum)

FICTILE, moulded of earth, clay, or other soft material

FORUM, open space in a town serving as a market or meeting-place

FRIGIDARIUM, room for cold baths in a Roman bath

FUMAROLA, volcanic spurt of vapour (usually sulphurous) emerging from the ground

GRAFFITI, design on a wall made with iron tool on a prepared surface, the design showing in white. Also used loosely to describe scratched designs or words on walls

HEPTASTYLE, temple with a portico of seven columns at the end

HERM (pl. *hermae*), quadrangular pillar decreasing in girth towards the ground, surmounted by a bust

HEXASTYLE, temple with a portico of six columns at the end

HISTORIATED, adorned with figurative painting or sculpture, usually comprising a narrative

HYPOGEUM, subterranean excavation for the interment of the dead (usually Etruscan)

ICONOSTASIS, a screen or partition that divides the public part of a church from that reserved for the clergy

INTARSIA, inlay of wood, marble, or metal

KORE, maiden

KOUROS, boy; archaic male figure

KRATER, antique mixing-bowl, conical in shape with rounded base

KYLIX, wide shallow vase with two handles and short stem

LARGO, an urban space resulting from the intersection of two or more streets or from the widening of a single street

LAURA, a monastery of the Eastern church

LOGGIA, covered gallery or balcony, usually preceding a larger building

LUNETTE, semicircular space in a vault or ceiling, often decorated with a painting or relief

MATRONEUM, gallery reserved for women in early Christian churches

MENHIR, a single upright monolith, usually of prehistoric origin

MESAPII, ancient inhabitants of Apulia, a fraction of the Iapigi (the others being the Daunii and Peucitii), who came from the Illyrian (east) shore of the Adriatic

METOPE, panel between two triglyphs on the frieze of a Doric temple

MITHRAEUM, a shrine of Mithras, a Persian sun-god worshiped in imperial Rome

MONOFORUM, a single-light window, without subdivisions

NARTHEX, vestibule of a Christian basilica

NAUMACHIA, a mock naval combat for which the arena of an amphitheatre was flooded

NYMPHAEUM, a sort of summer house in the gardens of baths, palaces, etc., originally a temple of the Nymphs, decorated with statues of those goddesses, and often containing a fountain

OCTASTYLE, a portico with eight columns

ODEION, a concert hall, usually in the shape of a Greek theatre, but roofed

OECUS (pl. *oeci*), generic term used to describe a room in a Roman building

OINOCHOE, wine-jug usually of elongated shape for dipping wine out of a krater

OPISTHODOMOS, the enclosed rear part of a temple

OPUS ALEXANDRINUM, mosaic design of black and red geometric figures on a white ground

OPUS INCERTUM, masonry of small irregular stones in mortar

OPUS MUSIVUM, mosaic decoration with cubes of glass (usually on walls or vaults)

OPUS QUADRATUM, masonry of large rectangular blocks without mortar; in *Opus Etruscum* the blocks are placed alternately lengthwise and endwise

OPUS RETICULATUM, masonry arranged in squares or diamonds so that the mortar joints make a network pattern

OPUS SECTILE, mosaic or paving of thin slabs of coloured marble cut in geometrical shapes

OPUS SPICATUM, masonry or paving of small bricks arranged in a herringbone pattern

OPUS TESSALLATUM, mosaic formed entirely of square tesserae

OPUS VERMICULATUM, mosaic with tesserae arranged in lines following the contours of the design

OSCHI, a nationality born of the fusion of the Samnites with the Opici following the elimination of Etruscan power in the second half of the 5C BC

PALAZZO, any dignified and important building

PALIOTTO, a vestment, hanging, or covering of any material that covers the front part of a Christian altar

PANTOKRATOR, the Almighty

PEDIMENT, gable above the portico of a classical building

PELIKE, a jug with round belly, narrow neck, and two handles

PERIBOLOS, a precinct, but often archaeologically the circuit round it

PERIPTEROS, a porch. A peripteral building (temple) is one that is surrounded by a single row of columns on all four sides

PERISTYLE, court or garden surrounded by a columned portico

PEUCITII, ancient inhabitants of Apulia, a fraction of the Iapigi (the others being the Daunii and Mesapii), who came from the Illyrian (east) shore of the Adriatic

PIETA, group of the Virgin mourning the dead Christ

PINACOTECA, an art gallery specialised in the exhibition of painting

PISCINA, Roman tank; a basin for an officiating priest to wash his hands before Mass

PITHOS, large pottery vessel

PLEISTOCENE, the earlier part of the Quaternary period (c 1.8 million years ago) or the corresponding system of rocks

PLUTEUS, a low wall that encloses the space between column bases in a row of columns

PODIUM, a continuous base or plinth supporting columns, and the lowest row of seats in the cavea of a theatre or amphitheatre

POLYPTYCH, painting or tablet in more than three sections

PREDELLA, small painting attached below a large altarpiece

PRESEPIO, literally, crib or manger. A group of statuary of which the central subject is the infant Jesus in the manger

PRONAOS, porch in front of the cella of a temple

PROPYLON, Propylaea. Entrance gate to a temenos; in plural form when there is more than one door

PROSKENION, the area before the stage of a Greek theatre

PROSTYLE, edifice with free-standing columns, as in a portico

PROTHESIS, the Byzantine rite of setting forth of the oblation, or the chamber north of the sanctuary where this is done

PROTHYRUM, Greek: a vestibule or space before a door or gate. Latin: a gate or railing before the door itself

PSEUDODIPTERAL, a temple with a double peristyle at the front and back

PSEUDOPERISTYLE, a false peristyle

PULVIN, cushion stone between the capital and the impost block

PUTTO, figure of a child sculpted or painted, usually nude

QUADRIGA, four-horsed chariot

RHYTON, drinking-horn usually ending in an animal's head

SAMNITE, of, relating to, or characteristic of an ancient people, an offshoot of the Sabines, in south-central Italy

SITULA, water-bucket

SKENE, the stage of a Greek theatre

SKYPHOS, a squat stemless cup with two opposing, rim oriented handles. A form particular to Athenian potters

STAMNOS, Big-bellied vase with two small handles at the sides, closed by a lid

STELE, Upright stone bearing a monumental inscription

STEREOBATE, basement of a temple or other building

STRIGIL, bronze scraper used by the Romans to remove the oil with which they had annointed themselves

STYLOBATE, basement of a columned temple or other building

SUDATORIUM, room for very hot vapour baths (to induce sweat) in a Roman bath

TELAMONES, see *Altantes*

TEMENOS, a sacred enclosure

TEMPIETTO, a small temple

TEPIDARIUM, room for warm baths in a Roman bath

TESSERA, a small cube of marble, glass, etc., used in mosaic work

TETRASTYLE, having four columns at the end

THERMAE, originally simply baths, later elaborate buildings fitted with libraries, assembly rooms, gymnasia, circuses, etc.

THOLOS, a circular building

TONDO, round painting or bas-relief

TRANSENNA, open grille or screen, usually of marble, in an early Christian church separating nave and chancel

TRICLINIUM, dining-room and reception-room of a Roman house

TRIFORA, a window divided into three lights joined by a common architectural motif

TRIGLYPH, blocks with vertical grooves on either side of a metope on the frieze of a Doric temple

TRIPTYCH, painting in three sections

TRULLO, rural dwelling of Apulia, built without mortar of local limestone and usually whitewashed, with conical roof formed of flat-pitched spiral courses of the same stone capped with diverse finials

TYMPANUM, the face of a pediment within the frame made by the upper and lower cornices; also, the space within an arch and above a lintel or a subordinate arch

VILLA, country-house with its garden; also, a Roman Farm or estate and, in some southern towns, an urban park

The terms Quattrocento, Cinquecento (abbreviated in Italy '400, '500), etc., refer not the 14C and 15C, but to the 'fourteen-hundreds' and 'fifteen-hundreds', i.e. the 15C and 16C, etc.

THE GEOLOGICAL DEVELOPMENT OF SOUTHERN ITALY

By Werner Heinitz

The topographical map of Italy shows that the Italian peninsula is built around a spine of mountain chains which extend south to the tip of the peninsula and which reach remarkable heights, bordered in the east by a parallel plain. The topography of the peninsula is the result of mountain-building processes that began in the Mesozoic era, and that are still active today, as the frequent earthquakes (Eboli, November 1980) and the active volcanoes of southern Italy demonstrate. Since the beginning of this century, many attempts have been made to explain the geological development of the region, but not all the problems have yet been solved.

Southern Italy is made up of four geological units: the true southern Apennines, the Calabrian massif, the Apulian platform, and the numerous volcanoes. The true southern Apennines stretch from Abruzzo in the north, to a line which runs from Sibari to Belvedere Marittimo in the south. The rocks that appear in this mountain chain are the remains of an ancient ocean floor. This ocean covered large areas of southern Italy in the Jurassic period (195–140 million years ago). Its floor was composed mainly of sedimentary rock, a rock resulting from the consolidation of loose sediment that has accumulated in layers. From west to east it had the following structure: Deep Basin (sedimentary rock deposited in deep water), Campano-Lucanian Platform (limestone, dolomite, etc., sediments deposited in shallow water), Lagonegro Basin (sediments deposited in deep water), Abruzzo-Campania Platform (shallow water sediments), Molise Basin (limestone, clay, float debris), Apulian Platform (limestone etc.). This ocean bed went through a series of complicated developments, the main one being a strong horizontal constriction. The reason for this squeeze is to be found in the position of Italy.

The predominant theory of the Earth's structure interprets the continents as plates that float like icebergs on a viscous substratum. This substratum is moved by so-called convection currents, and the continents move with it. Italy now lies at the point where the African plate, which is drifting north-east, pushes against the European plate. The result is a strong horizontal constriction causing rock units, which normally lie side by side, to come together like playing cards which are pushed together. These movements happen frequently as part of mountain-building processes (*orogenesis*) which last for several million years. The result of such movements is a complicated mountain chain where rock units are superimposed, the kind of structure that exists in the southern Apennines.

During the Jurassic era the whole ocean region was lowered, as is demonstrated by the presence of sediments deposited in deeper water. This development ended in the Middle Cretaceous period (90 million years ago), when parts of the Abruzzo-Campanian and the Apulian Platforms were raised. This process of elevation had its climax in the Upper Cretaceous period (88–65 million years ago), when the central units of these platforms emerged above sea-level. The edges, however, sank rapidly and were covered with the debris of the central units. During the Upper Tertiary period (22.5–5 million years ago) the whole region sank, and the true orogenesis started. It began in the west, where the deep basin was raised. As a result of this action, rock units of the deep ocean basin lying in the west were thrust over units of platforms in the east. The process shifted east during the Tertiary period (65–1.8 million years ago).

It is possible to distinguish three different phases in the orogenesis. Initially the ancient basins and platforms were raised and built up into a mountain chain by horizontal constriction. New basins developed at the edge of the newly-formed mountain chain, and the mountains shed debris into the newly-formed basins. In the Middle Pliocene era (3 million years ago) the westernmost part of the Apulian Platform sank, forming the Bradanic Trough, which is still detectable today in the long plain east of the Southern Apennines. In that trough, covered by the sea until one million years ago, the debris of the Southern Apennines was deposited next to limestone and clay.

The last large-scale movements, responsible for the present shape of the southern Apennines, began in the Late Pliocene epoch (3 million years ago). The movements formed two main faults (fractures or zones of fracture, along which the sides have moved relative to one another and parallel to the fracture) one parallel to the southern Apennines (north-west–south-east) and the other perpendicular to them (north-east–south-west). These faults are still active zones of weakness in the Earth's crust, as was shown by the severe earthquake in the region of Eboli in November 1980. The active volcanic zones of southern Italy also lie on these fault lines.

The main part of Calabria consists of a large mound of rocks of the Upper Palaeozoic age (c 280 million years old). The central part is made up of two large masses of granite, one in the Sila, the other at Serra San Bruno. Round these granite masses lay gneisses and phyllites, both rocks the appearance of which was changed by high temperatures and pressures. The mound stood largely above sea level during the Mesozoic era but in the Jurassic period (195 million years ago) much of the land mass was submerged, and in the Upper Cretaceous epoch (88 million years ago) it was completely covered by sea. The granite and the rock units that occur with it yield to younger sediments at the edge.

The volcanic regions of southern Italy are the zone of Roccomonfina and the Phlegraean Fields, north of Naples; and Vesuvius and Monte Vulture, further south. Today only the Phlegraean Fields and Vesuvius show volcanic activity.

The little-known volcanic region of Roccamonfina lies c 140km south-east of Rome, next to the Rome–Naples highway and autostrada. Today only the crater wall of Monte Frascara (933m) exists; this is open to the east. Within the wall are two intrusive domes: Monte Santa Croce and Monte Lattani. Extinct today, the last known eruption in this volcanic zone took place in 276 BC and was reported by the Roman historian Paulus Orosius who lived in the 5C AD.

The Phlegraean Fields cover an area of about 150 sq km and extend from Naples in the south to the beach of Limola Cuma in the north. They are part of the Campanian plain and encompass more than 50 known centres of eruption. To understand the origin of this large volcanic area it is necessary to look at its geological situation. The Tyrrhenian sea, between the gulf of Genoa and the straits of Messina, formed a mainland in the Tertiary period (65–1.8 million years ago). East of it lay the Apenninic sea mentioned above. During the orogenesis of the Apennines this mainland sank and was covered by the sea. Parts of the Earth's crust were dragged down into lower regions and, melted there by high temperatures and pressures, forming magma (a mobile rock material from which igneous rocks are thought to have been derived by solidification and related processes), which then ascended along zones of weakness in the Earth's crust.

The volcanism of the Phlegraean Fields is a result of the subsidence of the

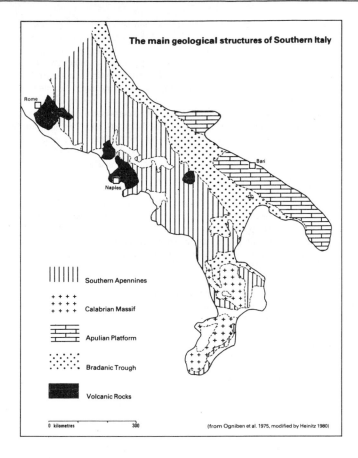

The main geological structures of Southern Italy

|||||| Southern Apennines

+ + + +
+ + + + Calabrian Massif
+ + + +

Apulian Platform

Bradanic Trough

Volcanic Rocks

0 kilometres 300

(from Ogniben et al. 1975, modified by Heinitz 1980)

Campanian Basin. There, the two fault lines of southern Italy cut across one another. The subsidence of the coastal region near Naples is still in progress. The volcanism of the Phlegraean Fields started in the Pliocene epoch (5–1.8 million years ago) and is still active today. The rocks produced by the several volcanoes have a thickness which varies from 1800m in the centre of the area to 250m in Naples. The magma chamber of the volcanic region lies c 3–4km below the Earth's surface.

It is impossible to describe all the volcanic phenomena of the Phlegraean Fields and so only three very spectacular places will be dealt with here. These are: Monte Nuovo, the Solfatara of Pozzuoli, and the Macellum (or Serapeum) of Pozzuoli.

Monte Nuovo, which rises to 133m above sea-level, is the youngest volcano of the area and was formed by an eruption in 1538. The volcano consists only of ashes, for no lava flows occured.

The crater of the Solfatara is today the most active volcano on the Italian mainland, after Vesuvius. It extends over an area of 2.2sq km. Twenty-five fields of fumaroles (vents from which gases and vapours are emitted, characteristic of a late stage of volcanic activity) are known in the area, nine of them in the crater itself.

The interior of the crater consists of lightly packed ashes, so that the soil sounds hollow if you stamp your foot. In the middle of the crater are depressions in which the muddy ground-water boils because of the high temperature of the fumaroles. Sometimes a mud volcano is formed: the mud starts to boil violently, and if the temperature of the fumarole increases, mud particles may be thrown out and deposited at the edge of the hollow. The temperature of the gases expelled, steam, carbon dioxide and hydrogen sulphide, is about 100°C and the sulphur sublimates at the edges of the fumaroles. A phenomenon often demonstrated by guides is the apparent increase of the steam activity if a lighted cigarette or something similar is held next to a vent. The activity is not really increasing, but the overheated steaming gases condense on the smoke particles and become visible. The same phenomenon can be repeated at every steam well in the world.

An excellent example of vertical movement above a magma chamber is provided by the Macellum of Pozzuoli. The three intact columns, 12.60m high (as well as the stouter, broken columns), are smooth and undamaged up to a height of 3.60m while in the 2.70m above this they have been bored by numerous molluscs. Archaeological evidence proves that the Macellum was intact up to the year 205 AD. In the following centuries it was covered up to 3.60m by waste and in the 10C the whole complex sank 5.60m. It was covered by water up to this height, and molluscs lived above the bed of waste. Later, the area rose again, the maximum height being reached in the 16C. After the eruption that formed Monte Nuovo, the whole region sank again—a movement which continues today.

The most notorious volcano is Mount Vesuvius near Naples, which reaches an altitude of 1281m and covers an area of about 480sq km. Vesuvius is a typical twin volcano. The outer wall, Monte Somma, is the remainder of a 4km wide crater which collapsed after the famous eruption of AD 79 which destroyed Pompeii and Herculaneum. The true Vesuvius emerged within the caldera of Monte Somma.

Vesuvius and Monte Somma are the most thoroughly known volcanoes in the world, their development having been studied since Roman times. The magma chamber of Monte Somma Vesuvius lies at a depth of 5–6km, according to current estimates. The volcanic activity started about 10,000 years ago. Periods of frequent eruption alternated with periods of absolute tranquillity that sometimes lasted more than 2000 years. Before the disastrous eruption of AD 79 the Monte Somma volcano had been quiet for more than 1200 years: only a few scientists knew that it was a volcano (cf. Strabo, *Geography*, V, 4; M. Vitruvius Pollio, *de Architectura*, 11, 62). The history of this, the most famous eruption in Europe, is known through a detailed description by Pliny the Younger in two letters to Tacitus. After AD 79 Monte Somma Vesuvius has been active at irregular intervals, but has seldom remained quiet very long. The last major eruption occured in 1944, but activity may start again at any moment.

PRACTICAL INFORMATION

Planning your trip

Climate

Southern Italy enjoys a typically Mediterranean climate: two rainy seasons (spring and autumn); hot, dry summers and mild winters, with mean temperatures almost always above 0°C (32°F) at the lower altitudes. The weather in the south—determined by the interaction of cool air masses from Central Europe and Turkey, humid ones from the Atlantic and warm ones from the Sahara and Central Asia—is usually warmer and sunnier than in the north, though from November to March it can be unexpectedly cool and wet, and inland in the mountains there is risk of snow and ice. In general, however, the climate is agreeable for much of the year and a succession of more than two or three bad days is unusual.

The heat in July and August is unpleasant in the towns and may be excessive on coasts sheltered from cooling breezes. Also, the region is subject to winds and to abrupt changes of temperature. The *maestrale* a cold, dry, northerly wind (whose name means 'masterful') often blows in winter; and the hot, dry North African scirocco is not uncommon in summer. The best time to visit the region is late spring (May–June) or early autumn (particularly September), when the temperature and rainfall are moderate and the droves of summer sun-seekers (Italian and foreign) that invade the coasts, especially between 15 July and 15 August, are still (or again) at home.

Formalities

Passports or visitor's cards are necessary for all British travellers entering Italy and must bear the photograph of the holder. American travellers must carry passports. British passports valid for ten years are issued at the Passport Office, Clive House, Petty France, London SW1, or by regional offices, or may be obtained for an additional fee through any tourist agent. American passports are issued by the passport offices located in most cities, or may be obtained for an additional fee through any travel agent. No visa is required for a British, US, or Canadian citizen holding a valid passport unless he or she expects to stay in Italy more than 90 days and/or to study or seek employment. Citizens of other countries and British or American travellers wishing to stay more than 90 days should check current visa requirements with the nearest Italian consulate before departure. Italian law requires travellers to carry some form of identification at all times.

Visitor registration

All foreign visitors to Italy must register with the police within three days of arrival. If you are staying at a hotel, this formality is attended to by the management. If staying with friends or in a private home, you must register in person at the nearest police station. For information or help (including interpreters), call the visitors' assistance numbers in Rome: 06 461950 or 06 486609.

Customs and duty free

Luggage may be examined on entering and leaving Italy. Free entry is allowed for personal effects (clothing, books, camping and household equipment, fishing tackle, one pair of skis, two tennis racquets, one portable typewriter or laptop computer, one portable radio, one tape or CD player with ten tapes/CDs, two still cameras with ten rolls of film for each camera, one movie/video camera with ten rolls of film/tapes, binoculars, personal jewellery, 400 cigarettes and a quantity of cigars or pipe tobacco not exceeding 1.1lb or 0.5kg), as long as they are not sold, given away, or traded. A maximum of two bottles of wine and one bottle of hard liquor, 4.4lbs (2kg) of coffee, 6.6lbs (3kg) of sugar and 2.2lbs (1kg) of cocoa per person may be brought in duty free. Overseas travellers arriving in Italy after visiting other countries are allowed to carry with them souvenirs (including 0.5 litre of perfume) up to a total value of $500, making only a verbal declaration.

Regulations on purchases abroad

There are no restrictions on gifts purchased in Italy except for antiques and works of art. These require the authorisation of the Ministero dei Beni Culturali e Ambientali.

All **EU subjects** must comply with EU limits:- Cigarettes 800; Cigarillos 400; Cigars 200; Smoking Tobacco 1kg; Spirits 10 litres; intermediate products 20 litres (e.g. port and sherry); wine 90 litres (of which not more than 60 litres sparkling); Beer 110 litres. These are guide levels and greater quantities may be deemed not to be for personal use.

US Citizens may bring back to the US duty free $400 worth of goods purchased abroad. The goods must accompany the traveller. A flat rate of 10 per cent is assessed on the next $1000 worth of goods purchased. Parcels containing gifts may be sent from abroad to the US duty free, providing the total value of such parcels received by one person on one day does not exceed $50. Each package should be marked 'Unsolicited Gift'. The amount paid and the contents of the package should be declared.

Canadian Residents returning from a trip abroad can qualify for personal exemption, though all articles acquired abroad, whether purchased or received as gifts, or purchased at a duty-free shop abroad or in Canada, must be declared on return to Canada.

Pets. Travellers entering Italy with a dog or a cat must have a veterinarian's certificate stating that the animal is in good health and has been vaccinated against rabies between 20 days and 11 months before entry into Italy. It must also give the breed, age, sex and colour of the pet and the name and address of the owner. The certificate is valid for 30 days. The forms are available from all Italian diplomatic and consular representatives and from the Italian travel office. Dogs must be on a leash or muzzled when in public. Customs officials may require a health examination of any pet if they suspect it is ill or has come directly from tropical regions.

Tourist information

Information may be obtained in the **UK** from the Italian State Tourist Board, 1 Princes Street, London W1R 8AY (tel. 0171 408 1254, fax 0171 493 6695); in the **USA** from the Italian Government Tourist Board, c/o Italian Trade Commission, 499 Park Avenue Avenue, New York, NY 10022 (tel. 212 843 6885, fax 212 843 6886); the Italian Government Travel Office, 401 North Michigan Avenue, Suite 3030, Chicago 1, IL 60611 (tel. 312 644 0996, fax 312 644 30197); or the Italian Government Travel Office, 12400 Wilshire Blvd, Suite 550, Los Angeles, CA 90025 (tel. 310 820 0098, fax 310 820 6357); and in **Canada** from the Italian Government Travel Office, 1 Place Ville Marie, Suite 1914, Montreal, Québec H3B 3M9 (tel. 514 866 7667, fax 514 866 0975). The London office issues free an invaluable *Traveller's Handbook* (in the USA, *General Information for Travellers to Italy*) usually revised every year.

Travel agents

Travel agents sell travel tickets and book accommodation and many offer inclusive tours and charter trips to Italy. In **Britain** tours are organised by Martin Randall Travel, Fine Art Courses Ltd, Pilgrim Air, Prospect Music and Art Tours Ltd, Special Tours, Swan Hellenic, Italian Escapades, and Italiatour, among others. International Chapters, 102 St John's Wood Terrace, London NW8 6PL, tel. 0171 722 9560, specialises in holidays to Italy. The many **North American** agents offering individual and group tours to Italy include The Travel Bug, 220 Montgomery Street, Suite 1034, San Francisco, CA 94104, tel. 415 981 1331 (toll free 1 800 221 2264), fax 415 296 0714; Donna Franca Tours, 470 Commonwealth Avenue, Boston, MA 02215, tel. 617 375 9400 (toll free 1 800 225 6290); and Central Holidays, 206 Central Avenue, Jersey City, NJ 07307, tel. 201 475 4559 (toll free 1 800 935 5000), fax 201 963 0966; Los Angeles Office 577 W. Century Blvd, Los Angeles, CA 90045, tel. 1 800 CHT WEST.

Disabled travellers

All new public buildings are now obliged by law to provide easy access and specially designed facilities for the disabled. Unfortunately the conversion of historical buildings, including many museums and monuments, is made problematic by structural impediments such as narrow sidewalks (which make mobility difficult for everyone). Barriers therefore continue to exist in many cases. Hotels that are able to give hospitality to the disabled are indicated in the annual list of hotels published by the local tourist boards. Airports and railway stations provide assistance and certain trains are equipped to transport wheelchairs. Access is allowed to the centre of towns (normally closed to traffic) for cars with disabled drivers or passengers, and special parking places are reserved for them. For further information, contact the tourist board in the city of interest.

Getting to Southern Italy

By air

Direct air services operate throughout the year between London and Naples and from several British and North American cities to Milan and Rome, where connections may be made with internal lines to Bari, Brindisi, Lamezia, Pescara, and Reggio Calabria. The carriers offering non-stop service between Britain and Italy are British Airways (tel. 0181 897 4000), Alitalia (tel. 0171 602 7111) and Meridiana (tel. 0171 839 2222). British Midland, Air France, Lufthansa and Sabena offer flights connecting through Paris, Frankfurt, and Brussels, respectively. These may cost less than the direct flights. Alitalia (tel. 1 800 223 5730) flies non-stop from New York (JFK or Newark) to Rome or Milan, from Boston and Chicago to Rome and from Los Angeles to Rome or Milan; American from Chicago to Milan; Canadian from Toronto and Montreal to Rome; Continental (tel. 1 800 2310856) from New York to Rome; Delta (1 800 241 4141) from New York to Milan and Rome; TWA (tel. 1 800 8924141) from New York to Rome and Milan and from Los Angeles to Rome; and United (tel. 1 800 5382929) from Washington DC to Rome. British Airways, Air France, KLM, and Sabena offer flights connecting through London, Paris, Amsterdam, and Brussels. These are often more economical than the direct flights. Charter flights are also now run to most of the main cities in Italy; the fare often includes hotel accommodation. See your travel agent for details.

Baggage allowance. Free baggage allowances vary from one airline to another. On Alitalia, for example, the following rules apply. On international flights except USA/Canada, allowances for checked baggage are determined by weight: 'P' and 'F' tickets, 40kg (88 lb); 'J' and 'C' tickets, 30kg (66lb); 'Y' tickets 20kg (44lb); in addition to the above, all passengers may carry on one bag maximum 45 x 35 x 18cm (18 x 14 x 7 in) and 5kg (11lb). There is no baggage allowance for infants not occupying a reserved seat. On flights to/from the USA and Canada, the allowance is by piece: 'P' and 'J' tickets, two pieces, each maximum 158cm (62in) and 32kg (70lb), plus one carry-on maximum 45 x 35 x 18cm (18 x 14 x 7in) and 5kg (11lb). Children under two years of age are allowed one piece maximum 115cm (45 in) and 5kg (11lb) plus one foldable pram/stroller.

By rail

The principal southern Italian towns are linked with Britain by a variety of rail routes, the most direct being from London to Paris, Turin, and Rome, or via Paris, Milan, and Ancona. Both take c 16hr. These services have sleeping cars (first class: single or double compartment; second class: three-berth compartments) and couchettes (seats converted into couches at night: 1st class: four; 2nd class: six) and connect with trains directed to the major southern cities. Information and tickets on the Italian State Railways (but not seat reservations) may be obtained in Great Britain from Citalia, Marco Polo House, 3–5 Lansdowne Road, Croydon, Surrey CR9 1LL (tel. 0181 686 0677), and Wasteels Travel, adjacent to Platform 2, Victoria Station, London SW1V 1JT (tel. 0171 834 7066); and in North America from CIT, 342 Madison Avenue, Suite 207, New York, NY 10173, tel. 212 6971482 (schedules), 212 697 2100 (rail pass information), 1 800 223 7987 (to order tickets only), or 1 800 CIT TOUR (general information), fax 212 697 1394; Los Angeles Office, 6033 West Century Blvd, Los Angeles, CA 90045, tel. 310 338 8616, fax 310 670 4269; Montreal Office, 1450 City Councillors Street, Suite 750, Montreal H3A 2E6, tel. 514 8459101, fax 514 845 9137; Toronto Office, 111 Avenue Road, Suite 808, Toronto M5R 3JH, tel. 416 927 7712, fax 416 927 7206.

By bus

A bus service operates in two days between London (Victoria Coach Station) and Rome (Piazza della Repubblica) via Dover, Paris, Mont Blanc, Aosta, Turin, Genoa, Milan, Bologna and Florence, daily from June to September, and once or twice a week for the rest of the year. Reductions are available for students. Information in London from the National Express office at Victoria Coach Station, from local National Express agents, and in Italy from SITA offices.

By car

The easiest approaches to Italy by road are the motorways through the Mont Blanc, San Bernard, Frejus or Mont Cenis tunnels, or over the Brenner Pass. British drivers taking their own cars by any of the routes across France, Belgium, Luxembourg, Switzerland, Germany and Austria need the vehicle registration book, a valid national driving licence, an international insurance certificate (the 'green card', valid for 45 days) and a nationality plate (fixed to the rear of the vehicle so as to be illuminated by the tail lamps). A Swiss Motorway Pass is needed for Switzerland, and can be obtained from the Royal Automobile Club, the Automobile Association, or at the Swiss border. Motorists who are not owners of the vehicle must possess the owner's permit for its use abroad. Foreign drivers hiring a car in Italy need only a valid national driver's licence.

The continental rule of the road is to drive on the right and overtake on the left. The provisions of the respective highway codes in the countries of transit, though similar, have important variations, especially with regard to priority, speed limits, and pedestrian crossings. Membership of the Automobile Association (tel. 01256 20123), or the Royal Automobile Club (membership enquiries, tel. 0345 33 1133; insurance, tel. 0345 121345; route information, tel. 0345 333 222) entitles motorists to many of the facilities of affiliated societies on the continent.

By sea

Adriatic Italy is connected by car-ferry and hydrofoil to Greece (Patras, Igoumenitsa, Corfu), Albania (Durres, Vlore), and Croatia (Split). Information and reservations from Società Adriatica di Navigazione, Zattere 1141, Venice (tel. 041 781611, fax 041 781894; branch offices in Ancona, Bari, Brindisi, Corfu, Durres, Igoumenitsa, Patras, Split, Trieste); Misano Alta Velocità, Via Tunisi 10, Brindisi (tel. 0831 562043, fax 0831 562005; branch offices in Milan, Genoa, and Rome); A.K. Ventouris, L. Posidonos 73, Piraeus (tel. 01 938 9280-7, fax 01 938 9289; branch offices in Patras, Igoumenitsa, and Brindisi); Agoumidos Lines, Kapodistriou 2, Piraeus (tel. 01 412 6680, fax 01 422 0595; branch offices in Brindisi, Corfu, and Igoumenitsa); Fragline, 5a Rethymnou St, Athens (tel. 01 821 4171, fax 01 821 3095; branch offices in Brindisi, Rome, Milan, Corfu, Igoumenitsa and Patras); and Illyria Lines, 5 Ifestou St, Athens (tel. 01 964 3124, fax 01 962 7042; branch offices in Brindisi, Durres and Vlore).

On Arrival

Tourist information

The Italian State Tourist Board (Ital. ENIT, Ente Nazionale Italiano per il Turismo) has information offices at the border crossings with Austria (Valico autostradale Lupo di Brennero) and France (Casello Roverino di Ventimiglia) as well as at Milano Linate and Napoli Capodichino airports. Within Italy each 'region' has information services organized on the regional, provincial, and local levels; where possible, these have been indicated in the text. A general reorganisation of the Italian tourist authorities begun in 1983 will, when completed, lead to the concentration of resources traditionally divided between the 'Enti Provinciali del Turismo' (EPT) and the Aziende Autonome di Cura, Soggiorno e Turismo (AA) under a single authority, the Aziende di Promozione Turistica (APT). In some areas this transition has already taken place.

Money

In Italy the monetary unit is the Italian lira (pl. lire). The rate of exchange in 1995 is approximately 2500 lire to the £ sterling and 1600 lire to the U.S. dollar. Notes are issued for 1000, 2000, 5000, 10,000, 50,000 and 100,000 lire; coins, for 50, 100, 200 and 500 lire. Travellers' cheques and Eurocheques are the safest way of carrying money while travelling and most credit cards are now generally accepted in hotels, shops, and restaurants (and increasingly at petrol stations). The commission on cashing travellers' cheques can be quite high. For banking hours, see under General Information below. Money can be changed at banks, post offices, travel agencies and some hotels, restaurants and shops, though the rate of exchange can vary considerably from place to place. Exchange offices are usually open seven days a week at airports and most main railway stations. A limited amound of lire can be obtained from conductors on international trains and at certain stations. For small amounts of money, the difference between hotel and bank rates may be negligible, as banks tend to take a fixed commission on transactions.

Where to stay

Hotels

Hotels in Italy are classified in five official categories, ranging from the most expensive (*****) to the cheapest and simplest (*). In this guide a selection of hotels has been given at the beginning of each route, with a view to making planning easier. The hotels listed, regardless of their cost, have been chosen on the basis of their personality or character: all have something special about them (beautiful surroundings, distinctive atmosphere) and even the simplest are quite comfortable. They have been listed with their official star rating in order to give an indication of price. Where no hotels have been indicated at the beginning of a route, the author has felt that none merit special mention; naturally, many establishments in the area will nonetheless be capable of providing satisfactory accommodation. Throughout Italy the provincial tourist boards publish official lists of hotels giving category, price, and facilities; and ENIT distributes a free annual list of accommodation in Italy (*Annuario Alberghiero*, listing hotels, residences, and camp sites), in one volume. Local tourist offices (APT/EPT in the larger towns, *Pro Loco* elsewhere) help travellers to find accommodation on the spot; nevertheless it is advisable to book well in advance, especially in July and August. A deposit should be sent to confirm the booking. Hotels equipped to offer hospitality to the disabled are indicated in the tourist boards' hotel lists.

More information about hotels and restaurants can be found in specialised publications such as the Michelin red guide to Italy (*Italia* revised annually) or, in Italian, *Alberghi e ristoranti* and *Guida Rapida d'Italia* (five volumes, of which numbers four and five cover the south), published by the Touring Club Italiano. The hotel and restaurant guides produced by the weekly newsmagazine *L'Espresso* are now issued (in a reduced single volume) in English every year. Other specialised guides include the *Charming Small Hotel Guide: Italy* (Duncan Petersen); or in Italian, *Gli Alberghi del Buongustaio* (Le Guide della Fenice), *Alberghi di Bell' Italia* (Giorgio Mondadori) and *Viaggiare Bene in Italia* (Pirelli/Mondadori).

Charges vary according to class, season, services available and locality. In all hotels the service charges are included in the rates, sales tax is added and the total charge is exhibited on the back of the door of the hotel room. Breakfast carries an extra charge, so when booking a room always specify if you want breakfast or not. Hotels are now obliged by law (for tax purposes) to issue a receipt to customers: you can be fined if you leave the premises without this document.

Camping sites

Camping is well organised throughout Italy. An international camping carnet is useful. Annual lists of camping sites are published by the APT/EPT (together with their hotel list), giving details of services provided, size of the site and so on. Sites are divided into official categories by stars, from the most expensive (****) to the simplest and cheapest (*). Their classification and rates must be displayed at the main office. Full details of the sites in Italy are published annually by the Touring

Club Italiano and Federcampeggio in *Campeggi e Villaggi Turistici in Italia*. The national headquarters of the Federazione Italiana del Campeggio, at 11 Via Vittorio Emanuele, 50041 Calenzano (Firenze), tel. 055 882391, fax 055 882 5918, has an information office and booking service.

Other forms of accommodation

A new type of hotel, called a *residence*, has recently been introduced into Italy. Often in a building of historic interest, such as a castle or monastery, this sort of establishment tends to have only a few rooms and can be a delightful place to stay. Residences are listed separately in the tourist boards' hotel lists, with their prices. Comfortable accommodation at very reasonable prices is offered by religious organisations in some cities; a complete listing is available from local tourist boards. Agriturismo, which provides accommodation in farmhouses in the countryside, is highly recommended for travellers with their own transport and for families. Terms vary greatly, from bed-and-breakfast to self-contained flats, and some farms require a stay of a minimum number of days. Cultural or recreational activities are sometimes also provided. Villas and farmhouses can be rented for longer periods through specialised agencies: details from your travel agent.

The Associazione Italiani Alberghi per la Gioventù (Italian Youth Hostels Association), Via Cavour 44, 00184 Rome (tel. 06 487 1152) runs 52 hostels, which are listed in its free annual guide. A membership card of the AIG or the International Youth Hostel Federation is required for access to Italian Youth Hostels. Details from the Youth Hostels Association, Trevelyan House, 8 St Stephen's Hill, St. Albans, Herts AL1 2DY and from the National Offices of American Youth Hostels Inc., Washington DC 20013-7613.

Food and drink

Restaurants

Italian food is usually good and inexpensive; a detailed description of southern cuisine follows. Generally speaking, the least pretentious *ristorante or trattoria* (there is now no difference between the two) provides the best value. In this guide a selection of restaurants has been given at the beginning of each route. The restaurants listed have been chosen for the quality and distinction of their cuisine and the extent of their wine lists; even the simplest are quite good. Like hotels, they have been graduated by price (from **** for the most expensive, to * for the cheapest). As a rule, the more exclusive eating places are considerably cheaper at midday. You should telephone for details *and* to reserve, as all the establishments listed provide good value for price and are likely to be crowded. Where no restaurants have been indicated at the beginning of a route, the author has felt that none merit special mention; naturally, many establishments in the area will nonetheless be capable of providing a satisfactory meal.

Restaurants are now obliged by law (for tax purposes) to issue a receipt to customers: you can be fined if you leave the premises without this document. Prices on the menu do not include a bread charge (shown separately, usually at the bottom of the page), which is added to the bill. The service charge is now almost always automatically added at the end of the bill; tipping is therefore not strictly necessary, but a few thousand lire are appreciated. Many simpler establishments do not offer a written menu, and here, although the choice is limited, the standard of cuisine is usually quite acceptable.

Several of the guides mentioned above list restaurants as well as hotels. Other specialised publications are *Guida ai Ristoranti d'Italia* (Rizzoli/Accademia Italiana della Cucina), *Ristoranti d'Italia* (De Agostini/Gambero Rosso Editore), and *Ristoranti di Bell'Italia* (Giorgio Mondadori).

Other eating places

Bars (or cafés) are open from early morning to late night and serve numerous varieties of excellent refreshments that are usually taken standing up. As a rule, you must pay the cashier first, then present your receipt to the barman in order to get served. Throughout southern Italy it has become customary to leave a small tip for the barman. If you sit at a table the charge is usually higher, and you will be given waiter service (so, you should not pay first). However, some simple bars have a few tables that can be used with no extra charge, and it is always best to ask, before ordering, whether there is waiter service or not.

Naples is considered to have the best coffee in Italy. *Caffè* (or *espresso* black coffee) can be ordered *alto* or *lungo* (diluted), *corretto* (with a liquor), or *macchiato* (with hot milk). A *cappuccino* is an espresso with more hot milk than a *caffè macchiato* and is generally considered a breakfast drink. A glass of hot milk with a dash of coffee in it, called *latte macchiato* is another early-morning favourite. In summer, many customers take *caffè freddo* (iced coffee).

Gelato (ice cream) is always best in a *gelateria* where it is made on the spot. *Panini* (sandwiches) are made with a variety of cold meats, fish, cheeses, or vegtables, particularly melanzane (aubergines) or zucchine fried in vegetable oil; vegetarians may also ask for a simple sandwich of *insalata e pomodoro* (lettuce and tomato). *Pizze* (a popular and cheap food throughout Italy), *arancini* (rice croquettes with cheese or meat inside), and other snacks are served in a *pizzeria, rosticceria* and *tavola calda*. A *vinaio* often sells wine by the glass and simple food for very reasonable prices. Sandwiches are made up on request at *pizzicherie* and *alimentari* (grocery shops), and *fornai* (bakeries) often sell delicious individual pizze, focaccie or schiacciate (bread with oil and salt), cakes and so on.

Southern Italian cooking

In Naples and throughout southern Italy, pasta is an essential part of most meals. Pasta is classified according to its composition and shape. A distinction is drawn between *pasta comune* (spaghetti, rigatoni, lasagne and so on) produced industrially and made of a simple flour and water paste, and *pasta all'uovo* (tortellini, ravioli and so on), made with an egg batter.

The forms that pasta may assume are numberless. An ordinary Italian supermarket usually stocks about 50 different shapes, but some experts estimate that there are more that 600 shapes in all. *Pasta corta* (ie rigatoni) is much more varied than *pasta lunga* (ie spaghetti). The latter may be tubular (like ziti or macaroni), or threadlike (spaghetti, vermicelli, capellini); smooth (fettucce, tagliatelle, linguine), ruffled (lasagne ricce), or twisted (fusilli). Pasta corta comes in a limitless variety of shapes—shells (conchiglie), stars (stelle), butterflies (farfalle) and so on—and may be smooth (penne) or fluted (rigatoni).

The differences of shape translate into differences of flavour, even when the pasta is made from the same dough, or by the same manufacturer. The reason for this is that the relation between the surface area and the weight of the pasta varies from one shape to another, causing the sauce to adhere in different ways and to different degrees. But even when pasta is served without a sauce, experts claim to perceive considerable differences in flavour, due to the fact that different shapes cook in different ways.

Naples is the classic home of *pastasciutta*, which is quite different from the *pasta fresca* preferred in northern Italy. The latter is usually home-made, from a dough composed of flour, eggs, and just a little water; and it is soft and pliable both before and after cooking.

Pastasciutta is generally factory-made, from a simple flour and water paste that is rolled into sheets, cut and moulded in the desired shape and then air dried. It is hard and brittle when bought, and when correctly cooked it remains *al dente* (chewy; never soggy), additional moisture being provided by the sauce. An early American appreciator of pastasciutta was Thomas Jefferson, who in 1787 brought a spaghetti-making machine from Italy to the United States.

A short history of pasta

Whereas the invention of egg pasta is generally credited to the Chinese, the origin of pastasciutta may well be Italian. The Etruscan Tomb of the Reliefs at Cerveteri, near Rome, has stucco decorations representing pasta-making tools: a board and a rolling pin for rolling out the dough, knives, even a toothed cutting-wheel for making decorative borders. References to lasagne may be found in Cicero and other Roman writers; the name itself is probably derived from the Latin *lagana* or *lasana*, a cooking pot.

By the end of the Middle Ages pasta was known throughout Italy. The fourteenth-century *Codice del l'anonimo toscano* preserved in the library of Bologna University, contains several serving suggestions; and the poet Boccaccio, in his masterpiece, the *Decameron* describes an imaginary land of grated parmesan cheese inhabited by people whose only pastime is the making of 'maccheroni e raviuoli'. Of course, tomato sauce was unheard of until the discovery of America: Boccaccio's contemporaries cooked their macaroni and ravioli in chicken broth and dressed them with fresh butter.

Regional dishes

Southern Italian cuisine can be very different from that of the north. The number and variety of regional dishes is so great that to describe them all in detail would require several hundred pages. What follows is therefore a brief summary.

Antipasti. *Crostini alla napoletana* are among the simplest and tastiest of all crostini. Small, thin slices of bread are covered with mozzarella, chopped anchovies and tomatoes; seasoned with salt and oregano; then lightly toasted in the oven. The *gatto* is fairly common in Neapolitan cooking, although the ingredients often change. It has little to do with the gâteaux of French haute cuisine, notwithstanding its Angevin origins. It is a humble dish, a sort of dumpling made of mashed potatoes, eggs, prosciutto, mozzarella and whatever else happens to be on hand. It is usually served piping hot.

Impepata di cozze is a simple Neapolitan dish of fresh mussels, poached and dressed with lemon juice, chopped parsley, and olive oil. *Mozzarella in carrozza* translates as mozzarella in a carriage. It consists of a slice of mozzarella fried between two slices of bread that are dipped in an egg batter, like French toast. *Pagnottine Santa Chiara*, as the name suggests, were invented by the nuns of Santa Chiara. They are savoury cakes made with anchovies, tomatoes, parsley, and oregano. *Panzanella alla napoletana* is a favourite salad dish made of crumbled bread, onions, tomatoes, anchovies, basil, and garlic (sometimes peppers and green olives are added)—all dressed with olive oil.

Peperoni farciti, stuffed baked peppers, is a peasant dish existing throughout the south in a variety of versions. Three common fillings are: olives, capers, parsley, and anchovies; aubergine and tomatoes; macaroni in a savoury sauce. *Taralli col pepe* are rings of crisp bread flavoured with pepper and almonds. Another version uses fennel seeds. *Zucchine a scapece* may be either an antipasto or a contorno (see below). Courgettes are sliced and fried in olive oil, then seasoned with vinegar and fresh mint leaves. Served cold.

Soups, pastas and **pizza.** *Fusilli alla napoletana* are served in a rich sauce made with meat drippings, tomatoes, onions, celery, carrots, ricotta, salame, bacon, garlic and seasoned pecorino cheese. Sometimes spaghetti or macaroni are used instead of fusilli. *Lasagne di Carnevale* is an especially rich dish, popular in Naples at Carnival time. Square lasagne are baked in a sauce containing sausages and meat balls, mozzarella, ricotta, and other cheeses, and hard-boiled eggs.

Minestra maritata, a very old, very typical Neapolitan speciality, is also known as *pignato grasso*. It is a classic winter dish consisting chiefly of beet greens or cabbage boiled with a ham bone and sausages, served hot as a soup. *Minestrone napoletano* is similar to all other Italian minestroni, with a predominance of yellow zucchine over all the other ingredients. Usually served with macaroni. *Maccheroni cacio e uova* is simply macaroni in a cheese and egg sauce, sprinkled with chopped parsley before serving. *Frittata di pasta*, or *pasta fritta*, originally a way of getting good mileage out of leftovers, is now a classic first course in its own right. Vermicelli or macaroni are seasoned with a rich sauce made with meat balls, chopped prosciutto, and cheese. The whole concoction, bound together by a few well-beaten eggs, becomes a fragrant and savoury omelette, often considered a complete meal.

Pasta e fagioli all'ischitana, a specialty of the island of Ischia, is made with spaghetti, tripolini, bucatini and linguine, or whatever leftovers one happens to have on hand. The sauce is made with lots of fresh beans, and is seasoned with hot red peppers. *Pasta alla sorrentina* adds diced scamorza cheese to the tomato sauce, to make it thick and stringy. The pasta thus seasoned is served with lots of grated caciocavallo or parmesan cheese.

Ragù alla napoletana, also known as *rrau*, is a delicious sauce for special occasions that is traditionally placed on the stove at dawn and left to simmer slowly all day. It is prepared by melting lard and ham fat in a pan, then adding slices of veal rolled around a filling of grated cheese, garlic, parsley, raisins and pine-nuts. As the sauce cooks, red wine and tomatoes are added. At the end the sauce is used to dress the pasta, while the meat rolls are served as an entrée.

Sartù is the richest of all Neapolitan dishes. Today only a few Neapolitan restaurants make it regularly, and to taste it at its best you should order it ahead of time. It is a rice pie stuffed with meat balls, sausage, chicken livers, mozzarella, mushrooms, peas, etc. Baked in a mould, it is not only tasty, but also very theatrical. *Spaghetti aglio e olio* is served in a sauce consisting of olive oil, garlic, parsley, and sometimes peperoncini, or hot red peppers. Best enjoyed after midnight.

Spaghetti alle vongole is spaghetti in a clam sauce flavoured with onions, tomatoes, cheese and aromatic herbs. When rice is used instead of spaghetti the result is *Risotto alle vongole*. *Timballo di maccheroni*, like *sartù* is a classic dish of the Neapolitan aristocracy. It gradually spread throughout the kingdom of the Two Sicilies to become one of the more characteristic dishes of southern Italy. It is made with macaroni baked in a pie with a sauce of chicken livers, mushrooms, and black truffles.

Vermicelli alla carrettiera (carters' vermicelli) belongs to a category of pasta (like *Spaghetti alla bucaniera* pirates' spaghetti, and *Maccheroni alla zappatora* (ditchdiggers' macaroni) whose names suggest that their seasoning is so strong that only he-men can be expected to cope with them. In vermicelli alla carrettiera a distinctive element is provided by the breadcrumbs that are sprinkled over the pasta instead of parmesan cheese. *Zite ripiene*, a speciality of Caserta, takes the pasta known as zite as a basic ingredient, although *conchiglie* or *lumache* (both called 'shells' in English) can also be used. The pasta is filled with diced pork, onions, salame or sausage, cheese, spices, and eggs, then covered with more cheese and baked. In a Lenten version the filling is made of ricotta, fresh basil, and other herbs.

Panzerotti, a kind of Apulian ravioli, is usually filled with anchovies, capers, and strong ricotta cheese (made from ewe's milk). *Spaghetti alla carbonara* (spaghetti with bacon, black pepper, eggs, and pecorino), and *Supplì* (rice croquettes stuffed with mozzarella cheese and minced meat) are among the specialties of Lazio; and Abruzzo is famous for *Maccheroni alla chitarra* (home-made pasta with pecorino cheese and tomatoes). *Zuppa di cardoni*, a rich, tasty dish from the Campanian hinterland, is made of cardoons (an edible thistle) cooked in chicken broth with meat balls, mozzarella, the boned chicken, and sausages. *Zuppa alla marinara* is made throughout the south with as many varieties of fish as possible, which are stewed together with clams and mussels in lots of tomato sauce, olive oil, garlic, and hot peppers.

Pizza is today at least as well known as spaghetti, and perhaps even more so. Suffice it to recall here that there is an infinite variety of pizza recipes, all based on bread dough. The secret of a successful pizza is a blazing hot oven. Only violent heat, in fact, is capable of cooking the pizza in such a way that it is soft, yet crunchy at the same time; if the oven is not hot enough, the dough becomes tough as shoe leather. A wood-fired oven is best, although it is possible to produce an acceptable pizza in an electric or gas oven.

Main courses. *Agnello pasquale* is a roast lamb seasoned with rosemary, bay leaf and sage and accompanied by tender new onions and potatoes. Considered traditional in the Easter period, it appears the year round on the menus of many restaurants. *Anguilla in umido* is a common dish in the Agro Pontino and the Caserta area, where it is still fairly easy to find eels (anguille) in the irrigation canals. The eels are cooked in tomato sauce and served on toast. *Anguilla alla griglia* is grilled and basted with a sauce of olive oil, garlic, vinegar and fresh mint leaves.

In the traditional *Baccalà alla napoletana* fillets of salt cod are first floured and fried, then stewed with tomatoes, capers, black olives, raisins, pine nuts, and, of course, garlic. *Braciola alla napoletana* is a rich dish usually reserved for special occasions. An immense slice of beef or pork is covered with chopped provolone, prosciutto, raisins, and eggs; then tightly rolled, tied with string and cooked in tomato sauce. *Cecenielli* literally means little chick-peas, but if you order cecenielli in a Neapolitan trattoria what you get is quite different: spicy little fish cooked in a flour and water paste, or served on a pizza. *Cervella alla napoletana* is brain of veal or lamb baked with capers, black olives, pepper, and breadcrumbs.

In *Coniglio all'ischitana* the delicate meat of the rabbit is cut into pieces, browned in olive oil and cooked in white wine, tomato sauce, and rosemary. *Costata alla pizzaiola* is a T-bone steak served in a tomato sauce flavoured with garlic and oregano. *Genovese* is the term used by Neapolitans to indicate a particular kind of beef stew—cooked slowly with much onion, olive oil, lard, and tomato sauce—that crept into the local culinary tradition through the colony of Genoese merchants who lived in Naples.

Polpo alla luciana: it seems that this manner of stewing octopus—with tomatoes, olive oil, garlic, and hot peppers—was developed by the wives of the fishermen of

Santa Lucia. When small octopuses are used, the dish is called *Purpetielle affocate*. *Ostriche* (oysters) and *Cozze nere* (black mussels) are specialities of Apulian cookery, as are *Tordi al solso*, thrushes cooked with fennel and bay leaves and conserved in white wine. In the mountains of Basilicata and Calabria, game dishes are plentiful, whereas in the mountainous regions of Abruzzo and Molise lamb dishes prevail. Also typical in the latter regions are *Pollo all'abruzzese* (chicken with sweet peppers), and *Trota alla brace* (grilled trout).

Vegetables. *Carciofi ripieni alla napoletana* is baked artichokes with a delicious filling of meat, mushrooms, onions, and tomatoes. *Cianfotta* is a sort of vegetable stew made with potatoes, yellow peppers, onions, tomatoes, aubergine, zucchini and celery. *Insalata di rinforzo*, a traditional Christmas dish, is a hodgepodge of cauliflower, olives, various pickled vegetables, anchovies and capers, mixed together and dressed with olive oil and vinegar. The name comes from the fact that the dish is eaten in more than one day and is continually 'reinforced' with other ingredients, which take the place of the ones eaten the day before. *Melanzane alla partenopea* is an aubergine casserole, like *Melanzane alla parmigiana* (which, despite its name, is a Campanian invention). Ingredients are aubergines, caciocavallo and parmesan cheese, tomato sauce, spices. *Peperoni in teglia alla napoletana* is yellow peppers fried in olive oil with capers and anchovies. In Basilicata and Calabria, aubergines are cooked in several different ways: *in agrodolce* (in sour wine with chocolate, cinnamon, walnuts, and raisins); *al funghetto* (baked with garlic, pepper, and oregano); or as *melanzane ripiene* (stuffed and baked).

No trip to Lazio would be complete without *Carciofi alla giudia* (tender artichokes fried crisp and sprinkled with lemon juice); and in Apulia grilled vegetables of all kinds, dressed in abundant olive oil (which here has a more aggressive flavour than the Ligurian or Tuscan oils) are often served as an entrée.

Desserts. *Coviglie* (*al caffè* or *al cioccolato*) is a traditional Neapolitan dessert much like a mousse. *Pastiera* is a classic that can be found in Campanian *pasticcerie* from November to March. It is a pie filled with fresh ricotta, grains of wheat, rice, or barley boiled in milk, candied fruit, eggs, sugar, spices and other ingredients. Some famous Neapolitan bakers make pastiera to order, packing it in such a way that it can stand up to long journeys.

Sfogliatelle are perhaps the most famous of Neapolitan breakfast pastries. There are two types, one made with a thin ribbon of crisp dough wound in tight spiral layers (*sfogliatelle ricce*) and the other a simple envelope of soft dough. Both types are filled with fresh ricotta, chopped candied fruit, cinnamon, vanilla, and other ingredients. *Sproccolati* are sun-dried figs filled with fennel seeds and preserved on wooden sticks. They are a speciality of Ravello and the Amalfi Coast. *Struffoli* a traditional Christmas dessert, has all the characteristics typical of ancient Greek sweets: it calls for very little sugar, relying for its sweetness on honey, and, to a lesser extent, on candied fruit. It comes in two shapes: the traditional cone and the more modern ring. *Susamelli*, s–shaped biscuits, were once made with flour, sesame seeds, sugar, honey, and candied orange and lemon peel. The fusion of the Italian words for sesame and honey (sesame and miele) gave rise to the name. These days, ground almonds are often substituted for the sesame seeds.

Southern Italian wines

Some southern Italian wines are universally known; others, highly popular at home, are seldom exported and may even be difficult to obtain outside their own province. The following list includes the more typical southern wines.

Southern Lazio. *Colli Albani* (dry or mellow white; the *superiore* is stronger, the *spumante* sparkling); served with antipasti, poultry and fish; *Colli Lanuvini* (dry or mellow white); served with antipasti, fish or dessert; *Cori Bianco* (dry, mellow, or sweet white); served with antipasti, poultry and desserts); *Cori Rosso* (dry red), served with poultry, pork, wildfowl; *Frascati* (dry white; the *superiore* is stronger, the *spumante* is sparkling, and the *novello* is fruity); served with antipasti, poultry, fish, desserts; *Genazzano Bianco* (mellow white), served with minestre, poultry and fish; *Genazzano Rosso* (mellow red); served with meats, cheeses and desserts; *Merlot di Aprilia* (dry red); served with roast meat and poultry, especially pork and boar; *Montecompatri Colonna* (mellow white; the *superiore* is stronger), served with antipasti and poultry; *Sangiovese di Aprilia* (dry rosé), served with pastasciutta, poultry, and mushrooms; *Trebbiano di Aprilia* (dry white), served with fish, minestre, vegetables, and cheeses; *Velletri Bianco* (dry or mellow white), served with antipasti, soups and fish; *Velletri Rosso* (dry red), served with roast meat and poultry and aged cheeses; *Zagarolo* (mellow white; the *superiore* is stronger), served with cold meats and poultry.

Campania: *Aglianico del Cilento* (dry red), served with roasted and grilled meats; *Aglianico di Guardia Sanframondi* (or *Guardiolo*; dry red; the *riserva*, aged two years, has a lighter bouquet and smoother flavour), served with roasted and grilled meat; *Aglianico di Sant'Agata dei Goti* (robust red rich in tannins; aged at least two years, *riserva* aged three years), served with roasts and stews; *Aversa Asprino* (dry, fruity white) served with fish or vegetables; *Aversa Asprino Spumante* (dry, sparkling white), served as an aperitif or with pastry; *Barbera di Castel San Lorenzo* (dry red), served with meats and aged cheeses; *Capri Bianco* (dry white), served with antipasti, risotti, zuppe and fritture di pesce; *Capri Rosso* (dry red), served with meat or poultry, pastasciutta and timballi. *Castel San Lorenzo Bianco* (dry white), served with fish or fresh cheeses; *Castel San Lorenzo Rosato* (delicate, dry rosé), served with antipasti di pesce, antipasti di prosciutto, poultry; *Castel San Lorenzo Rosso* (dry, fruity red), with meats and roast poultry; *Cilento Bianco* (delicate white), served with minestre, poultry, or fish; *Cilento Rosato* (intense rosé), with minestre and roast or grilled fish; *Cilento Rosso* (dry red), served with fried meat and stews; *Falanghina di Guardia Sanframondi* (or *Guardiolo*; dry, delicate white), served with fish; *Falanghina di Sant'Agata dei Goti* (dry, fruity white; the *passito* is more delicate), served with desserts or gelato; *Falerno del Massico Bianco* (dry white), served as an aperitif or with minestre and poultry; *Falerno del Massico Primitivo* (dry red), served with roasts and stews; *Falerno del Massico Riserva* (both *Rosso* and *Primitivo* aged two years); *Falerno del Massico Rosso* (dry red); served with meats, wild game and aged cheeses); *Fiano d'Avellino* (dry white), served with antipasti, fish, and poultry; *Greco di Sant'Agata dei Goti* (fresh, fruity white), served with poultry; *Greco di Tufo* (dry, delicate white; sometimes *spumante*), served with antipasti; *Guardia Sanframondi* (or *Guardiolo*) *Bianco* (delicate, dry white), served at with vegetables or poultry; *Guardia Sanframondi* (or *Guardiolo*) *Rosato* (dry rosé), served with shellfish and rich fish dishes; *Guardia Sanframondi* (or *Guardiolo*) *Rosso* (dry red; the *novello* is lighter and served at a lower temperature, the *riserva* is aged two years), served at with roast meat; *Guardia Sanframondi* (or *Guardiolo*) *Spumante* (delicate sparkling white), served as an aperitif, with shellfish or with pastry; *Ischia Bianco* (dry white; the *superiore* is stronger), served with fish and shellfish; *Ischia Rosso* (dry red), served with pastasciutta, poultry; *Lacryma Christi del Vesuvio Bianco* (dry white), served with fish; *Lacryma Christi del Vesuvio Liquoroso* (sweet amber), served at with desserts; *Lacryma Christi del Vesuvio Rosato* (dry rosé), served with antipasti and poultry; *Lacryma Christi del Vesuvio Rosso* (dry red), served with meat and poultry; *Moscato di Castel San Lorenzo* (sweet, mellow white; the *lambiccato* is stronger), served with pastry or gelato; *Moscato Spumante di Castel San Lorenzo* (sweet, sparkling white), served with pastry or gelato; *Piedirosso di Sant'Agata dei Goti* (robust red, rich in tannins) served with meats; *Sant'Agata dei Goti Rosato* (delicate rosé), served with poultry; *Sant'Agata dei Goti Rosso* (dry red), served with meats; *Solopaca Bianco* (dry white), served with pastasciutta, risotti, poultry and bolliti; *Solopaca Rosso* (dry, intense red), served with meats, especially lamb; *Taburno* (or *Aglianico del Taburno*) *Rosato* (delicate, dry rosé), served with pork, lamb and aged cheeses; *Taurasi* (dry red, the *riserva* is aged four years), served with fine roasts; *Vesuvio Bianco* (dry white), served with antipasti di mare, zuppe, risotti, fish; *Vesuvio Rosato* (dry rosé), served with antipasti, timballi, fresh cheeses; *Vesuvio Rosso* (dry red), served with roasts and stews.

Basilicata and Calabria. *Cirò Bianco* (dry white), served as an aperitif or with shellfish and swordfish; *Cirò Rosato* (dry rosé), served with fish; *Cirò Rosso* (robust, dry red; the *riserva* is aged three years), served with fine meats; *Donnici* (dry red), served with roasts and game; *Greco di Bianco* (sweet white; aged at least one year), served with pastry, fruit salad and gelato; *Lamezia* (delicate, dry red), served with poultry, rabbit and pork; *Melissa Bianco* (dry white), served with antipasti, fish; *Melissa Rosso* (dry red; the *superiore* is aged at least one year), served with stewed meats; *Pollino* (dry red; the *superiore* is aged two years), served with roast meats and poultry; *Sant'Anna di Isola Capo Rizzuto Rosato* (dry rosé), served with meats, especially lamb; *Sant'Anna di Isola Capo Rizzuto Rosso* (dry red), served with meats or roast poultry; *Savuto Rosato* (dry rosé), served with meats, poultry and fresh cheeses; *Savuto Rosso* (dry red), served with meats, game and aged cheeses.

Abruzzo and Molise. *Cerasuolo d'Abruzzo* (dry red), served with roast or grilled meats; *Montpulciano d'Abruzzo* (dry red; the *vecchio* is aged two years), served with meat and poultry; *Trebbiano d'Abruzzo* (dry white), served with fish and cheese. *Biferno Bianco* (dry white), served with poultry and vegetables; *Biferno Rosato* (dry white), served with poultry, rabbit and cheeses; *Biferno Rosso* (dry red; the *riserva* is aged three years), served with meats; *Pentro di Isernia Bianco* (dry white), served with vegetables, poultry, or cold meats. *Pentro di Isernia Rosato* (dry rosé), served with poultry, rabbit and game; *Pentro di Isernia Rosso* (dry red), served with roast meat and poultry.

Apula. *Aleatico di Gioia del Colle* (moderately sweet red), served with desserts; *Aleatico di Gioia del Colle Liquoroso* (robust, sweet red), served with desserts; *Aleatico di Puglia* (strong, sweet red), served with pastry or gelato; *Alezio Rosato* (dry rosé); served with minestre, fried and baked dishes, and cheeses; *Alezio Rosso* (dry red; the *riserva* is stronger), served with meats and poultry; *Brindisi Rosato* (dry rosé), served with pastasciutta, vegetables and cheeses; *Brindisi Rosso* (dry red; the *riserva* is aged two years); served with meats; *Cacc'e Mitte di Lucera* (dry red), served with meat, eggs and cheeses; *Castel del Monte Bianco* (dry white), served with fish and shellfish; *Castel del Monte Rosato* (dry rosé); served as an aperitif or antipasti; *Castel del Monte Rosso* (dry red; the *riserva* is aged three years); served with roasts; *Copertino Rosato* (dry rosé), served with pastasciutta and vegetables; *Copertino Rosso* (dry red; the *riserva* is aged two years), served with roasts; *Gioia del Colle Bianco* (dry white), served with fish and poultry; *Gioia del Colle Rosato* (dry rosé), served as an aperitif or with poultry; *Gioia del Collo Rosso* (dry red), served with meat and poultry; *Gravina* (dry or mellow white; the *spumante* is sparkling), served with poultry, fish and desserts; *Leverano Bianco* (dry white), served with roast or fried fish and shellfish; *Leverano Rosato* (dry rosé), served with soups, fried fish and cheeses; *Leverano Rosso* (dry red; the *riserva* is aged two years); served with meats; *Lizzano Bianco* (dry white), served with antipasti or fish; *Lizzano Rosato* (dry rosé), served with fish or shellfish; *Lizzano Rosso* (dry red), served with meats, cold meats and aged cheeses; *Lizzano Spumante Bianco* (dry sparkling white), served as an aperitif or with shellfish; *Lizzano Spumante Rosato* (dry sparkling rosé), served with fish and shellfish; *Locorotondo* (dry white; the *spumante* is sparkling), served with fish; *Malvasia Nera di Lizzano* (aromatic, sweet red), served with desserts; *Martina Franca* (or *Martina*; dry white; the *spumante* is sparkling), served with fish; *Matino Rosato* (dry rosé), served with pastasciutta, vegetables, and poultry; *Matino Rosso* (dry red), served with lamb, roast pork and aged cheeses; *Moscato di Trani* (sweet amber), served with pastry and gelato; *Moscato di Trani Liquoroso* (strong, sweet amber), served with pastry, fruit salad and gelato; *Nardò Rosato* (dry, almost bitter rosé); served with soups and roast fish; *Nardò Rosso* (dry, almost bitter red), served with lamb or aged cheeses; *Negroamaro di Lizzano Rosato* (dry, fragrant rosé), served with antipasti and minestre; *Negroamaro di Lizzano Rosso* (dry, fragrant red), served with meats and cold meats; *Orta Nova Rosato* (dry rosé), served with pastasciutta and cheeses; *Orta Nova Rosso* (dry red), served with meat and poultry and aged cheeses; *Ostuni Bianco* (dry white), served with antipasti, pastasciutta, fish, eggs and vegetables; *Ottavianello di Ostuni* (dry red), served with stewed and grilled meats; *Primitivo di Gioia del Colle* (dry red), served with meats; *Primitivo di Manduria* (dry or sweet red; can be *liquoroso*), served with roast meats; *Rosso Barletta* (dry red; the *vecchio* is aged two years); served with meat and game; *Rosso Canosa* (dry red; the *riserva* is aged two years), served with meats, especially lamb; *Rosso di Cerignola* (dry red; the *riserva* is aged two years), served with grilled meats; *Salice Salentino Rosato* (dry rosé), served at with soups, fried foods and cheeses; *Salice Salentino Rosso* (dry red; the *riserva* is aged two years), served with meats, especially lamb; *San Severo Bianco* (dry white), served with light antipasti, shellfish and fish; *San Severo Rosato* (dry rosé), served with antipasti, soups and poultry; *San Severo Rosso* (dry red), served with pork, lamb or wildfowl; *Squinzano Rosato* (dry rosé), served with antipasti, minestre and poultry; *Squinzano Rosso* (dry red; the *riserva* is aged two years); served with meats.

Travelling around

By rail

The Italian State Railways (FS—Ferrovie dello Stato) now run eight categories of trains. (1) EC (Eurocity), international express trains running between the main Italian and European cities. (2) EN (Euronotte), overnight international express trains with sleeping car or couchette service. (3) P (Pendolini), high-speed trains running between major Italian cities. (4) IC (Intercity), express trains running between major Italian cities. (5) E (Espressi), long-distance trains not as fast as the Intercity trains. (6) D (Diretti), intermediate-distance trains making more stops than the Espressi. (7) IR (Interregionali), the new name for Diretti. (8) R (Regionali), local trains stopping at all stations. M (Metropolitani), surface or underground commuter trains. Service in all categories is improving rapidly as the State Railways proceeds in its ambitious modernisation programme.

Seats can be booked in advance, as early as two months and as late as three hours before departure, from the main cities at the station booking office (open daily 07.00–22.00), or at travel agencies representing the Italian State Railways. Seats on a Pendolino can be reserved up to 30 minutes before departure at the Pendolino booking counter in the station. Couchettes and sleeping compartments should be booked well in advance, although those that are not occupied at the time of departure can be hired directly from the conductor without paying a supplement. Reciprocal booking arrangements exist with Austria, Belgium, Denmark, France, Great Britain, Hungary, Luxembourg, the Netherlands, Portugal, Spain, and Switzerland.

The timetable of the train services changes in late September and late May every year. Excellent timetables are published twice a year by the Italian State Railways (*In Treno*; one volume for the whole of Italy; trains with facilities for the disabled are marked) and by several private publishers. These can be purchased at news-stands and railway stations.

Tickets must be bought at the station (or from travel agents representing the Italian State Railways) before starting a journey, otherwise a fairly large supplement has to be paid to the ticket-collector on the train. Time should be allowed for ticketing, as there are often long queues at the station ticket counters. Some trains carry first class only; some charge a special supplement; and on some, seats must be booked in advance. It is therefore always necessary to specify which train you are intending to take, as well as the destination, when buying tickets. Before getting on the train, regardless of whether you are outbound or returning to your station of origin, you must stamp the date on the back of the ticket, using the meters located on or near the station platforms. In the main stations the better known credit cards are now generally accepted (although a special ticket window must be used when buying a ticket with a credit card). There are limitations on travelling short distances on some trains.

Fares in Italy are still much lower than in the UK or the USA. There is a 15 per cent discount on day return tickets (maximum distance, 50km) and on three-day return tickets (maximum distance 250km). Children under four travel free, and between four and 12 pay half price. There are also reductions for families and for groups of as few as three persons. For travellers over the age of 60 (with senior citizen railcards), the Rail Europ Senior card offers a 30 per cent reduction on Italian rail fares. The Inter-rail card (valid one month), which can be purchased in Britain or North America by young people up to the age of 26, is valid in Italy. In Italy the *Carta d'Argento* and the *Carta Verde* (both valid one year) allow a 20 per cent reduction on rail fares for those over 60 and between the ages of 12 and 26. A *Biglietto Chilometrico* (cumulative ticket) is valid for 3000 kilometres over a two-month period and can be used by up to five people at the same time. The Euro Domino and Euro Domino Junior cards, available to those resident outside Italy, gives freedom of the Italian railways for three, five, or ten days. These cards can be purchased in Britain or at main stations in Italy. The *Carta Blu* is available for the disabled.

Other forms of discounted travel are Rail Inclusive Tours, which offer transport, accommodation, excursions and so on in a single package; the *Tessera di Autorizzazione* (special concession card), which gives a 40 per cent discount and exemption from special supplements for frequent travel in first, second, or first and second class; the *Carnet di Biglietti a Tariffa Ridotta* (discount ticket pack), consisting of at least four tickets (valid for one month) at discounts of 10 to 20 per cent and various forms of periodic subscription.

Restaurant cars are attached to most international and internal long-distance trains. A lunch tray brought to the compartment (including three courses and wine) is a convenient way of having a meal. Some trains now also have self-service restaurants. Also, snacks, hot coffee and drinks are sold throughout the journey from a trolley wheeled down the train. At every large station, snacks are on sale from trolleys on the platform and you can buy them from the train window.

Carrier-bags with sandwiches, drink, and fruit (*cestini da viaggio*) are available, as are individual sandwiches (*panini*).

Sleeping cars with first- and second-class cabins offering one, two or three beds, are carried on certain trains, as well as Sleeperette cars with reclining seats (first class only) and Couchette cars (second class only), with four- and six-berth compartments.

Additional services available at main stations include assistance for the disabled, special car-hire offers automatic ticketing, porterage, and left luggage offices (open 24hr at the main stations; often closed at night at smaller stations). Porters are entitled to a fixed amount, shown on notice boards at all stations, for each piece of baggage.

By bus

Local and long-distance buses between the main towns in southern Italy are not as abundant as they are in the north, and as increasing numbers of residents become independently mobile, service is diminishing. Except in areas of particular interest to non-residents (such as Sorrento and the Amalfi Coast), most buses now carry school children from the villages to the towns in the early morning, and from the towns to the villages in the afternoon. Buses still serve most towns not reached by rail at least once a day, leaving major cities from a depot usually at or near the train station. Excellent timetables are published twice a year by the Italian State Railways. Accurate timetables for other areas can be obtained from the local tourist boards.

City buses are an excellent means of getting about in most towns, with the notable exception of Naples, where traffic is often paralysed; in this case, the Metropolitana is the swiftest and easiest means of moving across town. Almost everywhere, tickets must be purchased before boarding (at tobacconists, bars, news-stands, information offices and so on) and stamped on board.

By car

Regardless of whether you are driving your own car or a hired vehicle, Italian law requires that you carry a valid driving licence when travelling. You must also keep a red triangle in the car in case of accident or breakdown. This serves as a warning to other traffic when placed on the road at a distance of 50m from the stationary car. It can be hired from ACI for a minimal charge and returned at the frontier.

It is now compulsory to wear seat-belts in the front seat of cars in Italy. Traffic is generally faster (and often more aggressive) than in Britain or America, and as 80 per cent of the goods transported travel by road, lorries pose a constant hazard. Road signs are now more or less standardised to the international codes, and state-of-the-art technology is used to enforce speed limits (130kmh on motorways, 90kmh on major highways, 50kms in urban areas).

Certain customs differ radically from those of Britain or America. Unless otherwise indicated, cars entering a road or roundabout from the right are given precedence. Street cars and trains always have the right of way from either left or right. If an oncoming driver flashes his headlights, it means he is proceeding and not giving you precedence. In towns, Italian drivers frequently change lanes without warning. They also tend to ignore pedestrian crossings. In the south they view red lights with a certain contempt. Everywhere the drivers of motorbikes, mopeds, and Vespas weave in and out of traffic, snapping up the right of way. The concept of the safe following distance is unknown and if you leave a gap between your car and the vehicle in front of you, it will be filled immediately.

Roads in Italy. Italy probably has the finest motorways in Europe, called *autostrade*. They are indicated by green signs or, near the entrance ramps, by large boards of overhead lights. Tolls are charged according to the rating of the vehicle and the distance covered, except on the A3 south of Salerno, which is toll free. All autostrade have service areas open 24 hours a day, and most have SOS points every 2km. At the entrance to motorways, the two directions are indicated by the name of the most important town (and not by the nearest town), which can be momentarily confusing. Similar to autostrade, but not provided with service stations, SOS points, or emergency lanes, are the dual-carriageway fast roads called *superstrade* (also indicated by green signs).

Southern Italy has an excellent network of secondary highways (*strade statali* or *provinciali*, indicated by blue signs), usually good roads which provide fine views of the countryside. Local traffic can be extremely heavy in densely populated areas, such as the gulf coast between Naples and Castellammare di Stabia, and on main arteries, such as Highway 16 between Bari and Brindisi.

Throughout Italy, buildings of historic interest are often indicated by yellow signs (although there are long-term plans to change the colour to brown); townships (*comuni*) and their component villages (*frazioni*), by white signs. The territory of a comune is often much larger than the town of the same name that is its administrative centre—another source of confusion.

Fuel and service. Petrol stations are open 24 hours a day on motorways, elsewhere 07.00–12.00, 15.00–20.00; winter 07.30–12.30, 14.30–19.30. 24 hour self-service stations can also be found in or near the larger towns. Pumps are operated by 10,000 or 50,000 lire banknotes. All varieties of petrol (including diesel and unleaded) are now readily available in Italy, although they cost more than in Britain, and considerably more than in America. Most stations offer basic maintenance service (motor oil, brake fluid, and so on) but mechanical assistance must be sought from a *meccanico* (mechanic), *elettrauto* (auto electrician), *gommaio* (tyre shop), *carrozziere* (body shop), and so on. Temporary membership of the *Automobile Club d'Italia* (ACI) can be taken out on the frontier or in Italy (the headquarters of ACI are at 8 via Marsala, Rome, with branch offices in all the main towns). They provide a breakdown service (Soccorso ACI, tel. 116) and other advantages.

Parking. Many cities in southern Italy have taken the wise step of closing their historic centres to traffic (except for residents), which makes them much more pleasant to visit on foot. Access is allowed to hotels and for the disabled. It is always advisable to leave your car in a supervised car park, though with a bit of effort it is almost always possible to find a place to park free of charge, away from the town centre. However, to do so overnight, or even for brief periods in or around Naples and Bari, is not advisable. Always lock your car when parked, and never leave anything of value inside it.

Car hire is available in most Italian cities. Arrangements can be made before departure through the airlines (at specially advantageous rates in conjunction with their flights) or in Italy through any of the principal car-hire firms (the best known include Maggiore, Avis, and Hertz), which offer daily, weekly, and weekend rates. Special leasing rates are available for periods of thirty days and over. The State Railways also offers special rail-car combinations (see above).

Car and driver service is a convenient, though somewhat expensive way to visit southern Italy, especially metropolitan areas such as Naples and its environs, where traffic is harrowing and a knowledge of alternative routes saves time and fatigue. Details from ENIT or from the local tourist boards.

Maps. The Touring Club Italiano (TCI) publishes several sets of excellent maps, including *Carta Stradale d'Europa: Italia* on a scale of 1:1,000,000; the *Atlante Stradale Touring* (1:800,000); and the *Carta Stradale d'Italia* (1:200,000). The latter is divided into 15 sheets covering the regions of Italy. These are also published as an atlas (with a comprehensive index) called the *Atlante Stradale d'Italia*, in three volumes. The ones entitled *Centro* and *Sud* cover the southern mainland. These maps can be purchased from the TCI offices and at many booksellers. In London they are obtainable at Stanfords, 12–14 Long Acre, London WC2 9LP, and Robertson McCarta Ltd, 15 Highbury Place, London N5 1QP.

The Istituto Geografico Militare, via Cesare Battisti 10, Florence, publishes a map of Italy on a scale of 1:100,000 in 277 sheets and a field survey, partly 1:50,000, partly 1:25,000, which are invaluable for the detailed exploration of the country, especially its more mountainous regions; the coverage is, however, still far from complete at the larger scales and some of the maps are out of date. For the computer literate, Route 66 Geographic Information Systems BV of Veenendaal, The Netherlands, distributes software that calculates and displays routes from any origin to any destination in Italy.

By air
Frequent internal flights are operated between most main towns. Reductions are available for weekend travel.

Biking and walking
Biking and walking have become more popular in Italy in recent years and more information is now available locally. The local offices of the Club Alpino Italiano (CAI) and the World Wildlife Fund provide all the information necessary. Maps are published by the Istituto Geografico Militare (see above) and by CAI at a scale of 1:50,000.

Taxis
These are hired from ranks or by telephone; there are no cruising taxis. Before engaging a taxi it is advisable to make sure it has a meter in working order. Fares vary from city to city but are generally cheaper than London taxis. No tip is expected, but 1000 lire or so can be given. Supplements are charged for night service and for luggage. There is a heavy surcharge when the destination is outside the town limits (ask roughly how much the fare is likely to be).

General Information

Museums, sites and monuments
The opening times of museums, sites, and monuments have been given in the text, but they often change without warning. The provincial tourist authority in major cities keeps updated timetables of most museums. National museums and monuments are usually open Tuesday–Saturday 09.00–14.00, Sunday and holidays 09.00–13.00. In some cases they are now open also in the afternoon or evening, on at least one day per week. Archaeological sites generally open at 09.00 and close one hour before sunset. Naturally, as opening times are constantly being altered, care should be taken to allow enough time for variations in the hours shown in the text when planning a visit to a museum or monument.

Some museums are closed on the main public holidays: 1 January, Easter, 1 May,

15 August, and 25 December. Several smaller museums have suspended regular hours altogether and are now open by appointment only. Their telephone numbers have been included in the text, and visits may be reserved by calling ahead.

Entrance fees to Italian museums vary (from free to 10,000 lire) according to your age and nationality; British citizens under 18 and over 60 are entitled to free admission to national museums and monuments because of reciprocal arrangements in Britain. During the *Settimana per i Beni Culturali e Ambientali* (Cultural and Environmental Heritage Week), usually held early in December, entrance to national museums is free for all.

Churches in southern Italy open quite early in the morning (often for 06.00 mass), but are normally closed for a considerable period during the middle of the day (12.00 to 15.00, 16.00, or 17.00), although cathedrals and some of the large churches may be open without a break during daylight hours. Smaller churches and oratories are often open only in the early morning, but the key can usually be found by inquiring locally. The sacristan will also show closed chapels and crypts and a small tip should be given. Some churches now ask that sightseers do not enter during a service, but normally visitors may do so, provided they are silent and do not approach the altar in use. At all times they are expected to cover their legs and arms, and generally dress with decorum. An entrance fee is becoming customary for admission to treasuries, bell-towers, and so on. Lights (operated by 500 lire coins) have been installed in many churches to illuminate frescoes and altarpieces. In Holy Week most of the pictures are covered and are on no account shown.

Public holidays

The Italian national holidays when offices, shops, and schools are closed are as follows: 1 January, 25 April (Liberation Day), Easter Sunday and Easter Monday, 1 May (Labour Day), 15 August (Assumption), 1 November (All Saints' Day), 8 December (Immaculate Conception), Christmas Day '25 December' and 26 December (St Stephen). Each town keeps its patron saint's day as a holiday.

Health

British citizens, as members of the EC, have the right to claim health services in Italy if they have the E111 form (issued by the Department of Health and Social Security). There are also a number of private holiday health insurance policies. Italy has no medical programme covering US citizens, who are advised to take out an insurance policy before travelling. First Aid services (*Pronto Soccorso*) are available at all hospitals, railway stations, and airports. Chemist shops (*farmacie*) are usually open Monday–Friday 09.00–13.00, 16.00–19.30 or 20.00. A few are open also on Saturdays, Sundays, and holidays (listed on the door of every chemist). In all towns there is also at least one chemist shop open at night (also shown on the door of every chemist). For emergencies, dial 113 (State Police) or 112 (Carabinieri).

Useful addresses

Help is given to British, US, and Canadian travellers who are in difficulty by the British, US, and Canadian consulates in Italy, and by the British, US, and Canadian Embassies in Rome. They will help if your passport has been lost or stolen and will give advice in emergencies. The **British Consulate** in Naples is located at Via Crispi 122 (Atlas 4, 9; tel. 081 663 511); the **US Consulate**, in Piazza della

Repubblica (Atlas 4, 9; tel. 081 583 8111, fax 081 761 1869); the **Canadian Embassy** in Rome, at Via G.B. de Rossi 27 (tel. 06 445981, fax 06 445 98750).

There is an Anglican church at Via San Pasquale 18 (tel. 081 411842), a Baptist church at Via Foria 93 (tel. 081 554 6317), a Lutheran church at Via Carlo Poerio 5 (tel. 081 663207), a Methodist church at Via Vaccaro 20 (tel. 081 364263), and a Synagogue at Via Cappella Vecchia 31 (tel. 081 764 3480).

Crime
Pick pocketing is a widespread problem in towns all over Italy: it is always advisable not to carry valuables in handbags, and be particularly careful on public transport. Never wear conspicuous jewellery, including necklaces and expensive watches; women, when walking, should keep their handbags on the side of their bodies nearer the wall (never on the street side). Crime should be reported at once to the police, or the local *carabinieri* office (found in every town and small village). A detailed statement has to be given in order to get an official document confirming loss or damage (essential for insurance claims). Interpreters are provided. For all emergencies, dial 113.

Opera and festivals
The opera season in Italy usually begins in December and continues until June: the principal opera house in southern Italy is the San Carlo in Naples. Annual music, drama and film festivals take place in many towns, famous ones including the classical drama festival in the Roman Theatre at Pompeii (July and August), and the International Film Festival in Sorrento. Traditional festivals are celebrated in most towns and villages in commemoration of a local historical or religious event and are often very spectacular. The major festivals have been indicated in the text.

Telephone and postal services
Stamps are sold at tobacco shops and post offices. Correspondence can be addressed c/o the post office by adding 'Fermo Posta' to the name of the locality. There are numerous public telephones all over Italy, and card-operated phones are becoming increasingly common in major cities and resort areas. Local calls cost Lire 200. Cards offering 5000 or 10,000 lire in prepaid calls are available at post offices, tobacconists and certain news-stands. They are particularly convenient for phoning abroad. Long-distance calls in Italy are made by dialling the city code (for instance, 080 for Bari), then the telephone number; international and intercontinental calls, by dialing 00 plus the country code, then the city code (for numbers in Britain, without the initial zero), and the telephone number (for instance, the central London number 8552000 would be 0041 71 855 2000).

Newspapers
The most widely read newspapers are the *Corriere della Sera* of Milan, the *Stampa* of Turin, and the *Repubblica* and *Messaggero* of Rome. Among the principal papers in the south are the *Mattino* of Naples and the *Giornale di Sicilia* of Palermo. Foreign newspapers are sold at central street kiosks and railway stations.

Working hours
Government offices usually work Monday–Saturday, 08.00/09.00–13.00/14.00; businesses Monday–Friday, 08.30/09.00–12.30/13.00 and 14.30/15.00–18.00.

Shops generally open Monday–Saturday 08.30/9.00–13.00 and 15.30/16.00–19.30/20.00. Shops selling clothes and other goods are usually closed on Monday morning, food shops on Wednesday afternoon, except from mid-June to mid-September, when all shops are closed instead on Saturday afternoon. In resorts, during July and August, many shops remain open from early morning until late at night. Banks are open Monday–Friday, 08.30–13.30, 14.30–15.45. They are closed on Saturday and holidays and close early (about 11.00) on days preceding national holidays.

Public toilets
There is a notable shortage of public toilets in Italy. All bars (cafés) should have toilets available to the public (generally speaking, the larger the bar, the better the facilities). Nearly all museums now have toilets.

Language
Even a few words of Italian are a great advantage in the south of Italy, where English is not so widely spoken as in the north. Local dialects vary greatly and are usually unintelligible to the foreigner, but even where dialect is universally used, nearly everybody can speak and understand Italian. A simple series of instructions for pronouncing Italian words follows.

Words should be pronounced well forward in the mouth, and no nasal intonation exists in Italian. Double consonants call for special care as each must be sounded. Consonants are pronounced roughly as in English with the following exceptions: *c* and *cc* before e and i have the sound of *ch* in chess; *sc* before e and i is pronounced like *sh* in ship; *ch* before e and i has the sound of *k*; *g* and *gg* before e and i are always soft, like *j* in jelly; *gh* is always hard, like *g* in get; *gl* is nearly always like *lli* in million (there are a few exceptions, for example, *negligere*, where it is pronounced as in English); *gn* is like *ny* in lanyard; *gu* and *qu* are always like *gw* and *kw*. *S* is hard like *s* in six except when it occurs between two vowels, when it is soft, like the English *z* or the *s* in rose; *ss* is always hard. Z and *zz* are usually pronounced like *ts*, but occasionally have the sound of *dz* before a long vowel. Vowels are pronounced much more openly than in southern English and are given their full value. There are no true diphthongs in Italian, and every vowel should be articulated separately. The stress normally falls on the last syllable but one; in modern practice an accent-sign is written regularly only when the stress is on the last syllable, for example, *città*, or to differentiate between two words similarly spelt but with a different meaning: for example,(and); *è* (is).

Manners and customs
Attention should be paid by the traveller to the more formal manners of the Italians. It is customary to open conversation in shops and such places with the courtesy of *buon giorno* (good day) or *buona sera* (good evening). The deprecatory expression *prego* (don't mention it) is everywhere the obligatory and automatic response to *grazie* (thank you). The phrases *per piacere* or *per favore* (please), *permesso* (excuse me), used when pushing past someone (essential on public vehicles), *scusi* (sorry; also, I beg your pardon, when something is not heard), should not be forgotten. A visitor will be wished *Buon appetito!* before beginning a meal, to which he should reply *Grazie, altrettanto*. This pleasant custom may be extended to fellow passengers taking a picnic meal on a train. Shaking hands is an essential part of greeting and leave-taking. In shops and offices a certain amount of self-assertion is

taken for granted, since queues are not the general rule and it is incumbent on the inquirer or customer to get him or herself a hearing.

Begging and unwanted offers of guidance should be met with firmness but without harshness or rudeness. It should be borne in mind that in the south of Italy begging is regarded as a necessary stimulus to the virtue of charity; even the poor will give something, if only a few lire, to a beggar. In Naples the persistent attention of small boys should be firmly but kindly discouraged; further south, however, the local school children are frequently knowledgeable and genuinely anxious to show the beauties of their home town. Where this is done in the name of hospitality, no reward will be accepted.

There are few restrictions on photography in Italy, but permission is necessary to photograph the interiors of churches and museums and may sometimes be withheld. Care should also be taken before photographing individuals, notably members of the armed forces and the police. Photography is forbidden on railway stations and civil airfields, as well as in frontier zones and near military installations.

Weights and measures

Italians use a metric system of weights and measures. The metro is the unit of length, the grammo of weight, the ara of land-measurement, the litro of capacity. Greek-derived prefixes (deca-, etto-, chilo-) are used with those names to express multiples; Latin prefixes (deci-, centi-, milli-) to express fractions (kilometro=1000 metri, millimetro=1000th part of a metro). For approximate calculations the metro (or metre) may be taken as 39 inches and the chilometro (kilometre) as 0.6 mile, the litro (litre) as 1.75 pint, an etto as 3.5 oz, and the chilo (kilogram) as 2.2 lb.

The triumphal gateway of the Castel Nuovo, Naples, see p. 160

I THE TYRRHENIAN BIOREGION: LAZIO, CAMPANIA AND CALABRIA

The Tyrrhenian bioregion is made up of the regions on the western watershed of the Apennines: Lazio, Campania, and Calabria.

LAZIO

Lazio (anciently *Latium*) is a hilly region of 11,000 sq km lying between the Apennines and the Tyrrhenian Sea, at the west centre of the Italian peninsula. It consists of five provinces, Rome, Rieti, Viterbo, Frosinone and Latina, of which only the two last are included in this volume. The name, one of the oldest place names in Italy, originally designated a small area between the mouth of the Tiber and the Alban Hills. With the Roman conquest, Latium was extended south-east to the Gulf of Gaeta and west to the mountains of Abruzzo, forming the so-called *Latium novum* (or *adiectum*). The name, *Campania Romana*, dating from the time of Constantine and replacing that of Latium, was used to distinguish the area from that of the Campania Felix, which surrounds Naples (see below). It includes the Agro Pontino, formerly the Pontine Marshes, the region's only real plain of any extent.

To the south and east of this rise the Monti Lepini, Ausoni and Aurunci, set apart from the main body of the Apennines by the broad Valle Latina, which is crossed by the Rivers Sacco and Liri. The present region of Lazio was essentially formed in 1870, with the inclusion of the Papal States in United Italy. Its southern boundary was established in 1927 with the annexation of the area around the Gulf of Gaeta, which formerly belonged to the Province of Caserta.

CAMPANIA

Campania occupies the Tyrrhenian coast and the western slopes of the Apennines, between Lazio and Molise on the north, Apulia on the east and Basilicata on the south. It is a fertile, lovely region, with a charming variety of coast, plain, and mountain. Administratively it is divided into five provinces with capitals at Avellino, Benevento, Caserta, Salerno, and Naples. Anciently known as *Ausonia* or *Opicia* (from the Opici or Oscans), it received its civilisation from the Greeks and the Etruscans. Its present name (originally used to designate the fertile plain of Capua, the *Ager Campanus*) dates from the Samnite conquest (5C BC). Under the Romans, who occupied it after the Social War (88 BC), it rose to great prosperity and soon won the appellative Campania Felix on account of its beauty and fertility.

With the fall of the empire the region passed to the Goths, to the Byzantines, and finally to the Lombards, who partitioned it into the duchies of Benevento, Capua, Naples and, later, Salerno. In its subsequent history the region followed the fortunes of Naples, its chief city. Many of the more interesting places in Campania are conveniently visited from Naples.

CALABRIA
Calabria, the mountainous peninsula between the Tyrrhenian and the Ionian Seas, is the toe of the Italian 'boot'. Roughly 223km long, in the north it culminates in Monte Pollino (2248m), in the centre it expands into the granite plateau of the Sila (1928m) and in the south it terminates in the Aspromonte group (1955m). The rivers are short but copious. The vegetation along the coast is typically southern, but inland fine forests and mountain flora prevail.

As part of Magna Graecia, Calabria enjoyed an age of prosperity, and Croton (where Pythagoras taught), Sybaris, Locri and Rhegion were flourishing cities. Many traces of the past have been destroyed by the frequent earthquakes. The chief towns of the region are Cosenza, Catanzaro and Reggio, the provincial capitals.

On the whole Calabria is a poor country today, though emigration to Northern Italy, the United States, and Australia has largely been halted in recent years. The work of the postwar development programme known as the Cassa per il Mezzogiorno, in particular in encouraging hydroelectric schemes in the Sila, has brought considerable recent improvement; an excellent olive oil is produced in several places (the olive groves at Gioia Tauro are amongst the best in Italy); and a blossoming tourist trade along the Tyrrhenian 'riviera' has actually led to over–development, especially around Reggio and between Praia a Mare and Amantea. In spite of its charms, Calabria is still little known to the English-speaking traveller, though improvements in accommodation have brought most of the country within reach.

1 · Rome to Naples

A.   Via Frosinone, Cassino and Caserta

*This is the principal road route from Rome to Naples. It crosses the harsh, mountainous landscape of southern Lazio—an area dotted with ancient remains, such as the fortifications of **Alatri**, and remarkable medieval monuments, such as the churches of **Anagni** and **Casamari** and the renowned **Abbey of Monte Cassino**. Compania is entered near **Capua** and Santa Maria Capua Vetere, whose names recall the ancient Capua, one of the more important centres of Roman Campania. Modern Capua is interesting for its museum, the Museo Campano, which contains a unique collection of Italic Deae Matres (earth goddesses); and **Santa Maria Capua Vetere** is known for its ancient ruins, particularly the immense amphitheatre. At Caserta, Route 5F is joined to Naples.*

If you are arriving from Northern Italy on the Autostrada you can bypass Rome, diverging east before reaching the capital and joining the present route some 32km south.

The trip from Rome to Naples may be made non-stop in about 2hr; allow an extra hour or so for each place you wish to visit. State Highway 6 (the Via Casilina) weaves its way alongside the Autostrada for much of the way, though local lorry traffic can make the driving slow and frustrating.

ROAD 221km. Autostrada A1/E45 (Autostrada del Sole) and A2/E45—81km Frosinone—46km Cassino—51km Capua—18km Caserta (interchange with A2)—25km Naples.

RAILWAY from Rome (Termini) to Caserta in 1hr 45min–2hr 30min; to Naples (Centrale) in 30–45min more. Most trains stop at Frosinone and Cassino.

HOTEL EN ROUTE: Fiuggi Fonte, *****Palazzo della Fonte, Via dei Villini 7, tel. 0775 5081, fax 0775 506752.

RESTAURANTS EN ROUTE: Fiuggi Fonte, ****Hernicus (with rooms), Corso Nuova Italia 30, tel. 0775 55254, fax 0775 505502; Alatri, *La Rosetta (with rooms), Via Duomo 35, tel. 0775 434568.

THE VALLE LATINA

From central Rome, go to the *grande raccordo annulare*, or ring road, and follow it to the interchange with Autostrada A1 (Autostrada del Sole).

Exit at Valmontone or Colleferro for **Segni** (9000 inhab.), on the slopes of a hill (650m) to the south. This is the ancient *Signia*, founded by Tarquinius Priscus and noted for its wine, its pears and a kind of pavement called *opus signinum*. Here in 1173 Pope Alexander III canonised Thomas Becket. The town has some medieval houses, but it is particularly notable for its **cyclopean walls**, about 1km of which, including the Porta Sarcacena, are in good condition. There are also remains of the Temple of Jupiter Urius, for which Signia was famous.

Exit at Anagni-Fiuggi Terme to reach **Anagni** (20,000 inhab.), which stands on high ground (461m) just north of the Autostrada. The town preserves a strong feeling of the Middle Ages, with many fine 14C mansions, arched doorways, and trefoil windows.

History

It was the ancient Anagnia, capital of the Hernici; and Cicero had a fine estate here. It was also a favourite country residence of the popes, and the birthplace of Innocent III, Gregory IX, Alexander IV and Boniface VIII. The latter, following a quarrel with French king Philip IV, was insulted and imprisoned at Anagni in 1303 by Guillaume de Nogaret, Chancellor of France, but he was rescued by his fellow citizens three days later. The English pope Adrian IV died here in 1159.

At the entrance to the town, on the left, is the restored 14C Casa Barnekow, with the Romanesque tower of Sant'Andrea opposite. The **Palazzo Comunale**, further on, is an attractive 13C building with a vaulted passage beneath it, recently restored with great care. On the top of the hill (view) is the **Cattedrale** (Santa Maria), a large 11C basilica, altered in 1350, with an imposing campanile and a fine triple apse. A statue of Boniface VIII stands high up on the south flank. Within, on the north side, is the Caetani Chapel, with a Cosmatesque tomb. The fine tabernacle on the high altar dates from 1294. Nearby, in the choir, are a bishop's throne of 1263 and a candelabrum with mosaic decoration, both by Vassalletto. The crypt has a 13C Cosmatesque floor and some curious frescoes of the same period, in an old-fashioned Byzantine style. The treasury, on the right of the choir, contains the pontifical ornaments of Boniface VIII, chief among which is a cope embroidered in *opus anglicanum* with medallions representing the lives of Christ and the Virgin.

Some portions of a Roman rampart and remains of the Palace of Boniface VIII also survive at Anagni. The latter houses a small collection of documentary material on the town and its environs (Museo dell'Istituto di Storia e di Arte del Lazio Meridionale, open daily 09.00–15.00), of interest chiefly to historians.

11km south-east of Anagni on the Via Casilina, **Ferentino**, the *Ferentinum* of the Hernici, was colonised by the Romans in the Second Punic War. It is a maze of narrow alleys within a rampart of cyclopean walls with a later Roman superstructure, still pierced by four gates. At its highest point the **Bishop's Palace** rises on the massive foundations of the antique **citadel**. Adjoining is the **Cattedrale**, notable for a mosaic pavement of the 12C and for its transennae and a beautiful tabernacle and candelabrum of the13C. Lower down is **Santa Maria Maggiore**, a 13C church with a typical Italian Gothic façade. The Museo Civico, Piazzale del Collegio, is closed for restoration (1995).

The hills on either side of the road, in this area, are crowned by castellated villages.

81km **Frosinone** is a hilltop town (291m; 48,000 inhab.), the capital of the province of the same name and the chief place in the *Ciociaria*, a district once noted for the picturesque costumes of the peasantry (the name is taken from their traditional footgear, called 'cioce'. The area is now one of Italy's principal industrial centres.

■ **Information**. EPT, Piazzale de Matthaeis; tel. 0775 872525, fax 0775 27029 (branch office at Piazzale Vittorio Veneto 2).

■ **Post office**. Piazza della Liberttà.

Of the ancient *Frusino*, a town of the Hernici, only fragmentary walls and traces of an amphitheatre remain, together with a few finds of limited interest in the Museo Comunale (at the Palazzo del Comune; open Tue, Wed, Thu 09.00–13.00; Sat and Sun 09.00–12.00, 16.00–19.00). Today Frosinone is a bustling modern city, best avoided.

In the hills to the north-east, however, stands one of the region's finest medieval monuments, the ***Abbey of Casamari**, well worth a visit. Founded by the Benedictines in the 11C, the abbey passed to the Cistercians in 1151, to the Trappists in 1717, and in 1864 was returned to the Cistercians, who still hold it. The plan of the original abbey has been remarkably well preserved. The church, fine cloister, aisled chapter house, and guest house, all dating from the13C, adhere to the Burgundian Gothic types imported by the Cistercians and admirably embodied also at Fossanova (Route 1B). The conventual buildings house a photographic exhibit on Cistercian architecture, as well as a small Museo Archeologico and a *Cereatum Marianum* (open by appointment). Casamari was visited by Emperor Frederick II, when he was admitted to the brotherhood, an event that may be celebrated in the capital carvings of the cloister.

The scenic route to Frosinone

An alternative route from Rome to Frosinone touches on Palestrina and Fiuggi. It is both longer (116km) and slower than the one described above. From Rome to (38km) Palestrina, see Blue Guide Rome and environs. Beyond Palestrina the road gradually descends toward the south-east, with views on the right. 8km Genazzano is a picturesque little town situated north of the road. It was the birthplace of Martin V (Oddone Colonna; pope 1417–31). The church of the Madonna del Buon Consiglio contains a venerated Madonna, miraculously transported from Scutari

(Albania) in 1467; it is the scene of colourful pilgrimages on 25 March and 8 September. The village of Olevano Romano lies 6km north, on the road to Subiaco. A favourite resort of landscape painters, it preserves some cyclopean walls and remains of a medieval castle. The road now ascends nearly all the way to Fiuggi. 8km Paliano (271m) is a fortified town (7000 inhab.) on a rocky hill (439m) 3km south. It was a stronghold of the Colonna, whose simple tombs may be seen in the church of Sant'Andrea.

12km **Fiuggi** (8000 inhab.), situated in the among the Monti Ernici, consists of two separate places: **Fiuggi Fonte** or Fiuggi Centro, on the road from Palestrina; and **Fiuggi Città**, at the top of a hill, 4km north.

■ **Information.** AA, Via Gorizia 4; tel. 0775 55446, fax 0775 55766.

The lower resort is thronged in the season, which lasts from May to October. Because of its high altitude (621m at Fiuggi Fonte), the climate is agreeable and bracing, even in summer.

Fiuggi is known for its **mineral waters**, whose curative properties have been known from the13C. Their patrons have included Pope Boniface VIII (1294–1303) and Michelangelo. The waters issue at a temperature of 11°C from two springs, with a daily yield of nearly 2000 litres. Filtered through an extensive layer of porous volcanic tufa, they are tasteless and slightly radioactive.

The sea of Fiuggi Fonte is attractively situated on a wooded upland plain between two streams, the Fosso Pantano and the Fosso del Diluvio. Here are to be found most of the hotels and pensions, as well as numerous pleasant villas. The two springs are incorporated in separate spas, the Fonte Bonifacio VIII and the Nuova Fonte Anticolana. Both have gardens, with tennis courts, bowling greens, cafés and halls for concerts and art exhibitions. Delightful walks may be taken in the surrounding country.

From Fiuggi Fonte a road winds up to Fiuggi Città (747m), a medieval town without special character, known until 1911 as Antícoli di Campagna. In the Middle Ages it was under the Church, and in the 16C it passed into the hands of the Colonna.

At (14km) Vico nel Lazio Bivio, a turning leads north to Guarcino, the best starting point for the ascent of Monte Viglio (2156m, 11 km further north), the highest peak of the Monti Cantari. 3km Collepardo Bivio. The village, 5km north-east, is noted for its large stalactite grotto. About 5km farther north-east is the huge **Certosa di Trisulti** (established 1211 and several times rebuilt), with a17C pharmacy.

3km **Alatri** (502m), the *Aletrium* of the Hernici, is a picturesque town (25,000 inhab.) on a hill, with narrow winding streets and some interesting medieval remains. It possesses the most perfect example in Italy of the Pelasgic system of fortification. The great wall of cyclopean masonry that surrounded the town may still be traced, in some places with medieval or later additions. The crest of the hill is occupied by the **citadel**, c 180m round, built of immense polygonal blocks without mortar and still in perfect condition. Two gateways with monolithic architraves admit to the citadel, within which stand the **Cattedrale** and the bishop's palace. The church of **Santa Maria Maggiore**, in the main square, has a singular rose window (and enjoys a fine view). The Museo Civico, Corso Vittorio Emanuele 11 (closed for restoration 1995), houses local antiquities.

4km turning for (6km east) Veroli, the ancient *Verulae*, also with remains of polygonal walls. The church of Sant'Erasmo has a rich treasury of objects brought from the Cistercian Abbey of Casamari, 9km south-east. 9km Frosinone, join the route described below.

At (20km), **Ceprano**, Pope Gregory IX lifted the ban of excommunication from Frederick II on the emperor's successful return from Jerusalem (28 August 1230). The modern village, occupying the site of the Volscian *Fregellae*, guards the crossing of the copious River Liri (the ancient *Liris*), which further downstream becomes the Garigliano. These rivers formed the ancient boundary between the Kingdom of Sicily and the Patrimony of St Peter. Dating from Norman times, this remained in 1860 the oldest surviving frontier in Europe. Its strategic importance is underscored by the many battles that have been fought here: failure to destroy the bridge at Ceprano before the advancing Charles of Anjou was the first error of Manfred's last disastrous campaign (January–February 1266); and the Liri valley was the scene of intensive operations in January–May 1944 linked with the assault of Monte Cassino.

A shortcut to the sea

From Ceprano Highway 82 leads south across the Monti Aurunci to Itri and Formia, on the Tyrrhenian coast (53km; see Route 3). At Arce, 8km north-east on the Via Casilina, another road ascends the Liri valley to Avezzano. The fortified medieval village of **Rocca d'Arce** stands on the site of the citadel of *Fregellae*, just outside Arce. Roccasecca, to the south-east, is the birthplace of St Thomas Aquinas (1226?–74), son of Count Landolfo d'Aquino.

14 km exit for **Aquino**. The modern town, set between the Autostrada and the railway, is the insignificant successor of the famous Roman colony of *Aquinum*, the birthplace of Juvenal (c AD 55); the ruins of the ancient town extend into the vineyards and gardens far beyond the modern village. The church of **Santa Maria della Libera** (1125), which lost most of its roof in the Second World War, has a 12C mosaic; it stands on the foundations of a Temple of Hercules, and beside it is a charming little Corinthian arch. Beyond the Roman Porta San Lorenzo are the ruins of a basilica and of an amphitheatre, and two churches, **Santa Maria Maddalena** and **San Pietro**, incorporating the remains of temples of Diana and Ceres. Pontecorvo, 6km south, was named from the 'pons curvus' (crooked bridge) over the Liri.

On the left beyond Aquino appears the bare, stony Monte Cairo (1669m), the north bastion of two formidable defensive lines built by the Germans in 1943, the Gustav Line and the Hitler Line.

THE ABBEY OF MONTE CASSINO

12km **Cassino** (35,000 inhab.) was destroyed by fighting in 1944. It is dominated by the hill on which the famous abbey stands. The latter, by far the principal point of interest at Cassino, can be reached by car (the way is well marked), by bus, or on foot (a steep climb of about 1hr 30min). The ascent commands an uninterrupted series of magnificent *views. The **Museo Archaeologico Nazionale di Monte Casino** (open daily 09.00–19.00), at the beginning of the climb, houses Roman antiquities from local excavations.

■ **Information.** AA, Via Condotti 6; tel. 0766 21292, fax 0776 310946.

The ***Abbey of Monte Cassino**￼ (518m), perhaps the most famous monastery in the world, was founded by St Benedict of Norcia in 529, after he had left Subiaco guided by three tame ravens. Re-organised several times since then, it was a beacon of civilisation throughout the Middle Ages. Here in 790 Paulus Diaconus wrote his history of the Lombards and here the tradition of learning was kept burning by the devoted labours of the Benedictines. The tragedy of 15 February 1944, when Monte Cassino was bombed by the Allies, was the fifth in the abbey's history. The complex had previously been destroyed in 589 by the Lombards, in 884 by the Saracens, in 1030 by the Normans and in 1349 by an earthquake. The appearance of the abbey today still reflects the major building campaigns undertaken in the16C and 18C.

■ Open daily 09.00–12.00, 15.30–17.00; winter and Sun 09.00–12.00. Women must cover their shoulders and arms and men are required to wear long trousers. Shawls and other concealing garments may be had for a modest fee, at the entrance.

Access is through the ceremonial entrance in the south-west corner. A brief ascent leads to three communicating cloisters, rebuilt along the lines of those constructed in the 16C and18C. The cloister nearest the entrance contains a bronze Death of St

ABBEY OF MONTE CASSINO

Noviziato

Chiostro del Priore

0   50 m₅

1 Chapter Ho.
2 Court
3 Conference Hall
4 Church
5 Hall of Honour
6 Garden
7 Chiostro dei Benefattori
8 Refectory
9 Grand Prefettorio
10 Small Cloister

Entrance

Benedict by the modern sculptor Attilio Selfa. The lines of the destroyed church of San Martino, where the saint is reputed to have died, are marked in the pavement. In the central cloister is a well head of good design and, at the foot of the staircase, a statue of St Benedict (1736), which survived the bombardments unharmed. The staircase, of monumental proportions, leads to an elegant atrium and, beyond, to the **Chiostro dei Benefattori**, fronting the basilica, with statues of saints, popes and sovereigns, built to a design by Antonio da Sangallo the Younger.

The rebuilt **church** has entrance doors with bronze reliefs illustrating the first four destructions of the abbey. Its predecessor was itself a rebuilding in 1649–1717 from designs by Cosimo Fanzago. As richly Baroque as it was before, the interior is faced with marble intarsia which faithfully repeats the earlier design. Among the several paintings are works by Cavalier d'Arpino, Francesco de Mura and Francesco Solimena. Beneath the high altar, in a silver and bronze casket, are the remains of St Benedict and of his twin sister St Scholastica. In the choir of the old church were the tombs of Pietro de' Medici (died 1503) by Antonio and Francesco da Sangallo and of Guido Fieramosca by Giovanni da Nola (1535–48). The **crypt**, only the central vault of which was seriously damaged, is built in brightly coloured granite, with traces of old frescoes and decorations by the monks of Beuron in Germany (c 1898), executed with great severity of style.

The contents of the *****library and archives**—over 80,000 volumes, including 500 incunabula—were deposited in the Vatican in 1943. Among the precious documents are the Paulus Diaconus collection (8C), the 11C *Biblia Hebraica* of St Gregory the Great, and the *Liber Moralium* with notes in the handwriting of St Thomas Aquinas. Also preserved is the old main *****door** of the church, a wonderful piece of bronze work cast at Constantinople in 1066 and found damaged in the debris. A panorama famous throughout Italy can be enjoyed from the Loggia del Paradiso, above the portico.

The **town of Cassino** is one of wide streets and severe white buildings. Ruins have been left as a memorial, in the northern section. It takes its name from the Volscian *Casinum*, which was located somewhat to the south of the modern town. The site, known in the Middle Ages as Castel San Pietro or San Pietro al Monastero, was deserted in 866 by its inhabitants in favour of the newly founded settlement of *Eulogomenopolis* (or Town of St Benedict), later called *San Germano*, and since 1871 Cassino.

To the north-west of the town, the medieval ruin of Rocca Ianula tops a rocky peak that was a formidable obstacle in the fighting of 1944 (Castle Hill, 187m). The old Via Latina leads south to the remains of a Roman amphitheatre, above which are the ruins of the **Cappella del Crocifisso**, an antique tomb made over into a church dedicated to St Nicholas of Bari around the year 1000 and reconsecrated by Pope Innocent III in the later 16C. Within are remains of Byzantine frescoes. On the other side of the valley stood the villa of Terrentius Varro, where Mark Antony led a life of dissipation.

To the south of the railway line, c 1km along the road to Sant'Angelo in Theodice, is (right) **Cassino British Military Cemetery**, the largest British military cemetery in Italy, with 4267 graves of those who fell in operations in the vicinity. Here, too, is the memorial commemorating over 4000 officers and men of the Commonwealth who died in the Sicilian and Italian campaigns and who have no known grave. Designed by Louis de Soissons and unveiled in

1956, it consists of a formal garden with an ornamental pool in the centre. On each side rise 12 marble pillars on which the names of the dead are recorded.

THE PLAIN OF CAPUA
Beyond Cassino, the extinct volcano of Monte Roccamonfina is available on the right. At **Teano**, in 1860, Victor Emmanuel II on his march southward met Garibaldi returning from the Expedition of the Thousand and the overthrow of the Bourbon dynasty of Naples. The town occupies the site of the ancient *Teanum*, capital of the Sidicini, and possesses a Roman amphitheatre (near the road to the station), the Romanesque church of San Paride (just beyond), and a medieval cattedrale (restored). At nearby **Calvi Risorta**, the ancient *Cales* (famous for its wine), the little Romanesque cathedral, with a Cosmatesque pulpit and bishop's throne, is intact; likewise the small 10C castle and the **Grotta dei Santi** (30 min walk up the Rio de Lanzi), with its remarkable collection of 10C mural paintings of saints.

51km **Capua**, a town of 20,000 inhabitants, is situated within a narrow bend of the Volturno, 5km west of Monte Tifata (604m).

History
The town was founded in 856 by refugees from the ancient city, who built a new town on the ruins of *Casilinum*, noted for its heroic defence against Hannibal in 216 BC and deserted in the 2C AD. The new Capua became the medieval centre of the agricultural *Terra di Lavoro* and an important frontier town of the realm of Sicily. Its famous gate, designed by Freder ick II in 1247, was destroyed in 1557.

The town fell, after a bloody siege, to the French under D' Aubigny and their ally Cesare Borgia, in 1501. Honorius I (pope 625–638) and Ettore Fieramosca (died 1515; see below) were both natives. The plain and hills to the east of Capua were the scenes of the first Battle of the Volturno (1 October 1860), when Garibaldi defeated the Bourbons of Naples. Afterwards he entered and occupied the town.

The Via del Duomo crosses the town from Piazza dei Giudici, on the south, where the **Palazzo del Municipio** (1561) incorporates seven marble busts from the amphitheatre at Santa Maria Capua Vetere (see below), to Via Roma and the Museo Campano, on the north. The **Cattedrale**, founded in 835 and almost completely rebuilt, was destroyed in 1942 except for part of the apse, right outer wall, and side chapels. Of the 24 columns in the atrium (slightly damaged), 16 are original; the beautiful campanile dates from 861. The **crypt**, with 14 antique columns, contains mosaics.

The **Museo Campano**, in the former palace of the Dukes of San Cipriano, has been restored after bomb damage; the portal is in a late Catalan Gothic style. The collections (open Tue–Sat 09.00–13.30, Sun and holidays 09.00–13.00) include sculptures from ancient Capua, notably the extraordinary series of **Deae Matres** or Madri from the temple of Mater Matuta. These small women of stone, holding stone babies, are offerings to a female divinity, made in the hope of bearing pregnant or of giving birth safely, or offered in thanks after the birth. Uncovered in 1845 near Santa Maria Capua Vetere, they date from the 6C to the 1C BC.

Here are also inscriptions from the amphitheatre, a fine series of Campanian terracottas (mostly salvaged), a colossal head of Capua Imperiale and medieval sculptures. A small picutre gallery is devoted to Southern Italian art of the 15C to 18C. In the centre of the town is the Gothic palazzo of Ettore Fieramosca, one of the champions of the *Disfida di Barletta*.

A surprising country church

To the north-east of Capua the Cappella dei Morti commemorates the 5000 victims of the siege of 1501. Beyond the chapel (4km), at the foot of Monte Tifata, is the basilica of ***Sant' Angelo in Formis** (open by appointment; tel. 0823 960064), reconstructed in 1073 and adorned with 12 columns and 11C frescoes of Old and New Testament scenes, featuring prophets, kings, and saints. These are of the school of Monte Cassino and show a strong Byzantine influence.

The shortest (not the fastest) road to Naples (33km) runs from Capua via (15km) **Aversa**, a town of 58,000 inhabitants founded by the Normans in 1030 and little damaged in the Second World War. In the **castello** (rebuilt in the 18C), Andrew of Hungary, husband of Joan I, was murdered in 1345, and three years later Charles of Durazzo, who had instigated the murder, was killed by Louis of Hungary, Andrew's brother.

Aversa's cathedral preserves some original Norman work. **San Lorenzo** has a Lombard façade and a beautiful cloister. **San Francesco** houses a small collection of religious art. The white wine of Aversa, called Asprinio, is locally esteemed. Domenico Cimarosa (1749–1801), the composer, was a native of the town.

Sant' Arpino, a village 3km east, is near the ruins of *Atella*, the home of the *Fabulae Atellanae*, satrical farce in the Oscan language, which became traditional in the Roman theatre.

6km (from Capua) **Santa Maria Capua Vetere**, a town of 33,000 inhabitants, occupies the site of the ancient Capua.

History

An Oscan settlement here was transformed by the Etruscans into a city called *Capua* and soon became the most important place in Campania and the richest and most luxurious city in Southern Italy. Constanly assailed and sometimes defeated by the warlike Samnites, it placed itself under the protection of Rome in 343 BC.

It was always a hotbed of unrest, however, and it opened its gates to Hannibal in 216 BC. According to the legend, the Carthaginians were so softened by the luxury of the city that they never achieved another success. Capua was retaken by the Romans in 211 and severely punished. In 73 BC the revolt of the gladiators headed by the Spartacus broke out here in the amphitheare. Under the empire Capua was the most flourishing town in Southern Italy, but it was razed by the Saracens and its inhabitants fled in 856 to found the modern Capua. The present town on this site grew from a small settlement that clustered round the church of Santa Maria, which survived the Saracen raid.

Just outside the town are two interesting and well-preserved Roman tombs, the second of which is the largest in Campania. The imposing ***amphitheatre** (open daily 09.00–dusk) was built under Augustus and restored by Hadrian and Antoninus Pius. Although it has been exploited for building stone over the centuries, it escaped damage in the Second World War. It measures 170 x 140m, being second in size only to the Colosseum in Rome; it had four storeys and was surrounded by 80 arches, of which only two survive. Under the arena are three covered galleries, with a fourth around the circumference, and six vaulted passages lit by square apertures. Fragments of the building's sculptural decoration and other antiquities (notably a 2C mosaic pavement with Nereids and Tritons) are set in the part at the south side of the monument. Several statues have been removed to the Museo Archeologico Nazionale in Naples, and seven of the busts of deities that adorned the keystones of the arches have been incorporated in the façade of the town hall of Capua.

Explorations in 1976 revealed, in the vicinity of the amphitheatre, a military camp of the 2C BC, believed to be that of the Carthaginian forces engaged in the siege of Capua. In 1923 an interesting subterranean **Mithraeum,** with well-preserved frescoes, was discovered nearby; visitors are conducted (10 min walk) by the custodian. Further on, in Corso Umberto I, is a ruined arch erected in honour of Hadrian. The **Cattedrale** (Santa Maria), contains 51 antique columns from Capuan temples.

At San Prisco, 2km north-east, the church contains 5C and 6C mosaics in the tomb-chapel of St Matrona, princess of Lusitania.

6km Caserta, see Route 5F, and from there to Naples.

B.   Via the Monti Lepini

*This route, which follows the principal rail line from Rome to Naples, joins Route 1C at Terracina. The most interesting sights north of Terracina lie in the Monti Lepini, and seeing them may entail a diversion by bus if you are travelling by train. **Cori**, **Sermoneta**, and **Sezze** are famous for their ancient and medieval remains; and the impressive **Abbey of Fossanova** is the oldest conventual complex of the Cistercian Order in Italy. Its Burgundian Gothic forms would be imitated by Southern Italian builders again and again. Last but not least, if you are fond of Rationalist architecture you will be intrigued by the town plan and public buildings of **Latina**, built from the ground up in the 1930s. If you are not keen on this period in 20C architecture, Latina is best avoided.*

Local automobile and lorry traffic can be heavy on all main roads, especially the Via Appia between Rome and Terracina and in the vicinity of Naples. Travel time by car is about four hours. Rail travellers may reach Naples, stopping for two or three hours in Formia and Gaeta, in a long half-day. Direct and regional trains stop also at Sezze and Priverno-Fossanova stations. The latter is connected by a branch line (sometimes a bus service is substituted) to Terracina.

ROAD 256km. Highway 7 (Via Appia), 7dir, 7qu, and local roads—38km Velletri—17km Cori—26km Sezze—18km Priverno—30km Terracina—31km Gaeta—7km Fórmia—74km Pozzuoli—15km Naples.

RAILWAY from Rome (Termini, Tiburtina, or Ostiense) to Naples (Centrale) in 2hr–2hr 30min. The Pendolino from Rome (Termini) to Naples (Mergellina) makes the run in 1hr 45min. Most trains stop at Latina, Formia and Aversa. Frequent buses run between Formia and Gaeta and Terracina; and between Cisterna di Latina and Cori. Regional trains stop at Sezze and Priverno-Fossanova.

HOTELS EN ROUTE: Sperlonga, ***Parkhotel Fiorelle, tel. 0771 54092, fax 0771 549246; Gaeta, **Grand Hotel Le Rocce, tel. 0771 740985, fax 0771 741633. Youth Hostel at Sperlonga (under construction 1995).

RESTAURANTS EN ROUTE: Formia, ***Castello Miramare (with rooms), località Pagnano, tel. 0771 700138, fax 0771 700139; Fondi (Madonna della Civita), **Montefusco (with rooms), tel. 0771 727560.

Some pleasant hill towns

From Rome to Velletri, see Blue Guide Rome and environs. Then follow the posted indications for (17km) **Cori**, a little town (10,000 inhab.) combining two centres, Cori a Valle (220m) and Cori a Monte (398m). Famous for its ancient *walls, Cori suffered grievously during the Second World War, but the walls and Roman remains escaped unharmed. It is one of the oldest towns in Italy, its foundation being attributed to Dardanus of Troy or to Coras, brother of Tiburtus. The Roman colony of Cora suffered at the hands of Totila and Barbarossa and was rebuilt by the counts of Segni in the 13C. Its massive walls were constructed at four distinct periods and form a threefold circuit of the hill. The oldest portions date from the 11C BC.

At the entrance to the town is the surviving campanile of the church of Santa Maria della Trinità. From here Via Papa Giovanni XXIII, passing a section of Pelasgian wall, leads to the church of **Sant'Oliva**, which was formed by connecting two adjacent churches built, respectively, in the Middle Ages and in the 15C. In the beautiful cloister is a small collection of archaeological finds from local excavations. The road continues up to the so-called *Temple of Hercules, which despite its present name was probably dedicated to the Capitoline deities Jupiter, Juno, and Minerva. Behind the graceful Doric peristyle is the cella; this became the church of San Pietro, now reduced to a complete ruin. On a clear day the view spans the Monti Lepini and the Pontine Marshes to the sea. Descend to the Piazza San Salvatore, where there are fragmentary ruins of a Temple of Castor and Pollux and, nearby, remains of a cistern, a piscina and Roman walls. Outside the Porta Ninfina are more cyclopean walls and the Ponte della Catena, a boldly constructed Roman bridge attributed to Sulla.

Leave Cori from the south. At (9km) Doganella turn left, passing the *ruins of Ninfa (visits Apr–Oct, first Sat and Sun of month 09.00–12.00, 14.30–18.00), a medieval town abandoned in the 17C because of the malaria from the Pontine Marshes, an extensive swamp land that until recently occupied much of the coastal plain between Rome and Terracina. The remains of churches, houses and other buildings, surrounded by a ruined rectangle of walls, are all overgrown with luxuriant vegetation, making a park; a spring from the Monti Lepini has formed a little lake within the ruins.

Beyond Ninfa (6km) a road bends sharply to the left, ascending the slopes of the Monti Lepini (view of the Agro Romano) to the little town of Norma (433m). A road to the left at the entrance to the town leads to the remains of the Volscian city of *Norba, with massive towers and cyclopean walls. The view is magnificent.

The road to Terracina bends to the right. At the next junction turn right for (6km) **Sermoneta**, a charming medieval town (7000 inhab.) dominated by the well-preserved **Castello Caetani**. The latter was built in the 13C, enlarged in the 14C, and fortified in the early 16C, with the aid of Antonio da Sangallo the Elder. It culminates in a massive keep. The fortress was visited by Cesare and Lucrezia

Borgia, Charles V, and Pope Gregory XIII. The **Cattedrale** has a painting by
Benozzo Gozzoli, and the church of **San Giuseppe** has frescoes by Girolamo
Sicciolante of Sermoneta. A short distance beyond the junction is the 13C abbey of
Valvisciolo, with a fine Cistercian church of 1240.

12km (right) Bassiano (588m) was the birthplace of Aldus Manutius (Teobaldo
Mannucci, 1450–1516), the famous printer. The road descends for 6km to another
junction where you bear right for (2km south) **Sezze**, the Volscian *Setia*. It
preserves cyclopean walls and some Roman and medieval ruins, as well as a 14C
Cattedrale in the Cistercian style, the orientation of which was reversed in the late
15C or early 16C, making for the unusual main façade. The Antiquarium
Comunale (open daily except Mon 09.00–12.00, 16.00–18.00) contains archaeological material from local excavations and 16C and 17C paintings; the Museo
territoriale del giocattolo dei monti Lepini (open daily 08.30–12.30), an interesting
collection of locally crafted toys. The town is famous for its yearly **Passion play**,
enacted in the huge outdoor theatre.

Bear east at the junction for (9m) Roccagorga, and then continue south to cross
Highway 156, the Latina–Frosinone road. 9km **Priverno** (14,000 inhab.) has a
beautiful cathedral of 1283 and a Gothic Palazzo Comunale. Known until recently
as Piperno, it preserves the name of the Volscian Privernum, whose ruins lie 2km
north-east. On the left is a view of the valley of the Amaseno.

The road descends the valley alongside the Priverno branch railway to (5km) the
spendid Cistercian *****Abbey of Fossanova**, where St Thomas Aquinas died in 1274

FOSSANOVA ABBEY

while on his way from Naples to Lyons. The monastery is mentioned for the first time under the name of *Santo Stefano* in documents dating from the 11C. By order of Innocent II it passed in 1134–35 to the Cistercians, who built the present complex along the lines of Cistercian convents in France, in the last quarter of the 12C. It grew in wealth, becoming a leading intellectual centre and maintaining its position until the 15C, when it fell into decadence. The abbey at one time housed an important archive and library, but its documents and codices have since been dispersed.

The **church**, consecrated in 1208, has a plain façade that was meant to be preceded by a three-bayed portico, never built. It is dominated by a rose window and a Gothic door adorned with roll and fillet moulding and staggered shafts with beautifully carved capitals. The lintel bears a delicate interlace relief that is echoed in the tracery of the tympanum. The interior consists of a nave and aisles separated by compound piers, shallow transepts and a rectangular presbytery flanked by four chapels, two on each side. The ceiling is cross-vaulted, with pronounced transverse arches. In accordance with the early Burgundian style introduced to Italy by the Cistercians, the shafts attached to the piers are continued to the springing of the arches and the crossing is surmounted by an octagonal tower with mullioned windows, terminating in a lantern, also with windows.

Adjoining the church on the right is the **cloister**, striking in its harmony of proportion and detail. The older, Romanesque sections are distinguished by sequences of five arches carried by coupled columns. The side opposite the church, rebuilt in 1280–1300 in the Burgundian Gothic style, is articulated into groups of four arches, with a small aedicule projecting into the garden midway along. The sacristy, chapter house, refectory, and kitchen occupy the ground floor; the monks' cells, the floor above. Detached from the cloister are the Casa dei Conversi, the foresteria, and the Infirmary. The room where St Thomas died, later made into a chapel, has an 18C relief of the saint's death.

Just beyond the abbey, a road leads left for **Sonnino** (8km, 430m), which preserves a drum-tower of its castle and some 13C portions of the church of San Michele.

Descend into the Agro Pontino and (10km) turn left on the Via Appia. From here to (14km) Terracina, see Route 1C.

Following the Via Appia to Terracina
An alternative route, involving fewer curves (but more commercial traffic; express buses from Rome), follows the Via Appia to Terracina. From Rome to Velletri, see *Blue Guide Rome and environs*. Beyond Velletri cross the railway and descend the lower slopes of the Alban hills.

14km **Cisterna di Latina** is a town of 31,000 inhabitants with a station on the Rome–Naples railway. It lies near the site of *Tres Tabernae*, a stage of St Paul's journey to Rome (Acts xxviii, 15). The town is named after a reservoir built by Nero to supply Antrium (Anzio) with water. In the Middle Ages it was a fief of the Caetani, dukes of Sermoneta. It was one of the primary objectives after the Allied landing at Anzio and Nettuno in January 1944 and has been almost completely rebuilt since the Second World War. A local road branches to the right from the Via Appia after passing under the railway and runs south in a straight line through the reclaimed lands of the Agro Pontino. At Borgo Piave it meets the Strada Mediana from Pomezia, and you turn left.

16km **Latina** (104,000 inhab.), founded in 1932 and originally called Littoria, is the first and largest of the new towns of the Agro Pontino. Situated in the centre of the reclaimed Pontine Marshes, it is perhaps the best surviving example of *Rationalist town planning. Its orderly buildings, conspicuous lack of decorative detail, systematic street plan and large public spaces were intended to embody political principles dear to the Fascist regime, such as strength, authority, and regimentation.

■ **Information**. EPT, Via Duca del Mare 19; tel. 0773 480672, fax 0773 661266.

■ **Post Office**. Piazzale Bonificatori.

The Corso della Repubblica crosses the town from north to south, opening out into three squares—Piazza Roma, the spacious Piazza del Popolo (the town centre) and Piazza San Marco. In Piazza del Popolo are the **Palazzo Comunale** with a high tower, the Chamber of Commerce and other public buildings. Various important streets radiate from this square. On the west side of Piazza San Marco is the severe church of **San Marco**, which has a lofty campanile. On the east side of the Piazza del Popolo, Via Diaz and Piazza della Libertà, with the Prefettura, lead to the Parco Comunale. Further north, Viale Mazzini leads east to Piazza Bruno Buozzi, with the imposing **Palazzo di Giustizia**. A series of avenues encircles the centre of the town.

Near the town is Italy's first nuclear power station (1962), the first to be built abroad by a British firm.

After leaving the road to Latina on the right, the Via Appia approaches the railway, then diverges south-east. The road is now dead straight for 40km—the longest undeviating stretch in Italy—and is familiarly known as 'la fettuccia' (the ribbon). Flanked by canals on either side—that on the right is the Canale Linea Pio of Pius VI—the road crosses the Agro Pontino from end to end. On the left are the Monti Lepini, with their valleys opening into the plain and their picturesque villages. On the right are the reclamation roads of the Bonificia Pontina.

13km crossroad. Latina lies 6km right, its station 2km left on the road to Norma (13km). Near here was *Appii Forum*, on the Appian Way, where the brethren from Rome met St Paul (Acts xxviii, 15). Appii Forum was an interchange station for travellers from Rome who wished to continue their journey to Anxur (Terracina) by canal.

Monte Circeo rises ahead in the distance. 8km, Highway 156 leads left to Sezze (8km), which has been visible for some time on its hill. This road continues on to Frosinone (Route 1A). At 7km is a turning (right) for Pontinia (2km), another of the towns of the Agro Pontino, founded in 1935. At (4km) Mesa are the remains of a Roman tomb. After 3km cross a road from Priverno (16km) to Sabaudia (11km; see below). You now pass over the Canale della Selcella and two streams, tributaries of the Canale Linea Pio, to (14km) Terracina.

C. Via the Coast

*The chief sight on the northern leg of this route is the **Parco Nazionale del Circeo**, well worth a visit even if you are not an ornithologist (the area is one of Mediterranean Europe's largest bird sanctuaries). Hereabouts are several attractive seaside resorts—**Terracina**, with its imposing Temple of Jupiter Anxurus; **Sperlonga**, where the Roman élite goes; and **Gaeta**, a charming medieval town with a fine beach—not to mention some of the most breathtaking landscape on the Tyrhennian coast. From Minturno, where there are some interesting Roman remains, a diversion can be made to Sessa Aurunca, with its attractive 12C cathedral. The main route continues south-east after Minturno, bearing across the Phlegraean Fields (Route 3E) to Naples. Those who are driving will enjoy magnificent views after Terracina, where the road runs high above the sea.*

A word of warning: in summer this route is swamped by Romans (and Neapolitans) on their way to and from the seaside resorts. Traffic is congested and trains may be packed.

During the week, in all seasons, due account must be taken of commercial traffic and local commuters, especially in the vicinity of Naples. Like Route 1B, this itinerary calls for around four hours of driving. Rail travellers may reach Naples, stopping for two or three hours in Formia and Gaeta, in a long half-day.

ROAD 261km. Highways 148, 7 (Via Appia), 213, 7dir, 7qu and local roads—64km Nettuno—42km Sabaudia—11km San Felice Circeo—17km Terracina—31km Gaeta—7km Fórmia—74km Pozzuoli—15km Naples.

RAILWAY from Rome (Termini, Tiburtina, or Ostiense) to Naples (Centrale) in 2hr–2hr 30min. The Pendolino from Rome (Termini) to Naples (Mergellina) makes the run in 1hr 45min. Most trains stop at Latina, Formia and Aversa. Frequent buses run between Formia and Gaeta and Terracina; and between Terracina and points in the Parco Nazionale del Circeo. Direct and regional trains stop at Priverno-Fossanova, from where a branch line (sometimes replaced by a bus service) continues to Terracina.

HOTELS EN ROUTE: Sabaudia , ****Le Dune, tel. 0773 511511, fax 0773 55643; San Felice Circeo, ****Punta Rossa, tel. 0773 548085, fax 0773 548975; Sperlonga, ***Parkhotel Fiorelle, tel. 0771 54092, fax 0771 549246; Gaeta, **Grand Hotel Le Rocce, tel. 0771 740985, fax 0771 741633.

RESTAURANTS EN ROUTE: San Felice Circeo, ***La Veranda, Hotel Maga Circe, tel. 0773 547821, fax 0773 546224; Formia, ***Castello Miramare (with rooms), località Pagnano, tel. 0771 700138, fax 0771 700139; Itri (Madonna della Civita), *Montefusco (with rooms) tel. 0771 727560.

The beaches of southern Lazio

From Rome to Nettuno, see *Blue Guide Rome and environs*. Leave Nettuno by the Via Severiana and proceed east through gently rolling countryside. At (8km) Acciarella turn right and keep right until (11km) the road leading to (2km) **Torre Astura**, a castle on an islet joined to the mainland by a bridge and dominating the Via Severiana. Here Conradin, last of the Hohenstaufen, sought refuge after the battle of Tagliacozzo in 1268, only to be handed over by Giacamo Frangipani to Charles of Anjou, by whom he was put to death. Cicero, after his proscription, embarked at Astura on the flight that ended with his death at Formiae. The ***view** from the tower embraces the coast towards Nettuno and Anzio, with the Alban

Hills to the north and the Monti Lepini and Ausoni to the north-east and east. In the sea on the east side of the building, at water level, are ruins commonly called the Villa of Cicero, with a fish-pond in a good state of preservation.

Continuing along the coastline, here called the Lido di Latina, towards the south-east, you cross the Fosso Astura, formerly the Mussolini (now Moscarello) Canal, right flank of the Anzio beach-head. Beyond (4km) the Torre di Foce Verde, a road branches left for Latina (12km; Route 1B). Reclamation roads are seen on the left. You next reach the Idrovoro di Capo Portiere, after which the road enters the wild, beautiful *Parco Nazionale del Circeo.

> The park was set up in 1934 to preserve the natural beauty of the area, with its flora and fauna, and to provide a lasting reminder of what the Pontine Marshes were like before they were drained and improved. Extended in 1975 to an area of 8300 hectares, this vast preserve now includes the towns of Sabaudia and San Felice Circeo (see below) as well as the four coastal lakes of Fogliano, Monaci, Caprolace and Sabaudia. It extends from Capo Portiere, on the north, to Monte Circeo, on the south. Within are four 'riserve naturali integrali', specially protected areas to which entrance is granted only with the prior authorisation of the Azienda di Stato per le Foreste Damaniali at Sabaudia. These reserves are known above all for their oaks, ashes, horn-beams, elms, sorb-apples and black alders, for their eucalyptus groves and for the dwarf palms that grow on the steep slopes of Monte Circeo. Concerted efforts have been made to restore to the area the abundance of wildfowl for which the Pontine Marshes were either a resting place or a permanent abode, and the park now counts more than 200 species, among them, quail, wood-cocks, herons, seagulls, storks, woodpeckers and various birds of prey, including ospreys. Within the park limits are the ruins of a so-called Villa of Domitian (visits by special permission only), of Roman harbour works and of the walls and acropolis of Circeii (see below), as well as several medieval watch-towers.

The road runs through sand dunes 12–15m high, separating the **Lago di Fogliano** from the sea. The village of Fogliano is on the landward side. This lagoon is 5km long, with a maximum width of 1.5km and a depth of 4–5m; it is joined to the much smaller Lago dei Monaci by a short canal called La Fossella. Between the two lagoons is (9km) the Torre di Fogliano; here the road bends sharply inland to cross the Rio Martino. At Borgo Grappa you turn right, passing through the lowlands on the landward side of the Lago dei Monaci. Further on the road passes another lagoon, the Lago di Caprolace, 5km long, connected by the Fossa Augusta, built by Nero, with the Lago di Sabaudia, formerly Lago di Paola and in antiquity *Lacus Circeus*. This is a long narrow lagoon extending for 8km with a maximum width of 505m, as far as the base of Monte Circeo. It is separated from the sea by dunes, on which the highway runs. In places it is 15m deep. It has six branches or bays, called *bracci*, running inland. On the left are picturesque woods of the Selva del Circeo. In front are the wooded slopes of Monte Circeo and in the distance, rising from the sea, the Ponziane Islands: Ponza, Zannone, and Palmarola. 12km Turning for (2km) Sabaudia.

Sabaudia (15,000 inhab.), attractively situated between two of the arms of the Lago di Sabaudia, the Braccio Annunziata and the Braccio della Crapara, was founded in 1934. Its centre is the Piazza del Comune, with the **Palazzo Comunale**, from the tower of which there is a fine *view of the surrounding country. Largo Giulio Cesare leads to the **Annunziata**, a church with an imposing mosaic (1955) on the façade; inside is the chapel of Queen Margherita, formerly in the Palazzo Margherita in Rome.

Returning to the shore at Lido di Sabaudia, cross the Emissario Romano (also called the Porta Papale or Portocanale di Paola), an ancient outlet canal contained by walls in *opus reticulatum*. 6km Paola, at the south end of the Lago di Sabaudia, stands close to the canal. On the right is the cylindrical Torre Paola (26m), situated at the north-west end of Monte Circeo; the tower was built by Paul III (1534–49) to defend the canal. **Monte Circeo** (571m), wooded and rock-girt, rises abruptly from the south end of the tongue of land reaching into the sea between Anzio and Terracina. On its summit are the remains of a Temple of the Sun and a lighthouse to seaward. On its slopes are the cyclopean walls of the vanished town of *Circeii* and numerous caves; one of these, on the west coast, is called the Grotta della Maga Circe (**Circe's Cave**). In fact, Monte Circeo was once an island identified with *Aeaea*, the home of Circe, famous for her magic arts. Ulysses, who escaped the metamorphosis of his companions after they had been cast upon the island and forced Circe to restore them to human form, stayed for a year with the enchantress, who became by him the mother of Telegonus, reputed founder of *Tusculum* and of *Praeneste*, now Palestrina. Boats may be hired at Paola for a sea trip round the promontory.

The road now runs nearly due east across the base of Monte Circeo to (5km) a fork. The Via Severiana goes on from here to Terracina. You may turn right to reach (1.5km) **San Felice Circeo** (8000 inhab.), finely situated on the eastern slopes of Monte Circeo and an excellent excursion centre. Follow the coast, passing the ends of two canals built in the 16C to drain the Pontine Marshes. On the right, modern bathing establishments stretch along the beach. 5km Foce Sisto is the original outlet of the Fosso Sisto of Sixtus V. 8km Porto Badino lies at the end of the Canale Portatore, cut by Leo X. Ahead, Terracina is visible below the remains of the Temple of Anxur.

TERRACINA, GAETA AND FORMIA
15km leave the coast and enter **Terracina**, a town of 40,000 inhabitants situated between the last slopes of the Ausonian Hills and the Tyrrhenian Sea. The new town lies close to the sea; the old town, on the slopes above.

History
The Roman *Tarracina* succeeded the ancient Volscian town of *Anxur*: the names seem to have been interchangeable. Terracina was an important stage on the Appian Way from Rome to Capua and Brundisium and a favourite seaside resort of the Roman aristocracy. Ghalba, Roman Emperor AD 68–69, was born here in 3 BC. The town was noted for its Temple of Jupiter Anxurus, which crowned its fortified citadel.

■ **Information**. AA, Via Leopardi; tel. 0773 727759, fax 0773 727964.

■ **Ferries** to Ponza (2hr 15min).

In the principal street of the new town, built by Pius VI, is the early 19C church of the Santissimo Salvatore. At the east end of the town is the **Pisco Montano**, a rocky promontory cut away by Trajan to a height of 36m, to make an easier path for the Appian Way, which originally climbed over the summit of the rock. Horace,

who took the old road on his journey to Brundisium, refers to the three-mile crawl uphill in carriages to Anxur. The depth of the cutting is marked at intervals of 10 Roman feet, starting from the top; the lowest mark, near the present roadway, shows the figure CXX.

The street to the left of the Santissimo Salvatore ascends past a large (6.5m high) Roman arch of the first century AD to the **Piazza del Municipio**, a large (83 x 33m) square that occupies the site of the ancient forum. On the right rises the 14C Palazzo Venditti; on the left, the modern Palazzo Comunale. The Torre Frumentaria, adjacent, houses a small **Museo Archeologico** (open May–Sept 09.00–13.00, 17.00–19.00, closed Mon and the day after holidays; Oct–Apr 09.00–14.00, closed Sun and holidays), containing Greek and Roman statues and fragments.

At the far end of the square stands the **Cattedrale di San Cesario**, built amid the ruins of a Tempio di Roma e Augusto, of whose pavement much remains.

The cathedral, consecrated in 1074 and rebuilt in the 17C, is approached by a portico of antique columns on medieval bases, enclosing a 12C mosaic frieze. The fine campanile dates from the 14C. In the interior is a good mosaic pavement dating from the 12C or 13C; the pulpit and candelabrum are likewise decorated with mosaics. The two ciboria and the high altar are made up of antique fragments. The carved chest in the sacristy is thought to date from the 8C or 9C.

Along the right side and the rear of the church are vestiges of the ancient cella walls, which provided the foundation of the Christian building. The stones on the right flank bear a running acanthus-leaf pattern. Opposite is a largo containing ruins of the **Capitoline temple** dating from the first century BC and brought to light accidentally by fighting in 1944. Beside and behind the temple are well-preserved tracts of Roman street pavement. The curved segments of Roman masonry just north of this site suggest the presence of a theatre.

The ascent to the right of the cathedral takes 30–45 min to the summit of the hill (227m), dominating the town. Here are ruins of the walls of Anxur and of the ***Temple of Jupiter Anxurus** (possibly dedicated to Venus Obsequens, the bringer of good fortune). The temple is locally known as the Palazzo di Teodorico (Palace of Theodoric). The powerful arches of the foundation (33 x 20m) dominate the surrounding landscape. The ***view** is superb. To the south-west (17km) rises Monte Circeo.

From Terracina to Formia via Fondi

The inland route to Formia presents medieval hill-towns and superb natural scenery. Beyond the citadel of Anxur the Via Appia turns north-east with the foothills of the Monti Ausoni on the left. On the right is the outlet of the Lago di Fondi, the largest of the coastal lakes of Lazio (16km long), which you reach at Torre del Pesce. Beyond the railway you pass a turning for Monte San Biagio, a village on a hill (133m); on the right is its railway station.

18km **Fondi** is the *Fundi* of Horace's satires, which produced the famous Caecuban wine of antiquity. The old town is built along the traditional lines of the Roman battle camp. It is rectangular in plan, each side measuring about 400m. At the ends of the *decumanus* and *cardo maximi* are four gates; the forum stood at the centre of the grid, on the site now occupied by the church of Santa Maria. Although the town was sacked and burned by the Saracens in 866 and again destroyed by fire in 1222, its street plan still follows the ancient model, the city blocks being laid out along the cardi and decumani inferiori. The **Palazzo del Principe** and the **Castello**, once the seat of the Caetani and later of the Colonna, have been restored after war damage. The castle is note-worthy as the scene of the Conclave of 1378, when the dissident cardinals, outraged by the savage, erratic Urban VI, elected Clement VII as antipope, an act that marked the beginning of the Great Schism. In 1534 the corsair Barbarossa, fired by the fame of the beauty of Giulia Colonna, attempted to abduct her from the palace here; the lady, warned in time, fled inland. The baffled pirate sacked the town and massacred many of its people.

The church of **San Pietro** contains an early 14C Caetani tomb and a 13C pulpit and throne. Santa Maria Assunta and San Domenico (where St Thomas Aquinas taught) are also interesting.

The Via Appia now turns south-east, back towards the coast, and begins to climb into the Auruncian Hills, once notorious as a haunt of brigands, among whom were Marco Sciarra, the protector of Torquato Tasso (16C), and Fra' Diavolo (1771–1806), a murderous partisan of the Bourbons of Naples. The road winds up to a pass between Monte Grande (776m; left) and Monte Morano (517m; right) and then descends.

14km **Itri**, an important agricultural centre, was Fra' Diavolo's birthplace. It is divided by the Fosso Pontone in two: the upper town, huddled at the foot of the ruined castle; and the lower town, which fans out on the more level land below. Beyond, the road descends. Leave Itri station on the right and pass under the main railway, cross the valley known as the Conca di Sant'Angelo, and pass beneath the branch line for Gaeta (see below). Just beyond, a secondary road diverges for Gaeta, passing (left) the Tomb of Cicero. 9km Formia, see below.

The main road to Formia is now Highway 213, the Litoranea, between Terracina and Gaeta. Opened in 1958 to make viable a beautiful stretch of hitherto inaccessible coast, the road is well surfaced, has frequent lay-bys, viaducts and bridges, and is intelligently signposted. Seven years of building involved the excavation of 700,000 cubic metres of rock, the draining of 30 hectares of land and the construction of four tunnels more than a kilometre in total length. Traces of the ancient Roman road, the Via Flacca, can still be seen along the rock face.

On quitting Terracina leave the Via Appia on the left and continue to (16km) the road (right) for **Sperlonga**, a select resort 1km south-east consisting of an old quarter on a rocky headland and a new quarter behind. Just before the first tunnel, a bit further along the highway, is the charming **Grotta di Tiberio** (open daily 09.00–19.00, winter 09.00–16.00), with a circular pool, where Sejanus took the first step towards his pre-eminence by saving his emperor from a fall of rocks. A little inland, on the main road, is the **Museo Archeologico Nazionale** (open as above), which houses the sculptures, in the Hellenistic style of Pergamum and Rhodes, found during excavations in the grotto (1957–60). An inscription found in the cave, with the names of the three Rhodian sculptors responsible for the Laocoön group in the Vatican, did not lead to the discovery of its original. Instead, a huge group, *The Struggle with Scylla, has been reassembled, with Ulysses holding the Palladium as protection against the monster. A poem of Faustinus, a contemporary of Martial, extols the work as surpassing Virgil's lines on the Laocoön. Other notable sculptures include Ulysses Struggling with Polyphemus, and a bust of Aeneas as tutelary deity of the Julio-Claudian family group.

After passing through four tunnels the highway becomes most attractive. On the right, cliffs drop abruptly into the sea. On the major promontories stand medieval watch-towers.

13km **Gaeta** is a pleasant little town (24,000 inhab.) on a headland at the southern extreme of the gulf of the same name. Once an important fortress, it preserved its freedom throughout the Gothic and Saracenic invasions and reached a high level of importance under the Normans. The citadel was repeatedly attacked during the Middle Ages, but was taken only by treachery or by starving out the inhabitants.

Charles Edward Stuart 'won his spurs' here, aged 13, against the Austrian garrison in 1734. During his voyage from Gaeta to Naples with Charles of Bourbon, the Young Pretender's hat blew into the sea: when it was proposed that a boat should be lowered to recover it, the young Charles told the crew not to trouble, as 'he should be obliged before long to fetch himself a hat [the Crown] in England'.

Gaeta was the last stronghold of Francis II of Naples and fell to the Italian forces in 1861. Today it is famous for its beaches. It is also a NATO naval base.

■ **Information** AA, Piazza Traniello 4; tel. 0771 462767, fax 0771 465738.

The centre of town life is the modern Piazza del Municipio, which fronts on the harbour. From here the Lungomare follows the shore around the north slope of

Monte Orlando to the medieval quarter, passing two sets of defensive fortifications and the scanty remains of a 2C Roman villa. The church of the **Santissima Annunziata**, midway along on the right, dates from 1302, but was rebuilt in 1621. Within are a Nativity and a Crucifixion by Luca Giordano.

Continuing to the heart of the old quarter, you soon reach the **Cattedrale** (Sant'Erasmo). This suffered considerable damage in the Second World War. Dating from 1106 but rebuilt in the 17C and 18C, it has a fine campanile of 1148–1279 incorporating architectural fragments from antique buildings, particularly the tomb of Sempronio Atratino (see below). In the archway beneath the tower are steps leading to the interior. The passageway contains Roman sarcophagi and fragmentary reliefs from a 13C ambo. Within are the marble shaft of a candelabrum with 13C reliefs depicting the lives of Christ and St Erasmus and paintings by Southern Italian artists. The Museo Diocesano (open May–Sep daily 09.00–10.00, 17.00–19.00; Oct–Apr, Sun and holidays 09.00–10.00, 15.30–16.30), contains a small collection of sculptural and architectural fragments, and paintings.

Further west is the little 10C church of San Giovanni a Mare, commonly called San Giuseppe, surrounded by the most picturesque (or melancholy, depending on the season) of the quarter's narrow streets, vaulted passageways, and winding steps. Above to the south rises the **Castello**. The lower part dates from c 1289, the upper from c 1435. The prominent church of San Francesco, further inland, was rebuilt in 1850.

On the summit of Monte Orlando stands the **Tomb of Munatius Plancus** (died after 22 BC), founder of Lyons. The monument consists of a tower in *opus reticulatum* faced with travertine and crowned by a Doric frieze containing scenes of battle in the metopes. The hill itself is supposed to be the grave of Caieta, the nurse of Aeneas; the town was named after her. At the south-west point the cliff, riven by three narrow vertical chasms, is known as the *Montagna Spaccata*. The sanctuary of the Santissima Trinita, founded in the 11C, dominates the headland; the adjacent convent, founded by the Benedictines, is now a seminary.

> More ancient tombs may be seen in the environs. At the north end of the town, above the quarter of Porto Salvo, stands the Tomb of Sempronio Atratino, damaged by fighting in 1815. The marble facing was removed to build the campanile of the cathedral. Beyond Gaeta, between the coast road and Via Appia, stands the so-called Tomb of Cicero, recently restored.

7km **Formia**, with 34,000 inhabitants, was praised by the Romans for its wine. The town is the ancient *Formiae*, the fabled abode of Lamus, king of the savage Laestrygones.

History

After the murder of Julius Caesar on 15 March 44 BC, Cicero placed himself at the head of the republican party and in his Philippic orations assailed Mark Antony with immoderate vehemence. On the formation, on 27 November 43 BC, of the triumvirate by Octavian, Antony, and Lepidus, Cicero's name was put on the list of those proscribed. The orator fled to his villa at Formiae, but was there overtaken by Antony's soldiers and killed on 7 December, in his 64th year. At the time, Formiae was one of the chief residential centres of Italy, second only to Baiae (Route 7E) in terms of the number and opulence of its patrician villas. The area still contains numerous (though scanty) remains of farms and villages. As it was for the Romans, Formia is today a favourite bathing resort, and the sea views are enchanting. It was virtually destroyed in the Second World War and has been rebuilt since 1945.

■ **Information:** AA, Via Unità d'Italia 30/40; tel. 0771 771490, fax 0771 771386.

■ **Ferries:** daily for Ponza (2hr 30min).

■ **Hydrofoils:** daily for Ponza (1hr 20min)

In Piazza della Vittoria at the centre of the town, the municipio (in the former Convento dei Teresiani) houses a small **Antiquarium** (open 08.30–13.00, 15.00–19.00; closed Mon) containing statues and other material, mainly of the 1C AD, brought to light in local excavations. Some columns of a temple of Venus are to be seen in the piazza itself, which is planted as a public garden.

Below the square and separated from it by a modern viaduct is the Porto Nuovo, with ferries the year round to Ponza and Ventotene (Route 2). The medieval Torre di Mola rises to the south. Along the waterfront to the north on the grounds of the Giardini Colagrosso and the Villa Rubino, are the important remains (stuccoed vaults and fragments of wall paintings) of a Roman villa of the first or second century, commonly called **Cicero's Villa**, and a brief segment of defensive walls. The Porticciolo Caposele, nearby, incorporates part of the ancient harbour.

Along the Via Appia, further inland, can be seen the **Fontana Romana di San Rimigio**, a Roman fountain behind a well-preserved tract of the ancient road. The octagonal **Torre di Sant'Erasmo**, on the hillside to the south-east, marks the site of the Roman citadel. In the nearby Vico Anfiteatro is a private habitation built on the ancient theatre, the structure of which is still clearly visible (the amphitheatre, after which the street is wrongly named, stands in an orange grove near the station and awaits excavation). The small Roman Porticciolo di Gianola is reached by a road at the southern edge of the town.

The Campanian shore
At (6km) Santa Croce is a turning left for (14km) **Ausonia**, a village recalling the Samnite town of *Ausona* destroyed in the Second Samnite War. On a byroad just south of it is the church of **Santa Maria del Piano** (15C, restored), noted for the frescoes, possibly of the 12C, in its crypt. The surrounding ruins are probably those of Ausona. The road goes on to Cassino (Route 1A).

3km Scauri is another sea resort, with the ruins of the villa of M. Aemilius Scaurus, consul in 107 BC. It is connected with **Minturno** (3km east), a town of 18,000 inhabitants, where the church of San Pietro contains a Cosmatesque candelabrum and pulpit (1260–70), and the Annunziata has frescoes in the tradition of Giotto. Beyond (3km) Marina di Minturno the road emerges into open country. To the south the River Garigliano, the ancient *Liris*, divides Lazio from Campania.

On the west bank are the ruins of **Minturnae** (open 09.00–1hr before sunset), once an important town built amidst marshes formed by the overflowing of the river. Here the proscribed Marius, who had been taken prisoner in 88 BC, daunted the would-be assassin sent by Sulla.

History

The ancient *Minturnae*, the chief Tyrrhenian port of the Ausoni, became a major Roman colony in 295 BC. It is repeatedly described in the letters of Cicero, and a clue to its decline may be found in the *Metamorphoses* of Ovid (XV, 716), where allusion is made to its malaria-infested waters. The earliest settlement stood on the right bank of the Liris roughly 3km from the mouth of the river, and was enclosed within a rectangular enceinte in opus polygonale, with gates on the north and south sides and bastions at the four corners. The Roman town grew up to the west within its own wall circuit in *opus reticulatum*, with square and polygonal towers. The Appian Way, which crossed it from end to end, passed between the republican and imperial fora, forming the main street. A road flanked by tabernae ran along the river bank to the harbour, beyond which stood the chief sanctuary of the town, dedicated to Marica, the Italic goddess of fertility, to whom the waters of the river and its marshes were sacred.

■ **Information:** AA, Via Marconi 23, Scauri; tel. 0771 683783, fax 0771 683400.

Excavations conducted jointly by the University of Pennsylvania and the Soprintendenza alle Antichità in Naples in 1931–33 brought to light numerous ex-voto offerings, with archaic votive statues of Italic, Etruscan, and Greek workmanship, now at the Museo Archeologico Nazionale in Naples. More sculpture, pottery, and architectural fragments unearthed during the excavations are displayed in the Antiquarium Nazionale (Via Appia 7; opening times as the ruins).

The most conspicuous remains are located in the area of the Roman town. Chief among these is the **theatre**, built in the first century and later restored, of which the scena, orchestra, and cavea survive. Behind the theatre lies the **republican forum**, originally surrounded by a colonnade and incorporating two fountains on the side that faced the Appian Way. To the west stood temples dedicated to the Capitoline triad and, possibly, to Roma and Augustus; to the east another large temple extended over part of the Italic town. South of the Appian Way and separated from it by another arcade stood the **imperial forum**, flanked by the basilica and by public baths. Archaeologists have identified the site of an amphitheatre, beyond. Along the river bank are remains of the harbour and, 500m further on, part of a **Temple of Marica** (6C BC). Also visible are ruins of an aqueduct.

On the right bank of the river is **Minturno British Military Cemetery**, with the graves of 2049 men who fell in the Battle of the Garigliano, January 1944. The battle antedated by a few days the landings at Anzio and Nettuno. At an earlier battle of the Garigliano (1503), in which Gonsalvo de Cordova defeated the French, the Chevalier Bayard is said to have defended a bridge single-handed against 200 Spanish horsemen.

From Minturno to Capua

This is the fastest road route from Terracina to Naples. On the left bank of the Garigliano Highway 7 leads east to (20km) **Sessa Aurunca**. This small town standing on the saddle between the Monti Aurunci and the spur of Monte Massico, 2km north of the main road, is the ancient *Suessa*, capital of the Aurunci. Remains of a Roman theatre and baths, and the fine **Ponte degli Aurunci** (now largely walled-up) may still be seen. The **Cattedrale**, built in the 12C using fragments from the antique buildings, contains 13C Romanesque reliefs representing the lives of St Peter, Noah and Samson a mosaic pavement and a candelabrum, ambo (with the story of Jonah) and transennae of Cosmatesque work. The extinct volcano of Roccamonfina (1005m), c 11km north, is noted for its magnificent chestnut woods.

3km Cascano. **Carinola**, 6km south, has many charming 15C houses and a Romanesque cathedral. It is situated on the Piana di Carinola, the ancient *Falernus Ager*, renowned for its Falernian wine. 10km **Francolise** has a picturesque Angevin castle. The road goes on to join the Via Casilina 7km north of Capua (Route 3G).

The bridge across the Garigliano, with a span of 73m, replaces one destroyed in 1944. You enter Campania beyond. 22km Mondragone lies on the border of the *Falernus Ager*. At (12km) Castel Volturno, on the site of the town of *Volturnum*, you cross the Volturno. Anciently the *Vulturnus*, this is the chief river of Campania and the longest in Southern Italy (c 150km). It rises north-west of Isernia (Route 12). The highway follows the coast south, skirting (left) Lago di Patria and the ruins of *Liternum*, where Scipio Africanus died in self-imposed isolation. After a heavily developed resort area, a superstrada (expressway) winds across the Phlegraean Fields (Route 3E) to Pozzuoli and Naples.

2 · Ponza and its archipelago

The **Arcipelago Ponziano** *comprises two groups of islands, located approximately 35km apart and 32km from the coast of Lazio at Monte Circeo, arranged along a north-west–south-east axis. The north-west group includes* **Ponza***, the largest (7sq km) island and the chief centre of the archipelago; and the islets of* **Gavi, Zannone***, and* **Palmarola***. The south-east group comprises* **Ventotene** *and* **Santo Stefano***. All are of volcanic origin, the archipelago being linked geologically to the volcanic area of the Gulf of Naples. A collection of brilliant white rocks and pristine beaches, the islands are among the least spoilt in the Mediterranean, although their popularity as a resort is slowly eroding their primitive beauty. This development is most evident on Ponza, which nevertheless remains quiet and romantic out of season. The rocky coats, especially around Ventotene, are a skindiver's paradise.*

APPROACHES BY SEA: Passenger ferries serve Ponza daily from Anzio (2hr 30min, 15 Jun–15 Sep), Formia (2hr 30min), and Terracina (2hr). Hydrofoils run daily from Anzio (1hr 10min) and Formia (1hr 20min). Boats may be hired on Ponza to visit the other islands; commercial services are available Jun–Sep. Access for cars is severely restricted.

INFORMATION: Anzio, AA, Riviera Zanardelli 115; tel. 06 9845147, fax 06 9848135. Formia, AA, Via Unità d'Italia 30/40; tel. 0771 771490, fax 0771 771386. Terracina, AA, via Leopardi, tel. 0773 727759, fax 0773 727964.

Ponza is famous for its scenic beauty and its tiny rocky beaches dotted with Roman remains. The coast is steep and irregular and in most areas cliffs fall 100m or more into the sea. The chief town of the island is **Ponza** (3000 inhab.), which spreads out fan-like around its harbour. From here roads lead to (6km) Le Forna, a small village at the north end of the island and to Chiaia di Luna, a sandy beach 200m long on the west side. Paths ascend to the Punta dell'Incenso and to Monte della Guardia, respectively situated at the northern and southern tips of the island. Motor launches may be hired at the harbour for visits to the Grotte de Pilato and to the outlying islands.

Palmarola, located 5 nautical miles from the harbour is the largest of the uninhabited islands that surround Ponza and, with its jagged coastline and rich vegetation, the one most similar to the mother island. A small harbour with a restaurant operates on the island during the summer.

Zannone, about 3.5 nautical miles from Ponza, is a resting place for migratory birds and a showcase of Mediterranean flora and fauna. Among the latter may be counted the moufflon, a wild sheep peculiar to Southern Europe.

Ventotene, the larger of the two islands that make up the south-eastern part of the archipelago, differs from Ponza both in the reddish-brown tone of its rock and in the nature of its vegetation, which in contrast to the lush vegetation of Ponza, is dominated by prickly-pear and low macchia. Here Nero (son of Germanicus), Agrippina (sister of Caligula) and Flavia Domitilla (granddaughter of Domitian), lived in exile. Remains of a villa of the Imperial age may be seen near the PuntaEolo, at the northern end of the island. The town (700 inhab.) spreads southwest from the Cala Rossano, where the ferry from the mainland moors. At the Punta del Pertuso, the site of the Roman harbour, natural arches have formed in the tufa. The Antiquarium (Palazzo Municipale di Forte Torre; opened on request) has a small collection of local antiquities.

Near Ventotene lies **Santo Stefano**, a round island crowned by the *ergastolo* erected by Ferdinand IV in 1794–95, no longer in use. Both Ponza and Ventotene have been used as political prisons. Mussolini was interned for a short while on the former after his fall.

3–6 · Naples and environs

Naples, in Italian Napoli, is of the more populous cities in Italy (1,206,000 inhab.), the most important port after Genoa and the intellectual and commercial centre of the south. The animated and noisy town, bright with the southern sun, enjoys one of the more wonderful situations in the world, spread out fanwise above its beautiful gulf.

Naples is a unique city for several reasons, but the one that is most interesting for the visitor is that it bears traces of more than 20 centuries of continuous habitation. Its remarkably rich past is reflected, of course, in its architectural and artistic heritage; but it is evident also in the form and structure of the modern city, on which each civilisation that has occupied its soil has left a distinct, characteristic mark.

*In this Guide an effort has been made to strike a balance between Naples' vast topographical extent and its immense historical depth by locating the principal monuments in time as well as in space. The itineraries that make up Route 3 will take you through **ancient Naples**, as well as **Pompeii**, **Herculaneum**, **Vesuvius** and the **Phlegraean Fields**. Route 4 will concentrate on **medieval Naples** and on the once-powerful maritime republics of **Sorrento**, **Amalfi** and **Salerno**. Route 5 will deal with the grand building programmes of the **Spanish viceroys** and **Bourbon kings**. Finally, Route 6 will deal* with **Naples today**: *the contemporary city and also the islands of* **Capri**, **Ischia** *and* **Procida**, *which constitute one of modern Europe's more aristocratic resort areas.*

The mixture of walks in town and excursions into the environs has been designed to provide strategic getaways from what is, to put it mildly, an intense urban environment, as well as to enhance understanding of the city as a whole.

■ **Information:** Assessorato Regionale al Turismo, Spettacolo e Sport Via Santa Lucia 81; tel. 081 7961111, fax 081 7962027. EPT, Piazza dei Martiri 58; phone 081 405311, fax 081 401961 (branch offices at Stazione Centrale, Stazione Mergellina and Aeroporto Capadochino). AA, Piazza del Plebiscito (Palazzo Reale); tel. 081 418744, fax 081 418619 (branch office at Piazza del Gesù Nuovo 7). The AA publishes the useful monthly magazine *Qui Napoli*, in Italian and English (free).

■ **Airport. Capodichino** 4km north of the city centre, is the airport for both international and internal air services. Direct flights connect Naples with Athens, Brussels, Frankfurt, London, Marseille, Munich, Nice, Paris and Zürich; internal flights with Alghero, Ancona, Bergamo, Bologna, Cagliari, Catania, Firenze, Genoa, Lampedusa, Milan, Olbia, Palermo, Pantelleria, Pisa, Rimini, Rome, Turin, Trieste, Venice and Verona.

■ **Railway stations.** There are four main stations for State Rail services: **Napoli Centrale** (Atlas 3, 4); **Piazza Garibaldi** (in the same complex, but at a lower level); **Mergellina** (Piazza Mergellina); and **Campi Flegrei** (in the suburb of Fuorigrotta). There are also two minor stations where commuter trains serving the Gulf Area originate and terminate. These are: **Stazione Circumvesuviana** (Corso Garibaldi 387; Atlas 3, 8) for the Circumvesuviana line, which runs east and south to Pompeii, Sarno, Sorrento, Nola, and Baiano; and **Stazione Montesanto** (Piazza Montesanto; Atlas 2, 5), for the Cumana and Circumflegrea lines, which run west to Pozzuoli, Cuma, and Torregaveta

■ **Ships, boats, ferries and hydrofoils.** Naples harbour is one of the largest and busiest in the Mediterranean. **Cruise ships** moor at the Molo Angioino (Stazione Marittima Passaggeri; Atlas 3, 15); other vessels at the Molo Pisacane (Immacolatella Nuova; Atlas 3, 11) or within the inner harbour between the two. **Pleasure craft** may moor at Molosiglio (Atlas 2, 14), Santa Lucia (Atlas 4, 14), Mergellina (Atlas 4, 13), and Posillipo (Atlas 6). **Ferries** depart from Molo Beverello (Atlas 2, 14) to Capri (1hr 15min), Ischia (1hr 15min), Pozzuoli (30min), Procida (1hr), and Sorrento (1hr), daily; from the Stazione Marittima (Atlas 3, 15) to Cagliari, Thur and Sat 24 Jun–15 Sep, Thur only 16 Sep–23 Jun; to Palermo, daily; to Reggio Calabria–Catania–Siracusa–Malta, Thur; to the Aeolian Islands, Mon, Tue, Thur, Friday, Sat, and Sun 15 Jun–15 Sep, Wed and Fri 16 Sep–14 June. **Hydrofoils** run from Molo Beverello (Atlas 2, 14) and from Mergellina (Atlas 4, 13) to Capri (40–45min), Ischia (30-45 min), and Procida (35min), daily; to Sorrento (30min), daily; and to the Aeolian Islands (4hrs), daily Jun–Sep.

■ **Buses.** From Piazza Plebiscito to Pompeii and Salerno, with connections for the Amalfi coast; from Piazza Garibaldi (Stazione Centrale) to Caserta, Pozzuoli, and the Phlegraean Fields.

■ **Getting around town.** There is no easy way to get around Naples—except, of course, to walk. Traffic is so heavy that it practically stands still all day. Travellers who arrive by car should park in a safe place and use public transport while in the city. The **Metropolitana** offers frequent underground railway service along a single east–west axis, running from Piazza Garibaldi to Pozzuoli Solfatara in c 30min, with intermediate stops at Piazza Cavour (Atlas 2, 2), Montesanto (Atlas 2, 5), Piazza Amedeo (Atlas 4, 10), Mergellina (Atlas 4, 9), Fuorigrotta, Campi Flegrei, Bagnoli and Agnano Terme.

   Funicular railways climb to the Vomero from Piazza Montesanto (Atlas 2, 5), from Piazza Amedeo (Atlas 4, 10) and from Piazza Augusteo (Atlas 4, 13), the last two with intermediate stops at Corso Vittorio Emanuele; and to Posillipo from Mergellina and Campi Flegrei Station.

   Taxicabs tend to get stuck in traffic, as do buses. Cabs, with ranks in all the main squares, are equipped with meters, which should be carefully watched by passengers. Fixed supplements for holiday or night (23.00–06.00) service, for luggage, and for radio calls (tel. 570 7070, 556 4444 and 556 0202). A return fee must be paid for taxis dismissed beyond the city limits, and the fare from Capodichino airport is double the amount indicated on the meter. In Naples, as elsewhere in Italy, the horsedrawn **carrozza** is by no means extinct, but fares are rather high, and when hiring a vehicle it is advisable to make an exact agreement in advance as to charges.

■ **Hotels and restaurants.** The best hotels in Naples are on the waterfront over-looking Castel dell'Ovo and the Santa Lucia yacht basin, or on the hill above; both positions offer marvellous ***views** over the city and its gulf. Several of the finer establishments have roof gardens or terraces where the Neapolitan élite gather for an aperitif on warm evenings. Among the more pleasant hotels are: ****Britannique, Corso Vittorio Emanuele 133, tel. 081 761 4145, fax 081 660457; *****Excelsior, Via Partenope 48, tel. 081 764 0111; and ****Grande Albergo Vesuvio, Via Partenope 45, tel. 081 764 0044, fax 081 710 127. It is sometimes more economical to stay in Sorrento and commute.

   Youth Hostels at Salita della Grotta a Piedigrotta 23, tel. 081 761 2346, fax 081 761 2391; and Sorrento, Via Capasso 5, tel. 081 878 1783, fax 081 878 1783.

   The city's *restaurants* are among the finest in Italy. Try ****La Sacrestia, Via Orazio 116, tel. 081 761 1051, fax 081 664186; ****La Cantinella, Via Cuma 42, tel. 081 764 8684, fax 081 764 8769; ***A'Fenestella, Calata Ponticella, Marechiaro, tel. 081 769 0020, fax 081, 575 0686; and **Salvatore alla Riviera (for pizza), Riviera Chiara 91, tel. 081 680490, fax 081 680494.

■ **Special events. Religious and popular festivals**. Though in recent years the importance of the Neapolitan festivals has diminished, they still afford an inter-esting insight into the life of the people. On the *Festa di Sant' Antonio Abate* (17 January), horses and other animals are blessed at Sant'Antonio. At the *Liquefazione del Sangue di San Gennaro* on 19 September and 16 December in the cathedral and on the first Saturday in May at Santa Chiara, the phials are borne in colourful procession (late afternoon). On the *Ritorno dei Pellegrini da Montevergine* (Whit Monday), you can see interesting costumes and beribboned harness in the streets near the harbour. The people carry staves decorated with fruit and flowers as in the ancient Bacchanalia. The *Struscio*, so-called because of the rustling of the silk dresses worn on the occasion, brings a great crowd into

Via Roma on the Thursday and Friday before Easter to view the season's novelties in the shops. The *Festa della Madonna del Carmine* (16 July), features a mock burning of Fra' Nuvolo's campanile. New songs, specially prepared for the occasion, are sung at the *Festa di Piedigrotta* (September, in commemoration of the Battle of Velletri, 1744). In summer (Saturday night to Sunday night) the *Festivals of the Rioni* (quarters) follow one another at frequent intervals, with processions, fireworks, sports, and performances by the local musical clubs.

Concerts and drama. The major venues are: Teatro San Carlo (Atlas 2, 14), for opera and ballet; Auditorium della Radiotelevisione Italiana, Via E. Marconi (Atlas 1, 10) and Conservatorio di Musica San Pietro a Maiella, Via San Pietro a Maiella (Atlas 2, 6), for concerts. Opera and/or drama at the Politeama, Via Monte di Dio 80; Mediterraneo in the Mostra d'Oltremare; San Ferdinando, Piazza Teatro San Ferdinando; Cilea, Via San Domenico; Sannazaro, Via Chiaia 157 (with dialect plays); Bracco, Via Tarsia 40; Sancarluccio, Via San Pasquale 49; and Villa Patrizi, Corso Vittorio Emanuele. The latter, the exquisitely restored private theatre of an 18C patrician villa, merits a visit in itself. There is an **international film festival** (*Incontri Internazionali del Cinema*) at Sorrento in October; and an annual **music festival**, the *Luglio Musicale*, at Capodimonte in July.

■ **Sports**. Events include **football** at the San Paolo stadium in Fuorigrotta; **horse racing** at the Ippodromo di Agnano (Gran Premio) in April and harness racing in the summer; **motor racing** (Rally della Campania) in April–May; **cycling** (Giro della Campania) , also in April–May; **international regatta** (One Ton Cup) in June; **horse show** at Monte Faito, above Castellammare di Stabia, in July.

Tennis facilities include the Tennis Club Napoli, Villa Comunale; Tennis Club Petrarca, Via Petrarca 93; Tennis San Domenico, Via San Domenico 62; Tennis Vomero, Via Rossini. There is a **swimming pool,** Piscina Scandone, at Fuorigrotta.

■ **Cultural associations**. Fondazione Napoli 99, Riviera di Chiaia 202; Napoli Sotterranea (tel. 081 449821); and LAES, Via Santa Teresella degli Spagnoli 24, are actively involved in preserving the city's cultural-historical heritage and making it available to visitors, Fondazione Napoli 99 rehabilitating and opening monuments and engaging in a wide range of educational activities; Napoli Sotterranea and LAES offering **guided tours**. The Associazione Italo-Americana (American Studies Center), Via A. d'Isernia 36; British Council, Via dei Mille 48; Goethe Institut, Riviera di Chiaia 202; Istituto Francese di Grenoble, Via Crispi 86; Istituto Español de Santiago, Via San Giacomo 40, organise long-term cultural exchange (largely on the university level) and offer a number of foreign language study programmes.

■ **Consulates. British Consulate**, Via Crispi 122 (Atlas 4, 9), tel. 081 663511. **United States Consulate**, Piazza della Repubblica (Atlas 4, 9), tel. 081 583 8111.

■ **Post office**. Piazza Matteotti.

3 · Antiquity

PREHISTORY

The evidence of ancient life in the Naples area is overwhelming. Although there is little in the way of architectural remains in the city itself, the Museo Archeologico Nazionale possesses one of the largest and finest collections of Graeco-Roman antiquities in the world, and Pompeii and Herculaneum are justly famous for the insight they afford into ancient life. No less interesting, in this respect, are the Greek centres at Paestum and Velia; and the remains of Roman pleasure villas at Baia, Torre Annunziata, and Capri offer a unique look at upper-crust living in an area that was to Rome what the Hamptons are today to New York or the Côte d'Azur to Paris.

Today it is known with certainty that the area around Naples was inhabited as early as the **Stone Age**, the first known period of prehistoric human culture (before 3500 BC). Human remains and stone tools have been found on the island of Capri (the first of these were discovered in the time of the Roman Emperor Augustus), as well as along the coast and in the hills and valleys of the Neapolitan hinterland. Artefacts dating from the **Bronze Age** (after 3500 BC) and the **Iron Age** (after 1100 BC) are also common.

Many of these early inhabitants came to Italy by sea from the Eastern Mediterranean: traces of the Bronze Age cultures of Crete and Mycenae, for instance, are visible in burial artefacts from around the 15C BC onwards. In the period around 1000 BC, when archaeological deduction gives way to recorded history, references to the Naples area may be vaguely glimpsed in the myths and legends of ancient **Greece**. On the northern shore of the crescent-shaped gulf, for instance, stands *Cumae*, home of that ancient prophetess, the Sibyl; and the Phlegraean or Burning Fields, where the Olympian gods defeated the Giants and buried them beneath the earth (which stirs, in the earthquakes characteristic of the region, whenever the imprisoned monsters try to break free). To the south lie the Isole Sirenuse, the rocks into which the Sirens were metamorphosed after they had vainly enticed Ulysses to land.

The Greeks came to southern Italy from Ionia, a region of western Asia Minor from which they were driven by the non-Greek peoples who inhabited the neighbouring regions. The earliest Greek colonies in the Naples area were Cumae and Pithecusae (Ischia), founded by Chalcis in the 11C BC, according to tradition. These were soon followed by the neighbouring centres of Dikaearchia (Pozzuoli), Parthenope (Naples), and a little farther to the south, Poseidonia (Paestum). Greek colonisation of the Mediterranean eventually extended as far afield as France and Spain, but the Gulf of Naples marked for all practical purposes the outer edge of what came to be called *Magna Graecia* or Greece Beyond the Sea. Sybaris, Croton, Taranto, and Naples on the mainland, and Messina and Syracuse on the island of Sicily, became the chief centres of a flourishing Hellenic civilisation that attracted distinguished visitors from the homeland and gave rise to a splendid local culture.

Except on Sicily, the Greeks rarely ventured into the interior of the areas they settled. They were not colonialists in the strict sense of the term, but a seafaring people interested above all in securing safe and dependable lines of communication between their more distant outposts and their home ports in the Aegean. In southern Italy they also traded with the native tribes of farmers and herdsmen who inhabited the plains and mountains. These Italic peoples, though considerably less civilised than the Greeks, were quick to realise the mutual advantages of cooperating with the foreigners, whose customs they picked up and passed on to their neighbours further inland. For centuries both sides enjoyed the fruits of this relationship.

THE ETRUSCANS, THE SAMNITES AND THE ROMANS

Campania may have continued to flourish under Greek domination had it not been for the **Etruscans,** a powerful ethnic group that lived in the area coextensive with modern Tuscany and Umbria. The Etruscans, like the Greeks, had reached a high degree of political, social, and artistic development. Attracted by the mild climate and lucrative trade, they established their first colonies in south-central Italy in the 9C. Later, as their northern homeland was invaded by the Celts, they migrated to the region en masse. The Etruscans were more warlike than the Greeks, and perhaps more actively colonialist. As the years passed, they gradually consolidated their foothold in the south, conquering one Greek city after another. At one point their influence was so strong that new houses in Campanian towns were built almost exclusively in the Etruscan manner.

The tide finally turned against the Etruscans, however, as a consequence of two Greek victories at Cumae, in 525 and 474 BC. The resulting decline in their power was so rapid that between these dates the Etruscan kings were also chased out of Rome. Eventually, the expanding Roman republic interposed itself between the Etruscan homeland to the north and its extension in Campania; deprived of a land connection, the southern settlements dwindled.

The expulsion of the Etruscans and the involvement of the Greek colonies in the fratricidal Peloponnesian Wars created a power vacuum in Campania that was filled when the indigenous **Samnites** rose up and conquered the region, with relative ease, c 420 BC. The Samnites were a simple people who lived in the hills north and east of Naples. They were so keenly aware of the inferiority of their own civilisation with respect to those they had conquered, that instead of governing the occupied territory according to Samnite law and custom they created a federation of city-states, each governed by its own magistrate and faithful to its own traditions. In this manner they managed to maintain their hold over the area even while they were themselves gradually being conquered by the Romans in the series of conflicts generally referred to as the Samnite Wars (343–290 BC).

Under the **Romans,** who occupied it after the Social War (88 BC), Campania rose again to great prosperity and became known as the *Campania Felix* on account of its beauty and fertility. The alluvial plains and fruitful hills produced the finest grains, vegetables, olives, and wines. From Paestum came the famous roses whose essence—regarded as one of the more delightful and luxurious scents in the Roman world—was sold at the celebrated perfume market at Capua. The fertile slopes of Mount Vesuvius produced highly prized wines, as well as the more common *vinum vesuvium.* The forests yielded wood in abundance, the mountains provided numerous varieties of building stone, and the sea supplied fish from which the ancients made the sauces *garum, liquamen* and *muria,* which Pliny says were a special treat.

In the 1C AD the area developed its character as a rich man's playground. It became a place where Romans went to escape the tensions of the capital—to retire in their old age, or simply for a holiday. The main resort centres were Cumae, Baiae, Sorrento, the island of Capri, and the coast around Puteoli, Naples, and Pompeii. Herculaneum was known as a particularly healthful place, due to its position on a pleasant promontory. Pompeii was a bustling commercial, agricultural and resort town receiving gentle sea breezes in the day and cool mountain breezes from

Vesuvius at night. The coast along the Gulf of Naples was adorned with towns, residences, and plantations, which spread out in unbroken succession, presenting the appearance of a single city, as indeed is still very much the case today.

THE GROWTH OF NAPLES

Naples proper is the modern successor of two ancient towns that even before Roman times had merged to form a single metropolis. The colony of *Parthenope*, the more ancient of the two, was founded by Rhodian navigators in the 9C BC. It stood on Mount Echia, the volcanic hill now occupied by the quarter of Pizzofalcone. This site was chosen because it was easy to defend—it was surrounded by the sea on three sides, with steep cliffs, and was separated from the hinterland by a deep valley, today Via Chiaia.

After the Greek victory over the Etruscans the population of Parthenope grew rapidly, and it soon became clear that the city would have to be enlarged. This posed some serious problems: the lie of the land, which made Parthenope impregnable, also made urban development virtually impossible. Hence it was decided to build a new town, *Neapolis* (from which the Italian name *Napoli* derives), on a hillside on the other side of the harbour, with its highest point, the acropolis, in the area that would later become Caponapoli. Neapolis soon grew to surpass the older city in importance, swelled by the arrival c 450 BC of Greek colonists from Chalcis, Pithecusa, and Athens. Both towns were conquered by the Samnites c 400 BC and by the Romans in 326 BC.

Neapolis grew in population under the Romans but held on more tenaciously than any other city in Magna Graecia to its Greek customs, culture, and institutions. Greek games, in which musical competitions alternated with gymnastic events, were held by the Neapolitans every five years, and Greek was preserved as the official language. The emperor Nero was particularly fond of Naples' Hellenic culture, and he sang there several times before going to Greece.

Because of its Hellenic character, Naples was regarded as the city of learning. Roman youth flocked here to cultivate the arts of rhetoric, poetry, and music. Although the city lacked an amphitheatre, it did have a famous covered theatre, and the Neapolitan actors were renowned throughout the Roman world. Plutarch, the Greek biographer and moralist, tells that Brutus came personally to Naples to beg one of these actors, Canuzio, to come and recite in Rome. The theatres of Naples offered plays in Latin and in Greek; among the latter, that written by Claudius to honour his brother, Germanicus. The great masters included the orator Polemone, one of whose pupils was the Roman emperor and Stoic philosopher, Marcus Aurelius. Virgil, not yet famous, came to Naples in search of the atmosphere that his spirit demanded and that the hustle and bustle of the capital precluded. Here he wrote his exquisite *Georgics*, and when he died at an early age in Brindisi, on his way back from a fateful journey to Greece, he wished to be buried in Naples, and Augustus ordered that his wish should be fulfilled. According to Dante, his tomb is on the hill of Posillipo.

For the Romans, Naples and its splendid surroundings—the slopes of Vesuvius, the Capodimonte hill, the Phlegraean Fields, the harbours of Pozzuoli, Baia, Pompeii, Stabia and Herculaneum—afforded an extraordinary oasis of peace. Horace, the famous poet and satirist, wrote of 'restful Naples,' and another poet, Ovid, claimed that 'Parthenope was born in idleness.' Although modern Naples is anything but tranquil, the city and its magnificent environs still offer the visitor spectacles of immense cultural interest and unparalleled natural beauty.

A.   Ancient Naples

*Unfortunately, there are few ancient ruins in Naples to speak of—nothing, at least, as extensive as the Imperial Fora in Rome or as impressive as the Colosseum: most of Naples' ancient treasures lie buried beneath the fabric of the modern city. The few remains that can be seen have been camouflaged by time: incorporated into later structures, they crop up in unexpected places. The walk that follows offers a brief introduction to central Naples, following the line of the decumanus major the main street of the ancient town. A visit to the Greek and Roman remains beneath **San Lorenzo Maggiore** is highly recommended, as is the guided tour of the underground **aqueduct** conducted (in Italian) by LAES (see pp 97, 102). The total length of the walk (aqueduct excluded) is less than 1km; it can be covered in just over 1 hour.*

GREEKS AND ROMANS

The town plan of ancient Naples survives in the crowded lanes around the Via dei Tribunali (Atlas 2, 2 and 3, 3), which follows the course of the old *decumanus maximus*, the main street of the Graeco-Roman town. In this area are several buildings—mainly churches, but residential buildings, too—that incorporate vestiges of the very distant past. The 16C church of **San Paolo Maggiore** (Atlas 3, 3), for instance, stands on the site of a Roman temple dedicated to the Dioscuri—Zeus's twin sons Castor and Pollux, who were reunited after Castor's death by Zeus's decree that they live in the upper and lower worlds on alternate days. The front of the temple originally included six fluted Corinthian columns. It was used as the façade of the church until 1688, when it was destroyed in an earthquake. Today all that remains of the ancient edifice are two tall columns with their architrave and the bases of two more columns in front of the church, another column along the right side, and, beneath the statues of St Peter and St Paul, some weathered sculptures of the Dioscuri. The **Chiostro di San Paolo** incorporates 22 ancient granite columns, which, however, did not belong to the Temple of the Dioscuri.

Almost opposite San Paolo Maggiore, on the site of the Roman basilica, is the Franciscan church of **San Lorenzo Maggiore** (Atlas 3, 3), one of Naples' more important medieval churches, described in full detail in Route 4B. Here it is not so much the details of the church, as the form of the building as a whole, that is interesting. The ancient Roman basilica, an oblong building ending in a semicircular apse, was used as a court of justice and place of public assembly. During the first centuries of the Christian age, the Roman basilican form was taken by the Christians as the prototype for their meeting places, and the term is now used to refer to any Christian church consisting of nave and aisles and a large, high transept from which an apse projects. San Lorenzo Maggiore is, in this sense, a Christian basilica; its form corresponds almost perfectly to that of the Roman basilica of Neapolis. Its builders used the massive walls of the existing edifice as the foundation of their own building (a common practice in the Middle Ages), as may be seen in the **cloisters**, where archaeological excavations (open Mon–Sat 09.00–12.30) have brought to light the antique walls of the treasury, in the basement of the basilica, the remains of a Roman street flanked by shops, traces of Greek buildings made of large square blocks of tufa and the ruins, on a higher level, of a medieval public building.

Touring underground Naples

LAES with headquarters at Via Santa Teresella degli Spagnoli 24 (tel. 081 400256) leads tours of the ancient ruins. The same organization offers visits to the ancient *aqueduct that runs beneath the city. Begun by the Greeks and extended by virtually all those who came afterwards, the aqueduct was Naples' main source of water until the latter half of the 19C. It was used as a clandestine quarry during the period of the Spanish viceroys, when laws intended to curb new building inside the city walls prohibited the importation of building stone. The tour covers roughly 30,000sq m at a depth of 20–40m below the surface.

Across the street from San Lorenzo Maggiore, and running along the right flank of San Paolo Maggiore, the narrow Vico Cinquesanti leads to the Via dell' Anticaglia, which corresponds to the *decumanus superior* of Roman Neapolis. The street is crossed by two massive brick arches—the remains of the walls that joined the baths, which were located on the far side of the street, with the ancient theatre, which stood in the area between Vico Giganti, Via dell'Anticaglia, Via San Paolo and the former Convento dei Teatrini. The theatre was built to accommodate 11,000 spectators. Here Claudius had the play he had written in honour of his brother Germanicus performed, and Nero sang to an enthusiastic audience.

The **Cattedrale** of Naples, located just a few blocks to the east in the busy Via Duomo (Atlas 3, 3), was founded in the 4C on the site of a temple of Apollo. Inside, the piers of the nave incorporate no fewer than 110 antique columns of Oriental and African granite which, however, were taken from sources other than the temple over which the church was built. A stretch of ancient street pavement survives in a courtyard in the curia building, and there are other Graeco-Roman remains, including fragments of a mosaic pavement, in the basement.

THE MUSEO ARCHEOLOGICO NAZIONALE

By far the most extensive collection of ancient art in Naples is to be found in the **Museo Archeologico Nazionale** (Piazza Museo 18, Atlas 2, 2). This is one of the larger and more interesting museums of antiquities in the world. Universally famous for its magnificent series of exhibits of every kind from Pompeii and Herculaneum, it is also of prime importance for the study of Greek sculpture. The building that houses it, built as a barracks in 1586 but occupied by the university after 1599, was remodelled in 1790 to receive the antiquities from Pompeii and Herculaneum, the Farnese collections (inherited by King Charles of Bourbon from his mother, Elisabeth Farnese), and the picture gallery. Alexandre Dumas, père, held the office of Keeper in 1860–64.

During the Second World War the building suffered only superficial damage. Many of the treasures had been removed for safety; of those sent to Monte Cassino a few were lost, but most were carefully preserved. Unfortunately, recent investigations suggest that several thousand antique works of art have been pilfered over the years since the war. The picture gallery was moved to Capodimonte in 1957. The museum is open Tues–Sun 09.00–14.00. Ideally, it should be seen *after* Pompeii and Herculaneum, which provide a context for much of the work displayed. The museum operates on a rotating gallery basis, so not everything mentioned in the following description will be seen in a single visit.

Ground floor

The ground floor is devoted mainly to sculpture from the Farnese collection, the Borgia collection from Velletri, and the cities of Campania. The main entrance opens into the **Grande Atrio dei Magistrati**, containing statues and tombs of the Imperial Age of Rome, notably a *marble sarcophagus from Pozzuoli, with Prometheus moulding man out of clay in the presence of the gods (3C AD).

ROOM 1, the **Galleria dei Tirannicidi** (right), contains archaic sculptures, including severe style torsos, and the **Aphrodite Sossandra** from Baiae, the best surviving imitation of the celebrated work by Kalamis. The room takes its name from *Harmodius and Aristogeiton slayers of the tyrant Hipparchus, from Tivoli, a copy of the group made by Kritius and Nesiotes in 477 BC for the Agora at Athens. The present arrangement of the figures is of doubtful authenticity; various alternatives have been suggested, of which the most probable set Aristogeiton on the left of Harmodius, or the two statues on separate bases and at a distance from each other.

The rooms to the right contain sculpture of the golden age of Greek art (5C BC).

ROOM 2, *Athena, a copy of Imperial date, of a bronze statue of the school of Phidias; a low relief of Orpheus, Eurydice, and Hermes, the best of the three known copies of a work by Phidias; Aphrodite Genetrix, from Herculaneum; a Hellenic votive relief from Herculaneum; *Herm of Athena with a mild, youthful cast of features, probably from a Greek original of c 450–425, from Herculaneum; and Apollo, from the House of the Cithara Player at Pompeii.

ROOM 3. *Doryphorus (from Pompeii), the most complete copy of the famous spear-bearer of Polyclitus (c 440 BC), which was considered the 'canon' or perfect model of manly proportions. ROOM 5. Diomedes, from Cumae, from an Attic original (450–430 BC) attributed to Kresilas. ROOM 6. Nereids, possibly Greek originals of the 5C or 4C, from a Roman villa at Formia.

Returning to the Galleria dei Tirannicidi, pass through ROOM 7, which includes, among several marble works, a bronze Ephebe, from Pompeii. The next few rooms contain a new installation of sculpture from the Baths of Caracalla, formerly in the Farnese collection, together with other works. In the **Galleria di Flora** (ROOM 8) are two colossal figures from the baths: Neptune (?), a graceful copy of a 4C original, and Ganymede, with the eagle and a lifelike dog.

Stairs descend to the basement level, with the Egyptian and Epigraphical collections (see below).

On the right opens the Galleria del Toro Farnese, a long hall of six bays (ROOMS 11–16). At the far end (right), beyond a vestibule, are two small rooms (ROOMS 9, 10), containing, respectively, four statues, copies of originals commissioned by Attalus, King of Pergamum, to commemorate his victory of 239 BC; and the Venus Callipyge, from the Domus Aurea of Nero.

Returning through ROOM 11, pass a tomb from Atella with a relief of Achilles among the daughters of Lycomedes to ROOM 12, *Aphrodite of Sinuessa probably a 4C Greek original. The *'Farnese Heracles', another work from the Baths of Caracalla, is a copy by Glycon of a work by Lysippus; nearby is a Mars resting, a very fine replica (compare that in the Museo Nazionale Romano, Rome) from a 4C original. Also noteworthy is the second *Aphrodite in this room, an unusually beautiful torso attributed to Praxiteles.

ROOM 13 includes a colossal mask of Zeus, similar to the famous Vatican Jupiter, probably of the 4C BC; Eros, a copy of a Praxitelean bronze; the Vase of Gaeta with the myth of Hermes delivering the young Dionysus to the nymphs of Nysa, signed by the Athenian Salpion (1C BC); a relief panel showing the meeting of Paris with

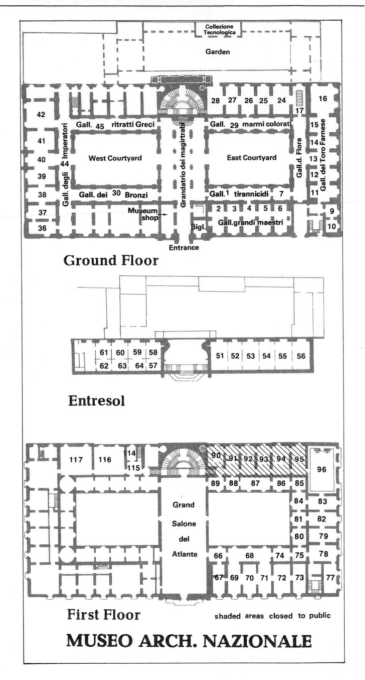

Ground Floor

Entresol

First Floor

shaded areas closed to public

MUSEO ARCH. NAZIONALE

Helen and Aphrodite; *Psyche from Capua, a copy of the 1C AD of a 4C BC original and a Venus from the amphitheatre at Capua, a reproduction perhaps of the
same original that inspired the Venus de Milo.

In ROOM 15 notice the Dionysus and satyr, a copy preserving all the liveliness
and exuberance of the original Hellenistic bronze; Pan and Olympus; and
Laughing Silenus, a most expressive head.

ROOM 16 hosts the work that gives its name to this section, the *Farnese Bull,
the largest known work of antique sculpture, representing the vengeance of Zethus
and Amphion on Dirce, Queen of Thebes. It also comes from the Baths of Caracala.

To the left is a gallery devoted to coloured marbles, mainly of Eastern deities.
Notice Apollo, in dark green basalt, a Hellenistic type; Diana of Ephesus, a Roman
work in alabaster, with face, hands and feet of bronze; and Apollo in porphyry with
white marble extremities.

The five rooms (ROOMS 24–28) leading from this gallery are occupied by a
collection of decorative sculpture and reliefs with interesting details of hunting and
other scenes. Note the fragment (in ROOM 28) showing two fighting biremes.

Basement

The Egyptian Collection, in the basement, is reached by the stairway at the end of the
Galleria di Flora. Here may be seen hieroglyphics, mummies, sculptures of sacred animals
and funerary statuettes (Uschebtia). Particularly noteworthy is a mummy case of the
Twenty-Second Dynasty, dating from the 9C BC. Also on this level is the Epigraphical
Section, beyond which another staircase ascends to the museum entrance. In the north
court is the Sezione Tecnologica, in which are gathered numerous ancient surgical and
scientific instruments, many of which have been reconstructed. The display of Farnese
Gems (including the famous *Tazza Farnese, a cup of veined sardonyx, one of the largest
known examples of the cameo-maker's art, of the finest Alexandrian workmanship of the
Ptolemaic age), temporarily located in the former Sale delle Veneri, may become permanent; and a partial display of the *Collection of Figured Vases was opened, in the
summer of 1995, in the Grande Atrio.

Entresol

From the Grande Atrio the main staircase ascends to the mezzanine floor. The east
wing contains mural paintings from Campanian cities. There are five rooms
(51–56), the last two containing the entire pictorial decoration from the Temple of
Isis at Pompeii. The finest exhibits in this genre, however, are on the first floor
(ROOMS 66–78, see below).

The west wing of the Entresol is occupied by *Pompeian mosaics. Among them
are some of the finer known examples of the art; all three types, tessellated, vermic-
ulated, and opus sectile are represented. Notice especially, in ROOM 59, comic actors
(or by a differing interpretation, begging musicians), a very fine mosaic from the
Villa of Cicero, representing two women, a man, and a dwarf, all masked and
playing musical instruments; *Consulting the sorceress a scene from a comedy,
both of these signed by Dioscorides of Samos; the Academy at Athens, seven figures
(Plato in the centre) with the Acropolis as background; a pattern of fish, crustacea,
and marine creatures, of more than 20 species, including an octopus, of considerable zoological realism (another may be seen in ROOM 60); also, panels showing
Nile scenes, with crocodiles, hippopotami, ibis and other creatures, originally the
frame of the Battle of Issus. ROOM 60 also contains winged boy riding a tiger.

ROOM 61 hosts mosaics from the House of the Faun, as well as the celebrated
Dancing Faun from which the house takes its name; a decorative band with

festoons and theatre masks; a still life in two registers, with a remarkably life-like cat catching a quail; and ***Darius and Alexander** at the Battle of Issus (333 BC). This, finely executed in minute tesserae, may be compared in scale with the hunting scenes at Piazza Armerina, in Sicily. The composition is thought to follow a 4C Greek painting probably by Philoxenos, and is one of the few ancient works that develops perpendicularly to the picture plane as well as horizontally. ROOMS 62–64 contain Roman portraits.

First floor

At the top of the stairs, between the east and west wings, is the immense **Salone dell'Atlante** now used for temporary exhibitions. The west wing hosts the **Sale della Villa dei Papiri**, in which are displayed art works and artefacts found in the celebrated villa at Herculaneum, excavated 1750–61.

ROOM 115. Cases 1, 2, and 3: small bronzes from the atrium. Case 4: small bronzes from a room on the west side of the villa. Case 5: small portrait busts, mainly from the 3C onwards; dancing and playing satyrs. In the adjoining rooms (110–114) are several murals and carbonised fragments of papyri. ROOM 116 is home to the so-called Dancers (1C BC), a sleeping satyr, a drunken Silenus and Hermes resting. ROOM 117. Portrait head (Seneca? 1C BC); Heracles, copy after Polycletus; and bust of an ephebe.

> The west wing will also house the new installation of **figuered vases** in the rooms facing the courtyard between the two circular halls.

The rooms in the **east wing** are numbered from front to rear of the building. Their contents fall into three groups: the south rooms are devoted to ***Campanian wall paintings;** the north rooms, to bronze objects; and in between are other miscellaneous objects including furniture, household utensils, images and so on, which give a very complete idea of ancient domestic life.

Cross the Grande Salone and turn into ROOM 67. Here are tomb walls with sacred vases, and horse and foot soldiers, from Paestum; a funeral dance, from Ruvo; and at the centre of the room, a painted tomb from Afragola (3C BC).

ROOM 70. Mural paintings including Hercules and Omphale; Bacchic scene, with a boy of charming vivacity; battle with a centaur.

ROOM 72. Coloured painting on marble, notably Perseus and Andromeda, considered the most faithful copy of the original painted by Nikias; Achilles discovered at Skyros, by the Greek painter Theon of Samos; Nuptials of Jupiter; Sacrifice of Iphigenia depicted in a manner similar to that of traditional representations of the sacrifice of Isaac; ***Medea** perhaps copied from a celebrated painting by Timomachus; Nuptials of Jupiter and Hera on Mt Ida; and ***girls playing with knuckle-bones** (The Astragal Players), signed by Alexander of Athens and executed in monochrome on marble, in the encaustic technique (the scene may represent the vengeance of Leto, as narrated by Ovid in *Metamorphoses* VI). ROOM 73. Meleager and Atalanta; Iphigenia in Tauris.

ROOM 74. Cupids at work and play; ***four small paintings of women**: Medea, Leda and the Swan, Diana, and a girl gathering flowers (so-called Spring), with delicate colouring, from Stabiae.

ROOM 77. Paquius Proculus and his wife, portraits of convincing realism; baker selling (or by another interpretation, a public official distributing) bread; Bacchus and Mount Vesuvius, generally considered an allegory of Pompeii; brawl in the amphitheatre at Pompeii between Pompeians and Nucerians (59 BC); view of the port of Puteoli, strangely reminiscent of the style of Canaletto.

ROOM 79. Arms and armour, trumpets and gladiators' helmets with delicate reliefs.

ROOM 80. Lamps, ivories, and enamelled terracottas, a style of ceramic decoration probably imported from Egypt. ROOM 81. Glassware. *Blue glass vase of fine workmanship, beautifully ornamented. ROOM 82. Tableware from the House of the Menander, cups and other vessels of silver (115 pieces in all), some produced by a late Hellenistic workshop, others by Roman workshops of the Augustan age. ROOM 83. Gold rings, necklaces and bracelets.

Pass to ROOM 96. In the centre, cork model of Pompeii on the scale of 1 to 100, showing the discoveries made up to 1879; models of Pompeian houses. The wall cases contain carbonised food, articles of domestic use such as soap and sulphur, textiles, rope-soled shoes; and triclinia or couches. Round the walls are Pompeian mural paintings (still life).

ROOMS 90–94 (closed 1995) contain *small bronzes from Pompeii and Herculaneum. ROOM 90. *Statue of a warrior perhaps Alexander; *Amazon, birds, beasts, and statuettes; crescent with Capitoline deities; mirrors and candelabra. ROOM 91. Putto; satyr with goatskin; iron strongboxes (arcae) with bronze plating and studs, decorated with relief panels; Fortune enthroned; Bacchic double hermae; wild pig assailed by dogs.

ROOM 92. Vases with ornamental handles; statuette of a Nike, of Hellenistic inspiration, wrongly restored on a globe and with a rod; vessels, lamps, door handles and locks; fine tripod vase. ROOM 93. Large situla; buckles and other ornaments; dice and knuckle-bones; theatre-tickets; mirrors and personal ornaments; fine Etruscan vase. ROOM 94. Various forms of heating apparatus; *krater adorned with silver chasing; lampholders and other objects.

The remaining rooms on this floor contain lesser works. ROOMS 84–85. Common glass objects. ROOMS 86–89. Closed 1995.

B.   Pompeii

Pompeii, one of the Roman Campanian towns that were buried by the Vesuvian eruption of AD 79 and painstakingly brought back to light during the last two centuries, has provided fundamental knowledge of the domestic life of the ancients. Here you see the greater part of a Roman town as it was when disaster overtook it more than 1900 years ago, in a setting sufficiently isolated from modern surroundings to preserve the illusion of antiquity. The contrasting beauties of white stone seen against a background of azure sky, and the ever-changing patterns made by sun and clouds on the slopes of the volcano, combine with the intrinsic interest of the ruins to make this one of the more fascinating archaeological sites in the world.

The excavations may be entered on the south by the Porta Marina, or by the Porta Anfiteatro. They are open daily from 09.00 until two hours before sunset. The official custodians, stationed in different quarters of the ancient town, open the closed houses on application and give all necessary information. They are not supposed to accept gratuities or accompany visitors. At least half a day is necessary for an adequate visit, which should at least touch upon the buildings around the forum; one of the three complexes of thermae; the two theatres the Fullonica Stephani; the houses of the Meander, of Loreius Tiburtinus, of the Faun and of the Tragic Poet; the Villa of Julia Felix and the Villa of the Mysteries. Lunch may be obtained at the Posto di Ristoro (near the forum). In hot weather the absence of shade is noticeable and some sort of hat is a must. Be sure, also, to wear comfortable shoes: the paving-stones of the street are notoriously uneven.

ROAD Autostrada A3, 26km from Naples, just below the slopes of Vesuvius, affording a good view of Camaldoli della Torre. Coach excursions daily. The Torre Annunziata road (Route 4C) is not recommended.

RAILWAY Circumvesuviana Railway (Sorrento line) to Pompeii Villa dei Misteri in 35–50 min, service at c 30min intervals; day return tickets valid by either route. The State Railway is more useful for visitors arriving from Salerno and the south.

INFORMATION: the AA operates an office at Piazza Esedra, Pompeii Scavi; tel. 081 861 0913.

POMPEII BEFORE THE ERUPTION
Although it is not known exactly when Pompeii was first settled, an Oscan village probably existed on the site as early as the 8C BC (the name *Pompeii* is of Oscan derivation, it seems). There is no archaeological or documentary evidence to support this date, however, and the oldest building that can be identified and reconstructed from its ruins—the Doric temple in the Triangular Forum—dates from the 6C, when Pompeii was already a flourishing commercial centre and one of the chief ports on the coast of Campania. Like the Greek coast towns of Cumae and Neapolis, Pompeii fell under the domination of the Etruscans c 530 BC. Certain aspects of the ruins, such as the layout of the oldest section and the design of the 6C city wall, as well as some family names (the Cuspii, for instance) are thought to be of Etruscan origin. The city fell to the Samnites c 425 BC and remained under their dominion for more than two centuries. In 200 BC it became a subject ally of Rome, but with the outbreak of the Social War it joined the Italic League and was besieged in 89 BC.

After the war's end Pompeii sank back into the near-anonymity of provincial life. As a token of Romanisation it was now called *Colonia Cornelia Veneria Pompeianorum* after the clan name of its conqueror, L. Cornelius Sulla, and the Venus Pompeiiana, patron deity of the city. In AD 59, after a brawl in the amphitheatre between the Pompeians and the citizens of Nuceria, the gladiatorial spectacles were suspended for ten years. It was possibly in compensation for this that, in AD 62, it was allowed to call itself *Colonia Neroniana*.

THE FINAL CATASTROPHE
The following year Pompeii was devastated by an earthquake, an unwelcome token of the renewed activity of Mount Vesuvius. Heedless of this warning, however, the town continued to flourish and even increased its wealth and influence. The final catastrophe took place on 24 August, AD 79, when the famous **eruption of Vesuvius** overwhelmed Pompeii, Herculaneum, and Stabiae. Pompeii, like Stabiae, was covered with a layer of fragments of pumice stone (lapilli), mostly very minute, and afterwards by a similar layer of ashes. The flow of lava stopped at the base of the mountain and did not reach the inhabited quarter.

All who had not left the city in the first hours died—from the accumulation of volcanic debris, the collapse of buildings, or in many cases, the poisonous vapours. It is estimated that of an approximate population of 20,000, 2000, who were trapped in the city or who for some reason chose to remain, perished. Among the victims of the catastrophe, the most illustrious was **Pliny the Elder**, a distinguished naturalist and commander of the Roman fleet at Misenum. Warned by his sister of the appearance of an ominous cloud in the east and by a letter from Popilla Rectina, wife of the magistrate Cn. Pedius Cascus, he hurried to the help of the fugitives, but could not reach Pompeii on account of the huge mounds of lapilli. He therefore sailed to Stabiae, where he found his friend Pomponianus, but was here overtaken and suffocated by the stifling vapours.

Pompeii was left a sea of ashes and lapilli, from which emerged the upper parts of the buildings that had not been totally destroyed. These, later, served as guideposts to the inhabitants who returned to dig among the ruins, and, still later, to the searchers for treasure and building material. By the 3C a number of buildings had been erected at *Civita*, to the north of Pompeii. This second Pompeii was, however, abandoned in the 11C because of the frequent earthquakes, the eruptions of Vesuvius, and the incursions of the Saracens.

UNEARTHING AND PRESERVING THE TOWN
Between 1594 and 1600 Domenico Fontana, the Roman architect, in constructing an aqueduct from the sources of the Sarno River to Torre Annunziata, tunnelled through the Pompeian mound and discovered some ruins and inscriptions. But it was not till 1748 that antiquarian excavations were begun. These, continued since with more or less activity, have laid bare the larger and more important half of Pompeii. In 1860 a regular plan of excavation was organised by the Italian Government; however, a chronic shortage of funds has made the task of unearthing and preserving the city a slow and arduous one. The site has now been systematically photographed, and the first comprehensive catalogue of its artistic assets is in preparation. Despite efforts to protect and preserve the city, however, the greatest threat to Pompeii remains that of the thievery and clandestine resale of artworks and artefacts, of which the worst recent example, the removal of three marble and two bronze statues from the House of the Vetii, is only too typical.

A high technology entry system, with automatic turnstiles at the entrances to the ruins, was introduced in spring 1995, at a cost of 1.4 billion lire.

THE ANCIENT CITY
The elliptical form of Pompeii was determined by the configuration of the prehistoric lava flow on which it is built, the southern fortifications following the natural bulwark made by the limit of the flow. The town was first surrounded by an *agger* (earthwork), buttressed by wooden boards and crowned by a palisade (*vallum*). About 450 BC this earthwork was replaced by a rampart of tufa and limestone, 3220m in perimeter, elaborated by the Samnites in the 4C BC and again in the 2C BC. In the late 2C or early 1C BC (just before the Social War) this was reinforced by towers. The entire enceinte has now been located, though the south-west wall remains to be excavated; all the eight gates are visible, the oldest being the Porta Stabiana.

The streets were paved in the Roman period with large polygonal blocks of Vesuvian lava and are bordered by kerbed pavements. In nearly all the roadways, at regular intervals, are stepping-stones for pedestrians. These stones did not interfere with the heavy vehicles that have left deep ruts in the roadway, because the draught-animals, attached to the end of a pole, enjoyed great liberty of action. When the Pompeian ladies or gentlemen did not wish to walk, they used litters.

The present names of the streets—Via di Mercurio, Via dell'Abbondanza, Vicolo del Gallo, and so on—have been taken from the street-corner public fountains, adorned with the heads of gods and goddesses, etc. On the outside walls of the houses and shops are numerous inscriptions, generally in red lettering; these include recommendations of candidates for the post of *aedile* or *duumvir,* dates, records, poetical quotations or short poems, the outpourings of lovers, jests and ribaldry. The character of Pompeii as an important maritime town is indicated by the numerous shops (sometimes attached to large private houses), taverns (*cauponae*), public bars (*thermopolia*), inns (*hospitia,* one with an elephant as sign) and stables (*stabula*), especially near the gates. The shops rarely have trade-signs, but frequently exhibit a phallus (carved, painted, or in mosaic), intended to ward off the evil eye, or one or two painted serpents, regarded as the genii loci.

The principal public buildings, grouped round the forum, lie not in the centre but in the most level part of the city, near the south-west corner. To the most ancient period of the town's history belong the houses built of large blocks of limestone, the Etruscan column, the Etruscan capitals, the Doric temple of the Triangular Forum and the Porta Stabiana. The Samnite monuments include the other gates and the walls, the temples of Jupiter and Apollo, the basilica, the portico of the forum, the Thermae Stabianae, the open-air theatre, the portico of the Triangular Forum and the gladiatorial barracks and palaestra. The Thermae of the Forum, the comitium, the covered theatre, the amphitheatre and the Temple of Zeus Meilichios are Augustan or earlier. The other public buildings are of later date. The Doric temple alone corresponds to the Greek model; all the others reveal an Etruscan scheme.

Pompeian houses

The dwellings at Pompeii exemplify the evolution of domestic architecture from the Italic model of the 4C and 3C BC to the Imperial Roman one of the 1C AD. The main feature of the **Pompeian house** was the *atrium* or interior court, surrounded by a roofed arcade. On the side opposite the entrance was the **tablinum** or chief living room, where the family dined and received their guests. To the right and left were the *alae,* the *cubicula* (bedrooms) and the *cellae,* used for various purposes. In front of the *tablinum* stood the *cartibulum* or table for the utensils used in serving meals. Near this was the *focus* or hearth. This, at least, was the early Italic plan, introduced by the Etruscans. Later, however, the chambers adjoining the façade, and sometimes also those at the sides, were converted into shops (*tabernae*) opening on the street. To the primitive house was added the Hellenic *peristylium,* and the tablinum ceased to be the general living room and was occupied by the family archives. Its former place was taken by the *triclinium,* one of the rooms opening off the peristyle. Some of the houses, even in the imperial epoch, maintained the simple original plan of atrium and tablinum. Even in the commercial districts of the last period, where its intimacy was encroached upon by shop and factory, the house remained a separate entity in Pompeii; nowhere does one find the blocks of flats typical of Ostia.

The characteristic dwelling of the fully developed style shows the rooms grouped round two quadrilateral spaces, the atrium and the peristyle, usually with the tablinum between them. Air and light were admitted through openings in the roof. The roof of the atrium sloped inwards so as to leave a quadrilateral opening in the middle (*compluvium*). Below this was the *impluvium,* a basin receiving the rain-water from the gutters of the *compluvium* and passing it on to the *puteus* or cistern.

The commonest form of the atrium, seen, for example, in the house of Lucretius Fronto, is the so-called *atrium tuscanicum,* in which the roof is borne by strong beams crossing from one side-wall to the other. A less frequent form (Houses of the Labyrinth, of the Silver Wedding, etc.) is the *atrium tetrastylum*, in which the roof is sustained by four columns at the corners of the impluvium. Still more rare is the Corinthian form, in which there are many columns (Houses of Castor and Pollux and of Epidius Rufus). Sometimes, as in the west or second atrium of the House of the Centenario, there is no opening in the roof.

Nearly every house had a second floor and some had a third; these were narrower than the first floor and were used by slaves or let out as lodgings. Few windows opening on the street have been discovered. In some cases the floor and ceiling of the upper rooms extended to form a small pillared loggia, the so-called *cenacula*. The second floor was reached by small flights of steps, either inside or outside. A small passage adjoining and parallel to the tablinum led in to the peristyle, which was in the form of a garden (*viridarium*) surrounded by an arcade, not invariably complete on all four sides.

Opening off the peristyle were smaller rooms for domestic purposes (*cubicula, triclinia, apothecae*) or for the reception of guests (*oeci, exedrae*). The triclinia are marked by their larger size, their mosaic pavements and the recesses in the lower part of their walls. The *lararium* or domestic sanctuary, in the form of an aedicula, or small temple, is found in the *atrium* in an adjoining chamber, or in the peristyle; sometimes, reduced to a mere painting, even in the kitchen. Nearly every house has a second entrance (*posticum*) near the peristyle.

The shops extended along the whole front of the house and were open to the street, though they could be closed by wooden shutters or sliding doors. The counting-house or cashier's office, in front of the entrance, is often lined with marble. Many of the shops have a back room for the use of clients or a bedroom for the shopkeeper on the mezzanine floor. The number of shops lent great animation to the principal streets. Lamps hung at the doors provided lighting for the town, along with others placed on municipal altars at the street-corners.

Wall paintings

Among Pompeii's most striking attractions are the **wall paintings** on its stucco-covered interior walls. These are disposed in three horizontal bands: dado, central zone and frieze. The colours are very vivid, predominantly red and yellow. The central field is occupied by small pictures, groups of flying figures or isolated figures. In this decoration four periods may be distinguished by their stylistic variations. In the first or Samnite period, the stucco ornamentation imitates the marble panelling of important Greek or Roman mansions; there are no human figures. In the second period (1C BC), the marble decoration is imitated in painting and figures are introduced in scenes depicting mythical, heroic, or religious subjects. In the third and best period (first half of the first century of the Roman Empire), the architectural framework takes on a distinctly decorative quality, and figures become more numerous. In the fourth period, the figures are accompanied by bizarre architectural effects, the colouring is less delicate, and the ornamental details are coarser.

THE SITE

Pompeii is divided (though not very regularly) into a chessboard of streets, the main thoroughfares being the Via Stabiana, Via di Nola and Via dell'Abbondanza. Archaeologists have devised a street plan that divides the town into nine regions, with varying numbers of *insulae*, or blocks. These generally consist of a group of dwellings, but may be wholly occupied by one building. The entrance to the exca-

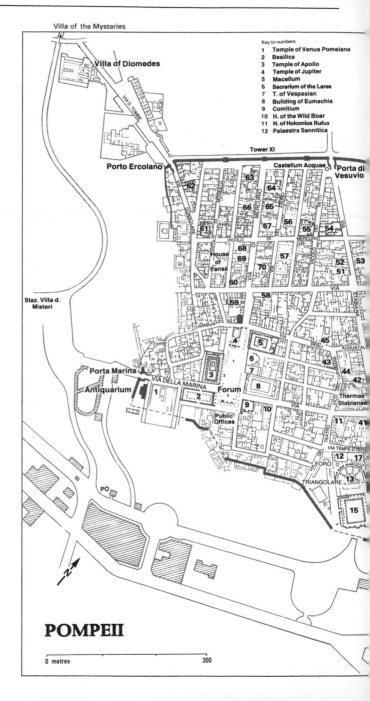

Villa of the Mysteries

Villa of Diomedes

VIA D. TOMBE

Tower XI

Porto Ercolano

Castellum Acquae

Porta di Vesuvio

Key to numbers

1   Temple of Venus Pomeiana
2   Basilica
3   Temple of Apollo
4   Temple of Jupiter
5   Macellum
6   Sacrarium of the Lares
7   T. of Vespasian
8   Building of Eumachia
9   Comitium
10 H. of the Wild Boar
11 H. of Holconius Rufus
12 Palaestra Sannitica

VICOLO   DI   MERCURIO

House of Pansa

VIA   DELLE   CONSOLARE

VIA   STABIANA

VIA   DEGLI   AUGUSTAL

Staz. Villa d. Misteri

Porta Marina

Antiquarium

VIA DELLA MARINA

Forum

Public Offices

Thermae Stabianae

VIA   TEATRO

VIA TEMPE D'ISIDE

FORO TRIANGOLARE

PO

POMPEII

0 metres   300

N

13 Teatro Grande
14 Teatro Piccolo
15 Quadriporticus
16 T. of Zeus Meilichios
17 T. of Isis
18 H. of the Cithara Player
19 H. of C. Pansa
20 H. of E. Sabinus
21 H. of P. Montanus
22 Verecundus
23 Fullonica Stephani
24 H. of Cryptoporticus
25 H. of the Menander
26 H. of Lovers

27 Thermopolium
28 H. of P. Paquius
29 H. of Priest Amandus
30 H. of Ephebus
31 Felix the Fruiterer
32 Weavers' Workshop
33 H. of J. Polybius
34 H. of C. Trebius Valens
35 Schola Armaturarum
36 H. of P. Cerialis
37 H. of the Moralist
38 H. of Loreius Tiburtinus
39 H. of Marine Venus
40 Villa Julia Felix
41 H. of C. Rufus
42 H. of Siricus
43 Lupanar Africani et Victoris
44 Inn of Sittius
45 H. of the Bear
46 H. of Marcus Lucretius

47 Casa delle Nozze d'Argento
48 Casa del Centenario
49 H. of M. L. Fronto
50 H. of the Gladiators
51 H. of Orpheus
52 Fullonica
53 H. of L. C. Jucundus
54 Casa degli Amorini Dorati
55 H. of the Vettii
56 H. of the Labyrinth
57 H. of the Faun
58 T. of Fortune
59 Thermae of the Forum
60 H. of the Tragic Poet
61 H. of Sallust
62 H. of the Surgeon
63 H. of Apollo
64 H. of Meleager
65 H. of Centaur
66 H. of Adonis
67 H. of Castor & Pollux
68 H. of the Little Fountain
69 H. of the Large Fountain
70 H. of the Anchor

vations for travellers arriving by road, or by railway from the Sorrento or Salerno lines, is the **Porta Marina**, the gate towards the sea. In antiquity this had an archway covering two passages, each with its own gateway: a steep track for mules and an easier pathway for pedestrians. The adjoining antiquarium, which once showed the historical development of the city, is now closed to the public.

The Via Marina leads directly from the Porta Marina to the forum. To the right can be seen the remains of the **Temple of Venus Pompeiana** (Map 1), guardian deity of the town. This building, having been partly destroyed by the earthquake of AD 63, was in process of restoration and enlargement when overtaken by the final catastrophe. Further on, on the same side, is the **basilica** (VIII, 1; Map 2), the most monumental of the city's public buildings, used as a court of law. This, in a distinctly Hellenistic style and probably dating from the 2C BC, is divided into nave and aisles by 28 Ionic columns of brick, covered with stucco. The Corinthian pilasters in tufa, now leaning against the wall, adorned the upper storey. At the end of the hall, badly damaged by the earthquake, was the raised tribunal for the judges (*duoviri jure dicundo*).

Leave the basilica by its north door and enter the **Temple of Apollo** (VII, 7; Map 3), a Samnite structure on the site of a 6C *sacellum*. The 48 columns of the portico were originally Ionic, with a Doric entablature, but after the earthquake they were converted into Corinthian columns by means of stucco, and the entablature took the form of a large zoöphorus. The stucco has now fallen off and the original design has come to light.

The portico was formerly decorated with paintings of scenes from the *Iliad*. The large tripod, painted on the first pilaster of the east wing, is one of the attributes of Apollo. In the middle of the uncovered area stood a large altar of travertine. The Ionic column to the left of the steps bore a sundial, emblematic of Apollo Helios. The bases placed against the columns of the portico supported statues, now in the Museo Archeologico Nazionale in Naples. At the sides are copies of the Apollo Sagittarius and Diana Sagittaria.

The actual temple stands on a high podium, accessible by steps in front, leading to the Corinthian pronaos. This enclosed the cella, which contained the statue of Apollo and the conical Omphalos, the symbol of the god. The latter is still in situ. An Oscan inscription in the pavement of the cella records that it was laid at the instance of Oppius Campanius, the Quaestor. Beside the rear door is the priest's chamber.

The *forum (VII, 8), the most perfect example known of a Roman central square, is planned so that Vesuvius dominates its major axis. When the basilica was built the opportunity was taken to furnish the square with a colonnade enclosing its two long sides and its southern extremity. Above this colonnade was a gallery, reached by small staircases (traces of which remain) designed to accommodate spectators of the fêtes and games held in the forum before the construction of the amphitheatre. The conversion of the colonnade from tufa to travertine, begun in the Imperial Age, was interrupted by the earthquake. The area enclosed by the colonnade, 142m long and 38m wide, was adorned with statues of officials and other distinguished people. Twenty two of the pedestals of these are extant, five with inscriptions. The larger base halfway down the west side is the orator's tribune. The passages leading to the central space were barred to vehicles. In a niche at No. 31 is a *tabula ponderaria* of travertine, showing the standard measures of capacity. Adjacent is the entrance to an inner court, and at No. 29 is a portico, possibly used as a vegetable market. No. 28 was a public latrine and No. 27 the municipal treasury.

At the north end of the forum stands the **Temple of Jupiter** (VII, 8; Map 4), built in the Italic manner, with a wide cella and pronaos enclosed by Corinthian columns. Later, it became the *capitolium* of the Roman town. The pronaos is reached by a flight of 15 steps, originally flanked by equestrian statues and interrupted by a platform on which stood an altar. The cella, with its Ionic columns, had a marble pavement bordered by mosaics. Apertures in the flooring of the pronaos and cella admitted light to some lower chambers (such as the *aerarium* or treasury), which communicated directly with the forum. The podium against the back wall, reached by steps, is believed to have borne statues of Jupiter, Juno, and Minerva. After the temple had been reduced to ruins by the earthquake, the cult of these deities was carried on at the small temple of Zeus Meilichios (see below).

To the right and left of the main steps were two triumphal arches. That on the right was demolished by the ancients to open up the view of the arch behind, which had an equestrian statue of Tiberius on its top and statues of Nero and Drusus in its niches.

Return by the east side of the forum, which was rebuilt in the 1C AD. The **macellum** (VII, 9, 4; Map 5), or provision market, was fronted by a graceful colonnade, with the shops of the *argentarii* or money-changers. Against the marble columns of the arcade and the pilasters between the shops are bases for statues. The interior court was enclosed by another colonnade, destroyed by the earthquake. The walls were adorned with frescoes: those surviving include Io guarded by Argus and Ulysses and Penelope. The frieze shows fish, game, amphorae of wine and the like. On the south are shops, with an upper storey. In the open centre of the court was a dome borne by 12 columns, of which the bases remain; it probably sheltered a tank or basin for fish. A chapel at the back contained statues of the Imperial family, to the right and left of this are the shops of a fishmonger and of a butcher.

The **Sacrarium of the Lares** next door (Map 6), is fronted by a marble colonnade and was originally paved and lined with marble slabs. A podium in the apse bore several statues. Around the walls are niches for eight other statues, probably representing the Lares Publici, or tutelary deities of the town.

The **Temple of Vespasian** (VII, 9, 2; Map 7) was begun after AD 63 but was never completed. In front was a columned portico. An altar, with bas-reliefs of the sacrifice of a bull, the sacrificial utensils and a civic crown between two laurels (the symbol of the imperial house), stands in the middle of the open court.

The **Building of Eumachia** (VII, 9, 1; Map 8), an imposing structure dedicated to Concordia Augusta and Pietas, was erected by the priestess Eumachia, acting also for her son, M. Numistrius Fronto. It was occupied by the *fullones* (fullers), bleachers of linen, who probably used it as a sale-room. In front is a *chalcidicum* or vestibule, with a portico of two rows of columns, at the ends of which are four niches for statues of Aeneas, Romulus, Julius Caesar, and Augustus. A covered corridor (*crypta*) runs round the other three sides.

A marble **portal* with splendid acanthus-leaf decoration gives access to an open court (*porticus*), surrounded by a colonnade with two rows of columns superimposed on each other without the intervention of a second storey. At the back stood the statue of Eumachia, erected by the fullers, now in the Museo Archeologico Nazionale in Naples.

On the other side of Via dell'Abbondanza stands the **comitium** (Map 9), or polling booth for the election of the civic magistrates. At the south end of the forum are three large halls, that in the centre probably used by the *ordo decurionum* (town council), the others by the *duumviri* and *aediles*.

Now descend Via dell' Abbondanza, the name of which is due to a misinterpretation of the bust of Concordia Augusta, on a fountain at the back of the Eumachia Building.

> Behind the comitium (Map 9) a steep quarter spreads down the slope of the lava flow; this represents one of the last expansions of the Augustan age, when the now superfluous walls on this side were demolished to make way for terraced houses of the Herculanean type (here somewhat ruinous).

To the right is the **House of the Wild Boar** (VIII, 3, 8; Map 10), named after the mosaic on the entrance floor. Further on, at the corner of Via dei Teatri, stands the **House of Holconius Rufus** (VIII, 4, 4; Map 11), one of the more prominent citizens of Pompeii, honoured by a statue at the neighbouring crossroad. The rich decoration of his elegant dwelling is unfortunately much faded. From here, Via dei Teatri leads south to the **foro triangolare** (triangular forum). This is reached by a fine Ionic portico giving access to two gates opening on the forum, which is surrounded by a Doric colonnade. Obliquely set within are the ruins of a **Doric temple** of the 6C BC, 30m in length and 20m in width. This is a heptastyle and pseudodipteral edifice, with 11 columns on each side. The remains include the elevated stylobate, a few capitals and fragments of the cella walls. Apparently dedicated to Hercules, it seems to have been already a ruin in the 2C BC and was used as a public dumping ground and as a quarry of building material. Towards the end of that century, however, the area appears to have been cleared for the erection of a sacrarium dedicated to Athena. Near the left rear of the temple was placed a semicircular seat, on the back of which was a sundial. Opposite the steps leading to the pronaos is an enclosure, perhaps a heroön to Hercules. To the left are three altars and (further back) a cistern, formerly covered with a cupola raised on eight Doric columns.

Adjoining the Triangular Forum, near the corner of Via del Tempio d'Iside, lay the **Palaestra Sannitica** (Map 12), where the young men trained for the games. To the south of this is a large reservoir for the water used in the theatre. Pompeii actually has two theatres, the larger open to the sky, the smaller with a roof. The *Teatro Grande (Large or Open Theatre; Map 13), which could contain 5000 spectators, dates from the 2C BC. Built on the model of the Hellenic theatres and especially resembling that of Antioch, it was provided with large tanks or basins, installed in the orchestra and communicating with the reservoir mentioned above, making it both a theatre and a nymphaeum. The water below the stage is said to have acted as a sounding-box. The theatre was restored in the reign of Augustus.

The *cavea*, or auditorium, is divided into three tiers: the *summa cavea* placed above a corridor and accessible by several staircases, the *media cavea* with 15 rows of seats arranged in five wedges, all also reached from the corridor, and the *ima cavea*, accessible from the orchestra only. The *ima cavea* consisted of four broad and low tiers, of the chairs (*bisellia*) of the municipal councillors (*decuriones*). After the restoration of the theatre, seats for distinguished spectators were also placed in the orchestra. The stone rings at the top of the wall were for the poles supporting the *velarium* or awning that protected the audience from the sun. The whole of the upper part overlooking the Triangular Forum is a modern reconstruction. Above the entrances to the orchestra are two small boxes (*tribunalia*), one of which was reserved for the President of the Spectacle, the other (perhaps) for the priestesses. The stage (*pulpitum*), which had a wooden flooring, was reached from the orchestra by flights of steps. Between the stage and the orchestra was a narrow slit for the curtain. The wall at the back of the stage (*scena*) represented the façade of a palace with three doors, the usual back-scene of an ancient theatre.

The *Teatro Piccolo (Small or Covered Theatre; Map 14), the roof of which was probably pyramidal, could hold an audience of 1000. It was constructed soon after 80 BC by the Duoviri C. Quintius Valgus and M. Porcius, and was used, as an *odeion*, for concerts. The cavea is crossed by one *praecinctio* or corridor. The lower part consists of four wide tiers, the upper of 17 tiers, arranged in five sections. The marble pavement was presented by the Duovir M. Oculatius Verus. Behind the building was a **quadriporticus**, a vast square piazza, surrounded by an arcade of 74 columns, that served originally as a foyer. Later this was converted into a barracks for gladiators, with two rows of cells, the upper ones being entered from a wooden gallery, part of which has been reconstructed. Here were found the fine weapons now in the Museo Archeologico Nazionale in Naples, also iron fetters and 63 skeletons. The palaestra of this building, the walks and colonnades of the Triangular Forum, and the Great Palaestra (described below) collectively formed the gymnasium of the Samnite period.

Emerge from the Small Theatre into the Via Stabiana, which leads to the right to the ancient Porta Stabiana. Following it in the other direction at the corner to the left you soon reach the **Temple of Zeus Meilichios** (Jupiter the Placable; Map 16). This is the smallest temple in Pompeii. The dedication indicates a Greek cult probably imported from Sicily. The temple had a tetrastyle vestibule. The cella had a small portico of two columns, and at the back were the terracotta statues of Jupiter, Juno, and Minerva now in the Museo Archeologico Nazionale. For a time, this temple was erroneously assigned to Aesculapius. A large altar stands in front of the steps.

Turn left along the side-street to reach the **Temple of Isis** (Map 17), which was almost entirely rebuilt, after the earthquake, by Numerius Popidius Celsinus. In keeping with the mysterious character of the cult of Isis, this temple is somewhat curious in form, with its lateral entrance provided with a triple door. The sacred enclosure was surrounded by a colonnade, the front walk of which has its central intercolumniation formed of two pilasters with half-columns, wider than the others. Opposite was a recess, the back of which bore a painted figure of Harpocrates (now the the Museo Archeologico Nazionale). In the open court is a small shrine, from which steps descend to a subterranean reservoir, intended for the lustral water. Small calcined bones were found on the main altar. Seven steps ascend to the pronaos, the roof of which is borne by six Corinthian columns. To the right and left of the entrance to the cells are niches for statues, and in front, to the left, is an altar. At the back, to the left, is a small staircase by which the priests entered the cella. Underneath this temple runs Fontana's aqueduct.

Now return to the Via Stabiana, in which, to the right (Map 18), is the large **House of the Cithara Player** (I, 4), or house of Popidius Secundus Augustianus, with two atria and three peristyles. Here was found the statue of Apollo Citharoedus now in the museum of Naples. On reaching the intersection of the Via Stabiana with Via dell'Abbondanza (once adorned with a statue of M. Holconius), turn to the right. No. 20 (left; Map 19) is the **House of Cuspius Pansa** or of the **Diadumeni** and No. 22 (Map 20) that of **Epidius Sabinus**.

NEW EXCAVATIONS

At this point begin the *new excavations (Nuovi Scavi), first undertaken in 1911. They stretch east for some 500m, to the Porta di Sarno or Urbulana, and include some of the more striking remains in the town. The original aim of these excavations was to trace the general line of the thoroughfare and to restore to their proper places the roofs, balconies, windows, stalls, doors, and the like which formed the street-front. On the north side little further has been, done and though the façade is complete for much of the distance, you cannot penetrate far into any building. To the south, however, every insula has now been excavated back to the next parallel street.

The characteristic feature of the new excavations is that the fittings and articles of domestic use, wall paintings, mosaics, statues and stucco ornamentation have all been left as far as possible in their original places. Fallen walls have been re-erected and rough-cast in their original colours; the painted stucco ceilings have been restored; some of the gardens have been replanted in accordance with what is known of classical horticulture, and water plays once more in the private and public fountains, some of the latter having several jets. Mural inscriptions, including unauthorised scrawls relating to the games or elections, are seen in full force. Here the ruins come nearest to capturing the atmosphere of everyday urban life in the Roman era.

The **House of Popidius Montanus** (No. 9; Map 21) was a great resort of chess-players (*latruncularii*), who were responsible for the notice to the left of the portal. The door, studded with large-headed bronze nails, was wide open at the moment of the catastrophe (plaster cast). Note also the cast of the closed door of No. 10 (left). Nos. 7–5, in front of which was a projecting penthouse, show the façade of the **Workshops of Verecundus** (Map 22), maker of cloth, woollen garments, and articles in felt (*coactilia*). The entrance of No. 7 is flanked by four paintings. Two of these show the patron deities of the work-rooms: Venus Pompeiana, in a quadriga drawn by elephants, and Mercury. The others represent the work of the *coactiliari* or felt-makers in full activity (right) and the sale-room for the products of the factory (left). The plaster cast of the door shows the iron mechanism for fastening it.

At No. 2, also with a penthouse, and surmounted by a pillared loggia, are the **Workshops of the Dyers** (*infectores*). To the right of the threshold is one of the vats used in dyeing, projecting from a furnace bearing phallic emblems. No. 1, above which is a large balcony used as a drying-room, was also (as a notice tells us) occupied by felt-makers. The painted frieze shows busts of Apollo, Mercury, Jupiter, and Diana, and the processional figure of Venus Pompeiana which was carried through the town.

The greater part of Insula 6, on the south, belonged to one owner who lived at No. 11 and converted the neighbouring house (Nos. 8–9) into domestic quarters. The *trapezophori* (legs) of a marble table, bearing the inscription P. Casca Longus, probably belonged to the fat conspirator who dealt the first blow at Julius Caesar and may have been acquired at auction after his banishment. No. 7 is the *Fullonica Stephani (Map 23). The double door was closed at the time of the eruption, but the small hatch in the right half had been left open, as is shown by the position in which its fastenings were discovered. Through this hatch were handed in the cloth and garments to be washed (in the impluvium or in the three tanks at the back), to be cleaned (in the five *saltus fullonici* adjoining the two hind-most tanks), to be bleached (by sulphur vapour), to be dried (on the wide terraces of the first floor), or to be pressed in the *pressorium* (by the wall to the left, on entering).

The house at No. 4 was being redecorated during the last days of Pompeii. This is suggested by the heaps of material for making stucco in the peristyle and the triclinium, by the plinths still waiting for their rough-casting, by the state of the rooms adjoining the entrance and by the one completed frieze, in the chamber at the south-east corner of the atrium. The decorations of the *cabinet (perhaps a *lararium*) to the right of the tablinum are unusually fine. The small vaulted roof, reconstructed from hundreds of minute fragments, is adorned with scenes from the last books of the *Iliad* executed in a band of white stucco against a blue background. At the top: Hector, driven by a Fury, resists the appeal of his parents at the Scaean Gate of Troy; Hector's combat with Achilles; Hector's corpse dragged at the chariot-wheels of Achilles. At the sides: Priam loading his treasures on the car and setting out, under the guidance of Hermes, to offer them to Achilles as a ransom for the body of Hector. On the south are a large hall and a *cubiculum* displaying the red colouring of the second style. The hall has a magnificent mosaic *floor and its walls show traces of an extensive wall painting.

No. 3 on this block is the **Shop of Verus the Blacksmith**, who dealt in bronzeware. The lamp and other objects on view here are just a few of those that were found. Among the technical instruments were the valuable fragments in bronze and iron, probably for repair, which enabled a reconstruction to be made of the *groma* the theodolite of the Roman surveyor.

By passing through House No. 2 you reach the **cryptoporticus** (Map 24), or underground portico, with its semicircular vaulting and elaborate decoration in white stucco. The walls, in the second style, are divided into vertical sections by female and phallic hermae. The frieze showed upwards of 50 pictures of scenes in the Trojan War, taken not only from the *Iliad* but also from the *Aethiopis* of Arctinus and possibly from other cyclic poems. Only about a score of these have been preserved, whole or mutilated. Latterly the cryptoporticus had been degraded to the status of a wine-vault (*cella vinaria*). The existing chamber is just a fragment of the whole, the rest having been filled up to enlarge the garden. In a glass case are shown plaster casts of the impressions made by the bodies of several occupants of this house. During the eruption they took refuge under the portico, but when the rain of lapilli ceased they climbed up to the garden with the aid of a ladder. Here, however, the showers of ashes overtook them, and they were all suffocated in one huddled group. Adjoining the east wing are some well-preserved rooms, including a striking *triclinium*, the vaulting of which, with fine white stucco-work, rested on painted caryatids of rosso antico. In the frieze are remains of paintings, in which heroic or mythical scenes alternate with banquets.

The door at the south-west corner of the cryptoporticus opens on a little street containing the **House of L. Ceius Secundus** (No. 15), notable for its beautiful façade with white rustication, protected by the original overhanging roof. In the vestibule are a plaster model of the door and a ceiling reconstructed from fragments. The tetrastyle atrium, admirably preserved, contains a plaster cast of a wooden cupboard. Beyond it is a pseudoperistyle, the walls of which are adorned with hunting scenes (*venationes*) and Nile landscapes, with pygmies.

Across the little street is the *House of the Menander** (I, 10, 4; Map 25), a fine dwelling belonging to a kinsman of the Empress Poppaea, where the silver plate now in the Naples Museum was found, in 1930. At the time of the catastrophe, this house too was being redecorated. At the onset of the eruption the family, with their slaves, took refuge in the room with the strongest roof, in which they were trapped by the fall of part of the peristyle and eventually killed when the roof collapsed about their heads. The beautifully appointed Tuscan atrium contains a lararium in the form of a tiny temple. In an exedra to the left are three Trojan scenes. The peristyle has stuccoed columns, and in the centre of the mosaic floor a panel depicting a Nile scene. On the north side are two elegantly decorated oeci. A series of exedrae contain a rich selection of paintings, including the seated figure of the poet Menander, from which the house takes its name. The calidarium of the private baths is well preserved.

No. 11 on the south-west corner of the insula is the **House of the Lovers** (Map 26), a charming small house with elegant decoration and a splendid inscription beneath the portico, reading '*amantes ut apes vitam mellitam exigunt*' (lovers, like bees, desire a honey-sweet life).

Return by the side lane between Insulae 6 and 7 to the *compitum* (crossing) where, under a canopy, figures of the 12 Dei Consentes are painted on the wall. Continue along Via dell'Abbondanza. On the north side (IX, 10, 2; Map 27) is a *thermopolium*, or tavern, that served hot and cold drinks on the ground floor, while on the first floor the wares included the favours of such complaisant *puellae* as Asellina, Smyrna, Maria, and Aegle. The objects found, including a phallic lamp, have been placed in their proper positions in the interior. The sign, to the right of No. 4, represents large wine jars, goblets and a wine funnel.

In contrast, the opposite side of the street (I, 7) consists of a series of residences of middle-class respectability. No. 1 (Map 28) is the imposing **House of P. Paquius Proculus** with rich mosaics in its vestibule, atrium, tablinum, and a room adjoining the peristyle. The restoration of the first floor, behind the tablinum, is noteworthy. An exedra on the north side of the peristyle contains the skeletons of seven children caught together by the catastrophe. Beyond the modest but tasteful **House of Fabius Amandio** (Nos. 2–3), is the **House of the Priest Amandus** (No. 7; Map 29), where the triclinium is decorated in the third style; the panels show Polyphemus with the ship of Ulysses and Galatea riding a dolphin, Perseus and Andromeda, Hercules in the garden of the Hesperides and the fall of Icarus. The charming garden was shaded by a tree, the stump of which remains.

Entered from the side lane is the **House of the Ephebus** (Nos. 10–12, Map 30), where the rich decoration added to an agglomeration of modest dwellings indicate the rise to wealth of its owner, the tradesman P. Cornelius Teges. Here was found the ephebus now in the Museo Archeologico Nazionale. Opposite (I, 8, 19) is a **dyeworks** with four boilers, washing vats and pressing-tables.

On the corner of the main street is the **Shop of Felix the Fruiterer** (Pomarius; I, 8, 1, Map 31). The sale room, in which the fruit was exhibited on wooden shelves, is adorned with Bacchic motives. Opposite, on the north side (Map 32), are *textrinoe* or weavers' workshops, with a high-columned upper storey. No. 6, the **Workshop of Crescens**, has a painted figure of Hermes-Priapus to the right of the entrance. Continue on the north side to the next insula (IX, 13). The plain façade of the **House of C. Julius Polybius** (Nos. 1–3, Map 33) has carved lintels over the side doors. Adjoining the entrance of No. 5 are paintings of Aeneas, Anchises, and Ascanius (right) and of Romulus with the spoils of King Acron (left). At the corner is an *amphora urinaria* (urinal) placed there by the fullers.

On the opposite side of the street, excavations behind the frontage were resumed in 1951, revealing (I, 9) three interesting dwellings. The **House of the Beautiful Impluvium** (entered from No. 2) has well-preserved decoration in the atrium and tablinum. In the **House of Successus** (No. 3) the painting of the boy being chased by a duck and the statue of the boy bearing a dove probably portray a favourite child of the house. The **House of the Fruit Orchard** (No. 5) is entered through the adjacent shop, as a plaster model of the original door closes the main portal. The walls of two cubicula are finely painted in the third style, with pictures of fruit trees, including the then rare lemon. In the alley beyond is the public altar of the serpent agathodoemon. Proceed past a thermopolium of the next insula, which ends with another crossroad altar, then return to the north side.

The **House of C. Trebius Valens** (III, 2, 1; Map 34) has no shops on its front. On the façade were three announcements of forthcoming shows at the amphitheatre and numerous electoral 'posters', with the householder's recommendations of different candidates: all these were destroyed by bombs in 1943. Among the interesting features of this large house are the black-walled room at the south-east angle of the atrium; a cubiculum, in the second style, to the left of the atrium; the tablinum, with its fine frieze (north wall) and its reconstructed east wall; the calidarium behind the *praefurnium* (kitchen), to the right of the tablinum; and the reconstruction of the east door in the portico. The garden has been replanted, and the 12 jets of the fountain again spout. At the end of the garden is a summer triclinium. The skeletons of the occupants were found under the portico (reconstructed).

On the same side, at No. 5 of Insula 3, are preserved many carbonised fragments of mats (*tegetes*). The **Schola Armaturarum** (No. 6) was probably the headquarters of a military organisation and not of the Collegium Juventutis Pompeianae, as was formerly supposed. The decorations of this building all refer to its function. On the exterior are two trophies of arms and on the door-jambs, two palm trees, the leaves of which were the reward of victory in the gymnasium. Inside are the Ten Female Genii, each holding a buckler and some kind of weapon. A plaster model of one of the cupboards, which contained gymnastic apparatus and fencing gear, stands by the west wall. The modern fastening of this armamentarium was made from a cast of the ancient one.

Cross the narrow *cardo orientalis* or Via Nuceria, which enters the city by the Porta Nuceria (see below). In this street to the left is the entrance (right) to the small but charming **House of Pinarius Cerialis**, identified from 114 gems found here (some uncut) as that of a lapidary. The fine decorations of a little room on the north side depict a theatrical representation of Iphigeneia in Tauris.

On the corner is the **Tavern of Zosimus**; the rest of the insula, known as the **House of the Moralist** (Map 37), consists of two inter-communicating houses belonging to the related families of T. Arrius Polites and M. Epidus Hymenaeus. In No. 2, two ceilings have been reconstructed: a coffered black ceiling in the triclinium, a yellow one in a cubiculum. The garden has been replanted. A wooden staircase (reconstruction) ascends to the rooms on the upper floor, the details of which have been reproduced as far as possible. The remains of the ornamentation have been affixed to the walls and ceilings. A small loggia, giving on the inside garden, is almost intact. At the south-east corner is a perfectly preserved windowledge. From the foot of the staircase, pass (without re-entering the street) into No. 3, skirting a black-walled room with flying female figures (left) and a small garden court (right). Below the loggia already noted, in immediate contact with the garden, is a summer triclinium in masonry, with the usual table in the middle. On the three black walls were painted, in white, three maxims for polite conduct at table. One of these was destroyed by bombs in 1943.

At the south corner of the crossroads is the **Hermes Caupona** (tavern) with the customary bar-room and a first-floor balcony (reconstructed). To the left is a private cistern (*castellum aquae*), the only one yet discovered, which retains the leaden tank from which pipes conveyed the water to the neighbour-members of the *consortium* or fellowship. On the walls of the next alley to the north are inscriptions in large white letters, almost literally fulminating against committers of nuisance, by invoking the thunderbolts of Jove against offenders.

On the right (II, 2, 5; Map 38), between two taverns, is the ***House of Loreius Tiburtinus**, one of those that give a perfect idea of patrician Pompeian life. A special charm is lent by the beautiful garden, now flourishing again after a rest of nearly 2000 years. A wide portal, closed by a door of bronze and flanked by benches, opens into the atrium where the water-jet of the impluvium plays again. A cubiculum in the east wing contains a Rape of Europa and a charming medallion of a girl. To the left is a room with two rows of paintings. The first, on a black ground, presents a summary of the *Iliad* in a series of 12 pictures. The other shows the Labours of Hercules, taken from a Hercules cycle. The peristyle is bordered on the garden-side by the north arm of the *euripus* (a series of communicating basins). At the east end is a cascade where the water gushes out between paintings of Narcissus and of Pyramus and Thisbe. Below is a *biclinium* the table of which seems to rise from the water. On the right couch of the biclinium is the signature of the artist Lucius, who executed the adjoining paintings. When the north arm of the euripus was full, it overflowed through conduits, passing under the little tetrastyle temple in the middle, into another branch, traversing the garden from north to south. Beneath the temple are ornamental carvings from which issued the water for a second cascade. In the large garden numerous plaster casts have been taken of roots of ornamental plants, shrubs, and trees. The euripus makes its final exit near the back door of the house, in the south alley.

The small house at No. 4 has over its entrance a painted stucco relief of the imperial emblem—a civic crown between two laurels. The **House of the Marine Venus** (II, 3, 3; Map 39) was damaged by a bomb in 1943 and not completely excavated until 1952, when the great painting of Venus was brought to light. The stuccoed decoration of the portico around the garden was completed just before the eruption.

The whole of the next insula, excavated in 1755–57 and reburied, and completely disinterred in 1952–53, is occupied by the ***Villa of Julia Felix** (II, 4; Map 40) and its magnificent garden. The villa seems to have served the function of a luxury hotel, being in three sections: the residential quarter of the proprietress; a bath for public use; an inn, a shop, and a series of rooms, some with independent street doors. The fine private rooms have big square windows overlooking the garden. They lost their decoration in the 18C; that of one room (Apollo and the Muses) is now in the Louvre. The **portico** has slender rectangular marble columns with delicate capitals; the tiled roof is a copy of the antique one. Below it the couches of the triclinium face the marble fish-ponds in the middle of the garden and the rustic stucco colonnade beyond. The **baths** are the most complete and perfect in Pompeii; their charming vestibule communicates by a hatch with the adjacent **inn**. The rented apartments, one still displaying its 'to let' notice, were on two floors.

Behind the villa rises the **amphitheatre** (I, 6), the most ancient structure of its kind known. Begun c 80 BC through the munificence of the Duoviri C. Quintius Valgus and M. Porcius, it was not completed until the time of Augustus (27 BC–AD14). The incriptions beneath the north entrance probably refer to restorations undertaken by C. Cuspius Pansa after the period of disuse that followed the fatal brawl of AD 59 and the earthquake. The axes of the amphitheatre measure

135 x 107m, and it held 12,000 spectators. The cavea was divided into three tiers, containing 5, 12, and 18 rows of seats. A space on the east side, as wide as two rows, was reserved for the President of the Games. In construction it differs from later amphitheatres in that the gallery from which the first and second tiers are reached is constructed in four unconnected sections, whereas the upper gallery, reserved for women and children, is entered from a corridor reached only by an external staircase. There are no subterranean chambers beneath the arena.

To the west lies the **Great Palaestra** a space c 110m square once shaded by great plane-trees, surrounded by a portico; in the centre is a large swimming pool. Here, after the Samnite palaestra had proved inadequate, the youth of the city exercised themselves and held their gymnastic competitions. In the latrine at the south-east corner were found many skeletons of youths who, during the eruption of Vesuvius, fled in vain to its shelter.

From the west side you may pass between Insulae 8 and 9 and, by turning left, descend to the **Porta di Nuceria**. Outside the gate modern excavations, removing an enormous quantity of earth, have exposed a street (Via Nuceria) running east–west and flanked by sumptuous tombs that date mainly from the second half of the 1C BC. Particularly worthy of note are (right) the painted announcements of games at neighbouring cities (Nuceria, Herculaneum, and so on), tombs with portrait statues and busts and the **Sepulchre of Eumachia**, the builder of the cloth market in the forum. Just outside the gate are casts of three further victims of the disaster. To the west the extramural view of the town is impressive.

Now return along the Via dell'Abbondanza to its intersection with the Via Stabiana. To the left is the **House of Cornelius Rufus**. To the right lie the **Thermae Stabianae** (VII, 1), the largest in Pompeii. They date originally from the Samnite era, but were enlarged soon after the establishment of the Roman colony and again under the empire. The entrance admits to the palaestra, enclosed by a portico, some of the beautiful stucco decorations of which are seen to the left. Along this stretch are the bowling alley and the swimming pool, with its appurtenances. Opposite are another bowling alley, a latrine and some private baths. To the right are the **men's baths**. These include the *apodyterium* (dressing-room), two chambers with marble floor, vaulted stucco and recesses for the clothes; the circular *frigidarium* or cold bath; the *tepidarium* with a plunge-bath; and (at the back) the *calidarium* or warm room, with a plunge-bath and a basin for washing. Hot air circulated below the tepidarium and the calidarium. Adjacent are the **women's baths**. From a corridor enter the dressing-room, with two entrances from the street and the usual recesses. Beyond the cold and tepid rooms is the calidarium, with hollow walls and flooring for the hot vapour to pass through. Between the two calidaria was the *praefurnium*, or heating apparatus, of which the furnace and the position of three cylindrical boilers are recognisable.

Beyond, to the right, diverges Vico del Lupanare, in which (right) stands the **House of Siricus** (VII, 1, 47; Map 42) composed of two communicating apartments. On the threshold is the inscription *Salve lucru(m)*, a candid salute to lucre. The handsome triclinium contains paintings of Neptune and Apollo helping to build the walls of Troy, Hercules and Omphale and Thetis with Vulcan. Opposite the entrance is a painting of two large serpents (agathodeomones), with the inscription (nearly effaced) *Otiosis locus hic non est, discede morator* (loitering forbidden).

Further on, to the left, is the **Lupanar Africani et Victoris** (Map 43) the coarse paintings and inscriptions on the ground floor of which place its character beyond a doubt. The first floor has a balcony (carefully restored after bomb damage). Opposite is the **Inn of Sittius** (Map 44), the sign of which was an elephant.

Vico del Lupanare ends at Via degli Augustali, where, almost opposite, is the **House of the Bear** (VII, 2; Map 45), so called from the mosaic at the entrance. To the right is a **Shoemaker's Shop**. Keeping to the right, regain the Via Stabiana and turn left. To the right (No. 12) is a restored **mill** (*pistrinum*). No. 5, on the same side, is the **House of Marcus Lucretius** (IX, 3; Map 46), priest of Mars and decurion of Pompeii. This was once one of the more luxuriantly decorated houses in the city. In the atrium, to the right, is the aedicula of the two tutelary deities of the house. Opposite is the tablinum. At the back is a pretty little garden, with a fountain and some marble figures among its flowers. The best of the well-preserved paintings, in the fourth style, are now in Naples.

The whole of the next insula on the right is occupied by the **Central Thermae** (IX, 4), built between the earthquake and the eruption, with the usual features on a more sumptuous scale and, in addition, a *laconicum* or *sudatorium*, a hot-air chamber of circular shape with domed vaulting. The building was unfinished at the time of its destruction.

Leave the thermae by the north side to emerge in the Via di Nola. On the right side of the lane opposite is a **tavern** in which were discovered three large bronze trumpets, apparently deposited here by the gladiators of the amphitheatre fleeing from the shower of lapilli. Further on, to the right, is the entrance to the **Casa delle Nozze d'Argento** (House of the Silver Wedding Anniversary; V, 2, Map 47), so called because the excavations were made in the presence of King Umberto and Queen Margherita in 1893, the year of their silver wedding. This is a real Pompeiian palace, with a spacious tetrastyle atrium. The front colonnade of the well-preserved peristyle is higher than the others. The triclinium is a large and handsome apartment. The cubicula on the south side have well-preserved decorations in the third style, and their private baths have been wonderfully restored; and the garden, with its stonework triclinium, is noteworthy.

Returning to the Via di Nola and following it to the left, you soon reach (right) the large, magnificent **Casa del Centenario** (House of the Centenary), so named because it was excavated in 1879, the 1800th anniversary of the eruption. It has two atria (that on the left handsomely decorated) and a spacious peristyle. A graceful fountain plays in a small court, now covered in and adorned with paintings of gardens, a fish-pond and scenes of the chase. To the west are the bathrooms and two chambers adorned with paintings. A secret chamber with erotic decoration opens from one. Of interest also are the decorations of two rooms entered from the front walk of the colonnade, one with white walls, the other with black.

Off the alley opposite stands the **House of Marcus Lucretius Fronto** (V, 4; Map 49), which dates from the early imperial period. The roof of the atrium is a modern restoration, in strict keeping with the maxims of Vitruvius. Among the notable paintings in this house are Neoptolemus slain by Orestes (first room on the right), Theseus and Ariadne, Toilet of Venus (second room on the right), Wedding of Mars and Venus, Triumph of Bacchus, landscapes (tablinum), Narcissus at the fountain, Pero and her father Micon condemned to death by starvation (room to the right of the tablinum), Pyramus and Thisbe, Bacchus and Silenus (first garden-room to the right).

Further on in the Via di Nola, to the left, is the **House of the Gladiators** (Map 50) with a four-sided porticus. The **Porta di Nola**, at the end of the street, dates from the Samnite era. It is decorated, on the side facing the city, with the head of Minerva.

Return to the Via Stabiana and turn right. At the corner on the left are a fountain, an altar to the Lares of the crossroads, and a pillar of an aqueduct. No. 20 (left) is the **House of M. Vesonius Primus** (VI, 14; Map 51), known as the **House of Orpheus** from the large painting in the peristyle. In the atrium is a portrait-herm of Vesonius. No. 22 is the **Fullonica of Vesonius**. The impluvium contains a marble table and a fountain, and there are three tanks behind the atrium. Opposite stands the **House of L. Coecilus Jucundus** (V, 1, 26; Map 53), the banker, where the famous receipts now in the Museo Archeologico Nazionale were discovered. In the atrium is a portrait-herm of the master of the house, a copy of the original at Naples; also two bas-reliefs representing respectively the north side of the forum and the destruction of the Porta del Vesuvio by the earthquake of AD 63. The tablinum has good decorations. The sign of the **Taberna Lusoria** (No. 28), a vase between two phalli, indicates its business, a gambling house below with rooms for hire above.

Beyond the next crossroads on the left, is the **Casa degli Amorini Dorati** (House of the Guilded Cupids) (VI, 16.7; Map 54), which belonged to the Poppaei, and which demonstrates the refined tastes of the age of Nero. The porticus has been restored on its old lines. The marble sculptures in the garden remain as they were. The marble bas-reliefs in the south wing of the colonnade represent satyrs, maenads, etc. At the south-east corner of the peristyle is a shrine devoted to the cult of Egyptian deities. The lararium in the north colonnade has the conventional form of a small temple. The mosaic on the floor of the interesting cubiculum to the right indicates the place occupied by the beds. On the walls, under antique glass, are the flying and gilded cupids that give the house its name. In the east colonnade is a large room with paintings of Thetis and Vulcan, Jason and Pelias, Achilles in his tent with Patroclus and Briseis. The stucco ceilings of two cubicula in the west colonnade are unusually fine.

The cardo ends at the **Porta di Vesuvio**, adjoining which is a *castellum aquae* or conduit-head, where water entering from an aqueduct was distributed to three channels. Outside the gate, beneath cypresses, is the ***Tomb of the Aedile Vestorius Priscus**, with scenes from his life painted on the inner walls.

To the right is a terminal cippus of the ancient *pomerium* (zone of defence) set up by T. Suedius Clemens, a military tribune. Further on are the ruins of the village, with factories, reoccupied in the 2C and 3C AD but afterwards abandoned. Turning back, notice the fine stretch of pre-Samnite wall, which is visible to the east; to the west are three fine towers.

Return by the Vicolo dei Vettii, No. 1 of which is the ***House of the Vettii** (VI, 15; Map 55), belonging to Aulus Vettius Restitutus and Aulus Vettius Conviva, two wealthy merchants of the Roman colony. Its beautiful paintings (still in their original positions) and the skilful reconstruction of its apartments make it one of the more interesting houses to visit.

To the right of the entrance, under lock and key, is a characteristically salacious image of Priapus. The atrium has delightful paintings of amorini and putti. To the right and left are strongrooms. On the right is the porter's lodge. In the corresponding little room to the left are paintings of Ariadne deserted, Hero and Leander, and a fish pond. The larger room to the left of the entrance has pictures of

Cyparissus, Amor and Pan wrestling for the entertainment of Bacchus and Ariadne, Leda and the Swan, and Jupiter enthroned. Opening off the atrium are two cubicula and the alae, in one of which (left) is a cleverly painted picture of a cock fight. To the right of the main atrium is a small rustic atrium (with a lararium), followed by the kitchen, with its fire-grate and boilers. Adjoining is a closed room with equivocal pictures and a statuette of Priapus.

The **peristyle** offers an enchanting spectacle. Against the columns surrounding it are statuettes, from which jets of water spouted into marble basins. Two other jets rise in the middle of the gaily coloured garden. In the east colonnade are two handsome rooms (*oeci*). In one of them are paintings of the infant Hercules and the serpents, Pentheus torn limb from limb by the bacchantes, Dirce and the wild bull; in the other, Daedalus showing Pasiphaë the wooden cow, Ixion on the wheel, Bacchus and the sleeping Ariadne, and beautiful arabesques.

In the north colonnade is a separate group of triclinium, cubiculum, and small garden. The triclinium is the exquisite ***Sala Dipinta** probably used for banquets on special occasions. On a black band round the room are charming little amorini at work and play (right to left): hurling at a target, weaving and selling wreaths, distilling perfume, driving a biga, forging metal, fulling cloth, celebrating the Vestalia, harvesting the grape, worshipping Bacchus, and selling wine. On the black panels below are winged nymphs gathering flowers; Agamemnon forcing his way into the Temple of Artemis to slay the sacred hind; Apollo as conqueror of the Python; Orestes and Pylades with Thoas and Iphigeneia. On the dado, Amazons and women with sacrificial vessels and a bacchante and satyr. On the large red panels, separated by candelabra-pilasters corresponding to the small black panels, are flying groups of Perseus and Andromeda, Dionysus and Ariadne, Apollo and Daphne, and Poseidon and Amymone. On the door-jambs, Hermaphroditus and Silenus.

Follow Vicolo di Mercurio to the right; at the corner on the left are the pillar of an aqueduct and some leaden pipes. No. 10 (right) is the **House of the Labyrinth** (VII, 11; Map 56), dating from the Samnite era and taking its name from a mosaic of Theseus and the Minotaur.

Turn south by Via del Fauno to reach Via della Fortuna. Here, to the right, is the entrance to the famous ***House of the Faun** (VI, 12, 2-5; Map 57). This house, belonging to the Casii, is 80m long and 35m wide, occupying a whole insula. Its popular name comes from the celebrated bronze statuette of the **Dancing Faun** found near the impluvium (it is now at Naples, and replaced here by a copy). On the pavement in front of the house is the salutation *have* (welcome). There are two atria and two peristyles. The beautiful stucco decoration successfully imitates marble. The fine pavement of the first peristyle has, unfortunately, been much injured. The mosaic pavements of the four triclinia (one for each season of the year) are now at Naples. The 28 Ionic columns of the peristyle are coated with stucco. The well-known mosaic of the Battle of Alexander (also at Naples) was found in the red-columned exedra. The second peristyle is in the form of a large garden, with a Doric porticus.

Continue to follow Via della Fortuna. To the left, at its intersection with the Strada del Foro and Via di Mercurio, stands the **Temple of Fortune** (VII, 4; Map 58), constructed in 3 BC by M. Tullius and restored after the earthquake. The Corinthian pronaos has two columns on each side. The architrave of an aedicula in the cella bears the name of the founder. At the north (right) corner is a **triumphal**

arch, also used as a reservoir. It bore an equestrian statue of Caligula. Refreshments are sold in the adjoining building.

Beyond the crossroad, to the left (No. 2), are the **Thermae of the Forum** (VII, 5; Map 59), built in the time of Sulla by the Duovir L. Cesius and the Aediles C. Occius and L. Niremius. The general arrangement resembles that of the Thermae Stabianae. The shelves for clothes in the apodyterium are decorated with a frieze of telamones. The large bronze brazier in the tepidarium and also the benches were presented by M. Nigidius Vaccula. The marble basin in the calidarium was placed here in 3 or 4 AD and cost (according to the inscription) 5250 sesterces. Within are plaster casts of victims of the eruption, in glass cases.

Opposite the thermae is the *****House of the Tragic Poet** (VI, 8, 5; Map 60), adopted by Bulwer Lytton, in his *Last Days of Pompeii*, as the dwelling of Glaucus. Among the valuable mosaics found here was one of a theatrical rehearsal, now at Naples. On the threshold is a mosaic dog, with the inscription *cave canem* (beware of the dog). Beyond the peristyle is the household sanctuary, in the form of an aedicula. In the triclinium are paintings of a youth and maiden looking at a nest of cupids, Marsyas teaching Olympus the flute, Theseus and Ariadne, Dido and Aeneas, and personifications of the seasons. Another important picture found here was the Sacrifice of Iphigeneia.

A little further on, to the right, is the large **House of Pansa** (VI, 6), *or Domus Allei Nigidi Mai*, notable for the regularity of its construction. Along the entrance wall and the wall to the left were rows of shops. The rooms on the right were to let.

Reached by following Vicolo di Modesto to the right, then taking the first turning

1 Entrance
2 Atrium
3 Alae
4 Tablinum
5 Peristylium
6 Oesus
7 Kitchen
8 Shed
9 Portico
10 Garden
11 Cubicula
12 Triclinium
13 Rented Rooms
14 Tabernae
15 Impluvium
16 Rooms with first floor
17 Piscina

CASA DI PANSA

on the left), is the misnamed **House of Sallust** (VI, 2, 4; Map 61), more properly known as the House of A. Cassius Libanus, a fine mansion of the Samnite period damaged by a bomb in September 1943, when its well-known picture of Diana and Actaeon was destroyed. A partial restoration was paid for by American funds.

Following the Via Consolare, which bears to the left, you pass a storehouse for salt (No. 13; right) and the **House of the Surgeon** (Map 62), a massive structure of Sarno stone. Several surgical instruments, now at the Museo Archeologico Nazionale in Naples, were found here.

The **Porta Ercolano** (Herculaneum Gate), at the end of the Via Consolare, dates from the close of the 2C BC and is the most recent and most important gate of the town. In antiquity it seems to have been called *Porta Salina* or *Saliniensis*. Of its three archways, that in the centre, for vehicles, was vaulted at the ends only; the lateral openings for pedestrians were vaulted throughout. Outside the gate runs the Via delle Tombe, or Street of Tombs. To the left is the tomb of the Augustalis (priest of Augustus) M. Cerrinius Restitutus, followed by those of the Duoviri A. Veius (in the form of a semicircular seat), M. Porcius (altar), and the priestess Mamia (seat with an inscription). Behind the last is the family sepulchre of the Istacidii.

To the left, at the end of a lane, is a terminal cippus marking the outer limit of the Pomerium. The chief tombs on the right side of this part of the street are those of the Aedile M. Terentius Felix Major, the Tomb of the Garlands and the Tomb of the Blue Glass Vase (No. 8). The semicircular red bench (No. 9), belongs to the House of the Mosaic Columns, which takes its name from four mosaic columns now at Naples.

> Keeping to the left, beyond the so-called Villa of Cicero, a building that was excavated in the 18C and covered up again, you pass a tomb in the form of an altar, a circular tomb with a columbarium, the tomb of the Augustalis C. Calventius Quietus, the enclosure of Numerius Istacidius Elenus and his family, the tomb of Noevoleia Tyche and the sepulchral triclinium of Cn. Vibrius Saturninus. On the other (right) side of the street is the fine sepulchre of M. Alleius Luccius Libella and his son. A little further on is a tomb with a marble door. On a low hill are the Monument of L. Ceius Labeo, the tomb of M. Arrius Diomedes and other unfinished sepulchres. Beyond this point lie the suburban villas (see below).

Returning to the gate, take the Pomerium road to the left, where a good idea may be gained of the fortifications. The **town rampart** is c 6m thick. It consists of an outer wall of the 2C BC and the pre-Samnite inner wall, with earth in the intervening space. The walls were originally of tufa or limestone, but they were repaired with blocks of lava shortly before the Social War. There were 12 towers between the Porta Ercolano and the Porta Marina, and several others on the north side, where the natural defences were weakest. It was this part of the wall that was chosen for attack by L. Sulla in 89 BC, and the damage caused by his missiles can still be seen.

Re-enter the city by the **Porta di Vesuvio** and return inside the wall to Tower XI, the top of which commands an extensive panorama. Follow Via di Mercurio downhill, passing, on the right, the **House of Apollo** (VI, 7, 23; Map 63), with a picturesque fountain, a handsome cubiculum, a mosaic of Achilles at Scyros, and a painting of Apollo and Marsyas. On the other side of the street is the **House of Meleager** (Map 64), with its tasteful fountain and Corinthian oecus. Beneath a marble table in the atrium is an apparatus for cooling wine and food in water. The **House of the Centaur** (Map 65) is decorated in the first style. In the **House of**

Adonis (Map 66), is a large painting of the wounded Adonis, tended by Venus and cupids. **The House of Castor and Pollux** (Map 67) possesses a Corinthian atrium with 12 columns and paintings of Apollo and Daphne, the Birth of Adonis, Minos and Scylla. Like many other dwellings, it is an amalgamation of several earlier buildings. At the east corner of the crossroads is a **caupona** (VI, 10, 1), in the back shop of which are scenes of tavern life. In the **House of the Little Fountain** (VI, 8, 23; Map 68), a mosaic fountain is adorned with a bronze group of a boy and goose (copies). The **House of the Large Fountain** (Map 69) has another mosaic fountain. Across the street is the **House of the Anchor** (VI, 10, 7; Map 70), so called from a mosaic on the threshold. The garden, on a lower level, is surrounded by a cryptoporticus. Here you are again within a short distance of the Posto di Ristoro and the forum.

THE SUBURBAN VILLAS
The two surburban villas are approached by the Via delle Tombe, or by the short avenue that leads north from Villa dei Misteri station. The famous **Villa of Diomedes** is so called on the slender ground that the burial place of M. Arrius Diomedes is on the opposite side of the road (see above). The villa had the largest

VILLA DEI MISTERI

1 Veranda	5 Atrium	9 Oecus
2 Tablinium	6 Peristyle	10 Vestibulam
3 Cubiculum	7 Kitchen	11 Former Entrance
4 Painted Hall	8 Small Atrium	12 Torculariam

garden in Pompeii, with a colonnade containing various chambers. Steps ascend to the peristyle, adjoining which are (right) a luxurious private bath with cold-water pool and (left) a large apsidal chamber, possibly a sitting room. The tablinum, opposite the entrance, opens onto a large terrace, from which steps and a ramp descend to the garden. In the middle are a piscina and a summer triclinium, with fountain, and an arbour borne by six colums.

In a vaulted cellar extending below three sides of the garden-colonnade were found amphorae of wine and 18 skeletons of adults and children who had vainly taken refuge in the cellar. The owner of the villa, probably a wine-merchant, was found near the garden door, with the key in his hand; beside him was a slave with money and valuables. A small staircase with two columns formed the main entrance from the Via delle Tombe and led directly to the peristyle.

About 200m to the west of the Villa of Diomedes stands the **Villa of the Mysteries** (Villa dei Misteri), a complex dwelling that started in the 2C BC as a town house, developed into a manor and declined into a farmhouse. It takes its name from a hall with 24 life-size ***painted figures** thought to have been executed by a Campanian painter of the 1C BC on a second style background. Entrance is gained from the rear of the villa, through what was once a broad gallery with a central exedra (1) and two lateral wings. Straight ahead is the tablinum (2), with black-ground paintings in a vauely Egyptian style. Here you turn right and walk through a cubiculum (3) adorned with Dionysiac figures (for example, a dancing satyr, a hallmark of the cult of the young god of excess) to reach the marble-paved Sala del Grande Dipinto (4). The paintings from a cycle, the meaning of which, although still under discussion, is probably connected with the rite of initiation into the Dionysiac mysteries, a practice that was common in Southern Italy despite prohibitory measures adopted by the Roman Senate.

According to the leading interpretation, the scenes, starting on the wall to the left of the door, represent (a) a child reading the rite before a young bride and a seated matron; (b) a priestess and three female assistants making a sacrifice; (c) sileni playing musical instruments in a pastoral setting; (d) the flight of the frightened initiate and a group of two satyrs and a silenus with a mask; (e) the marriage of Dionysus and Ariadne (damaged); (f) a kneeling woman unveiling (or, by a differing interpretation, protecting) the sacred phallus while a winged demon raises a flagellum to strike the young initiate, who seeks refuge in the lap of a companion; (g) the orgiastic dance of Dionysus; (h) the dressing of a bride for initiation and a seated woman who has undergone the initiation rite.

Returning to the tablitium, turn right through the atrium to the penistyle, then right again to the kitchen, with its two fireplaces. The adjacent small atrium gives access to an oecus gracefully decorated with architectural motifs. Around the peristyle are the vestibulam, leading to the former main entrance (opposite the atrium), and a torcularium, where grapes were pressed (across from the kitchen).

C. Mount Vesuvius

This is a literary itinerary, for armchair travellers. Those who wish to make the ascent of the volcano may do so, of course; the area was declared a National Park (a term used in Italy to indicate any protected natural district) in 1991. From Naples the expedition is most easily made, by car or by public transport, via the modern town of Ercolano, so it may conveniently be combined with a visit to Herculaneum.

*The road to the summit (marked) climbs to Eremo, site of the **Observatory** (597m) built in 1845 on a spur of the crater of Monte Somma and so far spared by lava flows. Luigi Palmieri, curator in 1872, remained at his post throughout the eruption of that year. The building houses a library, specimens of minerals thrown up by Vesuvius, relief plans and so on as well as seismic apparatus and meteorological instruments. The road ends at Colle Margherita (944m), a 10 min walk from the summit. Here vehicles are met by an official guide (fee) of the comune of Ercolano, who conducts parties by a path to the edge of the crater. The landscape is unsettling, to say the least; the views, spectacular.*

*Mount Vesuvius, the most familar feature in the Neapolitan landscape, is one of the smallest active volcanoes in the world (1277m; 1202m before 1944), but certainly the most famous. It is the only active volcano on the continent of Europe. It consists of a truncated cone, **Monte Somma**, which rises to the height of 1152m in **Punta del Nasone** on the north side. Within is an enormous crater, broken on the west, called the **Atrio del Cavallo** and **Valle dell'Inferno**. From the centre of this crater rises a smaller cone, variable in size and shape, which is Vesuvius proper.

Vesuvius and Monte Somma are the most thoroughly known volcanoes in the world, their development having been studied since Roman times. The volcanic activity started about 10,000 years ago. Ever since, periods of frequent eruption have alternated with periods of absolute tranquillity, sometimes lasting more than 2000 years. Before the disastrous eruption of AD 79, the volcano had been quiet for more than 1200 years. The name Vesuvius, or *Vesbius*, means 'the unextinguished'.

In ancient times the lower slopes of Vesuvius were planted with vineyards, above which was a thick belt of woods noted for their wild boar. Pliny the Elder wrote that no region on earth was more joyously touched by nature. Its volcanic nature was unsuspected except by men of science such as Diodorus Siculus, Vitruvius and, especially, Strabo, who inferred its igneous nature from its conical shape and the ashy nature of its barren summit.

'In early times', he wrote, 'this district was on fire and had craters of fire, and then because the fuel gave out, was quenched' (*Geography* V, 4). To this he attributed the fruitfulness of the lands around the mountain, saying that it had already been shown at Mount Etna that volcanic ash was particularly suited for the vine. Today the fertile soil of Vesuvius produces grapes for the excellent wine called Lacrima Christi.

The peak observed by Strabo was much higher than the present summit and was the completion of the now broken cone of Monte Somma. Within its seemingly dead crater, Spartacus and the rebel slaves took refuge in 73 BC, escaping by an unguarded rift from the besieging force of Clodius Pulcher.

In AD 63 a violent earthquake, mentioned by Seneca, caused serious damage in Pompeii, Herculaneum, Naples and Pozzuoli:

We have heard that Pompeii, the very lively city in Campania where the shores of Surrentum and Stabiae and that of Herculaneum meet and hem in a lovely, gently retreating inlet from the open sea, has been destroyed by an earthquake which also struck the entire vicinity. This occurred in winter, a time which our forefathers always held to be free from such perils...The region had never before been visited by a calamity of such extent, having always escaped unharmed from such occurrences and having therefore lost all fear of them. Part of the city of Herculaneum caved in, the houses still standing are in ruinous condition (*Naturales Quaestiones* VI, *De Terrae Motu*).

This was followed by other shocks, and in AD 79 the central cone blew out and Pompeii, Herculaneum, and Stabiae were destroyed, the first and last buried in cinders and lapilli, or small stones, while Herculaneum was drowned in a torrent of mud; the flow of lava does not seem to have extended very far. The catastrophe struck on the morning of August 24, ironically only a day after the annual celebration of the *Volcanalia*, the festival of the god of fire and forge, Vulcan. History owes an inestimable debt to Pliny the Younger, who witnessed the event, and left a description of his observations in two letters addressed to the historian Tacitus. This is altogether the oldest realistic description, in Western literature, of a major natural disaster:

To Tacitus:
Your request that I would send you an account of my uncle's end, so that you may transmit a more exact relation of it to posterity, deserves my acknowledgments; for if his death shall be celebrated by your pen, the glory of it, I am aware, will be rendered for ever deathless...

He was at that time with the fleet under his command at Misenum. On the 24th of August, about one in the afternoon, my mother desired him to observe a cloud of very unusual size and appearance. He had sunned himself, then taken a cold bath, and after a leisurely luncheon was engaged in the study. He immediately called for his shoes and went up an eminence from whence he might best view this very uncommon appearance. It was not at that distance discernible from what mountain this cloud issued, but it was found afterwards to be Vesuvius. I cannot give you a more exact description of its figure, than by resembling it to that of a pine tree, for it shot up a great height in the form of a trunk, which extended itself at the top into several branches; because I imagine, a momentary gust of air blew it aloft, and then falling, forsook it; thus causing the cloud to expand laterally as it dissolved, or possibly the downward pressure of its own weight produced this effect. It was at one moment white, at another dark and spotted, as if it had carried up earth or cinders.

My uncle, true savant that he was, deemed the phenomenon important and worth a nearer view. He ordered a light vessel to be got ready, and gave me the liberty, if I thought proper, to attend him. I replied I would rather study, and, as it happened, he had himself given me a theme for composition. As he was coming out of the house he received a note from Rectina, the wife of Basus, who was in the utmost alarm at the imminent danger (his villa stood just below us, and there was no way to escape but by sea); she earnestly entreated him to save her from such deadly peril. He changed his first design and what he began with a philosophical, he pursued with an heroical turn of mind. He ordered large galleys to be launched, and went himself on board one, with the intention of assisting not only Rectina, but many others; for the villas stand extremely thick upon that beautiful coast. Hastening to the place from whence others were flying, he steered his direct course to the point of danger, and with such freedom from fear, as to be able to make and dictate his observations upon the successive motions and figures of that terrific object.

And now cinders, which grew thicker and hotter the nearer he approached, fell into the ships, then pumice-stones too, with stones blackened, scorched, and cracked by fire, then the sea ebbed suddenly from under them, while the shore was blocked up by landslips from the mountains. After considering a moment whether he should retreat, he said to the captain who was urging that course, 'Fortune befriends the brave; carry me to Pomponianus'. Pomponianus was then at Stabiae, distant by half the width of the bay (for, as you know, the shore, insensibly curving in its sweep, forms here a receptacle for the sea). He had already embarked his baggage; for though at Stabiae the danger was not yet near, it was full in view, and certain to be extremely near, as soon as it spread; and he resolved to fly as soon as the contrary wind should cease. It was full favourable, however, for carrying my uncle to Pomponianus. He embraces, comforts, and encourages his alarmed friend, and in order to soothe the other's fears by his own unconcern, desires to be conducted to a bathroom, and after having bathed, he sat down to supper with great cheerfulness, or at least (what is equally heroic) with all the appearance of it.

In the meanwhile Mount Vesuvius was blazing in several places with spreading and towering flames, whose refulgent brightness the darkness of the night set in high relief. But my uncle, in order to soothe apprehensions, kept saying that some fires had been left alight by the terrified country people, and what they saw were only deserted villas on fire in the abandoned district. After this he retired to rest, and it is most certain that his rest was a most genuine slumber; for his breathing, which, as he was pretty fat, was somewhat heavy and sonorous, was heard by those who attended at his chamber-door. But the court which led to his apartment now lay so deep under a mixture of pumice-stones and ashes, that if he had continued longer in his bedroom, egress would have been impossible. On being aroused, he came out, and returned to Pomponianus and the others, who had sat up all night. They consulted together as to whether they should hold out in the house, or wander about in the open. For the house now tottered under repeated and violent concussions, and seemed to rock to and fro as if torn from its foundations. In the open air, on the other hand, they dreaded the falling pumice-stones, light and porous though they were; yet this, by comparison, seemed the lesser danger of the two; a conclusion which my uncle arrived at by balancing reasons, and the others by balancing fears. They tied pillows upon their heads with napkins, and this was their whole defence against the showers that fell round them.

It was now day everywhere else, but there a deeper darkness prevailed than in the most obsure night; relieved, however, by many torches and diverse illuminations. They thought it proper to go down upon the shore to observe from close at hand if they could possibly put out to sea, but they found the waves still ran extremely high and contrary. There my uncle having thrown himself down upon a disused sail, repeatedly called for, and drank, a draught of cold water; soon after, flames, and a strong smell of sulphur, which was the forerunner of them, dispersed the rest of the company in flight; him they only aroused. He raised himself up with the assistance of two of his slaves, but instantly fell; some unusually gross vapour, as I conjecture, having obstructed his breathing and blocked his windpipe, which was not only naturally weak and constricted, but chronically inflamed. When day dawned again (the third from that he last beheld) his body was found entire and uninjured, and still fully clothed as in life; its posture was that of a sleeping, rather than a dead man.

Meanwhile my mother and I were at Misenum. But this has no connection with history, and your inquiry went no further than concerning my uncle's death. I will therefore put an end to my letter. Suffer me only to add, that I have faithfully related to you what I was either an eye-witness of myself, or heard at the time, when report speaks most truly. You will select what is most suitable to your purpose; for there is a great difference between a letter and an history; between writing to a friend, and writing for the public. Farewell.

To Tacitus:

The letter which, in compliance with your request, I wrote to you concerning the death of my uncle, has raised, you say, your curiosity to know not only what terrors, but what calamities I endured when left behind at Misenum (for there I broke off my narrative). Though my shock'd soul recoils, my tongue shall tell.

My uncle having set out, I gave the rest of the day to study—the object which had kept me at home. After which I bathed, dined, and retired to short and broken slumbers. There had been for several days before some shocks of earthquake, which the less alarmed us as they are frequent in Campania; but that night they became so violent that one might think that the world was not merely shaken, but turned topsy-turvy. My mother flew to my chamber; I was just rising; meaning on my part to awaken her, if she was asleep. We sat down in the forecourt of the house, which separated it by a short space from the sea. I know not whether I should call it courage or inexperience—I was not quite eighteen—but I called for a volume of Livy, and began to read, and even went on with the extracts I was making from it, as if nothing were the matter. Lo and behold, a friend of my uncle's, who was just come to him from Spain, appears on the scene; observing my mother and me seated, and that I have actually a book in my hand, he sharply censures her patience and my indifference; nevertheless I still went on intently with my author.

It was now six o'clock in the morning, the light still ambiguous and faint. The buildings around us already tottered, and though we stood upon open ground, yet as the place was narrow and confined, there was certain and formidable danger from their collapsing. It was not till then we resolved to quit the town. The common people follow us in the utmost consternation, preferring the judgement of others to their own (wherein the extreme of fear resembles prudence), and impel us onwards by pressing in a crowd upon our rear. Being got outside the houses, we halt in the midst of a most strange and dreadful scene. The coaches which we had ordered out, though upon the most level ground, were sliding to and fro, and could not be kept steady even when stones were put against the wheels. Then we beheld the sea sucked back, and as it were repulsed by the convulsive motion of the earth; it is certain at least the shore was considerably enlarged, and now held many sea animals captive on the dry sand. On the other side, a black and dreadful cloud bursting out in gusts of igneous serpentine vapour now and again yawned open to reveal long fantastic flames, resembling flashes of lightning but much larger.

Our Spanish friend already mentioned now spoke with more warmth and insistancy: 'If your brother—if your uncle,' said he, 'is yet alive, he wishes you both may be saved; if he has perished, it was his desire that you might survive him. Why therefore do you delay your escape?' We could never think of our own safety, we said, while we were uncertain of his. Without more ado our friend hurried off, and took himself out of danger at the top of his speed.

Soon afterwards, the cloud I have described began to descend upon the earth, and cover the sea. It had already begirt the hidden Capreae [Capri], and blotted from sight the promontory of Misenum. My mother now began to beseech, exhort, and command me to escape as best I might; a young man could do it; she, burdened with age and corpulency, would die easy if only she had not caused my death. I replied, I would not be saved without her, and taking her by the hand, I hurried her on. She complies reluctantly and not without reproaching herself for retarding me. Ashes now fall upon us, though as yet in no greater quantity. I looked behind me; gross darkness pressed upon our rear, and came rolling over the land after us like a torrent. I proposed while we yet could see, to turn aside, lest we should be knocked down in the road by the crowd that followed us and trampled to death in the dark. We had scarce sat down, when darkness overspread us, not like that of a moonless or cloudy night, but of a room when it is shut up, and the lamp put out. You could hear the shrieks of women, the crying of children, and the shouts of men; some were seeking their children, others their parents, others their wives or husbands, and only distinguishing them by their voices; one lamenting his own fate, another that of his family; some praying to die, from the fear of dying; many lifting their hands to the gods, but the greater part imagining that there were no gods left anywhere, and that the last and eternal night was come upon the world.

There were even some who augmented the real perils by imaginary terrors. Newcomers reported that such or such a building at Misenum had collapsed or taken fire—falsely, but they were credited. By degrees it grew lighter; which we imagined to be rather the warning of approaching fire (as in truth it was) than the return of day: however, the fire stayed at a distance from us: then again came darkness, and a heavy shower of ashes; we were obliged every now and then to rise and shake them off, otherwise we would have been buried and even crushed under their weight. I might have boasted that amidst dangers so appalling, not a sigh or expression of fear escaped from me, had not my support been founded in miserable, though strong consolation, that all mankind were involved in the same calamity, and that I was perishing with the world itself.

At last this dreadful darkness was attenuated by degrees to a kind of cloud or smoke, and passed away; presently the real day returned, and even the sun appeared, though lurid as when an eclipse is in progress. Every object that presented itself to our yet affrighted gaze was changed, cover'd over with a drift of ashes, as with snow. We returned to Misenum, where we refreshed ourselves as well as we could, and passed an anxious night between hope and fear; though indeed with a much larger share of the latter, for the earthquake still continued, and several enthusiastic people were giving a grotesque turn to their own and their neighbours' calamities by terrible predictions. Even then, however, my mother and I, notwithstanding the danger we had passed, and that which still threatened us, had no thoughts of leaving the place, till we should receive some tidings of my uncle.

And now, you will read this narrative, so far beneath the dignity of a history, without any view of transferring it to your own; and indeed you must impute it to your own request, if it shall appear scarce worthy of a letter. Farewell (Melmoth–Hutchinson transalation, quoted in Wolfgang Leppmann's *Pompeii in Fact and Fiction*, London 1968).

In the centuries that followed the eruption of AD 79 only nine comparatively unimportant eruptions are recorded, and after 1500 a period of absolute quiescence set in, during which the mountain was again cultivated up to the cone and the crater covered with trees. On 16 December 1631, however, a violent eruption destroyed nearly all the towns at the foot of the mountain; the lava reached the sea near Portici and killed over 3000 people.

During the next 300 years there were 23 eruptions at intervals of one to 30 years. Sir William Hamilton forecast that of 1767 and went up the mountain while it was in progress. The most serious were those of 1794, which destroyed Torre del Greco; of 1871–72, which damaged San Sebastiano and Massa di Somma; and of 1906, in which Ottaviano and San Giuseppe suffered severely. In August 1928 and in June 1929 the lava descended into the Valle dell'Inferno, menacing Terzigno. An eruption in March 1944 altered the shape of the crater; the little inner cone disappeared, and in the following month the main fissure closed.

At Boscoreale, overlooking Pompeii, several Roman villas were unearthed in 1887–1907; they yielded a large find of silverware (now in the Louvre) and frescoes, some of which may be seen in Naples, others in the Metropolitan Museum of New York. A modest collection of finds from these and other sites may be seen in the *Antiquarium di Boscoreale, Uomo ed Ambiente nel Territorio Vesuviano* (Villa Regina, Boscoreale; open daily 09.00–18.00).

With reference to the tragic end of Pompeii, Herculaneum, and the other Campanian towns destroyed in AD 79, the poet Statius asked, 'Will future centuries, when new seed will have covered the waste, believe that entire cities and their inhabitants lie under their feet, and that the fields of their ancestors were drowned in a sea of flames?' As memory of the event waned and other misfortunes befell the empire, future generations did not believe because they did not know of the catastrophe. Pompeii was discovered inadvertently in 1592 and Herculaneum in 1709, but a systematic programme of excavation was not undertaken until the middle of the 19C.

D.   Herculaneum

Herculaneum *(Ercolano) destroyed with Pompeii in AD 79 and rediscovered in 1709, was a residential town without Pompeii's commercial importance, surrounded by villas of wealthy Romans. Though the excavations are small in extent compared with those of Pompeii and less immediately striking, the domestic buildings are better preserved, especially their upper storeys and wooden parts. Gardens have been replanted, contributing to a feeling of life and humanity not always achieved at Pompeii. Herculaneum also has the interest of a richer artistic life and of contrasting styles of house construction. The excavations are on an attractive terraced site.*

Visitors who have time to see only one of the two towns are advised to go to Herculaneum, where the most outstanding features can be seen in about two hours. These include the **House of Opus Craticium**, *the* **House of the Wooden Partition**, *the* **thermae**, *the* **Samnite House**, *the* **House of the Deer**, *and the* **House of the Relief of Telephus**. *The excavations are open daily, from 09.00 until 1 hour before sunset.*

ROAD. The modern town of Herculaneum is reached by Highway 18 (10km) or Autostrada A3 (13km); in Ercolano Highway 18 passes the entrance to the excavations.

RAILWAY. Circumvesuviana railway to Pugliano in 20–35 min, then by foot along the wide road descending seaward from the station (10 min walk).

HERCULANEUM THROUGH THE AGES

The foundation of Herculaneum, called *Herakleia* by its Greek settlers, was attributed by them to its patron deity, Hercules. The town passed through periods of Oscan and Samnite domination, before falling to Titus Didius, a lieutenant of Sulla, in 89 BC, after which a colony of veterans seems to have been established here. The damage done by an earthquake in AD 63 was being repaired, under the patronage of Vespasian, when the castastrophe of AD 79 overwhelmed the town. Unlike Pompeii, Herculaneum was submerged by a torrent of mud containing sand, ashes, and bits of lava, which raised the level of the soil by 12–25m and hardened into tufa, preserving many timber features and household objects which were burnt at Pompeii. Subsequent layers of volcanic matter buried the ruins to a depth of 39m and the town remained untouched for 1630 years.

The first discoveries were made in 1709 when Emmanuel de Lorraine, Prince of Elbeuf and cavalry commander of the Kingdom of Naples, came upon the back of the stage of the theatre while sinking the shaft for a well, and distributed a large group of statues and much of the scena among various museums. Charles III continued the exploration (1738–65), without any very clear plan, but the theatre, forum, and five 'temples' were located; the Villa of the Papyri was also explored and its treasure of sculpture and library recovered and transferred to Naples. The *Accademia Reale Ercolanese* founded in 1755 for the purpose of investigating the discoveries, published a work in eight volumes on the mural paintings and bronzes (1757–92) and a volume on the papyri (1797; by C. Rosini).

Desultory explorations were carried out in 1828–35 and in 1869–75, but not until 1927 was systematic excavation begun on any scale. This still continues, and you will probably have the opportunity to watch a 'dig' in progress. The new excavations have disinterred three cardines (III, IV, and V), the *decumanus inferior* and a part of the *decumanus maximus* as well as the suburban area which descends outside the walls, towards the harbour: houses are designated by insula and street numbers only.

THE ANCIENT CITY

The extent of the city is still uncertain, but in both area and population it probably attained only one-third of the size of Pompeii. With decumani running parallel with the coast (then much nearer the town than it is today) and cardines at right angles to the shore, the town suggests a Greek rather than a Roman plan and has affinities with Neapolis. The streets are paved with local volcanic stone, but are noticeably free from both the wheel ruts and the stepping-stones so characteristic of Pompeiian streets. On the seaward side the town ended in a terraced promontory, lined with patrician villas, beneath which the cardines descended abruptly through narrow archways to the extramural quarter round the harbour.

Herculanean houses

Unlike Pompeii, which was entirely dominated by the commercial classes, Herculaneum was a city of wealthy citizens, small artisans, and fishermen. The Herculaneum house is more evolved, freer, and further advanced in the adoption of new ideas than the Pompeiian house. The Samnite type of construction described at Pompeii exists also at Herculaneum, but frequently with the atrium daringly modified for the addition of an extra floor.

In the richer type of dwelling the Hellenistic plan of building round a peristyle is frequently followed, but the peristyle itself is often modified to a closed corridor with windows overlooking the central garden. In many middle-class houses the traditional plan has been abandoned and a central courtyard, more akin to the modern 'well', has been substituted. Finally there are apartment houses of several floors (though not on the scale developed in Ostia), in which the poorer artisans lived the crowded life of their modern Neapolitan counterparts.

THE SITE

The avenue that leads from the entrance gate to the excavations commands a wonderful *view across Herculaneum to the sea. This allows you to appreciate the natural beauty of the site, the magnitude of the disaster which transformed it, and the difficulties that face the excavators. Looking down on the city from above you can also see the variety of its dwellings and the topography of its streets.

Descend to Cardo III at the west corner of the site. To the left are Insula II and, beyond the decumanus inferior, Insula VII, both brought to light in 1828–35 when much of their interest was spoiled by inexperienced excavators. The **House of Argus** (II, 2; Map 1), indeed, must have been one of the finer mansions in the town: some idea of its grandeur may still be gained from the wall fronting the street and the noble columns of its peristyle. To the left of Cardo III is the back entrance to the house usually but wrongly called the **Hotel** (II, 1;). Occupying well over half the insula, this was the largest and perhaps the richest dwelling in the south quarter of the city. When the earlier excavations exposed its west side, it was assumed because of its proportions to be a hotel; but its plan, though complex, is almost certainly that of a private villa, designed to exploit all the advantage of its site. The house had already fallen on bad times and at the date of the catastrophe was undergoing modifications: the whole south wing had been converted into a self-contained dwelling and a room on the north side into a shop. The private bath of the Augustan period had been abandoned (hypocaust exposed). The house was badly damaged in the eruption and further mutilated by Bourbon excavators, but even in decay its extent is impressive.

You emerge by the main entrance (19) into Cardo IV. Opposite is the ***House of the Mosaic Atrium** (IV, 1-2; Map 2), another panoramic house beautifully disposed for the enjoyment of the view. From the street (No. 2), pass through the fauces to the atrium, both of which retain their pavements of geometric mosaic, though the floors were corrugated under the weight of the invading tufa. Facing the atrium are the unusual basilican tablinum, and, at right angles, a closed gallery formed by partially filling in the intercolumnar spaces of a peristyle. The door and window frames are remarkably well preserved. Off the narrow east walk are four cubicula with red walls, and a raised central exedra, adorned with mythological scenes, with a wooden table. This room enjoys a charming view of the garden with its marble fountain. The main living-rooms beyond, including a lofty triclinium paved in marble, open on to a terrace formerly shaded by a colonnaded roof, with a solarium, at either end of which is a diaeta, or siesta room, with low windows for the enjoyment of the view.

Continuing up Cardo IV, notice on the left the **House of the Bronze Herm** (III, 16; Map 3), with typical though diminutive characteristics of the Samnite house. The bronze portrait (temporarily removed) presumably represents the owner. The base of the stairs leading to an upper floor can be seen in the blind corridor leading off the atrium. On the other side of the street is the **House of the Alcove** (IV, 3; Map 4), its facade in opus reticulatum pierced with iron gratings and overhung by the remains of a first-floor balcony. The smaller door (No. 4) gave on to the stairs. The ground floor comprises two separate dwellings thrown into one, that to the left modest, and that to the right more distinguished with a tessellated atrium and a richly painted room with wooden couches. At the end of a long corridor is a small court with the alcoved room that gives the house its name.

The *House of Opus Craticium** presents a unique example of the wood and plaster construction, called *opus craticium*, used for plebeian dwellings, the defects and impermanence of which were noted by Vitruvius. The building, which consists of a shop with a back-parlour or work room, and two self-contained flats, preserves complete its upper floor with a balcony room over the pavement. The inner rooms overlook a small yard. The staircase (restored) still has several of the original steps. The houses on the other side of the street have points of interest; two rooms at the rear of No. 6, lit by circular windows, retain their barrel-vaulting, pavements, and mural decoration (of the first period; see Pompeii).

Next on the left is the *House of the Wooden Partition** (III, 11–12; Map 6), whose facade, rising to the second storey, gives a striking picture of the external appearance of the Roman private house. The open gallery above the cornice belonged to a second floor, added to the structure when the house declined in status; this was reached from a separate entrance in the decumanus. In the imposing atrium the double lining, in *opus signinum* and marble, of the impluvium tank should be noted; also the dogs'-head spouts (some original) of the compluviate roof. The most striking feature, giving its name to the house, is the wooden partition that closes the tablinum, reconstructed in situ with its ancient hinges and lamp brackets. Glass cases preserve remains of toilet articles, beans, etc., found in the house. The cubiculum to the right of the fauces has a geometrical pavement and a marble table, the further room on the left a well-preserved frieze. Behind the house is a charming small garden. The side of the house abutting the decumanus inferior was occupied by shops which, with one exception, communicate directly with the house. The corner shop (No. 10) contains a unique wooden *clothes-press** in an astonishing state of preservation.

Behind is the **House of the Skeleton** (III, 3; Map 7), so called from the remains discovered in 1831 on the upper floor. The small rooms are tastefully disposed and decorated.

Cross the Decumanus Inferior, passing a shop selling postcards. The greater part of Insula VI (left) is occupied by the *thermae**, erected early in the reign of Augustus on a plan similar to that used at Pompeii and decorated somewhat later; they survive, finely preserved and without modification, almost as they were planned. In the centre is the **palaestra**, the main entrance of which was in Cardo IV (No. 7). To the south, with separate entrances from the decumanus, was a covered hall with a penthouse roof, probably a sphaeristerium, where the ball game of *pila* was played. A second entrance to the palaestra from Cardo III (No. 1), flanked by a porter's lodge and a latrine, led also to the **men's baths**. From the corridor you enter the *apodyterium* (dressing room), with a convex pavement in *opus segmentatum*, shelves for clothes, and vaulted stucco. In an apse stands a cipollino marble basin. A vestibule, to the left, leads down marble steps to the circular *frigidarium* or cold bath, the domed ceiling of which is painted with fish on a blue ground and pierced by a skylight. From the other side of the apodyterium, pass through the *tepidarium* to the *calidarium* or warm room, with the usual plunge-bath and a scalloped apse for a hand basin; the fall of the vault has exposed the heating pipes and smoke vents.

The **women's baths**, entered from Cardo IV (No. 8), though smaller and simpler, are even better preserved. You enter a waiting-room and pass through a small linen-room to the *apodyterium*, whose mosaic, like that in the men's tepidarium, shows a triton surrounded by dolphins and cuttle-fish. Beyond, the small *tepidarium* and *calidarium* are virtually complete. Behind (No. 10) are the service quarters, where the well can be seen, and the staircase leading up to the attendant's living quarters and down to the *praefurnium* or heating apparatus, of which the heavy iron door and the poker survive, though the boilers were removed by Bourbon excavators.

> Further along (No. 11) is the **House of the Black Hall**, still largely buried, with an elegant tetrastyle portico. The paintings of the little vaulted rooms and of the black hall are particularly lively. The model temple, with wooden columns, surmounted by marble capitals, was a shrine for the Lares.

Visit next the houses on the other side of Cardo IV, starting at the crossroads. The ***Samnite House**, fronted by a stretch of fine paving, has an imposing portal and an open gallery (approached by a stair from No. 2) that led to a separate apartment added at a later date. The interior decoration is beautifully executed; that of the fauces in the first style of architectural imitation. The atrium has a blind gallery of graceful proportions. Beyond a simple **Weaver's House** (V, 3–4; Map 9) and work-shop, is the small but dignified **House of the Carbonised Furniture** (V, 5; Map 10), in the Samnite style, with an elegantly decorated triclinium and a delightful little court. The lararium is placed to be seen from the window of an inner room, the divan and table of which survive. Some furniture remains also in the upper rooms of the **House of the Neptune Mosaic** (V, 6–7, Map 11), which stand open to the street. Below is the best-preserved ***shop** in the town. A fine wooden partition separates the shop from the attractive living quarters behind, where a little court is enlivened by the fresh blues and greens of the mosaic of Neptune and Amphitrite that gives its name to the house, and of the nymphaeum. The **House of the Beautiful Courtyard** (V, 8; Map 12) has an unusual plan grouped around a wide hall that precedes the court. The **College of the Augustali** (Map 13), oppo-site, contains some very well-preserved wall paintings. The cardo continues between high pavements (once arcaded, as may be seen from the remaining columns) to the crossing with the usual public fountain and altar. A painted inscription on a pillar records rules of the street police.

Turn into the broad Decumanus Maximus, reserved for pedestrians, the left side of which still lies beneath the tufa. On the right is a **shop** (V, 10) with a little room over the pavement. Built into the counter and sunk into the floor are the dolia, or

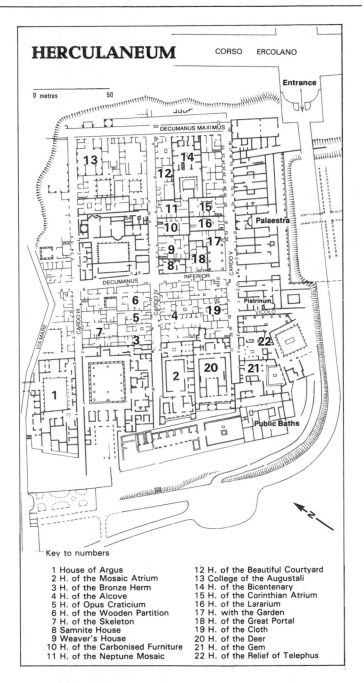

HERCULANEUM

CORSO ERCOLANO

Entrance

0 metres 50

DECUMANUS MAXIMUS

13

14

12

11

15

10

16

Palaestra

9

17

8

18

INFERIOR

DECUMANUS

6

CARDO IV

19

Pistrinum

5

VICOLO

4

CARDO III

7

3

22

VIA MARE

1

2

20

21

Public Baths

Key to numbers

1 House of Argus
2 H. of the Mosaic Atrium
3 H. of the Bronze Herm
4 H. of the Alcove
5 H. of Opus Craticium
6 H. of the Wooden Partition
7 H. of the Skeleton
8 Samnite House
9 Weaver's House
10 H. of the Carbonised Furniture
11 H. of the Neptune Mosaic

12 H. of the Beautiful Courtyard
13 College of the Augustali
14 H. of the Bicentenary
15 H. of the Corinthian Atrium
16 H. of the Lararium
17 H. with the Garden
18 H. of the Great Portal
19 H. of the Cloth
20 H. of the Deer
21 H. of the Gem
22 H. of the Relief of Telephus

large jars, in which foodstuffs could be preserved at an even temperature. This and the adjoining shops originally formed part of the **House of the Bicentenary** (V, 15–16; Map 14), a rich dwelling disinterred in 1938, two hundred years after Charles III began the excavations. Despite later modifications, the ground floor preserves its original plan. The fine atrium still has its lattice partition and the tablinum is decorated with mythical scenes and paved in mosaic. The outline of a cross on the wall of an upstairs room suggests that a private Christian oratory existed here, although the crucifix is not thought to have become established as a Christian symbol as early as AD 79.

Cardo V is admirably paved in limestone. To the left is a public fountain with a mask of Hercules; turn towards the the sea. The **corner shop** (V, 21) is interesting for the wooden window-fittings remaining in the dwelling above (entered from No. 22). Beyond on the right the houses continue to be in styles already familiar; three of them, preceded by a stretch of marble pavement once shaded by a portico, have features worthy of note.

In the **House of the Corinthian Atrium** (V, 30; Map 15), small but in good taste, the compluviate roof, supported by six tufa columns faced with stucco, feeds a graceful fountain. A mosaic, in a room to the right, shows in its pattern the sacred two-edged axe, or labrys. A glass case contains a wooden table and a small basket. Note also the elegant decoration of the cubiculum, lit by three skylights (two restored). Next door is the **House of the Lararium** (V, 31; Map 16), an earlier and smaller dwelling showing good examples of decoration in the first and third styles. Most wonderfully preserved is a wooden sacellum, which consists of a cupboard surmounted by a shrine in the form of a small temple in antis with Corinthian columns, where the Lares were kept. Beyond is the so-called **House with the Garden** (V, 33, Map 17), though the garden probably belonged to one of the more distinguished houses in the decumanus.

The other side of the street is quite different, foreshadowing the style developed at Ostia a hundred years later. The whole block (Insula Orientalis II), c 90m long, is of uniform construction in *opus reticulatum* and was apparently planned as a unit. The street frontage consists of shops with flats above, on a plan having no resemblance to the traditional Campanian house, but such as might be seen today.

The chief interest of the plain rectangular shops is in their use and contents. No. 16 contains a marble casket and an almost perfect wooden partition door; No. 13 has a counter with remains of its vegetable wares; No. 9 preserves its stove and sink and a little painting of Hercules pouring a libation between Dionysus and Mercury. No. 8 was a bakery, where two mills for grinding flour, 25 bronze baking pans, the seal of the proprietor and an oven carved with a phallic emblem were found. At No. 7 was the main staircase to the flats.

Behind this workaday façade a series of finely decorated and vaulted rooms overlook a huge open space surrounded by a portico, of which only the north and west sides have been unearthed. This area, the **palaestra**, where the public games were held, is approached by two great entrance halls (Nos 19 and 4), each with a prostyle porch. No. 4, by which you enter, had a black tessellated pavement and white walls and vault, a fitting entrance to the impressive colonnade within. Bourbon tunnels beneath the avenue give a vivid impression of the difficulties of excavation as well as of the size of the cruciform swimming-pool that occupied the centre of the palaestra. Its central *****fountain** of bronze cast in the form of a five-headed serpent entwined round a tree-trunk, has been re-erected.

Rejoin Cardo V by the Neptune fountain, the usual rectangular basin formed of limestone slabs joined at the corners by lead clamps. On the right side of the decumanus inferior is the imposing entrance of the ***House of the Great Portal** (V, 35; Map 18), its engaged brick columns surmounted by Corinthian capitals carved with winged Victories and an architrave decorated in terracotta; within are several good paintings, and, in the pavement of the diaeta, a picture executed in marble *opus sectile*. The other side of the street is occupied by shops. No. 14, a caupona well stocked with amphorae. The largest shop, on the corner (IV, 15–16), has an impressive counter, faced with polychrome marble and containing eight dolia for the storing of cereals.

Continuing the descent of Cardo V, note a small **shop** (right; IV, 17) with a priapic painting next to the counter, remains of nuts, lamps and utensils, etc., and a Judas window from the adjoining house. In the lane to the left, flanking the palaestra, is another *pistrinum*, or bakery, where the iron door of the oven remains closed despite the collapse of the vault, and with a stable for the asses that turned the mills. The **House of the Cloth** (IV, 19–20; Map 19) yielded pieces of ancient fabric in which the design is still discernible. The unusual arrangement of the stairs deserves notice. Beyond, you again approach the terraced quarter occupied by the houses of the rich. On the right is the ***House of the Deer** (Casa dei Cervi IV, 21; Map 20), the grandest dwelling yet discovered at Herculaneum, with a frontage of 43m. The entrance leads into a covered atrium, from which opens the spacious triclinium. The latter is painted with architectural motifs on black and red panels and paved in marble intarsia. Within are the two delicately executed groups of ***deer** at bay, after which the house is named. Behind, in an equally elegantly decorated oecus, stands a statuette of a satyr with a wineskin. The kitchen, latrine, and apotheca form a compact little block to the right. The garden is surrounded by an enclosed corridor, lit by windows and decorated with panels of cupids playing (most of these have been removed to the Museo Archeologico Nazionale in Naples); in this, the latest development of the peristyle, the columns have finally disappeared. In the centre is a summer triclinium flanked by two lovely smaller rooms, in one of which is a vigorously indelicate statue of the drunken Hercules. The far walk opens on to a terrace where an arbour, flanked by flower beds and siesta rooms, overlooks a sun balcony. Originally, this terrace opened directly on to the sea, commanding a view from Posillipo to Sorrento and Capri.

Cross the street to Insula Orientalis I. This consists of only two houses, both planned in an individual manner dictated by their situation; some of their rooms lie at a lower level and have yet to be explored. The **House of the Gem** (No. 1), named from an engraved stone found in it, has an unusual atrium with buttress-like pilasters and a side door that opens through a diplyon towards the irregular sunken garden. The latrine preserves an inscription (perhaps the work of a servant) recording a visit by a famous doctor. The floor of the triclinium is 'carpeted' in fine mosaic. The ***House of the Relief of Telephus** (No. 2–3), the most extensive of Herculanean mansions, is built around two sides of the House of the Gem and at two levels on the hillside. The walls were partially overthrown by the rush of mud that brought down the Quadriga reliefs (seen on either side of the entrance) from some higher public building. The atrium has colonnades on three sides; between the columns have been rehung the original oscilla, circular marble panels depicting satyrs. On the north side, small doors lead to the servants' quarters and stables. Descend a steep passage to the peristyle, which surrounds the garden, at the centre of which is an azure basin. Off the south walk are the ruins of a once grand room (8.5 x 6m), with a polychrome marble pavement; the reconstructed marble dado of one wall demonstrates the palatial standards of this rich dwelling.

In an adjacent room is a relief of the myth of Telephus, a late work executed academically in the classical manner.

Below the terrace are the public baths known as the **Terme Suburbane**, probably of late construction and surviving in a good state. Nearby is the plinth of a statue to M. Nonius Balbus, a celebrated citizen of the town. The base of another statue to his memory stands before the proscenium of the **theatre**, which lies partially buried to the west (entrance at No. 119 Corso Ercolano: apply at the office). The visit is interesting less for the theatre, the best of which was rifled by d'Elbeuf, than for the impression it gives of the daring of the 18C excavators. The great suburban **Villa of the Papyri**, from which came many works of art in Naples museum, was abandoned to the tufa in 1765.

E.   The Phlegraean Fields

*The **Phlegraean Fields** or Campi Flegrei (burning fields), is the name given to the volcanic region between Naples and Cumae. Eruptions have apparently ceased, but have left their trace in 13 low craters, some filled with water, which give the countryside its distinctive appearance, full of beauty and variety. It still abounds in hot springs and fumarole or steam jets (notably the Solfatara at **Pozzuoli**). The amenity of the seaboard attracted the first Greek colonists to the Italian mainland and the Romans were quick to appreciate the glorious climate and delightful surroundings. Innumerable villas sprang up at Baiae and Puteoli, which under the empire become a byword for unbridled luxury and the scene of the excesses of the imperial court. Of all this nothing remains except for a few ruined buildings and the names that evoke the memory of past glories.*

*By car a tour of the principal sights may comfortably be made in half a day (travel time 1hr); but if you can, spend a day or two on foot exploring this delightful country. The most important sites are the baths at **Baia**, the ruins at **Cumae** and the amphitheatre at Pozzuoli.*

CIRCUIT BY ROAD 60km, local roads. 9km Agnano Terme—6km Pozzuoli—7km Baia—3km Bacoli—6km Cumae—10km Pozzuoli—6km Bagnoli—13km Naples.

The old direct road to Pozzuoli (12km; followed by bus No. 152, and closely by the Cumana Railway) leaves Naples via Fuorigrotta and runs straight past a group of iron foundries to reach the Gulf of Pozzuoli at (8km) Bagnoli, from which point it follows the shore as described (in the opposite direction) below.

BY RAIL Cumana railway from Montesanto station every 20min to Pozzuoli (27 min), Baia (40 min), and Torregaveta (50min). Metropolitana (FS) from Piazza Garibaldi, every 30min, to Pozzuoli Solfatara (c 30min). Both railways go through long tunnels.

RESTAURANTS EN ROUTE: Bacoli, ****La Misenetta, tel. 081 523 4169, fax 081 868 8392.

Towards Pozzuoli

Leave Naples via Fuorigrotta and, beyond the zoo, continue along the Via Domiziana. 8km Agnano lies c 1km south of **Agnano Terme**, a spa with hot springs on the south side of the crater of Agnano. The crater, 6.5km in circumference, became flooded with water in the Middle Ages and was drained in 1866, the waters flowing out through a tunnel beneath Monte Spina, the south-west eminence. Its marshy surface abounds with mineral springs of varying composition and temperature.

The **spa** (open throughout the year) and the principal springs (mostly in the south-east part of the crater) are interesting even to the ordinary visitor. On the right of the central hall are the Stufe di San Germano, a series of rooms with gradually increasing temperature; at the left is a cave like the famous nearby **Grotta del Cane** or Dog Grotto, in which carbon dioxide covers the floor to the height of 0.5m, instantly extinguishing lights held in it and stupefying and killing animals. This phenomenon was formerly demonstrated to visitors at the expense of stray dogs. Of the sources, the most important are a hot spring near the spa (72.5° C), regulated in 1921, the intermittent Sprudel (70° C), further north, and the abundant Ponticello (87° C). Further on is the Fanghiera, or mud reservoir, kept moist by springs of which the most important is the Salvatore Tommasi (70° C). About 1km north near a hot chalybeate spring (39° C) is the **racecourse**, extending to the foot of the Astroni hills.

Adjacent to the spa are the ruins of the Roman **Thermae Anianae**, a six-storeyed building with passages leading to the sudatoria, or vapour-chambers, hollowed out in the hillside. Excavations have revealed some interesting mosaics and pipes for water and steam.

A road skirting the east side of the crater leads to the Parco degli Astroni, another extinct volcano.

The road climbs above Bagnoli (see below), under hills anciently called *Colles Leucogaei* on account of their white earth, which was used for bleaching barley. From the base of one of them issue the **Pisciarelli** (Pliny's *Fontes Leucogaei*), hot aluminous springs. Out to sea appears the island of Nisida with Capri behind, and ahead is Capo Miseno backed by Monte Epomeo on Ischia.

Turn away from the sea and pass the convent of **San Gennaro** built in the 16C on the supposed site of the beheading of St Januarius. In the church is preserved a stone stained with the martyr's blood, which turns bright red on the occasion of the liquefaction of his blood in Naples. The view from the convent over the gulf is very fine.

About 500m further on is the entrance to the **Solfatara di Pozzuoli** (open 07.00–sunset), a half-extinct volcano known to the ancients as *Forum Vulcani*. The huge elliptical crater, 752m across at its widest, has changed little in appearance since Roman times. The path along the bottom passes (left) a well of hot water 9m deep and soon reaches the **fumarole**, a number of violent jets of steam emerging from the ground at a high temperature (c 143° C) and charged with sulphurous vapour. The nature of the gas varies considerably. The ground is hot and makes a hollow sound when stamped on. About 100m south-east behind a small pavilion is the largest fumarola, or **Bocca Grande**, from which steam issues at a very high temperature (162° C) with a whistling noise. The barren north-west part of the crater is at the lowest level and was probably covered with hot muddy water until the 18C. At various dates since, funnel-shaped cavities containing hot mud have formed here. About 240m north of the Bocca Grande are the **Stufe**, more fumaroles in an artificial excavation.

POZZUOLI

Beyond the Solfatara the road curves back towards the sea and, passing beneath the railway and just to the left of the entrance to the amphitheatre (see below), descends to (6km) Pozzuoli, a curious town (28m, 77,000 inhab.) that stands partly on an isolated promontory of yellow tufa and partly on the slopes to land-ward, with its main street passing between on almost level ground. In 1970 part of the town was damaged by a 'slow earthquake' that raised the ground more than 75cm in six months. Further movement was registered in 1983.

History

Pozzuoli was the Greek *Dikaearchia*. Founded by colonists from Samos, it became a commercial post subject to Cumae and was afterwards conquered by the Samnites. The Romans established a colony here in 194 BC and the Romanised town, renamed *Puteoli* soon became the principal Italian port for trading with the East and was adorned with buildings appropriate to its wealth, so that Cicero was able to describe it as 'pusilla Roma'. Puteoli was the end of St Paul's perilous voyage from Caesarea in AD 62. The fall of Rome, the barbarian invasions, the eruption of Monte Nuovo, and the increase of malaria reduced the once prosperous port to the level of a fishing village and today only its ruins remain to testify to its former glory.

- **Information**. AA Via Campi Flegrei 3; tel. 081 526 5068, fax 081 526 1481.

- **Ferries** to Procida (30 min) and Ischia (1 hr)

- **Hydrofoils** to Procida (15 min)

At the east end of the town, just beyond the sea-girt **Capuchin Convent** where the composer G.B. Pergolesi (1710–36) died, is Piazza Matteotti (Porta di Città), where the buses from Naples terminate. Here Via del Duomo ascends to the **Cattedrale** (San Procolo), which incorporates a temple erected in honour of Augustus by the architect Cocceius. The church was completely rebuilt in 1643 by Bishop Martino de Leon y Cardenas, but a fire in May 1964 destroyed the Baroque structure, revealing the Roman building, in marble, as well as remains of a Samnite temple, in tufa, of the 3C to 2C BC. Within the church is the tomb of Pergolesi, undamaged by the fire.

From the Porta di Città Corso Vittorio Emanuele leads north and Corso Garibaldi leads west to the **public gardens**. Here are the theatre and busts of Pergolesi and of the native composer Antonio Sacchini (1734–86). To the left extends the harbour, which has engulfed the surviving remains of the **Roman port**. The *Moles Puteolana* or *Opus Pilarum* consisted of a breakwater of 25 piers connected by arches, cleverly arranged to prevent the silting up of the harbour. At the end was a triumphal arch to Antoninus Pius, who restored the harbour in AD 120 after a destructive tempest. In calm weather the foundations of a double line of piers and a number of columns can be discerned below the surface. The mooring rings by which ships were attached are now covered by more than a fathom of water, owing to the subsidence of the land. Offshore, on the south side of the town, are the remains of three submerged docks.

Continue beyond the Cumana station to arrive at the so-called **Serapeum**, set in a park along the waterfront, which was not a temple of Serapis, as the name implies, but a macellum or rectangular market-hall (75 x 58m). It dates from the

POZZUOLI

0 metres   400   *GULF OF NAPLES*

1C AD. Opposite the entrance on the seaward side was an apse, preceded by four Corinthian columns, three of which are still standing. These have been eaten away and perforated, from 3.5 to 5.5m above ground, by a species of shellfish (*Lithodomus lithophagus*) that still abounds in the Tyrrhenian Sea. This evidence suggests that the columns were at one time buried for 3.5m and submerged for another 2m. Perhaps during the eruption of 1538, they were again raised above the sea; they became dry early in the present century. Today water again covers the floor, although the 'slow quake' of 1970 raised the ground level by nearly 90cm. Within the building is a courtyard, 32m square, surrounded by a gallery of 48 cipollino and granite columns beneath which were 35 booths and two marble-lined public latrines. A second storey probably existed on the same plan. The central tholus, or domed circular edifice, was supported by 16 columns of *giallo antico* which are now at Caserta, only their bases remaining in situ.

Now cross the railway and mount by steps (5min) to join Corso Terraciano near the entrance to the *amphitheatre* (open daily 09.00–1hr before sunset). It is the best preserved of the monuments of Puteoli and rivals in size the Colosseum in Rome and the ampithectres of Capua and Verona. The present building (149 x 166m), finished under Vespasian, replaced an older amphitheatre whose ruins, discovered in the workings for the Direttissima railway line connecting Rome and

Naples in 1926–27, may be seen near the railway bridge to the north-east. It is built on three rows of arches and was originally surrounded by a brick arcade. The cavea had three ranges of seats divided by stairs into cunei. The arena (72 x 42m) has an open corridor along its greater axis, below which are substructures (dens for wild beasts and rooms for stage machinery) in a remarkably good state of preservation. These were added under Trajan or Hadrian. 60 openings connecting the substructures with the arena served for letting loose the wild beasts, for ventilation and for erecting the *pegma*, a wooden scaffold on which the gladiators fought and which could be run up very quickly. In Vespasian's time a conduit supplied water for flooding the arena on the occasion of a *naumachia* (mock sea battle). St Januarius and his companions were imprisoned here under Diocletian before their executions near the Solfatara. Here too Nero amazed the Armenian King Tiridates by his exploits among the beasts in the arena.

> To the north-west are remains of what was probably a Roman villa, the ruined **Tempio dell'Onore** and some fragments of thermae, known as the **Tempio di Nettuno**, dating from the time of Nero. Around the amphitheatre were reservoirs of water, the largest of which, the Piscina Cardito, still exists on the right of the Solfatara road.

THE LAKE DISTRICT
Continue by Corso Terracciano above the town. To the right, by the church of the Annunziata, Via Campana (the Roman Via Consularis Puteolis Capuam) diverges inland, lined on either side with sepulchral monuments, more of which came to light when the Direttissima railway was constructed parallel to the road. About 2km beyond Pozzuoli leave the new road (which continues towards Cumae, see below) and descend to the left, joining the old road; this, with the Cumana railway, follows the lovely coast of the Gulf.

To the right rises **Monte Nuovo** (140m), a volcanic cone of rough scoriae and tufa, entered (tip required) from about half way between Arco Felice and Lago Lucrino stations. It takes c 20min to reach the summit, and 10min more to descend into the crater (15m above the sea). This crater was thrown up during the earth-quake of 29 September 1538, when the Lucrine Lake was half filled up and Pozzuoli deluged with mud and lapilli.

4km, the **Lago Lucrino** (Lucrine Lake) is separated from the sea (fine beach) by a narrow strip of land, the Via Herculea, by which the hero drove the bulls of Geryon across the swamp. The lake is much shrunken since the time (c 100 BC) when Sergius Orata began the cultivation of the famous oysters. Cicero's villa, which he called *Academia*, stood on the shore nearby.

A road running straight inland leads to (10min) the **Lago d'Averno** (Lake Avernus), a crater 8km around and 34m deep, entirely surrounded by hills except for a narrow opening on the south side. It has been encircled by a stone edging to prevent the formation of malarial swamps. The surface of its waters is only 40cm above sea level.

> Surrounded, in the heroic age, by dense forest, which gave it a dark and gloomy atmosphere, Avernus was said to be the abode of the Cimmerians (Homer, *Odyssey* XI), who lived in eternal darkness, and the entrance to Hades. The Greek name *Aornos* (wrongly held to mean 'without birds') gave rise to the legend that birds flying over the lake fell suffocated by mephitic fumes. Hannibal, in pretended respect for local superstition but really for a reconnai-

sance of Puteoli, visited Avernus and offered a sacrifice; and the custom of making a propitiatory sacrifice to the Infernal deities of Avernus endured until after the days of Constantine. Agrippa, however, completely altered the appearance of the countryside. To counter the threat of Sextus Pompeius' fleet (37 BC) he cut down the forest and united Lake Avernus with the sea by a canal via the Lucrine Lake, and to Cumae by a tunnel (see below), thereby constructing a military harbour of perfect security, the Portus Julius. This was afterwards abandoned, and finally wrecked by the eruption of 1538. Despite Agrippa's improvements the legend, sung by Virgil and kept alive by Pliny and Silius Italicus, survived even among sixth century Byzantine writers.

On the east shore of the lake are ruins of **thermae**; the most remarkable remains, arbitrarily known as a Tempio d'Apollo, are of an octagonal building with a round interior broken by niches, the dome of which (now fallen) once spanned a space of over 36m. The overgrown ruins on the west side probably represent a shipbuilding and repair yard.

Agrippa's tunnel to Cumae, a passage more than 1km long executed by Cocceius, leads away from the north-west shore. It is known as the **Grotta della Pace**, after Pietro della Pace, who explored it in 1507. Straight and wide enough for chariots to pass, it is the most ambitious underground work attempted by the Romans and, being lighted at intervals by vertical openings, it could be travelled through with ease, even without a light, until it was damaged in the fighting of 1943.

A path along the south side of the lake, and rising above it to the left, leads in c 3min to a long gallery cut into the rock, off which opens a chamber blackened with torch smoke. Once a rival claimant to be the Sibyl's Cave, this is now thought to be part of Agrippa's defensive works.

Road and railway now follow the Via Herculea. The railway then tunnels through the Punta dell'Epitaffio, whereas the road follows the coast. Here must be placed the site of *Bauli*, where Agrippina, having escaped the previous day from a planned accident at sea, was done to death by her son Nero's orders in the bedroom of her villa. On the right of the road are some ruins of thermae, called the Stufe di Nerone or di Tritoli, including a remarkable **sudatorium** (vapour chamber) hewn out of the tufa. Modern quarrying has destroyed all but vestiges of the imperial villas of Pompey and Vespasian.

BAIA

3km Baia, the ancient *Baiae* extolled by Horace and Martial, is today a large village standing on the bay that bears its name and enjoying a splendid view across the Gulf of Pozzuoli.

History

In the early days of the Roman Empire, Baiae, which owed its name, according to legend, to Baios, the navigator of Odysseus, was the fashionable bathing resort of Roman society. Successive emperors rivalled each other in the construction of magnificent palaces, and here Caligula built his famous bridge of boats. However, the reputation of the town was stained by Nero's murder of his mother Agrippina and his sanguinary suppression of the conspiracy of Piso. Hadrian died here on 17 July 138. Baiae was plundered by the Saracens in the 8C and gradually deserted on account of malaria. The ruins of its palaces now extend some distance beneath the sea, owing to the subsidence of the ground. Finds made in the harbour in 1923–28 included statues and important architectural fragments.

Behind the station is the so-called **Temple of Diana**, like other 'temples' one of the thermal establishments for which Baiae was famous. Octagonal without and circular within, it preserves four niches and part of its domed roof. From the piazza, steps ascend to the **Scavi di Baia** (open daily 09.00–1hr before sunset). Systematic excavations, begun in 1941 and completed ten years later, have allowed the identification of a group of buildings, some of which were already known in the Middle Ages, comprising an **imperial palatium** built between the 1C and 4C AD. From the entrance, a long avenue leads to a portico where architectural fragments are displayed. From here steps lead to the upper terrace, one of several such areas set into the hillside at various levels. A row of rooms with shallow exedrae extends along the right. In the first of these was found the statue of Sossandra, a marble copy of a 5C Greek original, now in the Museo Archeologico Nazionale in Naples. The second contains a statue of Mercury, beheaded by thieves (who in antiquity enjoyed the god's protection!) in 1978.

A staircase descends to the central terrace, along one side of which a series of rooms forming a semicircle suggests the previous existence of a theatre-nymphaeum. From here, more steps descend to the lower terrace, occupied by a large (35 x 29m) rectangular bathing pool, surrounded by a graceful portico. To the east lies the complex of buildings traditionally called the **Temple of Venus**,

1 Upper Terrace
2 Central Terrace
3 Lower Terrace
4 Tempio dell'Eco

IL PALATIUM IMPERIALE

which includes numerous smaller rooms and a large vaulted hall surrounded by apsidal openings, also believed to be a nymphaeum.

Across the street, outside the park, is a hall of circular plan, 26m in diameter. Although the vault has collapsed, the rest of the structure is intact. From the north side of the pool a corridor partially covered by arches leads to the so-called **Temple of Mercury**. These buildings appear to have made up a **thermal complex**; principal among them is a great circular hall nearly 22m in diameter, similar in structure to the Pantheon in Rome. Like the smaller halls to the rear, it is filled with water to the base of the dome, creating the unusual acoustic effects from which it derives its nickname, 'Tempio dell'Eco'.

Beyond Baia, the road to Capo Miseno ascends a gentle slope along the shore, passing several columbaria (fine view). On the left is the 16C **Castello di Baia**, built by order of Don Pedro de Toledo. The castle houses the **Museo Archaeologico dei Campi Flegrei** (open Mon-Sat 09.00–16.00, Sun 09.00–14.00), with material from excavations at Baia and other area sites. At the end of a descent is (3km) **Bacoli** (27,000 inhab.), not, despite its name, the ancient *Bauli* (see above). The Via Della Marina, to the left at the entrance to the village, descends to the so-called **Tomb of Agrippina**, really the ruins of a small theatre. From the main road Via Ercole and Via Sant'Anna ascend to the church of Sant'Anna. Walking round this, you may go on to (15min) the **Cento Camerelle**, a two-storeyed ruin of which the upper part was a reservoir; the function of the lower storey is not known. At Via Creco 10 you may obtain the key of the *Piscina Mirabile (open 09.00–one hour before sunset; tip required). This, 10min south of the village, is the largest and best preserved reservoir in the district (70 x 25m). Its form recalls that of a basilica, with five pillared aisles of equal height. It lay at the extremity of an aqueduct and was used for supplying the fleet stationed at Misenum.

At the end of the town is (3km) the **Lago di Miseno** or **Mare Morto**. Leave the main road (see below), following to the south the causeway separating the lagoon from the picturesque harbour of **Misenum**. This was built by Agrippa in 41 BC as a temporary refuge for the Tyrrhenian fleet during the construction of the Portus Julius (see above); it was while stationed here with the fleet that Pliny the Younger witnessed the fatal eruption of Vesuvius in AD 79. The port consisted of two basins, of which the inner, the Mare Morto, is now shut off from the Porto di Miseno proper by the road causeway. The colony of Misenum was founded at the same time as the harbour, and its importance diminished as Roman naval power declined. It was destroyed by the Saracens in the 9C.

THE CAPO MISENO AREA

The byroad goes on to the village of Miseno (1.5km), beyond which cars cannot proceed. A path turns to the right near the church, to the right again just before a farmhouse, and then to the left, passing various ruins (see below). The ascent (1hr there and back) leads to *Capo Miseno (155m), a promontory commanding a wonderful view over the gulfs of Pozzuoli, Naples, and Gaeta, and the surrounding lakes and islands.

The cape itself is a segment of an ancient crater, the rest of which has sunk below the sea. The remaining portion so resembles an artificial tumulus as to have given rise to the legend that it was the burial-place of Misenus, the trumpeter of Aeneas. The headland was already covered with villas when the colony was founded and among its distinguished residents was Caius Marius, whose country house passed into the possession of Lucullus and later to the emperors.

Tiberius died there in AD 37. The ruins of Marius's villa are on the south side of the harbour; near the church are the remains of the circular baths; and to the north-west stands a theatre commanding a fine view of Ischia. On the west side of the headland is the **Grotta Dragonara**, an excavation supported by 12 pillars, probably a storehouse for the fleet. A lighthouse marks the extremity of the cape (78km). Walkers may follow the **Spiaggia di Miliscola** (*Militis Schola*), a narrow sand bar 2km long between the Mare Morto and the sea, and rejoin the main road c 1km before Cappella (see below).

Back on the main road, bear to the left along the north side of the Mare Morto, turning sharp to the right to reach (1km) Cappella, a village between Monte Grillo or Monte di Procida (144m) on the south, and Monte dei Salvatichi (123m).

About 1km beyond Cappella a road on the left leads to (1km) **Torregaveta**, the terminus of the Cumana railway. From here another road running south ascends to **Monte di Procida** (3km; bus from Torregaveta), a village on a tufa hill covered with ruined villas among vineyards which produce an excellent wine. **Acquamorta** on the end of the promontory beyond, commands a fine view of Procida and Ischia.

Leaving the Torregaveta road on the left you reach (1km) the semicircular **Lago di Fusaro**, the ancient Acherusian Swamp, separated from the sea by a sand bar pierced by two canals, one Roman and one modern (1858). On the slopes of the tufa hill north of Torregaveta is the ruined villa of Servilius Vatia. Since 1784 the lake has been a centre of oyster culture and fish breeding; the establishment, where oysters may be bought, is on the east shore near the road to Cumae. On the lake is a casino, built for Ferdinand IV by Vanvitelli (1782), now a marine biological station (admission to both establishments on application).

CUMAE

The road crosses the railway near Cuma Fusaro station. Leaving a road to Baia (2km) on the right, follow the lake shore and then pass through vineyards to reach (15 min. from the station) Cumae, perhaps the oldest Greek colony in Italy, now a mass of scattered ruins in a romantic situation where excavation fights a losing battle with nature.

History

By tradition, the foundation of Cumae dates from c 1050 BC, the first settlers being the Chalcidians and the Aeolians of Kyme. In fact, though it was one of the earliest colonies, there is no proof that it antedates Syracuse. Its prosperity and population increased rapidly, and colonies were dispatched to Dikaearchia (Pozzuoli) and, after the conquest of Parthenope, to found the settlement of Neapolis. Cumae was a centre of Hellenic culture, and from its alphabet all the other Italian alphabets were derived. Tarquinius Superbus (who later died in exile at Cumae) here purchased the Sibyline Books from the Cumaean Sibyl, according to Pliny, and regretted his attempt to bargain with her.

In 474 BC the Cumaeans, in alliance with Hieron of Syracuse, defeated an Etruscan fleet, a victory immortalised by Pindar in the first Pythian Ode. In 421 Cumae was conquered by the Samnites, passing later, with the rest of their possessions, to Rome. In the reign of Nero it was the scene of the voluntary death of Petronius Arbiter. No longer of importance, Cumae fell easy prey to the Sacracens in the 9C and was utterly destroyed by Naples and Aversa in 1207.

The ruins of the city lie for the most part beneath farmland; a visit requires at least two hours. A short distance before a fork, where the main road bears inland to the right, are the ruins of an amphitheatre, easily traced through the vineyards and olive groves that cover it. Taking the little road to the left at the fork you pass (right; on cultivated land) the **Temple of the Giants** and, farther away, the **Temple of the Forum**. Along the ascent towards Monte di Cuma (78m), the acropolis of the city, traces of many other buildings may be seen over a wide area.

Beyond the entrance to the excavations (refreshments; open daily 09.00–19.00), notice the massive **walls** of cyclopean stone, Greek in the lower courses, Roman above.

Go through a tunnel hewn through the rock. Beyond, to the left, is the entrance to the ***Cave of the Cumaean Sibyl**, one of the more famous of ancient sanctuaries, brought to light in 1932. Here Aeneas came to consult the Sibyl; on either side of the entrance marble plaques now recall the lines of Virgil (*Aeneid* VI 42–51). The cave consists of a dromos, or corridor, c 44m long, nearly 2.5m wide and c 5m high, ending in a rectangular chamber, all hewn out of the rock. The dromos, of trapezoidal cross-section markedly Minoan in style, runs due north–south in the shoreward side of the hill, and is lighted by six galleries opening to the west (so it is best visited in the afternoon). From the other side open three lower chambers, apparently designed for lustral waters and later used for Christian burials. The *oikos*, or secret chamber, at the end, probably redesigned in the 4C or 3C BC, has three large niches. At a lower level (reached by a path to the left) a huge **Roman crypt** c 180m long, tunnels through the hill; this lies on the same axis as the Grotta della Pace (cf. above) and is probably a continuation of it. Many dark passages leading from it show traces of Christian occupation.

A paved Via Sacra climbs to the first terrace where (right) are the remains of the **Temple of Apollo**, a Greek structure altered in Augustan times and transformed into a Christian church in the 6C or 7C. On the summit is the so-called **Temple of Jupiter**, a larger work of Greek origin also transformed (5C/6C) into a Christian basilica of five aisles. Behind the presbytery are remains of a large circular pool for baptism by immersion. Here the beauty of the ***view** and the stillness, broken only by the rustle of lizards and the murmur of the sea, make an indelible impression.

The chief **necropolis**, which has provided many interesting additions to the Naples museum, lies between the acropolis and Licola to the north, a modern village on the site of a drained lake. From the ruins a path (which you cannot enter from the other end) leads down to the deserted shore. Towards the sea the outer wall of the town is still traceable. An extension of the railway is planned from Torregaveta (4km), which may be reached by a pleasant walk along the beach or by a well-preserved stretch of the Roman road that linked Cumae with Misenum. This was a branch of the Via Domitiana, engineered in AD 95 to link Rome directly with Puteoli. Along its course to the north lie (8km) the **Lago di Patria**, once the harbour of the Roman colony of *Liternum* (scanty ruins), where Scipio Africanus died in 184 BC; and (20km) Sinuessa, near the modern Mondragone, where at the 106th milestone from Rome it joined the Via Appia.

Take the road running north-east (right) from Cumae; in 5 min a path (right) leads to the mouth of the Grotta della Pace (closed). The road then passes beneath (c 2km from Cumae) the **Arco Felice**, a massive brick archway, 20m high and 6m wide, in a deep cutting made in Monte Grillo by Domitian to secure direct communication between Cumae and Puteoli. To the west is a good stretch of Roman paving. Pass the north side of Lake Avernus and the Monte Nuovo, diverge right to reach (4km) Arco Felice station, then follow the shore road to (6km) Pozzuoli. Continue by the sea past thermal spas (hotels) and pozzolana quarries. 6km **Bagnoli** is a bathing resort and spa much frequented by the Neapolitans. From here the old road runs straight to (13km) Naples. Unhurried travellers may, however, continue round the coast past the huge chemical works of (11km) Coroglio, then climb in full view of Nisida to the **Rotonda** (2km), returning (6km) to Naples along the Posillipo peninsula (Route 5E).

4 · The Early Christian Period and The Middle Ages

THE FALL OF ROME

The decline of the Roman Empire is too complicated to go into in detail here. Suffice it to say very simply that the Romans were unprepared—economically, politically, and psychologically—for the enormous military effort that three centuries of barbarian invasions required of them. The eastern provinces, with their capital at Constantinople (or *Byzantium* as it was then called), managed to defend their borders and preserve imperial institutions of law and government. But the weaker provinces of the west were overrun one by one by the Germanic peoples who, driven from their homelands by other invaders, sought a safe refuge on Roman soil.These historical events found concrete expression in the art and architecture of our area. The early Christian churches and catacombs that grew up in Naples and its environs in the late Roman period reflect classical as well as medieval values. They set the spiritual tone of much of the art of later centuries. The finest of these works—the 5C mosaics in Naples (in the Baptistery of San Giovanni in Fonte and in the Catacomb of San Gennaro) and at San Prisco, near Santa Maria Capua Vetere (in the chapel of Santa Matrona, attached to the parish church)—are distinguished by an explicit naturalism that is rarely seen outside of Rome.

During the 5C Campania fell prey to the Goths, and for the next five centuries the region lacked both the financial resources and the political stability that are necessary for major artistic undertakings. In 535 the area was conquered by the Byzantine general, Belisarius. Totilla, another Gothic leader, drove the Byzantines from the region in 547; ten years later, it reverted to Byzantine rule. Then, toward the end of the century, the weak hold of the Eastern emperors relaxed under the pressure of another Germanic people, the Lombards, who in just a few years gained control of the important provinces of Capua, Benevento, Nola, Acerra, and Nocera, reaching the sea at Salerno in 646.

While the Lombards ruled over the interior of Campania, the part of the province remaining under the empire gave its allegiance to the duke of Naples, who was originally a Greek envoy, but in 661 became a Neapolitan. In 763 Duke Stephen II, while ostensibly maintaining his loyalty to Byzantium, secured for his family the privilege of hereditary power and gradually detached Naples from the direct domination of the empire. His allies in Sorrento, Amalfi and Gaeta soon followed suit. Their dukes, likewise separated by distance and political interest from their nominal allegiance to Byzantium, disengaged themselves from the Eastern

Empire in 768, 786, and 899, respectively. During this period, which historians call the age of the Independent Duchy (763–1139), Latin replaced Greek as the official language in Naples and the Roman image of St Januarius replaced the Greek effigy of the emperor on municipal seals and coins. The city developed one of the strongest fleets in Europe, and in the 9C it joined forces with Gaeta, Sorrento, and Amalfi to rid the Tyrrhenian Sea of the marauding Saracens, who terrorised the coasts and interfered with vital maritime trade. By so doing the Campanian cities avenged the Saracen sack of Rome (846), and with a famous victory over the Saracens three years later at Ostia, celebrated by Raphael in the Vatican Stanze, they saved the Eternal City from a new catastrophe.

THE NORMANS

The Norman conquest (1030–1130) restored political unity to Southern Italy. The Norman adventurers who first came to the area in 1016 to seek their fortunes in Apulia and Calabria seem to have had no political ambitions. Lacking organisation and experienced leadership, they were prepared to live as mercenaries in the service of the Byzantines or the Lombards. It was not until 1030 that Sergius of Naples, by awarding the Norman leader Rainulf the county of Aversa in payment for services rendered, gave them the opportunity to begin an organised conquest of the land. In the years that followed, Norman knights, led by the sons of Tancred de Hauteville, intervened in local conflicts and by so doing gradually gained control of Capua (1062), Salerno (1076) and Amalfi (1137). Naples was the last to fall: it maintained its independence until 1139, its citizens resisting even after the submission of its duke. By the middle of the 12C, Campania was completely in the power of the conquerors, whose dominion extended over all Southern Italy and Sicily. This vast territory became the Norman Kingdom of Sicily, with its capital at Palermo. It was administered efficiently and with great tolerance of the region's Arab, Jewish, Greek and Roman traditions. It is a pity that in this scheme of things Naples lost its primacy and was reduced to the status of a provincial town.

The Norman influence is most clearly seen in the maritime cities, which prospered through trade with Sicily and the Orient and were the chief channels through which the Norman court of Palermo administered its holdings on the mainland. Siculo-Norman artists, or local artists trained in the Norman schools of Sicily, were active at Salerno, Ravello, Sessa Aurunca, Gaeta and elsewhere in our area throughout the 11C and 12C. They have left an extraordinary series of sculptures—mainly decorated episcopal thrones, pulpits, paschal candelbra and altar screens—incorporated coloured glass inlay and marble tarsia work inspired by Saracenic sources. The Normans were also responsible for introducing to the area French architectural forms and styles, which find their most harmonious expression in the Abbey of Fossanova, consecrated in 1208 (Route 1B).

The rebuilding of the Benedictine abbey of Monte Cassino, which also took place in the 11C, under the enlightened direction of the abbot Desiderius, stimulated the renewal of artistic activity in the area. From Monte Cassino, Desiderius masterminded a real revolution of the arts. He brought in architects from Lombardy and artists from Constantinople and trained his monks in their methods, giving rise to a new artistic sensibility that combined the splendor of Oriental mosaic and allied crafts with revived early Christian narrative methods. Although Monte Cassino has lost most of its medieval grandeur, a reflection of this 11C blend of styles may be seen in the marvellous series of contemporary frescoes in the basilica at Sant'Angelo in Formis, near Capua (Route 1A).

Further contacts between Eastern and Western artistic cultures are evident in the bronze doors that appeared on Campanian cathedrals in the 11C and 12C. The first of these were installed at Amalfi in 1065. They had been commissioned in Constantinople by the wealthy Amalfitan merchant, Pantaleon, who had business interests in the Byzantine capital and must have seen by bronze doors on churches there. Desiderius of Monte Cassino was so impressed by these doors when he visited Amalfi that he ordered a pair for the abbey. The fashion spread from there to Salerno, Atrani, Ravello, Benevento and other Southern Italian cities.

FREDERICK II

In 1194 the crown of Holy Roman Emperor was claimed by Henry IV of Hohenstaufen in the name of his wife, Constance (daughter of the Norman king, Roger II). He was succeeded as emperor and as King of Sicily by his son Frederick II (1197–1250), whose splendid court at Palermo drew on Islamic and Jewish, as well as Christian, cultures. Frederick's belief in the principles of just government is reflected in the famous code of laws known as the *Constitutiones Augustales*. His interest in rational science and love of classical sculpture (visible in the remarkable series of classicising sculptures now on show in the Museo Campano at Capua, which he commissioned to decorate his Porta Romana outside that city) fore-shadow the Renaissance.

Naples initially challenged Frederick's sovereignty and suffered a humiliating defeat at the hands of an imperial army. In a gesture of calculated magnanimity, Frederick regained the favour of the Neapolitans by making their city, and not Palermo, the intellectual capital of his kingdom: in 1224 he founded the university, where many famous men of letters—including Pier delle Vigne, Andrea d'Isernia, Bartolomo Prignano, and Cino da Pistoia—were teachers.

Frederick's son, Conrad, died before he could inherit the kingdom, and Pope Urban IV at once set about finding a rival candidate for the Sicilian crown. He chose Charles of Anjou, the ambitious and ruthless young brother of St Louis of France. In two fortunate battles, at Benevento (1266) and Tagliacozzo (1268), Charles defeated the last of the Hohenstaufen, establishing himself as the first French king of Naples and Sicily. To mark the sharp contrast between his monarchy and that of his predecessors, he transferred his capital from Palermo to Naples, which naturally grew in importance.

THE ANGEVIN COURT

The Angevin court of Naples was as sophisticated and cosmopolitan as any contemporary court in Provence. As allies of the pope the French kings employed Florentine bankers and patronised Florentine intellectuals, many of whom, like the poet Giovanni Boccaccio, became quite fond of their adopted home. Boccaccio came to Naples as a young man, around 1327, to gain practice as a merchant and banker. He served a long (but fruitless) apprenticeship at the Bardi bank in the lively Portanova neighbourhood, an experience that brought him into daily contact with clients from all areas of the Mediterranean. Boccaccio's life could not have been that of an ordinary apprentice-clerk, for he was the son of a partner of the Bardi who in 1328 became a 'counsellor and chamberlain' of King Robert. The refined, gay life of the Neapolitan upper classes, divided between the aristocratic opulence of the city and the carefree, voluptuous idleness of the gulf-shore resorts (particularly Baia) is delightfully portrayed in his early works. In his *Rhymes*, for instance, he voices a curious lament:

If I fear the sky and sea of Baia,
the ground and waves and lakes and fountains,
the wild and the domestic places,
no one should be surprised.
Here one spends all one's time celebrating
with music and song, and with vain words
seducing wandering minds
or telling of love's victories.

Against this background he chose to set his great love novel, *Elegia a Madonna Fiammetta*.

The gaiety of the Angevin court unfortunately did not extend to the rest of the kingdom. Indeed, the political life of these years was as turbulent as the social life was exuberant. Charles initially enjoyed the favor of his subjects, but his political ambitions, which necessitated oppressive taxation, led to resentment. Revolt broke out spontaneously in Palermo on Easter Tuesday, 1282, in the Sicilian Vespers. Within a month the French garrisons on the island had been either expelled or massacred, and the Sicilian nobles had summoned the Catalonian Peter of Aragon to be their king. Charles died in 1286, and his heir, Charles II, was not crowned until two years later. He was succeeded in 1309 by his second son, Robert (the Wise), who proved a capable ruler and patron of the arts (it was he who financed Boccaccio's literary endeavours), but whose authority was limited by a turbulent and rebellious baronage. His death was followed by a whirlwind of coups and counter-coups. He was succeeded (1432) by his granddaughter Joan I, whose husband and crown prince, Andrew of Hungary, was assassinated in 1345, probably with the queen's complicity. Joan nominated Louis of Anjou her heir, and he was recognised by the anti-pope Clement VII. Pope Urban VI, however, named Charles of Durazzo, great-grandson of Charles II, king of Naples. Charles conquered the kingdom, took Joan prisoner in 1381 and had her murdered the following year. Louis died in exile three years later. The anarchic reigns of Charles III and his son Ladislas were followed (1414) by the dissolute rule of Joan II, which was torn by the rival claims of Louis III of Anjou and of Alfonso of Aragon to be her heir. Alfonso seized Naples at Joan's death in 1335 and the kingdom passed to the house of Aragon.

During the 13C and early 14C the artistic impetus in Naples, which came through the Angevin dynasty, was understandably French-oriented. The Angevins generally imported their architects from France, but they chose their artists from among the representative masters of the major Italian schools: Pietro Cavallini from Rome, Giotto from Florence, Simone Martini and Tino di Camaino from Siena. By so doing they established a pattern of patronage (privileging foreign artists or artists from farther north over local masters) that would continue, with rare exceptions, until the 17C.

FIFTEENTH-CENTURY NAPLES

During the brief reign of Alfonso V of Aragon, called 'the Magnanimous', Naples was again united with Sicily. The kingdom enjoyed a period of renewed splendour, for Alfonso was at once a brilliant ruler, a scholar and a patron of the arts. When he died (1458) his brother John II succeeded to the throne of Sicily, while Naples adopted his illegitimate son Ferdinand I (Ferrante) as king. Like his father, Ferrante surrounded himself with artists and humanists and was in this respect a typical

Renaissance prince, though often perverse and cruel (it was his policy to imprison his enemies in the Castel Nuovo until they died; they would then be mummified and exhibited to his guests, dressed in the clothes they had worn when living).

Ferrante was succeeded by Alfonso II, who in September 1491 surrendered the kingdom to Charles VII of France. Many months later Alfonso's son Ferdinand II (Ferrandino), with the help of Spain, returned to his capital, where he died in 1496. During the reign of his successor, Frederick, the country was torn by civil war and brigandage as both the French and the Spanish continued to press their claims. A series of victories of the Spanish forces under Gonzalo de Cordoba secured the kingdom for Spain in 1503. Naples was not united with Sicily, but governed by a separate viceroy, Gonzalo being the first.

While Renaissance painters in Florence, Rome, and Venice produced works of art that are known the world over, very little of note was done in 15C Naples. Like the Angevins, the Aragonese entrusted their most important commissions to the famous names of the north (notably the Florentines Donatello, Michelozzo, Antonio Rossellino and Benedetto da Maiano). This was only to be expected, as they could afford the best works and considered themselves to be on a level with the great families of northern cities.

The major Neapolitan painter of the 15C is Colantonio, whose style shows a debt to Flemish painting. Andrea da Salerno, too, has left many fine works throughout Campania. Despite the fine sculptured works by Northern Italian artists in the major churches of Naples, there was no local school of any merit. The most successful architects were Tommaso and Giovanni Tommaso Malvito and Giovanni Francesco Mormanno, whose creations we shall encounter shortly.

The itineraries that follow focus on the medieval monuments of Naples and on the territories of the former maritime republics of Sorrento, Amalfi, and Salerno, south of the city. A great deal of medieval art and architecture may also be seen north of Naples, at Sessa Aurunca, Gaeta, Fondi, Terracina and Cassino. These sites are described in Route 1.

A. Early Christian Naples

*Because this route involves sites outside the city centre, it is best covered by taxi (to cover it by bus would take hours, and on foot it is quite a hike). It begins at the **Catacomba di San Gennaro**, excavated in two storeys in the tufa beneath the church of San Gennaro extra Moenia (Atlas 4, 2), an 18C edifice built on 5C foundations. A second early-Christian burial ground, dedicated to **San Gaudioso**, lies beneath the 17C church of Santa Maria della Sanità (Atlas 4, 2)—which, incidentally, is the only design by architect Giuseppe Nuovo to survive intact. From here the walk along the Via della Sanità and the Via del Duomo to the **Cattedrale** (Atlas 3, 3) may be made in about 30min, but the neighbourhood is not the best in Naples, and due caution (see the Practical Information) is necessary. A look at the early Christian elements in the cathedral may be joined with the general visit described in Route 4B; the church of **San Giorgio Maggiore** (Atlas 3, 7), which incorporates some 5C architectural details, is just a few blocks south on the Via del Duomo. The Catacomba di San Gennaro may be seen on the same morning as the **Museo e Gallerie Nazionali di Capodimonte**, which is across the street, in a lovely park (see Route 5C).*

THE CATACOMBS

Some very old legends tell that St Peter visited Naples on his way to Rome, interrupting his journey to establish a diocese in the city and to name St Asprenus as its first bishop; numerous chronicles describe the martyrdom, near Pozzuoli, of the bishop Januarius; and unsubstantiated legends attribute the foundation of the city's first Christian churches to the time of Constantine (AD 306–377). But recent studies show that St Peter did not visit Naples, the birth date of the Neapolitan episcopate is still uncertain, and although there is evidence that followers of the new religion existed in the city shortly after the time of Christ, it is now known that Naples' first Christian churches were erected only at the end of the 4C.

The catacombs of St Januarius and St Gaudiosus are among the oldest Christian monuments of Naples. The ***Catacomba di San Gennaro**, located beneath the church of San Gennaro extra Moenia (Atlas 4, 2; entrance in Via Capodimente; open Sat, Sun and holidays, 09.30, 10.15, 11.00, 11.45) (dates from the 2C AD and seems to have developed around the family tomb of an early member of the Christian community. It probably became the official cemetery of Christian Naples after the burial here, in the 3C of the bishop-saint Agrippinus, over whose tomb a basilica was built. Later, when St Januarius, the 5C martyr and patron saint of the city, was entombed here, the catacomb became a place of pilgrimage. Here also are buried the first dukes of Naples, notably Stephen I (died AD 800) and Stephen III (died 832). In 831 Sicone, prince of Benevento, carried the relics of St Januarius off to his city; and around the mid 9C the bishop-saint John IV transferred the remains of his illustrious predecessors to the cathedral. But he, like his successor St Athanasius (died 877), was buried here, and the catacomb remained in use throughout the 10C and probably the 11C. The catacomb contains burial cells and fragmentary frescoes and mosaics, but is interesting above all for its extent and overall ambience.

The **Catacomba di San Gaudioso**, which lies beneath Santa Maria della Sanità (Atlas 4, 2; the sacristan takes you down), was named after the African bishop-saint Gaudiosus. According to a very old legend, Gaudiosus was deposed by the Vandal king Genseric and set adrift in a small boat, along with Quodvuldeus and several followers. After many vicissitudes, the ecclesiastics landed at Naples, where they founded a monastery. Gaudiosus died in 451 or 452 and was venerated as a saint. Around his tomb developed an extensive cemetery, of which only a small part remains today.

EARLY CHRISTIAN ARCHITECTURE

From the Catacomba di San Gaudioso, follow the Via della Sanità and Via del Duomo to the **Cattedrale**, inside which is the entrance (left) to the chapel of **Santa Restituta**, the city's oldest surviving church. Founded in the 4C, it was rebuilt after an earthquake in 1688. Recent restorations have revealed the bases of various columns and fragments of the early Christian mosaic floor. At the end of the right aisle is the ***baptistery**, or chapel of San Giovanni in Fonte. It is square in plan, with a small dome, and is believed to be the earliest (5C) example of this form of building in Italy. It preserves fragmentary 5C mosaics. In the centre of the dome is a gold Cross on a blue background with white and gold stars, flanked by the Greek letters Alpha and Omega (signifying that Christ represents both the beginning and the end) and surmounted by the hand of God holding a gold crown (a sort of warning that those who aspire to the crown must first bear the cross). Around this runs a band of flowers, fruit, and birds, including a phoenix with a halo, symbol of the Resurrection. Eight radial bands containing flowers, fruit, festoons, and birds divide the cupola into eight wedges, four of which are well preserved. The mosaics depict a turquoise drapery with gilded detail, a vase with two birds, the Women at the Sepulchre (largely ruined), Christ saving Peter from the waters, the Miracle of the Fish, the *tradito legis* (a bearded and haloed Christ giving the book of laws to St Peter), and St Paul (ruined).

From the cathedral it is a short walk to **San Giorgio Maggiore**, founded by St Severus in the late 4C, destroyed by fire in 1640 and rebuilt by the Baroque architect Cosimo Fanzago, who reversed its orientation. Just inside the entrance are the extensive remains of the apse of the early Christian basilica. These include a half-dome resting on three arches that spring from two columns. The Corinthian capitals were taken from ancient Roman buildings. The walls are made of alternating courses of brick and tufa, in the Roman manner.

B.   Anjou and Aragon

This route begins in the heart of the city, at the great **Castel Nuovo** *on the waterfront. From here you cross the Piazza del Municipio and follow the broad, modern Via Medina and Via Monteoliveto, busy with traffic, to the former convent of* **Monteoliveto**. *The Calata Trinita Maggiore then curves up to the old city centre, which you enter from Piazza del Gesù. From here you proceed along the street popularly known as the Spaccanapoli (the decumanus inferior of Neapolis), which changes its modern name several times during its length, but never its straight and narrow course, and the parallel Via dei Tribunali (the decumanus superior), emerging in the Via del Duomo (another modern thoroughfare) just south of the cathedral.*

This dark, crowded quarter gives you a feeling for medieval Naples. The major monuments of this period are the great conventual complexes of **Santa Chiara**, **San Domenico** *and* **San Lorenzo Maggiore**, *on the west side of the city centre; and the* **Cattedrale**, *the churches of* **Santa Maria Donnaregina** *and* **San Giovanni a Carbonara**, *and the* **Porta Capuana**, *on the east side.*

The route is roughly 3km long (the first km of which, from the Castel Nuovo to Santa Chiara, is uphill) and requires about 2hr. It may be combined with Route 5B, which follows the Via dei Tribunali, two blocks north.

THE CASTEL NUOVO
Above Naples harbour rises the royal residence of the Angevin kings, the ***Castel Nuovo** (Atlas 2, 14), commonly, but less correctly, called the Maschio Angioino.

Built for Charles I by Pierre de Chaulnes (1279–82), it was largely reconstructed under Alfonso of Aragon and rearranged by Ferdinand IV for use as the royal and viceregal residence. Now beautifully restored, it houses the offices and library of the Società Napoletana di Storia Patria, the **Biblioteca Comunale Cuomo**, and the meeting rooms of the City Council of Naples and the Regional Council of Campania, as well as a fine museum (see below).

Among the events that have taken place here are the abdication of Pope Celestin V and the mock marriage of Ferdinand I's granddaughter to a son of Count Sarno; the king arrested Sarno and other barons who were conspiring against him. The emperor Charles V stayed at the castle on his return from Tunis, and the revolt of Masaniello (see Route 5) was formally ended here in the pacts signed by the viceroy and the Prince of Massa.

Fronting the square across the dry moat is the long north wall between two massive 15C towers, the Torre del Beverello at the seaward end and the Torre di San Giorgio. Beyond this is the impressive main façade, which you enter between two further towers, under the famous *triumphal arch, erected between 1454 and 1467 to commemorate the entry of Alfonso I into Naples (1443). This masterpiece of the Italian Renaissance was most likely inspired by the celebrated Capua Gate of Frederick II. However, it differs from that monument in that it is not free-standing, but adapted to serve as the entrance to the castle. In this sense it is unique among the architectual inventions of its day, having no parallel in Tuscany or Lombardy. Many prominent sculptors, including Domenico Gagini, Isaia da Pisa, and Francesco Laurana, were brought to Naples to assist in its decoration. The large bas-relief shows the Triumph of Alfonso. Above the second arch stand the four Cardinal Virtues, followed by two large river gods and, topping the whole, St Michael.

The castle is best seen in the morning. Pass through the arch into a vestibule, then enter the polygonal courtyard. The **Museo Civico di Castel Nuovo** (open Mon–Fri 09.00–14.00, Sat 09.00–13.30) includes the **Cappella Palatina** or church of Santa Barbara, with a delicate Renaissance door surmounted by a Madonna by Francesco Laurana and 14C and 15C sculpture and frescoes within. There is also an extensive, if undistinguished, collection of 15C–19C painting, and silver and bronze objects in the south wing. The chapel is lighted by a large rose window of Catalan design and by tall Gothic windows, the splays of which contain frescoes attributed to Maso di Banco. The adjacent **Sala dei Baroni** a large (26 x 28m) hall damaged by fire in 1919, is now the meeting-place of the City Council. The door next to the entrance communicates with the **Viceregal Apartments**, which occupy the north side of the castle; on the wall opposite are a monumental fireplace and choir lofts of Catalan workmanship.

The seaward side of the castle affords an impressive view of the huge bastions, with the Torre del Beverello on the right and the Torre dell' Oro set back to the left; between them rises the restored east end of the chapel, flanked by two polygonal turrets.

TWO CHURCHES OF SANTA MARIA

From the Piazza del Municipio, north of the castle, take Via Medina. You soon reach (left) the Gothic doorway of **Santa Maria Incoronata** (Atlas 2, 10), a church built and named by Joan I (1352) to commemorate her coronation of 1351 and embodying the chapel of the old Vicaria, where she had married Louis of Taranto, her second husband, in 1345. The interior has kept its original form. In the vault are remarkable **frescoes** of the seven sacraments and the triumph of the Church by Roberto Oderisi (c 1370); the Cappella del Crocifisso contains others of like date. The street rises gently between huge new buildings of varying merit to an important crossroads of the reconstructed **Carità quarter**. Via Sanfelice leads right to Piazza Bovio; Via Diaz, realigned since 1945, leads left towards Via Roma, opening immediately into Piazza Matteotti (Atlas 2, 10), focal point of the quarter. Its north side is dominated by the post office, a vast edifice in marble and glass (1936), leaving which on the left you enter Via Santa Maria la Nova.

Santa Maria la Nova (Atlas 2, 10), built by Charles I for Franciscans expelled from the site of the Castel Nuovo (1279), was redesigned by Agnolo Franco in the 16C. The façade is a fine work of the Renaissance. The aisleless nave has a richly painted ceiling incorporating works by Fabrizio Santafede, Francesco Curia and others. The first chapel on the south side contains a St Michael by Marco Pino. The angels on the dome are by Battistello Caracciolo. The second chapel on the north side (San Giacomo della Marca), built by Gonzalo de Cordoba (1504), contains the tomb of Marshal Lautrec (died 1528 of plague while besieging Naples), by Annibale Caccavello, and statues by Domenico d'Auria; in the transept is a wooden *Crucifixion by Giovanni da Nola. The high altar, which combines complex and unusual architectural members with fine floral inlay, is one of the more important works of Cosimo Fanzago. The two cloisters contain 15C tombs and later frescoes.

MONTEOLIVETO AND SANTA CHIARA

Retrace your steps and turn right in Via Monteoliveto. Behind the post office is the cloister of Monteoliveto (the church is described below). The double order of arcades, built to compensate for the slope of the land (monks entering the cloister from the church emerged on the upper level), open directly onto the street, a reminder that the convent was once surrounded by gardens. In the former Olivetan monastery here, Torquato Tasso took refuge in 1588 from the persecution of Alfonso d'Este. On the opposite side of the street, a bit further on, is **Palazzo Gravina**, a beautiful Renaissance building in the purest Tuscan style, by Gabriele d'Agnolo and Giovanni Francesco Mormanno (1513–49), spoilt by the addition of a storey in 1839. It now houses the university Faculty of Architecture.

The church of **Monteoliveto** (Atlas 2, 6), or Sant'Anna dei Lombardi, stands in the piazza of the same name, with a Baroque fountain in front.

Begun in 1411, the church contains a wealth of Renaissance sculpture, mostly undamaged when the church received a direct bomb hit in March 1944. The façade, shorn of its 18C additions, has been reconstructed in its original style. The vestibule contains the tomb (1627) of Domenico Fontana, architect to Pope Sixtus V. Inside, on either side of the entrance, are marble *altars, by Giovanni da Nola (right) and Girolamo Santacroce. On the south side, the first chapel (Cappella Mastrogiudice) contains an *Annunciation and other sculptures by Benedetto da Maiano (1489) and the tomb of Marino Curiale (1490), in a similar style. The third chapel has an altar attributed to Giovanni da Nola. Beyond the fifth chapel a passage leads to the Chapel of the Holy Sepulchre, with a terracotta *Pietà by Guido Mazzoni (1492); the eight life-size figures are said to be portraits of the artist's contemporaries. A corridor on the right leads to the Old Sacristy, which is frescoed by Vasari and contains fine intarsia stalls by Giovanni da Verona (1510).

The apse contains 16C stalls and the tombs of Alfonso II (died 1495), by Giovanni da Nola, and Guerello Origlia, founder of the church. The sixth chapel on the north side was designed by Giuliano da Maiano; it also contains some repainted 16C frescoes. In the fifth chapel are a St John the Baptist by Giovanni da Nola and a Pietà by Santacroce. The third chapel has a Flagellation (1576) in marble relief and the first chapel, an Ascension (on wood) by Riccardo Quartararo (c 1492). From here entrance is gained to the **Piccolomini Chapel**, with a charming *Nativity by Antonio Rossellino (c 1475). The beautiful tomb of Mary of Aragon (died 1470), daughter of Ferdinand I, was begun by Rossellino and finished by Benedetto da Maiano.

Calata Trinità Maggiore climbs to the right, past the baroque church and piazza of the Gesù Nuovo, described in Route 5B. At the far end of the square are the great church and Franciscan convent of *Santa Chiara (Atlas 2,6), built in 1310–28 for Sancia, queen of Robert the Wise, who here died a nun. The church was completely burnt out by incendiary bombs on 4 August 1943, when the magnificent Baroque interior of 1742–57 was destroyed and most of the large monuments wrecked. The reconstruction has preserved the original Provencal-Gothic austerity, a quality so foreign to Naples as to be all the more striking. The Gothic west porch was undamaged.

The aisleless **interior**, the largest in Naples, has a new open roof 45m high and tasteful modern glass in the lancet windows. Of the glorious series of Angevin royal monuments, the principal survivals are the lower portions of the tombs of Robert the Wise (died 1343), the work of the Florentine brothers Giovanni and Pacio Bertini (behind the high altar) and of Charles, Duke of Calabria, by Tino di Camaino and his followers (to the right). Also undamaged is the extraordinary monument (1399) to their daughter, Mary of Durazzo (to the left). Every chapel has some tomb or Gothic sculpture that merits inspection.

Free access is allowed to the conventual buildings of the ground floor (open daily 09.00–14.00); the entrance is reached by passing between the north side of the church and the detached campanile (not finished until 1647), passing through the first court and turning right. The parts seen include a particularly fine 18C Nativity crib and the huge 14C ***cloister**, transformed in 1742 by Domenico Antonio Vaccaro into a rustic garden adorned with majolica tiles and terracottas. The austere refectory of the friars, with a charming fountain in the centre, lies off the east side.

SPACCANAPOLI
Via Benedetto Croce marks the beginning of the Spaccanapoli, whose decayed medieval and Renaissance palaces make it the most characteristic of old

CONVENTO DI SANTA CHIARA

Neapolitan streets. Beyond the house (tablet) where the eminent philosopher spent his last years, is Piazza San Domenico, with the Baroque Guglia di San Domenico (1737), enclosed by 16C mansions. On the left rises **San Domenico Maggiore** (Atlas 2, 6), a noble Gothic church built in 1289–1324, rebuilt after damage by earthquake and fire (1465 and 1506) and much altered since. The church of the Aragonese nobility, its chief interest is in its ***Renaissance sculpture** and monuments, which include some of the finest expressions of the Tuscan manner in Naples.

The **interior**, with aisles and transepts, is 76m long. In the south aisle, on the right of the entrance, is the Cappella Saluzzo, with decorated Renaissance arches (1512–16) and the monument of Galeotto Carafa (1507–15), all the work of Romolo di Antonio da Settignano. The tomb of Archbishop Brancaccio (died 1341) in the second chapel is by a Tuscan follower of Tino di Camaino. The seventh chapel leads to the **Cappellone del Crocifisso**. Here is the little painting of the Crucifixion that spoke to St Thomas Aquinas when he was living in the adjacent

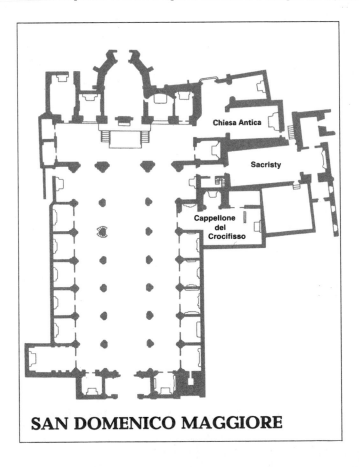

SAN DOMENICO MAGGIORE

monastery. To the left stands the fine tomb of Francesco Carafa (died 1470), by Tommaso Malvito, and behind is a side-chapel (1511) with other family tombs and frescoes by Bramantino. From the eighth chapel you enter the **sacristy** the ceiling of which hosts a brilliant fresco by Solimena. Above the presses are the coffins of ten princes of Aragon and 35 other illustrious persons, including the Marquis of Pescara (died 1525), hero of Pavia. The sacristan can be persuaded to show these.

The south transept contains the tomb of Galeazzo Pandone (1514), a fine work probably by a Tuscan artist; above, tomb slab of John of Durazzo (died 1335), by Tino di Camaino. Perhaps the best of the tombs in the **Chiesa Antica** (Sant' Angelo a Morfisa) is that of Tommaso Brancaccio by Jacopo della Pila (1492); note also that of Porzia, wife of Bernardino Rota, by Annibale Caccavello and Giovanni Domencio D'Auria (1559), in the vestibule. The beautiful altar and recessed seats at either side of the choir are adorned with inlaid marbles by Fanzago (1646); the paschal candlestick (1585) is supported by nine sculptured figures from a tomb by Tino di Camaino.

In the north transept, the first chapel contains a contemporary copy, by Andrea Vaccaro, of the Flagellation by Caravaggio (1607); the original, formerly on the opposite wall, is now at Capodimonte. Second chapel, Spinelli monument (1546) by Bernardino Del Moro. The north aisle chapels have many good 15–17C tombs, including that of G.B. Marino (died 1625), the poet, in the eighth, where the altar bears a lovely group by Giovanni da Nola. Fourth chapel, St John the Baptist by the same artist, with two paintings by Mattia Preti above. In the end chapel, Luca Giordano, Crowning of St Joseph.

The little church of **Sant'Angelo a Nilo** (Atlas 2, 6), on the south side of the square, has a fine Renaissance doorway. It contains the ***tomb of Cardinal Rinaldo Brancaccio**, the first work of Renaissance sculpture to be brought to Naples (1428). The architectural framework, the classical detail of which represents a clean break with Angevin Gothic aesthetic canons, is designed by Michelozzo; the relief of the Assumption is by Donatello. The tomb was executed in Pisa and sent by ship to Naples.

Keeping straight on, you pass (left) an antique statue of the Nile at the beginning of Via San Biagio ai Librai, in which are the former Palazzo Carafa, birthplace of Pope Paul IV, and (right; No. 121) the Palazzo Santangelo (1466), an elegant townhouse in the Tuscan style.

A little to the north, on the site of the Roman basilica (see Route 4A), is the Franciscan church of **San Lorenzo Maggiore** (Atlas 3, 3), begun by Charles I to commemorate the victory of Benevento and completed by his son. There is a fine door and doorway of 1325 in the 18C façade. Here on Easter Eve 1334 Boccaccio first saw Maria, natural daughter of Robert of Anjou, whom he immortalised as Fiammetta. Inside, the nave has been patiently restored to that Gothic simplicity retained unaltered by the transepts and the apse, which are by an unknown French architect of the late 13C. The ***apse** has nine radiating chapels; the high altar is by Giovanni da Nola. There are two chapels of inlaid coloured marbles by Cosimo Fanzago—the third chapel on the right, the Cappella Cacace, 1643-55, and the magnificent, bold Cappellone di Sant' Antonio, c 1638, in the left transept—and a number of good medieval tombs, notably that of Catherine of Austria (died 1323), first wife of Charles the Illustrious, possibly by Tino da Camaino. In the chapels are two large canvases by Mattia Preti: a Crucifixion with St Francis and Franciscan saints, and a Madonna and Child with St Clare and Franciscan saints. The monastic cloister, where Petrarch experienced the famous storm of 1345, is entered from outside by a 15C doorway to the left of the campanile (1507). The chapter house is supported on Roman columns.

San Lorenzo Maggiore stands on the corner of the Via dei Tribunali. Follow this street east (right) to the the Via del Duomo.

THE DUOMO

The *Duomo (San Gennaro; Atlas 3, 3), half a block to the north, was begun in the French Gothic style by Charles I in 1294 and finished by Robert the Wise in 1323. The façade, shattered by an earthquake, was rebuilt by Antonio Baboccio in 1407; only his portal remains, however, the rest being mainly from a Gothic revival design by Enrico Alvino (1877–1905). The remainder of the church was rebuilt after the earthquake of 1456.

Interior. The nave has an elaborate painted ceiling by Fabrizio Santafede (1621), supported on 16 piers incorporating over 100 antique columns. On the walls above the arches are 46 saints, painted by Luca Giordano and his pupils. Over the central doorway are (left to right) the tombs of Charles I of Anjou (died 1285), Clementina of Habsburg and her husband Charles Martel (King of Hungary and son of Charles II; died 1296), all moved from the choir in 1599, when the monuments were executed by Domenico Fontana.

In the south aisle, the **Capella di San Gennaro** or treasury, was built by Francesco Grimaldi in 1608–37 in fulfilment of a vow made by the citizens during the plague of 1526–29. It is closed by an immense grille of gilded bronze, based on a design by Cosimo Fanzago (1668). The luminous interior, faced with marble, has seven ornate altars, four of which have paintings by Domenichino (Domenico Zampieri), who began the frescoes; these were completed by Lanfranco after Domenichino had been hounded from the city. Above the altar on the right side is a large oil by Giuseppe Ribera. The balustrade of the main altar is by Cosimo Fanzago, with small doors by Onofrio d'Alessio. The sumptuous silver altar-front is by Francesco Solimena. In a tabernacle behind the altar are preserved the head of St Januarius (martyred at Pozzuoli), in a silver-gilt bust (1305), and two phials of his congealed blood, which tradition states first liquefied in the hands of the sainted Bishop Severus, when the saint's body was translated to Naples from Pozzuoli. The miracle has been documented since 1389 and repeats itself three times a year: on the first Saturday in May at Santa Chiara, and in the cathedral on 19 September and 16 December. The prosperity of the city is believed to depend on the speed of the liquefaction. The ceremony attracts an enormous crowd, and travellers who wish to be present should secure in advance a place near the altar by applying to the sacristan. The fifth chapel on this side of the church contains the tomb of Cardinal Carbone (died 1504) under a Gothic canopy.

Choir. The outer chapel on the right (Cappella Minutolo), paved with majolica, contains the tomb of Cardinal Arrigo Minutolo, by Roman marble-workers who came to Naples with Baboccio (1402–05), other tombs by a follower of Arnolfo di Cambio, and repainted 14C frescoes. The polyptych on the side altar is by Paolo di Giovanni Fei. The Cappella Tocco, adjoining, also Gothic, has frescoes (1312; restored). Below the high altar is the *Crypt of St Januarius or Cappella Carafa (apply to the sacristan if closed), by Tommaso Malvito (1497–1506), perhaps the masterpiece of Renaissance art in Naples. Entrance is gained through two fine bronze doors. Within, note the delicate ornamental carving; likewise the statue of the founder, Cardinal Oliviero Carafa, near the altar which covers the remains of the patron saint. In the north transept (right to left) are: the tomb of Innocent IV (died 1254), the opponent of Frederick II (*stravit inimicum Christi, colubrum*

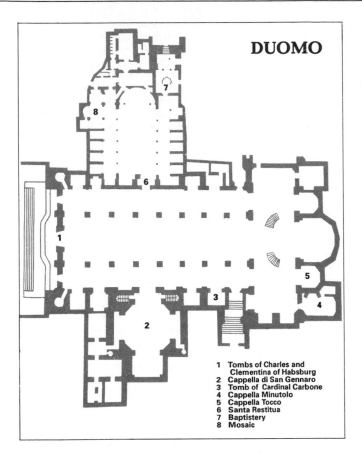

1 Tombs of Charles and
  Clementina of Habsburg
2 Cappella di San Gennaro
3 Tomb of Cardinal Carbone
4 Cappella Minutolo
5 Cappella Tocco
6 Santa Restitua
7 Baptistery
8 Mosaic

Federicum), a Cosmatesque work of 1315 partially reconstructed in the 16C; the tomb of Andrew of Hungary, murdered in 1345; and the cenotaph of Innocent XII (1703; buried in St Peter's, Rome).

Half-way along the north aisle is the entrance to the basilica of ***Santa Restituta**, founded in the 4C on the site of a temple of Apollo, rebuilt in the 14C and poorly restored in the 17C. The 27 columns may be relics of the old temple. The ceiling painting, showing the Arrival of Santa Restituta at Ischia, is by Luca Giordano. At the end of the right aisle is the **bapistery**, square with a small dome, the earliest example (late 5C) of this form of building in Italy; it preserves fragmentary 5C mosaics (described in Route 4A). The fifth and seventh chapels on the left contain beautiful 13C bas-reliefs in marble; in the sixth is a fine ***mosaic** (1322) of the Virgin Enthroned, by Lello da Roma, showing Byzantine influence.

North of the cathedral

From the cathedral, the Archbishop's Palace extends north to the church and convent of **Santa Maria Donnaregina** (Atlas 3, 3), often closed. Dating originally from the 8C, the church was reconstructed by Mary of Hungary, queen of Charles II of Anjou, following an earthquake of 1293. A second church, in the Baroque manner, was added when the nuns were incorporated in the Theatine Order. The 14C church is reached from the Vico Donnaregina. The presbytery, stripped in 1928–36 of later accretions, ends in a plain polygonal apse. To the right is the Cappella Loffredo, to the left the tomb of Queen Mary by Tino di Camaino and Gagliardo Primario (1326). In the nuns' choir, a rectangular gallery built over the west end of the church, are the celebrated **frescoes** by Pietro Cavallini and his pupils (begun 1308) representing the Passion, the legends of Sts Elizabeth of Hungary, Catherine and Agnes, and the Last Judgement. Another Cavallini fresco may be seen above the choir roof. The 17C church, elaborate but in good taste, has coloured marbles, majolica pavements and paintings by Luca Giordano.

Further north are the little chapel of **Santa Monica**, with a Gothic doorway and a fine tomb by Andrea da Firenze (1432), and, adjoining, ***San Giovanni a Carbonara** (Atlas 3, 3), built in 1343 and enlarged by King Ladislas at the beginning of the 15C. Within, facing the entrance, is the Cappella Maroballo, a richly decorated Renaissance monument with 15C statues. Behind the high altar towers the Tomb of Ladislas (died 1414), the masterpiece of Marco and Andrea da Firenze, a three-storeyed composition of trefoil arches, statues and pinnacles. Beneath this, entrance is gained to the Cappella Caracciolo del Sole (1427), with Andrea da Firenze's unfinished tomb of Ser Gianni Caracciolo, steward of Joan II, stabbed at the Castel Capuano in 1432. On the walls are 15C frescoes by Leonardo da Besozzo and Perrinetto da Benevento; the tiled floor dates from 1440. To the north of the sanctuary is the marble-lined Cappella Caracciolodi Vico, (1517), attributed to Tommaso Malvita; one of the more remarkable early 16C designs in Naples, this contains tombs and statues by Giovanni da Nola. In the sacristy is the tomb of Scipione Somma (died 1553).

Return to the Via dei Tribunali and continue east. The street ends on the west side of the **Castel Capuano** (Atlas 3, 3) also called La Vicaria. Begun by William I and finished by Frederick II, this was the residence of the Hohenstaufen and of some of the Angevin kings. Here, in 1432, Sergianni Caracciolo, lover of Joan II, was murdered. Much altered, the castle has been used as the Court of Justice since 1540.

Across the square to the north-east, near the little Renaissance church of Santa Caterina a Formiello, rises the beautiful ***Porta Capuana**, between two mighty Aragonese towers. The extant exterior decoration of this former city gate was begun by Giuliano da Maiano and completed, after his death in 1490, by Luca Fancelli. Smaller and more delicate than the triumphal arch of Alfonso at the Castel Nuovo, it is a rare and particularly fine application of the late 15C Florentine style in sculpture to a town gate. The only other project of the kind undertaken during the Renaissance was Agostino di Duccio's gate at Perugia, dating from around 1475. The open space in front of the gate is used as a market-place and is always animated and colourful.

C.   The Sorrentine Peninsula and Salerno

*This route focuses on **Sorrento**, **Amalfi**, and **Salerno**, the three great maritime republics that once vied with Venice, Genoa and Pisa for control of trade routes in the Mediterranean. From Colli San Pietro, above Sorrento, to Vietri, on the outskirts of Salerno, it follows the rugged, lofty **Costiera Amalfitana**, one of the more scenic roads in Italy. Deluxe coaches (SITA) make a circular tour of the Sorrentine Peninsula, closely following the itinerary described here. They leave from Piazza Municipio, in Naples, in the early morning, returning in the evening. For travellers without their own transport, this route may conveniently be combined with Capri (Route 6B); the night is spent at Sorrento, with departure next day by ferry or hydrofoil to Capri, returning from there to Naples. This journey may also be made in reverse, spending the night on Capri.*

ROAD 104km. Autostrada A3/E45, Highways 145 and 163 and local roads. 32km Castellammare di Stabia—18km Sorrento—17km Positano—12km Amalfi—25km Salerno.

RAILWAY to Sorrento, 44km, hourly by Circumvesuviana railway in 60–80 min; frequent buses run between towns on the peninsula.

SEA. Hydrofoils run several times daily from Mergellina to Sorrento in 30min, from where there are both hydrofoil and ferry connections to Capri (cf. below).

HOTELS EN ROUTE: Vico Equense, ****Capo la Gala, tel. 081 801 5758, fax 081 879 8747; Sorrento, ***Bellevue Syrene, Piazza della Vittoria 5, tel. 081 878 1024, fax 081 878 3963; Massa Lubse, ****Delfino, 081 878 9261, fax 081 808 9074; Positano****Le Sirenuse, tel. 089 875066, fax 081 811798; ****Le Agavi, località Belvedere Fornillo, tel. 089 875733, fax 089 770186; *****San Pietro, tel. 089 875455, fax 089 770072; Amalfi, *****Santa Caterina, tel. 089 871012, fax 089 871351; Rllo, *****Palumbo, tel. 089 857244, fax 089 858133; ***Villa Maria, tel. 089 857255, fax 089 857071.Youth Hostel in Sorrento, Via Capasso 5, tel. 081 878 1783, fax 081 878 1783.

RESTAURANTS EN ROUTE: Sant'Agata sui Due Golfi, ****Don Alfonso 1890 (with rooms), tel. 081 878 0026, fax 081 533 0226; Amalfi, **La Caravella, tel. 089 871070.

Towards Sorrento

Leave Naples by the quay, past the graving dock and the Granili, a huge red building 596m long, built in 1779 and now abandoned, and go through the dingy industrial suburb of San Giovanni a Teduccio (Route 6A) to Autostrada A3/E45.

Castellammare di Stabia, a modern town (68,000 inhab.) with an arsenal, lies on the south-east shore of the Gulf of Naples. It is visited as a climatic resort.

History

The ancient city of *Stabiae*, north-east of the present town, was destroyed by Sulla in 89 BC but was afterwards rebuilt, only to be swallowed up by the eruption of AD 79. On the beach at Stabiae the elder Pliny met his death. The site was repopulated and takes its name from a 9C castle, which Charles I of Anjou restored when he built the walls. In 1738 some ancient villas were brought to light by excavation, and further Roman remains are visible on the neighbouring hill of Varano.

■ **Information.** AA, Piazza Matteotti 34, tel. 081 8711334.

In the centre of the town, the shady park of the Villa Comunale gives a wide vista over the Gulf. To the left lies Piazza del Municipio with the Observatory, the **Duomo** (1587, much altered), and the **Municipio**, formerly Palazzo Farnese. Further south-west are the harbour with the yards of the **Arsenal** (1783), where some of the more powerful Italian warships have been built, and the **Terme Stabiane**, a spa. On a hill to the left is the **Castle,** enlarged by the Swabians (1197) and again by Charles I of Anjou (1266). A pleasant walk may be taken to (2km) the Villa Quisisana (now a hotel), a royal dwelling from 1310 to 1860, where the park commands a fine panorama.

Excursions

The ascent of **Monte Faito** (1100m) by cable railway, from the Circumvesuviana station, takes roughly 8 minutes, services connecting with the trains. The road (15km of switchback bends) climbs round the Villa Quisisana. The Belvedere di Monte Faito commands an extensive view; hence a track of 7km offers a magnificent circular walk along the ridge and round a fine wood. The ascent of **Monte Sant' Angelo** (1443m), the highest of the Monti Lattari, may be seen (guide desirable) either from Monte Faito or from Pimonte (see below); it takes 4–5 hours, the descent almost as much. The *panorama comprehends the whole of the Gulfs of Salerno and Naples, and northwards extends to the Gulf of Gaeta.

Agerola and **Amalfi**, 32km, can be reached by a beautiful road across the Altopiano di Agerola. You climb from the north end of the town to (4km) Gragnano, known for its excellent macaroni and wine. The road passes (5km) Pimonte, affording good views of the Monti Lattari beneath whose crest it passes in a tunnel, c 1km long, to emerge at (9km) Agerola, a village consisting of several 'frazioni' or hamlets, all frequented by summer visitors. From here the road descends the zigzag Vallone di Furore, with vistas over the Gulf of Salerno, to join the Costiera Amalfitana road near Vettica Minore, and then on to (2km) Amalfi, see Rte 8A.

A turning on the left at the beginning of the road for Gragnano (see above) leads to località San Marco, on the plain of Varano, where stand the extensive remains of two **Roman villas** (open daily, 09.00–one hour before sunset), both with remnants of fresco decoration, unfortunately damaged in the 1980 earthquake. The **Antiquarium di Stabiae** (Via Marco Mario 2, open daily 09.00–18.00) contains objects from the Bronze Age to the Middle Ages, and particularly material (frescoes, pavement fragments, Greek, Samnite, Italiot and Roman vases) from the excavations.

Beyond Castellammare the road hugs the shore, passing the pleasant beaches of Pozzano and Scraio, both with sulphur springs.

8km **Vico Equense** (90m, 19,000 inhab.) is the ancient *Aequana*, destroyed by the Goths and restored by Charles II of Anjou.

■ **Information**. AA, Via San Ciro 15; tel. 081 8798343, fax 081 8799351.

The 14C ex-cathedral church of San Salvatore contains the tomb of Gaetano Filangieri (died 1788), the jurist. In Corso Umberto is a small Museo Comunale (open Tue–Sun 09.00–13.00, 16.00–19.00) containing material from a necropolis of the 7–5C BC discovered beneath the present town. The Angevin Castello Giusso, rebuilt in 1604, is now private. Below the sheer cliff is a pleasant beach. The road rounds the head of the pretty valley behind Seiano; beyond, it turns the promontory of Punta di Scutolo, and you get a first view of the magical *Piano di Sorrento. This famous plain, with a general level of 80–100m above sea level, is a huge garden of perennial spring, covered with orange, lemon, and olive groves, interspersed with fig trees, pomegranates and aloes. The temperature is fresh and cool even in summer. It was a favourite resort of the emperors and other wealthy Romans, and its praises have been sung by numerous poets. The villages are rather closely crowded, but an indefinable spirit of peace broods over them all.

5km **Meta** (111m; 8000 inhab.), a pretty village, is connected by a lift with its two small harbours. The church of Santa Maria del Lauro is believed to occupy the site of a temple of Minerva. The road to Positano, Amalfi, and Salerno here diverges to the south. Our road winds across the plain, crosses some deep-set torrents and touches the villages of Carotto and Pozzopiano which, together with Meta, make up the comune of Piano di Sorrento. 3km Sant'Agnello (see below) is now almost an extension of Sorrento, which you enter by the Corso Italia; the views are restricted by the walls of the gardens and orange groves.

SORRENTO
2km Sorrento (18,000 inhab.), *Surriento* in Neapolitan dialect, surnamed *La Gentile*, is perched on a tufa rock rising 50m above the sea and bounded on three sides by deep ravines. Situated in a district of singular beauty, near the middle of the north side of the famous peninsula which bears its name, it is an enchanting place at all seasons. The district is noted for oranges, lemons, and nuts, and the town for inlaid woodwork (intarsio), lace and straw-plaiting. It is the seat of an archbishop.

History
In antiquity *Surrentum*, of Pelasgic, Etruscan, or Greek origin, was never a town of importance, but the Romans frequented it for the sake of its beauty of scenery and climate. In 1892 it fought a naval battle with Amalfi in defence of its rights as an independent republic. Its most illustrious son is Torquato Tasso (1544–95), the poet. In the 19C Sorrento was a favourite winter residence of foreigners; here in1867 Ibsen finished *Peer Gynt*, and here, some ten years later, Wagner and Nietzsche had their famous quarrel.

■ **Arrival by sea**. From the landing-place Via Luigi De Maio winds up to Piazza Tasso, also reached by a steep flight of steps.

■ **Ferries** daily to Capri (45min).

■ **Hydrofoils** daily to Naples (30min) and Capri (20min–1hr).

■ **Information:** AA, Via L. De Maio 35; tel. 081 8074033, fax 081 8773397.

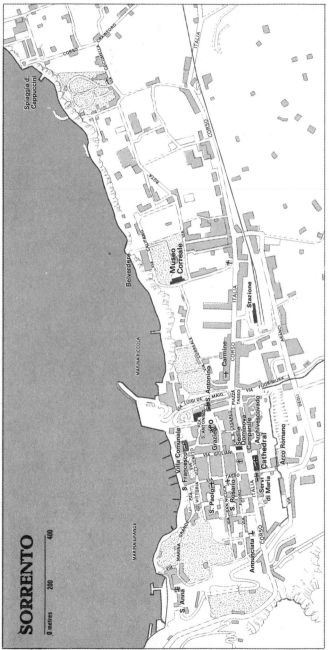

SORRENTO

0 metres   200   400

Spiaggia d. Cappuccini

CORSO

VIA COCUMELLA CRAWFORD

ITALIA

CORSO

TIOTA

VIA CHIPANO

Belvedere

VIA CHIPANO

Museo Correale

Stazione

CORREALE

CORSO

ITALIA

DEGLI ARANCI

MARINA PICCOLA

VIA. CORREALE

Carmine

VIA. LUIGI DE MAIO.

S. Antonino

S. ANTONINO

VIA A. CESAREO

PIAZZA TASSO

VIA FUORIMURA

VIA. GIULIANI

Grazie PO

Sedile Dominova

Campanile

Cathedral

Archivescovado

Arco Romano

VIA

DEGLI

Villa Comunale

S. Francesco

PZA. VENETO

S. Paolo

S. Rosario

Servi di Maria

ITALIA

TASSO

VIA. FUORO

DE VITTORIA

VIA. SAN NICOLA

CORSO

Annunciata

MARINA GRANDE

VIA. MARINA GRANDE

S. Anna
S. Francesco

■ **Festivities:** Sorrento is the site of an annual regatta (15 August), a film festival, and international tennis competitions. The Good Friday procession is particularly colourful.

The long Corso Italia leads past the railway station and Santa Maria del Carmine to Piazza Tasso, the centre of the town. Embellished with a monument to Torquato Tasso by Gennaro Cali (1870), it commands a view of the Marina Piccola, 48m below. The corso continues to the west, passing the campanile, with its four columns and antique ornamentation. The vault space beneath the Arcivescovado, leading to the neglected palazzi of Via Pietà, was once the scene of council meetings. The **Duomo** has a marble side-portal of 1479; the façade was rebuilt in 1913–24. Inside, the first chapel on the right has reliefs of the 14C or 15C. In the nave are the archbishop's throne (1573), with a marble canopy, and a pulpit of the same year, below which is a Virgin with Saints John the Baptist and John the Evangelist, a painting on panel by Silvestro Buono of Naples (1582). The stalls show typical local inlay work.

> Behind the cathedral is the south wall of the town, rebuilt in 1558–61, after a sack by pirates, on the line of the Greek or Roman wall; an arch of the Roman gate survives in Via Parsano.

Via Tasso, opposite the cathedral, leads towards the sea. In Via San Nicola (left, No. 29) is the Casa Fasulo (formerly Sersale), marked by a tablet as the house of Cornelia Tasso, who here received her illustrious but fugitive brother in 1577. In Via San Cesareo (right) is the **Sedile Dominova**, a loggia of the 15C with capitals in an archaic style. Beyond the Baroque church of San Paolo is Piazza della Vittoria, which overlooks the sea. Below, on the shore, are remains of a Roman nymphaeum. To the left a road descends, the last part in steps, through an arch (Greek ?) to the Marina Grande. Turning right you pass the Tramontano Hotel, which incorporates the remaining room of the house in which Tasso was born, and come to the church of San Francesco d'Assisi. The annexed convent, now a school of art, preserves a 14C cloister. Just behind the church is the little *Villa Comunale (view). Continue to Piazza Sant Antonino, with the church and statue of Sant'Antonino Abate (died 830), the patron saint of Sorrento, where he found refuge from the Lombards. In the little streets near the church of the Grazie are some attractive early 15C doorways. At the piazza join the winding Via Luigi De Maio on its way from the Marina Piccola to Piazza Tasso.

From the east side of Piazza Tasso, Via Correale leads to the **Museo Correale di Terranova** (open daily 09.00–12.30, 15.00–17.00) a charming old villa containing an important collection of Campanian decorative art of the 15C to the 18C, including furniture, intarsio and intaglio work, and porcelain; archaeological finds from the Sorrentine peninsula; medieval sculpture and a small library of Tasso's works. Among the pictures is a unique collection of works of the Posillipo School, in particular by Giacinto Gigante. The belvedere commands a superb view. On the coast 1.5km further east, near the Convento dei Cappuccini, is the Villa Crawford the residence of the novelist F. Marion Crawford, who died here in 1909. The villa stands above Sant'Agnello beach.

The neighbourhood of Sorrento affords opportunity for many excursions, a few of which are described below. Pleasant trips by small boats may also be made to the Grotte delle Sirene, the Grotta Bagno della Regina Giovanna (at the Villa Pollio Felix, see below), and other points, many showing vestiges of classical buildings.

Excursions

The **Piccolo Sant' Angelo**, a hill (440m) 1hr 15min south-east of Piazza Tasso, commands wide views of the plain of Sorrento and the gulfs of Naples and Salerno.

The walk (1hr 20min) to the Deserto and Sant'Agata sui Due Golfi combines breathtaking panoramas with local charm. Follow the Strada di Capodimonte, diverging to the left from the road to Massa Lubrense. At the second fork keep to the left. (To the right is Capodimonte, a fine viewpoint.) Beyond Priora, ascend to the left and then turn to the right. The *Deserto (454m) is a suppressed convent, commanding a wonderful view of Capri and the two bays. Descend from here on the south-east to (15min) **Sant'Agata sui Due Golfi** (390m), a favourite summer resort and an excellent centre for excursions. The church has a Florentine altar of inlaid marble, executed in the 16C and moved here in 1845 from the Girolamini in Naples. The road continues, offering a series of *views over the peninsula and the sea, to Positano.

Massa Lubrense is reached by a road running at some distance from the sea but so high up as to afford an uninterrupted series of delightful views. On leaving Sorrento cross the gorge of the Conca. A little further on the Strada di Capodimonte diverges on the left (see above). At Capo di Sorrento a track on the right descends to (7 min) the seaward extremity of the cape, with the ruins of the Roman Villa of Pollio Felix, worth visiting for the view alone. Next is Villazzano, at the landward end of the Punta di Massa; the *view of the Capo di Sorrento with its dense groves of olives is more extensive from the Telegrafo (239m), a hill 25 min to the left. On rounding the point you can see Capri and the Faraglioni.

The road turns inland and reaches **Massa Lubrense**, a village in an exquisite setting, deriving its name from Baebius Massa, a freedman of Nero, and the church of Madonna della Lobra. From the Villa Rossi, Murat watched the French assault on Capri in 1808. The lovely descent to the little harbour follows Via Palma, Via Roma (right) and Via Marina, passing the church of the Madonna della Lobra (1528), near the supposed site of the legendary temple of the Sirens. The fishing hamlet of Marina di Massa possesses remains of a Roman villa. Beyond Massa Lubrense the road passes below the Annunziata and the remains of a castello of 1389, leaves the attractive road to Termini on the right, and ascends to (4km) Sant'Agata (see above). The by road to Termini continues as a steep path (well-preserved sections of Roman paving) to the **Punta della Campanella** (47m; 1hr 30min. from Massa Lubrense), the *Promontorium Minervae* of the Romans, which takes its modern name from the warning bell of a tower built in 1335 by Robert of Anjou. The lighthouse commands an enchanting view of Capri.

THE AMALFI COAST

Return to Meta. Here you diverge from the Sorrento road, climbing abruptly over the spine of the Sorrento peninsula, to Colli di San Pietro (305m), with incomparable views in both directions, and drop steeply to the *Costiera Amalfitana. The road still remains high above the sea.

17km **Positano** (4000 inhab.) is a favourite resort, where the characteristic square white houses and luxuriant gardens descend in steep steps to the sea.

■ **Information.** AA, Via Saracino 2; tel. 089 875067, fax 089 875760.

■ **Special Events:** Sbarco dei Saraceni, when a mock landing from the sea is defeated amid fireworks, etc.

The road crosses the upper part of the town. Further on, the terrace behind the solitary little church of San Pietro offers an admirable viewpoint. Beyond Vettica Maggiore the road passes through Capo Sottile by the first of a series of short tunnels. Praiano, on the hillside above, has a good church. Delightfully situated on the shore is Marina di Praia, a fishing village with a fine sandy beach. On the steep slopes above the road lie the scattered hamlets of Penna and Furore, and between two tunnels a viaduct crosses the *Vallone di Furore, one of the more picturesque gorges in Southern Italy. Narrow and fjord-like, it runs inland between imposing rocky walls that rise almost vertically below the plateau of Agerola.

The road passes close above (8km) the **Grotta di Smeraldo**. The cavern may be reached by steps or by lift; a visit occupies c 1hr (open 09.30–17.00, winter 10.00–16.00). Its name derives from the apparent colour of the interior, which glows with a remarkable green light. It was dry before the sea eroded the coast. Stalagmites may now be seen under the water, and columns have formed where stalagmites have joined to stalactites.

The highway cuts across the Capo di Conca, beyond which it offers a vista of the Amalfi coastline stretching to the Capo d'Orso. Further on you pass Tovere and Vettica Minore, two villages amid vineyards and lemon and orange groves; between them a tortuous road winds inland to Agerola (see Route 2A).

AMALFI
6km Amalfi (6000 inhab.) nestles in the ravine of the Valle dei Mulini. Its churches, towers and arcaded houses, grouped together with attractive irregularity, rise above a small harbour, and are backed by precipices of wild magnificence.

History
Though known as early as the 4C AD, the city did not attain any degree of prosperity until the mid-sixth century, in the time of the Byzantine Empire. During the early Middle Ages it developed an important Oriental trade, its ships visiting the most remote seas. It has been the seat of an archbishop since 987 and its maritime republic once vied with Genoa and Pisa. Governed by its own Doges, it attained great wealth and a population of 70,000, but it was subdued by King Roger of Naples in 1131 and soon after twice captured by the Pisans (1135 and 1137). Much of the ancient town was destroyed by the sea in 1343. Its maritime laws, the *Tavole Amalfitane*, remained effective till 1570; and merchants from Amalfi maintained in Jerusalem the Hospital of St John the Almoner, the nucleus upon which the Crusader Knights built the Order of St John after 1099. Webster's *Duchess of Malfi* is based on the life of the hapless Joanna of Aragon (c 1478–1513), consort of Alfonso Piccolomini, Duke of Amalfi.

■ **Information:** AA, Corso Roma 19; tel. 089 871107, fax 089 872619.

From Piazza Flavio Gioia, on the waterfront, near which are the remains of the 13C republican arsenal (now used for temporary exhibitions), the Via del Duomo leads to the Piazza del Duomo, with a fountain of 1760. On the east side of the piazza stands the 19C *Duomo (Sant'Andrea), the richly coloured façade of which (1203) is approached by a lofty flight of steps. Both façade and steps were restored to their original Lombard-Norman style by Enrico Alvano, Luigi Della Corte, and Guglielmo Raimondi in 1875–94. The mosaic at the top is by Domenico Morelli.

The campanile, built in 1276 and restored in 1768, is partly Romanesque and partly Saracenic in form.

The imposing porch is divided by columns into two. The magnificent bronze *doors, with cross and saints in inlaid silver, were commissioned by the head of the Amalfitan colony in Constantinople and made there before 1066 by Simeon of Syria. The frescoes at either side of the entrance, executed in 1929 to a design by Domenico Morelli, add little to the decorative integrity of the whole.

The **interior**, thoroughly restored, consists of nave (fine ceiling), aisles, and chapels. From the fourth chapel on the right a flight of steps descends to the crypt, constructed in 1253 and restored in 1719 (knock on the door at the left of the gate for entrance). It contains an altar by Domenico Fontana and a statue of St Andrew by Michelangelo Naccherino. Below the altar rests the body of St Andrew the Apostle, brought here from Constantinople in 1208. At the entrance to the choir are two large columns from Paestum and two candelabra adorned with mosaic. Ancient ambones, also with mosaics, flank the high altar.

The 13C **cloister** (Chiostro del Paradiso; entered from the portico, open daily 09.00–16.00), with interlaced arches of marked Saracenic appearance, was once the burial-place of famous citizens. It is now a museum of architectural fragments.

Seaward of the duomo lies the Municipio, where the *Tavole Amalfitane* (see above) are displayed (in the Museo Civico, open daily 09.00–20.00; winter, Mon–Fri 09.00–14.00). From the main road west of the town (see above) you may climb the long flight of steps mounting to the former **Convento dei Cappuccini**, now a hotel. It was founded in 1212 and was originally a Cistercian house. The cloisters are picturesque, and the beautiful flower-screened verandah commands a justly famous *view.

For walkers
A pleasant walk may be taken in the cool **Valle dei Mulini**, with its water-operated paper mills and tall rocky sides. The favourite point is the Mulino Rovinato, c 1hr from the piazza. In the Palazzo Pagliara is a small **Museo della Carta** (open daily except Mon and Fri 08.00–13.00) with engravings, manuscripts, printed books, bills and posters, and tools and machines for making paper.

The Salerno road leaves Amalfi along the shore, passing between the Albergo Luna, in another convent with a good 12C cloister, and a 16C tower.

1km **Atrani** rises in an amphitheatre at the end of the valley of the Dragone. The road bridges the gorge between the village and the sea. From the bridge you may descend, passing under the arches, to the little piazza, with **San Salvatore de' Bireto**, a church of 940 restored in 1810. Its name refers to the capping of the Doges of the Republic of Amalfi; the handsome bronze doors, executed at Constantinople in 1086, resemble those of Amalfi. The church of **La Maddalena**, beyond the bridge, has an elegant campanile and a painting of the Incredulity of St Thomas by Andrea da Salerno.

RAVELLO
The road to (5km) Ravello diverges to the left beyond Atrani and ascends in windings, affording beautiful views of the Dragone valley.

Walkers may shorten the distance a little (making the climb in just over 1hr) by taking a mountain path from Atrani, but this is much less open than the road. Ascend the steps to the right of the church of La Maddalena, turn to the right, pass another church, follow a vaulted lane and climb a long flight of steps. Then enter the Dragone valley and join the road, profiting by various short cuts. At a fork, turn to the right around the small church of Santa Maria a Gradillo: here you get your first view of Ravello. Passing below the ruined castle, you then reach the piazza.

This isolated and markedly individual little town (350m, 2000 inhab.) in a situation of extreme charm, is the see of a bishop and one of the more famous beauty spots in Italy. The contrast between its bold situation and its seductive and richly coloured setting, between the rusticity of its hilly streets and the delicate perfection of its works of art, the gaiety of its gardens and the melancholy of its Norman-Saracenic architecture, is extraordinarily impressive.

History
Built in the 9C under the rule of Amalfi, Ravello became independent in 1086 and maintained its liberty until 1813. It enjoyed great prosperity in the 13C, and its wealthy citizens, forming relations with Sicily and the East, introduced the Norman-Saracenic style of architecture to their native town. Characteristic of the doorways of Ravello are the antique colonnettes, at the side, which give them the appearance of the Graeco-Roman prothyrum.

■ **Information**. Piazza Duomo 10; tel. 089 857096, fax 089 857977.

■ **Special events:** music festival in June–July.

The **Duomo** (San Pantaleone), built in 1086, was remodelled in 1786. The façade has three portals and four ancient columns. The fine bronze *doors in the middle (removed for restoration, 1994), by Barisano da Trani (1179), are divided into 54 panels with saints, scenes of the Passion, and inscriptions. They are protected on the inside as well as the outside by a double set of wooden doors, and are shown on request by the sacristan. In the nave (right) is a magnificent marble *ambo, borne by six spiral columns and adorned with mosaics. It was executed in 1272 by Niccolò da Foggia at the order of Niccolò Rufolo, husband of Sigilgaita della Marra. The beautiful *bust of a woman, which was above the door of the stairs, is now in the museum in the crypt. A smaller ambo on the left, of earlier date (c 1131), has a mosaic of Jonah and the whale. In the south aisle are two sculpted sarcophagi and in the choir, the bishop's throne (decorated with mosaics) and two paschal candlesticks. The largest chapel, on the left, is dedicated to St Pantaleon, whose blood (preserved here) liquefies on 19 May and 27 August. The sacristy hosts a Byzantine Madonna and two pictures by Andrea da Salerno, and the crypt contains a small collection of 12C and 13C sculpture and 13C and 14C goldsmiths' work.

Pass to the south side of the cathedral, noting its fine 13C campanile, and enter the grounds of the *Villa Rufolo (open daily, Jun–Sep 09.30–13.00, 15.00–19.00; Oct–May 09.30–13.00, 14.00–17.00), begun in the 11C and occupied in turn by Pope Adrian IV (1156; Nicholas Breakspeare), Charles of Anjou and Robert the Wise. An ensemble of Norman-Saracenic buildings, partly in ruins, the palace is enhanced by tropical gardens; here Wagner found his inspiration for the magic garden of Klingsor in *Parsifal*. The arcading of the tiny cloister-like court is striking. The terrace (339m) commands an extensive *panorama. The palace houses a small collection of antiquities and fragments from the cathedral.

Ascend to the right by the street behind the cathedral, past the old bishop's palace, to reach the Palazzo D'Afflitto with its bizarre portal (both these buildings are now hotels). Opposite is **San Giovanni del Toro**, a 12C church with a characteristic low campanile. Within, the nave is borne by ancient columns. The ambo, resembling those in the cathedral, has mosaics, tiles of Persian majolica (1175) and ancient frescoes. A chapel off the south aisle contains a statue of St Catherine, in stucco.

A little further on is a small piazza with a Norman fountain, enjoying a view of Scala (see below). From here you may return by the long Strada Vescovado, which passes the 12C church of Santa Maria a Gradillo and continues south from the cathedral, passing between Palazzo Rufolo and the post office. Beyond the churches of Sant'Antonio, with a Romanesque cloister, and Santa Chiara, is **Palazzo Cimbrone**, with an open vaulted terrace-room (reconstructed). At the end of a straight avenue through the lush gardens (open daily 09.00–dusk) is the *Belvedere Cimbrone, the most advanced point of the ridge on which Ravello lies. The open view of Atrani and the gulf is unrivalled.

Another walk

A short walk (1.5km) may be taken round the head of the valley to Scala (374m), once a populous, flourishing town, but ruined by pestilence and the rivalry of Ravello. The **Cattedrale** has a handsome Romanesque portal and contains a mosaic ambo, a mitre with enamels of the 13C, and a spacious crypt. The nearby villages of Santa Caterina, Campidoglio and Minuto all have interesting medieval churches, though that of Campidoglio has been extensively altered by Baroque additions. From Minuto walkers may cross via Pontone into the Valle dei Mulini (see above) to reach Amalfi.

Ravello to Salerno

From Atrani the road skirts the shore to (3km) **Minori**, a delightful village at the mouth of the Reginuolo. To the left of the road lie the remains of a 1C **Roman villa** (custodian, opens daily 09.00–16.00), excavated in 1954. The large peristyle, the nymphaeum and some vaulted rooms with frescoes are worthy of inspection. The antiquarium houses paintings found in the ruins of other Roman villas destroyed by the eruption of Vesuvius in AD 79, a lararium from Scafati, assorted pottery and architectural fragments.

At (2km) **Maiori**, a fortified village with a sandy beach at the mouth of the valley of Tramonti, a road leads inland across the Valico di Chiunzi (685m) to Angri (Route). The church of Santa Maria a Mare has a majolica-tiled cupola and an English alabaster altar-frontal.

■ **Information**. AA, Viale Capone; tel. 089 877452.

The scenery becomes wilder as the road twists away from the sea and back again round the Capo d'Orso, passing through a rocky defile. Beyond Capo Tomolo it makes a long detour round the savage valley of Erchie, affording the first glimpse of Salerno. The road crosses the wooded Vallone di San Nicola. From (10km) Cetara, a colourful fishing village, the road runs at so high a level that it commands the whole gulf as far as Punta Licosa, with a glorious prospect of Vietri and Salerno and enters (6km) **Vietri a Mare** by a lofty bridge. The **Museo della Ceramica**

Vietrese, in the Villa Guariglia (open Mon–Fri 09.00–13.00) contains a collection of local ceramics from the 18C to the 1930s. Beyond Vietri begins the approach, through scattered suburbs, to Salerno.

SALERNO

5km Salerno, a provincial capital of 151,000 inhabitants, is beautifully situated on the gulf to which it gives its name (the Roman *Paestanus Sinus*). The old quarter inland has narrow streets, and along the shore a modern quarter extends behind an excellent beach.

History

Salerno succeeds the ancient *Salernum*, which became a Roman colony in 194 BC. In the early Middle Ages it was subject to Benevento, but from the 9–11C it was practically an independent Lombard principality until it fell to the Normans in 1076. Pope Gregory VII, rescued by Robert Guiscard from the Castel Sant'Angelo, took refuge in Salerno, where he died in 1085. The city was destroyed by Henry VI in 1198, and soon after it became part of the Kingdom of Naples. The famous school of medicine of this *Civitas Hippocratica* reached its zenith in the 12C, before the rise of Arabic medicine. Petrarch calls it *Fons Medicinae*, and St Thomas Aquinas mentions it as being as pre-eminent in medicine as Paris was in science and Bologna in law. Salerno was the native town of John of Procida (1225–1302), a prominent figure in the Sicilian Vespers, and of Andrea Sabbatini da Salerno (1480–1545), the painter. Alfonso Gatto, the poet, was born here in 1909. In the Second World War, Salerno was the site of the Allied invasion of the Southern Italian mainland. Much of the town was destroyed in the heavy fighting.

■ **Information:** EPT, Via Velia 15; tel. 089 224322, fax 089 251844 (branch office in Piazza Ferrovia). AA, Piazza Amendola 8 (tel. 089 224744, fax 089 252576).

■ **Buses** to destinations throughout the province. From Piazza della Concordia to Paestum and the Costiera Amalfitana; to Pompeii from Piazza Ferrovia.

■ **Boats** to the Costiera Amalfitana (from the Molo Mattuccio Salernitano) and hydrofoils to Capri and Ischia (Molo Manfredi), daily Jun–Sep.

■ **Post office:** Corso Garibaldi.

Near the waterfront, the main Naples access road divides into two long streets that run parallel to the sea, passing left and right of the Teatro Verdi and the Villa Communale. 400m further on, the Via del Duomo leads into the old town, between the churches of Sant'Agostino (right) and San Giorgio (left) both of which contain paintings by Andrea da Salerno, and to the Via dei Mercanti (see below).

Further on is the ***Cattedrale** (San Matteo), founded in 845 and rebuilt by Robert Guiscard in 1076–85. The Porta dei Leoni, a fine Romanesque doorway, admits to the atrium, the 28 columns of which were brought from Paestum. To the right, the detached 12C campanile (55m) rises above the colonnade. The central doorway, decorated in 1077, has a bronze door with crosses and figures of niello work, made at Constantinople in 1099. In the nave are two spendid ***ambones** (1173–81) and a paschal candlestick, resembling in their mixture of Saracen and

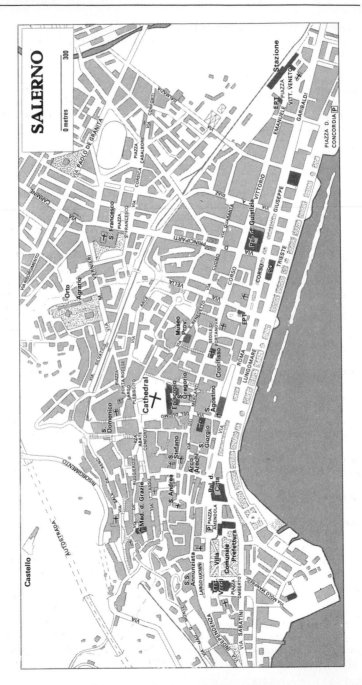

Byzantine styles those in Palermo. The north aisle contains the tombs of Margaret of Anjou (died 1412), wife of Charles III of Durazzo, by Baboccio da Piperno, and of Bishop Nicolò Piscicelli (died 1471), by Iacopo della Pila.

The **Museo Diocesano** (Palazzo Arcivescovile, Via Monsignor Monterisi 2; open daily 09.00–13.00, 16.00–19.00), contains a large *paliotto, or altar-front, of 54 ivory panels (late 11C), the largest known work of its kind. The high altar is decorated with 12C mosaic. The east end terminates in three apsidal chapels; in that to the left is a Pietà by Andrea da Salerno; that on the right contains, beneath a mosaic vault, the tomb of Gregory VII, the great Hildebrand, who died in exile in 1085 while the guest of Robert Guiscard. To the left Archbishop Carafa is buried in a pagan sarcophagus showing a relief of the Rape of Proserpine. Other interesting tombs should be noticed at the end of the south aisle. The little door, beside a curious relief of a ship unloading, leads to the crypt, in which is preserved the body of St Matthew, brought here in 954.

Behind the cathedral, Via San Benedetto leads past the **Museo Archeologico Provinciale e Galleria Provinciale d'Arte** (Via San Benedetto 28; open daily 09.00–13.00, 17.00-19.30), where a variety of finds from excavations in the surrounding province may be seen. The museum occupies two floors of the Lombard Romanesque convent of San Benedetto and contains medieval coins, paintings and a folklore section, as well as antiquities.

The Via dei Mercanti, typical of the old quarter, leads west from the Via del Duomo to the Arco Arechi, part of an 8C building, beneath which the road continues to the Fontana dei Delfini. From here a street to the right leads to the church of Sant'Andrea, with a small 12C belfry. It is worthwhile, for the sake of the *view, to ascend behind the town to the old **Castello degli Arechi** (273m), a Byzantine, Lombard and Norman fortress whose recently restored interior has been reopened to the public (open daily 09.00–13.00, 15.00–1hr before sunset).

East of Salerno

To the east are the unpopulated **Monti Picentini**, rising to 1790m, which derive their name from Picentine settlers who fled here (c 268 BC) before the Roman advance in the Marches. Their chief city, *Picentia* (see below), sided with Hannibal in the Second Punic War, and its people took refuge in the foothills on his defeat. At **Pontecagnano**, 10km south-east of Salerno, is a memorial chapel of the Hampshire Regiment (1945). Nearby excavations have brought to light 900 tombs in a large necropolis of the 9–4C BC, now visible in the Museo Nazionale dell'Agro Picentino (Piazza del Risorgimento 14; open daily 09.00–13.00, 17.00–19.30). Montecorvino, 10 km further east, is the site of **Salerno British Military Cemetery**, with 1850 graves of those who fell in the landings of 1943. The road continues to Paestum, Route 7A.

The return to Naples from Salerno (59km in 31min) may be made by Autostrada A3, which passes inland at the foot of the Sorrentine Peninsula. This is the route followed by the Ferrovia Dello Stato, which covers the distance in 30–90min. Motorists should bear in mind that local traffic between Naples and Salerno is notoriously heavy.

Leave Salerno by (3km) the Salerno Nord interchange. 8km Cava de' Tirreni (198m) is a busy town (53,000 inhab.) frequented by Neapolitans in summer. The cylindrical towers on the surrounding hills were used for netting wild pigeons by a curious local method now rarely seen. The main street, Corso Italia, is arcaded. The principal object of interest is the Benedictine abbey of **La Trinita di Cava**, 4km south-west, romantically situated near the hamlet of Corpo di Cava beneath a crag on the Bonea torrent. The abbey, founded by the Cluniac St Alferius, was built in 1011–25 and consecrated in 1092 by Urban II in the presence of Roger of Sicily, whose second wife Sibylla is buried here. So also are the founder and the antipope Theodoric (died 1102). The structure was radically altered in 1796; the campanile dates from 1622. The church contains a fine Cosmatesque ambo and a candlestick from the original building, as well as the 11C altar frontal. The crypt has 14C frescoes. The chapter house has carved and inlaid stalls, perhaps designed by Andrea da Salerno. An earlier chapter house is reached from the beautiful 13C cloister. The guest hall houses a museum (open Mon–Sat 09.00–12.30, Sun and holidays 09.00–10.30) containing items from the archives, which, with c 15,000 Lombard and Norman documents, makes this one of the most important centres for the study of the local medieval history.

7km **Nocera Inferiore**, the *Nuceria Alfaterna* destroyed by Hannibal in 216 BC and now an agricultural centre with 48,000 inhabitants. Here Queen Beatrice, first wife of Charles of Anjou, died in 1267. In captivity in the castello, Helena, Manfred's queen, died in 1271; and here Urban VI put six cardinals to the torture and was himself kept a prisoner by Charles of Durazzo (1384). Francesco Solimena (1657–1743), the painter, was a native. The Museo Archeologico dell'Agro Nocerino (open daily 09.00–13.00, 17.00–19.30) occupies the 14C church and convent of Sant'Antonio. Opened in 1965, it houses the Pisani collection of prehistoric material from the Sarno valley and material from recent local excavations. More finds may be seen in the Museo Archeologico at Nocera Superiore (Palazzo del Municipio; open Mon–Fri 09.00–13.00). Just outside Nocera is the village of Santa Maria Maggiore, which has a round **church* of the 4C or 5C, probably built as a baptistery. The double cupola, resting on 32 monolithic columns, covers a large octagonal font.

Just beyond (13km) Castellammare di Stabia (see above) exit for Pompeii, Route 3B. The modern village of **Pompei** (26,000 inhab.) has sprung up round the pilgrimage shrine of Santa Maria del Rosario, built in 1876–91 and enlarged in 1938 as a shrine for the Madonna of the Rosary, an old picture and framed with gold and precious stones that now adorns the high altar. The Museo Vesuviano (Piazza Longo 1; open daily 09.00–13.30) has Vesuvian stones, and prints and paintings representing the eruptions of the volcano.

2km **Torre Annunziata** (56,000 inhab.), the flourishing centre of the pasta industry, was founded in 1319 beside a chapel of the Annunciation. A bathing and thermal resort, it is crowded in summer. Here recent excavations have revealed two patrician villas, thought to belong to a residential suburb of Pompeii called *Oplontis* (open 09.00–1hr before sunset). The fertile coastal strip of black volcanic earth is thickly populated and dotted with pines, palms, prickly pears and Oriental-looking houses. On the right, on the summit of a small extinct volcano (184m) rises the monastery of Camaldoli della Torre. Both the motorway and highway cross the lava flow of 1767; on the left the coast stretches away to Sorrento, with Castellammare nestling in its bay.

8km **Torre del Greco** (107,000 inhab.), the most populous town in the province after Naples, is almost entirely modern. Perhaps taking its name from a tower of Frederick II, it has long been famous as the centre of the coral-carving industry. In the principal square are the Scuola d'Incisione sul Corallo, with a museum (open Mon–Sat 09.00–13.00), and the 19C church of Santa Croce, whose 16C predecessor was destroyed, except for its campanile, by the lava of 1794. Towards the sea is the old castello.

3km **Ercolano**, exit for Herculaneum (Route 3D). The modern town (63,000 inhab.) was built in the Middle Ages on the lava covering the stream of mud that overwhelmed Herculaneum. Just south of the excavations (Route 3D) is the Miglio d'Oro, where the road is flanked by sumptuous 18C summer homes. One of these, Villa Campolieto, has been restored to its original splendour and occasionally hosts special events.

1km **Portici** (72,000 inhab.), smoky with factories, is the alleged birthplace of the rebel leader Masaniello. It is noted for its **Palazzo Reale**, begun in 1739 by Canevari, which now houses the Faculty of Agriculture of Naples University; this was the birthplace of Charles IV of Spain (1748) and was occupied by Pius IX in 1849–50. Between Naples and Portici (Granatello) the first Italian train was inaugurated on 3 October 1839, by Ferdinand II. The **Museo Ferroviario Nazionale** (National Railway Museum; Corso San Giovanni a Teduccio, open Mon–Sat 09.00–14.00) occupies the recently restored premises of the railway works at Pietrarsa and is largely devoted to steam engines.

At (4km) San Giovanni a Teduccio interchange, leave the Autostrada for the Tangenziale. 8km Naples.

5 · The Viceregal and Bourbon City

THE SPANISH AND AUSTRIAN VICEROYS

During the period of the Spanish viceroys, and during that of the Austrian viceroys who followed them after 1707, Naples was oppressed by excessive taxation and delegated rule. Brigands terrorised the countryside, and pirates roamed the seas, discouraging trade and endangering travellers. The scarce attention that the Spanish governors dedicated to the provinces brought increasing numbers of immigrants to the capital, giving rise to a phenomenon of overcrowding—at the end of the century, Naples had 240,000 inhabitants; counting the suburbs, 300,000—that several viceroys, and especially Don Pedro de Toledo (1532–53), tried to alleviate by constructing new roads and new buildings. Population growth outpaced these measures, until the terrible plague of 1656 killed or dispersed half the population.

In the provinces, as in the capital, life was dominated by the nightmare of high taxes. Despite reduced profits, country dwellers devoted themselves as always to the cultivation of fields and orchards, and the sale of agricultural products remained their principal source of income. In the cities, an educated and ambitious middle class climbed steadily to wealth and political power, the successful buying titles and estates (it is estimated that 17C Naples had at least 119 princes, 156 dukes, 173 marquesses and several hundred counts). In contrast to these, and to the virtual army of clergy (which came to represent one-fortieth of the population), stood the hoards of ragged beggars known as *lazzeroni*. On one hand, they were considered as thieving, treacherous, seditious, lazy, and corrupt ('There is not such another race of rogues as the common people of Naples,' Henry Swinburne commented); but on the other their 'way of being satisfied with so little, of living on the air of time,' was idealised, especially by Northern Europeans, like Goethe, who attributed to them a peculiarly Mediterranean sense of freedom.

The French never fully accepted the idea that they had lost the kingdom of Naples to the Spanish (a French army under Lautrex de Foix, Viscount of Lautrec, laid siege to the capital in 1528), and the Neapolitans themselves considered the foreigners tyrants whose unjust rule was to be cast off at the earliest possible opportunity. When Viceroy Pedro de Toledo levied a new round of taxes in 1535, the people appealed in vain to the Spanish emperor Charles V, who passed through Naples on his way back from his Tunisian campaign. With more success the city rose up in 1547, when the Don Pedro was known, tried to revive an old project to introduce the Inquisition, in full swing at that time in Spain.and estates (it is estimated that 17C Naples had at least 119 princes, 156 dukes, 173 marquesses and several hundred counts). In contrast to these, and to the virtual army of clergy (which came to represent one-fortieth of the population), stood the hoards of ragged beggars known as *lazzeroni*. On one hand, they were considered as thieving, treacherous, seditious, lazy, and corrupt ('There is not such another race of rogues as the common people of Naples,' Henry Swinburne commented); but on the other their 'way of being satisfied with so little, of living on the air of time,' was idealised, especially by Northern Europeans, like Goethe, who attributed to them a peculiarly Mediterranean sense of freedom.

The French never fully accepted the idea that they had lost the kingdom of Naples to the Spanish (a French army under Lautrex de Foix, Viscount of Lautrec, laid siege to the capital in 1528), and the Neapolitans themselves considered the foreigners tyrants whose unjust rule was to be cast off at the earliest possible opportunity. When Viceroy Pedro de Toledo levied a new round of taxes in 1535, the people appealed in vain to the Spanish emperor Charles V, who passed through Naples on his way back from his Tunisian campaign. With more success the city rose up in 1547, when the Don Pedro, as he was known, tried to revive an old project to introduce the Inquisition, in full swing at that time in Spain.

Naples is nevertheless deeply indebted to this energetic viceroy, for he undertook the most ambitious (and successful) urban development programme in the city's history. He curbed ecclesiastical building (a sticky political problem throughout the viceregal period) by acquiring property in the city centre so that tenement houses would not be torn down and convents built in their place. He alleviated day-to-day 'commuter' traffic by moving administrative offices out of the downtown area (it was by his order that the law courts were moved to their present seat at the Castel Capuano). Most importantly, he doubled the area available for building within the city walls by constructing a new set of fortifications that ran from the Castel Capuano, on the east side of town, to the Castel Sant'Elmo (rebuilt in the form of a six-pointed star) on the Vomero hill, and from the latter to the Castel dell'Ovo, on the sea to the west. In place of the now obsolete Aragonese walls, he built the great thoroughfare known as Via Roma, and Via Toledo, in his honour.

To the west of this road he constructed a whole new quarter to house the Spanish garrison at Naples (the mazes of lanes and steep staircases that characterise this area have changed little since then and repay a visit). Via Toledo became the fashionable residential street of the aristocracy. At the southern end of the street, Don Pedro himself erected a new viceregal palace, which became known as the Palazzo Vecchio when, at the beginning of the following century, Viceroy Ferrante di Castro, in expectation of a visit that never took place by King Philip III, commissioned Domenico Fontana to build the magnificent Palazzo Reale.

ART AND ARCHITECTURE IN THE 16C–18C

By the end of the 16C, Naples bristled with churches and convents—at least 400 of the former, not counting private chapels, and about 200 of the latter. At the beginning of the 18C, a petition was sent to the viceroy, urging him to prevent the clergy from acquiring more property, which suggests that Don Pedro de Toledo's nightmare remained a major political concern of his successors.

Yet the construction of churches and convents gave rise to the great artistic flowering of the 17C and 18C, characterised by the presence of architects, sculptors, and painters who were famous throughout Europe—Cosimo Fanzago, Caravaggio, Giuseppe Ribera, Domenichino, Giovanni Lanfranco, Giovan Battista Caracciolo, Massimo Stanzione, Bernardo Cavallino, Salvator Rosa, Mattia Preti, Luca Giordano and others.

'That which seemed to us most extraordinary at Naples,' wrote one observer, 'was the number and magnificence of the churches. It may be justly said, that in this respect it surpasses imagination...If you would look upon rare pictures, sculptures, and the rarity of vessels of gold and silver, you need but go to the churches: the roofs, the wainscots, the walls are all covered with pieces of precious marble, most artificially laid together, or with compartments of basso relievo, or of joiner's work gilded, and enriched with the works of the most famous painters. There is nothing to be seen but jasper, porphyry, mosaic of all fashions, all masterpieces of art.'

Another connoisseur of the **Neapolitan Baroque**, the eminent British art historian Anthony Blunt, warns that 'the architecture of Naples is like its inhabitants: lively, colourful, and with a tendency not to keep the rules,' adding that 'if you go to Naples expecting its architecture to behave like that of Rome, you will be as surprised as if you expected its traffic to behave like Roman traffic, though you will be in less physical danger.' Many of the architects who worked in Naples at this time came from outside the city—Cosimo Fanzago, the most imaginative architect and sculptor of the period, was a native of Bergamo—yet they all seem to have become acclimatised. To a remarkable degree they ignored, and in some cases they anticipated, the accomplishments of their contemporaries in Rome and elsewhere in Europe.

In ecclesiastical architecture, the most characteristic examples of the Neapolitan Baroque style are those that combine simple ground plans with rich, varied decoration; for Neopolitan architects were accomplished at carrying out elaborate decorative schemes without bringing confusion to the overall form of their buildings. As a consequence, the great churches of the 16C and 17C lack the interest in new spatial forms that distinguishes ecclesiastical architecture in Rome during the same period. It was not until the 18C and the Rococo creations of Domenico Antonio Vaccaro and Ferdinando Sanfelice that Neapolitan church architects displayed inventiveness in planning.

In domestic architecture, the pressure of overcrowding caused Neapolitans to build higher than their counterparts in other Italian cities. This permitted them to move the *piano nobile*, the most sumptuous level of lordly palaces, from the first to the second floor and to introduce the vast, monumental doorways or *portes cochères* which, together with the magnificent external staircases, are the most striking and individual features of Neapolitan palaces.

In **painting**, the 17C was dominated by the dark, dramatic styles of the Spaniard **Ribera** and of **Caravaggio** (the latter, exiled from Rome where he had killed a man in a moment of rage, and from Malta, where he had insulted the Grand Master of the Order of St. John, took refuge in Naples until his involvement in a brawl in a waterfront tavern got him expelled from this city, too). Ribera and another foreigner, the Greek Corenzio, joined forces with the native Caracciolo in the 'Cabal of Naples' to exclude Northern competition. Using southern methods of intimidation, sabotage and the hired assassin, they hounded Annibale Carracci, the Cavaliere d'Arpino and Guido Reni from Naples and Domenichino to his death (1641). After Caracciolo's death in the same year, and Ribera's in 1652, the soul of Naples found its most perfect expression in the exuberant compositions of Luca Giordano, who also frescoed the rooms of the Medici-Riccardi palace in Florence. The first native school of **sculpture** in Naples arose in the 16C with Girolamo Santacroce and Giovanni da Nola and their pupils, alongside whom worked the Florentines Michelangelo Naccherino and Pietro Bernini, the father of Gian Lorenzo Bernini, of Vatican fame. In the 17C the fanciful Cosimo Fanzago was prominent, followed in the 18C by the disciples of Gian Lorenzo Bernini and the technicians of the Cappella Sansevero.

CHARLES III

The last years of Spanish rule were undistinguished. The usual burdensome taxation roused the Neapolitans to insurrection (1647) under Masaniello, an Amalfi fisherman who was used as a figurehead by liberal reformers seeking to undermine the power of the nobility. The ensuing Parthenopean Republic endured only a few months. In 1707, after the War of the Spanish Succession, Naples passed to the Archduke Charles of Austria (Charles VI), but the succession of viceroys was continued. In 1734, however, the Infante Charles of Bourbon (Charles VII, known as Charles III) seized Sicily and subsequently Naples and in 1744 defeated the Austrians at Velletri, near Rome, thus founding the Neapolitan Bourbon dynasty.

Charles (1734–59) was the first of the Bourbon kings who ruled Naples until the unification of Italy in the 19C. Although not without his faults, he was certainly the most generous and enlightened member of this controversial dynasty, whose name was later to become a byword for misrule. He restored order to public finance, curtailed ecclesiastical jurisdiction and immunities and taxed ecclesiastical property, then about one-third of the whole kingdom. He modernised the university and gave it a new home in the Palazzo degli Studi (now the National Museum). He also began the excavations at Pompeii and Herculaneum and published the finds in nine splendidly illustrated volumes. Sir James Gray, resident English minister at Naples, described him as follows:

> The King of Naples is of a very reserved temper, a great master of dissimulation, and has an habitual smile on his face, contracted by a constant attention to conceal his thoughts; has a good understanding and a surprising memory, as his father had, is unread and unlearned, but retains an exact knowledge of all that has passed within his own observation, and is capable of entering into the most minute detail. He is in many things his own Minister, passing several hours every day alone in his cabinet. (This and other contemporary accounts quoted in Sir Harold Acton, *The Bourbons of Naples*, London 1956.)

Charles was an absolute ruler. 'He has too good an opinion of his own judgement, and is so positive and obstinate, that he is seldom induced to alter his resolutions,' says Gray. 'He has very high notions of his prerogative and his independency, and thinks himself the most absolute monarch in Europe'. Yet the king chose his servants wisely, in spite of his autocratic character. Beginning with Bernardo Tanucci, the Tuscan law professor whom he made his prime minister, and the architect Vanvitelli, who designed the magnificent palace and gardens of Caserta, he appointed to high office men of competence and unquestioned personal integrity.

As a patron of the arts, Charles was uncommonly generous. His ambition to make Naples the most brilliant centre of musical culture in Italy (a position it would maintain throughout the 18C) culminated in the construction of the famous San Carlo Theatre, so named because it was inaugurated on his saint's day, November 4, 1738. These and many other improvements made in public and private life bear witness to this sovereign's acute mental vision, especially if one considers the briefness of his reign (25 years, compared to Frederick the Great's 46 and Louis XV's 59) and the sound political and economic position in which he left the kingdom at the end of it.

The numerous building projects undertaken during the reigns of Charles III and his successors changed the face of Naples. The architects who were most involved in these initiatives (which to a large extent gave the city the appearance that it has today) were Ferdinando Sanfelice, Domenico Antonio Vaccaro, Ferdinando Fuga and Luigi Vanvitelli.

The other art forms also played a major role in making Naples a truly European capital. Francesco Solimena was the last and perhaps the greatest of the Neapolitan Baroque painters, Giuseppe Sammartino made hundreds of statuettes for the presepi that filled the churches and palaces of the city, and the Capodimonte Porcelain Works turned out some of the finest porcelain in Europe.

Charles's son and heir Ferdinand IV (1759–1825), or Ferdinand I as he called himself after the Congress of Vienna, unfortunately possessed few of his father's virtues. He reigned with the enthusiastic approval of the Neapolitan mob, which fondly called him 'Nasone' on account of his bulbous nose. To his peers he was known as the Lazzarone King, 'beloved by the vulgar Neapolitans...from his having been born amongst them', and inclined 'rather to seek the company of menial servants and people of the very lowest class than those of a better education'. Ferdinand was famous for his indolent bonhomie, his love of the hunt, his inclination for crude practical jokes and his indifference to anything not directly related to his physical well-being. Sir William Hamilton, who succeeded Gray as resident English minister in 1764, called him insensitive, choleric, and obstinate, commenting that at the end of his regency 'the young King...seems to have been more desirous of becoming his own master to follow his caprices, than to govern his kingdoms'. When Ferdinand married Maria Carolina of Austria (daughter of Maria Theresa and sister of Marie Antoinette), Sir William described the young husband as follows:

> On the morning after his nuptials, which took place in the beginning of May 1768, when the weather was very warm, he rose at an early hour and went out as usual to the chase, leaving his young wife in bed. Those courtiers who accompanied him, having inquired of his majesty and how he liked her: 'Dorme come un'ammazzata', replied he, 'e suda come un porco' [she sleeps as if she had been killed, and sweats like a pig]. Such an answer would be esteemed, anywhere except at Naples, most indecorous; but here we are familiarized to far greater violations of propriety and decency... When the king has made a hearty meal and feels an inclination to retire, he commonly communicates that intention to the noblemen around him in waiting, to the favoured individuals, whom, as a mark of predilection, he chooses shall attend him. 'Sono ben pranzato', says he, laying his hand on his belly,

'adesso bisogna una buona panciatas' [I've eaten well, now I need to move my bowels]. The persons thus preferred then accompany his majesty, stand respectfully round him, and amuse him by their conversation during the performance.

WAR WITH FRANCE

On the outbreak of the French Revolution Ferdinand was not at first hostile to the new movement; but in the months that followed its outbreak he was compelled to move against republicanism at home and abroad. Every tremor that emanated from Paris was registered with particular anxiety in Naples, where the opposing forces had polarised more sharply than elsewhere in Italy. Rightly or wrongly, the Neapolitan liberals believed that they had suffered more under the Bourbons than the inhabitants of other regions of Italy had under their sovereigns; and they saw in the cause of revolutionary France the glimmer of hope for a free and united Italy.

The royalists, on the other hand, rallied in defence not only of their beloved Nasone, but also of their queen, the sister of the martyred Marie Antoinette. Sir John Acton, the French-born English baronet who became Ferdinand's prime minister, counselled prudence; but Maria Carolina, who exercised considerable influence over the king, maintained that the best defence was a strong offence. In 1793 Naples joined the first coalition against republican France, severely persecuting all those who were even remotely suspected of French sympathies. The eruption of Vesuvius in May 1794, widely regarded as an expression of divine wrath over the execution of Louis XVI and Marie Antoinette, won popular approval for the initiative.

In 1798, during Napoleon's absence in Egypt and after Nelson's destruction of the French fleet at the Nile, Maria Carolina persuaded Ferdinand to go to war with France. The king promptly sent an army against French-held Rome, which fell without resistance. For a few ecstatic days that December, the Neapolitans occupied the Eternal City; but the French under Championnet quickly counter-attacked, retook Rome and entered Naples so swiftly that the royal family had to be evacuated by Nelson himself, with the aid of Emma Hamilton, the lovely young bride of Sir William, who had her servants carry the crown jewels of Naples aboard the British flagship before it set sail for Sicily.

On 23 January 1799 the second Parthenopean Republic was proclaimed, but like its predecessor (which, it will be recalled, was instituted during the revolt of 1647), it was short lived. Governed by local liberals and precariously supported by the French army, it claimed dominion over the peninsular portion of the former kingdom while Ferdinand and Maria Carolina ruled Sicily from Palermo, protected by the British navy patrolling the Strait of Messina.

Although the republicans had noble aims, they were doctrinaire and unpractical, and they knew very little of the lower classes of their own country. A violent anti-French feeling in Southern Italy coincided with French defeats by Austro-Russian forces in the north. The following year the king and queen, with the aid of Nelson and of Cardinal Ruffo, who swept up from Calabria with a band of peasants, brigands, convicts and a few soldiers, managed to reconquer the mainland provinces of the kingdom. The French and their republican allies found themselves confined to Naples proper, and before long surrendered to a promise of amnesty. The foreigners were allowed to leave thanks to the implicit blessing of St Januarius, the liquefaction of whose blood was supposedly helped along in that year by the President of the Parthenopean Republic, who held the archbishop at gunpoint during the ceremony. Had the miracle not taken place, the French might well have been seized and lynched by the angry mob, whose sympathies were, as always, with their king.

NELSON'S SEVERE MEASURES
There followed a period of severe repression. Nelson, prompted by Emma Hamilton (now his mistress) and Maria Carolina, set out to eradicate all traces of the Parthenopean Republic, while the two husbands left him carte blanche. Sir William was lamenting the loss of much of his precious collection of antiquities, which had gone down with the ship that was transporting them to England, and Ferdinand had grown so fond of his Sicilian hunting grounds that he could barely be persuaded to return to the throne in Naples.

While the lazzeroni plundered the republicans' property to cries of *Chi tien pan' e vino ha da esser giaccobino* (He who has bread and wine is surely a Jacobin), Nelson unabashedly violated the terms of surrender, summarily executing the liberal leaders—among them the admiral Francesco Caracciolo, the philosopher Mario Pagano, the scientist Domenico Cirillo, and other prominent Neapolitan intellectuals.

BONAPARTE AND MURAT
After Napoleon's successful second Italian campaign, the king was forced to grant an amnesty to the surviving republicans, to close all the ports of his kingdom to the British fleet and to allow a French garrison to be stationed deep within his territory, at Taranto. Even so, the Neapolitans could consider themselves lucky, for Napoleon had treated them more leniently than his other and more powerful enemies. Only when he found out that they had been negotiating with Austria with a view to joining the third coalition, his patience gave out: after the Austerlitz campaign (1805), he issued the famous proclamation, 'the Bourbon dynasty has ceased to reign', and sent his brother Joseph to dethrone Ferdinand, who again fled to Sicily under the protection of a British fleet.

Joseph Bonaparte, though certainly no genius, was a cultivated and well-meaning man. He abolished the privileges of the nobility and the clergy and introduced several important reforms. But his taxes and forced contributions were resented, and royalist risings undermined his authority in much of the kingdom. In 1808 Napoleon gave Joseph the crown of Spain and appointed his colourful and flamboyant brother-in-law, Joachim Murat, king of Naples. Murat continued Joseph's reforms, put down the Bourbon guerilla bands in the provinces and instituted a programme of public works that included new roads to Posillipo and Capodimonte.

Meanwhile, in Sicily, where the king's extravagance and methods of police espionage rendered the royal presence a burden instead of a blessing, a bitter conflict broke out between the court and the parliament. In 1812 Sir William Bentinck, the British minister, obliged Ferdinand to grant a liberal constitution. But the wind changed as a consequence of Napoleon's defeat at Waterloo, and the king dissolved parliament in May 1815, after concluding a treaty with Austria for the recovery of his mainland dominions.

A month later Ferdinand re-entered Naples, amid some discontent, while Murat fled to Corsica. At first the king abstained from persecution and received many of the usurper's officers into his own army. Murat, believing he still had a strong following in the kingdom, landed with a few companions at Pizzo in Calabria, but was immediately captured, court-martialled and shot.

THE STRUGGLE FOR A CONSTITUTION
Ferdinand proclaimed himself king of the Two Sicilies at the Congress of Vienna, incorporating Naples and Sicily into one state and abolishing the Sicilian constitution of 1812. In 1818 he signed a Concordat with the Church, reinstating ecclesi-

astical juristiction over education and censorship. But ideas of national unity and personal gain continued to make progress throughout the country. In 1820 a spontaneous **insurrection**, which began in the army at Nola, quickly took fire under the leadership of General Guglielmo Pepe, the mutineers demanding a new constitution while assuring their continued loyalty to the king. Ferdinand, feeling himself helpless to resist, acceded to the demand. These events seriously alarmed the powers responsible for the preservation of the peace in Europe, who at the Congress of Troppau (October 1820) issued the famous protocol affirming the right of collective 'Europe' to interfere to crush dangerous internal revolutions.

The following year Ferdinand repudiated his engagements and the powers authorised Austria to march an army into Naples to restore the autocratic monarchy. General Pepe was sent to the frontier at the head of 8000 men, but was defeated by the Austrians at Rieti on 7 March. There followed a period of severe repression, the inevitable State trials resulting in the usual harvest of executions and imprisonments.

The conditions of the country continued to worsen under Ferdinand's successors, Francis I (1825–30) and Ferdinand II (1838–59). At the same time, the desire for a constitution became ever more fervent. Revolution broke out in Sicily on 12 January 1848, under the leadership of Ruggero Settimo; while demonstrations also shook Naples. On 28 January the king granted the constitution; but the following spring he refused to open the parliament and sent an army under Carlo Filangieri against the revolutionary government of Palermo, which fell on 14 April. Open despotism followed, during which liberal sympathisers were condemned to prison or the galleys for life. Thousands of respectable citizens were thrown into prison, including Luigi Settembrini, Carlo Poerio and Silvio Spavento. The kingdom, reduced by indolence to squalor and by corruption, persecution, and fear to moral decay, provoked Gladstone's famous denunciation of it as 'the negation of God erected into a system of government'.

GARIBALDI'S VICTORY

Francis I refused several opportunities to strike an alliance with Victor Emmanuel, king of Piedmont and Sardinia, for the division of Italy. On 5 May 1860 Garibaldi embarked at Quarto, near Genoa, with 1000 picked followers on board two steamers, and sailed for Sicily. On the 11th the expedition reached Marsala and landed without opposition. Garibaldi was somewhat coldly received by the astonished population, but he set forth at once for Salemi, where he issued a proclamation assuming the dictatorship of Sicily in the name of Victor Emmanuel, with Francesco Crispi as secretary of state. On the 15th he attacked and defeated 3000 of the enemy under General Landi at Calatafimi. The news of this brilliant victory revived revolutionary agitation throughout the island. By a clever ruse, Garibaldi avoided General Colonna's force, which expected him on the Monreale road, and entering Palermo from Misilmeri, received an enthusiastic welcome. After three days' street fighting the Bourbonist commander, General Lanza, not knowing that the Garibaldians had scarcely a cartridge left, asked for and obtained a 24-hour armistice (3 May). Garibaldi went on board the British flagship to confer with the Neapolitan generals Letizia and Chrétien; then he informed the citizens by means of a proclamation of what he had done, and declared that he would renew hostilities on the expiration of the armistice. Lanza became so alarmed that he asked for an unconditional extension of the armistice, which Garibaldi granted, and 15,000 Bourbon troops embarked for Naples on 7 June, leaving the revolutionaries masters of the situation.

The news of Garibaldi's astonishing successes entirely changed the situation in the capital, and on 25 June 1860 the king again granted a constitution. The king appealed to Great Britain and France to prevent Garibaldi crossing the Strait of Messina and only just failed. On 19 August Garibaldi crossed with 4500 men and took Reggio by storm. He was soon joined by the rest of his troops, 15,000 in all, the Neapolitan army collapsed before Garibaldi's advance, and the people rose in his favour almost everywhere. Resistance dissolved as the march became a race for Naples, which Garibaldi entered with a small staff 48 hours ahead of the vanguard of his troops, although the city was still full of troops, and was received with delirious enthusiasm. Francis II fled to Gaeta, to take the field with his still loyal army. Two months later a successful campaign on the Volturno opened the way to Garibaldi's meeting with Victor Emmanuel II, which sealed the unity of Italy.

A.   From Piazza del Municipio to Via Partenope

*This route leads through the historic area south and west of the Castel Nuovo. The first part of the walk takes in some of the city's more notable public buildings, which grew up as the Spanish viceroys and their Austrian successors, anxious to mark the distinction between their rule and that of the Aragonese, moved the civic centre of Naples from the Castel Nuovo to the area immediately to the south–west. Highlights in this area include the **Palazzo Reale**, the centre of viceregal government, and the monumental church of **San Francesco di Paola** with its square, today called Piazza del Plebiscito. The latter is now closed to traffic, allowing one to imagine the immense visual and symbolic impact that such an immense open space had, when first built, for the inhabitants of the crowded city.*

*The second part of the itinerary explores the city's finest old residential quarter, **Pizzofalcone**, which stands on a hill (the site of the ancient Parthenope) between the gulf shore and Via Chiaia, Naples' elegant shopping street. Here some truly spectacular examples of Neopolitan palace architecture (as well as one or two small churches supported by aristocratic families) can be seen. Finally, the walk ends on the busy Via Partenope, a scenic boulevard carved out of the slums when the old fishing port of Santa Lucia was 'improved' in the late 19C and now home to many of the city's luxury hotels.*

The total length of the route is about 3km; it may be walked comfortably in just over two hours. Care should be taken when crossing the street in Piazza del Plebiscito and at all major intersections, as Neopolitan drivers rarely stop at crossings.

PIAZZA DEL MUNICIPIO

The long Piazza del Municipio (Atlas 2, 10), with a central monument commemorating Victor Emmanuel II, overlooks the harbour. On the west side stands the **Palazzo Municipale** (or di San Giacomo; 1819–25), the Palace of the Ministers under the Bourbons, which incorporates the church of **San Giacomo degli Spagnoli**. The latter, founded by Don Pedro de Toledo in 1514 and rebuilt in 1741, follows a Latin cross plan. The first chapel in the south aisle contains a Madonna and Child by Marco Pino. Above the altar in the south transept is a Martyrdom of St James by Domenico Antonio Vaccaro, who also painted the Dead Christ in the frontal above the main altar. In the apse can be seen the *Tomb of the founder, executed in his lifetime by Giovanni da Nola.

Above the square, to the south, rises the Castel Nuovo, described in Route 4B. Keeping the castle on your left, follow Via Vittorio Emanuele II south-west to Via

San Carlo, which branches right. On the left, at the entrance to the Giardino Reale and the Biblioteca Nazionale (see below), are groups of Horse Trainers, by Baron Clodt, presented by Czar Nicholas I. Further along on the left lies the **Teatro San Carlo** (Atlas 2, 14).

The Teatro San Carlo

This, the largest opera house in Italy, was built for Charles of Bourbon by the contactor and impresario Angelo Carasale on a plan by court architect Giovanni Antonio Medrano. Begun in March 1737, it was finished in the following October and opened to the public on 4 November, the King's saint's day. In the decades that followed it was remodelled a number of times, notably in 1762 by Giovanni Maria Bibiena, in 1768 by Ferdinando Fuga, in 1797 by Domenico Chelli and in 1812 by Antonio Niccolini (who added the courtyard and loggia). Destroyed by a fire on the night of 12 February 1816, the old theatre was rebuilt in its present form by Niccolini (who, it is said, inserted hundreds of clay pitchers in the walls in order to improve the acoustics). The foyer on the garden side was added in 1938.

Interior (open 09.00–12.00). The **concert hall**, seating 3000, is famous for its perfect acoustics. The 185 boxes are arranged in six tiers; above the centrally situated Royal Box, the fifth and sixth tiers open up in the manner of an amphitheatre. Throughout the theatre red upholstery and gold trim combine to create a rich, festive atmosphere. The ceiling is adorned with a painting of Apollo introducing the Greek, Latin, and Italian poets to Minerva, by Giuseppe Cammarino, and the curtain bears a representation of Homer and the Muses with poets and musicians, the work of Giuseppe Mancinelli. The prémiers of Rossini's *Lady of the Lake* and *Moses*, Bellini's *Sonnambula* and Donizetti's *Lucia di Lammermoor* were performed on this stage.

At the time the San Carlo was built, Italy was the centre of European musical culture and Naples was the centre of music in Italy, thanks to Charles III's generous patronage of composers and performers. Rousseau, in his famous essay on Genius, advised the aspiring musician to go to Naples to study; his eminent contemporary Lalande declared that music could be discerned in the gestures, the inflection of the voice and even the cadence of everyday conversation in Naples. 'Music is the triumph of the Neapolitans', he wrote. 'Everything there expresses and exhales music'.

In the light of these considerations it is hardly surprising that Charles should have desired to provide his capital with a large, splendid opera house, even though he had no personal passion for this particular art form. Indeed, as one observer noted, the king often talked during one half of the performances and slept during the other—a habit that scandalised his foreign guests. The 18C English traveller Samuel Sharp has left a description of the original appearance of the theatre (which today is lost), as well as an amusing account of the Neapolitan manner of enjoying a performance.

'The King's Theatre, upon the first view, is, perhaps, almost as remarkable an object as any man sees in his travels' he writes. 'The amazing extent of the stage, with the prodigious circumference of the boxes and the height of the ceiling, produce a marvellous effect on the mind...Notwithstanding the amazing noisiness of the audience during the whole performance of the opera, the moment the dances begin there is a universal dead silence, which continues so long as the dances continue. Witty people, therefore, never fail to tell me, the Neapolitans go to see not to hear an opera...It must be confessed that their scenery is extremely fine; their dresses are new and rich; and the music is well adapted, but, above all, the stage is so large and noble, as to set off the performance to an inexpressible advantage...It is customary for gentlemen to run about from box to box between the acts, and even in the midst of the performance; but the ladies, after they are seated, never quit their box the whole evening. It is the fashion to make appointments for such and such nights. A lady receives visitors in her box one night, and they remain with her the whole opera; another night she returns the visit in the same manner. In the intervals between the acts, principally between the first and second, the proprietor of the box regales her company with iced fruits and sweetmeats.' (Acton, cit.)

Opposite the Teatro San Carlo is the main entrance to the arcades of the cross-shaped **Galleria Umberto** I (1887–90, rebuilt since 1945), less animated than in former days. The dome is 56m high and is one of the first major iron-and-glass constructions in Italy. The street ends in the busy Piazza Trieste e Trento (Atlas 2, 14), still generally known as Piazza San Ferdinando, with a modern fountain in the centre. The square lies at the junction of several important streets: to the north runs Via Toledo (Route 5B); to the west, Via Chiaia (described below). Turning south you come immediately to Piazza del Plebiscito (Atlas 2, 14), a wide hemicycle with a Doric colonnade and frigid equestrian statues of Charles III of Bourbon and Ferdinand IV, by Antonio Canova and Antonio Calì. Here rises the church of San Francesco di Paola, founded by Ferdinand IV to celebrate the restoration of the Bourbon dynasty after the Napoleonic interlude and designed by Pietro Bianchi (1817–32) in obvious imitation of the Roman Pantheon. The north and south ends of the piazza are occupied respectively by the Prefecture and the Palazzo Salerno, residence of the military commandant.

THE PALAZZO REALE
On the east is the majestic façade (167m wide) of the ***Palazzo Reale** (Atlas 2, 14), built by Domenico Fontana in 1600–02, in anticipation of a visit by Philip II of Spain. Occupied only by viceroys, it was restored in 1838–42 after a fire, and again after damage in the Second World War. The statues in the ground-floor niches represent the eight dynasties of Naples: Roger the Norman, Frederick II the Swabian, Charles I of Anjou, Alfonso of Aragon, Charles V of Austria, Charles III of Bourbon, Joachim Murat, and Victor Emmanuel II of Savoy. In the interior (Museo dell'Appartamento Storico del Palazzo Reale, open Tue–Sat 09.00–14.00; Sun and holidays 09.00–13.00) the **chapel**, attributed to Cosimo Fanzago (1668), stands at the foot of the **grand staircase** (1651, restored 1837), which ascends to various fine halls with period furniture, tapestries, paintings, and porcelain, preceded by the small **Teatro di Corte**, built by Ferdinando Fuga in 1768 and restored after war damage in 1950. Here also are the original bronze ***doors** of the Castel Nuovo, by Guillaume le Moine and Pietro di Martino (1462–68), on which six reliefs depict Ferdinand of Aragon's struggle with the barons. The cannon-ball lodged in the lower relief on the left door is a relic from the naval battle between the French and the Genoese, in which the doors and other booty en route to France from Naples were recovered and returned to the city.

Part of the great building houses the **Bibliotecca Nazionale**, or National LIbrary, (open weekdays 09.00–18.30, Sat 09.00–13.30; entrance in Via Vittorio Emanuele III), founded in 1734, and including 1,500,000 volumes and over 17,000 incunabula and manuscripts. Annexed are the Lucchesi-Palli Library of Music and Dramatic Literature, and the J. F. Kennedy Library of American Studies.

PIZZOFALCONE

From the north-west corner of Piazza del Plebiscito the steep quarter of Pizzofalcone (Atlas 2, 13) is reached by Piazza Carolina and Via Serra, which lead to the piazza and church of **Santa Maria degli Angeli**, by Francesco Grimaldi. The church, begun in 1600, is built to one of the more daring designs of its day. The architect's clear, decisive treatment of solids and voids and his handling of architectural ornament are well ahead of contemporary developments in Naples or even in Rome. The third south chapel contains a Holy Family by Luca Giordano; the second on the north an Immacolata by Massimo Stanzione.

From the piazza, turn left and ascend Via Monte di Dio. In the Middle Ages this street was lined with convents, but in the 18C it became the centre of a fashionable residential area. Today it is known for its aristocratic palaces, the most noteworthy of which is **Palazzo Serra a Cassano** (Nos 14–15), built in the early 18C to plans by Ferdinando Sanfelice and recently restored. With two courtyards and a scenographic double staircase, it is one of the most impressive of all Neapolitan palaces. Also interesting are **Palazzo Sanfelice** (Nos 4–5), **Palazzo Caprocotta** (No. 74), and **Palazzo Carafa di Nola**, the courtyard of which gives onto a lovely garden. Via Parisi leads west to the former convent of the Nunziatella, now a military college, with an 18C church begun by Ferdinando Sanfelice.

Returning by Via Parisi and continuing along the north side of Palazzo Serra a Cassano, turn left into Via Egiziaca a Pizzofalcone. Just beyond the church of **Santa Maria Egiziaca a Pizzofalcone**, attributed to Cosimo Fanzago and sumptuously adorned with marble (over the high altar is a painting of the saint by Andrea Vaccaro), Via della Solitaria descends to the Istituto d'Arte, with a small museum of applied arts (open by appointment; tel. 081 764 6133). From here, steps go back down to Piazza del Plebiscito.

VIA CHIARA AND THE BORGO MARINARO

Turning to the west from Piazza Trieste e Trento you enter Via Chiaia (Atlas 2, 13) and pass under a bridge linking Pizzofalcone with Via Nicotera. Nearby a lift ascends to Santa Maria degli Angeli (see above). Further on, **Palazzo Cellamare**, begun in the 16C and restored in the early 18C, stands on a bend in the street, beyond which (right) is the church of **Santa Caterina** (c 1600), with the simple tomb of Cleotilde of France (1755–1802). From here Via Santa Caterina opens immediately into Piazza del Martiri, with a column by E. Alvino (1868) comemorating the martyrs of four revolutions (1799, 1820, 1848, and 1860). To the left Via Morelli leads to the west end of the Galleria della Vittoria (see below), where you turn south to the waterside and follow the shore eastward along Via Partenope (Atlas 4, 14), a broad promenade enjoying a magnificent view across the gulf. On the right is the **Borgo Marinaro**, the ancient island of *Megaris*, once the site of a villa of Lucullus, later joined by a mole to the shore to form the little Porto di Santa Lucia. Restaurants line the quay. On the island rises the **Castel dell'Ovo** (Atlas 4, 14), a fortress of 1154, once the prison of the luckless Conradin and of Beatrice, daughter of Manfred, the last of the Swabians. It is now used for meetings, lectures, and exhibitions. The Museo di Etnopreistoria, operated by the Club Alpino Italiano, is open by appointment (tel. 081 764 5343). At the end of Via Partenope stands the Baroque **Fontana dell'Immacolatella** (1601), with statues by Pietro Bernini and caryatids by Naccherino. Turn left into the straight Via Nazario Sauro, which affords a further splendid *view right across to Vesuvius. Halfway along, a wide terrace overlooks the sea.

Reached by any of the streets leading inland is the quarter of **Santa Lucia**, the site of the old shellfish market and once highly characteristic, but now much changed. It is crossed by the broad Via Santa Lucia, which receives its name from the church of Santa Lucia, rebuilt since 1945.

At the end of Via Nazario Sauro, from which Via Cesario Console ascends back to Piazza del Plebiscito, go down by Via F. Acton with a view, to the right, over the public gardens, to the Molosiglio, embarkation point for pleasure boats. To the left, at the bottom of the hill, is the mouth of the Galleria della Vittoria, a tunnel 623m long, opened in 1929, beneath the hill of Pizzofalcone. Via Acton bears right, skirting the south side of the Palazzo Reale, to the Porto Beverello, from which ferries serve Ischia, Procida, Capri, and Sorrento. With the Castel Nuovo high above, you reach the wide forecourt of the **Stazione Marittima Passeggeri** (Atlas 3, 15), where the largest passenger liners dock; this was built on the Molo Angioino to the design of C. Bazzani in 1936 and rebuilt after 1945.

B. From Piazza Trieste and Trento to the Cathedral

*This route explores the neighbourhoods of central Naples that were transformed, during the 17C and 18C, to accommodate the numerous new inhabitants—soldiers, aristocrats, and clergy—who thronged the city. In addition to visiting the area's major religious monuments—the **Gesù Nuovo**, **Santo Spirito**, **San Pietro a Maiella**, the **Cappella Sansevero**, **San Paolo Maggiore**, **San Gregorio Armeno**, **San Lorenzo Maggiore** and the **Girolamini**—look into doorways along this walk to discover the magnificent interior courts and open staircases of Neopolitan patrician homes. Keep an eye open as well to the details of religious architecture. In Piazza del Gesu Nuovo and Piazza San Domenico Maggiore, for instance, stand two 'guglie'—respectively the **Guglia dell'Immacolata** and the **Gugilia di San Domenico**—fanciful Baroque spires typical of Neopolitan taste, erected as neighbourhood ex votos for deliverance from the plague of 1656.*

The route parallels the course of Routes 3A and 4B, and if followed in reverse may be used as the return leg of a round-trip exploration of the city centre. The walk is just over 2km long and requires about 2hr.

VIA TOLEDO

From Piazza Trieste e Trento, **Via Toledo**, so called after its founder Don Pedro de Toledo, opens from the north side of Piazza Trieste e Trento (Rte 5A) and forms, with its continuations, an almost straight thoroughfare 1.5km long, rising gradually from south to north. Closed to motor traffic, it is the high street of Naples and all day is filled by a noisy and lively throng, especially in the late afternoon. Numberless streets and alleys diverge from it: those on the right, broad and modern to the south of Piazza della Carità, descend through the business district towards the harbour; those on the left, narrow and often squalid, ascend steeply, sometimes in steps, towards Corso Vittorio Emanuele. A parallel highway is projected to the west, which may eventually cut through the chessboard of populous streets with their lofty tenements.

On the corner facing Piazza Trieste e Trento is **San Ferdinando** (Atlas 2, 14), a Jesuit church begun by Giovanni Giacomo Conforto and altered by Cosimo Fanzago, but again modified and renamed, after their expulsion in 1767, in honour of Ferdinand I, whose morganatic wife Lucia Migliaccio (died 1826) is buried within. Beyond the Galleria Umberto I, on the right, is the church of **Santa Brigida** (Atlas 2, 10), built in 1612 in honour of St Brigid of Sweden. Here Luca Giordano is buried; his ingenious perspective paintings add apparent height to the dome. The painting of St Francis receiving the Stigmata, in the transept, is by Massimo Stanzione.

The Banco di Napoli, further on, boasts a continuous existence since the 16C. Behind its modern building lies the new but architecturally uninteresting business quarter centred on Piazza Matteotti (Atlas 2, 10) but taking its name from Piazza della Carità. The church of **Santa Maria della Carità**, at the north-west corner of the piazza, contains paintings by various 18C artists.

THE GESÙ NUOVO AND ITS NEIGHBOURHOOD

Via Toledo now changes its name to Via Roma. Where it crosses the Spaccanapoli (Route 4B) stands the Baroque **Palazzo Maddaloni** (right), an ancient building redesigned by Cosimo Fanzago. Follow Via Benedetto Croce right to Piazza del Gesù Nuovo (Atlas 2, 6). In the centre stands the **Guglia dell'Immacolata**, a fanciful Baroque column (1747–50) typical of Neapolitan taste, its ornate marble emphasised by the severe west front of the church of the *Gesu Nuovo (also called Trinita Maggiore), built between 1584 and 1601 by order of Isabella della Rovere. The embossed stone façade, once a wall of the palazzo of Roberto Sanseverino (by Novello da San Lucano, 1470) is pierced by three sculptured doorways. Those at the sides date from the sixteenth century, the central doorway from 1685.

The rich *interior (1601–1631), ornate with coloured marbles, has frescoes by Corenzio, Stanzione and Ribera. That of Heliodorus Driven from the Temple, above the entrance, is by Francesco Solimena (1725). The original design, by Giuseppe Valeriano, one of the more distinguished architects working in Naples at the end of the 16C, was much more severe, calling for white plaster walls and a discreet use of coloured marble and black piperno. A highly original design, it differs considerably from the Roman Gesù, which served as the model for many Jesuit churches of the day. Its centralised plan and the flat, continuous wall surface which defines the space with maximum clarity, are still visible beneath the beautiful decoration of inlaid coloured marbles, the inventors of which, working under the direction of Cosimo Fanzago, seem to have gone to great lengths to respect the intrinsic qualities of the spatial design. The original dome was damaged by an earthquake in 1688 and replaced by the present structure in 1744.

Retrace your steps to Via Roma. On the opposite side of the street a few blocks up is the church of **Santo Spirito**. Altered between 1757 and 1774 by Mario Gioffredo, it rivals Vanvitelli's Annunziata as the most masterful expression of the new Classical taste that grew up in Naples under Charles III. Within, Gioffredo's main order of powerful columns almost swamps the earlier interior. But the architect remains faithful to the Neapolitan tradition in such devices as the choir gallery above the main altar, the design of the altar itself and the overall proportions of the building. At the sides of the entrance are the tombs of Ambrogio Salvio and Paolo Spinelli, by Michelangelo Naccherino. In the south transept, a Madonna and Saints by Fedele Fischetti. In the apse, Pentecost, by Francesco de Mura. The first north chapel has a Purification, Conversion of St Paul, and Fall of Simon Magus, by Fischetti; the fourth chapel, a Madonna del Soccorso by Fabrizio Santafede. The tomb on the left is also by Naccherino. In the fifth chapel is a Baptism of Christ, by Santafede. The façade, which is much less advanced than the interior, adheres to the contemporary Roman type.

Opposite Santo Spirito is the **Palazzo d'Angri**, by Luigi and Carlo Vanvitelli (1755), where Garibaldi stayed in 1860. Continuing, you pass (left) Via Tarsia, which leads to Montesanto Station and the Montesanto Funicular, opposite which, in the church of **Santa Maria di Montesanto**, Alessandro Scarlatti is buried. Via Roma ends in Piazza Dante (Atlas 2, 6), enclosed on the east side by Luigi Vanvitelli's hemicycle and the 17C Port'Alba; the monument to the poet dates from 1872.

Also in the area

Via Pessina and its continuations lead northwards to the Museo Nazionale Archeologico (Route 3A) and the Galleria Nazionale di Capodimonte (Route 5C). Three blocks on, Via Conte di Ruvo leads right to Via Bellini and the Accademia di Belle Arti (with a small gallery, open daily 09.00–14.00), across the street from which stands the little church of **San Giovanni Battista**, with paintings by prominent 18C artists. These include St Mary Magdalene, by Mattia Preti, above the entrance; Annunciation, by Andrea Vaccaro and Immacolata, by Bernardo Cavallino, in the first south chapel; Crowning of the Virgin by Massimo Stanzione, in the south transept; St John the Baptist, by Luca Giordano, above the high altar; and St Luke painting the Virgin, by Andrea Vaccaro, in the first north chapel. In Via Santa Maria di Costantinopoli, the church of the same name has a noteworthy ceiling by Belisario Corenzio.

THE CONSERVATORY OF MUSIC AND FAMILY PALACES

From Piazza Dante pass under Port' Alba to enter Via San Pietro a Maiella. To the right, in the former convent of the same name, is the **Conservatorio di Musica**, the oldest in existence, founded in 1537 and removed here in 1826. The conservatory grew out of the gradual merger of four institutions—Santa Maria di Loreto, the Pietà dei Turchini, Sant'Onofrio a Capuana, and the Poveri di Gesù Cristo—that grew up in the 16C and 17C as homes for foundlings. In these institutions catechism and singing were taught. Later on, when the private donations that were their only income dwindled or ceased altogether, the young musicians began to offer their services in churches, theatres, and the homes of nobles. In time the conservatories became great markets for singers, instrumentalists, virtuosi, and composers, the demand for which was insatiable. Domenico Cimarosa, Nicola Antonio Porpora, Giovanni Paisello, Domenico and Alessandro Scarlatti, and Giovan Battista Pergolesi all graduated from the Conservatory of San Pietro a Maiella and its illustrious predecessors. Today the library (with an extraordinary collection of autograph manuscripts) and the museum (portraits of eminent musicians and historical items such as Martucci's piano and Rossini's desk) repay a visit. Both are opened by request.

The church of **San Pietro a Maiella**, adjoining, built in 1313–16, contains a magnificent series of *paintings** by Mattia Preti (1656–61) depicting the life of Celestin V and the legend of St Catherine of Alexandria.

Pass the Policlinico, with its 17C chapel and the ruined church of Santa Maria Maggiore, in front of which is the graceful chapel (1498), in the Tuscan Renaissance style, of Giovanni Pontano (1426–1503), the poet and humanist. Immediately beyond is a decayed tower of Roman material and early construction, called the Campanile della Pietrasanta.

Continue along Via dei Tribunali, which corresponds to the decumanus major of the Graeco-Roman city. Reached by the Via N !o (right) and Via De Sanctis is the *Cappella di Santa Maria Della Pietà dei Sangro (Cappella Sansevero; 1590), the tomb-chapel of the princes of Sangro di San Severo (open as a museum, 10.00–13.00, 17.00–19.00). It is remarkable for its 18C interior decoration, a profusion of frescoes, marbles and statuary. Most notable among the allegorical figures are those of Modesty (Pudicizia; completely veiled), by Antonio Corradini, and Disillusion (a man struggling in the net of vice), by Francesco Queirolo, a marvel of technical ability. The Dead Christ, a veiled statue in alabaster, by Giuseppe Sammartino (1753), is a work of astounding realism.

The neighbourhood is dominated by the Sangro **family palaces**. In Piazza San Domenico Maggiore (Atlas 2, 6; Route 4B), at No. 3 is the Palazzo Del Balzo, built in the early 15C and renovated after the earthquake of 1688; the marble doorway and the courtyard, with its low arches and elegant first-floor portico, elements typical of the Catalan architectural style brought to Naples by the Aragonese, belong to the original building. To the right, at No. 17, is an 18C palace of the Sangro family designed by Mario Gioffredo and remodelled by Luigi Vanvitelli. The impressive portico is carried by Greek columns unearthed during the construction of the building. Across the square, at No. 12, is the palace of Giovanni di Sangro, with a fine 18C doorway. No. 9 is the Neapolitan residence of the main line of the family, dukes of Torremaggiore and princes of Sansevero. It was built in the early 16C and later enlarged. The magnificent portal was made by by Vitale Finelli, on a design by Bartolomeo Picchiatti (1621). The stucco bas-reliefs of the entry foyer were executed by Giuseppe Sammartino, when the palace belonged to Raimondo di Sangro (1711–71), well known for his mechanical inventions.

SAN PAOLO MAGGIORE
Return to Via dei Tribunali. In Piazza San Gaetano a flight of steps mounts to the church of **San Paolo Maggiore** (Atlas 2, 2), rebuilt by Francesco Grimaldi (1603) on the site of a temple of the Dioscuri, whose hexastyle portico remained until the earthquake of 1688 overthrew all the columns but two. The spacious interior has alternating large and small bays in the nave arcade that create an unprecedented sense of movement. The transept and apse are less ingenious. The church is decorated with frescoes by Stanzione (1644), and (in the sacristy) by Solimena. There are also two interesting Baroque chapels: the first chapel left of the high altar, the Cappella Firrao (1641) by Dionisio Lazzari, decorated with inlaid coloured marbles and mother of pearl; and the fourth south chapel, the Cappella della Purità (1681) by Giovanni Domenico Vinaccia, again with inlaid coloured marbles and paintings by Massimo Stanzione.

SAN GREGORIO ARMENO
A little to the south lies **San Gregorio Armeno** (Atlas 3, 7), a convent of Benedictine nuns, whose charming **cloister**, an oasis of tranquillity in contrast with the noise of the streets outside, is overlooked by the 17C campanile and a tiled cupola. At the centre of the garden is a Baroque glorification of the well of Samaria, with figures of Jesus and the Samaritan woman, carved by Matteo

Bottiglieri in 1730, which from a distance appear to be walking among the orange trees.

The **church** has a fine gilded ceiling of 1582, a gilded bronze comunichino (1610), and frescoes by Luca Giordano of the life of the saint. The nuns here were traditionally the daughters of noble families, accustomed to a life of luxury which they could hardly be expected to renounce. An 18C English traveller provides an account of a royal visit to the convent, and of the somewhat unusual conventual cuisine:

> The company was surprised, on being led into a large parlour, to find a table covered, and every appearance of a most plentiful cold repast, consisting of several joints of meat, hams, fowl, fish, and various other dishes. It seemed rather ill-judged to have prepared a feast of such a solid nature immediately after dinner; for those royal visits were made in the afternoon. The Lady Abbess, however, earnestly pressed their Majesties to sit down; with which they complied...The nuns stood behind, to serve their royal guests. The Queen chose a slice of cold turkey, which, on being cut up, turned out [to be] a large piece of lemon ice, of the shape and appearance of a roasted turkey. All the other dishes were ices of various kinds, disguised under the forms of joints of meat, fish, and fowl, as above mentioned. The gaiety and good humour of the King, the affable and engaging behaviour of the royal sisters (Queen Maria Carolina and the Princess of Saxe-Teschen), and the satisfaction which beamed from the plump countenance of the Lady Abbess, threw an air of cheerfulness on this scene; which was interrupted, however, by gleams of melancholy reflection, which failed not to dart to mind, at sight of so many victims to the pride of family, to avarice, and superstition. Many of those victims were in the full bloom of health and youth, and some of them were remarkably handsome.

Via San Gregorio is famous for its craftsmen, who make the figures for Neapolitan presepi.

Almost opposite San Paolo Maggiore, on the site of the Roman basilica, is the Franciscan church of San Lorenzo Maggiore (Routes 3A and 4B). Further on the street broadens before the church of **Girolamini** (or San Filippo Neri), built in 1592–1619 by Giovanni Antonio Dosio and Dionisio di Bartolomeo, with a façade by Fuga (c 1780), now blocked up. You enter from the side facing the cathedral. The interior is well and richly decorated and has 12 monolithic granite columns; the fine wooden ceiling was damaged in 1943. Over the principal entrance is a fresco by Luca Giordano of Christ driving the moneylenders from the temple. Near the last column on the left is the tomb of Giovanni Battista Vico (1668–1744), pioneer of the philosophy of history. The apse contains paintings by Corenzio; the chapel of St Philip Neri (left), frescoes by Solimena. In the convent is a small pinacoteca (closed 1995) with paintings by Andrea da Salerno, Guido Reni, Massimo Stanzione, and others.

Turn left along the Via del Duomo, where No. 142 gives access to the cloisters of the Girolamini; the library occupies a fine room by Marcello Guglielmelli (1727–36). Immediately opposite is the cathedral (Atlas 3, 3, Routes 4A, 4B), just south of which is the **Monte della Misericordia**, a charitable foundation of 1601; in its octagonal church (1658–78; entrance in Via dei Tribunali) is a huge painting by Caravaggio of the *Seven Acts of Mercy (1607). The recently reordered pinacoteca has paintings by Fabrizio Santafede, Francesco de Mura, Luca

Giordano and others (church and pinacoteca open by appointment; tel. 081 446944).

The Botanic Garden

About 1km north-east along Via Foria lies the **Botanic Garden** (Atlas 5, 3), founded by Joseph Bonaparte in 1807; it covers about 12 hectares (open by appointment, tel. 081 449759) and contains an early 19C neo-Classical greenhouse in addition to numerous varieties of **exotic plants**. Opposite its north end, Sant'Antonio Abate, the church of a 14C hospital for lepers, retains frescoes of the 14C and 15C. Just beyond is the Albergo dei Poveri, a workhouse built by Ferdinando Fuga in 1751, of which the immense façade, 345m long, occupies the north side of Piazza Carlo III. From the other side Corso Garibaldi, a busy thoroughfare, descends in a straight line to Piazza Garibaldi (1km) and the docks (Route 6A).

C.   Palazzo Reale di Capodimonte

*The **Palazzo Reale di Capodimonte** (Atlas 5,3), a plain Doric building begun in 1738 and completed in 1838, is magnificently situated in a fine park, enjoying a wide view of Campania and of Naples itself. In May 1957 the palace was opened as the new seat of the Museo e Gallerie Nazionali di Capodimonte, comprising the National Gallery of Naples, formerly in the Museo Nazionale, and a large collection of Italian art of the 19C, formerly in the Accademia delle Belle Arti, as well as important exhibitions of armour, porcelain, and ivories from the royal collections.*

APPROACHES. The palace is situated at the north end of Via Toledo and its extensions (Route 5B), 4km from Piazza del Municipio and 3.5km from Piazza Garibaldi (Stazione Centrale). City bus services (Nos 110 and 127) run from the latter to the Tondo di Capodimonte, where pedestrians mount the tree-lined flight of steps. No. 24, from Piazza Vittoria (Atlas 4, 10), continues to ascend Via di Capodimonte, in a long curve, passing the dome of a huge new church. To the left, in Via Miano, is the Porta Piccola; to the right, the Porta Grande, the more usual entrance to the magnificent *PARK (open 09.00–dusk, free). Within may be seen the kilns from the famous porcelain works founded by Charles of Bourbon in 1739, which were working until 1805. The entrance to the Palace is through the most northerly of the three courts.

VISITS. After two years of renovation and restoration, the museum reopened in Sept 1995 with a temporary arrangement of its celebrated collections of old master paintings and decorative arts. By the end of 1996 these works will be installed in a permanent manner, and the traditional collections will be supplemented by a fine collection of 19C art (in storage while work proceeds) and a new gallery of contemporary art, on the top floor. The following description is based on the transitional installation and may not reflect the final order, unknown at the time of writing. The museum is open Tue–Fri 10.00–18.00, Sat 10.00–21.00, Sun 09.00–15.00.

Intended by Charles of Bourbon as the most important summer hunting-lodge in Europe, the ***Palazzo Reale di Capodimonte** was begun in 1738 by Giovanni Antonio Medrano, and the park was designed by Ferdinando Sanfelice. The construction by Joachim Murat of the Sanità bridge and of a new approach road stimulated further enlargements, which were completed by Antonio Niccolini for

Ferdinando IV in 1834–38. After the decline of the Bourbons the palace became a favourite haunt of Victor Emmanuel II, and in 1906–47 of the Dukes of Aosta.

While renovation work continues elsewhere in the building, the fabulous **Farnese collections**, which constitute the core of the museum's holdings, have been brought together, in the monumental rooms of the main floor, in a special exhibition entitled 'I Farnese. Arte e collezionismo' (The Farnese, Art and Collecting). The exhibition highlights the museum's oldest and most important collection of master paintings and drawings, inherited by Charles of Bourbon from his mother, Elisabetta Farnese. The rooms are reached by the monumental main staircase.

ROOM 1: Girolamo Mazzola Bedoli, allegorical figures of a Man Measuring a Column (Euclid) and a Seated Man with Scale and Hammer (Pythagoras); Guglielmo della Porta, Portrait of Pope Paul III.

ROOM 2: Cesare Aretusi, Portrait of Duke Ranuccio I; Girolamo Mazzola Bedoli, **Allegory of Parma Embracing Prince Alexander Farnese** (1555–58), commissioned by Margaret of Austria on her son's departure for Flanders to be educated at the Spanish court; Giulio Campi, **Portrait of Duke Ottavio Farnese** (c 1560), in which Ottavio wears the collar of the French Order of St Michel, conferred upon him for switching the family's loyalty from Spain to France in 1551–56; Sanchez Coello, Portrait of Prince Alessandro Farnese; Gervasio Gatti, Portrait of Prince Ranuccio Farnese; anonymous 17C Parmesan artist, Portraits of Duke Ranuccio I and Margherita Aldobrandini; Anthonis Mor, Portrait of Duke Alessandro Farnese as a Young Man; Guglielmo della Porta, two busts of Pope Paul III; **Infant Hercules Throttling the Serpents**, a bronze of 1555–60 based on ancient Roman models and long considered itself an antiquity; busts of Antinoos; Caracalla as an adult; Caracalla as a child; Lucius Verus; Scipione Pulzone, Portrait of Cardinal Alessandro Farnese; Raphael, **Portrait of Cardinal Alessandro Farneese, Future Pope Paul III** (1509–11), executed on the occasion of Alessandro's election as bishop of Parma, the first step in his climb to power; Sebastiano del Piombo, Portrait of Pope Paul III with a grandson (Ottavio Farnese?); Titian, **Portrait of Cardinal Ranuccio Farnese as a young man** (c 1542), the painter's first commission for the Farnese, showing the twelve-year old Ranuccio as Gran Priore of the Order of the Knights of Malta and brilliantly depicting the contrast between the young man's innocence and the social role he was summoned to play; Portrait of Duke Pierluigi Farnese; two portraits of **Pope Paul III**, **Pope III with His Grandsons Alessandro and Ottavio Farine** (1545–46), in which the young men are shown as the continuers of the family's ecclesiastical and secular traditions; **Portrait of Cardinal Alessandro Farnese** (1545–46), famous for the detail of the gloves, the presence of which suggests that Alessandro (cardinal at the age of fourteen) was something of a dandy.

ROOM 3: Giorgio Vasari, Allegory of Justice, Truth and Vice. ROOM 4: Michelangelo, **Group of Soldiers** (c 1546), a cartoon for the fresco of the Crucifixion of St Peter in the Vatican; copies after Michelangelo and executed by Pontormo; Giovan Francesco Penni, Madonna del Divino Amore; Raphael, **Moses before the Burning Bush** (c 1514), a cartoon for another Vatican fresco, in which the scale and sculptural quality of the figure recall Michelangelo's Sistine Ceiling, unveiled in 1512. ROOM 5: Botticelli, **Madonna and Child with Angels** (c 1468–69), one of the artist's early works, combining the soft transparency of Filippo Lippi with the sculptural quality of Verrocchio; Sebastiano Mainardi, Madonna and Child, the Young St John and Three Angels; Masolino, **Assumption of the Virgin** and **Foundation of the basilica of Santa Maria Maggiore** (c

1428), two panels of a triptych commissioned by Pope Martin V from Masolino and Masaccio (the latter died before they were completed for that church.

ROOM 8: Giovanni Bellini, **Transfiguration** (1478–79), perhaps the artist's masterpiece, showing perfect command of light and atmosphere and an extraordinary humanisation of Christ; Dosso Dossi, Sacra Conversazione; Holy Family; Garofalo, Madonna and Child with St Jerome; Circumcision; St Sebastian; workshop of Garofalo, Adoration of the Magi; Lorenzo Lotto, **Madonna and Child with St Peter Martyr** (1503), the artist's earliest known work, commissioned by Bishop Bernardo de' Rossi as a votive offering for having escaped a murder plot; *Portrait of Bernardo de Rossi, Bishop of Treviso* (1505), a work of unmiti-

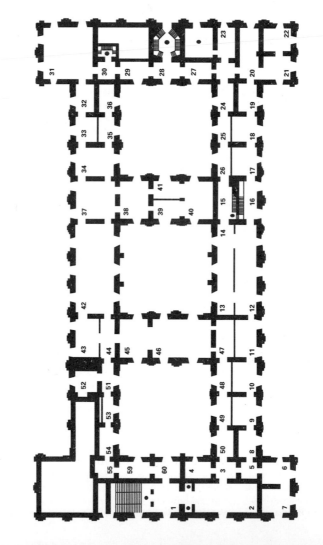

CAPODIMONTE

gated realism; Andrea Mantegna, *Portrait of Francesco Gonzaga (1406–62), cardinal at seventeen, later portrayed by the artist in the *Camera Picta* in Mantua; Filippo Mazzola, Pietà; Giovan Girolamo Savoldo, St Jerome.

ROOM 9: Andrea del Sarto, *Portrait of Leo X with Two Cardinals (1525), a copy of the famous portrait by Raphael, secretly ordered by Ottaviano de' Medici and sent in guile to Federico Gonzaga instead of the original, which Federico had demanded as a gift from Clement VII; the composition shows Leo X with his cardinal-grandsons Giulio de' Medici (the future Pope Clement VII) and Luigi de' Rossi and is intended to sanction the transmission of ecclesiastical power along blood lines; Daniele de Volterra (attr.), Portrait of a Young Man; Giulio Romano, *Madonna della gatta (c. 1523), showing a clear debt to Raphael in the compositional scheme; Scipione Pulzone, Portrait of a Lady in Red; Portrait of a Lady in Black; school of Raphael (Giovanni Francesco Penni), Madonna del Divino Amore; school of Raphael, Holy Family ('Madonna of the Veil'); Madonna del Passeggio; Sebastiano del Piombo, two portraits of Clement VII; *Madonna of the Veil (1533–35), drawing on the styles Raphael and Michelangelo; copy after Sebastiano del Piombo, Portrait of Giulia Gonzaga; Marcello Venusti, copy after Michelangelo, Last Judgment.

ROOM 10: copy after Andrea del Sarto, Madonna and Child with the Young St John; Agnolo Bronzino (attr.), Portrait of a Lady; Cigoli, Deposition; Peter De Witte, Holy Family with the Young St John, Madonna and Child with the Young St John; Franciabigio, St Bartholomew; St Bruno; Girolamo da Carpi, Portrait of a Gentleman in Black (Girolamo de Vincnti?); Maso da San Friano, Two Men; Iacopo Pontormo, Scene of sacrifice (c. 1540), a mysterious exercise in anticlassicism executed in grisaille; Domenico Puligo (?), Madonna and Child with the young St John; Rosso Fiorentino, *Portrait of a young man (c 1527), thought to represent Parmigianino; Francesco Salviati, *Portrait of a Gentleman (c 1545), a work of singlular psychological intensity.

ROOM 11: Sofinisba Anguissola, Self-Portrait at the Spinet; El Greco, Healing of the Blind; *Portrait of Giulio Clovio (1571–72), the famous Croatian illuminator, holding his *Golden Book* now in the Pierpont Morgan Library in New York; the freedom of the brushwork suggests the influence of Titian, under whom El Greco worked on his arrival in Venice in 1567; *Young Man Lighting a Candle with a Coal ('El soplón', c 1575), in which the artist brings Venetian colourism to bear on a subject celebrated by Pliny in the *Naturalis Historia*; Pordenone, Disputa of the Immaculate Conception; Titian, *Danäe (1544–46), painted for the private apartments of Cardinal Alessandro Farnese and representing the story, from Ovid's *Metaorphoses*, of a young princess seduced by Zeus in the form of a shower of gold; the provocative sensuality of the figure contributes to the ambiguity of the scene, which some scholars believe depicts Alessandro's mistress; Portrait of Filippo II; *Portrait of a Young Lady (1545–46), thought by some to represent the artist's daughter, Lavinia Vecellio, and by others, Alessandro's young lover, subject of the Danäe; Mary Magdalen.

ROOM 12: Michelangelo Anselmi, St Claire; St Anthony of Padua; Madonna and Child, Mary Magdalen and St Apollonia; Nativity; Adoration of the Shepherds; anonymous (Michelangelo Anselmi?), Portrait of a Gentleman (Giovan Battista Castaldi); Bagnacavallo (?), Madonna and Child with the young St John; Bastianino, Madonna and Child; Girolamo Mazzola Bedoli, Holy Family with St John the Baptist and Angels; St Claire; Portrait of a Taylor; Portrait of Anna Eleonora Sanvitale; Annunciation; Jacopo Bertoja (attr.), Madonna and Child; Jacopo Bertoja, Rape of Helen; Mars and Venus; Correggio, Madonna and Child ('la

Zingarella'); Marriage of St Catherine; St Joseph and a Devotee; Nicolò dell' Abate, Portrait of a Young Man with Book; Giambologna, ***Rape of the Sabines** (1578), a small bronze prototype of the marble group in Florence, commissioned by Duke Ottavio for his study; Lelio Orsi, St George and the Dragon; Parmigianino, ***Portrait of Galeazzo Sanvitale** (1524), showing the spatial ambiguity and disquieting effects of light and shadow on which the artist built his reputation; Holy Family; ***Portrait of a Young Woman** (1530–35) identified with the courtesan Antea, possibly the artist's mistress during his years in Rome; Lucretia; Francesco Maria Rondani (?), portrait of a musician; Pellegrino Tibaldi, Holy Family with St John the Baptist and St Catherine of Alexandria.

ROOM 13: Girolamo Mirola, Intervention of the Sabine Women in the Battle Between the Romans and Sabines; Girolamo Mirola (?), Portrait of Ludovico Orsini; Jan Sons, Tabula Cebetis Thebani; Baptism of Christ; St Cecily and the Vision of St John, Loves of the Gods (ceiling).

ROOM 14: Tapestry from the Medici manufacture (after 1524), designed by Francesco Salviati; plaques, ivories, ambers; small bronzes, notably Francesco di Giorgio Martini, *David (1475–85), combining iconographic traditions of the Middle Ages (David as elderly prophet) and the Renaissance (as young hero); majolicas from the Castelli manufacture (1574–1589), Farnese dining service; goldsmith's art, notably Manno di Bastiano Sbarri and Giovanni Bernardi da Castelbolognese, *Farnese Casket (1548–61), a box in gilt silver, lapis lazzuli, enamel and carved crystal made for Cardinal Alessandro Farnese; Iacob Miller the Elder, *Diana the Huntress (1610), a gilt silver centrepiece; Francesco Villamena, from a design by Annibale Carracci, *Farnese Bread-Tray (c 1600), with drunken Rilenus; incised crystal by Giovanni Bernardi da Castelbolognese; medals, including Pisanello, Giovanni VIII Paleologo; precious stones and curiosities.

ROOM 15: Jacques de Backe, The Seven Deadly Sins (Avarice, Lust, Wrath, Sloth, Gluttony, Pride, Envy); Arnout De Muysser, Market with Woman Selling Game; Market with Woman Selling Flowers; 16C Roman school, busts of Roman emperors.

ROOM 16: Cesare da Sesto, Christ of Sorrow and Cardinal Oliviero Carafa in Prayer; Cesare Magni, Virgin of the Rocks; Giampietrino, Madonna and Child, St John the Baptist and St Jerome; anonymous 16C Lombard artist, Lucretia; Alessandro Buonvicini (Moretto da Brescia), Christ at the Column; Callisto Piazza, Three Half-Figures and a Child (allegory of marriage?); Ercole Procaccini, Marriage of St Catherine; Camillo Procaccini, Jesus at Gethsemane; Giulio Cesare Procaccini, Madonna and Child with Angel; Jan Sons, Marriage of St Catherine.

ROOM 17: Peter Bruegel, ***The Misanthrope** (1568); the Flemish proverb at the bottom reads, 'As the world is so untrustworthy, I am in mourning'; ***The Blind Leading the Blind** (1568), illustrating the well-known New Testament parable ('when one blind man leads another, both will fall into the ditch'); Civetta, two Landscapes with the Good Samaritan; Coastal Landscape; Landcape with Temptation of Christ; Landscape with Storm at Sea; Moses before the Burning Bush; Lucas Cranach the Elder, Christ and the Adultress; anonymous Italianizing Flemist artist, Deposition; anonymous Franco-Flemish artist, Portrait of a Young Prince; copy after Van Der Goes, Pietà; Bernard van Orley, Portrait of Charles V as a Young Man; Marinus van Reymerswaele, The Avaricious; Marten de Vos, Jesus Among the Youths; workshop of Konard Zitz, Sacra Conversazione.

ROOM 18: Joachim Beuckelaer, Street Market; Country Market; Vendor of Exotic Animals; Game Vendor; Butcher's Shop; Fishmonger's Shop; Fish Market.

ROOM 19: Agostino Carracci, Portrait of a Lute Player (Orazio Bassani?);

*Arrigo Peloso, Pietro Matto and Amon Nano (c 1598), representing three
characters from the Roman court of Cardinal Odoardo Farnese, Pietro the buffoon,
Rodomonte the dwarf, and Arrigo Gonzalez, the 'wild man of the Canary Islands';
Democritus; Annibale Carracci, *Marriage of St Catherine (c 1585), a master-
piece of classicism commissioned by Ranuccio Farnese as a gift to his brother,
Cardinal Odoaro; Vision of St Eustachio; Portrait of a Musician (Claudio Merulo);
St Francis of Assisi; Male Portrait; St Jerome; Christ and the Canaanite Woman;
workshop of Annibale Carracci, Annunciation (recto); Madonna and Child with St
Francis (verso); Ludovico Carracci, *Rinaldo e Armida (1593), an entertaining
literary subject drawn from Tasso's Gerusalemme Liberata.

ROOM 20: Sisto Badalocchio, Deposition; Agostino Carracci, St Jerome; Holy
Family with St Margaret; Annibale Carracci, *Satyr (perhaps directed against
Caravaggio; the smiling head in the corner is a portrait of the artist); Bacchus;
River Allegory; River Landscape; Ecce Homo; *Hercules at the Crossroads
(1596), showing the choice between the 'easy way' of earthly pleasure, indicated
by Voluptuousness, and the rocky path to glory, pointed out by Virtue; *Pietà
(1599–1600), a painterly homage to Michelangelo's sculpture in St Peter's;
Rinaldo e Armida; Annibale Carracci (?), Rape of Europa; Giovanni Lanfranco,
Jesus Served by the Angels; Assumption of the Virgin; Noli Me Tangere; Marriage
of St Catherine.

ROOM 21: Bartolomeo Schedoni, St Jerome and the Angel; St Mary Magdalen in
Ectasy; Ecce Homo; Announcement of the Massacre of the Innocents; Cupid; Holy
Family with Saints Lawrence, Francis of Assisi, Pellegrino and John the Baptist;
Holy Family; Charity; Portrait of Vincenzo Grassi; St Sebastian Healed by the Pious
Women.

ROOM 22: Michele Desubleo, Ulysses and Nausicca; Guercino, St Jerome; David
with the Head of Goliath; Giovanni Lanfranco, Adoration of the Child with Sts
Francis of Assisi and Rusticus; Saving of a Soul; Madonna and Child with Sts
Charles Borromeo and Bartholomew; Madonna and Child with Sts Mary of Egypt
and Margaret.

ROOM 27: Francesco Albani, St Elisabeth in Glory; Giulio Cesare Amidano, St
Lawrence; Sisto Badalocchio, Madonna and Child in Glory and Sts Crispino and
Crispiniano; Lionello Spada, Cain and Abel; Alessandro Tiarini, Madonna and
Child with Angels.

ROOM 28: Luca Cambiaso, Venus and Adonis; Death of Adonis; Carlo Saraceni,
landscapes with scenes from Ovid's Metamorphoses.

ROOM 29: Jan Ranc, Portrait of Elisabetta Farnese; Sebastiano Ricci, the Virgin
Interceding on Behalf of the Souls in Purgatory; Assumption of St Mary Magdalen;
Pope Paul III Inspired by Faith to Call the Ecumenical Council; Pope Paul III
Naming His Son Pier Luigi Duke of Parma and Piacenza.

ROOM 30: Giuseppe Piamontini, Bust of Charles of Boubon. From here you pass
directly to the elaborately decorated Royal Apartments, an overwhelmingly rich
showcase of European decorative arts. ROOM 31, the Sala della Culla, has tapestries showing episodes from Cervantes's Don Quixote, Neapolitan clocks and furniture, a model of the Temple of Isis at Pompeii, and a marble floor from a villa of
Tiberius on Capri. ROOMS 35–26 display china of various provenance, including
the fabulous *Servizio dell'Oca from Capodimonte (1739–95). ROOM 37 is the
*Salone delle Feste, adorned in blue and gold by Salvatore Giusti (1835–38); the
adjoining rooms contain an elaborate Aurora in Capodimonte biscuit, by Filippo
Taliolini (c 1807), paintings of Vesuvius by Pierre Jacques Volaire, and a beautiful

anonymous *Presepio. ROOM 45 has tapestries with stories of Henry IV and a display of precious objects in cases. From here you enter the famous *Armoury of the Farnese family (ROOM 46), notable for its fine examples of ceremonial armour of the 15–17C. ROOM 52 is the *Salottino di Porcellana, a pretty little room in the Chinese style, executed in Capodimonte porcelain in 1757–59, intended for the Palace of Portici but moved here in 1866. Portraits of Napoleon and Murat hang in ROOM 54; the following room contains Canova's Letitia Bonaparte, c 1808.

The **Gabinetto dei disegni e delle stampe**, on the mezzanine floor, displays drawings from the Farnese collections, including Parmigianino, Portrait of a Seated Lady, Madonna and Child, Studies for a Pentecost, Male Nude with Garland, Cupid Drawing his Bow, Young Men Wrestling, Study for the Madonna of the Long Neck, Study for a Female Figure, Study of Three Female Heads, Madonna and Child, Seated Woman with Book; Girolamo Mazzola Bedoli, Seated Man in a Niche with Cello; St Cecily at the Organ; Sofonisba Anguissola, Child Pinched by a Shrimp; Jacopo Bertoja, Study for Christ Entering Jerusalem, Jacob's Dream; decorative motifs; figure studies; Study for a Beheading; Study for a Bust of a Woman; Ercole Setti, Meeting of Sts Anne and Joachim; anonymous 16C Venetian artist, Christ in Glory; Bartolomeo Schedoni, Adoration of the Magi; anonymous 17C artist, Compositions of Flowers and Butterflies; anonymous late 17C artist, Chinese Oranges; anonymous 16C Bolognese artist, Study for a Putto.

The rooms on the ground floor, across the courtyard from the main entrance, house a temporary selection of works belonging to the museum but not to the Farnese collections. Highlights include ROOM 1, Raphael, *Eternal Father; Masaccio, *Crucifixion, Filippino Lippi, *Annunciation; ROOM 2: Mantegna, *St Eufemia, drawings by Titian and Tintoretto; ROOM 5, Ribera, *Drunken Silenus, and Caravaggio, *Flagellation, from the church of San Domenico.

The **Osservatorio di Capodimonte** has a small Museum (Salita Moiariello 16; open by appointment, phone 081 293266) featuring astronomical instruments in use from the observatory's establishment (1819) until the early twentieth century. The collection is displayed, in part, on the original premises.

D.   Castel Sant'Elmo, San Martino and Villa Floridiana

This itinerary takes in three of Naples' finest museums, all of which are set in splendid surroundings on the slopes of the Vomero hill. The best way to do the route is to take a bus, taxi or funicular to the top of the hill, then walk down. The approach can also be made by foot: from the Museo Nazionale, Via Salvator Rosa diverges left to climb to Piazza Mazzini, from where Corso Vittorio Emanuele starts its winding course round the slopes of Sant'Elmo. Just west of the piazza stands the church of Santa Maria della Pazienza (or La Cesarea; 1636).

Via Santacroce leads to Piazza Leonardo, from where Via Michelangelo runs to the **Vomero**, *a huge modern quarter built to a regular plan. Its north–south axis, Via Bernini, leads directly to Piazza Vanvitelli, the centre of the quarter. From here Via Alessandro Scarlatti mounts to the upper station of the Montesanto funicular railway.*

If you are following the route by car you can reach the same point by turning left in Via

Raffaele Morghen. The bus terminates in Via Tito Angelini, beyond which the road ends at the Castel Sant'Elmo, on the summit of the hill.

CASTEL SANT'ELMO AND SAN MARTINO

The ***Castel Sant'Elmo**, built in 1329–43 and altered to its present form in the 16C by Pier Luigi Scrivà of Valencia, was originally intended to discourage popular insurrection. Long used for political prisoners, it has recently been restored and reopened to the public as an exhibition space. It hosts many of the city's larger temporary exhibitions and commands an extensive, magnificent ***view**.

Adjoining is the Carthusian monastery of ****San Martino** (Atlas 2, 9), founded in the 14C but transformed in the late 16C and early 17C. Architecturally beautiful in themselves, the conventual buildings now also provide an admirable setting for the treasures of the **Museo Nazionale di San Martino** (open Tue–Sun 09.00–14.00). The museum, occupying 90 rooms, illustrates the history, life, and art of Naples.

From the outer gate you enter the Cortile Monumentale and the ***church**, one of the few instances in which a later decorative scheme has been satisfactorily applied to a Gothic building (the original ribs of the nave vault can still be discerned) and certainly the most cogent expression of the Baroque aesthetic in Naples. The **monks' choir** is decorated with frescoes by the Cavalier d'Arpino; at the back a Crucifixion by Lanfranco and a Nativity by Guido Reni; on the left, ***Institution of the Eucharist** by Ribera and Washing of the Disciples' Feet by Caracciolo; on the right, Last Supper by Stanzione and Institution of the Eucharist by a son and pupils of Paolo Veronese. Leading off the choir is the **sacristy**, with ceiling-paintings by the Cavalier d'Arpino, from which an antechamber with frescoes by Stanzione and Giordano opens into the **treasury**. Above the altar, ***Descent from the Cross**, Ribera's masterpiece; the vault-fresco of Judith was Luca Giordano's last work (1704).

From the choir pass by the side of the high altar (a gilded wooden model by Francesco Solimena for a final design that was to be executed in *pietre dure*) into the **nave**. Begun by Dosio and finished by Fanzago, it is rich in inlaid marble work, notably the door by Bonaventura Presti. The Ascension on the ceiling is by Lanfranco; the 12 ***prophets**, by Ribera; and the Descent from the Cross, over the principal door, by Stanzione. The chapels on both sides (not always accessible) contain many notable works of art. Those at the west end of the nave were decorated c 1700 by Lorenzo and Domenico Antonio Vaccaro; those at the east end are variously ascribed to Giuseppe Sammartino and Antonio Tagliacozzi Canale. Their marble balustrades and bronze grilles are by Cosimo Fanzago. The two central chapels, with frescoes by Massimo Stanzione, were begun by Fanzago in 1656 and completed in the late 18C.

The door to the right of the high altar opens into the **choir of the Frati Conversi**, with inlaid stalls of the 15C. From here a passage leads to the Cappella della Maddalena, adorned by Fanzago, the **parlour**, and the **chapter house**, with frescoes by Corenzio.

The little 17C **Chiostrino dei Procuratori** gives access to the **Salone Carozze e Stemme** (carriages and coats of arms; ROOM 1), from where you may enter the beautiful convent gardens, which amply repay a visit. The adjacent **pharmacy** displays antique glass from Murano and other European factories. The other rooms

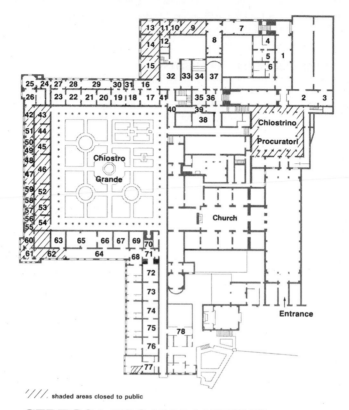

///// shaded areas closed to public

CERTOSA DI SAN MARTINO

in this section house the Maria Teresa Orilia bequest of porcelain, biscuit, and so on; and 15C and 16C polychrome wood sculpture from Neapolitan churches.

Returning to the Salone Carozze e Stemme you enter the *Quarto del Priore (the former prior's apartment), with ceilings frescoed by Micco Spadaro. Here is displayed an outstanding series of artworks representing four centuries of Carthusian patronage in Naples. The works range from 15C Catalan painters to the major figures of the 17C and 18C (Bernini, Santacroce, Caracciolo, Corenzio, Guarino, De Rosa, Vaccaro and others).

From here, you enter the *Sezione Presepiale, with a celebrated collection of presepi (or representations of the Nativity, elaborate compositions with hundreds of statuettes), some by prominent Neapolitan sculptors.

The corridor that you followed earlier to the Chiostrino dei Procuratori, in the opposite direction opens onto the *Chiostro Grande which, with its white and grey marble ornamentation and beautifully kept gardens, is undoubtably one of the more striking achievements of Italian Baroque architecture. The original conception of the cloister, its general layout and the form of the arcade, are due to Antonio Dosio (16C), but its present character is largely a result of the sculptural and architectural programme developed by Cosimo Fanzago in the 17C. His design, conceived in 1623, is strongly conditioned by the style of Buontalenti (note especially the curved and twisted framework of the **niches** above the doors), introduced to Naples in the first quarter of the century by Michelangelo Naccherino and other Florentine artists. Five of the six **busts** (St Martin of Tours, Bishop Nicola Albergati, St Bruno, St Hugh, and St Dionysius) are by Fanzago's hand, whereas the sixth (St Januarius) is an early work of Domencio Antonio Vaccaro. Fanzago is also partly or wholly responsible for the eight **statues** at the corners and centre of the arcade (that of the Resurrected Christ was begun by Naccherino).

VILLA FLORIDIANA

Return to the Montesanto funicular station (see above) and continue to descend by Via Raffaele Morghen. The second street to the left leads into Via Cimarosa. This runs parallel to Via Scarlatti, passing the upper station of the Chiaia funicular, to the shaded park of the **Villa Floridiana** (Atlas 4, 9). The gardens (open 09.00–1hr before sunset), beautifully sited on a spur overlooking the sea, are famous for camellias; the view from the terrace is particularly fine.

The mansion houses the *Museo Nazionale della Ceramica Duca di Martina** (open Tue–Sun 09.00–14.00), based on the original **porcelain collection** of Placido di Sangro, Duke of Martina, augmented by his nephew, Count De Marzi and presented to the city by the widow of the latter, Maria Spinelli. The museum now contains over 6000 pieces of European and Asiatic porcelain and pottery, as well as goldsmiths' work, ivories, and 17C and 18C 19C paintings.

From the foyer, a stair ascends past a marble bust of Ferdinand IV. On the landing are two columns of African marble and Oriental granite, with Oriental vases and bronze decorations of the nineteenth century. From here, pass through the ante-camera to reach ROOM 1, containing assorted porcelain, precious stones, ivories, and the cane collection, with a variety of interesting carved handles. ROOMS 2–4 are dedicated to Meissen porcelain, including many fine miniatures. ROOM 5. Bourbon (Capodimonte and Naples) porcelain. ROOMS 6–7. More Meissen ware. ROOM 8. Viennese and Meissen ware. ROOM 9. Pieces from the Ginori works at Doccia and other Italian manufactures. ROOM 10. French porcelain of various manufacture. ROOM 11. German porcelain from manufactures other than Meissen. ROOM 12. English (Chelsea, Wedgwood, Burslem, Bow Essex, Worcester) and Swiss porcelain. ROOM 13 Oriental (China and Japan) porcelain. ROOM 14. Donazione Riccardo Di Sangro, a rich, varied collection given to the museum in 1978.

The small room adjacent (13) contains Chinese and Japanese items of varied provenence. On the ground floor, beyond the ticket counter, is ROOM 18, with Italian Renaissance and Hispanic-Moorish majolicas. ROOM 17 has Baroque majolicas from the Manifattura di Castelli. ROOMS 19-20. Murano glass and Bohemian crystal. ROOMS. 21-22. Medieval and Renaissance collections; enamels, ivories, etc.

Via Cimarosa goes on to join the winding Via Falcone, which can be reached on foot much further down the hill by taking the Via Luca Giordano (left). Continue the descent, turning left into Via Tasso, to the Ospedale Internazionale, where you emerge into Corso Vittorio Emanuele. To the left the Corso returns to Piazza Mazzini (see above); to the right, skirting the Rione Amedeo, it leads to the Piazza Piedigrotta and Mergellina station (see below). At No. 292 is the **Raccolta d'Arte della Fondazione Pagliara**, part of the university institute of Suor Orsola Benincasa, with paintings by Neapolitan masters, mainly of the 18C and 19C (closed for restoration 1995).

E.   Mergellina and Posillipo

Throughout Italy, in the early and mid 19C, the romantic fashion for broad, open spaces and breathtaking views led to the construction of parks and panoramic carriage roads in and around major cities. The Pincio in Rome is one such project; the Viale dei Colli in Florence is another. In Naples the old mule tracks to Posillipo were improved to make a parkway, and the waterfront at Mergellina, west of Pizzofalcone, was developed as a wooded quayside promenade, for the benefit of the chic new residential quarter on the hillside to the north. Both areas correspond extremely well to the romantic ideal; a stroll through the park at Posillipo, in particular, is rewarding.

The itinerary described here is 5–6km long, so good walking shoes and a free morning or afternoon are musts. Using public transport, the best procedure is to take bus 140 from Piazza della Vittoria to its terminus at Capo Posillipo (Rotonda) and make the tour of the park on foot. Bus 152 crosses the city from Corso Garibaldi to the Mostra d'Oltremare, continuing to Pozzuoli (Route 3E).

THE RIVIERA
From Piazza dei Martiri (Route 5A), the short Via Calabritto leads south to the fine Piazza della Vittoria (Atlas 4, 10). On the seaward side a column of ancient marble commemorates Neapolitans who lost their lives in the various revolts against the Bourbons. From the landward side of the piazza the Riviera di Chiaia, a broad, busy street, extends westward for c 1.5km. Along the left side of the street lies the Villa Communale, a favourite public garden beautifully shaded by sub-tropical trees. In the centre is the Zoological Station (Atlas 4, 10), founded in 1872 for research into the habits of marine flora and fauna. Its chief attraction is the famous ***Aquarium** (open Tue–Sat, 09.00–17.00; Sun 09.00–18.00), remarkable for the perfection of the arrangements by which water is supplied directly from the sea, enabling the most delicate marine organisms to be preserved alive. The collection includes more than 200 species from the water of the gulf.

Across the Riviera di Chiaia, set in a walled garden, is the neo-Classical Villa Pignatelli, which houses the ***Museo Principe Diego Aragona Pignatelli Cortes** (Atlas 4, 10), opened to the public in 1960. The collection (open Tue–Sun 09.00–14.00) includes Italian and European porcelain (from Capodimonte, Venice, Doccia, Vienna, Berlin, Meissen, Thuringen, Bow, Chelsea and Zurich); biscuits from Naples, Vienna and Sèvres; Chinese vases; period furniture, and some works of painting and sculpture, including family portraits. Villa Pignatelli also hosts masterpieces from the collection of the Galleria Nazionale di Capodimonte, while renovation on the Capodimonte Palace (Route 5C) proceeds. The works are shown on a rotating basis, and there are also temporary exhibitions of contemporary art. In the garden is the Museo delle Carrozze Mario D'Alessandro Marchese di

Civitanova, with English, French and Italian **carriages** of the 19C and early 20C.

Between the Villa Comunale and the sea runs Via Caracciolo, a wide promenade skirting the sea all the way to Mergellina, with an uninterrupted view all round the bay. Halfway along it stands the Armando Diaz Monument (1936).

> To the right of the Riviera di Chiaia rises the **Rione Amedeo**, a modern, fashionable quarter. Ascending Via Santa Maria in Portico, leave to the left the church of Santa Maria in Portico (begun 1632, with a façade of 1862) and climb to that of the **Ascensione a Chiaia**. Begun in the 14C but rebuilt by Cosimo Fanzago in 1645, the church contains canvases by Luca Giordano. Further on another church, designed by Cosimo Fanzago but ruined by later restorations, Santa Teresa a Chiaia (1650–62), also contains paintings by Giordano. To the west lies Piazza Amedeo, the centre of the quarter. From here the Parco Margherita winds up to join Corso Vittorio Emanuele.

The Riviera di Chiaia passes the north side of Piazza della Repubblica, with the Monumento allo Scugnizzo by Mazzacurati (1969), commemorating the Quattro Giornate di Napoli. Shortly afterwards, it ends at Largo Torretta (Atlas 4, 9), an open space called after a former tower erected as a defence against pirates. Here the road divides, Via Piedigrotta (right) leading direct to Piazza Piedigrotta. On the far side, where Corso Vittorio Emanuele enters the piazza, lies Mergellina station. To the left stands **Santa Maria di Piedigrotta** (Atlas 4, 13), a 14C church remodelled in 1822 and restored at the beginning of the 20C; the façade is by Enrico Alvino with a campanile rebuilt in 1926. Within are a 15C Neapolitan painting on wood, and, in the large chapel near the choir, tombs of the Filangieri family. On the high altar stands the wooden figure of the **Madonna**, after the manner of Tino di Camaino, much restored and much venerated. On the night of 7–8 September this forms the focal point of an animated **festival**.

On the hill

Beneath the railway viaduct and to the left of the entrance to the Galleria Quattro Giornate (a tunnel leading to Fuorigrotta), steps give access to the **Parco Virgiliano**. Here a pillar marks the remains of Giacomo Leopardi, moved here from a church in Fuorigrotta recently demolished. Nearby is a Roman columbarium in *opus reticulatum* traditionally known as the **Tomb of Virgil**, restored in 1927. Immediately below the columbarium is the mouth of the **Grotta Vecchia** or **Crypta Neapolitana** (710m long; closed), a remarkable feat of Roman engineering, planned by Cocceius for Agrippa and Octavian to provide a direct road from Neapolis to Puteoli. It is described by Seneca, Petronius and John Evelyn.

Turning south, join Via Mergellina (from the Torretta; see above) and enter Piazza Sannazaro. To the right is the entrance to the Galleria della Laziale (or di Posillipo), a straight modern tunnel 900m long, leading to Fuorigrotta.

The Quartiere Flegreo

At the far end of the tunnel, Via Fuorigrotta leads directly into the Quartiere Flegreo, a new quarter developed since 1938 from the little village of Fuorigrotta. The broad principal thoroughfare, Viale Augusto, and the parallel Via Giulio Cesare both terminate to the south on the vast Piazza Vincenzo Tecchio, in the north–west corner of which is the entrance to the **Mostra**

d'Oltremare. This is a modern precinct, set in gardens below the north slope of the Phlegraean hills, comprising a number of pavilions designed to house exhibitions, fairs, congresses and places of entertainment of all kinds. Among the more important constructions are the Arena Flegrea (10,000 seats), the Teatro Mediterraneo, a large swimming pool, and the Palazzo dei Congressi; there are also ice- and roller-skating rinks, a dance hall and restaurants.

To the south, Viale Kennedy leads (1km more) to the ***zoo** (open daily 09.00–19.00; refreshments, no restaurant), opened in 1950 in a beautiful park set with tropical trees and containing a fine collection of well-housed animals. Viale Kennedy continues across the Campi Flegrei to Pozzuoli (Route 3E).

MERGELLINA
You reach the shore again at the little bay of Mergellina (Atlas 4, 13), much sung by poets and affording a good view back to Santa Lucia. Here is the lower station of the funicular to Via Manzoni. Above the south end of the bay rises the church of **Santa Maria del Parto**, or del Sannazaro, founded in the 16C by the Neapolitan poet Jacopo Sannazaro, containing the well-known Diavolo di Mergellina (St Michael Overthrowing Satan), by Leonardo da Pistoia (1542). At the back of the apse, which is decorated with paintings and stucco, is the tomb of Iacopo Sannazaro, by Fra Giovanni da Montorsoli (1537).

POSILLIPO
From the church, Via Posillipo hugs the shore for some way and then climbs away up the slopes of the hilly promontory known as ***Posillipo**, a name said to be derived from *Pausilypon* (sans-souci), a villa belonging to Vedius Pollio and afterwards to Augustus. This picturesque road, begun in 1808 under Murat, passes many handsome villas amid rich vegetation and commands lovely views, especially fine at sunset. Hereabouts, in 1839, the two-year-old W.S. Gilbert was kidnapped by brigands and ransomed, an incident which finds an echo in *The Gondoliers*.

On the left side of the road is the **Palazzo di Donn'Anna**, built in 1642–44 by Fanzago for Anna Carafa, wife of the Duke of Medina, viceroy of Naples. Perhaps the most ingeniously planned and dramatically situated of all Neapolitan palaces, its construction was interrupted by the death of the patron in 1642. Further on is the Ospizio Marino, a home for old sailors and fishermen, with a monument to Ludovico da Casoria, its founder. The view becomes increasingly fine as the road climbs to Piazza San Luigi (c 85m; restaurants), on the far side of the Parco della Rimembranza, which contains an Egyptian-style mausoleum, the memorial to the dead of the First World War. The exceptional ***view** gives its name to the church of Santa Maria di Bellavista. Close to the church Via Ferdinando Russo leads down in 10 min. to **Capo di Posillipo** (view) near which is the sumptuous Villa Rosebery, Neapolitan residence of the President of the Republic. Continue to the Quadrivio del Capo, a central point for excursions to the area.

Marechiare
To the south Via Marechiaro, a road through villas and vineyards, leads down to (1km) **Marechiaro**, an unspoilt fishing hamlet with stone houses rising in steps from the sea. A plaque marks the window celebrated by Salvatore di Giacomo in the song set to music by Tosti. From here an excursion may be made by boat to the **Grotta dei Tuoni** (where the waves produce thunderous echoes) and La Gaiola, a rock near which the remain of Pollio's villa (see

above) may be seen. The road to the right from the Quadrivio, Via Boccaccio, climbs directly to Via Manzoni (see below).

About 150m beyond the Quadrivio, Viale Tito Lucrezio Caro, to the left, winds up to the entrance to the **Parco di Posillipo** (153m) on the top of Monte Coroglio. A road encircles the park; at the point nearest the sea a **belvedere** offers a splendid view of Capri and Vesuvius, as well as Ischia and Capo Miseno. Nisida lies immediately below. From the park entrance, you may go directly to Posillipo Alto by Viale Virgilio (see below).

Return by Via Caro and turn left, passing under the Viaduct of Montagna Spaccata to reach the **Rotonda di Posillipo**, another famous viewpoint overlooking the Campi Flegrei, the Gulf of Pozzuoli and Procida. The view is somewhat marred by the railway sidings and chemical works in the foreground. The road turns towards the sea and descends, passing the entrance to the Grotto of Sejanus, a tunnel c 950m long leading to Pollio's Villa, which in spite of its name is believed to have been cut in AD 37. At the foot of the hill a byroad crosses the modern causeway to the island of **Nisida**, an extinct volcano known to the ancients as *Nesis*. The castle, now a school, was the prison of Carlo Poerio, whose plight horrified the visiting Gladstone.

Nesis belonged to Lucullus and was afterwards the retreat of Marcus Brutus, who was visited here by Cicero, The **conspiracy against Caesar** was here planned by Brutus and Cassius; and here Brutus bade farewell to his wife Portia.

Viale Virgilio from the park crosses the viaduct to join Via Boccaccio above the Quadrivio del Capo, from where you ascend Via Manzoni (left; view towards Agnano) or Via del Casale (right) to arrive at the Torre Ranieri crossroads. From here Via Petrarca drops gradually to Mergellina, offering unimpeded *views towards the sea and Via Manzoni (left) runs along the whole length of the Posillipo hills through magnificent country dotted with modern villas. The road passes the upper station of the funicular from Mergellina (see above).

At the Quadrivio di Posillipo Alto (160m) Via Stazio descends in steep bends to Mergellina. Via Manzoni continues, still affording pleasant views, to the Villa Patrizi, where a road diverges (left) for Agnano, and Largo Europa. From here another road to the left, Via Tasso, drops down (with a great part of the city spread out below) to join Corso Vittorio Emanuel, and Via Falcone ascends to the Vomero.

F.   The Royal Palace of Caserta

Caserta, a town of 69,000 inhabitants, is known as the Versailles of Naples from the royal palace built here by Charles III of Bourbon. This is one of the grandest neo-Classical edifices in Europe; its park is both immense and fascinating. Both are conveniently visited from Naples in half a day. Alternatively, they may be combined with Routes 1A.

ROAD (29km). Autostrada A2 to Caserta Nord.

RAILWAY. A choice of two routes (the old main line to Rome via Cassino, and the line to Benevento and Foggia) provides a good service from Naples (Centrale) to Caserta in 30–45 min.

INFORMATION: EPT, Palazzo Reale; tel. 0823 326832, fax 0823 326300 (branch office at Piazza Dante 35).

THE PALACE
The *Royal Palace (or Reggia), overlooking a huge square, is one of the more sumptuous buildings of its kind in Italy. The building was begun by Charles III in 1752 and completed by Ferdinand I in 1774 from the plans of **Luigi Vanvitelli**. The first stone was laid by the king on his 36th birthday, January 20 1752; for the occasion the perimeter of the future palace was marked by regiments of infantry and squadrons of cavalry, and two cannons with artillerymen were placed at each corner. The army of workmen engaged on the building was swelled by convicts and galley-slaves.

Construction proceeded briskly until 1759, the year in which Charles left Naples to take the throne of Spain. Work then slowed, coming to a complete halt in 1764 when, in the midst of a severe plague and famine, the half-finished building was occupied by the poor and homeless. After the death of Vanvitelli in 1773 his son, Carlo, continued the construction, but he ran into difficulties of various kinds and was unable to complete the building according to his father's plan. Eliminated from the design were four corner towers and a central dome, which undoubtedly would have relieved the gravity of the building's present configuration, and the guards' quarters, which were to enclose the vast forecourt on all sides.

During the long reign of Ferdinand IV the palace was enlivened by balls, receptions, hunting parties and theatrical performances. It was the favourite residence of Ferdinand II and after the unification of Italy it was visited by the Savoyard kings. It was presented by Victor Emmanuel III to the State in 1921. On April 29 1945, it was the scene of the unconditional surrender of the German forces in Italy to Supreme Allied Commander in the Mediterranean, Field Marshal Harold Alexander.

The two principal façades, 247m long and 36m high, are pierced by 243 windows and several monumental entrances. The two other sides are 108m in length, and have 135 windows. The palace consists of five storeys—a ground floor, mezzanine, first floor, second floor, and attic—containing 1200 rooms served by 43 staircases, all arranged around four monumental courtyards, whose decoration was never finished. The design of the building was controversial even in its own day. Although many contemporaries regarded it as one of the nobler edifices of its kind in Europe, some considered it a megalomaniac construction. Henry Swinburne visited it in the 1770s and left this account:

> The vast dimensions of its apartments, the bold span of their ceilings, the excellence and beauty of the materials employed in building and decorating it, and the strength of the masonry, claim the admiration of all beholders, who must confess it is a dwelling spacious and grand enough to have lodged the ancient masters of the Roman world. It is a pity that its enormous bulk drowns the minuter members of its architecture, and gives too much the idea of a regular monastery, where the wealthy chief of some religious order presides over long dormitories of segregated monks; by the gigantic range, and the number of windows, too great a sameness is produced, the few breaks in the front become imperceptible, and the lines too long and uniform, consequently fatiguing to the eye; the colonnades sink into the

walls, and variety is in vain sought for in the prodigious expanse; bolder and greater projections, massive towers, arcades or porticoes, would have shown the parts of this great building to more advantage, and formed those happy contrasts that are so necessary in works of so very large a dimension. Upon a nearer approach, the parts and proportions are better distinguished, and the objection ceases.

The **interior** (open daily 09.00–18.00) is of great interest. The main portico is divided into three vestibules by 64 columns. The **state staircase** ascends to the first-floor vestibule, an octagon surrounded by 24 pillars of yellow marble. Opposite the head of the stairs is the **Palatine Chapel**, usually closed. Modelled on the chapel of the Palace of Versailles, it contains the finest marble ornaments and several noteworthy paintings, including an Immaculate Conception by Giuseppe Bonito, a Presentation in the Temple by Antonio Raffaele Mengs and five works by Sebastiano Conca.

A door on the left gives entrance to the **Royal Apartments**, beautifully decorated with tapestries, paintings, frescoes, and period furniture. The **Room of the Halabardiers**, the first to be entered, has a Bourbon coat of arms borne by Virtues in the ceiling. The **guard room**, following, is decorated with the apotheosis of the Farnese family (of which, it will be recalled, Charles's mother was an eminent member) and the 12 provinces of the kingdom, in the ceiling; and with scenes from ancient history in the bas-reliefs around the walls. On the right is a marble statuary group of Alexander Farnese crowned by Victory, carved, according to tradition, out of a column from the Temple of Peace in Rome.

The adjacent **Room of Alexander**, which corresponds to the centre of the main façade, enjoys a good view of what was once the tree-lined high road to Naples. The ceiling fresco and the stucco reliefs show scenes from the life of Alexander Farnese; the other paintings celebrate deeds of Charles of Bourbon. The portrait medallion in porphyry over the fireplace is of Alexander the Great. The room is furnished in the Empire style; particulary noteworthy is the large clock on the right wall, made in Naples in 1828.

The **New Apartment**, so-called because it was the last to be completed (1845), is reached by a door on the right. It consists of three rooms, furnished in the Empire style and decorated with paintings and reliefs of mythological subjects. Notice, in the centre of the first room, an Oriental alabaster cup presented by Pope Pius IX to Ferdinand II.

The **throne room**, the largest room of the palace, is adorned with a frieze containing medallions of the kings of Naples from Roger the Norman to Ferdinand II (Joseph Bonaparte and Joachim Murat have been tactfully omitted). The ceiling painting shows Charles III laying the first stone of the palace. Beyond the throne room extend the living quarters of the king. The **council room** contains a fine table given by the city of Naples to Francis I as a wedding present. An antechamber, where majolicas are displayed, gives access to the **Bedroom of Francis II**, containing a magnificent mahogany bed and the first known example of a **roll-top desk**. The ceiling painting of Theseus killing the Minotaur is by Giuseppe Cammarano. Adjoining the bedroom are the king's **bathroom** and **study**. Beyond two handsome **drawing rooms** decorated with mythological subjects lies the **Bedroom of Joachim Murat**, containing perhaps the finest Empire-style furniture in the palace; on the far side of the room are an antechamber and a small chapel.

Returning to the central Room of Alexander, enter the east wing of the palace, inhabited by Ferdinand I from 1780 until his expulsion in 1806, and from 1815 until his death in 1825. The **reception room**, **drawing room**, **dining room**, and **fumoir** are decorated with allegories of the Four Seasons, by Antonio De Dominici and Fedele Fischetti. Here Maria Carolina held her famous receptions, one of which is recorded in a particularly delightful manner by an English guest, Lady Anne Miller:

> After mounting a staircase, you enter several large rooms, hung and adorned in the Italian taste with crimson damask, velvet, etc., and amply illuminated. The chairs are placed all round against the walls, and each sits down where they choose. These rooms were so full, that there was a double row of chairs placed back to back down the middle. Accident placed me exactly opposite the Queen, who took the first chair she found empty. There are no tables in any of the rooms; but every person being seated, the supper is served thus: The best looking soldiers, chosen from the King's guards, carry about the supper with as much order, regularity, and gravity as if they were performing a military manoeuvre. First appears a soldier bearing a large basket with napkins, followed by a page, who unfolds and spreads them on the lap of each of the company as they happen to sit; but when it comes to the Queen's turn to be served, a lord of the Court presents her majesty's napkin. The first soldier is immediately followed by a second, bearing a basket of silver plates; another carries knives and forkes; then follows a fourth, with a great pâté, composed of macaroni, cheese, and butter; he is accompanied by an ecuyer tranchant, or carver, armed with a knife a foot long, who cuts the pie, and lays a large slice on the plate (which has been placed on the lap of each of the company); then a fifth soldier, with an empty basket. to take away the dirty plates; others succeed in the same order, carrying wine, iced water, etc.; the drinkables are served between the arrival of each eatable: the rest of the supper consisted of various dishes of fish, ragouts, game, fried and baked meats, perigord-pies, boar's-heads, etc. The dessert was formed into pyramids, and carried round in the same manner; it consisted of sweetmeats, biscuits, iced chocolate, and a great variety of iced fruits, creams, etc. The Queen ate of two things only, which were prepared particularly for her by her German cooks; she did me the singular honour to send me some of each dish.

Beyond the public rooms is the **study**, with lacquered furniture from Frankfurt am Main, and a small **drawing room**. The **Bedroom of Ferdinand II** follows. From here you enter the rooms of the queen: first her **sewing room**, with a small **bathroom** adjacent; then a tiny **dressing room**, beyond which lie the **drawing room** and a room for the queen's ladies-in-waiting. From the latter a series of richly decorated rooms leads to the **library**, containing some 10,000 volumes and a huge presepio, with over 1200 pieces made by Giuseppe Sammartino and other eminent sculptors.

The next ten rooms comprise the **gallery**, where an extensive but dull collection of still-lifes, historical scenes, and family portraits is displayed. The small Museo Vanvitelliano contains the architect's original drawings and models for the palace.

> The palace is the temporary home of the *Terraemotus collection** of international contemporary art, assembled by the Neapolitan dealer/collector Lucio Amelio following the 1980 earthquake. The collection is shown on request.

Return to the ground floor and cross the second courtyard to the **Palatine Theatre**. This charming eighteenth-century period piece hosted concerts, plays, and balls. Lady Anne Miller describes the original appearance of the theatre and the use that was made of it during a ball she attended in 1771:

> There is no precedence observed at these balls, the King and Queen go in and out promiscuously, which is the reason why the company is not so numerous as one might expect to find it. None but such as the Queen esteems proper to receive and converse with sans cérémonie are ever admitted; and there are many of the Neapolitan nobility, even to the rank of dukes, who are allowed only to see the ball from the upper boxes...The theatre is in the palace; it is approached through spacious courts, and then through large passages lined with a double row of guards under arms. The plan is circular, the proscenium appeared to me to cut off about a third from the circle; the boxes are larger than those in any other I have yet seen, they are lined, gilt, and decorated with a profusion of ornaments...The stage was covered with the musicians upon benches, rising pyramidically one above the other, the top of the pyramid is crowned by the kettle-drums. The musicians are all in a livery, their coats blue, richly laced, their waistcoats red, and almost covered with silver, small black hats, with long scarlet feathers stuck upright in them: large wax candles are placed between, so that they form a striking coup d'oeil upon our entering the theatre; the whole is so artfully illuminated that the effect is equal, and seems as if the light proceeded from a brilliant sun at the top...The pit (which is more like an antique arena) is floored with a composition coloured red, very hard, and rather slippery; here it is they dance. The boxes are appropriated to the foreign ministers and great officers belonging to the Court.

Inaugurated by Ferdinand IV in 1769, the theatre has been recently restored to its original form, with a horseshoe-shaped auditorium and five tiers of boxes. The ceiling painting, by Crescenzo della Gamba, shows Apollo killing the Serpents.

THE GARDENS

From the main portico you enter the *gardens (open 09.00–1hr before sunset), which extend to the north, east and west sides of the palace. Among the more enchanting achievements of Italian landscape architecture, they were laid out by Martin Biancour under the supervision of Luigi Vanvitelli. They are famous for their fountains and ornamental waterworks adorned with statuary groups. The crowning glory of the gardens is the **Great Cascade**, a waterfall some 75m high which can be seen clearly from the palace 3km away (shuttle bus). The central promenade leads across a broad lower garden bordered by holm oaks and camphor trees (paths diverge into the woods on the left and right) to the circular **Fontana Margherita**, which is linked by a bridge over a sunken highway to the impressive **Pescheria Superiore**. Beyond, a long, narrow lawn ends at the semicircular **Fontana di Aeolo**, inhabited by statues of 29 zephyrs and wind gods (54 were originally planned). This is followed by the **Fontana di Cerere**, containing seven stepped cascades and statues of Ceres, nymphs, tritons, and river gods; then more lawn and the **Fontana di Venere**, with its group of Venus and Adonis.

From here a scenographic staircase flanked by men and women in hunting garb leads up to a basin with groups of Diana surrounded by nymphs and Actaeon being turned into a stag, into which the Great Cascade plunges. The water is brought from Monte Taburno by a lofty aqueduct. The view from the top of the wooded hill is especially fine.

To the east of the cascade is another, later garden laid out in the so-called English style; visitors are accompanied by a custodian. Here are more modest fountains and romantic groves of holm oaks, artificial ruins adorned with statues from Pompeii and Herculaneum, a large fish-pond, a miniature fort for Prince Ferdinand's mock battles, a swan lake, an apple orchard, a Classical temple, a bath of Venus, covered walks and greenhouses.

Excursions

San Leucio, 3km north-west of Caserta, was built as a model town and social experiment by Ferdinand IV, who here built the Casino Reale di Belvedere (also called the Casino di San Leucio) and introduced the culture of silkworms and silk manufacture. The industry (now artificial silk and nylon), continues in the vast Palazzo dello Stabilimento Serico, much of the work being done on ancient hand looms.

About 2km north-east of Caserta a turning off Highway 87 leads to (1km) **Caserta British Military Cemetery**, with 769 graves. It is immediately east of the civil cemetery.

Caserta Vecchia (399m), 10km north-east (bus) by the road passing the cemetery, was founded in the 8C, and preserves the aspect of a medieval town. The *Cattedrale, a fine example of Southern Norman architecture, dates from 1123–53; the central cupola and campanile (the latter with a roadway through it) were added c 100 years later. The exterior is adorned with sculptures; inside, note 18 antique columns, a paschal candlestick and (in the transepts) the tombs of Count Francis II (died 1359) and Bishop Giacomo (died 1460), as well as many mosaic details. The ruins of the 13C Castello lie to the east.

6 · Naples from the late nineteenth century to today

In 1884 a terrible epidemic of cholera swept Naples, taking a high toll of lives particularly in the crowded alleys and tall tenements of the medieval city centre. As a result special laws were passed to hasten urban renewal. Wide thoroughfares were driven through the slums, the waters of the Serino river were brought into the city, and complete new quarters were built. Naples lost much of its picturesqueness without gaining in improved health, as the population evicted from the condemned buildings was housed in neighbouring blocks, increasing density even further.

The greatest achievement of the Risanamento, as the urban renewal programme was called, was the construction of the Corso Umberto I (popularly the Rettifilo) from Piazza Garibaldi and the railway station to the Piazza del Municipio, the centre of local government. Other 'improvements' included the rebuilding of the quarter of Santa Lucia, the founding of a new residential district on the Vomero hill and the establishment of the first industries in the Vasto Arenaccia area, the most easterly link in the chain of industrial suburbs that encircles Naples today, presenting a serious obstacle to the successful expansion of the city.

Quite independently of the Risanamento, wealthier Neapolitans began, around the end of the century, to build their luxurious villas in the area around the Riviera di Chiaia (Piazza Amedeo, Parco Margherita). Many of these elegant dwellings, which continued to be built up till the eve of the First World War, are in a curious local variant of the Art Nouveau style.

The period between the wars witnessed a revival of building without any precise guidelines. During the Fascist period both urban expansion and rebuilding activity in the city centre were important. The suburban quarters grew rapidly, particularly at Fuorigrotta, where development was stimulated by the construction of the Mostra d'Oltremare fairgrounds and of the tunnel under the hill of Posillipo.

In central Naples the most striking changes took place in the Carità quarter, between Via Toledo, Via Monteoliveto, and Via Medina. Here the central post office, the provincial office building and the police headquarters were erected, concentrating administrative services even more in an already overburdened area. Finally, in 1939 the need for an organic design stimulated the drafting of a general town plan, which, however, was not applied until many years after the war.

Meanwhile, the events of the Second World War nullified many earlier improvements. Naples was heavily bombed on 4 August 1943 by the advancing Allies; and it was attacked and captured by the Germans after the armistice of 8 September. A Neapolitan rising (Le Quattro Giornate, 28 September–1 October) drove out the Germans, who before retreating destroyed the port, utilities and public archives. A typhus epidemic followed by a bad winter added to the distress and aggravated the age-old problem of the 'scugnizzi', unfortunate children who managed to survive only by resorting to crime.

Commercial and industrial development has radically changed the aspect of the city in the post war years. The gulf coast from Pozzuoli to Castellammare di Stabia and the inland suburbs host an array of industrial plants (including ironworks, food processing plants, an oil refinery, cement works, aircraft and automobile assembly plants), and residential building has expanded over the hill zones as well as to the eastern plains. This apparent burgeoning of wealth and activity is illusory, however: it does not truthfully reflect the economic condition of the city, which, notwithstanding costly and elaborate plans for development, remains substantially poorer than its northern counterparts.

Overcrowding has further aggravated the century-old problem of economic malaise, creating more troubles of its own. Naples has the highest population density of any European city and is severely lacking in social services. Despite the efforts of the local authorities to provide adequate housing, many Neapolitans still live in 'bassi'—street-level, single-roomed dwellings in which light and air are admitted by a double door alone. At the same time, illegal building activity has altered the appearance of the town beyond recognition; and faulty construction has led to death and injury in more than one instance. A special investigatory committee of the Ministry of Public Works revealed in 1971 that almost everything built in Naples since 1945 is in violation of the law, and blamed 'the frivolity and the incapacity of the civil authorities, the impudence of speculators and the ever-growing greed of building contractors' for having 'trampled upon the right of Neapolitans to an orderly form of civil society, blindly transforming the ancient and marvellous capital of the Mediterranean into the present, most uninhabitable provincial capital in Italy'. Judiciary action in 1975 resulted in the incrimination of a former mayor, the demolition of 22 buildings erected on lands destined for parks, schools, and other public facilities and the arrest of several contractors. In spite of intimidatory actions brought by the profiteers and their sympathisers, the effort to restore to Naples her natural grace and beauty continues.

The task is not an easy one, for even the force of nature must be taken into account. On 22 November 1980 a violent earthquake rocked Campania and the neighbouring region of Basilicata, claiming more than 3000 victims and causing incalculable damage. In Naples, the largest city affected by the quake, 200,000 people were left homeless. An effort is now being made to make reconstruction activity coincide with an overall design for urban renewal, and the city is beginning to show signs of recovery. Particularly in recent years, countless monuments have been cleaned, renovated, or restored; an endeavour has been made to extend the areas in which automobile traffic is restricted; and major renewal programmes have been launched in the area behind the Stazione Centrale (the Centro Direzionale or management centre, an office quarter designed by the internationally acclaimed architect Kenzo Tanje) and at the former steel works at Bacoli (destined to become parkland). If work proceeds at the present pace, walks through both areas will be included in the next edition of this Guide.

When Goethe visited Naples in 1787, he exclaimed: 'Naples is a paradise, in it every one lives in a sort of intoxicated self-forgetfulness. It is even so with me...Were I not impelled by the German spirit, and desire to learn and to do rather than enjoy, I should tarry a little longer in this school of a lighthearted and happy life, and try to profit from it still more'. In the 19C, Sorrento, Capri, Ischia and the villages of the Amalfi coast came into their own as alternative resorts for visitors to the south. Sorrento and Ravello were favorite haunts of Wagner and Nietzsche. Residents of Capri have included Emil von Behring (1854–1917), discoverer of a successful inoculation against tetanus, and Axel Munthe, the Swedish physician; Maxim Gorky (1868-1936), who lived here in 1907–13 and ran a school for revolutionaries visited by Lenin, Stalin, and Chaliapin; C.C. Coleman (1841–1928), American painter of genre scenes; and Norman Douglas (1868–1952), the writer. Positano is frequented by a certain sort of jet set, Gore Vidal spends several months of the year at Ravello, and Ischia is virtually a German colony. Today these areas, which are known principally for their natural beauty, attract hundreds of thousands of visitors each year. And no wonder: these luxurious paradises of sea and sand possess a subtle magic, under the spell of which one readily forgets oneself and the world.

A.   The Rettifilo and the Harbour

*The area of the city between the medieval Castel Nuovo and the modern Stazione Centrale is dominated by the busy Corso Umberto I, popularly called the **Rettifilo**. This long, straight thoroughfare is a typical example of late 19C town planning in Italy, which as a rule had little regard for local needs or traditions. The Rettifilo cuts through Naples' eastern quarters in a merciless manner, destroying the area's medieval flavour and introducing an academic, pretentious architectural style vaguely related to the neo-Classicism of the Bourbon era. A few impressive monuments of the city's past do survive, however, and amply repay a visit. Two hours are more than enough for the 4km-long visit to this living example of how not to treat a city.*

THE RETTIFILO

From the Piazza del Municipio the wide Via Agostino Depretis leads straight to Piazza Giovanni Bovio (formerly Piazza della Borsa; Atlas 2, 10) in the centre of which is the graceful **Fontana del Nettuno**, designed in 1601, in all likelihood, by Domenico Fontana. The sea-monsters are by Pietro Bernini, and the figure of

Neptune by Michelangelo Naccherino. To the left stands the **Palazzo della Borsa** (1895), engulfing the 8C chapel of **Sant'Aspreno al Porto**, which was transformed in the 17C and incorporates columns from San Pietro ad Aram. From the north-east side of the piazza starts the busy Corso Umberto Primo, or Rettifilo, laid out in 1888–94 to connect the city's civic and financial centre with the main railway station.

Via Mezzocannone leads left to **San Giovanni Maggiore**. The church, built in the 6C on the ruins of a pagan temple, but remodelled in 1685 and again in 1870, retains its basilican plan. A chapel on the south side contains an 18C terracotta presepio; the third chapel on the north a Baptism of Jesus, attributed to Giovanni da Nola; the fifth chapel a late 16C bas-relief of the Beheading of John the Baptist. The magnificent high altar (1732–43) is the work of Domenico Antonio Vaccaro.

The church of **San Pietro Martire**, built in 1294–1347 in a small square to the right of the corso, and much damaged during the Second World War, contains a number of 14–16C works of art, including (in the third north chapel) a naïvely realistic 15C Catalan painting on wood of St Vincent Ferrer, as well as paintings by Solimena and Stanzione.

Immediately opposite the church is the imposing façade of the **University of Naples** (Atlas 3, 7) by Pier Paolo Quaglia and Guiglielmo Melisborgo (1897–1908), with a pediment sculptured by Francesco Ierace. The university was founded in 1224 by Frederick II. In 1777 it was established in the 16C rooms of the former Jesuit convent behind the present building. Located here are the **Musei di Antropologia, Mineralogia, Zoologia e Paleontologia** (Via Mezzocannone 8 and Largo San Marcellino 10, open Mon–Fri 09.00–13.00, Sat and Sun 10.00–13.00), with the study collections of the faculty of science.

Three blocks further along the Corso, on the left, a crooked alley and a flight of steps leads up to the church of **Santi Severino e Sossio**, built over an earlier structure in 1494–1561 and decorated in the 17C. The interior has ceiling paintings by Corenzio, who fell to his death while retouching them and is buried near the entrance to the sacristy. In the fourth chapel on the south side is a 16C polyptych. On the same side is the sacristy vestibule, in which are two Cicaro *tombs of the 16C, both with inscriptions by Sannazaro. The **Cappella Sanseverino** (right of the choir) contains the tombs by Giovanni da Nola of three Sanseverino brothers, all of whom were poisoned on the same day (1516) by their uncle. The *choir stalls (1560–75) are by Bartolomeo Chiarini and Benvenuto Tortelli. The **Benedictine Convent**, with four cloisters, was the repository of the State Archives; these, removed for safety during the war, were wantonly destroyed as a reprisal by the Germans. The **Chiostro del Platano**, named after a plane tree said to have been planted by St Benedict, is accessible by a door at the left of the vestibule. It is frescoed by Andrea Solario.

With the church behind you, turn immediately left to the Via del Duomo. One block up, on the left, is the Palazzo Cuomo (Atlas 3, 7), a severely elegant Florentine building of 1464–90, that now houses the attractive **Museo Civico Gaetano Filangieri** (open Tue–Sat 09.00–14.00; Sun and holidays 09.00–13.00), established in 1881. The original collections of Prince Gaetano Filangieri (1824–92) were burnt by the Germans in 1943, but a new collection has since been formed. On the ground floor are objects from various excavations and Oriental arms; above, sculpture (notably a boy's head by the Della Robbia) and paintings by Ribera, Mattia Preti, Luca Giordano, Bernardo Cavallino and others. Note particularly Ribera's gruesomely realistic head of St John the Baptist; Mattia Preti, Meeting of

Peter and Paul at the Gates of Rome; Bernardino Lanino, Madonna and Child; Battistello Caracciolo, Ecce Homo. The gallery has a good collection of porcelain, and the library has a number of manuscripts and documents dating from the 13–19C.

Return to the corso by way of San Giorgio Maggiore, rebuilt in the 17C but retaining its 5C apse (see Route 4A) and Sant'Agostino alla Zecca (Atlas 3, 7), a church of the 14C transformed in the mid 17C by Bartolomeo Picchiatti and Giuseppe Astarita with the tomb of Francesco Coppola, Count Sarno. The fine 14C **chapter house**, opening off the Baroque cloister, is reached by a door beneath the 17C campanile.

On the corso, further on to the left, is the little church of **Santa Maria Egiziaca** (Atlas 3, 7), originally of the 14C, but in its present form designed by D. Lazzari (1684), with paintings by Andrea Vaccaro, Luca Giordano and Francesco Solimena. The oval plan is rare in Naples.

By taking Via Egiziaca to the left and then turning right in Via dell'Annunziata you reach the **Santissima Annunziata** (Atlas 3, 3), rebuilt by Luigi Vanvitelli and his son Carlo in 1761–82 after a fire, important as one of the first examples of the new Classical taste in ecclesiastical architecture that was championed by Vanvitelli and Fuga as official architects of Charles III. The **interior** is a Latin cross with barrel-vaulted nave and choir and short transepts. The nave arcade is replaced by a colonnade bearing a flat entablature. The crossing, the choir, and the semicircular apse, as well as the gallery at the west end of the nave, provide interesting variants in the use of **columns**. The white and grey stucco underscores the severity of the design. The slender cupola, badly damaged in 1943, has been well restored. The **treasury**, containing frescoes (in a bad state) by Corenzio, and the **sacristy**, on the south side (likewise decorated by Corenzio and containing sculptured 16C presses), are relics of the former church of 1318, in which Joan II was buried (plain tomb before the high altar). The altars of the unusual, circular crypt are adorned with 17C terracotta statues.

Turn right and, by Via Antonio Ranieri, regain the Rettifilo near the church of **San Pietro ad Aram**, which has a finely stuccoed interior. The 17C façade faced Via Santa Candida, but the usual entrance is by the south door from the corso. The church stands on the site where St Peter is said to have baptised St Candida and St Asprenus, who later became first Bishop of Naples. A fresco in the porch depicts St Peter celebrating mass with them. The high altar is decorated with mosaics, and the presbytery is adorned with early works of Luca Giordano. Restorations in the crypt in 1930 uncovered remains of an aisled church of the early Christian era.

Corso Umberto I terminates in the vast Piazza Garibaldi (monument by Cesare Zocchi, 1904) in front of the modern **Stazione Centrale** (Atlas 3, 4). From here the broad Corso Garibaldi leads shortly into Piazza Nolana, where the massive **Porta Nolana**, part of the ancient enceinte, has a 15C relief of Ferdinand I. From the piazza, Corso Garibaldi continues southwards, passing the Stazione Circumvesuviana, to Piazza Guglielmo Pepe. Here Via del Carmine, to the right, leads to the church of **Santa Maria del Carmine** (Atlas 3, 8), rebuilt at the end of the 13C. The campanile was begun in the 15C, but not completed until 1631, when Fra Nuvolo added the spire; the façade, by Giovanni del Gaizo, dates from 1766. The interior of the church is decorated with polychrome marble; the modern roof replaces a 17C coffered ceiling destroyed in 1943. On the north side is the monument, to a design of the Danish sculptor Thorvaldsen, to Conradin of Swabia, who is buried behind the altar. Under the transept arch stands a 13C wooden crucifix and above it a painting, God the Father, by Luca Giordano; the frescoes in the north transept and in the sixth chapel on the north side are by Solimena; in the south transept is an Assumption, also by Solimena. Behind the high altar a much-venerated 14C painting, the Madonna della Bruna, occupies a 16C marble shrine. In the north transept is a 15C crucifix.

THE MARKET AND THE HARBOUR

To the west, in the noisy Piazza del Mercato, centre of old Naples, Conradin and his kinsman Frederick of Baden were beheaded by Charles I of Anjou in 1269. Here also Masaniello's rebellion broke out in July 1647. In the church of **Santa Croce al Mercato** is preserved a porphyry column from a chapel erected on the site of Conradin's scaffold. On the west side of the piazza stands **Sant'Eligio**, restored after war damage, with a good Gothic doorway showing French influence. On the south side lie the remains of the Castello del Carmine.

The Porta del Carmine, with massive pillars, gives access to the Via Nuova della Marina, along which you turn to the right. This busy street skirts the extensive installations of the **harbour**. Already famous in Greek and Roman times, this was developed greatly under Charles II of Anjou and went on expanding as the volume of shipping increased. The enormous damage sustained during the Second World War reduced it to a third of its pre-war efficiency, the passenger terminal being all but destroyed. Reconstruction began in 1946 and the city rapidly regained its former status as a major Mediterranean port, only to lose it again by not converting promptly to container shipping. Among the more notable modern works is the 330m-long **Graving Dock** (1955), by the Molo Cesario Console at the east end of the harbour. Immediately facing the south end of Via del Duomo is the Immacolatella Nuova landing stage.

Continuing to the west, you approach an area through which Via De Gasperi leads to Via Depretis. Emerging from the tenements, beneath which it has long been buried, is the church of **Santa Maria di Portosalvo**, erected in 1544. To the left Via Cristoforo Colombo passes another pier, the Immacolatella Vecchia, with the seat of the Capitaneria di Porto and enters the seaward end of Piazza Municipio.

B.   Capri

*Unfortunately you are not the only one who knows that **Capri** is one of the more beautiful spots on our small planet. Obviously, the best time to visit the island is out of season (Nov–Mar), or at mid-week, when the crowds are elsewhere. But in all fairness it must be said that the island's appeal as a resort is a boon as well as a burden to the modern traveller: it was Capri's natural beauty that led an eminent Roman, probably the emperor Tiberius, to build a luxurious beach house here (the famous **Villa Jovis**); and Swedish physician Axel Munthe's **Villa San Michele**, which stands on the site of another Roman patrician home, is hardly less impressive. Development in the late 19C and early 20C has given the towns of **Capri** and **Anacapri** an aristocratic air that other Southern Italian resorts lack; and everywhere the views over sea and coast more than compensate for any inconvenience that sharing them with varying numbers of fellow travellers may cause.*

Automobile traffic on the island is severely restricted, so if you are driving, leave your car on the mainland and use the bus to get around on the island. It is possible to visit Capri from Naples in one day by using an early morning hydrofoil, taking the bus to Anacapri at midday and returning by a hydrofoil leaving Marina Grande in the late afternoon or evening. It is better to combine Capri with Sorrento by spending the night on the island and leaving for Sorrento by an early-morning boat. All who can, however, should devote two or more days to Capri, to allow the ascent of **Monte Solaro** *and a trip by boat along the east coast of the island.*

APPROACHES BY SEA: Passenger ferries go daily to the Marina Grande from Naples (1hr 15 min), Sorrento (45 min) and Ischia (1hr, Apr–Oct). There is also a daily hydrofoil service to the Marina Grande from Naples (40–45 min), Sorrento (20min-1hr.) and Ischia (50min, Apr–Oct).

HOTELS: Capri, *****Grand Hotel Quisisana, via Camerelle 2, tel. 081 837 0788, fax 081 837 6080; ****Scalinatella, Via Tragara 8, tel. 081 837 0633, fax 081 837 8291; ****Punta Tragara, Via Tragara 57, tel. 081 837 0844, fax 081 837 7790; ****Luna, Viale Matteotti 3, tel. 081 837 0433, fax 081 837 7459; ****Villa Brunella, Via Tragara 24, tel. 081 837 0122, fax 081 837 0430; ***Villa Sarah, Via Tiberio 3a, tel. 081 837 7817.

RESTAURANT: Anacapri (La Migliara), **Da Gelsomina, tel. 081 8371499.

THE ISLAND
Capri, a small island 6km long and 3km wide, lies 5km from the Punta della Campanella, of which it forms the geological continuation. It is a mountainous island, with a precipitous and almost inaccessible coast, abounding in caves and fantastic rocks. With its perennial sunshine, its pure air, and its luxuriant, almost tropical vegetation, it is the pearl of the Gulf of Naples. Its beauties are, however, best enjoyed out of season.

The appearance of the inhabitants, especially of the women (who wear a highly picturesque costume on special occasions), is distinctly Greek. The population is c 12,000 and the chief town is also called Capri. Anacapri, in a somewhat less sheltered position, is the only other centre of any size. Monte Solaro (59m) is the highest point. The chief products of the island are fruit, oil and wine.

History
Capri was inhabited in prehistoric times; later, it became Greek and then Roman. Augustus, who visited it personally, obtained it from the Neapolitans in exchange for the larger and more fertile island of Ischia. His contributions to Capri included roads, aqueducts and villas (29 BC).

The wider fame of the island began with Tiberius, who retired to Capri in AD 27. The story of the magnificence, profligacy, and horrors of his ten years' residence was unknown before the writings of Tacitus and Suetonius, but the publicity value of these undoubted exaggerations ensures their perpetuation. On the dominant points of the island Tiberius erected several villas, dedicated (probably) to the major deities of the Roman Pantheon. The most important of these structures was the Villa Jovis. In 182 the emperor Commodus, son of Marcus Aurelius, assigned the island as a place of exile for his wife Crispina and his sister Lucilla.

During the Middle Ages Capri was occupied at length by the Saracens, whose lasting influence can be seen in local building conventions, especially the barrel-vaulted roofs of many homes and churches. In 1806 the island was taken by the British fleet under Sir Sidney Smith and strongly fortified; Sir Hudson Lowe was appointed governor. In 1808, however, it was retaken by the French, under Lamarque, and in 1813 it was restored to Ferdinand I of the Two Sicilies.

The island is much frequented by foreigners, and for more than 150 years has provided a home for expatriates, artists and eccentrics.

The town

Travellers arriving in Capri generally land on the north coast, in the bay of the Marina Grande. From this point you get to the town of Capri by funicular railway, by road (3km), or by footpath (Strada Campo di Pisco).

Capri (142m, 7000 inhab.), a small, quaint town with vaulted houses and labyrinthine streets, lies in the saddle between Punta del Capo on the east and Monte Solaro on the west. Hard by rise the hills of San Michele and Castiglione.

■ **Information**. AA, Piazzetta Ignazio Cerio 11; tel. 081 8370424, fax 081 8370918 (branch offices at Piazza Umberto I, Capri; Via Orlandi 19a, Anacapri; Banchina del Porto, Marina Grande).

■ **Transport**. Frequent buses from the Piazza to the Marina Grande, to the Marina Piccola, and to Anacapri. Funicular railway between the Piazza and the Marina Grande, every 30min.

■ **Special events**. San Costanzo (patron saint of the island) 14 May; Sant'Antonio (at Anacapri) 13 June; Festival of the Madonna (on the Tiberio and Solaro) 7–8 September; Madonna della Liberta (Marina Grande) mid-Sep.

The road from the Marina Grande passes the church of **San Costanzo**, built in the 10C and 11C and enlarged c 1330, with a Byzantine dome and small, characteristic campanile. Within, the crossing is marred by the loss of its ancient cipollino columns, four of which were removed in 1755 to decorate the royal chapel at Caserta (four remain); these came originally from the nearby **Palazzo a Mare** (surviving exedra below the cliff to the west). The road joins further on with those from the Marina Piccola (south-west) and Anacapri (north-west), and in 7min more it ends on Piazza Umberto Primo. Here stands the 17C church of **Santo Stefano**, approached by a flight of steps. The interior contains, at the foot of the high altar, a fragment of inlaid pavement from the Villa Jovis (see below) and the tombs of Giacomo and Vincenzo Arcucci by Naccherino.

Adjacent is the **Palazzo Cerio**, once a residence of Joan I. The mansion now houses a small private museum of antiquities and fossils (**Museo del Centro Caprese Ignazio Cerio**; open Tue, Thu, and Sat 17.00–20.00, Wed and Fri 10.00–13.00) found in excavations on the island at the turn of the century by the physician and naturalist Ignazio Cerio, as well as an interesting library and archive. Close to the upper station of the cable railway from the Marina may be seen remains of a megalithic wall.

Walks around Capri

Several fine walks may be taken in the environs of Capri. To the south-west are (20 min) the ruins of the Castiglione (249m; closed to the public), a medieval castle constructed with ancient materials, and the **Punta Canone**, which affords a superb view of the Faraglioni and the Marina Piccola. To reach the latter, you ascend the steps of Santo Stefano, follow (right) Via Madre Serafina and pass the church of Santa Teresa. About 500m further on, a narrow path to the right climbs to the Castiglione. Bear left. More steps and a shaded path lead to the scenic overlook. On the north slope of the hill, in 1786, Hadrawa the antiquary, secretary to the Austrian ambassador, discovered five ancient rooms with painted and marble decoration.

To reach the **Certosa di San Giacomo** (6 min), leave the piazza by a vaulted passage in the south corner and follow Via Vittorio Emanuele to the Quisisana Hotel. Via Federico Serena, to the right of the hotel, climbs, and then descends to the Carthusian monastery founded in 1371 by Giacomo Arcucci, secretary to Joan I; it was sacked by Torgud in 1553 and suppressed in 1807. The conventual buildings house the Museo Diefenbach (open 09.00–14.00, Sun and holidays 09.00–13.00), with works by the 19C German artist. The fresco above the portal of the Gothic church, showing the Madonna and Child with the founder and his queen, might be a work of Andrea Vanni. From Via Federico Serena (see above) Via Matteotti leads to Via Augusto, a paved path built by Friedrich Krupp, the German armaments manufacturer, which descends to the Marina Piccola.

The **Punta Tragara**, like the Punta Canone, can be reached in about 20 min. Via Camerelle, to the left of the Quisisana Hotel (see above), skirts a series of brick vaults known as the Camerelle, probably the arches of a road connecting the villas of Tragara and Castiglione. Ascend slightly to reach the Belvedere di Tragara (view of the Faraglioni and towards Marina Piccola); steps by the café and a path lead from here to the **Punta Tragara**, from which the view includes (to the east) the flat rock known as Il Monacone from a species of seal once native to Capri. From the steps another path continues east to the Arco Naturale (see below).

What is perhaps Capri's most famous nature walk leads to the **Arco Naturale** (20 min) and the **Grotta di Matromania** (10 min more). From the north-east corner of the piazza follow the narrow Via Botteghe, Via Fuorlovade, and Via Croce. Where the latter divides take Via Matromania (right); after 8 min keep to the left, and after 8 min more descend the steps (left) to the Arco Naturale, a fantastic archway in the rock (view). Returning to the path continue to descend to (10 min) the Grotta di Matromania, which opens towards the east. The cave ends in a semicircular apse, and there are various small chambers with walls in *opus reticulatum*. This is probably a **sanctuary of Cybele**, the Mater Magna; the erroneous belief that it was a Mithraeum was exploded when it was learned that a Mithraic relief in the Naples museum, supposedly discovered here, had in fact been found elsewhere on the island.

VILLA JOVIS

A lovely walk of just under an hour leads to the ***Villa Jovis**, known to the Capriotes as the Palazzo di Tiberio. From Via Croce (see above) take the rising Via Tiberio (left; follow the central strip of paving) and pass the small church of Santa Croce. Further on bear to the right, passing near the remains of a pharos, or **lighthouse**, probably built by Augustus and overthrown by an earthquake after the death of Tiberius. Here is the **Salto di Tiberio** (296m), the almost vertical rock off which, it is fabled, Tiberius pushed his victims. A few more paces lead to the ruined villa, a residence of palatial proportions with several storeys. It was systematically explored for the first time in 1932–35, by which time most of its mosaic pavements and other decorative elements had already been carried off. The ruins cover an area of 7000sq m, centring around a rectangular zone occupied by four large cisterns hewn out of the rock and divided into intercommunicating cells.

From the entrance to the archaeological park a brick path mounts to the **Vestibule**, conserving the bases of four marble columns. Adjacent are the rooms of the guard corps, converted during the Middle Ages into cisterns. A corridor ascends to a second vestibule, from where a corridor on the right climbs to the **thermae**, consisting of a dressing room, a frigidarium, a tepidarium, a calidarium (with two semicircular apses), and rooms for the heating and distribution of the water. To the east, built in a hemicycle, are the **state rooms**.

Retracing your steps, go along the west wing of the palace, past servants' quarters, to the **imperial apartments** (remains of mosaic pavement), from where a corridor and steps descend to the Loggia Imperiale or Belvedere, a long (92m) straight porch set into the north rim of the cliff, 20m below the level of the palace. Steps along the west (inland) flank of the villa descend to vaulted store rooms and to the kitchens, set apart from the rest of the structure.

At the highest point, on an ancient substructure, is the chapel of **Santa Maria del Soccorso**, commanding the finest *view in Capri, embracing the island itself, the sea, the Punta della Campanella, and the two gulfs. Restored in 1979, the church stands behind an enormous bronze Madonna brought to the site by a United States Navy helicopter and solemnly blessed by Pope John Paul II.

ANACAPRI

The trip to from Capri to Anacapri is a mere 3km and may be made on foot or by bus. The road, constructed in 1874 and restored in 1923, ascends in long windings hewn in the rock and affords a series of beautiful views. On the way you pass the Torre Quattro Venti, near which is the **Palazzo Inglese**, built c 1750 by Sir Nathaniel Thorold and a key point in the French assault of 1808. Formerly the only means of communication between Anacapri and the rest of the island was by the **Scala Fenicia**, a flight of 800 steps attributable to the Greeks or to Augustus, descending to the Marina Grande. This (now, however, with fewer steps) crosses the road at the chapel of Sant'Antonio, above which are the ruins of the Castello di Barbarossa, destroyed in 1535 by the corsair of that name. Near the top of the steps is the Villa San Michele (see below).

Anacapri (284m), a village of 5000 inhabitants, recalls Sicily with its white houses and quasi-oriental roofs.

From Piazza della Vittoria the main street bears right. To the north, in Piazza San Nicola, the octagonal church of **San Michele**, finished in 1719, possesses a majolica pavement (Story of Eden), executed by Leonardo Chiaiese (1761) to a design of Solimena. The plan of the church is ascribed to Domencio Antonio Vaccaro. The four sides on the main axes are slightly longer than those on the diagonals, and the vestibule and choir are deeper than the other areas leading off the central space, imparting a longitudinal emphasis to the plan which is not unlike that of the Concezione in Naples. The architect also uses the pilasters at the points where the vestibule and choir join the central space to lead the eye from one area of the church to the next, placing them at an angle to the main axis.

The centre of the town is Piazza Armando Diaz with the **Chiesa Parrocchiale** (parish church, or Santa Sofia; 1510, enlarged 1870), from where the street continues (left) to the smiling village of Caprile (500m). Via San Michele mounts (15 min) from Piazza della Vittoria to the **Villa San Michele** (open daily 10.30–15.30), built by the Swedish doctor Axel Munthe (1857–1949) on the site of a villa of Tiberius and containing a small collection of antiquities.

Walks around Anacapri

The plateau of **Migliara** (304m), reached in 40 min, commands a striking *view of the Faraglioni and the precipices of Monte Solaro. To reach it, take the stony path from the road's end at Caprile, joining the mule track that leads to the Belvedere di Migliara. Then return via the Torre della Guardia, above the Punta Carena, and the 15C Torre di Materita.

A road runs west from the Chiesa Parrocchiale to the Mulino a Vento and to the 12C Torre di Damecuta, near which another **Roman villa** (open daily 08.00–14.00), smaller but similar to the Villa Jovis, has been excavated. Damaged in AD 79, it was fortified by the French and British in the 19C. From the long belvedere the *view of the Phlegraean Fields is particularly fine at sunset. A path descends to the Blue Grotto (described below).

The ascent of **Monte Solaro** may be made in about 1hr (or by chair-lift from Piazza della Vittoria in 12 min). From the Strada della Migliara, skirt the garden wall of the Villa Giulia to reach the path (signpost), along the slope, which winds south. A steep ascent passes by remains of the English fortifications of 1806–08 to the Crocella saddle (45min), where a shrine of the Virgin stands. It takes c 15min more to attain the summit of Monte Solaro (589m), which is crowned by a ruined castle. The wonderful *panorama extends over the gulfs of Naples and Salerno to the Ponziane Islands (north–west), the Apennines (east), and the mountains of Calabria (south).

On the north coast of the island is the famous *Grotta Azzura** (Blue Grotto), a visit to which is the most popular excursion on Capri. The approach is made by sea (daily 09.00–early afternoon, except when strong north or east winds blow, making entrance to the cave impossible), from the Marina Grande. The boat skirts the north side of the island, affording a view of the ruins known as the Bagni di Tiberio. The light effects are best 11.00–13.00.

A marine cavern, the Blue Grotto owes its geological formation to gradual subsidence of the coast, probably since the Roman epoch. Though known in antiquity, it seems then to have lacked the curious effects of light that are now its great charm. Its possibilities were realised in 1822 by Augusto Ferrara, a Capri fisherman, who in 1826 led Kopisch, a German poet, and some others to its 'accidental' discovery. Kopisch entered the facts in the register of Pagano's hotel, and these were published in Hans Christian Anderson's novel, *The Improvisator*.

Once a nymphaeum of Tiberius, the cavern has, in recent years, yielded a wealth of archaeological material, including several large stàtues (these objects are awaiting collocation in the planned archaeological museum). In addition, underwater explorations in 1976 revealed the existence of niches, platforms, and broad apses hewn out of the rock, in c 2m of water. The mouth of the cave is barely 1m high, so that even in calm weather, heads have to be ducked.

The **interior** is 57m long, 30m wide, and 15m high. The sun's rays, entering not directly but through the water, fill the cave with a magical blue light and objects in the water have a beautiful silvery appearance. Near the middle of the grotto is a ledge where boats can land. An adjoining cleft, once supposed to be the beginning of an underground passage to the villa of Damecuta, has been proved to be a natural orifice. Outside the grotto is the beginning of a path ascending to Anacapri.

Boat tours

The *giro or voyage around the island by boat takes 3–4 hr and may be begun at the Marina Grande or the Marina Piccola (excursions daily Apr–Sep; on request at other times). Heading east from the Marina Grande, you pass in succession the Grotta del Bove Marino, the strangely shaped little point of Fucile (musket), and the rock named La Ricotta (cream-cheese). After doubling round Il Capo, you reach the Grotta Bianca and Grotta Meravigliosa, both with stalactites (the second accessible also from the land). Further on are the Faraglione di Matromana and Il Monacone, the latter with Roman remains.

Off the Punta Tragara are three gigantic rocks called the *Faraglioni, one of which, La Stella (90m), is connected with the island. The outermost, Lo Scopolo (89m), resembles a sugar-loaf and is the habitat of a rare species of blue lizard.

The boat passes through a natural arch in the central rock. Next comes the Grotta dell'Arsenale, supposed to have been used for repairing ships. Beyond the Marina Piccola, at the foot of Monte Solaro, is the **Grotta Verde**, with beautiful green light effects (best 10.00–11.00 am; inaccessible in a strong south wind). Not far off comes the Grotta Rossa. The voyage along the west side of the island to the Blue Grotto is less interesting.

C.   Procida and Ischia

*'Capri or Ischia?' is a dilemma that faces every first-time visitor to the Naples area, and the answer is: 'Procida'. Perhaps because it is nearer to the mainland than the other islands in the gulf, or perhaps because it is the least dramatic, **Procida** has suffered less from the domesticating influence of tourism. For this reason it remains the most characteristic—the noisiest and most chaotic, but also the most colourful—of the three islands. **Ischia**, alas, is a prime destination of package tours; fortunately these focus on the thermal resorts of the north coast—**Casamicciola Terme**, **Lacco Ameno** and **Forio**—leaving the west and south of the island relatively untouched. You will not find Ischia as rich in history as Capri, but the geology of the island is thoroughly fascinating: its volcanic origin is responsible for the hot mineral springs that are its chief claim to fame, as well as for the rich soil that yields the excellent Ischia Bianco and Ischia Rosso wines.*

APPROACHES BY SEA: Passenger ferries go daily to Procida from Naples (1hr), Pozzuoli (30min), and Ischia (30min). There is also a daily hydrofoil service to Procida from Naples (35min), Pozzuoli (15min) and Ischia (15min). Passenger ferries run daily to Ischia from Naples (1hr 15min), Pozzuoli (1hr), Procida (30min), and Capri (1hr, Apr–Oct); and there is a daily hydrofoil service to Ischia from Naples (30–45min.), Procida (15min), and Capri (50min, Apr–Oct). Automobile traffic is severely restricted on both islands.

HOTELS: Ischia: ****Grand Hotel Excelsior, Via Emanuele Gianturco 19, tel. 081 991020, fax 081 984100; ****Grand Hotel Punta Molino Terme, Lungomare Cristoforo Colombo 25, tel. 081 991544, fax 081 991562; ****La Villarosa, Via Giacinto Gigante 5, tel. 081 991316, fax 081 992425; Lacco Ameno, ****San Montano, tel. 081 994033, fax 081 980242; Forio, ***La Bagattella, località San Francesco, tel. 081 986072, fax 081 989673; Cuotto, ***Paradiso Terme, tel. 081 907014, fax 907913. Sant'Angelo (Serrara Fontana), ***San Michele, tel. 081 999276, fax 081 999149, ****Miramare, tel. 081 999219, fax 0811 999325.

RESTAURANTS: Ischia: ***Damiano, Via Nuova Circonvallazione, tel. 081 983032 (open Apr–Oct, evenings only, all day Sunday); **Giardino Eden, Via Nuova Cartaromana 68, tel. 081 993909 (open May–Sep).

PROCIDA

Procida, Ischia and the tiny islet of Vivara constitute the archipelago known as the Phlegraean Isles; they can be considered a continuation of the Phlegraean Fields, whose volcanic origin they share.

The island of **Procida** (3.5km long, 11,000 inhab.), the ancient *Prochyta*, is formed of four craters of basaltic tufa and pumice stone partly destroyed by the sea to form semicircular bays. The islet of Vivara represents a fifth crater. The chief occupations are fishing and vine growing and the islanders have long been famed for their seamanship.

■ **Information**: AA, Via Marina; tel. 081 810 1968.

The little town of **Procida**, with flat-roofed white houses of Eastern aspect flanked by steep cliffs, stretches along the north coast and rises in terraces on the hills beyond. The winding streets have changed little since the Middle Ages. The popular feast days are 26 September and 8 May, both dedicated to St Michael.

Ferries and hydrofoils land at the Marina. In Piazza dei Martiri are a tablet commemorating 12 of the inhabitants of Procida executed after the rising of 1799, and a statue of Antonio Scialoia, the statesman, who died on the island in 1877. The **Castello** (now a prison) commands in one direction a fine view over Ischia and Monte Epomeo and in the other of Cape Miseno and the Gulf of Naples. In bygone days, escaped prisoners were famous for their appetites; hence the term *sprocidato*, 'escaped from Procida', but also, in popular slang, 'famished'.) Via San Michele climbs to the Terra Murata (91m), highest point of the island, where the abbey church of San Michele features, in the ceiling, Luca Giordano's St Michael defeating Lucifer. At the south–west end of the island (carriage), beyond the castle of Santa Margherita is the Bay of Chiaiolella, facing the olive-clad islets of Vivara and Ischia.

ISCHIA

Ischia is a collection of craters and lava streams of which the highest point is the conical Monte Epomeo (788m), the north side of an extinct volcano. Adjoining its slope are other craters—Monte Rotaro and Monte Montagnone on the north-east, Monte Trippiti on the east and Monte Imperatore and the hills extending to the Punta dell'Imperatore on the west. Lava streams formed also the promontories of Monte Caruso and Punta Cornacchia on the north-west. About 34km in circumference, Ischia is the largest island in the Gulf of Naples. It has a mild climate, and its volcanic slopes are richly covered with sub-tropical vegetation. Its beauty, interest, and variety prompted Bishop Berkeley to describe it, in a letter to Pope (1717), as 'an epitome of the whole earth'. Celebrated for its hot mineral springs (season May–Oct; some open year-round) and for sea-bathing, boating and its delightful walks, Ischia is everywhere well supplied with hotels, restaurants and bathing establishments.

History

According to the ancient poets, Ischia was the abode of the giant Typhoeus who, when struck by Jupiter's thunderbolts, expressed his revengeful fury in volcanoes and earthquakes. The Greeks who colonised it called it *Pithecusa* or *Pithecusae*, the Latins *Aenaria* or *Inarime*. In the 9C it was known as *Iscla*, a corruption of *insula* or, simply, The Island, from which its modern name is derived.

The earliest recorded volcanic eruption on the island dates from c 500 BC; the last was in 1301. Ischia was seized in 474 BC by Hieron of Syracuse, c 450 by the Neapolitans, and in 326, by the Romans. Augustus exchanged it with the Neapolitans for Capri. It was later taken by the Saracens in 813 and 947, by the Pisans in 1135, by Henry VI and Frederick II. Finally it came to share the fortunes of Naples.

Ischia was the birthplace of the Marquis of Pescara (1489), and his widow Vittoria Colonna retired here in 1525. The island was sacked by the pirate Barbarossa in 1541 and captured in 1547 by the Duke of Guise; it was occupied by Nelson, and in 1815 provided a brief refuge for Murat. The self-portrait of Allan Ramsay in the National Portrait Gallery in London was executed on the island in 1776 and the sculptor Canova was rewarded in 1816 with the title of Marquis of Ischia.

The town

The comune of **Ischia**, the chief town (18,000 inhab.) of the island, consists of Ischia Ponte, extending picturesquely along the shore for c 2km north of the castle, and the modern Ischia Porto around the harbour to the north-west, the two separated by a fine beach backed by pine woods.

■ **Information**: AA, Corso Colonna 116, Ischia; tel. 081 991464, fax 081 9819041 (branch office at the Stazione Marittima).

■ **Principal thermal establishments.** Ischia Thermal Centre, Ischia; Terme Belliacci and Terme Piro, Casamicciola; Regina Isabella, Lacco Ameno. Many hotels on the island have thermal swimming pools.

Most ferries and hydrofoils land at Ischia Porto. The town was built around a crater lake, the seaward side of which was pierced in 1854 to form the circular harbour, 1.5km across. The Punta San Pietro on the east and the public park and the mole on the west side command good views. Via Roma and its continuation, Via Vittoria Colonna, lead to **Ischia Ponte**, beyond which the Ponte Aragonese (1438), a causeway 228m long, leads to the rocky islet fortress of Alfonso the Magnanimous (private).

On the island is the 14C **Cattedrale**, ruined when the English fleet bombarded the invading French in 1806, with a huge crypt (frescoes). The **Castello**, where Vittoria Colonna stayed, rises 111m above the sea (open summer, 09.00–1hr before sunset).

From Ischia Ponte follow the Via del Seminario and Via Sogliuzzo through pine woods to the little Piazza degli Eroi, from where Via Alfredo De Luca leads back to Ischia Porto.

A road diverging to the south from the main road, about 600m west of Ischia

Porto, leads to (35min) **Fiaiano** (198m; view) and (north) in 10min more to the top of Monte Montagnone (311m).

The island

A tour of the island by road (30km; bus) may be made comfortably in half a day. The road climbs steeply from Ischia Porto to the hamlet of Perrone and turns south-west.

5km **Casamicciola Terme**, on the north slope of Monte Epomeo, is a pleasant bathing resort and spa, the first on Ischia to be frequented for its mineral waters. The town (7000 inhab.) was rebuilt after the earthquake of 1883 in which 1700 people perished. The mineral waters (80°C) of the Gurgitello, prescribed for arthritis and rheumatism, are used in the establishments of Manzi and Belliazzi, and similar waters feed those of the Castagna. At the Villa Ibsen, then Piseni, Ibsen started *Peer Gynt* in 1867. The Osservatorio Geofisico on the Grande Sentinella commands a fine view.

2km **Lacco Ameno** (4000 inhab) is another thermal resort, with the most radio-active waters in Italy. At the little church of Santa Restituta, dedicated to the patron saint of the island (died 284), traces of an early sanctuary have come to light (open daily 09.00–12.00 and afternoons on request; apply to the parish priest). The 18C Villa Arbusto houses a Museo Archeologico containing finds from the excavations of Pithecusa, remains of which occupy the gardens (apply for admission to the, AA). In addition to Greek and Italic material, the finds include Egyptian and Syrian objects which demonstrate the colony's ancient commercial ties with the eastern Mediterranean. St Restituta's day (17 May) is celebrated by fireworks and bonfires on Monte Vico, etc. The thermal establishments of Lacco Ameno are considered the most exclusive on the island.

The road now ascends steeply over the lava stream of 464 BC and descends to (3km) **Forio** (12,000 inhab.), centre of production of Epomeo wine and the centre of the foreign (particularly German) colony on the island. The Pensione Nettuno occupies a convent of 1742, with a picturesque medieval tower. The Santuario del Soccorso, above the village, commands an enchanting view.

The road passes above the radioactive sands of Citara, traversing Cuotto, where a path diverges to the right for the Punta dell'Imperatore (232m; lighthouse), the south-west extremity of the island. 4km Panza; view of Capri. To the south lie the rich orchards of Succhivo, and **Sant'Angelo** (2.5km), a health resort with submarine springs, from whose sandy beach, the Marina dei Maronti, issue plumes of stream.

Beyond Panza the road turns east and ascends, with many turns and magnificent views all the way, to (4km) Serrara Fontana (331m); higher up is Parrocchia, a hamlet with a colour-washed church. 2km **Fontana** (449m) has a church of 1374. This is the best starting place for the ascent of Monte Epomeo (788m; 1hr; mules for hire), the summit of which commands a *view extending from Terracina to Capri. The prominent iron crucifix commemorates 44 people killed in an air crash. The descent to Forio, Casamicciola or Ischia Porto takes 2hr.

Descend through a ravine to (1.5km) Buonopane (286m), separated by another ravine from (2km) Barano d'Ischia, among its vineyards. To the south is the village of Testaccio from which you may descend on foot to the Marina dei Maronti (see above). Turn north-east and Procida, Capo Miseno and the castle of Ischia come into sight ahead. Beyond Molara leave Sant'Antuono on the right, and, following the Lava dell'Arso, rejoin the coast between Ischia Ponte and Ischia Porto at (5km) the Piazzetta di Ferrocavallo.

7 · Naples to Reggio Calabria

A. Via the coast

*This is the main rail route from Naples to Reggio Calabria and Sicily. By car it is considerably slower than Route 7B, which passes inland. To save time at the start of the journey (and to avoid heavy local traffic in the Naples–Salerno area), you follow the Autostrada as far as Battipaglia, from where minor roads lead across the **Cilento**, a broad mountainous peninsula between the Gulfs of Salerno and Policastro. This is still one of the more beautiful and unspoilt areas of Campania (a considerable part of the peninsula was declared a National Park in 1991), where local journeys are sometimes made by mule or by the traditional cart. Known in ancient times for its unpredictable winds and currents, the coast is particularly rich in literary allusions. The **Punta Licosa** (the ancient Enipeum or Posidium Promontorium) takes its name from the siren Leocosia, who threw herself into the sea from the headland after failing to enchant Ulysses; and **Capo Palinuro** recalls Aeneas' pilot Palinurus who, overtaken by sleep, fell into the sea and drowned, and here appeared to the hero asking to be buried. The Cilento is also the site of two of the more important colonies of Magna Graecia, **Paestum** and **Velia**. The former is known primarily for its well-preserved Doric temples and its excellent museum,modern home of the remarkable set of Greek wall paintings from the so-called Tomb of the Diver; the latter, though considerably less spectacular, is attractive because of its position and its curious layering of Greek, Roman, and medieval remains.*

*Beyond the lovely resort of **Maratea** the highway runs the whole length of Calabria. The scenery is varied, the vegetation luxuriant, and there are spectacular views of the coastline,the Aeolian Islands, Sicily and the Strait of Messina. The white sand beaches around **Tropea**, on the Monte Poro headland, are among the finest in the south.*

Motorists should bear in mind that traffic can be quite slow during the summer, when the beaches are crowded. In ideal conditions a full day of driving (8hr) is necessary. The best places to interrupt the journey are Paestum, Maratea and Tropea. The latter is also a good place to stay for those wishing to visit Reggio (which is large and noisy) and the Aspromonte (Route 9).

ROAD 538km. Autostrada A3/E45 to Battipaglia, then Highways 18, 267, 447, 562, 278 and local roads. 77km Battipaglia—33km Agropoli 70km Palinuro—42km Sapri—18km Maratea—85km Paola—113km Tropea—89km Villa San Giovanni—11km Reggio Calabria.

RAILWAY. From Naples (Centrale) to Reggio Calabria (Centrale), 476km in 4hr 30min–5 hr. To Villa San Giovanni (where through trains to Sicily cross the Strait of Messina), in c 15min less. From Naples (Centrale) to Maratea, 193km in c. 2hr 30min, with a change of trains at Sapri. Beyond Battipaglia the road follows the coast, whereas the railway cuts inland between Agropoli and Marina di Ascea and again between Pisciotta and Policastro. From Maratea to Reggio, 283km in c 2hr 45min, with a change of trains at Paola. To (139km) Lamezia Terme Centrale, junction for Catanzaro in c 1hr 15min. With a few exceptions, the main express trains bear inland again after Lamezia, returning to the coast at Gioia Tauro. A branch line serves Tropea and the picturesque towns of the Monte Poro headland. From Naples to Paestum, 95km in c 1hr 30min (a change is usually necessary at Salerno or at Battipaglia; only slow trains stop at Paestum).

HOTELS EN ROUTE: Palinuro, ****King's Residence, tel. 0974 931324, fax 0974 931418; Maratea, *****Santavenere, tel. 0973 876910, fax 0973 877654; Acquafredda, ****Villa Cheta Elite, tel./fax 0973 878134; Scalea, ****Grand Hotel De Rose, tel. 0985 20273, fax 0985 920194; Cetraro, *****Grand Hotel San Michele, tel. 0982 91012, fax 0982 91430; Parghelia, ***** Baia Paraelios, tel. 0963 600004, fax 0963 600074; Capo Vaticano (Tropea), ***Punta Faro, tel. 0963 663139, fax 0963 663968. Youth Hostel at Scilla (under construction 1995).

RESTAURANTS EN ROUTE: Paestum, **Nettuno, Zona Archeologica, tel./fax 0828 811028; Vibo Valentia (Marina), **L'Approdo, tel./fax 572640.

Naples to Paestum
From Naples, take Autostrada A3/E45 past Salerno to (77km) Battipaglia, then follow Highway 18 south.

23km ****Paestum** has been for a thousand years a romantic ruin in the midst of a solemn wilderness. Its Doric temples, unsurpassed even by those of Athens in noble simplicity and good preservation, produce an incomparable effect of majesty and grandeur.

History
Originally called Poseidonia, the city of Neptune, it was founded by Greeks from Sybaris in the 6CBC, its name being Latinised to Paestum when it came into the hands of the Lucanians in the 4C. In 273 BC it was taken by the Romans. Paestum was famed in antiquity for its roses, which flowered twice a year, and for its violets. Malaria gradually killed or drove off much of the population, and c AD 877 the city was destroyed by the Saracens. All but overgrown by tangled vegetation, it was rediscovered during the building of the coach-road in the 18C.

The ancient ruins comprise remains of numerous public, private and religious buildings, including four major temples, a forum and an extensive residential quarter. The town walls are constructed of square blocks of travertine and are 4750m in circumference. Their extant ruins rise to a height of 5–15m and include four gates (of which the most important is the Porta Sirena on the east side) and several towers. The town is crossed by a *cardo* and a *decumanus*, both of which preserve paved segments. Recent excavations have shown that the temples belong to two groups, that to the south (dedicated to Hera) including the so-called basilica and Temple of Neptune and 11 smaller temples, that to the north (dedicated to Athene) focusing on the Temple of Ceres. Between the two ran the Via Sacra, now brought to light. In the middle, immediately east of this main street, are the forum and other neighbouring buildings, while the residential area develops to the north and west.

■ **Information:** AA, Paestum, Via Magna Grecia 151; tel. 0828 811016, fax 0828 722322.

From the Porta della Giustizia, on the south side of the excavations, the Via Sacra leads first to the ***basilica**, the earliest temple at Paestum, misnamed by its discoverers in the 18C. Measuring 60 x 24m, it is an enneastyle peripteros with 50

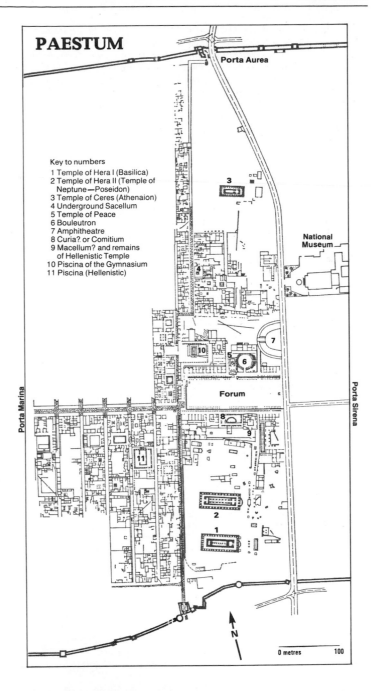

PAESTUM

Porta Aurea

Key to numbers
1 Temple of Hera I (Basilica)
2 Temple of Hera II (Temple of
  Neptune—Poseidon)
3 Temple of Ceres (Athenaion)
4 Underground Sacellum
5 Temple of Peace
6 Bouleutron
7 Amphitheatre
8 Curia? or Comitium
9 Macellum? and remains
  of Hellenistic Temple
10 Piscina of the Gymnasium
11 Piscina (Hellenistic)

National
Museum

Porta Marina

Porta Sirena

Forum

N

0 metres 100

fluted columns, nine at the ends and 18 along the sides. The colonnade is still standing, as are the entablature and part of the inside of the frieze. The columns are 6.5m high, with a lower diameter of 146cm and an upper diameter of 98cm. They belong to the Doric order and show distinct features of the early style: rapid tapering, a marked entasis (or swelling profile) and a bulging moulding of the capital. These and other features enable archaeologists to date the temple to c 550 BC.

Inside the colonnade stood the cella, or sanctuary, formed by a porch-like structure (or pronaos in antis) formed by three columns standing between two great pilasters at the ends of the cella walls. A colonnade at the centre of the cella divided the interior into two small naves; three columns are still standing and the capital of two others are lying on the ground. There were probably seven in all, and also perhaps a half-column against the end wall, which separated the cella from the treasury.

About 50m farther north stands the ****Temple of Neptune**. This temple, built in the 5C BC, is the largest in Paestum and ranks with the Theseion at Athens and the Temple of Concord at Agrigento as one of the three best-preserved temples in Europe. It stands on a basement (or stylobate) of three steps and is 60m long by 24m wide. It is a hexastyle peripteros with 36 fluted columns (14 at the sides, six at the ends). These are 9m in height and taper from 270cm at the base to 146cm at the top. The cella, with a pronaos in antis, and opisthodomos (enclosed rear part) is divided into three aisles by two rows of two pilasters and seven columns 1m in diameter, with smaller columns above, of which three remain on the north side and five on the south. The entablature is well preserved and the pediments are almost intact. The roof, however, has gone. Shelley, the English Romantic poet, wrote that 'the effect of the jagged outline of the mountains through the groups of enormous columns on one side, and on the other the level horizon of the sea, is inexpressibly grand'. To the east are the remains of a large sacrificial altar.

Continuing to the north, the Via Sacra crosses the *decumanus maximus* (which joins the Porta Sirena to the Porta Marina) on the site of the **forum**, which replaced the earlier Greek agora. Measuring 157 x 57m, it was surrounded on all four sides by a fine Doric portico, of which some fragments are still visible on the three remaining sides. On the south side are the remains of baths of the Imperial age, of the curia, of a Hellenistic Greek temple and of what may have been the macellum. On the north side are a Roman temple of an early period with later additions (the so-called Temple of Peace), a Greek theatre (bouleutron) and, farther to the right and partly under the modern road, a Roman amphitheatre.

Adjoining the Via Sacra just north of the forum is a large building with a central cistern or piscina and a portico, possibly the gymnasium. From here the Via Sacra leads past the **underground sacellum**, a tomblike structure whose exact significance is a matter of dispute among archaeologists. It is generally believed to have been a sacred edifice consecrated to the deities of fertility; but it might also have been an empty tomb dedicated to Is, the mythical founder of Sybaris, erected at Paestum by Sybarite refugees after their city was destroyed in 509 BC.

Further north along the Via Sacra stands the **Temple of Ceres** (more accurately an Athenaion, a temple dedicated to the goddess Athena), of a date intermediate between the two surviving southern temples. It is the smallest of the three, a hexastyle peripteros of 34 fluted colums (6 x 13), 6m high; it is raised on a stylobate of two steps and measures 33 x 14m. The cella is quite simple and the pronaos of unusual depth. The architrave is the only remaining part of the entablature, but much remains of the pediments. Near the south wall of the cella are three

The Temple of Ceres at Paestum, viewed from the west

Christian tombs of the early Middle Ages, when the temple was used as a church. To the east are traces of a large sacrificial altar and of a votive column, suggesting that the temple once stood at the centre of a small sanctuary.

Excavations on the west side of the Via Sacra have brought to light an extensive residential quarter in which some homes appear to have been quite luxurious; at least one had a private *piscina*, probably of Hellenistic workmanship.

The **Musco Nazionale**, adjoining the archaeological area (open daily, Sep–Jun 09.00–18.30, Jun–Aug 09.00–22.00, closed first and third Mon of each month; a ticket to one gives admission to the other), was designed in 1952 to display many fine objects from recent excavations, including prehistoric and protohistoric material, burial treasures, an important group of tomb paintings, architectural and sculptural fragments, and votive terracottas, of Greek, Lucanian, and Roman provenance. Most notable is the collection of archaic sculpture from the sanctuary of Argive Hera at the month of the Sele, including 33 ***metopes** with Homeric and other scenes; and the truly extraordinary cycle of mural paintings from the so-called ****Tomb of the Diver**, perhaps the only extant examples of Greek painting (c 480 BC). The four panels forming the coffin are decorated with a funeral banqueting scene in which singing, games, lovers, and music accompany the deceased into the other world. The fifth panel, the lid, shows the Diver from whom the tomb takes its name—a naked youth who executes a perfect dive into a blue sea, in an unusual allegory of death.

Around Paestum

The atmosphere of Paestum may best be appreciated by a tour of the **walls** (c 4km). The lower and outer courses are of the 5C B C, the inner parts date from the Lucanian period. The Porta Sirena retains its arch and the Porta Marina its towers and bastions. From the latter the Torre di Pesto, a medieval watch-tower, lies c 1km south-west. It commands a good view of the magnificent sandy beach, unfortunately marred by bathing establishments, extending in both directions. About 9km to the north, near the mouth of the Sele, lie the remains of another Greek temple, referred to by Strabo and Pliny but undiscovered until 1934.

Across the Cilento

About 4km beyond Paestum, Highway 18 crosses the Solofone. Here turn right onto Highway 267 to (6km) **Agropoli**, a popular resort. The medieval town stands on a headland above a small, picturesque bay. Just west of the town is the convent of San Francesco, situated on a cliff 60m above the sea.

The old road to Calabria

The traditional route across the Cilento (Highway 18, 73km) bypasses Agropoli and the coastal towns to Policastro, crossing the mountainous interior of the peninsula, where some of the wildest landscape in Campania is to be found. Although the scenery is magnificent, the driving is slow and difficult. South of Paestum the road climbs away from the Sele plain to (13km) Ogliastro Cilento (350m), which commands a view over the Gulf of Salerno to Amalfi and Capri. 4km Prignano Cilento was the birthplace of Urban VI (Bartolomeo Prignano, 1378–89). The road descends the west side of the valley of the Alento. At Procoio the railway and a byroad diverge towards the coast. The main road climbs to (31km) **Vallo della Lucania** (8000 inhab.), where the church of Santa Maria delle Grazie contains a polyptych by Andrea da Salerno. To the east rises Monte Sacro (1705m) with a sanctuary already a place of pilgrimage before 1323. Beyond the town, the view over the hills to the sea opens up to embrace Pioppi and the Torre di Punta (see below). The road continues through oak woods to Laurito (475m, 1000 inhab.), perched on a spur of Monte Bulgheria (right). 39km Torre Orsaia is known for its textile industry. Beyond, the highway descends to (11km) Policastro, where it rejoins the coast.

From Agropoli bear south-east; the road runs inland, to the east of Monte Tresino, returning to the coast near the village of Santa Maria di Castellabate. Further on lies (14km) **San Marco**, a fishing village and a growing resort, with remains of ancient walls and, in the sea, of a Roman breakwater carved out of the rock. Mule tracks lead along the coast via (3.5km) **Punta Licosa** (the ancient *Enipeum* or *Posidium Promontorium*), which takes its name from the siren Leucosia, who threw herself into the sea from the headland after failing to enchant Ulysses, to (3.5km) Ogliastro Marina, on the south side of the peninsula. Opposite the point stands the tiny isle of **Licosa**, containing remains of ancient walls and the modern navigational light, visible at a distance of 12 miles.

From San Marco the road cuts inland once again to the tiny hamlet of Case del Conte, then returns to the coast, offering good views over the sea, punctuated by groves of maritime pine. Beyond (10km) Agnone, the highway hugs the coast to

(6km) **Acciaroli**, on a lovely promontory, a favourite resort of Ernest Hemingway. Leave the town to the right and wind past the houses of Pioppi, where there are fine views of Capo Palinuro. At Marina di Casal Velino, cross the valley of the Alento (the *Hales* of the ancients). Above the river, now marked by a medieval ruin, lie the remains of the ancient *****Velia**.

History

Elea, as the city was called by the Greeks, was founded in the mid 6C by Phocaean colonists driven from their homeland by the attacking Persians. One of the last Greek colonies to be founded on the Italian peninsula, it retains the typically Phocaean system of town planning, by which the residential quarters are divided into independent zones separated by walls.

The town derived its livelihood from fishing and commerce, as the rocky, arid hinterland was unsuitable for agriculture. Its ties with Massalia (the modern Marseille) developed to such an extent that at one time Elea was considered a sub-colony of the latter. In the 3C BC the inhabitants threw in their lot with Rome; nevertheless the city retained its Hellenic culture, language, and customs, supplying the capital with priestesses of Ceres, who tradition dictated must be Greek. Although it never attained great civic or economic importance, Elea became a leading intellectual centre, giving its name to the Eleatic school of philosophy of Xenophanes, Parmenides, and Zeno. Its decline became evident in Roman times, as its harbours (there were apparently two, on the north and south sides of the headland, which once projected into the sea) filled with silt. By the 12C it had disappeared altogether, and the medieval town of Castellammare della Bruca had grown up in its place. This in turn was abandoned in the 17C.

The ruins were discovered in 1883. They may be visited (open 09.00–1hr before sunset) comfortably in about an hour. On the south side of the archaeological site are a sea wall, later fortified when the area beyond filled with silt; and remains of Roman tombs. Just beyond stands the Porta Marina Sud, one of the two gates (the other is at the north end of the town), which initially opened onto the harbours. Within extends the south quarter, the centre of residential and political life. On the right lies the **palaestra**, with its cryptoporticus; notice, near the entrance to the latter, the collection of bricks, of a type peculiar to Velia, impressed with the town's mark. Numerous statues, including a portrait of Parmenides, were found here.

In an olive grove to the east are **Roman baths** dating from the 2C AD, of which some rooms preserve their mosaic pavements. Farther on, on the right, is the **agora**, the central square and marketplace of the Greek town, dating, as it is to be seen today, from the 3C BC. Along the right side stalls were attached to the walls and pillars on market days. The main street now ascends more sharply, the paving stones (which are laid endwise in the characteristic Greek fashion) being staggered somewhat to provide a better foothold.

Near the top of the hill stand the Porta Arcaica, built in the 6C BC, in a position of obvious defensive importance; and the **Porta Rosa**, a remarkable structure of the 4C BC brought to light in 1964. Toward the end of the same century the lofty arch was walled up and this tract of the road, threatened by landslides, was replaced by another road that runs along the viaduct above to the **acropolis**. Here remains of a medieval tower overlie the foundations of an Ionic temple dating from the second half of the 5C BC. Excavations in the area have revealed a small

Hellenistic temple and an open sanctuary dedicated to Poseidon. At the north-east corner of the site the walls come together to form the Castelluccio, a tall tower dating from the 4C BC.

A series of curves leads through wild valleys and groves of giant olives, past the villages of Ascea and Pisciotta to (37km) **Palinuro**, a fishing centre and a popular resort splendidly set in a small bay. An antiquarium (closed 1995) contains finds from the necropolis of Molpa (2km east). At the entrance to the harbour you can see the ruins of what popular belief holds to be the cenotaph erected to Palinurus who, overtaken by sleep, fell into the sea and drowned and here appeared to the hero, asking to be buried (*Aeneid*, V, 838–871; VI, 337–383).

A walk along the coast
An excursion may be made to (2km, 30min) the ruins of **Molpa**, originally an outpost of the Greek colony at Velia, later made over into a castle, where Emperor Maximian withdrew after renouncing his title. The path, which runs through olive groves and along the beach, is difficult in places.

The Capo Palinuro headland contains numerous **caves** accessible from the sea (boats may be hired at the harbour), some of which were occupied in prehistoric times. Also of interest are the **natural arches** at Foce del Mingardo and Archetiello.

Leaving Palinuro, bear south-east on Highway 562 to (10km) Marina di Camerota, a modern resort. Here, as at Palinuro, excursions may be made to numerous caves along the coast. The road leaves the coast, penetrating the rocky hinterland in a series of tortuous bends. Beyond the village of Lentiscosa the going improves somewhat, offering a view to the left of the sheer face of **Monte Bulgheria** (1225m). Beyond (14km) San Giovanni a Piro, the descent to the sea begins. Rejoin highway 18 on the west slope of the Valle del Bussento and cross the river to reach (10km) **Policastro** (the Greek *Pixous*), situated, with a beautiful backdrop of hills, on the bay of the same name. The cathedral of **Santa Maria Assunta** dates from 1177. Follow the rocky coast east.

10km **Sapri**, a pleasant resort (7000 inhab.) on a sheltered bay, achieved fame during the Risorgimento, giving its name to the daring expedition of Carlo Pisacane and Giovanni Nicotera, who landed on the beach to the west of the town in 1857 with a handful of patriots freed from the political prison on the Isle of Ponza in the hope of stirring a popular rebellion against the Bourbons. Their plans were thwarted; after a brief clash with the Bourbon troops the party dispersed and was largely cut down by local peasants. Today the town is known for its fine beaches, its olive oil, and its wood and marble industries.

Into Calabria
With Sapri behind you, leave Campania and cross the short Tyrrhenian seaboard of Basilicata. The road, one of the more beautiful in Italy, affords breathtaking *views in all directions, with imposing cliffs on the left and steep drops down to the sea on the right.

8km Acquafredda is a small resort. 10km Fiumicello lies on the sea below **Maratea**, pleasantly situated on a hill-slope. The town (5000 inhab.), reached by a winding road on the left, commands a marvellous *view of the Gulf of Policastro.

■ **Information**. APT, Piazza del Gesù 32, tel. 0973 876425.

At Maratea Inferiore is the church of **Santa Maria Maggiore** containing very fine 15C Gothic choir stalls, a marble Virgin in Glory and paintings of the Neapolitan school. The former church of the Francescani has an interesting cloister. From Maratea Superiore the road continues for c 1km to the sanctuary of **San Biagio**, with good views back to Capo Palinuro and Monte Bulgheria. Maratea hosts a drama festival in August.

Inland to Lagonegro via Rivello

From Maratea an excellent new highway winds inland, via Castrocacco, to Lagonegro (27km, Route 7B), passing (right) **Rivello**, a picturesque village on a cliff overlooking the River Noce. Here the Greek Orthodox rite was practised until the 13C, and several of the village's churches show traces of a Byzantine origin. Notable among these are San Nicola dei Greci, which overlooks the town, Santa Barbara, with a single nave and semicircular apse adorned by arched corbels, and the Convento dei Minori with 16C frescoes by a local painter, Giovanni De Gregorio, called Pietrafesa. Rivello Castle is now a restaurant.

You enter Calabria just before (16km) **Praia a Mare** (6000 inhab.), reached by a turning on the right. Above the town you can see the Santuario della Madonna della Grotta (reached by steps), containing a medieval wooden statue of the Madonna and Child, and another marble Madonna of the school of Gagini. Off the coast lies the **Isola di Dino**, a triangular plateau rising 65m above the sea, with grottoes showing the same light effect as at the Blue Grotto of Capri. The island may be reached by boat from Praia a Mare in c 20 min.

The road continues along the coast to (8km) San Nicola Arcella, a charming little town (1000 inhab.) on a hilltop, then it crosses Capo Scalea and descends once again to the sea. A turning on the left ascends in 4km to **Scalea** (62m, 9000 inhab.), an attractive old town rising in steps above a good beach, now largely spoilt by development, and commanding good views of the cape, the sea and the fertile Lao delta. The latter is believed to be the site of the Sybarite colony of Laos, a flourishing commercial centre of the 6C and 5C BC that later fell to the Lucanians. A Lucanian necropolis has recently come to light south of the river, near the site of the Roman *Lavinium*, remains of which are no longer visible. The church of **San Nicola** contains a tomb of 1343 that recalls the Pisan style of Tino di Camaino.

Some prehistoric cave drawings

On the road from Scalea to Mormanno (Route 16) lies (23km) Papasidero, near which (1hr walk) is the rock shelter of **Il Romito**, with Palaeolithic graffiti of bulls and oxen (c 10,000 BC) discovered in 1961.

Leaving the old road on the left, proceed south from Scalea across the Lao delta. Above (12km) Cirella, the ruined medieval town (Cirella Vecchia), destroyed by the French in 1806, is prominent on its hill. South of the town, on the beach before the fortified Isola di Cirella, are the remains of a Roman tomb.

4km Diamante, a fishing centre and resort, is noted for its cedar trees. Beyond, the road hugs the narrow coastal plain to (10km) **Belvedere Marittimo** (203m, 9000 inhab.), which commands a splendid view of the sea and the coast. The town contains several churches, including the **Chiesa Matrice**, with a 15C Tuscan relief above the main door and the **Chiesa del Crocifisso**, which contains a great wooden crucifix; and a ruined medieval **Castello**.

Near Cittadella del Capo, the road passes through four short tunnels. 15km

Cetraro has three statues by Giovanni Battista Mazzola (1533) in the church of the Ritiro. About 8km further on, in the hills to the left, is Guardia Piemontese. Like Montalto Uffugo, further inland, it was colonised by Waldensians in the late 14C, but these Protestant colonies were destroyed with great cruelty in 1559–61. Nearby is Terme Luigiane, a sulphur spa. 15km from Cetraro a road on the left climbs to Fuscaldo (378m, 9000 inhab.), with a ruined castle and several Baroque churches.

7km **Paola**, once an attractive town (18,000 inhab.), has been entirely transformed by unchecked development as a resort. It was the birthplace of San Francesco da Paola (1416–1507), founder of the Minims, the strictest order of the Franciscans. The **Santuario di San Francesco**, above the town to the north, dates from 1435 and is fronted by a long piazza with a modern statue and an obelisk commemorating the Holy Year of 1950. The basilica, dedicated to Santa Maria degli Angeli, has recently been restored; its façade is an unusual mixture of Renaissance and Baroque motifs. The interior contains the 16C Cappella del Santo and 15C and 16C artworks of the Neapolitan school; adjacent is a small cloister. In central Paola are several churches of minor interest. The **Santissima Annunziata**, high in the town, built in the 13C and later redecorated in the Baroque manner, has been restored to its former state. Above the high altar, with its marble inlay, is a 16C painting of the Annunciation. A descent may be made by steps (left), passing a pleasing Baroque fountain, through the Porta San Francesco, with another fountain at its centre. Rising at the back you can see the Baroque façade of the church of Santa Maria di Monte Vergine. Santa Caterina, with a Gothic portal of 1493, houses a painting of the Madonna delle Grazie attributed to Domencio Beccafumi.

A mountain road to Cosenza

Highway 107 runs inland from Paola to Cosenza (32km). A bus runs several times daily from Paola Station to Cosenza in 1hr 30min–2hr, substituting for the train. The appeal of this route lies in the striking views from the high mountains of the **Catena Costiera**, the range that separates the Tyrrhenian seaboard from the plain formed by the rivers Crati and Busento. After leaving Paola the highway climbs steeply up the west slope of the Catena Costiera among vineyards and orchards, and through dense forests of oak, chestnut, and beech trees. There are splendid *views through the trees to the sea. 17km **Passo della Crocetta** (950m) offers a breathtaking panorama that extends from the volcanic cone of Stromboli and the other Aeolian Islands to the west across the broad valley of the Crati to the Sila to the east. Here begins the descent to Cosenza, again through fields and the forests that dominate the Crati valley.

7km San Fili (550m, 3000 inhab.) enjoys a good location on a hilltop, among woods and farms. The Chiesa Parrochiale dell'Assunta has a Baroque portal and interesting choir stalls of inlaid wood (1801). 7km a road diverges right to (3km) Rende, where the Palazzo Municipale was built in the 12C or 13C by remodelling a castello initially dating from 1095. The Palazzo Zagarese (Via del Bartolo; open daily 09.00–13.00) contains a small museum of religious art. The descent continues among woodlands and olive groves to the valley floor. 10km turn right onto Highway 19 and enter Cosenza (Route 7B) from the north.

Beyond Paola, the highway parallels the main railway line past the convent of Sant'Antonio to (7km) San Lucido, a charming little town (6000 inhab.) on a promontory overlooking the sea. In its castello was born Cardinal Fabrizio Ruffo (1744–1827), the Bourbon politician and collaborator of Fra' Diavolo. 8km a minor road leads left to **Fiumefreddo Bruzio** (220m, 4000 inhab.), where parts of the medieval town walls and two gates can still be seen. The church of the Matrice possesses an 18C wooden crucifix. **Santa Chiara** has a wooden coffered ceiling, coloured majolica-tile floors and three carved and gilded wooden altars. In San Francesco da Paola is a tomb of the Mendoza family. The church of the **Carmine**, on a hill east of the village, has a 15C Gothic portal and remains of a cloister. A dirt track to the north leads in c 1hr to the ruined **Abbey of San Domenico** or Fonte Laurato, originally dating from 1020–35, interesting for its mixture of Byzantine and Norman architectural elements.

19km **Amantea** (12,000 inhab.) extends downward from its ruined castello to the beach. A modest centre in Roman times, the town has been identified with the *Clampetia* of Livy. It was vehemently defended against the French under Verdier in 1806, but has resisted less successfully the recent onslaught of builders and holiday-makers. The ruins of the medieval church and convent of **San Francesco d'Assisi**, in the upper part of the town, and those of the vast **Castello** on its hilltop, offer splendid views of the sea and the coastline. In the lower town, the 15C church of **San Bernardino da Siena** is fronted by a portico with five Gothic arches on octagonal piers, with ceramic decorations. The first north chapel contains a Madonna by Antonio Gagini (dated 1505) and other sculpture.

Beyond Capo Suvero, where you have a view of the whole curve of the Gulf of Eufemia and, on a clear day, of Stromboli and the Aeolian Islands, you enter the Piana di Sant'Eufemia. This intensely cultivated plain is encircled by beautiful mountains, the lower slopes of which are covered with olive groves. 40km **Sant'Eufemia Lamezia**, a modern town, is the road and railway junction for Catanzaro (Route 10) and for the Ionian resort areas. It is the sum of five distinct villages, the most impressive being **Nicastro** (11km north-east), the old *Neocastrum* of Byzantine or Norman origin, almost entirely destroyed by earthquake in 1638. Charmingly built up the side of a mountain, it is dominated by the ruins of the **Castello** of Frederick II, the prison of his rebellious son Henry, who escaped only to die mysteriously at Martirano, 16km north-west. The local costumes of the women are beautiful. From here you may join the Cosenza–Catanzaro road at Soveria Mannelli or Tiriolo.

To the east rises the plateau of Maida. The Battle of Maida, by which the British under Sir John Stuart expelled the French from Calabria in 1806, gave its name to Maida Vale in London. This battle proved the value of the rifle and the 'thin red line' tactics put to successful use in the Peninsular War.

THE SOUTHERN CALABRIAN COAST
19km Ponte Angitola lies at the narrowest point of the Calabrian peninsula. A road to the left ascends to Serra San Bruno (see below). Our road bears right to (6km) **Pizzo**, a prosperous little town (9000 inhab.) traditionally engaged in fishing for tuna and swordfish and now also a resort. In the old **Castello** (erected in 1486 by Ferdinand I of Aragon and partially restored) Joachim Murat, ex-king of Naples, was tried by court-martial and shot on 13 October 1815, five days after he had landed in an attempt to recover his throne. The church of **San Giorgio** contains a number of marble statues, among which may be noted a 16C St John the Baptist and a regal figure of St Catherine of Alexandria. From the narrow streets of the

medieval town there are extensive views of the coast; below, the rock on which the settlement stands (*Lu Pizzo* in local dialect) plunges straight into the sea.

Beyond Pizzo, Highway 19 climbs inland to (10km) Vibo Valentia, described in Route 7B.

The coast road continues along the sea, past the busy industrial port of Vibo Marina to Briattico, a farming and fishing town located between two lovely beaches, La Rocchetta to the north and Le Galere to the south. From here the road follows the railway to (35km) **Tropea** (61m, 7000 inhab.), still perhaps the most picturesque of the several small fishing towns that line the rocky coast between Sant'Eufemia Lamezia and Gioia Tauro. Huddled on a cliff above the sea, it commands stunning views of the coast and, on clear days, of the Aeolian Islands. Below, broad white sandy beaches extend to the north and south for more than 4km.

History

The origin of the town is uncertain. The most likely hypothesis holds that it was founded by the Greeks, whose initial interest probably focused on its natural harbour (which Pliny the Elder calls *Portus Hercules*, in reference to the popular belief that the hero was the first to realise its importance), now largely filled with silt. Excavations have revealed remains of Greek and Roman settlements, now chiefly in the archaeological museum in Reggio Calabria, as well as an extensive proto-Villanovan necropolis. A Siculan centre has recently been identified at Torre Galli, c 4km south-east of the town. During the Middle Ages Tropea provided a natural fortress for those members of the lesser nobility and the middle class who sought respite from their feudal obligations. The numerous extant **palaces**, with fine sculpted doorways, attest to this tradition.

From Piazza Ercole, at the centre of the town, Via Roma leads north to Largo Duomo and the **Cattedrale**, a Norman construction rebuilt several times in the 17C and 18C and restored to its 'original' state in 1926–32. The east flank, with its false arcade and inlaid ornamentation, and the Gothic arcade adjoining the main façade, give the church a rare grace and beauty. The three-aisled interior is impressive in its simplicity. It contains a 14C wooden crucifix, a marble ciborium of Tuscan workmanship and an interesting double tomb with effigies of a brother and sister, to which the tondos representing the Annunciation, now mounted on the interior walls, also belonged. At the end of the south aisle stands an extremely fine statue of the Madonna and Child by Giovanni Angelo Montorsoli. Behind the high altar, enclosed in a silver frame, can be seen the Madonna di Romania, supposedly painted by St Luke.

Throughout the old town are the once luxurious residences constructed by the lesser nobility and the rising middle class, now largely reduced to flats. The houses, distinguished by their carved granite doorways (often crowned by **grotesque masks** to ward off the evil eye) follow a common plan, with living quarters on the second and third floors and a spacious atrium on the ground floor. Although originally medieval, most were redesigned and rebuilt to Baroque canons; others, such as the Palazzo Toraldo di Francia (via Lauro 12), were done over at the turn of the 19C in the Liberty style, an austere variant of Art Nouveau. More such designs may be seen in the early modern villas at the south-west edge of the old town.

Corso Vittorio Emanuele, the main street of Tropea, connects Piazza Ercole with the **affaccio**, a scenic overlook on a clifftop at the seaward end of the town. Opposite, on a steep rock, are the remains of the Benedictine sanctuary of **Santa Maria dell'Isola**. This is reached from the belvedere del canone, another scenic overlook just a few blocks south of the affaccio, from where steps descend to the beach. The path that climbs to the church is lined with fishermen's caves; the garden behind offers outstanding views of the town, the coast and the Aeolian Islands. In mid-August the sun sets directly over Stromboli.

Tropea to Stilo
A good day trip can be made from Tropea to **Serra San Bruno** and **Stilo**, 91km away by Highways 522, 18, 182, 110, and local roads, returning via **Locri**. Stilo and Locri are described in Route 10.

Leave Tropea by the road to the station, passing beneath the railway and bearing left into open country, with good views back to the town and the sea. The road winds upward through switchback turns amid woods and farmland; to the north-east the Serre Calabre range, dominated by the wedge-like mass of Monte Cocuzzo (1030m), is visible in the distance. A small road leads left to Drapia; further on, another leads right to Brattirò, known for its vineyards. At Caria, follow a sharp bend to the left and climb through a second series of curves to the Monte Poro plateau, an isolated formation rising little over 700m above the sea, particularly rich in archaeological finds. At Torre Galli, excavations conducted in 1922–23 brought to light an extensive **necropolis** dating initially from the 9C BC and used for some 300 years thereafter. Over 330 trench or pit tombs were unearthed, as well as a few instances of cremation attributed to the infiltration of Greek influences. The artefacts found at the site are now in the National Museum in Reggio Calabria.

The road is crossed by another leading to Zungri (4km) and Spilinga (9km). At the former airport of Vibo Valentia (now a military airfield) turn left on Highway 18 then right on Highway 182 to (45km) **Soriano Calabro** (3000 inhab.), an important centre for agriculture and handicrafts, founded by the Normans and acquired in fee by the Dominican Order in the mid 17C. The monastery of San Domenico, founded in 1501, was one of the wealthier and more illustrious houses of the Order in Europe; it produced four popes and was visited by Charles V on his return from Tunisia (1535) as well as by the philosopher Tomaso Campanella. The convent was destroyed by earthquake in 1659 and 1753, rebuilt and destroyed by fire in 1917, and restored on a smaller scale in the 1920s. The earthquake of 1783 also devastated the town, causing extensive landslides and altering the course of the river. The main street ascends to the town hall, then turns abruptly left. Steps at the right of the turning descend to the former main façade of the monastery, now a solitary ruin. The new church of **San Domenico**, constructed in the 19C, contains portraits of Benedict XIII and Innocent II (two of the four monks of Soriano who became pope) by a follower of Caravaggio, handsomely carved choir stalls and a painting depicting St Dominic dating from the late 15C or early 16C. The road continues to the village of Sorianello (in the church of San Giovanni, wooden Crucifix by the Flemish artist David Müller), then it ascends, in a series of curves, through dense forests of chestnut and holm oak. Higher up, firs and pines predominate.

13km **Serra San Bruno** (803m, 7000 inhab.) lies on a broad, wooded plateau. Founded in the late 11C by Bruno of Cologne, founder of the Carthusian Order, the town was originally intended to house the families of the lay dependants of the nearby monastery of Santo Stefano del Bosco and was held in fee by the latter until 1765. It now enjoys relative prosperity as a consequence of its woodworking industry. Its small wood and stone houses, often entered from external steps; the lace-like decoration around eaves and gables; and the graceful balconies with 17C ironwork make this one of the more charming mountain towns of Calabria. The Baroque churches are notable for their carved granite façades. Chief among them is the **Chiesa Matrice** (also called San Biago) at the north end of the wide main street, constructed in 1795. Within, marble statues of St Stephen, St Bruno of Cologne, the Madonna and Child, and St John the Baptist, originally in the Certosa, stand against the first and third piers on either side of the nave. On their bases are bas-reliefs depicting the Stoning of St Stephen, St Bruno making peace between Count Roger and Robert Guiscard, the Nativity, and scenes from the life of St John the Baptist, signed by David Müller and dated 1611. The figure of the Matrice (above the high altar), a fertility figure identified by the fruit or grain that she holds or that decorates her image, is rich in pagan allusions.

Further along the main street stands the church of the **Addolorata**, built in 1794. The bold curvilinear façade, with its broken lines and unusual proportions, reflects a taste that prevailed earlier in the century in more cosmopolitan centres. The interior contains a ciborium with bronzes and coloured marble reconstructed from the one designed for the certosa by Cosimo Fanzago in 1631 and destroyed by earthquake in 1783 (other fragments are in the cattedrale of Vibo Valentia). Continue down the main street to the church of the **Assunta** (also called San Giovanni), which dates from the 13C. The Baroque façade, with its campanile and clock, was added in the 18C. In the suburb of Spineto, the church of the Assunta allo Spineto dominates a long, narrow piazza.

The abbey of **Santi Stefano and Brunone** (women not admitted) enjoys a spendid location in a valley 2km south-west. Founded by St Bruno of Cologne at the end of the 11C on land donated by Roger, brother of Robert Guiscard, it houses an independent community of Carthusians. The members are bound by vows of silence, permanence, poverty and solitude, in emulation of the primitive monks of Egypt and Palestine. The present abbey, with its low walls and cylindrical towers, was built in the late 18C and early 19C. It adheres to the canons of Carthusian architecture, with two cloisters adjoining the church, surrounded by the living quarters of the lay brothers and the monks' cells. Within (men can visit 11.00–12.00, 16.00–17.00, accompanied by a monk) are the ruins of the magnificent buildings of the earlier monastery destroyed by the earthquake of 1783. On top of the free-standing Doric façade of the former abbey church stand two massive stone pinnacles, turned out somewhat by the tremors. Behind rise the first two arches of the nave arcade (the church was built to a Greek cross plan with three aisles on double Doric piers and a dome at the crossing); in front and to one side stand the remains of the cloister. The new abbey is built in an austere neo-Gothic style. The church contains interesting woodwork by local craftsmen and a silver bust of St Bruno, containing the founder's skull.

Further along the road that leads from the village to the abbey is the little church of **Santa Maria del Bosco**, set in a charming valley and surrounded by a dense fir forest. Here Bruno of Cologne lived and died, in the company of a handful of followers from the Chartreuse of Grenoble. At the foot of the broad stairway before the church is the pool into which the saint plunged as penance. The waters of the pool are held to be miraculous. More walks, interesting for the lush vegetation and splendid views, may be made to Colle di Arena (locally, *La Crista*, 1104m) in c 3hr and to Monte Crocco (1268m), in c 4hr; both with broad views of the Serre, Monte Poro and the bays of Gioia Tauro and Sant'Eufemia.

From the certosa return toward the village, bearing sharply right at the Parco della Rimembranza onto Highway 110 for Monasterace. The road ascends through a magnificent forest of firs, pines and beech to a broad, open plateau occupied chiefly by farm and pasture land. At Passo di Pietra Spada (1335m) begins the descent to the Ionian sea, with spectacular views of the rocky, arid landscape that characterises the east side of the Serre. A road on the right diverges to Nardodipace (1086m), a new town built in 1955 to accommodate the inhabitants of a village destroyed by floods. The descent continues; after crossing a beech wood the road winds in interminable curves through some of the wildest and most dramatic land-scape in Italy. On a clear day the *view reaches as far as the sea. Throughout the route, there are good prospects of Monte Consolino to the north–east and of the steep, vertiginous slopes of Monte Stella, ahead. 31km Pazzano (410m) develops vertically along the slope of the latter; you leave Highway 110 on the left and mount to (2km) Stilo, Route 10.

Head south from Tropea along the coast, following the road signs for Capo Vaticano. On the outskirts of the town, leave the cemetery on the right, following the road around to the left through verdant farmland, with good views to the sea, to (4km) Santa Domenica, where pleasant excursions may be made along the beaches at the base of the cliffs (footpath from the station). Soon after the road turns inland toward (6km) Ricadi, a village (4000 inhab.) among fields of olives, wheat and onions. **Capo Vaticano**, a magnificent headland with good bathing beaches, lies to the south-west (overlook). After Coccorino the highway hugs the coast, the cliffs falling straight into the sea on the right. The *view is one of the more striking in all of Calabria. 8km Ioppolo is a charming little village with a splendid prospect over the coastline to the south.

8km **Nicotera** (8000 inhab.) is an old town on a hill, with magnificent views of the sea and the plain of Gioia. Built on its present location by Guiscard, it retains unaltered a name recorded in the ancient itineraries. A walk through its winding streets can be rewarding. The **Cattedrale** (1785) has a Madonna della Grazia by Antonio Gagini, some fragments of bas-reliefs, and a wooden crucifix, often displayed in the Museo Diocesano di Arte Sacra (Piazza Duomo 10; open by appointment; tel. 0963 82175). The Museo Civico Archeologico (also open by appointment; tel. 0963 82175) on the main road, houses a collection of objects unearthed nearby, in the area between Marina di Nicotera (6km, bus) and the mouth of the Mesima. Here archaeologists hypothesise the existence of a Roman emporium that may have served the Greek Medma (Rosarno). Iron Age tombs similar to those at Torre Galli have also been found in the area.

Beyond Nicotera you leave the coast and descend to 'La Piana', entering the area (extending south to Scilla) devastated by the earthquake of 1783. 11km the road meets up with Highway 18 and enters **Rosarno** (14,000 inhab.), a busy modern town much ruined by unchecked building. The ancient colony of Medma is believed to have stood at Pian delle Vigne, nearby. Founded by the Locrians in the 6C BC, it passed back and forth between its parent city and Croton before finally gaining independence in the late 5C. It was the home of Philip of Medma, friend of Plato and possibly the author of the latter's posthumous works.

Across the plain lies (11km) **Gioia Tauro**, a sprawling city (18,000 inhab.) with a small harbour and a frequented beach, known principally for its olive production. The city is thought to stand on or near the site of the Locrian colony of Metauron, and excavations have revealed traces of the Greek necropolis and remains of Roman buildings.

In the foothills of the Aspromonte

15km inland lies **Seminara**, once the most formidable fortress in Calabria and now a centre of ceramic production, situated on a hill commanding a good view. Here, in 1495, the Sieur d'Aubigny, general of Charles VIII, defeated Gonzalo de Cordoba in the only battle that Gran Capitan ever lost, and in 1503 was himself defeated by the Spaniard, Ugo de Cardona. The battles are commemorated in four contemporary bas-reliefs in the Casa del Comune. Sinopoli, 12km further on the same road, is a good starting-point for the ascent, by bridle path and footpath, of Montalto (1955m), the highest peak of the Aspromonte (Route 14).

Leave Gioia amid the heavy traffic that will characterise the route from here to Reggio Calabria. Cross the Petrace, beyond which the foothills of the Aspromonte reach to the sea. The road, offering wide views across the Strait of Messina to Sicily, passes east of (10km) **Palmi** (19,000 inhab.), which lies among olive groves half way up the north slope of Monte Sant'Elia. Here can be seen more early 20C Liberty designs.

■ **Information**. APT, Via Dante 30.

The centrally located **Casa della Cultura** houses several museums. The Museo Calabrese di Etnografia e Folklore Raffaele Corso'(open Tue, Thu, and Fri 08.00–14.00; Mon and Wed 08.00–14.00 and 15.00–18.00) has an extensive collection of ceramic materials, hunting and fishing equipment, tools and articles related to shepherdry, and sections devoted to religious life, popular superstitions, weaving and costumes. In the same building is a museum dedicated to Francesco Cilea, composer of *Adriana Lecouvreur*, born in Palmi in 1866. Also of interest are the Museo d'Arte Moderna and Museo Guarisi (open as above) with a collection of materials from Taurianum, an ancient city destroyed by the Saracens, of which scant remains are visible between Palmi and Lido di Palmi.

A good viewpoint

5km south of Palmi a road (marked) on the right mounts to the summit of Monte Sant'Elia, commanding a splendid *view* across the Strait of Messina to Sicily. On a clear day, Stromboli is also visible. To the south the high cliffs drop sheer into the sea.

18km **Bagnara Calabra**, in a lovely position on steep slopes terraced and planted with vineyards, is known for its sword-fishing in Apr–Jun. It has been destroyed several times by earthquakes, most recently in 1908.

9km **Scilla** (6000 inhab.) is on a spur behind the famous **rock of Scylla** which, crowned by a castello (now a youth hostel) rises 73m sheer from the sea. It faces the Punto del Faro, in Sicily, across the Strait of Messina, here four nautical miles wide.

History

Although the rock of Scylla, personified in the *Odyssey* as a marine monster with seven heads, and the whirlpool of Charybdis were placed by the ancient poets exactly opposite each other, modern geographers have transferred Charybdis to a spot nearer the harbour of Messina. At certain tides there are still strong currents and whirlpools off the Faro point, but these are not very dangerous, even to small craft. The conditions may have been changed since antiquity by earthquakes.

Scilla fell to the Saracens in the 9C and to the Normans in the 11C.

The **Castello** was fortified by Pietro Ruffo in 1225; in 1282 the fleet of Charles I of Anjou took shelter here after failing to take Messina. The castello was occupied by the British after the Battle of Maida and defended for 18 months against the French. Huddled around the northernmost of the two small bays is the fishermen's quarter; the main bathing beach is on the south side of the headland. The recently rebuilt church of the Immacolata, at the foot of the road leading to the castello, was once an important Basilian monastery.

Beyond Scilla the scenery, with its luxuriant vegetation characterised by aloes, prickly pears and orange groves, becomes even more beautiful. At (10km) Villa San Giovanni (13,000 inhab.) there are train and car ferries to Messina (see *Blue Guide Sicily*). From here, habitation is continuous to (16km) Reggio Calabria (Route 9).

B.   Via Castrovillari and Cosenza

*This is the principal road route from Naples to Reggio. The main rail line follows the coast (see Route 7A). If you are arriving from Rome by Autostrada you can bypass Naples, diverging east at Caserta and joining the present route at Salerno. Highlights on this route include the magnificent **Certosa di San Lorenzo** at Pudula, one of the larger monastic complexes in Italy and a singularly successful example of Neopolitan baroque architecture; the breathtaking landscape of the **Monte Pollino** massif, between Basilicata and Calabria; **Mormanno** and **Morano Calabro**, two charming old towns forgotten by time; and the imposing Greek walls of Hipponium, the ancient predecessor of **Vibo Valentia**.*

Traffic permitting, the trip may be made non-stop in about five hours. State Highway 19 weaves its way alongside the Autostrada for much of the way, offering a pleasant alternative, especially in the areas between Eboli and Polla and between Lagonegro and Castrovillari.

ROAD 519km. Autostrada A3 (Autostrada del Sole)—101km Contursi —58km Padula—35km Lagonegro Nord—21km Lauria Sud—41km Morano-Castrovillari—69km Cosenza Nord—51km Lamezia-Catanzaro—34km Vivo Valentia—41km Rosarno—51km Villa San Giovanni—17km Reggio Calabria.

RAILWAY. From Naples (Centrale) to Reggio Calabria (Centrale), 476km in 4hr 30min–5 hr. To Villa San Giovanni (where through trains to Sicily cross the Strait of Messina), in c 15min less.

HOTELS EN ROUTE: Maratea, *****Santavenere, tel. 0973 876910, fax 0973 877654; Acquafredda, ****Villa Cheta Elite, tel./fax 0973 878134; Parghelia (Exit Pizzo Calabro), ***** Baia Paraelios, tel. 0963 600004, fax 0963 600074. These localities are described in Route 7A.

RESTAURANTS EN ROUTE: Castrovillari, *** La Locanda di Alìa, Via Jetticelle 69, tel. 0981 46370, fax 0981 46370; Altomonte, **Barbieri (with rooms), Via San Nicola 30, tel. 0981 948072, fax 0981 948073; Vibo Valentia Marina (exit Pizzo Calabro), **L'Approdo, tel./fax 0963 572640.

THE VALLE DI DIANO

From Naples to (55km) Salerno, see Route 4C. Beyond Salerno the Autostrada proceeds east, then turns south–east, leaving the road to Potenza (Route 17C) on the left and entering the long Valle di Diano, the ancient bed of a lake, drained when the River Tanagro was canalised. The next two exits give access to the **Grotta di Pertosa** (open 08.30–12.00, 14.30–17.00; June-Sep 14.30–19.00; Pertosa station lies c 1km west), an extensive cavern 2.5km long that may be explored by boat and on foot; the stalactites are impressive.

89km Sala Consilina-Teggiano exit. Across the valley to the south stands **Teggiano** (8000 inhab.) on its hillside. The **Cattedrale**, rebuilt after an earthquake of 1857, has a richly carved portal, ambo and paschal candlestick, all of the 13C; the 14C tomb is by followers of Tino di Camaino. Above the town stands the Castello, erected by the Sanseverino in 1285 but later rebuilt. **Sala Consilina** (13,000 inhab.), dominated by its castello, is set against a backdrop of mountains rising well above 1200m. The Museo Archeologico (Via Cappuccini; open daily 09.00–19.00) contains finds from local excavations dating from the 9C–6C BC.

THE CERTOSA DI SAN LORENZO

About 9km further south a by-road (left) leads to (3km) **Padula**, below which is the magnificent *****Certosa di San Lorenzo** (open daily, Apr–Oct 09.00–19.30, Nov–Mar 09.00–16.30).

It was founded in 1306 by Tommaso Sanseverino, who paid for and erected the Carthusian monastery on his own land. The decision to found a monastery for a French order is likely to have been made for political reasons, as Tommaso was close to the Angevin kings of Naples and the valley, situated between the capital and the remote province of Calabria, was of considerable strategic importance: through the feudal organisation of its land, the certosa maintained a strong influence over the entire area. The monastery retained its importance until its suppression in 1816.

The plan of San Lorenzo follows the standard pattern of a Carthusian monastery, in keeping with the order's religious and administrative organisation. A long wall, once acting as an enceinte, encloses the complex. The arrangement of building within is determined by the rigorous division between 'lower' and 'upper' houses—or in lay terms, between communal and secluded activity. The main gate opens onto the outer court, which gave access to the stables, storage rooms, granaries, pharmacy and living quarters of the lay brothers. The second entrance, the principal one in architectural terms, leads into the monastery itself, where visitors were only rarely admitted. One eminent visitor was Charles V, who stayed here in 1535, while on his way from Naples to Reggio Calabria. For the occasion the monks are said to have prepared the emperor and his train an omelette made with 1000 eggs.

The **main façade**, built in the second half of the 16C, has more the appearance of a secular building than of a religious one. It has a two-storeyed, rusticated front with engaged Tuscan columns. The attic balustrade, the urns, the pinnacles, and the elaborate crowning niche with a statue of the Virgin and Child are all 17C additions. They reflect a Neapolitan tradition of terminating a façade with a horizontal line broken in the centre by an emphatic vertical element.

Inside begins a long corridor, terminating in the monumental staircase (described below). To the right is the small Chiostro della Forestiera, or guest cloister, made up of a double loggia with a fountain in the middle. From here the **church** is entered through a door dated 1374 and decorated with carved reliefs of the life of St Lawrence, from the same period. The interior has cross-vaults borne by ogival arches. Its Baroque decorations fortunately do not mask its simple Gothic structure. Magnificent intarsia **choir stalls** (c 1507) grace the nave and chancel. The Coro dei Laici, or lay choir, has stalls decorated with landscapes, architecture and saints; whereas the Coro del Padri, for the monastic brothers, depicts New Testament scenes, saints and hermits, scenes of martyrdom, and architecture. There is a fine majolica floor. The high altar is made of plaster with inlaid coloured marbles and mother of pearl, here set in swirling floral patterns. The door to the sacristy has intarsia panels depicting the entrance to the monastery and church as it was at the beginning of the 16C.

A door on the left of the high altar gives entrance to the treasury, with fine Baroque stucco work. Passing out of the treasury, turn left into the **Sala del Capitolo** (with more good 17C stucco work and frescoes), or right into the **old cemetery** (1522), rebuilt in the 17C to resemble a cloister. Around the portico are antique architectural fragments found on the site during building work. The Cappella del Fondatore, at the far end, contains a 16C tomb of Tommaso Sanseverino. Next to the chapel is the refectory, with a splendid 18C Baroque portal, a much worn majolica floor, a fresco of the Marriage at Cana by Francesco d'Elia (1749), and a marble pulpit. The cemetery also gives access to the interesting and well-preserved kitchen complex, with canteens and a giant oak and pine press (1785).

The narrow **staircase** is formally quite bold, winding up like a ribbon, without balustrades. At the top is the **library**, with exquisite Baroque doors of inlaid coloured marbles and a good majolica floor. The ceiling is decorated with allegorical canvases from the 18C.

Now descend to the immense *great cloister, which measures a staggering 104 x 109m and is articulated by 84 pilasters of smoothly rusticated stone. A heavy Doric frieze, decorated with scenes of martyrdom and of the Passion of Christ, runs between the upper and lower storeys. In the centre is a fountain, and on the south side the monks' cemetery, enclosed by an elegant balustrade. Although its architects are unknown, the sense of space, peace, and melancholy the cloister imparts is memorable. Its atmosphere and poetic charm were recorded by François Lenormant in 1883. He writes:

> I went to sit in the Great Cloister. There were many clouds, driven by a violent wind, passing swiftly in front of the full moon, producing continuous sudden changes that ranged from profound darkness to brilliant light...There is nothing more enchanting than the effect of these drops of nocturnal light which at times reveal the architecture in all its extraordinary purity down to the smallest detail, and at times conceal it completely. These sudden changes in light seemed to conjure up white phantoms in the depths of the porticos, as though the ghosts of the old inhabitants of the monastery had risen, as was their custom, to celebrate night office.

The **monks' quarters** and gardens open onto the cloister. On the north side is an octagonal tower containing the elliptical **grand staircase** by Gaetano Barba (1761–63), a structure of singular elegance leading to an upper gallery now closed to the public. Also accessible from the cloister is the **Museo Archeologico della Lucania Occidentale** (open as the Certosa), set up in 1957 to display material from local sites. It contains interesting finds from a nearby Villanovan necropolis.

To the Ionian Sea

A few kilometres south, near Montesano station, a road to the left gives a choice of two mountainous routes to the Ionian Sea, crossing into Basilicata by the Sella Cessuta (1028m) to (32km) **Moliterno**, an interesting old town with a much altered Lombard castello. Beyond (7km) **Grumento Nova**, above the River Agri (right) is the Roman **Grumentum**, site of two Carthaginian defeats in the Second Punic War. The extensive ruins, not systematically explored, yielded in 1823 the Siri Bronzes now in the British Museum. Beyond another ridge at (54km) Corleto Perticara the road is joined by Highway 92 from Potenza.

The steep, lonely continuation of Highway 103 (left) touches (46km) Stigliano, a superbly sited old town, then descends via (56km) Montalbano Ionico to (13km) Scanzano. Highway 92 (right) recrosses the Agri, then joins the Latronico road (see below) in the valley of the Sinni, reaching the coast near Nova Siri (Route 10). Both roads are remarkable for the the the dramatic quality of the ****landscape**, which increases its power and beauty as you near the sea.

The autostrada may be re-joined at the Buonabitacolo Padula interchange. The road climbs out of the Valle di Diano, through conifer forests, and crosses a brief stretch of Basilicata.

28km Lagonegro Nord, exit for **Lagonegro** (666m, 6000 inhab.), a small town somewhat bleakly situated in the high mountains, with Baroque churches. In the wooded Piazza Grande are three of these: Sant'Anna (1665), San Nicola (1779-1839), and the Madonna del Sirino. The latter is flanked by an open chapel containing Romanesque pillars and two lions from another building. Monna Lisa del Giocondo (died 1505) is said to be buried in the 10C church of San Nicola, in the old town. Monte del Papa (2005m), to the east (ascent in 3–4 hr), commands views to the Tyrrhenian and Ionian Seas.

> Both coasts may be reached from here with relative ease. To the south Highway 585 descends the Castrocuoco valley to join the Tyrrhenian coast road (33km) between Maratea and Praia a Mare. From Lago Sirino, a winding road diverges right to Sapri (Route 7A).

At Lauria Sud a fine new road runs east via (14km) Latronico and the Parco Nazionale del Monte Pollino, a nature reserve established in 1990 to protect the wilderness highlands of this great massif (2248m), to the Ionian Sea at Nova Siri. It commands exceptional ***views** down the valley of the Sinni to the coast, passing through (37km) Chiaromonte, where the parish church contains a medieval crucifix, two paintings of the Neapolitan school and a good inlaid marble altar; and Senise, where the church of San Francesco has a polyptych by Simone da Firenze and good choir stalls. Senise stands on a lake formed by Europe's first earthwork dam, visible from the road just east of the town. Lonely but singularly beautiful roads lead north to the valley of the Agri, which is crossed by a faster highway from Atena Lucana (where there is a small Museo Comunale, closed for restoration 1995) to the sea.

On a ridge between the Sinni and Agri valleys near where these reach the coast stands the isolated church of ***Santa Maria di Anglona**, a Romanesque construction initiated in the 11C, but as it appears today, consisting mainly of alterations and additions of later epochs. It has a good west portal, a fine apse and a number of interesting but crude carvings let into different parts of the building. The interior contains frescoes of the 11C, 12C and 13C and the curious Madonna Nera, of uncertain date and provenance.

About 10km west lies **Tursi**, to which the See of Anglona was transferred in 1546. In the lower town is the Cattedrale, which has two interesting representations of the Annunciation, a good painted ceiling, and a majolica floor. A fine monstrance of 1741 can be admired in the sacristy. In the upper town, reached by a stiff climb, the Chiesa della Rabatana, once the cathedral, dates from the 16C but was much altered in the 18C. It has a fine inlaid marble high altar and a 14C triptych representing the Madonna dell'Icona, with scenes from the life of Christ and the Virgin. Steps lead down to an earlier crypt, where a chapel contains 16C frescoes and, in an adjoining room, a Nativity composed of carved stone figures. It dates from the 16C and has great, though somewhat naive charm.

Lauria is also connected with Maratea (Route 7A), on the Tyrrhenian coast.

Into Calabria
You enter Calabria just short of (40km) **Mormanno** (840m, 4000 inhab.), a popular refuge from the heat of summer, where the church of **Santa Maria del Colle** contains much good gilded and carved woodwork, fine Baroque altars, a Tuscan relief to the right of the main altar and, in the sacristy, a good painting of the 18C Neapolitan school. The narrow side streets provide brief but interesting walks.

A mountain road descends via Papasidero to Scalea, on the Tyrrenhian coast (Route 7A).

From Mormanno, cross the Passo di Campotenese, a rich pastoral plateau nearly 900m high. The road descends abruptly, into the valley of the Coscile, passing just east of **Morano Calabro** (694m, 5000 inhab.), dominated on its conical hill by the church of **San Pietro**, which contains, at the first altars on the north and south sides, marble statues of *Santa Caterina* and *Santa Lucia* by Pietro Bernini; and, to the left and right of the high altar, statues of Sts Peter and Paul by followers of Bernini. Also of fine workmanship are the late 18C and early 19C choir stalls. A fine 15C processional cross in silver gilt is kept in the sacristan's house (and produced on request). At the bottom of the hill stand the church of La Maddalena, with its tiled cupola, and that of **San Bernardino**, with a superb carved wooden pulpit of 1611 and a polyptych of Bartolomeo Vivarini, signed and dated 1477. The town is served by (16km) the Morano–Castrovillari interchange.

Castrovillari (362m, 23,000 inhab.), 7km away, stands on a smiling upland plain at the south end of the Pollino massif. The old town or *civita* has a castello of 1490 near which, in the Biblioteca Comunale, is housed a small collection of the results of local excavations including prehistoric, protohistoric, Roman and medieval material (open daily 08.30–13.00, Tue and Thu 08.30–13.00 and 15.00–18.00). Sooner or later this is to be moved to Palazzo Gallo. A long winding road leads on, past the church of San Giuliano, with its pleasing Renaissance façade, to **Santa Maria del Castello**, a church of 11C origins, reconstructed in the 14C. Here, in the Cappella del Sacramento, a fine Baroque altar encloses a fresco of the Madonna del Castello, a much revered image of Byzantine taste. On the right wall of the staircase leading up to the cantoria you can see the remains of frescoes, possibly dating from the 13C. The church also contains two paintings by Pietro Negroni, 17C choir stalls and, on a pillar in the south aisle, a 17C olive-wood figure of the Crucified

Christ. The Baroque high altar and the bishop's throne likewise merit attention. The sacristy houses a minute museum, which includes a 15C copper plate of Nuremburg work and a cope given to the church by Pope Pius IV.

Highway 105 winds south to (23km) Firmo, beyond which a turning on the left leads in 9km to Altomonte, where the splendid Gothic church of *Santa Maria della Consolazione is to be seen. It is one of the more interesting Gothic buildings in Calabria, constructed, possibly by Sienese architects, under the patronage of Filippo Sangineto, Count of Altomonte, during the Angevin period. The simple façade, which dates from 1380, contains a large rose window. Within are the splendid tomb of the founder, by a follower of Tino di Camaino (c 1350). The former Dominican convent adjoining the church houses a small museum (open daily 08.30–13.00, 16.00–20.00) with works of art removed from the church during a recent restoration. These include small remains of frescoes, three parts of a triptych by an artist close to Bernardo Daddi, a Madonna and Child of the 15C Neapolitan-Catalan school, and two small panels in alabaster of 1380, related to French art of the period.

Followed in the opposite direction (east), Highway 105 cuts over to the Ionian coast, here only 23km away. You reach it just north of Sibari.

Beyond Castrovillari the Autostrada and the State Highway descend to the Coscile valley. 15km **Spezzano Albanese** interchange. Spezzano itself (320m, 8000 inhab.) is pleasantly spread out on a hillside and the local medicinal springs are exploited as a spa. The costume and dialect of the inhabitants proclaim their descent from Albanian refugees who fled before the Turks and settled here in the 15C. The people are noticeably tall and fair among the small, dark Calabrians.

A few kilometres south of Spezzano on Highway 19, a road (Highway 106b) leads left to (7km) **Terranova**, where the convent of Sant'Antonio contains rich Baroque work and the cloister has charming rustic frescoes. The road continues to the Ionian coast via Corigliano Calabro and Rossano (Route 10).

The Autostrada enters the valley of the Crati, notable for its wide expanses of gravel. In the summer, the temperature here can reach scorching heights. In the hills to the east lie (11km) Bisignano and (14km) Acri, both towns of growing importance in the Calabrian hydroelectric scheme. At Bisignano can be seen the remains of a Byzanto-Norman castello and, in the church of the Riformati, a Madonna della Grazia of the school of Antonello Gagini (1537).

Isolated in the mountains 15km north of Acri is **San Demetrio Corone** (4000 inhab.), the most important Albanian colony in Calabria, with an Italo-Albanian college founded in 1791 by Ferdinand I. The 11C or 12C church of **Sant'Adriano** contains a Norman **font** with a representation of a monkey sitting on two dragons (?) and four pieces of pavement with snakes, birds and leopards, also dating from the Norman construction.

COSENZA

39km Cosenza (240m, 104,000 inhab.), a provincial capital of Calabria, stands at the confluence of two rivers.

History

It succeeds *Cosentia*, the capital of the Bruttians, which came early under the influence of the Greek settlements of Magna Graecia. Taken by Rome in 204 BC, in imperial times it was an important halt on Via Popilia, linking Rome with Reggio and Sicily. In AD 412 Alaric the Visigoth died here (probably of malaria) on his way back to Sicily after the Sack of Rome. Legend holds that he was buried along with his treasure in the bed of the Busento, the waters having been diverted for the occasion and then restored to their natural channel. Twice destroyed by the Saracens, the town was conquered by Robert Guiscard, but it rebelled against the rule of his half-brother Roger, who managed to restore his authority only after a siege (1087). In the 13C, 14C, and 15C the city shifted its loyalties several times in the struggle between the Aragonese and the Angevins, and Louis III of Anjou died here in 1434 while campaigning against the Aragonese. A notable centre of humanistic culture in the 16C, Cosenza was the birthplace of Bernardino Telesio (1509–88) the philosopher, whose thought was instrumental in freeing scientific research from theological restrictions. The city contributed freely to the liberal movement in the 19C and participated in the uprisings of 1848 and 1860. It was damaged by earthquake in 1783, 1854, 1870 and 1905, and frequently bombed in 1943. Today it is an important commercial and agricultural centre. The University of Calabria, Italy's newest and most modern, lies on the outskirts to the north.

■ **Information**: APT, Corso Mazzini 92; tel. 0984 27821 (branch offices at Piazza Pasquale Rossi, Stazione Centrale, Autostrada A3–Frascineto Ovest Service Area).

■ **Airport**: At **Lamezia Terme**, on the Tyrrhenian coast 61km south. Direct flights to Naples, Palermo and Rome.

■ **Railway stations**: **Centrale** (Ferrovie dello Stato), Piazza IV Novembre, with lines for Paola and Sibari; **Cosenza Città** (Ferrovie Calabro-Lucane), Via Catanzaro, just east of the central station; **Cosenza Casali**, Via dei Martiri, lines for Catanzaro and San Giovanni in Fiore.

■ **Post office** on Via Vittorio Veneto.

The old town, overshadowed by its castello, descends to the Crati, whereas the growing modern city lies to the north, beyond the Busento, on level ground. Entering Cosenza from the north, follow the long Viale del Re through the modern town past the municipal hospital, then turn left and descend to Piazza della Vittoria, with its austere memorial to the victims of the First World War. Ahead lies Piazza XX Settembre, adjoining the Central Station. Further south the church of San Domenico retains a 14C rose window. The Ponte San Domenico crosses the Busento to the old town, which is crossed by the winding Corso Telesio.

The ***Cattedrale**, in the Gothic style of Provence, was consecrated in 1222 in the presence of Frederick II. The interior was reworked in the Baroque style in

1750 and the façade made over in 1831; both, however, have been restored to their original states. The façade, with its three Gothic portals, large central rose window and two smaller rose windows at the sides, is one of the more graceful in Calabria. It is ideally complemented by its surroundings. The **interior** is simple, with a nave and two aisles divided by piers, and an elevated presbytery. The apse was restored in a neo-Gothic manner and frescoed at the end of the 19C. In the south aisle, at the foot of the stairs to the presbytery, is a Roman sarcophagus; in the north transept is the lovely *tomb of Isabella, wife of Philippe la Hardi, who died in 1270 after falling from her horse while returning to France from Sicily (some authorities say her body was returned to Saint-Denis).

Behind the cathedral, in Piazza Giano Parrasio, the **Tesoro dell'Archivescovado** (visible on request) contains an extraordinary *Byzantine reliquary cross** in gold and enamel work with Greek lettering, presented by Frederick II on the occasion of the consecration of the cathedral. The small enamel panels depict the four Evangelists, the Madonna, and the symbols of Christ. The pedestal dates from the 18C. Further on is Piazza XXV Marzo, with monuments commemorating Telesio and the brothers Bandiera, martyred patriots of the Calabrian rising of 1844. Here stand the Biblioteca Civica and the Museo Civico Archeologico (open daily 09.00–13.00), housing a modest collection of antiquities from excavations in the city and in the environs.

From a point in Via Telesio opposite the cathedral, Via del Seggio climbs to an old quarter with many interesting details. The church of **San Francesco d'Assisi** has a 13C doorway and a plain cloister. Within (open daily 09.00–13.00) is a small collection of paintings by local artists of the 15C to the 18C. The ruined **Castello** (383m) was the site of Louis II of Anjou's marriage to Margaret of Savoy (1434). It commands good views. A steep staircase at the right of the church of San Francesco descends to the confluence of the two rivers. The 16C church of San Francesco di Paola stands beyond the Crati.

A scenic route to Catanzaro

Beyond Cosenza, Highway 19 leaves the Autostrada and crosses the peninsula to Catanzaro (Route 10), 81km south-east. Though highly scenic, this route is known for its hills and bends and requires attentive driving. Proceeding south, leave on the left a road offering alternative routes across the Sila via either Lago Arvo or Lago Ampollino to Santa Severina (Route 8A). 18km **Rogliano** has an elegant church of 1544, restored in 1924. The road descends in curves to the Savuto (the *Sabutus flumen* of the ancients), then mounts to (7km) **Carpanzano,** where the chiesa parrocchiale has a Renaissance façade and inlaid wooden altars. The vista opens over the Savuto valley, known for its wines.

The road climbs steeply to the Passo di Agrifoglio, 928m, then through dense forests to a second pass 936m high, beyond which it crosses the wooded Borboruso highlands. At (18km) Soveria Manelli, a road diverges right to (25km) Nicastro and (11km) Sant'Eufemia Lamezia, Route 7A. Bear south-east, crossing the watershed between the Ionian and Tyrrhenian seas. The view extends over broad woodlands and, at a certain point, embraces the Gulfs of Sant'Eufemia and Squillace in a single glance. The road continues to wind, offering magnificent *views** over the two seas. Ahead lies the Monte di Tiriolo. 25km **Tiriolo** (690m, 4000 inhab.) is delightfully situated on a ridge. The women wear a charming native costume. The road descends in zigzags, affording more beautiful views.

The fast way to Catanzaro follows Autostrada A3 from Cosenza to (61km)

Sant'Eufemia-Lamezia, from where Highway 280 crosses the narrow Isthmus of Catanzaro, reaching the city in 34km.

VIBO VALENTIA AND SOUTH

From Cosenza, the road winds through a narrow valley, reaching the sea near Sant'Eufemia-Lamezia (Route 7A). Beyond (19km) Pizzo Calabro it climbs high along a steep ridge, affording a series of fine sea views before turning inland. 10km **Vibo Valentia** (34,000 inhab.), the *Hipponium* of the Greeks, was a place of some military importance described by Cicero as an 'illustre et nobile municipium'. An important intellectual centre in the late 18C, it was the provincial capital under Murat, a status it has recently regained. It contributed enthusiastically to the cause of unity during the Risorgimento.

■ **Information**, APT, Piazza Diaz, 8; tel. 0963 42008.

The church of **Leoluca** (or Santa Maria Maggiore) is splendidly decorated with fine 18C stucco work and large bas-reliefs of an excellent Baroque exuberance. The last chapel on the north side contains a superb *marble group of the Madonna between St John the Evangelist and the Magdalen (notice the fine bas-reliefs on the bases). These are the last works of Antonio Gagini (1534). In the chapel opposite can be seen statues of the Madonna and Child, and St Luke, of the school of Gagini. On the high altar is a Madonna and Child attributed to Girolamo Santacroce. Two Romanesque lions in the sacristy once formed part of an earlier façade of the church. The **Chiesa del Rosario** (1280, rebuilt in the 18C) contains a strange Baroque wooden pulpit rising from a confessional. Beyond the balustrade to the high altar, on the right, stands the Cappella Crispo, a Gothic construction dating from the 14C. **San Michele** is an exquisite little Renaissance church dating from the early 16C with a fine but somewhat overshadowing campanile of 1671. The Castello Normanno is slowly being restored. In Piazza Garibaldi the **Museo Archeologico Statale di Vibo Valentia**, established in 1994, preserves an interesting collection of finds from the necropolis of Hipponium (open daily 09.00–19.00).

A cypress-lined road at the north edge of the town leads to the cemetery; halfway along a small gate on the left opens onto the imposing remains of the **Greek walls** (best seen at sunset), which include the foundations of several large towers. The first 100m are obscured by vegetation. On the other side of the highway, in the Parco della Rimembranza or Belvedere, can be seen the somewhat scanty remains of a late 6C or early 5C Doric temple.

South of Vibo Valentia the Autostrada crosses rolling countryside with farms and olive plantations, returning to the coast near (54km) Palmi. From here it runs high above the coast towns described in Route 7A, offering more stunning *views of the Tyrrhenian Sea and, finally, of the Strait of Messina and Sicily before entering (44km) Reggio Calabria, (Route 9).

8 · La Sila

The plateau of **La Sila**, peopled by the descendants of the Bruttians, is an irregular expanse of gneiss and granite 1000–1300m above the sea. It occupies the area between the Ionian Sea on the east, the steep Crati valley on the north and west and the Marcellinara ridge beyond the Corace valley on the south-west. It is divided into three parts: the *Sila Greca* on the north, with the majority of the Albanian colonies in Calabria; the *Sila Grande*; and the *Sila Piccola*, divided roughly by the Rogliano–Crotone road. The highest peak is Monte Botte Donato (1928m).

The forests of the Sila were famed by the ancients for the wood they supplied for shipbuilding, but deforestation has left much of the area free for pasture. This condition is being slowly corrected by controlled cutting and careful replanting. The climate is harsh in winter (snow does not disappear from the mountain tops until May) and mild in summer, offering a pleasant escape from the often stifling heat of the Calabrian coast. Olive, oak, poplar and fruit trees grow at the lower altitudes, intermixed with vineyards and the typical, low macchia mediterranea. Above 700m these give way to chestnut, turkey oak and broad expanses of cereal crops. The area above 1200m is characterised by alders, aspens, maples and a native pine (*Pino larico calabrico*) that grows to a height exceeding 40m, often in dense groves. On the higher peaks grow beech trees and, in some areas, silver fir, once much more common. Snowdrops bloom in Feb–Mar, followed, in late Apr–Jun by daffodils, jonquils, violets and small orchids. In June–July the pine forests abound with wild strawberries, and in Sep–Oct, with exquisite mushrooms. In autumn the red beech trees against dark firs are splendid. Woodland animals, particularly foxes, hares, martens, wild boar, roe deer, squirrels and a rather ferocious variety of wolf, are still present in large numbers. Wildfowl include interesting native species of partridge. Vipers may be found in all the wilder areas. The lakes and streams abound with trout.

A.   Cosenza to Crotone

*This is the main road across the Sila to the Ionian coast. It crosses some of the finest countryside in Calabria. The first part of the journey passes through rolling green highlands, touching upon the lovely **Lago di Cecita** and running near **Lago Arvo**. Beyond **San Giovanni in Fiore** the landscape becomes more arid and dramatic as the road descends to the sea and Crotone. Travel time is roughly 2hr.*

ROAD 126km. Highways 107/E93 and 106—36km Camigliatello Silano—25km San Giovanni in Fiore—35km Santa Severina—30km Crotone. Travel time c 2hrs.

RAILWAY to San Giovanni in Fiore only, 85km in 2hr 30min.

RESTAURANT EN ROUTE: Camigliatello Silano, **Aquila-Edelweiss, tel. 0984 578044, fax 0984 578753.

CLIMBING TO CAMIGLIATELLO

Leave Cosenza (Route 7B) from the north. Presently the road begins to mount the west slope of the Sila. The air becomes noticeably cooler on approaching (13km) Celico (805m, 3000 inhab.), birthplace of the Abbot Gioacchino (see below).

Immediately afterwards, you touch upon Spezzano della Sila (850m, 5000 inhab.), a locally important centre in a splendid position overlooking Cosenza. The Sanctuary of San Francesco has a 15C Gothic door and 17C wooden choir stalls. 3km Spezzano Piccolo (750m), with its unusual campanile, is reached by a turning on the right. The landscape takes on a more alpine appearance. 18km **Camigliatello Silano** (1275m) is a summer and winter sports resort.

The old State Highway leads west to (5km) Fago del Soldato, a village of small wooden houses among pine woods, from which the Botte San Donato may be climbed in c 3hr. **Springs** along the way offer excellent mineral waters. The combined use of timber and corrugated steel is characteristic of local architecture.

Across the Highland

Leave Camigliatello from the south, bearing east along Highway 107. The woods gradually give way to broad fields of grain and pasture, affording views to the left of **Lago di Cecita** (or **di Moccone**) and the magnificent Bosco di Gallopane, beyond. Further to the right can be seen the verdant slopes of Monte Pettinascura. The landscape is relatively flat here—you are crossing the highland plain at an altitude of roughly 1350m. 5km Croce di Magara is a small hamlet. From here a secondary road follows the Neto valley to (20km) Germano, at the foot of Monte Ruggiero. The route continues through rolling countryside, paralleled by the one-track railway. 7km the highway is joined by the road from Lorica (Route 8C), beyond which you follow the valley of the Garga. 10km a turning on the right winds south-west to (12km) Lago Arvo, shortly after entering the valley of the Arvo River, and the vista opens up to the Ionian Sea.

5km **San Giovanni in Fiore** (1008m, 21,000 inhab.), the chief town of the Sila, is somewhat mean and shabby in appearance. It grew up in the 12C around the Badia Florense, founded by Abbot Gioacchino, who enjoyed a wide local reputation as a prophet. The attractive costumes of the women are famous and the town celebrated for its textile trade. The abbey, a 13C Cistercian Gothic edifice of bare aspect, stands in the lower part of the town.

Continuing to the east, you cross the Neto (the *Neaethus* of Theocritus) and reach (10km) the turning for Caccuri, birthplace of Cecco Simonetta, secretary to Francesco Sforza, and of his brother Giovanni, who wrote a biography of the prince. 12km bear right, leaving the new road for Crotone on the left. Across the valley of the Neto lies Strongoli Petilia, on a ridgetop; ahead is the Ionian Sea. The deeply eroded landscape is known for its **conical formations of clay**, called timpe.

10km **Santa Severina** (325m, 3000 inhab.), on an isolated outcrop of sheer rock, was a Byzantine and Norman fortress with a scholastic tradition. John of Salisbury notes that its inhabitants helped him with difficult passages of Aristotle. The sainted 8C pope Zacharias was a native. Here in 1950 began the expropriation of latifondia estates under the Sila reform act. The church of **San Filomeno** is built to a Byzantine plan, with three apses (only one being visible from the exterior). The high cupola is reminiscent of Armenian constructions. Underneath is the church of the Pozzolio, the exterior of which is adorned with good carved surrounds. The Norman **Cattedrale** has been largely rebuilt; it has a main portal of the 13C enclosed in a later surround showing provincial Renaissance-Baroque taste. To the north flank of the church is attached a Byzantine *Baptistery (8–9C) built to a circular plan and incorporating pillars from a pagan edifice. The old cathedral, or

Addolorata, dates from the 10C; the Castello, of the same period, rebuilt by Robert Guiscard, is now a school.

Beyond Santa Severina, the road descend then climbs out again, offering views of the Neto valley and the coast, to the east. 11km you pass the village of Scandale (350m, 4000 inhab.), built on a site inhabited since prehistoric times. After a brief stretch in view of Crotone and the sea, the road ends; turn right onto Highway 106 and proceed south to **Crotone**, Route 10.

B.   From Rossano to Longobucco and Camigliatello

*This route ascends from the Ionian coast to Camigliatello, the chief centre of the Sila, from which the descent to Cosenza and the Tyrrhenian coast may be made by following Route 8A in reverse. If you are looking for the atmosphere of Old Calabria (or simply some fine gifts) stop at **Longobucco**, where the craft tradition (fabrics and lace are the local specialities) is both strong and genuine. Beyond, the century-old **Gallopane Forest** and **Lake Cecita** provide unexpected alpine scenery—and temperatures. Travel time is about 1hr 20min.*

ROAD   83km.   Highway   177—23km   Cropalati—18km   Longobucco—42km Camigliatello.

*RESTAURANT EN ROUTE: Camigliatello Silano, **Aquila-Edelweiss, tel. 0984 578044, fax 0984 578753.*

Through the Sila Greca

Leave Rossano (Route 10) from the south–east, cross the valleys of the Celadi and Colognati Torrents and begin the ascent of the Sila Greca. Near (13km) Paludi, excavations have revealed Bruttian walls and a theatre. 10km Cropalati (367m, 2000 inhab.), is the Byzantine *Kouropalates*. Leave the village on the left and enter the broad valley of the Trionto. Ahead, Longobucco stands between sheer rock walls, above a narrow gorge. The road descends to the wooded valley floor, then climbs steeply through a series of curves to the opposite rim.

18km **Longobucco** (780m, 6000 inhab.) is a very old town with a distinctly alpine character. Here and in the neighbouring villages textiles are handwoven to traditional designs embodying Byzantine and Saracenic influences. The work is done exclusively by women and most colours are made from vegetable dyes.

The road continues to climb. The wooded slopes of Monte Paleparto (1481m) dominate the vista to the north. Further on, pines grow among large masses of granite; in the distance can be seen the Capo Trionto headland and the sea. The road winds up the forested east flank of Monte Altare, 1651m. The ascent becomes milder beyond the last great curve. Shortly afterwards the descent begins across the ancient and magnificent **Bosco Gallopane** to the Sila Grande. To the left, the forest extends virtually without interruption to the summit of Monte Pettinascura, 1708m. 24km a road on the right diverges to Acri (Route 7B). Ahead, the view broadens to embrace the entire Cecita basin, bounded on the south by Monte Botte Donato.

Lago di Cecita, also called Lago di Moccone, is set in a wide valley among pastures and fields of grain, at an altitude of 1135m. It was created by damming the Moccone, and like Lakes Arvo and Ampollino, its waters are used to generate electricity. To the south lies Monte Botte Donato, to the east Monte Pettinascura, to the north Monti Altare and Sordello, to the west the Serra la Guardia.

The road winds along the east shore of the lake. At (6km) Forge di Cecita, a turning on the left leads through dense forests to (4km) La Fossiata, a hamlet named after the nearby torrent. Planted with a variety of Silan flora, it is the showcase of the Forest Administration and a starting point for the ascent of the Serra Ripollata (1682m). The highway follows the south shore of the lake past the modern Colonia Montana di Camigliatello, from where it bears south–east across wheat fields and pastures. You climb along the wooded Serra Lunga, with views to the right to the Serra la Guardia and the Catena Costiera. 12km the road passes beneath the Cosenza–San Giovanni in Fiore railway and enters Camigliatello, Route 8A.

C.   From Catanzaro to Camigliatello

*Not for those who suffer car sickness, this road winds up in an unending series of curves through magnificent landscape, past **Taverna**, birthplace of the 17C painter Mattia Preti (several examples of whose work may be seen in the town's churches), and **Villagio Mancuso**, where residents of Catanzaro go to escape the heat, to the dark pines of the Pesaca Forest and the verdant shores of **Lakes Arvo** and **Ampollino**. Medieval villages untouched by time (or almost: a vogue for mufferless mopeds is fast taking root) dot the landscape of this magnificent plateau. Travel time is roughly 1hr 50min.*

ROAD 110km. Highways 109b, 179d and 108b and local roads—26km Taverna— 16km Villaggio Mancusa—68km Camigliatello.

The climb to Taverna

Leave Catanzaro (Route 10) from the north. The road begins to climb into the hills. 8km Sant'Elia (664m, 2000 inhab.) enjoys a broad vista over the coast to Capo Rizzuto. As you gain altitude, the character of the vegetation changes, the olive groves gradually mixing with oak and chestnut woods. 2km pass the small church of Termine. Further on, Taverna comes into view below. Descend into the valley, cross the Alli River, and climb out again among chestnuts and terraced olive groves.

16km **Taverna** (521m, 3000 inhab.) is set among the foothills of the Sila Piccola. Its name suggests that the village might have been a post-stage on the road from the Ionian coast to the Sila. The old town, which was located to the east of the present centre, was destroyed once by the Saracens and again by the condottiere Francesco Sforza.

Mattia Preti (1613–99), the 'Cavalier Calabrese', one of the more renowned painters of the 17C Neapolitan school, was a native of Taverna and several of the town's churches contain paintings by him. The former conventual church of **San Domenico** houses the most notable of these, including, on the north side (first altar), St John the Baptist, in the lower right corner of which is a self-portrait of the artist dressed as a Knight of Malta (which honour was accorded him by Pope Urban VIII after he had worked in the cathedral on the island); second altar, Madonna with Saints; third altar, ***Crucifixion**; fifth altar, Madonna of the Rosary; behind the main altar, ***Christ in Majesty**, possibly inspired by Michelangelo's Christ of the Last Judgement; on the south side (first altar), Martyrdom of St Peter; second altar, St Francis de Paola, resembling the painting of the same subject in the church of Sant'Agata degli Scalzi in Naples; third altar, St Sebastian (patron of the town); fourth altar, Madonna and Saints, an early work; fifth altar, the Infant Christ. The furnishings of the church also merit inspection, as does the wooden ceiling. In the sacristy are Neapolitan paintings of later date as well as furnishings of the 17C and 18C.

Above the high altar in the nearby church of **San Nicola** is the handsome Madonna della Purità, commissioned by Giovanni Antonio Peorio and Lucrezia Teutonica, his wife, and probably executed in Emilia between 1636 and 1644. The painting is movable; in a niche behind is a large carved and painted bust of St Nicholas of Bari (1699).

The church of **Santa Barbara**, which formerly belonged to the Order of the Minims, contains several more of Preti's paintings, including a Baptism of Christ, St Barbara being received into heaven (reminiscent of Guercino) and the large Patrocinio, sent by the artist from Malta, in which the dead Christ is supported in the arms of his Father. In the lower part of the painting appears a portrait of Marcello Anania, Bishop of Sutri and Nepi, once priest at Santa Barbara and Preti's first master. The church also contains finely crafted Baroque altars and figures, especially that of St Sebastian to the right of the entrance; and a Crucifix of the school of Fra' Umile da Petralia. On the outskirts of the village, in the church of San Martino, is a panel by Preti and his school.

Through forest and field

Beyond Taverna, the road proceeds through loops and turns to (2km) San Giovanni. Here turn left onto Highway 179d and begin the ascent of the Sila proper, crossing the magnificent pine forest of Pesaca.

Eastwards via Mesoraca

Highway 109 leads right to (3km) **San Pietro** (479m, 1000 inhab.), where the church of Santa Maria della Luce contains an interesting 17C wooden crucifix. At (11km) **Zagarise**, the church of the Assunta has a fine Gothic façade of local granite, with an ogival portal and rose window. Beyond, the road winds among the hills, with good views at times to the coast. 10km **Sersale** enjoys a position dominating the hills of the Marchesato. From here Highway 180 leads south–east to Cropani and the Gulf of Squillace. Alternatively, you might bear north to (5km) Cerva, from where a byway leads south–east to the Albanian colony of Andali.

18km **Mesoraca** (415m, 10,000 inhab.) is built on a ridge between two mountain torrents. The former conventual church of the **Ritiro** (the monastery was destroyed by earthquake in 1783) contains some unusual paintings of the late Neapolitan school. The church of the **Annunciata** has a good 16C Madonna and Child above its central portal. It contains a series of marble inlaid Baroque altars, of which the finest is the high altar, upon which stands a silver tabernacle. The sacristy has 18C woodwork. In the environs are the ruins of the Basilian monastery of Sant'Angelo di Frigilo and the **Santuario del Santissimo Ecce Homo**, which contains a Madonna and Child by Antonio Gagini (1504) and, in a chapel to the right, a venerated wooden figure of Christ attributed to Fra' Umile da Petralia (1600).

The road ascends in a series of curves, with views ahead to Petilia and back to Mesoraca. 7km Foresta is linked to Highway 109 and the sea by a road leading off to the right. 2km a turning on the left mounts to **Petilia**

Policastro (436m, 11,000 inhab.). Initially called simply Policastro (from the Byzantine *palaiokastron*, old castle), the second name was added in the mistaken belief that the town stood on the site of the Greek settlement of Petilia, now believed to have been located near Strongoli. Petilia Policastro can be reached by railway from Crotone, 41km in c 1hr. Just north of the town you are joined by a road from Lago Ampollino (see below); turn right to (19km) Santa Severina, Route 8A.

The road continues to wind upward. 15km, leave on the right a byroad for (16km) Buturo, headquarters of the Amministrazione Forestale della Sila Piccola. Further on lies Villaggio Mancuso (1300m), a much-frequented summer resort. The road climbs among dense pines, then descends to (3km) Villa Racise, another tourist centre. The descent continues through dense woodlands. Leaving on the left a road to Panettieri and Carlopoli, begin to climb again, frequently along steep slopes. 11km another road diverges right to Buturo (see above). Beyond, the forest grows thinner as you descend to (4km) the junction with Highway 179. Here there is a choice of two routes both equally interesting.

Turning left on Highway 179, you follow the Savuto valley westward. As the valley broadens, you come upon (6km) the junction with Highway 108b. Here bear north, crossing the Savuto again after a brief descent. After a climb through the forest, the view opens up on all sides as you reach Colle Ascione (1384m). Beyond, the descent begins to **Lago Arvo**, visible to the right. The lake (1280m) was created by damming the Arvo River near Nacelle. Tunnels convey its waters, together with those of Lago Ampollino to the hydroelectric plants at Orichella, Timpa Grande and Caluria, on the Neto River.

An alternative route via Lago Ampollino
Bearing right, you follow the valley of the Savuto east to its headwaters, crossing woods, pastures and fields planted with wheat and rye. You then descend the wooded valley of the Ampollino, which widens below the forested crest of Montenero (1881m) to form **Lago Ampollino**, 1279m. The lake, created by damming the Ampollino at the foot of Monte Zigomarru, is approximately 13km long. Its waters are used to generate electrical power. The road winds around the wooded south bank. The view over the water is splendid. At the east end of the lake you leave on the right a road to (19m) Cotronei and cross the Ampollino. The road climbs steeply through pine forests to the Valico di Croce di Agnara, a pass 1371m high, it descends, then mounts again to the Neto valley. Cross the River Neto; beyond, the ascent is again steep and tortuous. At (30km) San Giovanni in Fiore join Route 8A to Camigliatello.

11km Highway 178 diverges left to (22km) **Aprigliano** (720m, 3000 inhab.), the medieval *Aprilianum*, birthplace of the poet Domenico Piro. Nearby is the hermitage of San Martino, where the Abbot Gioacchino is believed to have died. The church, with its single nave, wide transept and three semicircular apses, recalls French monastic architecture of the eleventh century.

Follow Highway 108b around the north shore of Lago Arvo, with occasional views through the trees to the water. 9km Lorica, 1350m, is a small summer and winter resort set on the north shore of the lake, between dense forests and rolling fields of grain. Just east of here a secondary road (left) ascends Monte Botte Donato (1928m), descending to Camigliatello via Fago del Soldato. Although somewhat longer than the main road, it affords some of the finest *views in all of Calabria. If you remain on the main road, at (5km) Rovale (1322m), leave Highway 108b, turning left toward Silvana Mansio and Monte Volpintesta (1730m). 11km a road diverges left to (500m) Silvana Mansio. 3km the highway ends; turn left on Highway 107 to (12km) Camigliatello Silano, Route 8A.

9 · Reggio Calabria and the Aspromonte

Reggio Calabria is the regional capital and the last major city on the Italian peninsula before crossing to Sicily. It is known above all for its **Museo Nazionale della Magna Grecia**, which houses an extraordinary collection of prehistoric, Graeco-Roman and medieval antiquities. The city stands at the foot of the **Aspromonte**, a wild, mountainous region for centuries isolated from the rest of the world. Here, in some villages, the dialect spoken is still based on ancient Greek. Interesting day trips may be made from Reggio and its environs, the usual starting points being Melito di Porto Salvo, on the south coast, and Bagnara Calabra, to the north.

■ **Restaurants**. Reggio Calabria, *Da Giovanni, Via Torrione 77, tel. 0965 25481; Melito di Porto Salvo, **Casina dei Mille (with rooms), Highway 106; tel. 0965 787434, fax 0965 787435.

REGGIO CALABRIA
Reggio is a flourishing city (178,000 inhab.), with wide streets and low buildings constructed in reinforced concrete.

History
Its name still carries a reference to *Rhegion* or *Rhegium*, founded c 723 BC by the Chalcidians, who were afterwards joined by the Messenese. The colony grew in size and wealth under Anaxilas, but it was sacked by Dionysius the Elder of Syracuse in 387 BC and was later subject to the Mamertines and repopulated by the Romans. Its propitious situation secured it continuous prosperity and enabled it to survive the repeated ravages of both pirates and earthquakes.

Reggio was rebuilt with wide and regular streets after the earthquake of 1783, only to be practically demolished again on 28 December 1908, when 5000 of its 35,000 inhabitants perished and every house that was not completely ruined was seriously damaged. Heavily bombed in 1943, it was occupied on 3 September by the Allies, who crossed the Straits practically unopposed.

■ **Information**: APT, Via Demetrio Tripepi 72; tel. 0965 858496, fax 0965 890947 (branch offices at Via Roma 3, Corso Garibaldi 329, Stazione Centrale, Airport, Autostrada A3—Rosarno Ovest Service Area).

■ **Airport**: At Ravagnese, 4km south, with daily service to Rome and to Palermo.

■ **Railway stations: Centrale**, Piazza Garibaldi, at the south end of the town, for all trains; **Lido**, more centrally placed near the hotels and the museum is served by most; **Marittima** is the terminus of trains from the east, but is not served from the north.

■ **Ferries**: To Messina, daily in 45 min from the Stazione Centrale.

■ **Hydrofoils**: To Messina and the Aeolian Islands, daily (15min–2hr), from the Stazione Marittima.

■ **Post office**: Via Miraglia.

Corso Garibaldi, roughly parallel to the sea, forms the main thoroughfare of the city, with Piazza Italia at its centre. To the north–east of the piazza the severe Tempio della Vittoria (1939) serves as a war memorial. Two massive towers of the castle survive, further south, and afford a fine view over the city and the straits. There is a mosaic pavement of the Norman period, taken from two ancient Calabrian churches destroyed, like so many others, by earthquakes, in the nearby **Chiesa degli Ottimati**.

THE MUSEO NAZIONALE DELLA MAGNA GRECIA

To the north-east, in Piazza De Nava, is the ***Museo Nazionale della Magna Grecia** (open Tue–Sat 09.00–13.00, 15.00–19.00; Sun and Mon 09.00–13.00), by far Reggio's chief attraction for the visitor. It contains an extensive collection of antiquities, including beautiful terracottas, marbles, and small bronzes of fine workmanship, from Sibari, Locri, Medma and other sites throughout Calabria. The museum building is under perennial reconstruction and displays are moved or closed as work progresses.

Ground Floor. Neolithic, Iron and Bronze Age collections (flint implements, iron and bronze swords, spear heads, pottery, bones), well displayed and clearly labelled. At the beginning of the section are large cases containing instructive scale models of prehistoric villages. and a cast of a graffito representing a bovid from Papasidero, the only such Italian find dating from the Upper Palaeolithic period. The rooms that follow are dedicated to prehistory: Neolithic on the left, Upper and Lower Palaeolithic on the right, with material from localities throughout the region: from Favella della Corte, Cosenza, Girifalco, Catanzaro, Cassano Ionio, Praia a Mare, Opido Momentina, Tropea, Drapia, Cirò, Calanna, Torre Galli, Grotterie, Serra Aiello.

Mezzanine. On the landing, treasures of the 7–4C BC from Caulonia and Locri Epizephyrii, notably an extraordinary series of votive ***Pinakes**. Also from Locri (Sanctuary of Persephone), 7C terracottas, ointment jars, mirrors, fibulae, jewellery and bronze statuettes; and some very interesting clay tablets intended as ex-voto offerings to the goddess. There are 176 different types, here assembled into ten groups according to subject. Notice also the reconstructed fictile acroterion, revetment of coping and pediment cornice from the Temple of Zeus (5C BC), and 38 bronze tablets inscribed in Locrian dialect (350–250 BC) from the temple archive. These were the accounting books. The ***equestrian group** from the Marafioti Temple at Locri, and the other celebrated group featuring the ***Dioscuri**, in Parian marble from a nearby sanctuary, have both been removed for restoration (1995). Here also is a fine collection of ***coins**, nearly all Greek and Roman, well displayed, and representative of all sites. It includes the silver stater, typical of Magna Graecia, of standard weight (8g), stamped with the symbol of the mint and the name of the city where it was made (tripod = Croton; bull = Sybaris; hipogriff = Locri; eagle and serpent = Hypponion; wheat = Metapontum).

First Floor. Finds from Rhegium, including architectural terracottas, some bearing traces of the original painting, and a large Hellenistic sarcophagus in the

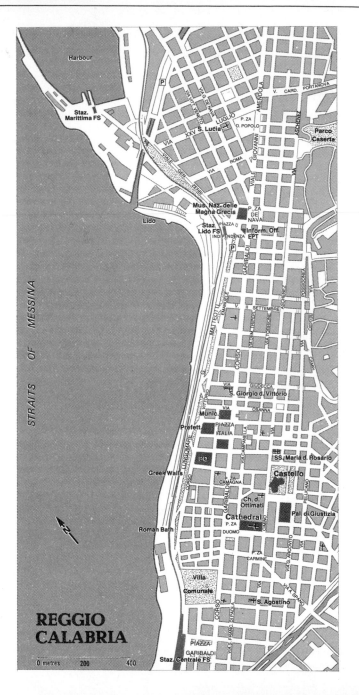

Harbour

P

Staz.
Marittima FS

V. CARD. PORTANOVA

AMENDOLA

ASCHENEZ

Parco
Caserta

XXV LUGLIO S. Lucia

P.ZA
D. POPOLO

VIALE GIOVANNI

VIA GEN. DE NAVA

VIALE VITT. VENETO

VIA ROMA

VIALE GEN. ZERBI

Mus. Naz. delle
Magna Grecia

Lido

Staz.
Lido FS

PIAZZA
INDIPENDENZA

P.ZA
DE
NAVA

Inform. Off.
EPT

GARIBALDI

MATTEOTTI EMANUELE

V. II SETTEMBRE

VALORE TRIPEPI

VIA TORRIONE

ASCHENEZ

POSSIDONIA

VIA

REGGIO CAMPI

STRAITS OF MESSINA

CORSO VITTORIO

VIA GIUDECCA

S. Giorgio d. Vittorio

VIA OSANNA

Munic.

Prefett.

PIAZZA
ITALIA

VIA CAMPANELLA

SS. Maria d. Rosario

Greek Walls

LUNGOMARE

CORSO GARIBALDI

VIA CAMAGNA

Castello

Ch. d.
Ottimati

Cathedral

P.ZA
DUOMO

VIA GIUDICE

PELLICANO

Pal. di Giustizia

Roman Bath

P.ZA
CARMINE

VIA ACQUAVIVA

VIA A. SPANÒ

Villa
Comunale

CORSO

VIA S. FRANC. DI PAOLA

S. Agostino

REGGIO
CALABRIA

PIAZZA
GARIBALDI

Staz. Centrale FS

0 metres   200   400

form of a foot (the deceased was buried in a sitting position); Alexandrian glass and gold goblet from Tresilico, with hunting scenes of gold leaf set in the glass. Metaurus: imported ceramics from Attica and Chalcis. Medma: fictile votive offerings and moulds for making them (notice the small statue of a seated deity holding a dove); bronze objects, including a mirror handle with a Silenus approaching a seated nude youth. Laus: treasure from a 4C chamber tomb used for the burial of a Lucanian warrior and his wife, including a fine ceremonial suit of armour and diadem. Caulonia: clay lion-head decoration of a temple, head of a statue, and coloured mosaic with a sea monster from a patrician house. Crimisa (Cirò): 5C head of Apollo attributed to Pythagoras of Rhegium, and fragments of feet and hands.

Second Floor. Byzantine artefacts: reliquary crosses and medals of the 6–11C. Arabo-Norman gesso-work: columns and panels with peacocks, etc. Two small panel paintings by Antonello da Messina, St Jerome and Three Angels. Two late 15C panels by Pietro Cararo. A fine but small late 14C St Lucy. Mattia Preti, Return of the Prodigal Son. Fede Galizia, Judith and Holofernes. Various 17C canvases, dark and anonymous. Paintings of the 18C and 19C by Vincenzo Cannizzaro, Adrian Mangland and others.

Basement. Marine archaeology section, with finds from a Greek ship discovered at Porticello, at the north entrance to the Strait of Messina. These include an extraordinary bronze **Head of a Philosopher* (5C BC), considered the only Greek portrait head in existence. The ****Riace Bronzes**, the celebrated heroic nude statues discovered off Riace in 1972, are viewed from a platform overlooking the glass enclosure in which they are undergoing restoration. The scenario is curiously like that of an operating theatre: restorers are opening the statues to remove the earth used in casting, now a source of corrosion. The Bronzes were first revealed to the public in Florence in 1980. Statue A, 205cm tall and weighing 250kg, originally held a shield and lance and wore an Attic helmet. The statues have been attributed to Phidias (460 BC) and Polyclites (430 BC) respectively, and they have been associated with the temple at Delphi built by the Athenians to commemorate the victory of Marathon.

Near the post office are remains of the Greek walls and of a Roman bath. The **Lungomare**, described by D'Annunzio as the most beautiful kilometre in Italy, or in Europe, though now busy with traffic commands a magnificent panorama.

THE ASPROMONTE

The **Aspromonte**, the last great spur of the Apennines, is an old massif with soft contours descending in several terraces to the sea. The name denotes the district bounded by the Tyrrhenian Sea, the Strait of Messina and the Ionian Sea on the west, south, and east; and by the Petrace, Plati and Careri rivers on the north. At the centre of the Aspromonte rises Montalto (1956m), the highest peak of Calabria; from here, numerous ridges radiate in all directions. Most of these drop abruptly into the sea. The longest, which extends to the north-east, forms the main watershed.

The four terraces or *Piani dell'Aspromonte*, as they are known locally, were made by bradyseisms and reflect successive alterations in the relative levels of land and sea. Earthquakes have afflicted the area with uncommon frequency, the most disastrous being that of 1783, which destroyed much of the inhabited area between Palmi and Reggio.

Almonds, peaches, figs, and citrus fruit flourish in the coastal areas, and the lowlands between Scilla and Capo Spartivento are celebrated for their plantations of bergamot orange, used for scent and eau de cologne. Jasmine is grown in the area around Brancaleone. In the hill zones are groves of giant olives. Above 650m chestnuts and oaks prevail, then beech and conifers. The highland areas were once covered by dense forest, unfortunately destroyed over the centuries, so that much of the region is now given over to pastures and to the cultivation of grain and potatoes. The forests of the Aspromonte are constantly expanding, however, due to an active reafforestation programme. Together with the spectacular views—which at some points span the north and west coasts of Sicily—and with the winter sports at Gambarie (see below), these woodlands are the district's chief attraction. A considerable part of the area was set aside as a National Park in 1991.

Garibaldi's untimely advance on Rome was checked by Cialdini at the battle of Aspromonte in September 1862 and in later years its fastnesses were the haunt of Musolino, a nineteenth-century Robin Hood. Even today, they are a favourite hiding-place of fugitives from the law.

From Reggio Calabria to Gambarie

Leave Reggio from the north following Highway 18 along the coast as far as (5km) Gallico Marina, then turn inland on Highway 184 and cross broad citrus orchards to (1km) Gallico Superiore. The road climbs through the foothills of the Aspromonte, offering good views across the Strait of Messina and along the densely populated coast north of Reggio.

5km Sambatello (286m) is known for its dry rosé wine. Beyond, the road follows the valley of the Gallico, dominated by the ruined castle of Calanna, a structure of strategic importance in Byzantine, Norman and Swabian times. Below, the river bed is strewn with small orchards protected against the violent winter currents by dykes. The highway crosses the river and is joined by the road from (2km) **Calanna**, perched on the ridge above. The village (510m, 2000 inhab.) enjoys a splendid view. In the Chiesa Parrocchiale can be seen fragments of medieval sculpture from a ruined Byzantine church, as well as a 15C bell and sculptural fragments dating from the 16C and 17C. Nearby, excavations in 1953 revealed a necropolis dating from the 9–6C BC. The material recovered is now in the Museo Nazionale in Reggio.

As the valley narrows the ascent becomes more tortuous. 3km Laganadi is set among olive groves. The road crosses a deep ravine, then resumes its climb, with views of the villages of Cerasi and Ortì in the distance. 3km Sant'Alessio in Aspromonte (565m). Continue through wooded glens and past a river bed graced by flowering junipers in summer to (7km) **Santo Stefano in Aspromonte** (714m, 2000 inhab.), a small town with a distinctive mountain character (the upper floors of many houses are in wood), the birthplace of Musolino (see above). Beyond, the road loops back to the west. The *view spans the Strait of Messina and the Sicilian coast from Punto Faro to Mount Etna. 9km the road terminates at **Gambarie** (1300m), a popular summer and winter resort in a magnificent position among beech and fir forests.

■ **Information**. APT, Piazzale Mangiaruca.

From Bagnara Calabra to Gambarie

From Bagnara Calabra (north of Reggio, see Route 7A), follow Highway 18 north. 5km turn right onto Highway 112, which winds up to a broad plain covered with olives and dwarf oaks. Through further loops and turns, the road mounts to (10km) Sant'Eufemia d'Aspromonte (440m). Here leave the main road on the left and cross the Piani dell'Aspromonte. The *view to the west is magnificent. 10km you emerge onto Highway 183, which is followed to the south. A dirt track on the left leads to the site of Garibaldi's capture at the battle of Aspromonte (see above). Beyond, ascend steeply to (8km) **Gambarie**.

From Melito di Porto Salvo to Gambarie

Melito is on the south coast (Route 10). Follow the coast road east to the outskirts of the town, then turn left onto the road (marked) to Gambarie. The highway follows the west bank of the Fiumara Melito; beyond the turning for Prunella (right) begins the ascent of the Aspromonte. At (9km) Chorio the valley narrows. 2km you pass a small hamlet. A road on the right diverges to San Lorenzo and (16km) Roghudi. 5km **Bagaladi** (475m) derives its name from the Arabic Baha' Allah, 'the beauty that comes from God'. The road continues to climb through several curves, with views over the Pristeo and Melito valleys. At the head of the latter, the Punta d'Atò rises sheer to a height of 1379m. Continue the ascent through forests of oak and chestnut, with broad views over the sea and the Strait to Etna and the Monti Peloritani and cross a rolling plain planted with forage and grain, followed by a forested glen between two high mountains. Further on, the view to the left embraces the Campi di Sant'Agata and the Calopinace valley. The Strait, with Mount Etna beyond, become visible once again. 33km the road to Reggio via the Passo di Petrulli (1056m) branches left. Continue across a broad pasture, then descend rapidly between beach trees to a large clearing and (3km) Gambarie.

Excursions from Gambarie

To Puntone di Scirocco, 1660m, c 2km by chairlift from Bivio di Gambarie, where the road from Gallico meets that from Delianuova.

To Montalto summit, 1985m, 4hr (steep) by mule-track. Also on muleback, May–Oct, conditions permitting. On the summit stands a large bronze Christ turned toward Reggio in benediction. From the top of the mountain the Strait of Messina is out of sight, and Sicily and Calabria appear to form a single, continuous land mass. Just below the summit, a track to the north leads to (3hr) Delianuova. A steep path to the north-east winds through forests of beech, fir, oak and chestnut to the Santuario di Santa Maria dei Polsi, of Byzanto–Norman origin.

To the Cippo di Garibaldi. From Bivio di Gambarie, Highway 183 crosses a plateau. A signpost indicates the way through the woods to the so-called Cippo di Garibaldi, 1204m, a modern monument built on the site where the general was captured.

10 · Taranto to Reggio Calabria

*This route follows the instep of Italy, remaining within four or five kilometres of the Ionian Sea throughout its length. Although the shore is itself uninteresting, the villages in the hills to the north and west, particularly **Stilo** (with the little Byzantine church of the Cattolica) and **Gerace** (with its magnificent cathedral), are well worth visiting. In addition, major archaeological sites, **Metapontum**, **Policoro**, and **Locri**, where excellent museums afford insight into life in the Greek colonies of Magna Graecia, lie on the plain near the sea.*

Motorists should bear in mind that the road along this route is perennially under construction, and roadwork can cause major delays. Where there is no interruption, the flow of traffic is fast and wild, an oncoming vehicle rarely being viewed as an obstacle to overtaking. Travel time is about 5hr 30min.

ROAD 499km. Highway 106—48km Metaponto—112km Rossano—93km Crotone—63km Catanzaro Marina—86km Locri—68km Melito di Porto Salvo—29km Reggio Calabria.

RAILWAY 471km in c 6hr. To Metaponto, junction for Potenza and Naples, 44km in c 30min. To Catanzaro Lido (junction for Lamezia Terme and the Tyrrhenian coast line) in c 3hr 30min.

HOTEL EN ROUTE: Castellaneta Marina, ***Golf Hotel, tel. 099 6439251, fax 099 6439255.

RESTAURANT EN ROUTE: Melito di Porto Salvo, **Casina dei Mille (with rooms), Highway 106; tel. 0965 787434, fax 0965 787435.

Through ancient Lucania

Taranto, see Route 19B. Quitting the town by the Ponte di Porta Napoli, keep right beyond the Borgo and follow the deserted shore of the Gulf of Taranto. A characteristic feature of the landscape is the series of parallel dunes covered with low brush, which are separated by marshy valleys.

42km you cross the Bradano and enter Basilicata. On the river bank, to the right, is the acropolis of the ancient **Metapontum**, the entrance to which is marked by the disused antiquarium.

History

Founded in the 7C BC possibly from Pylos in the Peloponnesus, Metapontum may have served initially as a buffer state between the Achaean colony at Sybaris and the Spartan Taras (Taranto). Archaeological evidence suggests that it was built on the site of an earlier, indigenous settlement. The city grew in wealth due to the suitability of the surrounding land to agriculture and to its excellent location for trade with Poseidonia (Paestum) and the Tyrrhenian colonies. **Pythagoras** transferred his school here after his expulsion from Croton, giving rise to a philosophical tradition that was carried on long after his death in 497. Alexander, King of Epirus, killed in battle against the Bruttians and Lucanians, was buried at Metapontum. During the Second Punic War the city sided with Hannibal, who, on his retirement from Italy in 207 BC, evacuated the inhabitants to save them from Roman vengeance. Later it was sacked by Spartacus.

Air surveys of the area have revealed the limits of the city walls (c 6km in circumference); the grid-like street plan, with wide avenues at regular intervals and rectangular insulae measuring c 190 x 38m; the agora; and an artificial harbour at the mouth of the Basento, linked to the town by a canal.

The *Tavole Palatine, a peripteral hexastyle temple of the Doric order, is the most extensive remnant of the ancient colony and one of the better-preserved monuments of Magna Graecia. Built in the late 6C as a sanctuary, probably dedicated to Hera, it stands 3km from the urban centre. Of its 32 Doric columns, 15 are still

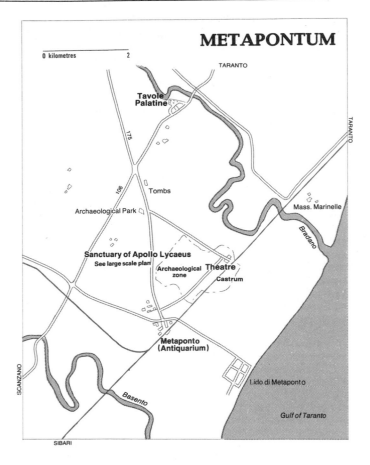

METAPONTUM

0 kilometres 2

TARANTO

Tavole Palatine

175

106

Tombs

Archaeological Park

Mass. Marinelle

Bradano

Sanctuary of Apollo Lycaeus
See large scale plan

Archaeological zone

Theatre

Castrum

Metaponto (Antiquarium)

Lido di Metaponto

SCANZANO

Basento

Gulf of Taranto

SIBARI

TARANTO

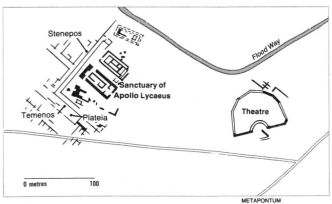

Stenepos

Flood Way

Sanctuary of Apollo Lycaeus

Temenos

Plateia

Theatre

0 metres 100

METAPONTUM

upright; some bear traces of their original stucco. Although parts of the lower course of the architrave have been preserved, the entablature has disappeared altogether. Much remains, however, of the stilobate and the foundations of the cella, which seems to have been divided into two unequal parts.

The remainder of the town may be reached by following Highway 106 south to the junction with Highway 175 and turning left (immediately on the left, remains of a monumental tomb from the Hellenistic period; further on, on the right, another tomb from the 5C). From the modern village of **Metaponto**, where there is a new **antiquarium** (open daily 09.00–19.00) mounting temporary exhibitions of finds from the excavations, a country road follows the railway north to (c 3km, left) the **theatre** and the **Temple of Apollo Lycius**, a Doric construction of the 6C BC. From the fragmentary remains archaeologists have deduced that this temple, like that of the Tavole Palatine, had 32 columns, 6m high. Numerous sections of these, as well as several Doric capitals and pieces of the architrave, have been found on the site, and a reconstruction is under way. Excavations around the perimeter of the temple have revealed traces of smaller religious buildings and numerous archaic votive statuettes.

Lido di Metaponto is a pleasant resort.

■ **Information**: APT, Piazzale Lido; tel. 0835 741933.

Beyond (20km) Scanzano Ionico, where you are joined by a road from Sala Consilina, the highway crosses the Agri.

A brief diversion

The Agri valley road is one of the more spectacular in Southern Italy; the landscape, deeply eroded by wind and rain, affords *views of a strange and wild beauty that certainly merit a side-trip (20 minutes up and 20 minutes back are sufficient to get a taste of what the countryside can offer, here). Along the road are numerous villages, of little artistic merit but fascinating by virtue of their strong intrinsic character. Another road of equal interest runs up the valley of the Sinni, and a loop of 122km may be made via **Tursi**, returning to the coast near Nova Siri, 8km south of Scanzano. This area is described in detail in Route 7B.

Just west of (3km) **Policoro**, excavations after magnetic soundings in 1961–67 have located the site of *Heracleia*, a joint colony of Taras and Thurii founded in 433 BC at the end of a ten-year struggle for control of the fertile Siri valley. Here the painter Zeuxis was born in the 5C BC, and Pyrrhus achieved his virst victory over the Romans (280 BC), who were terrified by the appearance of a squadron of elephants.

The *Museo Nazionale della Siritide (open daily, 09.00–19.00) contains the result of excavations from the site of Siris-Heracleia and others in the Valle d'Agri (Roccanova, Sant'Andrea, Castranova, Chiaromonte, etc.). The museum follows an open plan: the rooms to the left of the entrance are mostly concerned with diggings from the Siris-Heracleia and those to the right with the Valle d'Agri excavations. The rooms are excellently laid out and clearly labelled, with an abundance of plans and photographs to show the sources of the excavations.

To the left terracottas from the 6–1C BC, including a disc with a votive inscription; an ivory figure (4C BC); fictile bust of Hephaistos (second half of the 4C BC); results of excavations in the Sanctuary of Demeter at Heracleia, including heads of divinities; fragments of painted vases; several bronze plates with dedicatory inscriptions and the representation of the divinity Eleusinie (late 5C BC); a large Laconic krater (archaic) used in Classical times for libations and filled with small votive vases, coins, etc.; terracotta fragments and remains of metal-work from archaic times up to the Roman; prehistoric fragments.

To the right: two fine burial treasures, one from the tomb of a man, the other from that of a woman; Corinthian helmet, remains of armour and other bronze ware of the 7C and 6C BC; Roman glass; skull of a young girl still bearing her jewellery; lekythos (black figure) by the Painter of Edinburgh; coins from the Sanctuary of Demeter and Bendis; metal axe and agricultural implements; terracotta statuettes, etc; Greek vases, including a *Hydria showing a conversation between young people in the presence of Eros, by the Painter of Amykos, *group of vases by the Painter of Policoro; and a superb *pelike (wide-mouthed jar) portraying Poseidon and Athena, attributed by some to the Painter of the Carnee, and by others to the Painter of Policoro.

The museum is customarily used as a way-station for burial treasures excavated in the environs and awaiting restoration. The entrance hall often holds entire tombs, complete with earth, in open crates.

A road leads inland to the isolated church of *Santa Maria di Anglona, Route 7B.

IONIAN CALABRIA
The road now traverses the Pantano di Policoro, a thicket of myrtle, oleander and lentisk, crosses the Sinni (formerly the Siris) and enters Calabria. 10km Nova Siri station, the hills come close to the sea. 5km Rocca Imperiale, with a castello built by Frederick II, stands on an eminence 4km west of the road. Beyond (30km) Trebisacce is the large alluvial plain of Sibari around the mouth of the Crati. At Sibari the railway to Cosenza diverges from the main line.

The ancient **Sybaris**, from which Sibari takes its name, probably stood on the left bank of the Crati (*Crathis*). This Achaean colony, whose luxury and corruption have become a byword, was destroyed by the men of Croton (510 BC), who flooded it with the waters of the Crathis. The descendants of the survivors, with the help of a band of Athenian colonists, founded Thurii in 443, 6km further inland, near Terranova di Sibari. Among the Athenians were Lysias, the orator (died 402) and Herodotus, who died at Thurii between 430 and 425 BC.

Romanised after 290 BC under the name of *Copiae*, the town endured until the decline of the empire. Recent drainage operations, which have greatly improved the former malarial condition of the plain, have brought some traces of Copiae to light, though the exact site of Greek Sybaris remains a mystery. Some of the material discovered to date may be seen in the Museo della Sibaritide e Parco Archeologico (Strada Statale 106, open 08.30–12.30, 15.00–19.00).

To the south there is a splendid view of the mountains of the Sila and, to the north, the steep limestone crags of Monte Pollino, snowcapped except in the height of summer. The road runs further inland leaving (right) turnings to Spezzano Albanese and San Demetrio Corone (Route 7B).

At (17km) **Corigliano Calabro** (207m, 40,000 inhab.) the large church of

Sant'Antonio di Padova has a decorative Baroque interior and a good inlaid marble high altar. About 6km beyond, you pass below the **Convento del Patire** (Santa Maria del Patirion; 609m), founded by St Nilus (see below) on a rugged peak in magnificent surroundings. In the 12C it rivalled Mount Athos as a seat of monastic learning; the church preserves traces of a mosaic pavement.

12km **Rossano** (275m, 35,000 inhab.) lies 6km south of the road. The little town was the birthplace of St Nilus (910–1001), founder of Grottaferrata and Patire. The cattedrale has a Baroque altar attached to a pillar on the north side of the nave, which encloses a Byzantine Madonna of the 8C or 9C; and a wooden ceiling. In the archbishop's palace, attached to the cathedral, is the Museo Diocesano (open daily 09.00–13.00) in which you can see the celebrated *Codex Purpureus, an extremely rare Greek work of the 6C.

The narrow Via Arcivescovado, to the right of the cathedral, leads down to the small church of the **Panaglia**, a 12C building with an interesting apse containing *opus spicatum*. Within is a fresco of San Giovanni Crisostomo. At the top of the town stands the 10C church of *San Marco, built to a Byzantine plan with five domes and three apses. The Passeggiata di Santo Stefano commands a view across the Gulf of Taranto.

From Rossano to Camigliatello Silano, see Route 8B.

Cross the Trionto and gradually turn south between the Sila and the sea. 33km Cariati Marina, a road turns inland to the old town of **Cariati**, where you can make a circuit of the old walls and bastions into which houses have been built. The **Cattedrale**, whose tiled cupola can be seen from the marina, has an impressive interior and contains 18C choir stalls by Girolamo Franceschi. The **cemetery church** (just outside the town) is a bare and pleasing late Gothic building with a well proportioned ribbed dome, completely vested inside with patterned tiles of Moorish inspiration.

30km Torre Melissa is known for its excellent Cirò wine. About 4km beyond, a road diverges right to **Strongoli**, 9km inland, the ancient *Petilia* which, faithful to Rome, held out against Hannibal in 206 BC. Here and in neighbouring villages textiles are handwoven to traditional designs.

CROTONE

Cross the Neto and enter the Marchesato, a former fief of the Ruffo family. 21km **Crotone** (62,000 inhab.) stands on a promontory c 2km east of the road. An industrial centre of some importance, it has the only harbour between Taranto and Reggio.

History

The Achaean colony of *Croton*, founded in 710 BC by settlers sent, as legend narrates, by the Oracle of Delphi, became the most important city of the Bruttians. Its dominion, together with that of Sybaris, extended over much of Magna Graecia and included colonies on both the Ionian and the Tyrrhenian coasts. Pythagoras (c 540 BC) made it the chief centre of his school of philosophy, but was expelled some 30 years later when the oligarchy that he supported and justified was overthrown. In the same century, Croton was conquered by the Locrians but, thanks to the prowess of its champion Milo (one of a series of famous Crotonian athletes), it vanquished the Sybarites in 510. It submitted to Agathocles of Syracuse in 299. Here Hannibal embarked after his retreat from Rome.

In the 13C it reached a second eminence as capital of the Marchesato. Most of its ancient buildings were used by Don Pedro of Toledo in the construction of his castello. From the 11C to 1929 the town was known as *Cotrone*. George Gissing wrote much of his *Ionian Sea* here in 1897.

■ **Information**. APT, Via Torino 148; tel. 0962 23185.

On the road to the town are storehouses for olives, oranges and liquorice. The castle dates from the 16C. The church of San Giuseppe has a decorative façade with two domed chapels. Nearby is the excellent Museo Archeologico Statale (closed for renovation 1995). When open, the ground floor houses (right) a large collection of small votive terracottas from the 5C and 6C BC; and (left) prehistoric remains and Greek, Crotonian, Italic and Roman coins. On the first floor are displayed various types of antefix (4–3C BC); small bronzes (7–4C); various decorative terracotta pieces from temples; Crotonian ceramics (6–4C); a Roman copy, in marble, after a Greek original of Eros and Psyche; a Hellenistic female bust and other marble remains.

An interesting excursion may be made to (11km) Capo Colonna and (25km) Le Castella, see below.

From Crotone, the road turns inland across a hilly peninsula, off the coast of which Calypso's island of Ogygia was supposed to lie. 17km Isola di Capo Rizzuto was one of the centres of post-war agrarian reform. 8km there is a choice of two turnings, both of which lead left to **Le Castella**, the name of which derives from the Aragonese fortress built on an island just offshore. Near (9km) Steccato, the highway returns to the coast, where it is joined by the railway. 6km Cropani (347m), in the hills 7km north of the road, has a church with a 15C portal of singularly Classical simplicity.

CATANZARO

16km an expressway (Highway 19b) diverges inland to **Catanzaro** (12km), an animated city of 104,000 inhabitants, capital of its province. Situated on a height between the gorges of two mountain torrents, it boasts a glorious record of opposition to tyranny.

■ **Information**: Assessorato Regionale al Turismo, Santa Maria di Catanzaro, Pal. Europa; tel. 0961 8511 61940, fax 0961 63143. APT, Galleria Mancuso; tel. 0961 743901 (branch office in Piazza Prefettura).

■ **Airport** at Lamezia Terme, on the Tyrrhenian coast 61km west, with direct flights to Naples, Palermo, and Rome; air terminal in Piazza Matteotti.

■ **Railway stations**: **Catanzaro** (Ferrovie dello Stato), with lines for Catanzaro Lido and Sant'Eufemia Lamezia; **Catanzaro Città** (Ferrovie Calabro–Lucane), with lines for Cosenza and Catanzaro Lido.

■ **Post office**: Corso Mazzini

From Catanzaro station a unique funicular tramway ascends through a tunnel to Piazza Roma and crosses Corso Mazzini. To the west of the Corso, near the rebuilt cathedral, is the church of the **Rosario** (or San Domenico), a Baroque edifice with paintings of the Madonna del Rosario and the Madonna della Vittoria, celebrating the victory of Lepanto; as well as some marble altars, all of the 17C. On the south flank of the church is the Oratorio della Congrega del Rosario, with elaborate stucco work. The **Museo Provinciale**, in the public gardens of the Villa Trieste (open Thu and Fri 10.00–12.00), contains a Madonna and Child, signed by Antonello da Messina; an Assumption by the school of Preti and a collection of later paintings; the remains of an equestrian monument of the second century AD; prehistoric material; a marble head from Strongoli and a Greek helmet from Tiriolo, of fine workmanship. Most of this material was away for restoration in 1995, leaving very little to see. Adjacent to the museum is the Villa Margherita, a public park commanding an exceptional view to the sea. More views may be obtained on all sides of the town from the *circonvallazione*, or ring road.

From Catanzaro to Camigliatello, see Route 8C.

Between Catanzaro and Locri

Return to the coast and Highway 106 at Catanzaro Marina, an important industrial town and a crowded, built-up resort. Just off the road, c 2km south of Catanzaro Marina, is the ruined church of **Santa Maria della Roccella**. Although its date of construction is disputed, it is generally believed to be an 11C building modelled on the large Cluniac churches of the north and conditioned by local building traditions. It is built to a Latin cross plan, with a simple nave, three semicircular apses, and a broad transept. The crypt follows the plan of the presbytery and apses. The façade, nave walls and transept have largely fallen down, and access to the crypt is difficult; nevertheless the contrast between the warm red brick of the remaining walls and the cool silver-green of the olives that grow around the ruin is striking. Excavations nearby have begun to bring to light the ruins of the Roman settlement (see below).

Descend along the coast. Ahead, high up on the right (290m) appears the town of **Squillace** (7km, 3000 inhab.), the Greek city of *Schilletion*, which became *Scolacium* under the Romans. It was the birthplace of Cassiodorus (480–575), the secretary of Theodoric, and of General Guglielmo Pepe (1782–1855), commander of the Neapolitan army in Lombardy. The cathedral contains 16C sculptures and the castle commands a view.

17km *Soverato* stands below **Soverato Superiore**, where the Chiesa Arcipretale contains a fine Pietà by Antonio Gagini (1521) and, on the right of the main entrance, a 16C bas-relief also depicting a Pietà.

■ **Information**: APT, Via San Giovanni Bosco 1; tel. 0967 25432.

29km Monasterace Marina stands about 1km south of the ruins of *Caulonia*, an Achaean colony destroyed by Dionysus I in 389 BC, consisting of a rampart and a fragmentary Doric temple. From Monasterace Marina Highway 110 winds up the valley of the Fiumara Stilaro to (15km) **Stilo** (400m, 3000 inhab.), beautifully situated on the flank of Monte Consolino. The town is overlooked by the *Cattolica, a gem of Byzantine architecture resembling San Marco at Rossano (see above), perhaps the best-preserved monument of its kind in Europe.

The Cattolica survived the earthquake of 1783, which destroyed much of the town, and was restored in the first quarter of the 20C. Built to a square plan, it has five conical domes on circular drums. The **interior** measures 6 x 6m and is divided into nine quadrants by four rough columns. The latter, taken from antique buildings, have been placed on top of their capitals to symbolize the defeat of paganism.

The Byzantine Cattolica, Stilo

The first column on the right bears the Greek inscription, 'God is the Lord who appeared to us', surmounted by a carved cross. On the walls and ceiling can be seen traces of Byzantine frescoes in three strata corresponding to three different epochs, discovered and restored in 1927.

Tommaso Campanella (1568–1639), the philosopher, was a native of Stilo, and its environs were a favourite resort of Basilian anchorites. Emperor Otho II was defeated by the Sicilian Saracens here in 982. From the vantage point of the Cattolica, other interesting remains of domed churches can be seen. These include the ruined convent of San Domenico, where Campanella lived and worked.

Beyond Stilo the road continues to (37km) Serra San Bruno, Route 7A.

13km cross the Allaro, the former Sagras, where 10,000 Locrians defeated 130,000 Crotonians (c 540 BC). **Caulonia,** 8km inland, was founded by the refugees from ancient Caulonia. The church has a Carafa tomb (1488). At (6km) Roccella Ionica, the ruined castello stands on a striking cliff overlooking the sea. Near (7km) the station of Gioiosa Ionica are remains of a small Roman theatre. The ruined castle commands a good view. The road passes through plantations of bergamot trees. 4km Siderno is a sprawling modern town with a frequented beach.

LOCRI AND GERACE
5km **Locri** (14,000 inhab.) lies 5km north of the ruins of its ancient namesake. This, the famous *Locri Epizephyrii*, was founded by colonists, probably from the Opuntian Locris in Greece, in either 710 BC or 683 BC, on a site that had already been inhabited by native Siculian peoples for several centuries.

History
The Greek colony flourished, perhaps by virtue of its location on a major highway (the *dromos*, which bisects the site) and of its contacts with Sicily and Tyrrhenian colonies. Locri was the first Greek city to possess a written code of laws, attributed to Zaleucus (664 BC), and it was praised by Pindar as a model of good government. Religious life centred on Persephone, and the city contained a celebrated sanctuary dedicated to that goddess. The Locrians conquered the Crotonians (see above), allied themselves with Dionysius I and finally surrendered to Rome (205 BC). The town dwindled and was eventually destroyed by the Sarcacens.

■ **Information**: APT, Via Matteotti 90; tel. 0964 29600.

Although the richest remains from the site are housed in the Museo Archeologico Nazionale in Reggio Calabria, the recently constructed **Museo Statale di Locri** (open daily 09.00–13.00) contains clear plans and photographs illustrating the history and artistic development of the city, as well as a well-displayed collection of pottery and bronzes from Greek and indigenous tombs, architectural fragments, a vast assortment of small votive statues (the craftsmen of Locri specialised in producing these), Roman inscriptions and Locrian and Greek coins. Visits to the **ruins** (open daily 09.00–1hr before sunset) begin at the museum, from where a dirt path leads inland to (500m) the remains of an Ionic temple believed to have

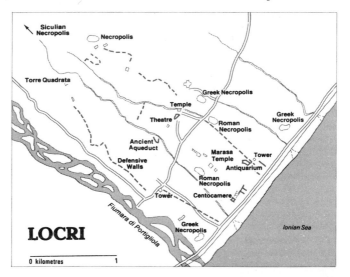

been dedicated to Zeus. Originally constructed in the 7C BC, it was enlarged in the 6C and completely rebuilt in the following century.

Further on, a footpath leads from a modern hamlet situated on the dromos to a Doric temple (called Marafioti) and the neighbouring Hellenistic theatre, much altered in Roman times, where in 1959 30 bronze tablets of the 3C BC recording civic expenditures were found. The visible stretches of the town walls (behind the antiquarium and c 1km further south, along a track perpendicular to the coast road) date in all likelihood from the 6C. Traces of the earlier walls may be seen at the Centocamere, an area only partially excavated, entered from a dirt track (marked Locri scavi) c 500m south of the museum on Highway 106. Here too are the foundations of houses and parts of a water system, as well as the beaten-earth streets dividing the insulae. The shrine of Persephone stands in a ravine outside the city wall, just above which are the foundations of a small temple of Athena. Little, however, remains to be seen of these monuments, and access is difficult. Greek and Roman tombs are to be found in the vicinity of the dromos; and a Siculian necropolis, further inland.

From the centre of modern Locri, Highway 111 climbs inland through olive groves to (9km) **Gerace** (479m, 3000 inhab.), situated on an impregnable crag overlooking the road. Founded by refugees from Locri in the ninth century, it possesses a remarkable *Cattedrale*, the largest church in Calabria. Consecrated in 1045, this was rebuilt under Swabian rule and restored after an earthquake in the 18C. The spacious **interior** is built to a Latin cross plan. The nave and aisles are divided by 20 granite and coloured marble columns possibly from Locri, above which rounded arches of differing heights spring from high stilt-blocks. At the end of the south aisle is the Gothic Cappella del Sacramento (1431); in the adjacent south transept can be seen the 14C tomb of Giovanni and Battista Caracciolo and of Niccoló Palazzi. Antique columns also support the vault of the much-restored crypt.

The church of the Sacro Cuore has a distinctive dome and contains pretty Baroque decoration. San Francesco d'Assisi (1252) has two fine portals, of which the larger bears Arabic and Norman decorative elements. Within are a tomb of Niccoló Ruggo (died 1372), of Pisan influence; and a marvellous inlaid marble high altar. The small church of San Giovanello is also of Byzanto-Norman construction.

Beyond Gerace, the road continues to climb, through an area once ruled by outlaws, to a broad, flat highland, from where it descends via (23km) Cittanova and (6km) Taurianova to (13km) Gioia Tauro, Route 7A.

On to Reggio

Continue south along the coast. Just before (9km) Ardore Marina, a road turns inland to (5km) **Bombile**, near which lies the **Santuario di Bombile**, constructed in a most astonishing way inside a large cave. The sanctuary, reached by a track through olive groves, has a charming façade into which an attractive Baroque portal, dated 1758, is set. Inside, the edifice is completely built and vaulted as would be any free-standing church and exhibits somewhat later decoration. Over the high altar stands the Madonna della Grotta, a fine marble statue, possibly by a close follower of Antonello Gagini.

At (3km) Bovalino Marina a turning on the right mounts to (5km) **Bovalino Superiore**, where the church of the Matrice contains a marble Madonna della Neve by the school of Gagini. Set into the south wall is a fragment of a marble

Madonna and Child mutilated by Turkish pirates. Also to be noted is the Madonna of the Rosary, clothed in fine 18C garments. The Chiesa del Rosario has a rich 14C portal.

Beyond (22km) Brancaleone you round Capo Spartivento, the *Heracleum Promontorium* of the Romans, at the south-east extremity of Calabria. Some of the villagers in this area retain a dialect of Greek origin, though scholars dispute whether from a period BC or AD. Garibaldi landed in 1860 and again in 1862 at (32km) Melito di Porto Salvo, the southernmost town (10,000 inhab.) on the mainland. A beautiful mountain road ascends to Gambarie (Route 9). Etna and the east coast of Sicily come into view. On the right rises the five-pronged crag of **Pentedattilo**, whose name translates from the Greek as 'five fingers', with a picturesque ruined village at its foot. Further on, the road winds around the Punta di Pellaro and Messina appears across the Straits. 29km Reggio Calabria, see Route 9.

II THE ADRIATIC BIOREGION: ABRUZZO, MOLISE, APULIA AND BASILICATA

The Adriatic bioregion, or the lands on the eastern watershed of the Apennines, includes the regions of Abruzzo, Molise, Apulia (*Puglia* in Italian), and Basilicata.

ABRUZZO AND MOLISE

These occupy the east centre of the Italian peninsula, with their seaboard on the Adriatic. They are bordered on the north by the Marches, on the west by Lazio and on the south by Campania and Apulia. With a total area of 15,232sq km, they comprise the hilly provinces of L'Aquila, Teramo, Pescara, Chieti, Campobasso and Isernia. Formerly a single region, they became administratively independent in 1963.

Within the confines of Abruzzo are the highest peaks of the Apennines, which here diverge slightly from the main north-west-south-east axis to form the Meta Massif, in the Abruzzo National Park. The Lago-Gran Sasso-Maiella range, which culminates in the Corno Grande (2912m), the 'roof' of the peninsula, divides the region into two fundamentally different districts, characterised by maritime and alpine climates. Between this and the central range lies the so-called Abruzzo highland, with the basins of L'Aquila and Sulmona.

The first human presence in Abruzzo seems to date from the Lower Palaeolithic period, after which habitation is continuous to the present. Evidence from the Upper Palaeolithic and Neolithic periods has been found throughout the region, particularly in the Fucino basin, rich in cave finds, and at Corropoli, where the so-called Ripoli culture, distinguished by a particular type of painted ceramics, appears to have lasted over a millennium.

The Apennine culture was introduced at a fairly advanced stage (Middle Bronze Age), probably by small groups of shepherds from Apulia or the Marches; and even in the sub-Apennine phase, Neolithic traditions persisted. Especially in the mountain areas, the sub-Apennine cultures maintained their autonomy, contributing later to the formation of numerous allied tribes of mixed origin, who were subdued by the Romans only after a long, bitter struggle culminating in the Social War (91–82 BC).

After the fall of the empire, the region was partitioned between the dukes of Spoleto and Benevento and was later united by the Normans to the Duchy of Apulia. Frederick II Hohenstaufen transformed Abruzzo into an independent province with Sulmona as capital, but since the advent of the Angevins the region has followed the fortunes of the Kingdom of Naples. The Bourbons in 1684 divided it into Abruzzo Citeriore, Ulteriore Primo and Ulteriore Secondo (corresponding to the three northern provinces of today), and Molise.

The name, Abruzzo, originally *Aprutium*, seems to be derived from that of the Praetuttii, one of the aboriginal tribes. The Tronto river, which today separates Abruzzo from the Marches, is the historical border between the Kingdom of Naples and the Papal States. On the west, the boundary with Lazio still follows the line of division between the ancient IV Regio Samnium and I Regio Latium. The title of Duke of Abruzzi was borne by Luigi Amedeo, grandson of Victor Emmanuel II, the distinguished explorer and mountaineer (1873–1933). Medieval Abruzzan art is characterised by severe simplicity and Abruzzan churches are distinguished by their flat, gableless façades. The region is noted for its pottery and goldsmiths' work and for its attractive local costumes; and the people are famous for their pride, their industry and their hospitality. The origin of the name Molise, which is first heard of as a region in the thirteenth century, is uncertain.

APULIA

Apulia (Puglia) occupies the extreme south–east of the Italian peninsula, from the 'spur' (Monte Gargano) to the 'heel' (Salentine or Iapygian Peninsula) of the 'boot'. For the most part it is flat, rising gently inland to a long plateau (**Le Murge**), with no considerable elevations except the Gargano Promontory. It is the ancient *Apulia*, originally inhabited by the Pelasgians and the Oscans. Among its towns were several Greek colonies, including Taras. It flourished under the Roman rule which followed upon the defeat of Pyrrhus, and with the rest of southern Italy it has passed through the hands of innumerable overlords, its most prosperous period being under the Swabians.

The great period of church building in Apulia was under the Normans, who combined diverse influences from France, Pisa, the Lombards and the Orient into the style known loosely as Apulian Romanesque. This style is generally characterised by the massive solidity, rounded arches and flat ceilings found in the contemporary architecture of Northern Europe, though here embellished with delicately detailed ornamental features of Byzantine or Saracen origin. The details of these churches and of Frederick II's fine castles amply repay study.

As in Abruzzo and Lazio, there are still nomad shepherds in parts of Apulia. In these three provinces together there are about 3000km of grassy 'drove-roads', known as 'tratturi' (with side-tracks known as 'tratturelli' or 'bracci', under the administration of the State, by which the sheep are driven up to the lofty pastures of Abruzzo in spring, returning to the Apulian lowlands in autumn.

Apulia largely consists of flat expanses of limestone, almost destitute of rivers, as the surface water disappears in the limestone fissures. The rainfall is very light, and the country deserves its epithet of 'seticulosa' or thirsty. In general, however, the soil is well cultivated. Wheat is the chief crop in the almost treeless plain of the Tavoliere della Puglia, known also as the Capitanata, around Foggia. Further south, vineyards predominate, with groves of olives, almonds, and figs.

The great **Apulian Aqueduct**, the largest in the world, with 2700km of channels, supplies drinking water to 268 communes in the region. From the sources of the Sele, on the west side of the watershed, it conveys into Apulia c 15,000,000 litres of water per hour.

BASILICATA

A region corresponding roughly to the ancient *Lucania*, this occupies a three-cornered area between the Gulf of Taranto, the Tyrrhenian Sea and the lowlands of Apulia. The country is almost entirely composed of steep parallel ranges of limestone and dolomitic mountains, precluding easy communication. It was colonised from Greece in the 7C BC and reached a high degree of prosperity, but later it was drawn into the struggles between Rome and the Samnites and the campaign against Pyrrhus and Hannibal, and in the Middle Ages it suffered from the continual vicissitudes of the Kingdom of Naples.

Its present name was assumed in honour of Emperor Basil II (976–1025), who overthrew the power of the Saracens in Sicily and southern Italy. Despite recent progress the region is one of the poorest in Italy: the soil does not favour cultivation, and industries remain undeveloped. Potenza and Matera, the only towns of any size, are the provincial capitals. In the forests, wild boar and wolves are not uncommon.

11 · Ancona to Bari

This route, which skirts the sea, gives access to regions remarkable for their natural beauty, their magnificent castles and their austere medieval churches. Particularly fine examples of the latter may be seen at **Atri** *and* **Lanciano**. *Pescara and Foggia are busy provincial capitals, of little interest to visitors, but the area between* **Barletta** *and* **Bari** *possesses the richest architectural heritage on the Adriatic south of Venice. Here are the splendid Terra di Bari cathedrals, great churches that combine Northern and Eastern influences in a unique way, giving rise to a characteristic local style broadly referred to as the Apulian Romanesque. The first and, in a sense, the most typical expression of this local tradition is the magnificent basilica of San Nicola in Bari, for it is to this model that the builders of later churches turned for inspiration, at least initially.*

In its last phase, the Apulian Romanesque style aspired to an elegance and grace of form which in Northern Europe was to become a guiding aesthetic principle. This architectural taste, coupled with rich and eclectic decorative schemes that unabashedly combine Byzantine, Norman, Pisan, Lombard and Provençal motifs, makes these some of the more interesting and curious churches in Southern Italy. Also characterisitic of the area are the conical rural constructions called 'caselle'.

Travel time by car is about 3hr 45min. You can visit a selection of the intermediate sites (stopping, say, at Lanciano, Trani, and Ruvo) in a single day, reserving Bari for the following day. In Bari the greatest care should be taken to protect personal property (including automobiles), as petty thiefs, locally known as 'topini' (little mice), are quite active.

ROAD 462km, Autostrada A14. From Ancona, 116km Giulianova—30km Pescara Nord—73km Vasto Nord—39km Termoli—77km Foggia—74km Andria/Barletta—11km Trani—15km Molfetta/Ruvo di Puglia—27km Bari. Because of nimble-fingered petty thieves, motorists should keep windows up and doors locked while driving in Bari.

RAILWAY 446km in c 4hr 30min, with frequent trains. To Pescara, 146km in 80–90min. From Pescara to Foggia, 177km in c 2 hr. From Foggia to Bari, 123km in c 1hr. This is the main rail line connecting Milan with Bari and points south. It keeps close to the road all the way.

HOTELS EN ROUTE: See Routes 16 and 19. Youth Hostel in Bari, Via Nicola Massaro 33; tel. 080 320282.

RESTAURANTS EN ROUTE: Pescara, **La Cantina di Jozz, Via delle Caserme 61, tel. 085 690383, fax 085 65295; Vasto, ***Villa Vignola (with rooms), Highway 16, tel. 0873 310050, fax 0873 310060; Foggia, **Il Ventaglio, Via Postiglione 6; tel. 0881 661500; Barletta, **Antica Cucina, Via Milano 73, tel. 0883 688 05349, fax 0883 688 05349; ****Bacco, Via Sipontina 10, tel. 0883 521718; Santo Spirito (Bari), **L'Aragosta, Lungomare Colombo 235, tel. 080 533 5427.

PESCARA AND THE COAST OF ABRUZZO

From Ancona follow Autostrada A14 south. This area of the Marches is described in *Blue Guide Northern Italy*. Beyond San Benedetto del Tronto you cross the River Tronto and enter Abruzzo.

116km **Giulianova**, a seaside resort of 23,000 inhabitants, was founded in 1470 by the people of San Flaviano (the ancient *Castrum Novum*) and named in honour of Giulio Antonio Acquaviva, Duke of Atri. It consists of a medieval town set on a hill 1km from the coast and a new quarter, Giulianova Lido, which stands between the highway and the sea. The Renaissance **Duomo**, built to an octagonal plan, contains a 14C reliquary. The fine Romanesque church of Santa Maria a Mare was ruined in 1944, but has been restored. The modest Pinacoteca Comunale Vincenzo Bindi (Via Garibaldi 14) is temporarily closed to the public.

■ **Information**: AA, Alba Adriatica, Piazza Aldo Moro 6; tel. 0861 712426. Giulianova, Via Galilei 18; tel. 085 800 4840. Roseto degli Abruzzi, Piazza della Libertà 25; tel. 085 1157; Pineto, Viale Gabriele D'Annunzio 123; tel. 085 949 1745. Silvi, Viale Garibaldi 158; tel. 085 930343.

From Giulianova to Teramo and L'Aquila, see Route 12

Beyond Giulianova you cross the Tordino and, near (9km) Roseto degli Abruzzi, the Vomano. In the distance on the right rises the Gran Sasso d'Italia (Route 13).

8km Pineto, exit for **Atri** (442m, 11,000 inhab.), on a hill to the west. This is the legendary *Hatria*, which became a Roman colony in 282 BC. Its coins are among the heaviest known, exceeding in weight the oldest Roman coins. The *Cattedrale (1285), with a graceful campanile and a beautiful though simple façade, contains 15C frescoes of Old and New Testament scenes, evangelists, doctors, and saints, by Andrea Delitio, and a fine tabernacle (1503) by Paolo de Garvi. The crypt, entered from the handsome cloister behind the church, is a Roman *piscina;* in the sacristy are two carved polyptychs. The Museo Capitolare (open daily 10.00–12.00, 15.00–16.30), also in the cloister, houses a small collection of medieval art. An archaeological museum with finds from local excavations is to open in autumn 1995.

The churches of Sant'Agostino and Sant'Andrea have good portals. The severe façade of the **Palazzo Acquaviva dei Duchi** (town hall and post office) masks an attractive 14C courtyard.

You cross the River Saline beyond Silvi Marina. From (13km) Montesilvano, served by the Pescara Nord interchange, country roads run west to Citta Sant' Angelo (10km; 317m), with a 14C church, and south-west to (30km) Penne.

On the latter, south-west, road is (11km) **Moscufo**, situated on a hilltop with views over the sea and the mountains, from the Gran Sasso to the Maiella. The church of Santa Maria del Lago, 5km south of the road, has a fine pulpit of 1158. To the south of (10km) **Loreto Aprutino** (250m) the church of Santa Maria in Piano contains notable frescoes (Last Judgement, stories from the life of St Thomas Aquinas, New Testament scenes and saints) by 13C and 14C artists. 30km **Penne** (438m, 12,000 inhab.) is an ancient city of the Vestini. The church of San Giovanni contains a processional cross attributed to Nicola da Guardiagrele (in the treasury). The 14C cathedral, almost completely destroyed in 1944, has been restored. Santa Maria in Colleromano, 1km south-east, has fragmentary 15C and 16C frescoes; and at Pianella, 18km south-east near the road to Chieti, is an interesting little Romanesque church.

8km **Pescara**, with 129,000 inhabitants, capital of the province of the same name, is the most active commercial town in Abruzzo, as well as an important fishing port and a frequented bathing resort.

■ **Information**: Assessorato Regionale al Turismo, Viale Bovio 425; tel. 085 7671, fax 085 767278. EPT, Via Nicola Fabrizi 171, tel. 085 421 2939, fax 085 298246; AA, Piazza della Rinascita; tel. 085 422 5021, fax 085 422 5020.

■ **Airport**: Pasquale Liberi, 6km north, with daily service to Ancona and Milan.

■ **Railway stations**: **Centrale**, the main station and the terminus of the line from Rome via Sulmona; **Porta Nuova**, for the south part of the town.

■ **Post office**: Via Potenza.

■ **Special events**: San Cetteo (10 Oct); Stagione Teatrale e Musicale (Nov–May); Stagione Estiva di Prosa (open-air theatre, Jul–Aug); Festival Internazionale del Jazz (July); Concorso Ippico (July); Premio Internazionale Ennio Flaiano (international theatre, cinema, literature, and television prize, July).

The town, completely modern and charmingly situated among pinewoods, is divided into two parts by the River Pescara. The northern section, known as Pescara Riviera, was formerly the separate commune of Castellammare Adriatico. Pescara proper, on the south, is on the site of the Classical *Aternum*, the common port of the Vestini, Marrucini, and Peligni, and at the seaward end of the Via Valeria (today Highway 5).
Pescara was the birthplace of Gabriele D'Annunzio, the poet (1864–1938), whose life and work may be admired in the **Museo Gabriele d'Annunzio** (Corso Manthonè 101; open daily 09.00–13.00, Sat and Sun 09.00–13.00, 15.00–18.30). The Museo Civico e Pinacoteca Basilio Cascella (Via Guglielmo Marconi 45; open daily except Sun 09.00–13.00; Thu 09.00–13.00, 16.00–1930) contains paintings, sculpture, and prints by three generations of the Cascella family, likewise natives. The Museo delle Genti d'Abruzzo (Via delle Caserme 22; open daily except Sun 09.00–13.00) has sections devoted to ethnography, prehistory and protohistory, religion, popular festivities, and (opening in 1995) agriculture.
From Pescara to Chieti and Rome, see Route 14.

South-east of the city centre is the attractive Pineta di Pescara. Beyond, the range of the Maiella comes into view on the right. **Francavilla a Mare**, another seaside resort, was the home of the painter Francesco Paolo Michetti (died 1929). In the treasury of the modern church of Santa Maria Maggiore is a monstrance by Niccola da Guardiagrele.

■ **Information**: AA, Piazzale Sirene; tel. 085 817169, fax 085 816649.

39km **Ortona** (68m, 23,000 inhab.), a town several times devastated by earthquakes and badly damaged in the Second World War, is the most important port of Abruzzo.

■ **Information**: AA, Piazza della Repubblica; tel. 085 906 3841, fax 085 906 3882.

The Palazzo Farnese, begun in 1584 by Giacomo della Porta for Margaret of Parma, was left unfinished on her death here in 1586. It lies between the municipio and a piazzetta called after the composer F.P. Tosti (1846–1916), a native. The cathedral is a restoration, having been half demolished in the Second World War. The adjacent Pinacoteca e Museo, with works by regional artists and material from local archaeological sites, is opened on request. About 3km south, to the east of Highway 16, beyond the Moro River, is **Ortona (Moro River) British Military Cemetery**, with 1614 graves.

A pleasant country road

From the Ortona exit a road (Highway 538) runs inland along the ridge of the north–west side of the Moro valley, crossing most of its Second World War battlefield. At (25km) Guardiagrele station the railway turns left for Lanciano, to regain the coast at San Vito (see below). Bear right on the Chieti road for (3km; left) **Guardiagrele**, a little town noted in the 15C for its goldsmiths, of whom Nicola di Andrea was the most famous. The 14C Romanesque church of **Santa Maria Maggiore** was damaged in 1943, but the external fresco of St Christopher, by Andrea Delitio (1473) survived. The noted silver *crucifix by Nicola di Andrea (1431) has been stolen from the treasury. The 14C church of **San Francesco** has a carved Romanesque-Gothic portal and a 15C cloister. The Biblioteca Comunale (open Tue–Sat 15.30–19.00) has a small collection of architectural fragments and sculptures from area churches.

A scenic road leads to (40km) **Chieti** (Route 14) via (5km) the Bocca di Valle, where a huge inscription on a cliff and a cave chapel, serve as the Abruzzo Memorial for the First World War. At Fara Filiorum Petri the Sagra di Sant'Antonio Abate (16 January) is celebrated by burning a forest of 'farchie', bamboo columns up to 12m high. To the south rises the Maielletta.

From (10km) the Lanciano interchange it is a short drive inland to **Lanciano** (283m, 35,000 inhab.), the *Anxanum* of the Romans, originally a city of the Frentani. The handsome cathedral, with its 17C campanile, is built on a bridge dating from the time of Diocletian and restored in 1088. The church has been closed indefinitely for restoration. **Santa Maria Maggiore**, a Cistercian edifice of 1227, has a Gothic portal of 1317 and, in the handsome Burgundian Gothic interior, a crucifix by Nicola da Guardiagrele (1422) and a triptych by Polidoro di Renzo (1549). Sant'Agostino contains other interesting examples of goldsmiths' work. The 13C church of San Francesco is traditionally held to contain evidence of the first eucharistic miracle recorded by the Church, which took place around the year 700 during a mass celebrated by a Basilian monk who doubted the eucharistic presence. The reliquary is kept in a marble tabernacle over the ciborium and is composed of a silver monstrance (1713) and a chalice below it in crystal, the former containing the flesh, the latter the blood into which the bread and wine were transubstantiated. The 11C **Porta San Biagio** is the only remaining town gate; near it is the 14C campanile of the disused church of San Biagio.

From Lanciano to Roccaraso

At (23km) a road fork beyond the Aventino bridge, the turning on the left follows the valley of the Sangro to (69km further) Castel di Sangro (Route 12). On the way is (13km) **Bomba**, with a monument to Silvio Spaventa (1822–93), a native hero of the Risorgimento, and remains of cyclopean walls. From here a winding country road ascends to Fallascoso (27km), near which lie the ruins of the Roman *Iuranum*. The extensive remains include a forum, a theatre, foundations of several temples and numerous houses and streets. A parallel road on the east passes **Atessa**, where the church of San Leucio contains a monstrance by Nicola da Guardiagrele.

Next you reach (8km) Fossacesia Marina, with the village of **Fossacesia** 4km inland. Here the magnificent conventual church of **San Giovanni in Venere** over-looks the Adriatic above the railway station. Documented from the 8C, it was rebuilt in 1015 by Trasmondo II, Count of Chieti, and after 1165 it was enlarged in the Cistercian style by Abbot Oderisio II. The lower part of the façade is in stone, the upper part in brick. The remarkable marble *Portale della Luna (1225–30) has a tall quatrefoil archivolt with, in the lunette, Christ enthroned between the Virgin and St John; and below, the remains of small statues of St Benedict and Abbot Rainaldo. At the sides of the door are broad, flat engaged pilasters with bas-reliefs depicting Old and New Testament scenes, of Apulian Romanesque inspira-tion. Above rises the tympanum, divided into three parts like a triptych and probably conceived in relation to a group of frescoes that was never executed.

The basilican **interior** (1165) has a nave and aisles separated by cruciform piers. Above, in the nave, are attached shafts designed to support a vaulted ceiling that was never carried out. The raised presbytery is covered by cross vaults; in the apses are frescoes of the 12C, 13C, and 14C. Steps in the aisles descend to the crypt, which contains some late 12C frescoes and columns from a temple of Venus that occupied this site in antiquity. At the rear of the church are visible the three elegant apses. The **cloister** (ring for entrance) was rebuilt in 1932–35.

Across the Sangro on Highway 16 is (5km) Torino di Sangro Marina, south of which lies the **Sangro River British Military Cemetery**, with 2619 graves. Beyond (8km) Casalbordino Station a road diverges for (4km; right) the much frequented Santuario della Madonna dei Miracoli (festival, 11 June).

16km Vasto Nord exit for **Vasto** (34,000 inhab.) a pleasant town 3km from its railway station.

■ **Information**: AA, Piazza del Popolo 18; tel. 0873 801751 (seasonal branch office at the Rotonda Lungomare Dalmazia).

■ **Hydrofoils**: From Punta Penna for the Tremiti Islands (2hr 45min), 15 June–15 Sep.

Vasto is the mythical *Histonium* and for centuries was subject to the D'Avalos. Dante Gabriel Rossetti, the painter, was the son of a blacksmith of Vasto and is honoured by a statue in Piazza Diomede. The church of San Pietro contains a picture painted at the age of 80 by Filippo Palizzi (1818–99), a native of the town. The **Castello** dates from the 13C. The plain **Duomo** (1293) has a Gothic portal. Across the square, the Museo e Pinacoteca Civici, in the 18C Palazzo D'Avalos (opened on request) contains antiquities, including Oscan inscriptions, and works by Palizzi.

Through Molise and into Apulia

You now cross the Trigno, the boundary between Abruzzo and Molise.

39km **Termoli**, probably the ancient Buca of the Frentani, has suffered repeatedly from earthquakes and was largely destroyed by the Turks in 1566, though it was little damaged in the Second World War.

■ **Information**: AA, Via Bega: tel. 0875 706754.

■ **Ferries and hydrofoils**: daily the Tremiti Islands (1hr 40min and 45 min respectively).

The town, with 27,000 inhabitants, has medieval walls, a **Castello** built in 1247 by Frederick II, and a 13C **Duomo**. The striking stone façade, in the Apulian Romanesque manner, dates from the 12–15C; the arcading continues along the right flank of the church to the apse. The views from the promontory on which the old town stands are exceptional: to the west is the Maiella Range; to the east the mountainous Gargano Promontory; seaward, 25m distant, the Tremiti Islands, for which Termoli is the chief departure point.

From Termoli to Naples via Campobasso and Benevento, see Route 15.

A diversion via Serracapriola

A country road (Highway 16b) forges south-east through magnificent countryside to rejoin the motorway at (60km) San Severo. 31km **Serracapriola**, with a castle, stands on a hill. Between the Ponte di Civitate over the Fortore and (16km) San Paolo di Civitate the road passes the scanty ruins of the Roman *Teanum Apulum*, and, higher up (left) those of the medieval *Civita*, where the Normans defeated and captured Pope Leo IX in 1053, immediately afterwards imploring his pardon, which was accorded and accompanied with a grant of the suzerainty of Apulia, Calabria and Sicily to Humphrey and Robert Guiscard.

You enter Apulia shortly after Termoli and the motorway bears inland, across the foot of the Gargano headland. 58km **San Severo**, the ancient centre (55,000 inhab.) of the area known as the Capitanata, is noted for its vines (Sansevero white is particularly dry and delicate). It is a starting-point for exploring the Gargano. The church of **San Severino** has an elegant rose window in its Romanesque façade. The Biblioteca Comunale (Via Zannotti) includes the small **Museo Alessandro Minuziano** (open daily, 08.30–13.30, 16.00–19.00; Sat 08.30–13.30), with Stone, Bronze and Iron Age finds, Daunian material of the 4C and 3C BC, Roman inscriptions (from Teanum Apulum), and medieval ceramics.

To the left rises the huge mass of Monte Gargano. Ahead lies the great plain of Foggia, an area rich in prehistoric sites, of which few have been systematically excavated. In Roman times the plain was centuriated, i.e. partitioned into farms of uniform area with a regular network of roads between them. This pattern can still be traced and gave the district the name of 'Tavoliere' (chessboard). Its modern prosperity was greatly increased by an improvement scheme of 1934–38. Photographic reconnaissance in 1945 revealed upwards of 2000 settlements, many confirmed as Neolithic by excavation. Passo di Corvo, which is the largest known Neolithic site in Europe, has yielded tools and implements, and masses of pottery.

32km **Foggia** (160,000 inhab.) a city of modern aspect with important paper and textile mills, the marketing centre of a vast agricultural region, is also the focus of communication for northern Apulia.

History

Founded by the people of the abandoned Italic town of Arpi (the site of which may be traced 3km north), Foggia probably takes its name from the *foveae* or trenches made to store corn. Frederick II often resided here; here on Palm Sunday in 1240 he summoned the Third Estate to a *colloquia*, an event almost certainly noted by Simon de Montfort, who passed through Apulia shortly afterwards, embarking from Brindisi to join Richard of Cornwall's crusade. Frederick's third wife, Isabella, daughter of King John of England, died here in 1241, as did Charles I of Anjou in 1285.

In 1528 Lautrec took the town and massacred the inhabitants. It was almost totally destroyed by an earthquake in 1731, when the casket containing Frederick's heart was lost. Foggia became an important airbase in the Second World War and was much damaged by bombing, the remaining portions of Frederick's palace being destroyed. Umberto Giordano (1867–1949), composer of *Andrea Chenier*, was a native.

■ **Information**: EPT, Via Senatore Emilio Perrone 17; tel. 0881 723650, fax 0881 676864.

■ **Post office**: Viale XXIV Maggio.

From Piazza Cavour, the older part of the city lies to the north-west. Follow Via Lanza and Corso Vittorio Emanuele to Via Garibaldi. Here turn left, then immediately right in Via Duomo. The **Cattedrale**, built in 1172, retains part of its Romanesque façade and crypt; the remainder, shattered in 1731, was rebuilt in the baroque style. An interesting portal with primitive bas-reliefs, brought to light in 1943 when bombs levelled the building which adjoined the cathedral, can be seen along the north flank.

The **interior**, built to a Latin cross plan with a single nave, has modern (1932) stained-glass windows and, above the door, a painting of the Miracle of the Loaves, by Francesco De Mura. The Cappella dell'Icona Vetere, to the right of the presbytery, contains a Byzantine icon which, according to tradition, was found in a pond in 1073. The restored crypt has vaulted ceilings and stout columns with delicate Romanesque capitals, possibly by Nicola di Bartolomeo da Foggia.

Via Arpi, to the north, leads (right) to Piazza Nigri, where the small **Museo Civico** (open daily, 09.00–13.00, 16.30–19.00) has several rooms devoted to archaeology, displaying finds from the Belgian excavations at Ordono, from Arpi; and from Ascoli Satriano. There is also material from Siponto, a section devoted to folk traditions and a modern picture gallery.

From Foggia the motorway turns south-east across the monotonous Tavoliere plain. 35km **Cerignola** (120m, 55,000 inhab.) is an important market town with a school of agriculture and a modern cathedral. Near here Gonzalo de Cordoba defeated the French in 1503. To the east are San Ferdinando di Puglia, an important wine-producing centre founded by Ferdinand II in 1843; and Margherita di

Savoia, a town on the edge of a very important **salt field**. There is a good beach and the bromo-iodide salts are used for medicinal cures.

A fast road to Bari

From Cerignola, the coastal towns are conveniently reached by a new expressway, Highway 16b, which parallels the old coast road to Bari. The new highway is slowly being extended southward (beyond Bari it replaces, rather than complements, Highway 16) and tracts are open as far as Maglie, in the Salentine Peninsula (see. Route 20). Between Cerignola and Bari, the new highway represents an excellent alternative to the route described below.

15km our road is joined by Autostrada A16 from Naples (Route 17). 7km beyond exit for (5km) **Canosa di Puglia** (105m, 31,000 inhab.) a flourishing agricultural and trade centre on a hilltop overlooking the Tavoliere. This is the ancient *Canusium*, which legend holds was founded by Diomedes. It might indeed have been of Greek origin, as archaeological evidence (chiefly silver and bronze coins inscribed in Greek) and later records (its inhabitants were bilingual at the time of Augustus) suggest. In antiquity the town was well known for its polychrome and red-figure pottery and large askoi decorated with relief figures, examples of which may be seen in the museums of Ruvo, Bari and Taranto. An early and steadfast ally of Rome, it stood for her in the Hannibalian wars, taking in the survivors from the battle of Cannae. This was its most prosperous moment and it was at this time that its commercial activities reached their peak. The town retained its importance after the opening of the Via Traiana and in the 4C AD it became the capital of the region. Its diocese, documented from AD 343 but moved to Bari following the destruction of the town by the Saracens, is the oldest in Apulia.

The **Cattedrale**, dating from the 11C, is uninteresting externally. Within, the *chiesa antica* or old church is readily identifiable despite 17C alterations and modern additions (the latter corresponding to the first three bays of the nave). It is built to a Latin cross plan, with five domes in the Byzantine manner and cross vaults in the aisles, carried on arches that spring from 18 antique columns. The columns, taken from the ancient monuments of Canusium, have beautiful white marble capitals with carved volutes and acanthus leaves. On the north side of the nave stands a masterfully carved pulpit of the 11C. Behind the altar, with its modern tabernacle and 13C silver-gilt icon of the Madonna della Fonte, is a splendid ***bishop's throne** borne by elephants and decorated with plant and animal motifs, carved by the sculptor Romualdo for Ursone, Bishop of Bari and Canosa (1079–89). Steps in the aisles descend to the crypt, rebuilt in the 16C. A door in the south transept leads to a small court where the remarkable ***tomb of Bohemond** (died 1111), son of Robert Guiscard, has a fine door fashioned from solid bronze by Roger of Melfi. The walls of the tomb are faced with marble. Within are two columns with good capitals and the simple tomb slab, inscribed *Boamundus*. Around the walls of the court can be seen architectural fragments, inscriptions, and a Greek torso of the 4C BC.

Adjacent to the church are the public gardens of the Villa Comunale, containing more architectural fragments. Across the town, Via Cadorna leads to the three **Ipogei Lagrasta**, whose underground chambers, excavated in 1843, yielded a number of gold, ivory and glass objects; and a variety of vases, including the famous Anfora dei Persiani, now in the Museo Archeologico Nazionale in Naples. The largest of the tombs has nine chambers and an interesting atrium with painted and stuccoed Ionic columns.

The **Museo Civico Archeologico** (open Mon–Sat 09.00–13.00) has a small

The 11C throne carved by the sculptor Romualdo for Ursone, Bishop of Bari and Canosa

collection of Canosan ceramic ware, Hellenistic and Roman material from the district and finds from the nearby Tomba Diurso, which also yielded objects in the Museo Nazionale in Taranto. The ruined medieval **Castello** incorporates large (1.5 x 1m) blocks of tufa from the ancient acropolis; the ***view** ranges across the Tavoliere from the mountains of the Basilicata to those of the Gargano.

A famous battleground

On the banks of the Ofanto, the ancient Aufidus, some 10km nearer the sea, lies the site of **Cannae** where, in 216 BC, Paullus Aemilius and Terentius Varro, the Roman consuls, were defeated by Hannibal. Many Romans perished in the battle. The **Museo di Canne della Battaglia** (open by appointment; tel. 0883 33600) houses finds from the immense necropolis and the scanty remains of the ancient city, including native Apulian painted vases (among the oldest painted ceramic ware in Italy), ivories, bronzes and coins and numerous other objects demonstrating the continuous importance of the site from prehistoric times to the Middle Ages. The Cittadella di Canne, situated on a hill above the museum, has been excavated in the more superficial strata only and shows mainly medieval remains.

About 7km east of Canosa, a road diverges (right) to (13km) **Minervino Murge** (429m, 11,000 inhab.), known as the Balcony of Apulia on account of its panorama. The road continues to (68km) Gravina di Puglia, Route 17C.

THE CATHEDRAL TOWNS OF THE TERRA DI BARI

16km exit for **Barletta**, an agricultural centre (89,000 inhab.) and port, with a considerable trade in vegetables and wine, which has recently regained some of the prosperity it enjoyed in the Middle Ages, when it was Manfred's favourite residence.

History

Archaeological evidence has demonstrated the existence of an indigenous centre on the site dating from the 4C or 3C BC. However, the first mention of the town—which was variously known as *Barduli, Baruli, Bardulo, Baretum* and finally, in common speech, *Barletta*—dates from Roman times. Under the Normans it became an important trade centre and fortress. Its population was increased in 1083 by refugees from Cannae, when that city was destroyed by Robert Guiscard. Here in 1228, before going on crusade, Frederick II proclaimed his son Henry heir to the throne. The inhabitants rebelled after the king's death, but the uprising was put down by Manfred, who established his court here. The city was the seat of the Archbishop of Nazareth from 1291 until 1818. It reached greatest prosperity under the Angevins, from whom it received special privileges and concessions, becoming in a brief time one of the more important fortresses of the kingdom. During this period it traded actively with the Orient, and its merchant fleet was one of the finest in the region. Here in 1459 Ferdinand I of Aragon was crowned King of Naples, and later suffered an Angevin siege.

On 13 February 1503, while the French were besieging the town, took place the famous Challenge or *Disfida di Barletta*, when 13 Italians and 13 Frenchmen met in mortal combat. Prospero Colonna and Bayard were the umpires of the struggle which ended in victory for the Italians. The champions were greeted by the clergy in procession bearing aloft Serafini's Madonna, now in the cathedral.

Barletta was damaged by earthquakes in 1689 and 1731, and stricken by plague in 1656–57, after which it suffered a long period of decay. Since 1860 it has grown rapidly in wealth and size. Today it hosts several important industries.

■ **Information**: AA, c/o Comando Vigili Polizia Urbana; tel. 0883 331331.

From the west side of town, follow Corso Vittorio Emanuele, passing (right) **San Giacomo**, with its eccentric plan, pyramidal tower, and pointed arches. At the far end of the avenue stands (right) the **Colosso**, a 5C bronze statue, over 5m high, possibly representing the emperor Marcian. The head and torso are original; the hands and legs were recast, somewhat clumsily, in the 15C. The statue was restored in 1980.

Behind is the 13C **Chiesa del San Sepolcro**, built over an earlier church documented from the 11C. The north flank has blind arcades with pointed arches enclosing monoforum windows and a good Gothic portal. The Baroque façade conserves, on the right, a small Gothic doorway; at the left corner stand the remains of the campanile brought down by the earthquake of 1456. The church was completely restored in 1972.

The **interior** is built in the Burgundian Gothic style with three aisles, three apses and a shallow transept preceded by a vestibule or narthex incorporating a gallery in the upper part. The aisle ceilings have simple cross vaults, whereas those of the nave and transept are ribbed. Over the presbytery is an octagonal dome, possibly of Byzantine inspiration. In the gallery are 14C frescoes representing the life of St Anthony Abbot, the Annunciation, and saints. The south apse contains a 16C panel portraying the Madonna di Costantinopoli, of Byzantine taste. The baptismal font, near the entrance-door, dates from the 13C.

From the rear of the church, Corso Garibaldi leads towards the harbour, passing (right) the pleasant Baroque façade of San Domenico. The former convent (entrance at 8 Via Cavour) houses the **Museo Civico** (closed for renovation except for the De Nittis collection, open daily except Mon and holidays 09.00–13.00). In the vestibule are a Roman milestone from Cannae and a mutilated statue of Frederick II, the only surviving likeness. The rooms to the left contain mementos of the Risorgimento; a collection of coins ranging from the 8C BC to the present; and antique pottery (5–3C), chiefly from Daunian sites in the Barletta area (note especially the decorated askoi). The rooms to the right contain works by the native artist Giuseppe De Nittis (1846–84).

On the second floor are paintings by leading Neapolitan artists (Luca Giordano, Massimo Stanzione, Andrea and Nicola Vaccaro, Francesco Solimena, Francesco de Mura, Domenico Morelli, etc.) and many fine Tuscan works, including a Head of Bacchus by Benvenuto Cellini.

The **Duomo**, further on, was built in the 12C, enlarged in 1307 and again in the 15C. The tripartite façade has blind arcades, a rose window and a profusely carved monoforum window in the central section flanked by elegant bifora windows on either side. The main entrance dates from the 16C. The lateral entrances, which belong to the original building, have historiated arches. An inscription above the left portal records the participation of Richard Coeur-de-Lion in the building's construction. The Romanesque campanile has monoforum, bifora and trifora windows on successive levels. The campanile, with its octagonal spire, is an addition of 1743.

The first four bays of the basilican **interior**, carried on antique columns, are built in the Apulian Romanesque style, with decorative bifora above the nave arcade. They date from the 12C and reflect the plan and character of the original church. The remaining bays, which date from the 14C, have pointed or rounded arches on compound piers and ribbed cross vaults. The polygonal apse, with its ambulatory and shallow radiating chapels, was erected during the following century and shows French Gothic influence. It contains carved tomb slabs of various ages. The 13C tabernacle above the high altar was dismantled in the 17C and reassembled, with modern additions, in 1844.

In the ambulatory can be seen the Madonna della Disfida by Paolo de' Serafini da Modena (1387), the only signed work of that artist. The fine pulpit on the south side of the nave was executed in 1267. Steps at the end of the north aisle descend to the crypt, where the semicircular apses of the 12C cathedral have been brought to light by recent excavations. In a room adjoining the church is a small collection of paintings and ecclesiastical objects, including some 13C illuminated codices.

To the north-west of the cathedral is the little church of **Sant'Andrea**, with a fine 13C portal signed by Simeone da Ragusa and a Madonna by Alvise Vivarini (1483). The massive **Castello**, to the east, was built in the 13C on top of the earlier construction that hosted the court of Manfred as well as Frederick II's assembly of barons and prelates at the time of the Third Crusade. It was enlarged by Charles of Anjou to a design by Pierre d'Agincourt later in the 13C; and fortified again some 200 years later by the Aragonese, in the face of the impending Saracen invasion. The four corner bastions were erected in 1532–37 by Charles V to a plan by Evangelista Menga, architect of the castle of Copertina.

Within, the impressive court is lined by vaulted rooms no doubt used as workshops, stables and barracks. On the east side a ramp mounts to the bastions; a fine **staircase** gives access to the first floor rooms, opposite. Along the walls are three 13C windows, two of which bear reliefs of eagles in the tympana.

To Castel del Monte

4km south of the motorway is **Andria** (151m, 90,000 inhab.) the most populous city of the province after Bari. Founded by the Normans in c 1046, it was sacked by the French in 1527 and again in 1799. Its earlier fidelity to Frederick II is recalled by the inscription on the Porta Sant'Andrea. The Gothic **Cattedrale**, several times restored (the façade is a modern reconstruction), has a large crypt with remains of sculptures and frescoes; here lie Yolande of Jerusalem and Isabella of England, two of Frederick's consorts. The Museo Diocesano (open by appointment, tel. 0883 592719) houses paintings, sculptures and decorative objects from several of the town's churches. Sant'Agostino (1230) has a highly individual 14C portal with rich decoration. In San Domenico is a bust of Francesco II del Balzo (1442), perhaps by Francesco Laurana.

By far the most important monument in the territory of Andria, however, is *Castel del Monte, 18km further south, a massive octagonal castle with Gothic corner towers, crowning an isolated peak (540m) of the Murge and known as the Spia delle Puglie. It was built by Frederick II c 1240 and for 30 years was the prison of Manfred's sons. It is notable for its harmony of proportion, its fine windows in the Italian style and the principal entrance in the form of a Roman triumphal arch, most unusual for the 13C. The **interior** (open

Castel del Monte, perhaps the finest of the castles built by Frederick II in Southern Italy

daily except Mon, Apr–Sep 09.00–13.00, 14.00–18.30; Oct–Mar 09.00–13.00, 14.00–16.30), built round an octagonal court, has two storeys with spacious rooms virtually identical in plan and decoration. The capitals of the pillars are remarkable for their beauty and variety.

The motorway and railway now run side by side along the coast, through olive groves and vineyards. 11km **Trani**, a pleasant white town (51,000 inhab.) with a small harbour, is an important centre of the wine trade, its strong, dark red wines being mostly exported for blending.

History
It succeeds the ancient city of *Tirenum* or *Turenum*, which probably dates from the 3C or 4C AD, although popular legend attributes its foundation to Tirenus, son of Diomedes. Before the year 1000 it was, together with Bari, one of the easternmost outposts of the Roman church.

Under the Normans it was an important embarkation point for the Orient. Its commercial activity drew considerable colonies of merchants from Genoa, Pisa, Ravello and Amalfi, as well as a large Jewish community; and its *Ordinamenta Maris*, of 1063, is the earliest maritime code of the Middle Ages.

The town enjoyed its greatest prosperity at the time of Frederick II, when it rivalled Bari in importance. It suffered greatly from the struggle that shook Apulia under the Angevins, and in 1308–16 it engaged in a political and economic conflict with Venice. It repeatedly shifted its loyalty between the Angevins and the Aragonese, siding with the latter, finally, in 1435. Here in 1259 Manfred married his second wife, Helena of Epirus; here also (a few days after Conradin's execution) Charles of Anjou married Margaret of Burgundy. Trani was the birthplace of Barisano, the sculptor (late 12C) and of Giovanni Bovio (1841–1903).

■ **Information**: AA, Via Cavour 140, tel. 0883 43295.

The ****Cattedrale** (San Nicola Pellegrino), next to the sea, was begun at the end of the 11C, over an earlier church. Its imposing form and refined decoration, together with the dramatic beauty of its position (best appreciated at dawn) make it one of the more striking churches of Apulia.

The façade, reached by a flight of steps preceded by a porch with a finely carved frieze, has a richly sculptured portal with bronze ***doors** by Barisano da Trani (1175–79), who also cast the doors of the cathedrals of Ravello (Route 8A) and Monreale. The iconographic and decorative schemes of both the bronze and the stone reliefs reflect Byzantine, Saracenic and Romanesque models. The door jambs are decorated with bas-reliefs of biblical scenes, plant and animal motifs, and geometric patterns that are carried over into the arch above. To either side, blind arcades with cylindrical shafts and finely carved capitals traverse the façade to enclose the lateral portals.

The upper storey consists of a broad, smooth surface of warm stone pierced by a fine rose window and several smaller windows, all with carved surrounds. The beautiful, tall, 13C campanile stands upon a graceful archway open to the sea. The octagonal belfry and spire date from 1353–65.

The flanks of the church are traversed by prominent blind arcading surmounted by a double clerestory. High up on the south transept are a second rose window and two large bifora, above a curious sculpture of two men and a bull. The triple apsidal ending, like the transepts, has finely carved eaves with projecting animal corbels and, at the centre, a great window with a rich surround. More windows and carving can be seen on the north transept.

The **interior**, recently restored to its original Romanesque form, has a nave arcade of six semicircular arches supported by double columns. Above runs a triforium, the left and right halves of which are joined by a characteristic gallery spanning the west façade; and a clerestory with simple monoforum windows. The ceilings of the nave and transept are in wood, whereas those of the aisles have stone cross vaults.

At the sides of the presbytery can be seen fragments of a 12C mosaic pavement; in the chapel on the north side is a 13C relief of the Crucifixion. The crypt has an interesting vaulted ceiling carried on 28 marble columns with intricately carved capitals. A door in the west wall admits to the lower church of Santa Maria della Scala, which may also be entered from the archway beneath the porch of the façade.

The area of this church corresponds to that of the nave above, and is divided into three narrow aisles by Roman columns, probably brought here from Canosa, supporting low cross vaults. Here are to be seen a Gothic tomb, Lombard sarcophagi (under the porch), some 14C and 15C frescoes and fragments of an early mosaic pavement. Beneath is the interesting **Ipogio di San Leucio**, preserving fresco fragments. At 4 Piazza del Duomo is the Museo Diocesano (open daily 08.30–13.00), with architectural and sculptural fragments and paintings, chiefly from the Middle Ages.

Use as a prison has spoilt much of the **Castello**, which was built for Frederick II in 1233–49, by Phillip Chinard, Stefano di Trani and Romualdo di Bari, as an inscription on the sea wall records. Near the harbour are the 15C Palazzo Caccetta, the Baroque chapel of Santa Teresa (adjacent); and, by an arch over the street, the church of **Ognissanti**, erected by the Knights Templar in the 12C. The latter is preceded by a sort of pronaos with a double file of piers and columns, beyond which three sculpted 13C doorways admit to the simple interior.

Of the four surviving Romanesque churches, Sant'Andrea, in the form of a Greek cross, is the oldest. San Francesco has a quaint, pleasant façade with a modest portal and an oculus; the interior has been redecorated in a Baroque style and contains three little Byzantine domes. Rising from the shore at the south edge of the town is the 11C Benedictine abbey of Santa Maria della Colonna, now a museum for temporary exhibitions.

7km south of the motorway, **Corato** (232m, 43,000 inhab.) is built to a radial plan around a circular medieval quarter.

7km **Bisceglie**, a town of 49,000 inhabitants which exports excellent cherries, has a Romanesque **Cattedrale**, begun in 1073 and completed in 1295. The façade, altered by Baroque additions, has an ornate central portal with a shallow porch borne by griffins on columns. Along the south flank is a Renaissance doorway with crude sculptures; more interesting is the apsidal end, with its richly decorated window and blind arcades. The interior, completely restored in 1965–72, is basilican in plan with compound piers and a graceful triforium above the nave arcade. Over the main entrance is a 13C relief of Christ with Sts Peter and Paul. The Renaissance choir stalls, brought here from the Abbey of Santa Maria dei Miracoli, are carved with the likeness of 70 eminent figures of the Benedictine Order.

The Museo Civico Archeologico (Via Monte San Michele; open by appointment,

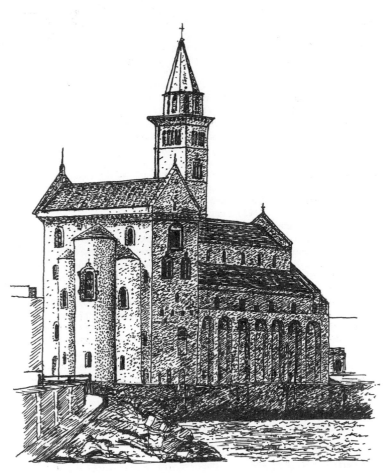

Trani Cathedral, fortress of the Roman Church in the Southern Adriatic

phone 080 991099), contains Paleolithic and Neolithic material as well as paleontological finds. The little church of **Santa Margherita**, set in a courtyard in Via Santa Margherita, is one of the simpler achievements of the Apulian Romanesque style (1197). Along the south side are three tombs of the Falcone family, the largest of which dates from the 13C.

8km **Molfetta** is an active commercial centre (64,000 inhab.) with light industries and one of the larger fishing fleets on the Adriatic. On the sea at the edge of the old town stands the **Duomo Vecchio** (San Corrado), an unusual building begun in 1150 but not completed until the end of the 13C. The highly original design, probably of Byzantine inspiration, has a short nave covered by three domes, on polygonal drums, with pyramidal roofs. Compound piers with rounded arches separate nave and aisles; on top of the engaged columns are intricately carved capitals. More carvings (dating from the 13C) may be seen in the second chapel on the south side. The west front of the church is without a façade, whereas the apsidal end, which presents, as elsewhere in Apulia, a flat wall masking the semi-circular apse, has delicate interlacing blind arches, a fine window with a sculptured archivolt flanked by columns supported by lions, and two tall campanili of Romanesque design. You enter the church from the court of the episcopio, adjacent.

The Baroque Duomo Nuovo dates from 1785. The interior, asymmetrical in plan, is of harmonious design. The Museo Diocesano (in the bishop's palace), and the Museo Archeologico (Seminario Regionale Pugliese) house local archaeological finds including Peucetian and Hellenistic ceramics (open by appointment; tel. 080 911559).

8km south of the motorway, **Ruvo di Puglia** (265m, 25,000 inhab.) succeeds the ancient *Rubi*, famous for its terracotta vases (5–3C BC), of which an excellent collection may be seen in the Museo Jatta (Piazza Giovanni Bovio 35; open by appointment, tel. 080 811042).

The 13C ***Cattedrale** is a fine example of the late Apulian Romanesque style, richly ornamented. The vertical thrust of the façade, evident in the tall central gable and steep roof line, has been somewhat lessened by the widening of its base to accommodate the chapels added to the interior in later centuries. Along the edges of the roof, blind arcades spring from delicate human- or animal-head corbels, a motif that continues along the right flank of the building. High up at the centre of the façade is a superb 16C rose window, surmounted by a seated figure that some identify with Frederick II, others with an Apocalyptic personage. Below are a mullioned window (in the lunette, St Michael in bas-relief) and an oculus surrounded by angels' heads. On the ground level, the three portals stand beneath supporting arches that redistribute part of the weight of the massive wall above. The jambs and archivolts of the doorways are carved with figurative and decorative reliefs by local artists, in a style that fuses Lombard, French and Oriental elements. On either side of the main entrance are unusually slender columns borne by crouching telamones and surmounted by griffins. The sculptural decoration of the apse, transept and south flank of the church also merits close inspection. The campanile, set apart at the rear of the church, was originally a defensive tower.

The **interior**, like the façade, foreshadows the Gothic sensibility for soaring height and delicate ornamentation. It is built to a basilican plan with semicircular apses and high wooden ceilings in the nave and transept. Above the nave arcade runs a balcony on sculptured corbels; higher up is a graceful triforium articulated, as is the nave arcade, by pilaster strips. Recent restoration has closed off all but two of the lateral chapels. The tabernacle above the main altar is a modern construction.

11km **Giovinazzo** (21,000 inhab.), on the coast, has an interesting and well preserved old quarter and a 12C cathedral (rebuilt in 1747) with a large crypt. About 7km south-west of the town, near the motorway, you can see a group of dolmens discovered in 1961.

The same interchange serves **Bitonto** (3km south), a town (54,000 inhab.) producing olive oil. It is famed for its Romanesque ***Cattedrale** (1175–1200), the most complete and harmonious in Apulia. The church follows a T-plan, the apse being concealed behind a single uniform wall surface that unites the arms of the transept and that is a recurrent characteristic of the Apulian Romanesque style. The façade, the design of which faithfully follows that of San Nicola in Bari, is divided into three parts by bold pilaster strips. Blind arcades surmounted by a chessboard cornice run along the pointed gable and the eaves above the aisles.

The upper portion of the façade is dominated by the magnificent rose window, protected by a foliated archivolt on hanging columns. Below are bifora windows. The central portal has strongly projecting foliated arches resting on griffins atop columns borne by lions and surmounted by the pelican pecking her breast, a symbol of the Passion. Above the door are reliefs of the Annunciation, Visitation, Epiphany and Presentation at the Temple, in the lintel; and of the Descent into Limbo, in the lunette. The lateral portals have door-joints and architraves carved with plant motifs. A loggia on the left connects the façade with the 16C Palazzo De Lerma, now a tenement. Along the right flank, deep arches enclose lancet windows and, in the last bay, the Gothic Porta della Scomunica, with sawtooth mouldings of Siculo-Norman workmanship. Above runs a graceful hexaform gallery, with splendidly carved arches, columns and capitals; and a clerestory with intricate tracery in the windows.

The south transept is adorned with tall blind arcades surmounted by bifora and a rose window, with a handsomely carved architrave. On the east wall is a finely carved window, similar in form and workmanship to the main portal, and, higher up, a broad Moorish arch. The 13C campanile was remodelled in 1488 and in 1630.

The **interior**, simple and dignified, is built to a Latin cross plan with three semicircular apses and a shallow transept. The nave arcade is borne by columns alternating with compound piers in a rhythmic order of two to one. The capitals are profusely carved. Along the aisle walls are half columns from which spring simple cross vaults. The nave arcade is surmounted by a triforium, the two parts of which are joined by a 19C balcony on the west wall. Along the south side of the nave are a pulpit made with fragments of the high altar of 1240 and a magnificent *ambo by Maestro Nicola (1229) with a bas-relief representing Frederick II and his family. Stairs in the aisles descend to the crypt with 30 fine columns.

The church of **San Francesco** has a façade of 1286; that of the **Purgatorio**, bizarre reliefs of human skeletons above the portal (cf. Gravina di Puglia, Route 17C). Several good Renaissance palazzi survive in the town.

The Museo Civico E. Rogadeo (52 Via Rogadeo; open Mon, Tue, and Thu 09.00–13.00, 16.30–19.00), houses a small collection of antiquities from local excavations as well as a recently opened gallery of paintings by 19C regional artists. The Museo delle Tradizioni Popolari (28 Via Amendola; open Tue–Sat, 18.00–20.00) has a modest collection of folk art, utensils, costumes, etc.

BARI

16km Bari, the capital of Apulia, is the second largest town in Southern Italy (353,000 inhab.) and a frequented port of call for ships bound for the Eastern Mediterranean. It has important oil refineries.

History

The ancient *Barium* was founded by the Illyrians, civilised by the Greeks and an important commercial centre under the Roman Empire. Taken from the Romans by the Ostrogoths and from the Ostrogoths by the Byzantines, it eventually came into the sphere of the Lombard dukes of Benevento. In 847 it became a Saracen emirate, only to be liberated, some 34 years later, by Emperor Louis II. After the fall of Sicily to the Saracens it became the capital of the Byzantine province of Lombardy and, in 975, the seat of the 'catapan' or Byzantine governor.

In the 11C the city rose to be one of the more important Adriatic ports of Italy, rivalling Venice, with whose help it was freed from a Saracen siege in 1003. The anti-Byzantine revolts that shook the town and much of north-central Apulia in the first half of the century paved the way for the Norman conquest of the region, which was made final in 1071 with the fall of Bari to Robert Guiscard. In 1087 the remains of St Nicholas of Myra, patron saint of Russia, stolen from Asia Minor by sailors from Bari, were brought here to be deposited in the crypt of the basilica of San Nicola, which was begun in 1089. In the following years the city became a major religious centre: at the Council of Bari in 1098, St Anselm of Canterbury defended the doctrine of the procession of the Holy Ghost against the Greek Church. In 1156 the town rose against the Normans. As a reprisal William the Bad levelled it to the ground, except for the shrine of St Nicholas.

Bari flourished under Frederick II (who granted it considerable powers and privileges, despite the dubious loyalty of the townspeople), but it declined under the Angevins. At the end of the 15C it passed into the hands of the Sforza, and Isabella of Aragon, widow of Galeazzo Sforza, held her court here. At her daughter Bona's death in 1558 it became part of the Kingdom of Naples and, like many southern Italian towns, suffered the grievous effects of absentee government. Torn by famine (in 1570 and 1607), class strife and internal political struggles, it fell into a century-long period of decay. The plague of 1656–57 claimed the lives of four out of five inhabitants, reducing the population to a mere 3000. In the 18C Bari was subject to the Austrians, then to the Bourbons; the latter, under Ferdinand IV, drew up an ambitious plan for enlarging the city. This, however, was not to be carried out until 1813, when Joachim Murat issued a decree authorising construction of a Borgo Nuovo outside the old town walls.

■ **Information**: Assessorato al Turismo, Industria Alberghiera, Turismo Termale, Cultura, Sport, Tempo Libero, Beni Culturali, Musei, Archivi e Biblioteche, Via Bozzi 45c; tel. 080 558 9752, fax 080 540 4784. EPT, Piazza Moro 33a; tel. 080 524 2361, fax 080 524 2329. AA, Corso Vittorio Emanuele 68; tel. 080 521 9951.

■ **Airport** at Palese, 8km west with daily service to Rome, Trieste, and Venice.

■ **Post office**: Via Amendola.

■ **Special events**: San Nicola (8 May and 6 Dec), celebrated with a colourful historical parade of St Nicholas and procession on the sea (Processione dei Pelligrini) on 7–8 May; Processione dei Misteri (Easter Week). The Fiera del Levante, inaugurated in 1930 to increase Bari's trade with the Levant, is held annually in Sep near the Punta San Cataldo.

Bari has grown steadily in wealth and population over the last century and a half, expanding to over ten times its previous size. The present city consists of three parts. The 'Città Vecchia' or old town, which stands compactly on a peninsula, is characterised by a maze of narrow, winding streets where life is still closely tied to

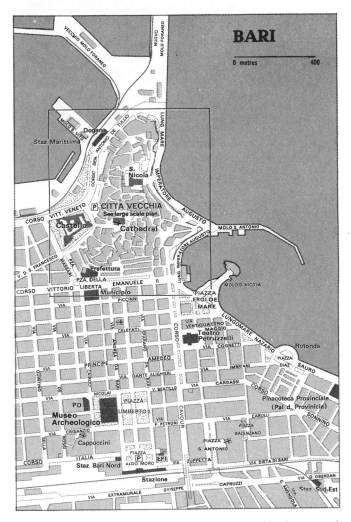

the maritime activities of the adjacent port. Its peculiar and baffling town plan (it is almost impossible to wind your way from one end of the quarter to the other without getting lost) afforded the inhabitants protection from the wind as well as from their enemies (Saracen invaders were lured into the narrow streets and blind alleys and attacked from the windows and rooftops above). It is here that the major medieval monuments are located. The 'Città Nuova' or modern quarter, broadly laid out to a chessboard plan with wide, straight avenues, is the financial and administrative centre of the city as well as the seat of its museums, theatres and concert halls. The university, one of two in Apulia (the other being at Lecce), is also located here. The industrial area spreads inland and to either side, between the city proper and the semi-circular ring of satellite towns by which it is surrounded. Via

Sparano da Bari, the high street of Bari, bisects the new town, connecting the Citta Vecchia with Piazza Umberto I and the railway station.

Corso Vittorio Emanuele, running east and west, divides the modern city from the old town. In Piazza della Libertà, an expansion of the corso, are the municipio with the Teatro Piccini, the prefettura and a monument to Piccini.

To the north, beyond Piazza Massari, stands the *Castello (Castello Normanno-Svevo), built by Frederick II over an earlier fortress, in 1233–39 and extended with massive bastions by Isabella of Aragon. Its predecessor saw the traditional meeting of Frederick and St Francis in 1221. The earlier structure, which stands at the centre of the complex, is readily distinguishable from the 16C additions. It is trapezoidal in plan, with a tall enceinte made of warm brown tufa laid in rusticated rows, and block-like corner towers. You reach it by crossing the moat (now a public garden) to a vaulted entrance hall, from where an archway on the right leads to the outer court. You make a circuit of the massive south tower to a second archway with 13C bas-reliefs, entrance to the elegant atrium. Beyond lies the inner court. The more monumental rooms are used to house the **Gipsoteca del Castello** (open daily 09.00–15.30; with special exhibitions 09.00–19.00). The vaulted hall on the west side contains a collection of plaster-cast reproductions of sculptural and architectural fragments from Romanesque monuments in Apulia. On the floor above are the offices of the Soprintendenza ai Monumenti e Gallerie di Puglia and laboratories for the restoration of paintings. The nearby Molo Pizzolo hosts a modest aquarium (open Mon–Sat 09.00–13.00) with examples of local marine life.

To the east lie the narrow streets of the old town. One block west is the *Cattedrale, an apsidal church of the 12C, built over the remains of an earlier church destroyed by William the Bad in 1156. Basilican in plan, with shallow transepts surmounted by an octagonal drum, it is one of the more noteworthy medieval cathedrals of Apulia. The façade is Romanesque in spirit, with a modern rose window and three Baroque portals incorporating the simpler 12C doorways. Deep arcades run along both flanks, surmounted by a gallery that corresponds to the triforium level of the interior. Two towers, of which that on the south side was damaged by earthquake in 1613, rise just east of the transepts and are joined at the rear of the church by a wall that masks the apse. The east window, a masterpiece of Apulian sculpture, is set beneath a hanging baldachin and ornamented with plant and animal motifs of Oriental inspiration. The cylindrical Trulla on the north, now the sacristy, was built in the 11C as a baptistery and converted to its present function in 1618.

The **interior** has been restored to its original simplicity, with a nave and two aisles supported by tall, slender columns probably taken from the earlier church. Above the rounded arches of the nave arcade runs a false matroneum, which opens directly onto the side aisles. The nave contains remains of a 14C marble pavement with a rose design matching that of the façade. Steps in the crossing mount to the raised presbytery; above, the dome stands to a height of 35m.

In the semicircular main apse are to be seen marble choir stalls and a bishop's throne recomposed from fragments of the original. The ciborium on the high altar and the marble pulpit in the nave are likewise modern reconstructions. The north apse contains remains of 13C and 14C frescoes and the tomb of Bishop Romualdo Grisone (died 1309). A door in the north aisle opens onto the sacristy and steps at the ends of both aisles descend to the Baroque crypt.

Excavations below the floor of the church have brought to light an early Christian basilica dating from the 8–10C, with extensive remains of a **mosaic**

SAN NICOLA

pavement, now visible in the south apse. In the archives is a precious exultet of the early 11C, an illuminated scroll with medallions of Greek saints and, on the verso, liturgical scenes. Also of interest are the late 11C Benedizionario of Apulian workmanship and two smaller exultets. More works from the cathedral and the diocese are preserved in the bishop's palace (shown by appointment, tel. 080 521 2725).

From the north flank of the cathedral follow Strada del Carmine and Strada delle Crociate to (right) the **Arco di San Nicola**, a large Gothic arch adorned with a relief of the saint. (This is an area of town dear to pickpockets: watch out!) Pass beneath and emerge in a small piazza dominated by the Romanesque basilica of **San Nicola*, the first great church built by the Normans in Apulia, founded in 1087 to receive the relics of St Nicholas, stolen from Myra in Lycia by 47 sailors from Bari. It stands in the centre of four piazze, known as the Corti del Catapano, after the Byzantine governor's palace, which once stood here. Owing something to the churches of Caen, but deriving more from Lombard models, San Nicola became the model for the cathedral and the inspiration of later Apulian churches. The majestic façade, flanked by unfinished towers, is clearly divided into three parts reflecting the tripartite division of the interior. The tall central section terminates in a steep gable, whereas the lateral sections end in gently sloping semi-gables. The entire roof line is edged with blind arcading that culminates in the large, slightly pointed arch at the apex. The vast surface of the façade is enlivened by an oculus and eight arched windows, of which the uppermost are mullioned. Lower down its flatness is relieved by blind arches and attached columns. The central portal is set beneath a shallow porch with a pointed gable surmounted by a sphinx and carried by two bulls. The surface surrounding the door and the arch and gable above are richly carved with ornamental and symbolic motifs combining Arabian, Byzantine and Classical influences.

Tall, deep arcades, which become noticeably shallower in the arms of the transept, run along both flanks of the church, surmounted by a graceful gallery below the eaves of the roof. In the third arch on the north side is the magnificent **Porta dei Leoni**, so-called after the lions that support the columns at the sides of the doorway. The sculptural decoration, including two figures of Months on the impost blocks and scenes of chivalry below the arch, are signed by the sculptor Basilio. Another fine doorway is to be seen on the south side. The east wall, like that of the cathedral, masks the apsidal endings of the nave and aisles. The bas-relief of the Miracles of St Nicholas below the central window dates from the 15C.

Interior. The nave and aisles are separated by tall stilted arches on marble columns with elaborately carved capitals. The three great transverse arches were added in 1451; the church seems to have been completed c 1105, although it was not consecrated until 1197. An arched choir screen on tall columns with fine Romanesque capitals (note particularly that on the left) separates the nave from the transept. Beyond, stands the high altar. The *****bishop's throne**, probably made for the council of 1098, stands in the apse below the monument (1593) of Bona Sforza, Queen of Poland and Duchess of Bari.

The crypt, reached by steps in the aisles, has 28 columns with diverse capitals; the vaulted ceiling was freed of its stuccoes in 1957. The altar contains the relics of St Nicholas, said to exude a 'manna' to which is attributed miraculous powers; the silver and gold reliefs were executed in 1684 by Domenico Marinelli and Antonio Avitabili over a Byzantine icon donated in 1319 by the King of Serbia. Notice the mosaic detail of the floor and the low bench in the apse. In the galleries above the aisles are housed the remains of the Treasure of St Nicholas, together with fragments of paintings and sculpture brought to light during the recent restoration.

On the north side of San Nicola is **San Gregorio**, an 11C church with fine windows and façade, and three semicircular apses. The Romanesque interior has particularly good capitals. The Museo di San Nicola (Largo Abate Elia 13, open by appointment; tel. 080 5211205) preserves a small collection of religious and historical objects.

A walk through the old streets of Bari is still rewarding, though they are cut off from the sea by the modern Lungomare Impero Augusto, part of the promenade (9km) that now extends the length of the city, joining the Porto Nuovo to the reconstructed Porto Vecchio. The little church of **Sant'Agostino** (popularly Sant'Anna), rebuilt in 1508, has a façade incorporating fragments of the 12C church over which it stands. Nearby, in Piazza Mercantile, can be seen the **Sedile dei Nobili**, the meeting-hall of the town's patrician rulers, originally of 1543 but remodelled in the 17C and 18C. The **Colonna della Giustizia**, at the end of the square, is flanked by a stone lion upon which debtors were exposed to public ridicule. **Santa Maria dei Maschi**, further west, has a 17C façade. The 11C and 12C church of the **Vallisca** or Madonna della Purificazione, has a fine porch and a simple interior.

Lungamore Imperatore Augusto meets Corso Vittorio Emanuele II at the vast Piazza Eroi del Mare. From here, Lungomare Nazario Sauro diverges south–east past the Rotonda, a semicircular terrace overlooking the sea, to the Palazzo della Provincia.

On the top floor of the Palazzo della Provincia is the **Pinacoteca Provinciale** (open Tue–Sat 09.30–13.00, 16.00–19.00; Sun 09.00–13.00) containing works of the 11–19C, mainly by Southern Italian artists. ROOM 1. Medieval sculptural fragments and paintings of local provenance, including low reliefs, fragments of capitals, a charming polychrome wood Madonna and Child from Basilicata, and two fine icons of the 13C, representing St Margaret and St Nicholas, from Santa Margherita, Bisceglie.

ROOM 2. In the first part of the room, more sculpture and paintings of the 11C,12C and 13C, notably architectural details that fell from the rose window of San Nicola in 1943, when an American ammunition ship blew up in the harbour. The second part of the room hosts 15C panels for altarpieces produced by the Venetian painters Antonio and Bartolomeo Vivarini for the churches of Surbo, Altamura, Andria, and Modugno, notably Bartolomeo Vivarini , *Annunciation, for the Chiesa Matrice, Modugno, a small work commissioned by the Venetian clergyman Alvise Canco; at the end of the room is a presepio composed of fragmentary figures that were once painted in naturalistic colors, by the Apulian sculptor Stefano di Putignano.

ROOM 3 is dominated by Giovanni Bellini's *St Peter Martyr, painted for the Indelli Chapel in the church of San Domenico in Naples; the painting is set away from the wall, to

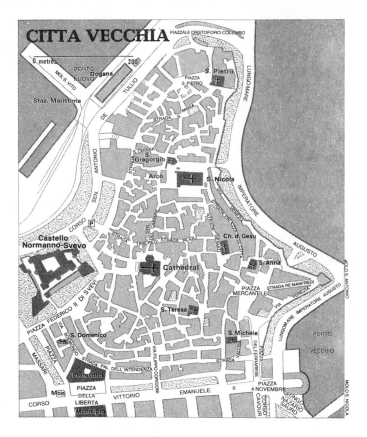

give a glimpse of the fine drawings by the artist on the back. Also in the room are a small St Peter, a Pietà with Saints, and a Head of a Saint, minor paintings by anonymous artists.

ROOM 4 is devoted to Apulian Renaissance painting showing affinities with Neapolitan trends of the period; whereas ROOM 5 highlights a particularly fascinating neo-Byzantine trend fostered by artists who worked in the Terra di Bari during the 16C, many of whom came to the area from the Eastern Mediterranean after the fall of Constantinople. The works include a Madonna and Saints by Donato Bizamano, showing a mixture of Oriental and Venetian elements, a fine panel with miniatures of the lives of Christ and the Virgin by Giovanni Maria Scupula; and a polyptych by an anonymous Eastern Adriatic artist known by the initials ZT. The other great 16C trend, Mannerism, is represented by Marco Pino (Holy Trinity).

The Venetian School returns in ROOM 6 with three outstanding paintings executed for the cathedral of Bari: ***Sacra Conversazione** by Paris Bordone, ***Virgin in Glory with Saints** by Paolo Veronese and a ***St Roch** by Jacopo Tintoretto, completed after the artist's death by Palma the Younger and Leonardo Corona. The Ascension of Christ by Garofalo, also displayed in this room, has been removed for restoration (1995).

The next group of rooms (ROOMS 7–9) is devoted to 17C painting by Neapolitan artists and local painters trained in Naples, which eventually replaced Venice as the leading point of reference for the cultural élite of Apulia. Conventional painters working in the tradition of Domenichino, for whom local patrons expressed a preference, and the more radical 'caravaggeschi' (Andrea Vaccaro, Matteo Stomer) are both represented.

Access to the Baroque collections is through ROOM 10, a corridor lined with glass cases displaying examples of popular ceramics, and ROOM 11, with a (woodblock) printed tapestry by Petrus Wouthers of Antwerp. ROOM 12 is occupied by two large genre scenes of the early 18C Neapolitan painter Giuseppe Bonito and, in a small showcase, a composition of statuettes (of shepherds) possibly inspired by the paintings.

Theatrically placed to be framed by the marble doorway is (ROOM 13) ***St Peter of Alcantara**, by Luca Giordano, who was Apulian by birth; the original study for the painting is also displayed. In addition, the room contains other works by Giordano (Deposition of Christ, Departure of Rebecca) and by his follower Andrea Miglionico, altarpieces by the local painter Nicola Gliri, and, in a large glass case, an Adoration of the Magi with putti and shepherds from the Caleno Presepioe.

ROOMS 14–15 are devoted to Rococo painting, represented particularly by the Apulian artists Corrado Giaquinto, who worked in Rome, Naples, Madrid, Turin, and Vienna; and Oronzo Tiso, a follower of the Neapolitan master Francesco Solimena.

The tone changes abruptly as you enter ROOM 16, which hosts 19C works of more secular subjects and smaller scale made for middle-class patrons. Here can be seen several paintings by the local artist Francesco Netti (1832–94), as well as works by Telemaco Signorini, the Macchiaiolo; Francesco Galante, of the Posillipo School, and a small Wooded Landscape attributed to Corot. A separate section of the gallery, dedicated to the ***Anna and Luigi Grieco Collection**, provides an outstanding panorama of 19C, and early 20C Italian painting by artists ranging from Giovanni Fattori to Giovanni Boldini, Tranquillo Cremona, Giuseppe De Nittis, Silvestro Lega, Filippo Palizzi, Pellizza da Volpedo, Raffaello Sernesi, Telemaco Signorini, Massimo Campigli, Carlo Carrà, Felice Casorati, Giorgio De Chirico,

Filippo de Pisis, Mario Mafai, Giorgio Morandi, Ottone Rosai, Mario Sironi and Lorenzo Viani.

Returning to the Rotonda, follow Via Imbriani, then Via Dante Alighieri west, turning left in Via Andrea da Bari to reach the Palazzo dell'Universita (or dell'Ateneo), which houses the **Museo Archeologico** (closed for renovation 1995). The **vestibule** contains Roman inscriptions; Tarentine and indigenous antefixes (6-4C BC); large vases recovered from a sunken Roman ship; in cases (left of centre), coins from the Greek colonies at Sybaris, Metapontum, Croton, Laos, Caulonia (6-4C BC); right of centre, coins from Nuceria, Bruttiorum, Petelia, Hippnium, Vibo, Bretii, Paestum and Lucania (3-1C BC); Apulian coins from Arpi, Barium, Ausculum, Butuntum, Azetium, Brundisium, Rubi, Caelia, Canusium, Uria, Graxa, Salapia, Mateola and Venusia, showing the transition from the Tarentine to the Roman type; against the pillar, on the right, Campanian coins from Cumae, Neapolis, Poseidonia, Velia, Thurii and other centres (6-1C BC); at the right of the central window, Tarentine coins from the 6-2C BC; on either side, cases with Byzantine coins; in the case opposite the window, various objects in bone and amber, mainly from Taranto and Canosa.

Turn left to enter the **Corridoio delle Terracotte Figurate**; against the corner pier, terracotta statue of a woman in prayer, from Canosa (3C BC) in glass cases, bronze objects fibulae, of the 7–5C; Apulian vases of various types and provenance; classical and Hellenistic statuettes in terracotta.

There follows the **Corridoio degli Scavi Recenti**, displaying a sampling of material brought to light in excavations conducted since 1950, mainly sculptural fragments and small vases from Egnatia, proto-Italic ceramic vases from Bitonto, Peucetian vases and bronzes from Monte Sannace (Gioia del Colle) and Apulian material from necropoleis at Bari and Conversano.

Now turn right to the **Corridoio della Ceramica Apula**. This collection is arranged topographically and embraces Attic black figure (5C BC) and red figure (4C BC) vases; indigenous geometric ceramics, including Peucetian ware, bichrome and monochrome vases from Gioia del Colle, and proto-Italic vases from Ceglie del Campo; a bronze Apollo of Greek workmanship, also from Ceglie; a krater decorated by the Amykos painter, from Ruvo, and geometric and red figure vases from Canosa. Particularly noteworthy for their beauty and rarity are 2736, Gnathian pelike (4C BC); 1627, Messapian trozzella with deer-hunting scene; and (no number) a large Apulian krater with battle and theatrical scenes.

Retrace your steps to the beginning of the corridor and enter ROOM 1, **Sala dei Bronzi**. Beginning on the entrance wall: bronze objects of various date and provenance; armour, spear heads, Corinthian helmets; bronze humeral, preserving original gilt (6C BC); *complete suit of armour of an Apulian warrior, from Canosa. The glass cases at the centre of the room contain glass and alabaster ware; jewellery in bronze, gold, coral and precious stones; bronze mirrors. ROOM 2, **Salone**: material from private collections, arranged by type; note particularly Case 12, Gnathian ware, and (at the centre of the room) bronze armour of Corinthian workmanship, including a fine embossed belt bearing a representative of a chariot race. ROOM 3, **Sala di Canosa**: material from the tombs at Canosa, including vases with characteristic sculptural decoration (more of these are in ROOM 2).

Return to the **Corridoio della Ceramica Apula** and follow it to its end, then turn right to the **Corridoio della Preistoria**, containing Protoapennine (early 2nd millennium BC) and Apennine ceramics (18–17C BC), bronze and ceramics from Bari, Monte Sannace, Andria and Bisceglie and neolithic material from Molfetta. From here return to the vestibule.

The Facoltà di Agraria (via Amendola) has a modest Orto Botanico that is shown on request (open by appointment; tel. 080 242152); and the Museo Etnografico Africa Mozambico (Convento Cappuccini, via Gen. Beltomo 9, at Poggiofranco; open by appointment, tel. 080 5510037), houses a small but interesting collection of ethnographical material from East Africa.

12 · Campobasso to L'Aquila and Ascoli Piceno

This is perhaps the most spectacular nature itinerary in south-central Italy. It winds its way northward through the wooded mountains and fertile valleys of Molise and Abruzzo, through wild countryside and past medieval castles and villages that economic development have not yet had time to spoil. The road from L'Aquila to Teramo, in particular, affords unequalled views over the **Gran Sasso d'Italia** *and the Vomano valley.* **Roccaraso**, **Sulmona**, **Popoli**, *and* **Campli** *are fine old cities that amply repay a stroll and* **L'Aquila**, **Teramo** *and* **Ascoli Piceno** *remain pleasant places despite being bustling provincial capitals.*

The trip requires about 4hrs 30min. The driving may be difficult in winter because of snow. An alternative route passes through the newly opened Gran Sasso Tunnel. Walkers have excellent chances of encountering the small wolves and brown bear native to the region, as well as the abundant deer and chamois.

ROAD 288km. Highways 87 and 17 from Campobasso to L'Aquila, then Highway 17, Autostrada A24, and local roads to Teramo and Highway 81 and local roads to Ascoli Piceno.—51k—Isernia—39km Roccaraso—34km Sulmona—17km Popoli.—49km L'Aquila—60km Teramo—10km Campli—28km Ascoli Piceno.

RAILWAY from Campobasso to Isernia, 59km in c 1hr (a change is necessary for Sulmona, and may be made at 48km Carpinone, saving 11km and 15min each way). From Isernia to Sulmona, 129km in 2–3 hr. Sulmona to L'Aquila, 60km in 1hr–1hr 15min.

HOTELS EN ROUTE: Assergi, **Campo Imperatore(2130m, at the foot of the Gran Sasso), tel. 0862 411289, fax 0862 413201. Youth Hostel at Pescocostanzo, Via Roma 23; tel. 0864 641247.

RESTAURANTS EN ROUTE: Cantalupo del Sannio, *Del Riccio, tel. 0865 814246; L'Aquila: ***Tre Marie, Via Tre Marie 3, tel. 0862 413191; Teramo, **Duomo, Via Stazio 9, tel. 0861 241774, fax 0861 241774; **Moderno, Coste Sant'Agostino, tel. 0861 414559; Civitella del Tronto, **Zunica (with rooms), tel./fax 0861 91319.

Through Western Molise

Campobasso, Route 15. Beyond the city the road twists, climbing and then descending to (16km) Vinchiaturo, an attractive little town (51,000 inhab.) rebuilt after the earthquake of 1805. A road to the east leads through splendid landscape to (16km) **Cercemaggiore**. Above the town, near the summit of Monte Saraceno (1086m) are the walls of a Samnite village intermixed with the ruins of medieval fortifications. The view from the summit spans vast areas of Molise, Campania and Apulia.

Continue south; on the left rise the **Monti del Matese**. The group constitutes one of the more beautiful and unspoilt areas of Southern Italy, a large, high massif extending crescent-like between the Volturno on the north, the Calore on the south, the Tammaro on the east and the Biferno on the north-east. On the south or Campanian side, it rises like a steep wall, whereas the north slopes ascend more gradually. The central region, which contains highland plains at altitudes of 1400–1900m, culminates in the triple peaks of Colle Tamburo (1982m), Monte Gallinola (1923m) and Monte Miletto (2050m). The latter is the *Tifernus Mons* of Livy and the site of the last Samnite struggle against the Romans.

The valleys and gorges of the interior are largely calcareous, and the porosity of the rock permits the absorption of large quantities of water, giving rise to numerous springs at various altitudes and, on the south side, to the large Lago del Matese. The smaller lakes of Gallo and Latino are man-made. The Matese is covered by vast forests, chiefly of beech-trees, with lesser numbers of oaks, maples, ashes, spruces, chestnuts, walnuts, hazel-trees, hornbeams, etc.; and by pastures.

The native fauna include wild pigs, roe-deer (rare), wolves, foxes, badgers, wild-cats, hares, weasels, martens and squirrels. Eagles nest on the Miletto and Gallinola as well as in the Tre Finestre district. Moorhens, ducks, lapwings, woodcocks and snipe inhabit the areas along the lakes and streams, and trout abound. The more isolated villages preserve traditional customs and dress. Campitello, Boiano and San Massimo in Molise, and Piedimonte Matese, San Gregorio and Letino in Campania, are the best starting-points for excursions and climbs. San Gregorio and Campitello are year-round resorts.

The road is joined by the expressway from Termoli; a few metres further, bear right towards Isernia.

Over the Matese to Naples

A scenic route to Naples, which virtually bisects the Matese, zigzags up the north slopes of the massif via Guardiaregia (732m) to the Sella del Perrone (1257m), on the watershed, the administrative boundary between Molise and Campania. From here it descends, in view of the Lago del Matese, to (30km) San Gregorio Matese. Another steep descent leads to (11km) **Piedimonte Matese** (138m), a summer resort with two interesting baroque churches. 5km Alife preserves a rectangle of Roman walls in a fairly good state. Beyond you join a road (Highway 372) that runs up the Volturno valley from Telese to Venafro, and proceed to Naples.

Carry on to the north-west. 2km a turning on the left mounts to (4km) **Campochiaro**, a medieval village with walls and an Angevin keep. Excavations have brought to light nearby an Italic sanctuary of the 2C BC, incorporating the largest known Samnite temple after that of Pietrabbondante (described below). Evidence of earlier buildings, dating from the 4–3C BC, has also been found.

Beyond the turning, the highway runs between tall poplars. 5km **Boiano** (482m, 8000 inhab.), a chilly place, is the ancient *Bovianum*, one of the main centres of the Samnites and the meeting place of the Italic chiefs during the last phase of the Social War, before the capital was moved to Isernia. The upper town preserves some megalithic walls and remains of a castle.

The ascent of Monte La Gallinola

From Boiano you may ascend Monte La Gallinola (1923m) in c 2hr. A road mounts to the Rifugio Sant'Egidio, from where a steep trail, later a footpath, climbs through the forest to the Costa Alta, a pass 1680m high (***view**). The way crosses ski slopes at Sogli di Boiano, to the base of Monte la Gallinola. A narrow path climbs to the summit. The ****view** is extraordinary, embracing the entire peninsula from the Gulf of Naples to the Adriatic, with the Lago del Matese directly below. You may also climb Monte Miletto in c 3hr, from Sogli di Boiano.

The road runs parallel to the railway. 4km a turning on the left climbs to San Massimo (3km) and Campitello Matese (14km). The latter, a winter sports centre (1417m), has a refuge maintained year-round by the EPT in Campobasso. The ascent of Monte Miletto (2050m) takes roughly 1hr.

Continue north-west. 5km Cantalupo del Sannio rises above the road on the left. Further on, Pesche, on the right, has medieval walls with cylindrical bastions; and Carpinone has a handsome castle of the Caldora family. Beyond, the road meets Highway 85.

18km **Isernia** (423m, 22,000 inhab.) is the Samnite *Aesernium*, headquarters of the Italics after the fall of Corfinium. Though a provincial capital, it is a modest town with one main street. It is well known for its onions and lace.

■ **Information**: EPT, Via Farinacci 1; tel. 0865 3992.

The Romanesque Fontana Fraterna was damaged in the Second World War. Bomb damage to the church of **Santa Maria delle Monarche** exposed a 14C fresco of the Last Judgement which was covered with 18C plaster. The church complex now houses a museum documenting prehistoric settlements in the area (**Museo Archeologico Sannitico Romano**; open daily 09.00–13.00, 15.00–19.00). The tower of the cathedral (rebuilt after the earthquake of 1805) stands on a medieval archway. One of the Roman bridges is partially intact. Recent excavations nearby have revealed some monumental tombs.

From Isernia to Venafro

From Isernia Highway 85 turns south-west past Macchia d'Isernia and Monteroduni, both with fine castles, to (16km) Ponte a Venticinque Archi, by which you cross the Volturno. A road runs north up the Volturno valley to Alfedena (40km, Route 12). 9km **Venafro** (222m), with its cyclopean walls and the remains of an amphitheatre, is the ancient *Venafrum*, praised by Horace for its olive oil. The 18C **Chiesa del Purgatorio** contains a Madonna and Child with saints by Fedele Fischetti. In the adjacent Piazza Cimorelli is the 15C Palazzo Caracciolo, a fortified residence built by Maria di Durazzo, who also enlarged the castle. Beneath the baroque veneer of the church of the **Annunziata** is a Romanesque building of 1387. Within, the second south altar incorporates seven English alabasters dating from the 15C and representing scenes from the Passion. The former convent of Santa Chiara houses the **Museo Nazionale** (closed for restoration 1995), containing inscriptions, statues, architectural fragments and miscellaneous objects relating the Roman colony of Venafrum. On the south-west edge of the town is the 15C **Cattedrale**; in a transitional Romanesque-Gothic style, it is a conglomerate of several churches, the oldest of which dates from the 5C. Recent excavations have revealed remains of a Roman theatre on Monte Croce, near the ancient walls. Highway 85 continues from Venafro to Capua (Route 1A) and Naples.

Beyond Isernia the road climbs north-west, then descends to cross the Vandra valley. At (14km) Forlì del Sannio Bivio (770m) Highway 86 branches right and runs generally north-east to (138km) Vasto, on the Adriatic (Route 11). On this road are (26km) Carovilli and (28km) Agnone, where the cathedral has a good Romanesque portal. Midway between the two towns a turning on the right leads to (16km) *Pietrabbondante, near which lie the ruins of a religious sanctuary of Samnite construction (open 09.00–1hr before sunset), the largest yet discovered, consisting of two temples and a theatre, and dating from the 2C BC. Beyond Agnone the road passes (16km) Castiglione Messer Marino, 10km south of which is Schiavi, where St Anselm retired in 1098 after his attendances at the conclave of Bari. Here you can see two Italic temples of the 3C and 2C BC.

North into Abruzzo
Highway 17 continues to climb. 6km Rionero Sannitico a turning leads south to Cerro al Volturno (10km), with a ruined castle in an imposing position above the town. The nearby Badia di San Vincenzo, a Benedictine abbey dating from the 8C, possesses a small *crypt containing frescoes of the life of Christ and martyrdom of Sts Lawrence and Stephen, the only surviving examples of the 9C Benedictine school. In the hills to the west lies the beautiful lake of Castel San Vincenzo.

From Rionero Sannitico there is a descent to (6km) Ponte Zittola. From here, Highway 83 runs west to Alfedena (6km), on the Sangro, with a 15C church. On the opposite side of the river are the cyclopean walls of the Samnite town of *Aufidena* and, beyond the station, the Madonna del Campo, with frescoes by Cola dell'Amatrice. Beyond the Vallico de Barrea, a pass 1164m high, lies the Abruzzo National Park.

THE ABRUZZO NATIONAL PARK
The *Parco Nazionale dell'Abruzzo, the second of Italy's national parks, was established in 1923 and enlarged in 1925 and 1976. It now occupies an area of 400sq km in one of the wilder and more spectacularly beautiful zones of the Apennines. Its grassy valleys, vast beechwoods and alpine meadows compare favourably with those of the Alps or the Pyrennees. Its rare wildlife, which includes the Abruzzo brown bear (*Ursus arctos marsicanus Altobelli*), the highest concentration of wolves in Italy and a sub-species of the chamois (about 500 of which inhabit the so-called Camosciara between Monte Amaro and the Meta Massif) is known to naturalists throughout the world.

Within the park lie the sources and upper valleys of the Sangro, Giovenco and Melfa. The east boundary is formed by the Montagna Grande range, the south and south–west boundary by the watershed between the Sangro and the Liri, which also includes the highest peak of the park, Monte Petroso (2247m).

A threat to the natural environment was posed in the early 1960s by private speculation; but this trend has recently been brought to a halt, largely due to the awakening of public opinion, in which a leading role was played in Italy and throughout the world by the World Wide Fund for Nature. Hunting, fishing, and the gathering of native flora are forbidden; and special hunting regulations are enforced in a wide area around the park. The park is a refuge for golden eagles, wrynecks, firecrests, Sardinian warblers, blue rock thrushes, middle spotted, great spotted and white-backed woodpeckers, alpine choughs, snow finches and the most southerly breeding population of dotterel in Europe. Among the small predators present may be counted wild cats, foxes, otters, badgers and pine martens. There are numerous red squirrels and a significant number of wild pigs.The park is also rich in wild flowers and butter-flies.

At (25km) **Pescasseroli** (the birthplace of Benedetto Croce, 1866–1952) is a Park Visitors' Centre with an excellent small **Museo e Area Faunistica** (open daily 10.00–12.00, 15.00–19.00). Maps and camping permits may be acquired at the Ufficio di Zona, viale Santa Maria; information is available from the AA, Via Piave (tel. 0863 910461). Other park-related museums and wildlife areas may be seen at *Civitella Alfedena (Museo del Lupo Appenninico e area Faunistica*, Centro di Visita del Parco d'Abruzzo, open daily 09.00–12.00, 15.00–19.00); *Opi (Museo del Camoscio e Area Faunistica*, Centro di Visita del Parco d'Abruzzo, open 09.00–12.00, 15.00–19.00); and *Villavallelonga (Museo del Cervo e Area Faunistica*, Centro di Visita d'Abruzzo, open daily 09.00–12.00, 15.00–19.00).

4km **Castel di Sangro** (793m) is a picturesque town of 5000 inhabitants situated partly on a hill and partly on level ground, at the confluence of the Sangro and the Zittola. A developing resort, it is also known for its traditional ironworking, woodworking and woollen industries. The town was reduced to ruins during the Second World War and has been largely rebuilt. In the central Piazza del Plebiscito stands the modern Palazzo del Municipio, in the left flank of which is the entrance to the **Biblioteca Civica** (open Mon–Fri 08.00–14.00, 15.00–20.00; Sat 08.00–14.00), which contains, at the bottom of the stairs, two headless Roman statues and, in the rooms above, architectural fragments and a collection of antique bronzes unearthed along the river Zittola in 1957. Also in the square is the church of the Annunziata (or San Domenico), originally of the 15C and rebuilt after the Second World War, opposite which steps ascend to the upper town. Here the two-towered church of **Santa Maria Assunta**, rebuilt in 1695–1727 over an earlier edifice, escaped the war with minor injuries. The Baroque façade incorporates modern statues. At the far end of the portico on the right there is a 14C Pietà in a Gothic aedicule. The interior, entered from the sides, is built to a Greek cross plan with four small domes in the arms and a large dome at the crossing. In the south arm are a Madonna and Child with Saints by Paolo De Matteis, and Adoration of the Shepherds and Disputa by Domenico Antonio Vaccaro. Behind the marble high altar (1738), Last Supper by De Matteis, Ecce Homo and Christ on Calvary by Francesco De Mura. In the north arm are a painted wooden altar frontal of the 16C and minor paintings.

Several medieval and Renaissance houses can be seen in the upper town. A mule track mounts through pine woods to the ruined castle, near which are traces of cyclopean walls.

The road continues to climb. 9km **Roccaraso** (1236m) is a pleasant summer resort and winter sports centre, connnected by rail with Sulmona. It has a ruined castle.

■ **Information.** AA, Viale Roma 60; tel./fax 0864 62210.

About 2km beyond Roccaraso there is a road-fork where Highway 17 bears left (north-west) and Highway 84 right, beyond which the descent becomes very steep, with many acute bends. Just before (23km) Pettorano sul Gizio the road crosses the railway and the descent is easier.

From Roccaraso to Lanciano

At (2km) the road-fork (see above) turns into *Highway 84. The magnificent views afforded by this road on its descent have won for it the name of Ringhiera dell'Abruzzo (Balcony of Abruzzo). To the left of the fork lies Rivisondoli (1320m), a summer and winter resort. 3km Turning for (2km left) **Pescocostanzo** (1395m). The little town, once famous for its lace and other peasant arts, with its characteristic deep eaves and porches, is also frequented for holidays, in winter and summer. The church of **Santa Maria del Colle**, a remarkable work of the 16C, 17C and 18C, has elaborately carved wood detailing. Particularly noteworthy are the ceiling of the nave and the high altar, the latter incorporating, in a central niche, an 11C Madonna and Child, the so-called Madonna del Colle. In Rivisondoli the AA operates an information office in Via Patini (tel. 0864 69351); that of Pescocostanzo has an office in Piazza Umberto I (tel. 0864 641440). A station on the Sulmona railway serves both resorts.

6km Palena station (1270m) lies in the grassy hill-girt plain called Quarto di Santa Chiara, where the railway bears off into the hills on the left. 10km Palena village (767m). Beyond (9km) Lama dei Peligni (669m) the road spirals down towards the Sangro valley. About 8km beyond (18km) Casoli Highway 84 makes a right-angled turn at a fork; the road to the right leads to Torino di Sangro, whereas the present road, further on, crosses the Sangro. 31km **Lanciano**, see Route 11. Lanciano may also be reached by road (96km) and railway (2hr 45min) from Castel di Sangro via Bomba, Route 11.

SULMONA AND ENVIRONS

9km Sulmona (405m) is a pleasant town of 25,000 inhabitants delightfully situated in a ring of mountains, on a ridge between two small streams. Its many attractive old houses, medieval or later, give it a charming air of antiquity.

History

The *Sulmo* of the Paeligni, this was the birthplace of the poet Ovid (P. Ovidius Naso, 43 BC–AD 17) and of Innocent VII (Cosimo de' Migliorati, 1339–1406), collector of Peter's Pence in England in 1376–86. Emperor Frederick II made Sulmona the capital of an independent province. It was bestowed by Charles V as a principality upon Charles de Lannoy (1487–1527), viceroy of Naples, to whom Francis I surrendered at Pavia. In the 14C and 15C, the goldsmiths of Sulmona were famous. Today Sulmona is renowned for its sweets and liqueurs.

■ **Information**: AA, Via Roma 21; tel./fax 0864 53276.

The **Duomo** (San Panfilo), at the north end of the town, is built on the ruins of a Roman temple and has a Gothic portal and an 11C crypt. Cross the Villa Comunale to enter Corso Ovidio, the main street of the town, and proceed to (right) Via Ciofano, where the 15C **Palazzo Tabassi** (No. 44) has a fine Gothic window. In the corso are the church and palazzo of the *Annunziata, founded in 1320 and showing a happy combination of Gothic and Renaissance elements. The left portal is surmounted by a richly carved Gothic arch embracing statues of St Michael and, in the lunette, the Madonna and Child, originally gilded, painted and set against a fresco background. Inscribed in the architrave is the date 1415. The monumental central portal recalls the Tuscan Renaissance style. It dates from 1483, as does the central portion of the façade. The smaller right portal is somewhat later. Along the base of the façade, on tall plinths, are statues of the doctors of the Church (Saints Gregory the Great, Jerome, Ambrose and Augustine); St Pamphilus, titular of the cathedral; and the Apostles Peter and Paul. Above, a delicately carved frieze runs the length of the façade, forming the base of the ornamental windows, which offer the same interesting contrast of styles as the portals below. On the first floor is a museum of local antiquities and paintings (open daily 10.00–12.30, 17.00–19.30), including the church treasury, with interesting examples of goldsmith's work. The church, rebuilt after an earthquake in 1706, preserves a campanile of 1565–90.

In the nearby Piazza XX Settembre is a 20C statue of Ovid. Further on, opposite a fountain of 1474, is a rich Romanesque portal leading to the presbytery of the church of San Francesco della Scarpa. Here terminates the aqueduct that powered local industries during the Middle Ages. Behind this lies the broad Piazza Garibaldi, containing the church of San Filippo Neri, at the far end. Still further is Santa Maria della Tomba, mainly of the 15C and 16C.

> About 6km north is the abbey of **Santo Spirito**, or Badia Morronese, founded in the 13C by Pietro Angeleri, afterwards St Celestine V, who dwelt in a hermitage high upon the Montagna del Morrone. The convent (dating from the 17C and 18C, with a fine chapel of the original foundation) and hermitage can be visited by appointment with the tourist board in Sulmona (tel. 0864 53276). On the way to the hermitage are the remains of a Temple of Hercules, called the Villa of Ovid.

From Sulmona to Scanno

Leave Sulmona by the imposing 14C Porta Napoli and cross the Gizio River. Near (11km) Anversa-Scanno station the road passes beneath a lofty railway viaduct. At (5km) **Anversa degli Abruzzi** (660m) the church of the Madonna delle Grazie in the piazza has a doorway dated 1540 and a painting of Sts Michael and Francis, of the 15C Sulmona school, in the sacristy. San Marcello has a Gothic portal. The road beyond Anversa threads through the deep, narrow gorge known as the *Gola del Sagittario**. 12km Lago di Scanno, c 2km long, is stocked with trout.

5km **Scanno** (1015m), an ancient little town in a striking situation, is popular for summer holidays. The peasant women still wear their handsome local costume. The peasant New Year, 11 November, is celebrated by igniting immense bonfires (the *Glorie di San Martino*) in the hills around the town. The AA operates an information office at Piazza Santa Maria della Valle 12 (tel. 0864 74317, fax 0864 747121). The road goes on over the watershed to (17km south) Villetta Barrea, 6km west of Alfredena.

The road crosses the undulating upland plain of Sulmona, the 'fresh land of copious springs' of Ovid's lament for his homeland. Its characteristic growth of poplars is encouraged by its many streams.

9km Pratola Peligna lies to the left. Just beyond, on the right, is Roccacasale, crowned by a castle finely placed against the flanks of the Cunza, a barren peak of the Montagna del Morrone, which rises to a height of 2061m. From the road junction near Corfinio station to (8km) Popoli, the road coincides with Highway 5 (town and road in Route 14). Bear left and cross the railway and the Autostrada just short of Popoli station, from where Highway 17 begins an immediate, steep and winding ascent, called the Strada delle Svolte, reaching a height of 746m. From Navelli (760m) a byroad descends on the right for **Capestrano** (8km), the birthplace of St John Capistran (1386–1456). The fine 15C castello, built by the Piccolomini, dates from the 15C, as does the nearby Convento di San Giovanni.

From here a new road descends to Bussi, passing near (right) the ruined abbey of Santa Maria di Cartignano and (left) the lonely Romanesque church of **San Pietro ad Oratorium**, with 12C frescoes and 13C sculptures. Another road crosses the hills to Penne (59km, Route 11) via the Forca di Penne (918m), a pass marking the south–east limit of the Gran Sasso range.

THE FRESCOED CHURCHES OF BOMINACO

To the left of the road, beyond Navelli, a turning ascends to **Bominaco** (3km), where two remarkable *churches, relics of a fortified monastery, have been preserved. The lower church (San Pelegrino) was rebuilt in 1263 and has a small porch with three rounded arches. The rectangular interior is covered by a pointed barrel-vault divided into four bays by transverse arches and reflects on a humble scale the Burgundian Gothic style introduced to Southern Italy with the abbey of Fossanova (Route 1B). The walls and ceiling are completely decorated with murals of the period, of which the most extraordinary are those above the cornice, which form a cycle representing the Calendar of the Diocese of Valva, with the months, the signs of the Zodiac and feast days. Two stone plutei, carved with a dragon (left) and a griffin (right), and originally painted, separate the nave from the sanctuary. Hidden on the north side of the altar is a small hole through which, according to tradition, you can hear the heartbeat of the saint, buried below. The upper church (Santa Maria Assunta) is a splendid example of 12C architecture (note in particular the sculptural decoration of doors, apse, capitals, etc.). It contains a contemporary pulpit, signed and dated 1180, and paschal candlestick.

Onwards to Teramo

From (15km) Barisciano (891m) a road on the right ascends to Forca di Penne (44km, see above), whereas at (8km) San Gregorio (586m) the highway is joined on the left by the road from Molina. From (4km) Bazzano a road leads north to Paganica (3km) affording an approach to Assergi and the Gran Sasso. Just beyond, lies L'Aquila, Route 13.

On the outskirts of L'Aquila Highway 17 feeds into Autostrada A24. This goes on to Assergi, then passes immediately below the main peaks of the Gran Sasso in a tunnel, descending towards (60km) Teramo by the Mavone valley.

To Teramo

An alternative route from L'Aquila to Teramo, 10km longer but incomparably more beautiful, climbs over the Gran Sasso d'Italia (Route 13) by the Passo delle Capanelle (1299m). Highway 80 branches to the right of Highway 17 just west of L'Aquila and at first ascends the valley of the Aterno. 8km **San Vittorino**, a 12C village on a hill, is reached by a turning on the right. Beneath the Romanesque church of San Michele (1170, rebuilt 1528), can be seen the **Catacomba di San Vittorino**, with walls in *opus reticulatum* and *opus incertum*, 14C and 15C frescoes and the presumed tomb of the saint. The church, which is broken into two parts by a dividing wall, contains 13C frescoes and reliefs.

Near (2km) Ponte Cermone are the ruins of *Amiternum*, comprising a theatre, an amphitheatre, and the remains of a building with frescoes and mosaics, excavated in 1978. This ancient Sabine town was the birthplace of Sallust. 4km Arischia, you begin to ascend the north-west flank of the Gran Sasso. 8km Taverna della Croce (1270m) marks the beginning of a saddle preceding the road's summit-level at (4km) the Passo delle Capannelle, the west–north-west limit of the Gran Sasso range. 4km beyond, a secondary road left to the lovely **Lago di Campotosto* (3km), an artificial lake 64km round taking its name from the village of Campotosto, on the north shore. The fishing in the lake is excellent.

Beyond (5km) La Provvidenza (1100m), a starting-point for the ascent of the Gran Sasso, the descent of the narrow, picturesque valley of the Vomano begins. At 19km a by-road climbs south to Pietracamela (1005m), passing the village of **Fano Adriano** (745m), where the 12C church of San Pietro has a simple, characteristic façade of 1550. Monte Corvo and other peaks of the Gran Sasso appear on the right. 8km **Montorio al Vomano** is dominated by its ruined castle. In the main square stands the church of San Rocco, with a curious composite façade, added piecemeal over the centuries. About 16km south, on a byroad, is Isola del Gran Sasso (415m), one of the approaches to the Gran Sasso. 10km to the south-east is Castelli, another approach to the mountains.

From Montorio the road climbs out again, then descends, in view of the Monti della Laga, to (14km) Teramo.

Teramo (265m, 52,000 inhab.), the modern-looking capital of the province of the same name, is situated between the Tordino and the Vezzola rivers. It was the ancient *Interamnia Praetuttiorum*, which became a Roman city in 268 BC. Under the Angevin dukes of Apulia it flourished in the 14C; but later, distracted by feuds between the Melatini and the Antonelli, it became part of the Kingdom of Naples.

■ **Information.** EPT, Via del Castello 10, 0861 244222, fax 0861 244357.

■ **Airport.** At Pescara, 66km south-east, with daily service to Ancona and Milano.

■ **Railway station.** Viale Crispi.

■ **Post office.** Via Pannella.

■ **Special events.** San Berardo (19 Dec); Giugno Teramano (theatre, opera, folklore and cuisine; Jun); Stagione Lirica e del Balletto (Nov–Dec); Mostra–Mercato dell'Agricoltura (May).

The **Cattedrale*, at the centre of the town, has a good campanile and a singular Romanesque-Gothic **portal** incorporating mosaic decoration, a rose window, and statues of Sts Bernard and John the Baptist, and Christ Blessing. In the architrave is the date 1332. On either side of the door are statues of the Archangel Gabriel and the Virgin Annunciate, by Nicola da Guardiagrele, on columns borne by lions; several other lions scattered about the façade probably belonged to the porches of the lateral doorways, now destroyed.

The austere **interior** was begun in the 13C and extended in the following century. The two parts meet at a slight angle, with steps separating the earlier church from the Gothic addition. The high altar is faced with a fine silver frontal by Nicola da Guardiagrele (1433–48), with 34 relief panels depicting New Testament scenes, apostles and saints. On the south wall of the presbytery is a notable polyptych by Jacobello del Fiore, formerly in the church of Sant'Agostino; and in the south transept, a fine, 13C wooden Madonna in a marble tabernacle. The church incorporates numerous antique architectural fragments and part of the wooden ceiling of the original building. Above the arches of the nave are the arms of the churchmen who aided in its reconstruction. The holy-water stoups at the west end of the nave arcade have been recomposed from medieval sculptural fragments.

Near the east end of the town are the **Madonna delle Grazie**, with a 15C wooden *Virgin** attributed to Silvestro dall'Aquila; Sant'Antonio, with a portal of 1309; and the 14C Casa dei Melatini. Remains of the walls of a Roman amphitheatre may be seen in Via San Bernardo, on the left side of the cathedral, and in Via Vincenzo Irelli, which branches south to the recently excavated Roman theatre. In the Villa Comunale is the **Pinacoteca Civica** (open Mon–Sat 9.30–13.30), containing works by local artists of the 15C and by 17C and 18C Roman and Neapolitan artists.

> Giulianova can be reached from Teramo in 40 min. The route descends the valley of the Tordino to the Adriatic, where it joins Route 11.

Leave Teramo by Viale Bovio and cross the Vezzola, then climb among the hills to the north. At 8km Campli Bivio is a turning for the little town of **Campli** (2km, 393m), where a museum in the former convent of **San Francesco** (open daily, 08.30–13.30, 15.30–19.30) houses material from an Italic necropolis discovered at Campovalano, nearby. Excavation of the site, which began in 1967, has revealed more than 200 pit tombs dating from the 7–5C BC. The church, a Romanesque edifice of the early 14C, has a fine portal and simple but elegant decorative details. Within are a 14C crucifix, 15C frescoes, and a panel depicting St Anthony of Padua by Cola dell'Amatrice (1510).

The **Palazzo del Comune**, erected in the 14C, was rebuilt in 1520 and restored in 1888. It has a portico on heavy piers and mullioned windows. The little church of **San Giovanni** also dates from the 14C and contains a 14C wooden crucifix and 15C frescoes, as well as two 16C wooden altars. Just beyond is the Porta Orientale, part of the medieval walls. From the centre of the town a dirt track leads to (c 1km) the church of **San Pietro**, founded together with the adjacent ruined Benedictine convent in the 8C and rebuilt at the beginning of the 13C. The three-aisled interior, restored 1960–68, has votive frescoes on the piers and, on the north wall, a panel, from an early Christian sarcophagus, with bas-reliefs of biblical scenes.

Continue north through mountainous country. At 6km a turning on the right mounts to **Civitella del Tronto**, a town in a magnificent position on a hillside below its ruined castle, which was almost the last stronghold of the Bourbons to yield to the Italian troops (1861). It also resisted Guise's attack in 1557 after he had taken Campli in his campaign against Alva's Spaniards. Civitella is interesting for its Renaissance mansions.

Descend, with good views back to Civitella, and cross the Salinello by a tall bridge; a road diverges left to Ripe (627m), near which have been found caves inhabited from the Upper Palaeolothic to the Bronze Age. Beyond (5km) Lempa you enter the Marches and a long, winding descent begins. The road passes beneath the expressway linking Ascoli Piceno and San Benedetto del Tronto, then turns west, followed by the railway, to (17km) Ascoli Piceno, a handsome town with an extraordinary main square, described in *Blue Guide Northern Italy*.

13 · L'Aquila and the Gran Sasso d'Italia

L'Aquila *is a regional capital in a setting of great natural beauty. Its air of detached serenity is still largely unspoilt, notwithstanding Baroque and neo-Classical attempts to redesign the city and the modern building that has invaded the surrounding countryside. In the city and its environs may be seen some of the finest churches in Abruzzan, notably* **Santa Maria di Collemaggio**, *the highest achievement of Abruzzo religious architecture. The 16C castle houses a truly outstanding collection of* **polychrome wood statues** *removed for safekeeping from these churches, many of which are in a state of partial or total abandon. Above the city rises the* **Gran Sasso d'Italia**, *which is largely responsible for L'Aquila's chilly climate. The peaks of this chain are the highest in the Apennines, rising to 2912m at the Corno Grande. The area has recently become a national park and certainly repays a visit. Wild horses roam the grasslands of the Campo Imperatore plateau. The Gran Sasso is icy in spring or autumn, and can be cool even in mid summer.*

The approach to L'Aquila may be made from Rome by Autostrada A24. This goes on to Assergi, then it passes immediately below the main peaks of the Gran Sasso in a tunnel, descending towards Teramo by the Mavone valley. An alternative approach may be made by the Via Salaria to Antrodoco (see Blue Guide Northern Italy) from where Highway 17 (here called the Via Sabina) runs across the Apennines to L'Aquila. This route is followed by a secondary railway linking L'Aquila to the Rome-Ancona trunk line (Rome to L'Aquila in c 3hr, with a change of trains at Terni). The road from Antrodoco to L'Aquila is described in reverse order below.

HOTELS EN ROUTE: *Assergi (2130m, at the foot of the Gran Sasso),* **Campo Imperatore, tel. 0862 411289, fax 0862 413201

RESTAURANTS EN ROUTE: *L'Aquila:* ***Tre Marie, via Tre Marie 3, tel. 0862 413191; Teramo, **Duomo, Via Stazio 9, tel./fax. 0861 241774; **Moderno, Coste Sant'Agostino, tel. 0861 414559.

L'AQUILA

L'Aquila (721m) is the capital (68,000 inhab.) of Abruzzo, as well as of the province that bears its name. Prosperous despite frequent earthquakes, the town is notable for its broad streets and imposing public buildings. There are two seasons for visitors: from June to September and a fortnight at Christmas. The summer climate is delightfully cool. L'Aquila is the main centre from which to ascend the peaks of the Gran Sasso d'Italia (see below).

History

Founded in 1240 by Frederick II as a barrier to the encroachments of the popes, L'Aquila was peopled with the inhabitants of the numerous castles and fortified villages that had grown up in the valley and on the surrounding hills following the destruction of the ancient centres of *Amiternum, Forcona, Foruli* and *Peltuinum*. In 1423 the combined armies of Joan II, Pope Martin V and the Duke of Milan successfully assaulted the town, and Braccio Fortebraccio, the famous condottiere, who held the place for Alfonso of Aragon, was killed. Attendolo, first of the Sforza, was drowned in the Pescara, nearby, in the same action while fighting for the allies.

In later years L'Aquila became, on the strength of its wool trade, one of the chief cities of the Kingdom of Naples, extending its commercial ties to the major centres of north Italy and of Europe. It was at this time that the Franciscan Sts Bernard of Siena, John of Capestran and Giacomo della Marca came to the town, increasing its importance as a centre of religious activity. L'Aquila suffered especially severely from the earthquakes of 1461 and 1703.

- **Information.** EPT, Piazza Santa Maria di Paganica 5; tel. 0862 410808, fax 0862 65442. AA, Via XX Settembre 8; tel. 0862 22306, fax 0862 27486.

- **Railway station.** 2km south-west of the town (bus in 15min).

- **Post office**. Piazza Duomo.

- **Special events**: *Teatro Internazionale dei Burattini* (Jun–Jul), *Rassegna Musica e Architettura* (Jul–Aug); historical-religious pageant of the *Perdonanza Papale* (28–29 Aug).

The main approaches to the town unite at Piazza delle Acacie, where Via XX Settembre comes in from Rome (and the railway station), Viale Francesco Crispi enters from the south-west and Corso Federico II leads north-east to Piazza del Duomo, the town centre and market-place.

Pedestrians coming from the station may turn to the right and go through the town wall by Porta Rivera, inside which is the **Fontana delle Novantanove Cannelle**, a singular fountain with 99 spouts (an allusion to the 99 castles from which the town was formed) in the shape of a courtyard of red and white stone. The water issues from 93 grotesque masks (six of the spouts are unadorned) of human, animal and fantastic figures, each of which differs from the others. Set into the end wall is a tablet inscribed 'Magis. Tangredus de Pontoma de Valva fecit hoc opus' and dated 1272. Tancred's fountain is believed to have included two sides only; the third, that on the left of the entrance, is generally held to have been added in 1582. The complex was restored and the right wall rebuilt in the 18C (as the Baroque character of the masks attests), probably following damage in the earthquake of 1703. Further restorations were carried out in 1871 and 1934.

On the west side of Piazza del Duomo is the **Duomo** (San Massimo), dating from 1257 and rebuilt after 1703. The neo-Classical façade is a work of the 19C; the upper storey, with its twin bell-towers, was added in 1928. The original wooden doors are covered by an awkward bronze composition of 1976. Traces of the 13C church can be seen along the right flank. Within is a monument to Cardinal Amico Agnifili by Silvestro dall'Aquila (1480), reconstructed after the earthquake of

1703. Other fragments may be seen at the left of the door to the sacristy and above the portal in the south flank of the church of San Marciano (see below).

On the south side of the square stands the 18C church of the Suffragio. The church of San Giuseppe, on the right in Via Sassa, contains the Camponeschi tomb (1432) by Gualtiero Alemanno.

> On the immediate right of the cathedral Via Roio leads past Palazzo Dragonetti De Torres and Palazzo Rivera (left) to Palazzo Persichetti, all three 18C mansions. Other fine houses from this and earlier centuries may be seen in the neighbourhood. The churches of Santa Maria di Rio, across the street from Palazzo Persichetti, and San Marciano, behind Palazzo Rivera, have plain Romanesque façades.

From the piazza return along Corso Federico II and take a side street to the right to Piazza San Marco, in which are the churches of **San Marco**, preserving two portals dating respectively from the 14C and 15C, and Sant'Agostino. In the other direction is the church of **Santa Giusta** (1257), the simple façade of which incorporates a Romanesque portal and a splendid rose window adorned with grotesque figures. The uninteresting interior contains, in the first south chapel, a Martyrdom of St Stephen by Cavalier d'Arpino. In the choir are Gothic stalls. Opposite the church is the 18C Palazzo Conti, a sumptuous building with an unusual balcony.

Returning to Corso Federico II, you reach again Piazza delle Acacie (see above), and cross it into Viale Francesco Crispi, which runs alongside the Villa Comunale. Turn left into Viale di Collemaggio, an avenue that leads east to ***Santa Maria di Collemaggio**, a majestic Romanesque church (1287) founded by Pietro dal Morrone (1221–96), who was crowned here as Pope Celestine V in 1294 and canonised as St Peter Celestine in 1313. The façade is a graceful composition of red and white stone, with three doors and three rose windows, of which that in the centre is particularly splendid. The large central portal, embellished with spiral moulding and delicate carvings, is flanked by Gothic niches, some of which retain fragments of statues. The wooden door dates from 1688. Carved surrounds also adorn the lateral portals. The façade is divided horizontally by a prominent frieze, the linear value of which lends emphasis to the flat roof line, a recurrent characteristic of the churches of Abruzzo. The low octagonal tower at the south corner was possibly intended for open-air benedictions. On the north side of the church is a Holy Door, unusual outside Rome.

The impressive **interior** was restored in 1973. The floor is paved with red and white stones in square and diamond patterns. The graceful nave arcade, consisting of broad pointed arches on massive piers, carries a wooden ceiling. In the aisles are 15C frescoes brought to light during the restoration, a 15C terracotta statue of the Madonna and paintings by the 17C artist Charles Ruther. The church also contains the Renaissance tomb (1517) of Celestine V, in a chapel at the right of the apse.

Leaving the church, go back along Viale di Collemaggio for a short distance and then take Strada di Porta Bazzano to the right. This road leads to the Porta Bazzano, from where Via Fortebraccio leads to a flight of steps at the head of which rises ***San Bernardino** (Pl 8), an imposing church of 1454–72 with an elaborate Renaissance façade by Cola dell'Amatrice (1524). The Baroque interior, with a splendid, 18C carved ceiling by Ferdinando Mosca, contains (south aisle, second chapel) a Coronation of the Virgin, Resurrection, and Saints, by Andrea Della Robbia; further on, ***Tomb of San Bernardino** (1505) and (in the apse) ***Monument of Maria Pereira** (1496), two fine works in stone by Silvestro dell'Aquila, the latter showing the influence of Antonio Rossellino. Behind the altar (right) is a huge Crucifixion by Rinaldo Fiammingo.

From the piazza in front of the church, Via San Bernardino leads left to a cross-roads called Quattro Cantoni, a traffic centre of the town. Keep straight on here, across the corso, to Piazza del Palazzo, in which is a statue, by Cesare Zocchi (1903), of the historian Sallust (Sallustius Crispus, 86–34 BC), a native of Amiternum. Dominating the piazza is the Palazzo di Giustizia with its tower, whose bell sounds 99 strokes every day at vespers. It was rebuilt in 1573 for Margaret of Austria, illegitimate daughter of Charles V, wife of both Alessandro de'Medici and Ottavio Farnese, and Governess of the Abruzzi.

On the opposite side of the square is the **Biblioteca Provinciale Salvatore Tommasi**, the most important library in Abruzzo, with over 100,000 volumes including 150 incunabulae, among them two books printed at L'Aquila in 1482. Adjacent is the Convitto Nazionale, in which St Bernard of Siena (1380–1444) died.

Returning to the corso and proceeding north (left) you pass, in the side streets, the churches of **Santa Maria di Paganica** (1308) on the left and Santa Maria del Carmine on the right. Both have 14C façades, the former with a handsomely carved portal. From the end of the corso cross the busy Piazza Battaglione Alpini, with its rhetorical fountain, to the Parco del Castello. The **Castello** (Pl 4), built by Pier Luigi Scriva in 1530, now houses the ***Museo Nazionale d'Abruzzo** (open Mon-Sat 09.00–14.00, Sun 09.00–13.00) and the Auditorium, one of the halls used by the Societa Aquilana dei Concerti. The museum, the finest in east Central Italy, incorporates the collections formerly held by the Museo Civico and the Museo Diocesano d'Arte Sacra, as well as works from ruined churches throughout the region.

You enter through a monumental doorway surmounted by the arms of Charles V and huge horns of plenty carved by Salvato Salvati and Pietro di Stefano and dated 1543. Beyond the entrance hall lies the large, rectangular court; turn right and proceed beneath a vaulted portico to the large, domed room in the southeast bastion, at the centre of which stands a **prehistoric elephant** (*Archidiskodon Meridionalis Vastinus*), partly reconstructed with plaster casts, found at Scoppito. Against the wall are plant fossils in glass cases.

Return to the courtyard and, passing the entrance, turn right to the **Archaeological Section**. Outside the entrance are various architectural fragments of Roman manufacture and a large Roman Hercules from 1C AD. Highlights of the collection include inscriptions; tomb relief from Coppito (Pitinum); stele of Q. Pomponius Proculus, from Scoppito (Foruli); calendar from Amiternum; mile stone of the Via Claudia Nova (Foruli); tympanum with head of Medusa from Preturo; headless lion holding the head of a ram; bas-relief with a funeral procession; ***tympanum** with butcher's tools; tympanum with relief of carpenter's tools; vases in terracotta and impasto, bronze jewellery, painted vases, Etruscan ware in bucchero and clay (6C BC); terracotta votive statues (3–2C BC); and a fine collection of small cups, plates and bowls (1C BC–1C AD).

Also on the ground floor are a group of works donated to the museum in 1993 by the contemporary artist **Emilio Greco**, and the **Sala del Gonfalone**, displaying the banner of the City of L'Aquila, adorned with representations of the Redemption and Annunciation.

Steps ascend to the first floor, where the **Religious Art Section** occupies the corridor and the rooms adjoining. In the corridor are: (left) fresco of Christ with the Virgin and St John (13C) by Armarino da Modena, for an apse; below, stone altar frontal with plant and animal reliefs, and a large Baptism of St Augustine by Mattia Preti; (right) detached frescoes from ruined churches of Abruzzo: Madonna del Latte (14–15C), Madonna and Child, St Sebastian, Madonna in Glory (15C), Byzantine fresco with Saints, Madonna and Child, Archangel, Crucifixion by Francesco da Montereale (15C–16C).

ROOM 1: polychrome wooden crucifix (13C); enthroned Madonna and Child (13C); 12–13C fresco fragments. ROOM 2: panel painting of the Madonna and Child (dated 1262); polychrome Madonna and Child (13C); Byzantine Madonna del Latte (1270–80); panel of the Madonna and Child (signed Gentile da Rocca and dated 1283). ROOM 3: St Balbina; polychrome Madonna and Child (late 14C); wooden statue of St Catherine of Alexandria between panels representing episodes from her life; enthroned Madonna; polychrome wooden statue of ***St Leonard** (late 14C) ROOM 4: more polychrome wooden statues, including a poorly preserved b ut evocative Santa Coronata; in the glass case, gilded silver processional cross (dated 1434 and signed by Nicola da Guardiagrele). ROOM 5: Tree of the Cross (early 15C); triptych (15C); Madonna and Child with Saints, altarpiece by Jacobello del Fiore (15C); St Bernardino of Siena, by Sano di Pietro; ***triptych**, with Madonna and Saints, Nativity, Annunciation to the Shepherds and Transito della Vergine, showing Sienese influence (15C). ROOM 6: ***Madonna and Child**, by Silvestro dell'Aquila (late 15C); minor sculptural works; St Setastian (1478) by Silvestro dell'Aquila; panel paintings of the 15C and 16C; note the painted ceilings in this and the following room. ROOM 7: 15C panel paintings: St John Capestran with episodes from the life of the saint, by the Master of St John Capestran (15C); Stigmatization of St Francis, by the Master of St John Capestran (15C); a poorly preserved terracotta Madonna and Child (16C); at the centre, terracotta Nativity (late 15C). ROOM 8: 15C and 16C stained glass; church furnishings and 16C panel paintings. ROOM 9: assorted paintings by local artists of the 15C, including two paintings by Pietro Alemanno, one of Carlo Crivelli's disciples. ROOM 10: other assorted paintings by local artists of the 15C, including two paintings attributed to Saturnini Gratti.

The recently established **Coin Collection**, also reached from the first-floor loggia, displays over a hundred pieces offering a good sample of Abruzzan numismatics from the 4C BC to the unification of Italy. The **Gold Room**, on the landing between the first and second floors, contains an arrangement of objects (notably processional crosses and shrines) from Sulmona, Teramo, and L'Aquila.

The Religious Art Section continues on the second floor, with works from the 16C up to the 18C, including, in the corridor, several paintings by Carl Ruther, a Benedictine monk of Flemish origin, member of the community of Santa Maria di Collemaggio. The Cappelli collection follows, with works by Neopolitan artists, including Madonna and Child with St Augustine by Fabrizio Santafede; Christ and the Adulteress, Martyrdom of St Bartholomew, Job in the Dung Pile and The Tribute Money by Mattia Preti; Tobias and the Angel, Adoration of the Shepherds and Presentation of Tobias by Bernardo Cavallino; St Agatha, by Andrea Vaccaro; Madonna and Child with Saints and Trinity with Saints, by Francesco De Mura;

Pietà, attributed to Francesco Solimena; Madonna of the Rosary, by Fabrizio Santafede. The following rooms are dedicated to Roman painters of the 17C and 18C, Carl Ruther, minor Flemish painters, Giulio Cesare Bedeschini (16–17C), and to artists native to L'Aquila, chief among whom is Francesco da Montereale.

The **Modern Art Collection** contains works by contemporary painters such as Mino Maccari, Giuseppe Capogrossi, Mario Mafai, Domenico Cantatore, and Giovanni De Santis, as well as numerous minor artists.

The road to the right of the castle leads to (15 min) the Madonna del Soccorso, with a good Renaissance façade (1496) and two early 16C tombs in the style of Silvestro dall'Aquila.

From the end of the corso, Via Garibaldi leads north-west to the 14C church of **San Silvestro**, with an elegant rose window in its simple façade and 15C frescoes in the apse. From here, Via Coppito and Via San Domenico lead to San Domenico, a church dating in part from the 14C, now used as an auditorium. Of the many 18C mansions, perhaps the most interesting is the **Palazzo Benedetti**, in Via Accursio (near Santa Maria Paganica) with its finely proportioned courtyard. The Convento di San Giuliano, just outside the town, houses a small Museo di Scienze Naturali (open 09.00–12.00, 15.30–19.00; Sun and holidays 09.00–12.00 and 16.00–19.00).

From L'Aquila to Amatrice and Poggiovitellino

To (10km) *Ponte Cermone* by Highway 80, see Rte 23. The road, branching from Highway 80, continues up the Aterno valley. 19km Montereale (823m). At (6km) Aringo the road reaches 955m and keeps about this height for several km. You enter Lazio. 16km **Amatrice** (950m) was the birthplace of Niccolo Filotesio (born 1559), known as Cola dell'Amatrice. 3km Poggiovitellino, on the Via Salaria, see *Blue Guide Northern Italy*.

From L'Aquila to Celano and to Molina Aterno, see Route 14.

From L'Aquila to Rieti

From L'Aquila, the railway accompanies Highway 17 to its end at Antrodoco. Both ascend the valley of the Raio, a tributary of the Aterno. The *views of the Gran Sasso and of L'Aquila beyond (10km) Sasso-Tornimparte station (663m) are especially fine. You pass the ruins of the Sabine city of *Foruli* (right) before reaching (6km) Vigliano station. Beyond (4km) the **Sella di Corno** (1005m), the highest point on the road, you cross from Abruzzo into Lazio, and further on begins the descent of the fine ravine called the Gola d'Antrodoco (which the railway circumvents by a series of short tunnels and curved viaducts), offering fine views of the town. 14km Antrodoco, and from there to (24km) Rieti by the Via Salaria, see *Blue Guide Northern Italy*.

THE GRAN SASSO D'ITALIA

The Gran Sasso d'Italia, a predominantly limestone formation, containing the highest mountains in Italy (apart from Etna), is part of the east wall of the Abruzzo mountain group. With an average depth of c 15km, it extends in a west north-west–east south-east direction for c 35km from the Passo delle Capannelle, on Highway 80 from L'Aquila to Teramo (Route 12), to Forca di Penne, on a secondary road from Popoli to Penne (Route 11).

The Gran Sasso comprises two almost parallel chains separated by a central depression interrupted by peaks of its own. The south chain is a uniform rampart extending from Monte San Franco (2132m) in the west to Monte Bolza (1904m) in the east, with the Pizzo Cefalone (2533m) in the centre. The north chain includes the formidable peaks of Monte Corvo (2623m): the Pizzo Intermesoli (2635m), the Corno Piccolo (2655m), the Corno Grande with its three summits, one of them the highest of all (2912m), Monte Brancastello (2385m), Monte Prena (2561m) and Monte Camicia (2570m). Deep valleys extend from this chain to the north: the Venacquaro, between Monte Corvo and the Pizzo Intermesoli; the Valmaone, between the Pizzo Intermesoli and the Corno Grande; the Valle dell'Inferno, between the Corno Grande and Monte Brancastello. To the south are the Passo di Portella (2260m) and the Vado di Corno (1924m).

The ski runs of the Gran Sasso compare favourably with the most famous Alpine runs. Of the shelters, the Duca degli Abruzzi Refuge (2388m) is habitable (key at the Albergo Campo Imperatore); that of Carlo Franchetti (2433m) was built in 1959 (key with Lino d'Angelo at Pietracamela); the old Garibaldi Refuge is derelict.

Much of the central depression consists of the **Campo Imperatore**, a vast tableland (2130m) inhabited by herds of wild horses. It is connected with the road from L'Aquila by aerial ropeway (see below). Other approaches include those from La Provvidenza, on Highway 80 from L'Aquila to Teramo; Pietracamela, at the foot of the Corno Piccolo; Isola del Gran Sasso, below the Corno Grande; and Castelli, below Monte Prena. All these localities are mentioned below.

Ascent of the Gran Sasso

The *Funivia del Gran Sasso d'Italia* (Gran Sasso Aerial Ropeway; operative 08.00–17.00 except in high winds), enables travellers to reach the Campo Imperatore and return to the town in a day. An alternative approach may be made in fair weather by an extension of Highway 17b, which links the upper and lower stations of the ropeway.

The ropeway's lower station is at Fonte Cerreto, above Assergi. The Viale del Gran Sasso d'Italia leads out of L'Aquila, past the castle, to become Highway 17b. Its direction is generally east to (9km) Paganica (660m). An alternative exit from L'Aquila is by the Porta Napoli and Highway 17 to (9km) Bazzano (Route 12) and from there by a secondary road to (3km further) Paganica. From Paganica the road ascends north-east to (7km) Assergi (867m), a tiny village of importance to mountaineers; its church has a Gothic façade and a 12C crypt. Beyond Assergi the road climbs sharply to (4km) Fonte Cerreto (1120m), location of the Stazione Inferiore Funivia.

Autostrada A24 follows roughly the same course to Assergi. Buses from L'Aquila (50–60 min) connect with the ropeway services.

The ropeway climbs several times daily to (3km) Campo Imperatore (2130m) in 30min. Above the terminus is the Albergo di Campo Imperatore. The hotel is at the top of a ski-lift or sciovia, 600m long, which ascends from Le Fontari (1980m) during the winter season (Dec–Apr). It was the scene of the daring German 'rescue' of Mussolini in 12 September 1943. Now it is the usual starting point for itineraries and ascents.

Tunnels link the hotel to the little church of the Madonna della Neve and to the astronomical observatory and the adjacent Giardino Botanico created for the study of high altitude pastures.

From the Albergo di Campo Imperatore there are several recognised hiking trails across the Gran Sasso and to its various summits. Those who desire the services of a guide should apply to the APT in L'Aquila. Detailed information about the area is given in the *Guida dei Monti d'Italia*, volume *Gran Sasso*, published by the CAI and TCI. A selection of the recognised itineraries, all starting from the Albergo di Campo Imperatore, is given below. The times shown for each excursion are for one way only.

To La Provvidenza via the Sella dei Grilli

7 hr skiing possible all the way. From the hotel turn round the left of the observatory and follow the mule track to reach the Passo di Portella (2260m). From the pass, a track descends to the Capanne di Val Maone. From here continue to the left to the Sella dei Grilli (2110m). Skirting the south slopes of the Pizzo d'Intermesoli, the way passes through the Fonte dei Grilli to reach the Casa Venacquaro, from where there is an easy climb to the Sella Venacquaro (2300m). A track leads to the Masseria Vaccareccia (1503m). Cross the Piano del Castrato and, keeping left, descend the Valle del Chiarino to the Masseria Cappelli (1262m). A road follows the aqueduct past the source of the Vomano to the village of La Provvidenza.

To La Provvidenza via the Sella dei Cefalone

6hr 30min. From the Passo di Portella (see above) climb the crest that ascends towards the Pizzo Cefalone for c 500m, passing over the summit (2163m), which looks out over the wide valley on the east flank of Pizzo Cefalone. Descend into the valley and keep left to reach a second crest which, with the first, forms a small valley and which leads easily to the head. A steep slope leads to the Sella del Cefalone. Descending beneath the Sella dei Grilli, turn left to reach the Casa Venacquaro (2001m). From here to La Provvidenza, see above.

To Pietracamela via the Valmaone

3hr 45min, skiing possible. From the Passo di Portella, descend to the Capanne di Vale Maone, continuing with the east wall of the Pizzo d'Intermesoli on the left and the north-east slope of the east peaks of the Corno Grande and the east summit of the Corno Piccolo on the right. Pass under the Grotta d'Oro, leave the Valle dei Ginepri on the right and reach the Sorgenti di Rio d'Arno. From here you go down, avoiding a branch to the left. Advancing through the wooded Valle di Rio d'Arno, you have an easy descent to Pietracamela, see below.

To Pietracamela via the Sella dei Due Corni

6hr 15min; skiing practicable for experts; route for the ascents of the Corno Grande. From the hotel climb to the Duca degli Abruzzi Refuge (2388m), then north to the Sella di Monte Aquila, see above. Cross the Campo Pericoli and climb steeply to (2 hr) the Sella di Brecciaio. You now cross a wide plateau to the north-east of the Conca degli Invalidi. After another steep climb you reach (1hr 15min) a fork. The right branch leads up in 3hr 15min hrs by the north-west slope to the west peak of the Corno Grande, the highest of the three summits (2912m).

Climb up to the Passo del Cannone (2697m) and descend (care needed) to the Sella dei Due Corni. From the saddle descend on a steep path into the Valle delle Cornacchie, and, keeping left, reach the Franchetti Refuge (2613m), facing the east wall of the Corno Piccolo. From here the route is to the Passo delle Scalette and into the Regione Arapietra. Enter the Prati di Tibo and descend.

Via the Sella dei Due Corni to Isola del Gran Sasso
7hr 45min. To the Regione Arapietra, see above. Turning right, descend by a steep mule track past the little church of San Nicola (1096m). An easy descent follows to Casale San Nicola, at the beginning of a motor road. Isola del Gran Sasso, see below.

Via the Vado di Corno to Isola del Gran Sasso
5 hr, practicable on skis. Descend a little valley to the east of the hotel as far as Le Fontari. Here bear left and take the path skirting the slopes of Monte Aquila. Vado di Corno (1294m) with a *view of the Valle dell'Inferno. Hence there is a climb of 3 hr to Monte Brancastello (2385m), to the east From Vado di Corno the route leads to Vaduccio; you then descend through woods to Fosso Vittore. Cross the river, reach a roofless shed and descend by track to the bridge of Casale San Nicola. Isola del Gran Sasso is 8km from here.

To the Garibaldi Refuge via the Passo di Portella
2 hr. From the pass descend and follow a track to the right which at first descends and then gently ascends to a hump, on which is a rain-gauge. From here, you go through a valley to the Garibaldi Refuge (2231m).

14 · Pescara to Rome

This is a pleasant way to reach Rome from the Adriatic coast. It touches upon two charming cities, **Chieti** *(with an award-winning archaeological museum) and* **Tagliacozzo** *(a quiet medieval town), offering all the while excellent diversions (to the church of* **San Clemente in Casauria, Celano** *and its castle, or the ancient ruins of* **Alba Fucens***, for instance) and an unparalleled series of magnificent views. Trains also stop at* **Sulmona***, another interesting town, described in Route 12.*

Motorists should allow four hours driving time, plus stops. Autostrada A25/E80 closely accompanies the highway, diverging somewhat to the south beyond Popoli, and to the north beyond Avezzano, where it joins up with A24 from L'Aquila. From Pescara to Rome by Autostrada is 210km, driving time 1hr 50min. Both roads pass through beautiful scenery. The Chieti interchange, which also serves Pescara, is reached by an expressway that runs just north of the Via Valeria.

ROAD, Highway 5 (Via Valeria), 233km. From Pescara, 16km junction for Chieti— 37km Popoli—68km Avezzano—18km Tagliacozzo—64km Tivoli—31km Rome.

RAILWAY, 240km in c 3hr 15min; to Sulmona, 68km in c 1hr; to Avezzano, 133km in c 2hrs. Several fast trains daily, each stopping at Chieti, Sulmona and Avezzano. Passengers for L'Aquila and Rieti change at Sulmona.

THE PESCARA VALLEY
Pescara, Route 11. The Via Valeria ascends the valley of the Pescara River, with the railway at first on the left, then on the right. At (12km) the Madonna delle Piane, Highway 81 (from Chieti to Teramo) crosses the road. Chieti itself lies 5km to the left on this road; just outside the town the road passes the octagonal church of Santa Maria del Tricalle (built about 1498). 2km Chieti station; trolley-bus to the town (5km east) in 10 min by another side road.

Chieti (330m), capital of the province of the same name, is a lively little town of 58,000 inhabitants. It is famous for its wide *views of Abruzzo from the Gran Sasso and the Maiella to the sea.

■ **Information.** EPT, Via Spaventa 29; tel. 0871 65231, fax 0871 65232.

■ **Airport.** At Pescara, 10km north-east, with daily service to Ancona and Milan.

■ **Railway station.** Chieti Scalo, 5km west; bus.

■ **Post office.** Via Spaventa.

■ **Special events**: *Stagione di Prosa e di Musica,* Teatro Marruccino (Nov–May); Good Friday Procession; *Sagra di San Giustino* (May); *Vivi l'Estate,* various cultural and folk events (July–Aug).

Chieti stands on the site of the ancient *Theate Marrucinorum.* Gian Pietro Carafa, Bishop of Chieti (afterwards Paul IV), gave the name of his see to the Theatines, the religious order that he founded in 1524, with St Cajetan (Gaetano da Thiene). The **Cattedrale,** many times rebuilt, has a graceful campanile (1335–1498); within are a Baroque pulpit and stalls, and (in the treasury) a silver statue of St Justin, by Nicola da Guardiagrele. Behind the post office are interesting remains of three small Roman temples. The Palazzo Municipale, in the cathedral square, was erected in 1517, as the palace of the Valignani, and rebuilt in neo-Classical style in the 19C. The Pinacoteca Provinciale (open Mon–Fri 08.00–14.00, 15.00–20.00; Sat 08.00–14.00; closed Sun) has a few unimportant paintings; the Museo di Arte Sacra, adjoining the Baroque church of San Domenico (1642), is mainly notable for its examples of local woodcarving; Santa Maria Mater Domini (to the south-east) contains a Madonna carved in wood, by Gagliardelli.
    In the Villa Comunale is the ***Museo Nazionale Archeologico degli Abruzzi** (open daily 09.00–19.00), which won the European Community's European Museum of the Year award in 1984 for its extraordinarily rich and well-displayed collections of Italic and Graeco-Roman antiquities.
    ROOMS 1, 3, and 4 are devoted to **Burial Cults in Pre-Roman Abruzzo**, ranging from the 9–4C BC. The objects displayed were found at grave sites throughout the region; their provenance is labelled and they are numbered progressively. Although most are made of inorganic materials (which do not decay), rare fragments of fabric, leather, and wood (see below, ROOM 4) also survive. The finds include vessels for food and drink, arms and armour, jewellery, and personal adornments, which testify to the social status of the deceased as well

as to the commercial and cultural ties that the Italic communities of Abruzzo enjoyed with other Mediterranean and continental European populations.

Especially interesting, in ROOM 1, are two of the 272 tombs excavated at Campovalano (Province of Teramo). The first, belonging to a man, yielded a bronze helmet of the Corinthian type and a bronze shin-guard; the second, of a woman, contained embossed bronze sandals imported from Etruria and a glass sceptre. Both are 'patrician' tombs of the 7C or 8C BC. In the same room are burial treasures from the excavations conducted at Penna Sant'Andrea (Teramo) in 1973, including masks and pearls of Phoenician–Punic origin; similar objects have been found only at Carthage, in Spain, and in Sardinia. Particular importance is given to the stone stelae from the same site, which bear the first written evidence (7C or 6C BC) of the ethnic term Safin (Sabines).

ROOM 2, devoted to **Italic Sculpture**, holds the famous *****Warrior of Capestrano**, the burial stele of an Italic monarch of the 6C BC, flanked by a series of presumably contemporary archaic sculptures: the so-called Devil's Legs from Collelongo (L'Aquila), the Atessa Torso (Chieti), the Leopardi Head from Loreto Aprutino (Pesaro), and a fragment from Rapino (Chieti). ROOM 3 contains a variety of material from Iron Age necropoleis, notably the treasures of several tombs unearthed at Capestrano (one is probably that of the warrior); a stele from Guardiagrele (Chieti); material from Paglieta and Torricella Peligna (excavated in the 19C but never before displayed); finds from the necropolis of Alfedena (L'Aquila); an iron sword and bronze belt with traces of fabric from the necropolis of Pennapiedimente (Chieti), dating from the 4C BC and treasures from two of the 300 tombs identified in 1983 at Le Castagne, dating from the 7C or 6C BC and representing one of the larger necropoleis of Abruzzo.

In addition to the 'cultural' material of the archeological collections, the museum houses a number of human remains of importance, mainly from Iron Age necropoleis, housed in the **Anthropological Section** (ROOM 5). Explanatory panels outline how knowledge about a person (sex, age at death, degree of isolation, state of health, blood group, nutritional habits, etc.) is obtained centuries or even millennia after the individual's death from an examination of his or her bones. Fundamental in evolutionary terms is the Ortucchio jaw (8000–9000 years BC) which, compared to other specimens of the late Iron Age, demonstrates a marked decrease in the size of teeth.

ROOMS 6–9 are temporarily closed (1995).

Pansa Collection (ROOMS 10–11). This private collection, recently left to the museum, reflects the tastes and interests of an *amateur* of the late 19C and early 20C, an eminent local solicitor with a predilection for small bronzes, objects from daily life, jewels, glass, and ivory. Next comes the **Numismatic Collection** (ROOMS 12–13), where the exhibits have been selected from among c 15,000 coins from various areas of Abruzzo, ranging in date from the 4C BC–18C AD. The coins have been arranged to reflect the economic history of the region from pre-Roman times onward; the thematic display cases and panels show the provenance, technical characteristics, and site of each find. The coins are color coded (yellow = Greece and Magna Graecia, red = republican Rome, and so on) to increase clarity. Expecially interesting are the Roman Aureo of Gauda (Case 7), one of three known examples of this type (the other two are in the British Museum); and the medieval pieces, many of which were minted in Northern Italy and illustrate the prosperity brought to the region by the trade in wool, silk and spices. Magnifying glasses are provided on request.

ROOMS 14–16 are devoted to **Roman Portraiture**, public, private, and funerary; whereas ROOMS 17-18 constitute the **Lapidarium**, with Roman funerary and honorary epigraphy, including two extraordinary *burial beds in bone and ivory.

At the eastern edge of the town, in the shadow of a high-rise development, lie the remains of **Roman thermae**, consisting of a large (60 x 14m) cistern and numerous rooms, one of which retains its mosaic pavement. The complex probably dates from the early Imperial Period.

Return to the Via Valeria and turn south. To the left of the road, above (12km) Manoppello station, is the Cistercian church of **Santa Maria d'Arabona** (1208), containing a noteworthy aumbry and paschal candlestick (ring for admittance).

At (8km) Scafa, with asphalt works, a power-station, and an oil well (at Alanno, just to the north) the valley narrows beneath the slopes of La Plaia (right).

An approach to the Maiella Massif

A road with fine views runs south from Scafa–San Valentino station to (27km) Sant'Eufemia a Maiella. 6km San Valentino is near the ancient *Interpromium*. 10km San Tommaso (right) has a fine 12C church. 6km **Caramanico** (556m) is a summer resort with sulphur baths on the west slopes of the Maiella range. Its church of Santa Maria Maggiore has a fine portal of 1476 and a reliquary by Nicola da Guardiagrele; San Domenico has two good doorways. The APT operates an information office at Via della Libertà 19. Beyond 6km Sant'Eufemia a Maiella a fair road, rising to 1282m, leads south over the mountains to (20km) Campo di Giove, a mountain village (1064m), with a station on the railway from Roccaraso to Sulmona (see Route 26).

6km Torre dei Passeri (172m) is a picturesque village, bypassed by the main road. About 2km south is the church of ***San Clemente in Casauria**, rebuilt by the Cistercians in the 12C, but retaining its original crypt of 871, the date of its foundation by Emperor Louis II. The façade is fronted by a magnificent portico, with three broad arches (that at the centre is rounded, whereas the others are slightly pointed) on compound piers. The capitals and archivolts are richly carved. Above, two orders of attached shafts terminate in a delicate band of arched corbels, above which rises the fenestrated upper storey, an addition of 1448.

The main portal, with its complex sculptural programme, is a splendid work of the 12C. The bronze doors, with 72 relief panels (some of which are missing), are roughly contemporary. The interior, built to a Latin cross plan with shallow transepts, ends in a semicircular apse, unusual in Cistercian architecture, but in keeping with the Romanesque tradition. The first four bays of the nave arcade are taller than the others and are lighted by clerestory windows. Above the door is a Gothic loggia. The magnificent ambo (right), candlestick (left) and altar canopy are of the same date as the sculptures of the portal. Steps lead down to the crypt.

Castiglione a Casauria, 4km west, has a fine 14C church and palazzo.

Rejoining the main road, with the village of Tocco high up (355m) on the south side of the valley, enter the Gola di Popoli, with steep cliffs on either side. From (10km) Bussi a road ascends the Tirino valley to Capestrano (15km; Route 12).

Beyond another gorge the valley widens as you approach (3km) **Popoli** (254m), a town of 6000 inhabitants, 3km below the junction of the Aterno and the

Sagittario, which unite to form the Pescara river. The town is dominated by the ruined castle of the Cantelmi, dukes of Popoli. The war-damaged church of **San Francesco** preserves its important façade and a good medieval Crucifixion group above the high altar. The 14C Gothic Taverna Ducale was built as a storehouse for the ducal tithes; adjoining is the so-called Taverna dell'Universita, added in 1574. From Popoli to L'Aquila, see Route 12.

Over the mountains to Avezzano

Beyond Popoli the Via Valeria, leaving the Sulmona road on the left after 7km, passes the station and then (6km) the village of **Corfinio**, known until 1928 as Pentima. Beyond the village is the 13C Romanesque basilica of San Pelina, with a characteristic apse and a finely carved ambo. The church of Sant'Alessandro, adjoining on the south, incorporates antique architectural fragments. The former seminary, on the north side of the church, contains the small Museo delle Antichità Corfiniensi (open by appointment; tel. 0864 728350), with antiquities from the widely scattered ruins of *Corfinium*. This was the chief town of the Paeligni: in 91 BC, at the beginning of the Social War, it became the capital by the insurgent Italic tribes, who renamed it Italica and intended that it should supplant Rome. In 49 BC, after Julius Caesar had crossed the Rubicon, L. Domitius Ahenobarbus held out against him for a short time at Corfinium.

4km Raiano (395m) has a station on the railway from Sulmona to L'Aquila. The road follows this line up the Gola di San Venanzio, the steep gorge of the Aterno, as far as (7km) Molina Aterno (448m).

> Another road, parallel with the railway, leads north from Molina to (47km) L'Aquila, passing (15km) Beffi on its castle-crowned height, and the oil well of (9km) Vallecupa, and joining Highway 17 at (14km) San Gregorio.

The Via Valeria turns south-west past (10km) Castelvecchio Subequo, with an interesting church, after which, rising in sharp curves, it reaches the summit at (15km) Forca Caruso (1107m). At (10km) Collarmele (835m) cross the Pescara–Rome railway and motorway, to reach the north side of the Lago Fucino (see below). On the left is the road (Highway 83) to Pescina and Alfedena (see Route 12). 6km Celano Bivio.

A scenic road to L'Aquila

The road from Celano Bivio to L'Aquila (53km), served by bus from Avezzano to L'Aquila, runs north from its junction with Via Valeria. 4km **Celano** which stands on a hill (800m) crowned by a castle of the Piccolomini, was the birth-place of Tomaso da Celano (died 1253), the first biographer of St Francis of Assisi and author of the hymn 'Dies Irae'. Its churches have been well restored after an earthquake in 1915, as has the imposing **Castello**. The latter was begun in 1392 and completed after 1463, and consists of a rectangular core with four square towers and projecting battlements, surrounded by an irregular enceinte with cylindrical towers at the corners and square bastions along the ramparts. The attached loggie and mullioned windows were added in the 15C, possibly by Antonio Piccolomini. Within, a ramp ascends to the keep, at the centre of which is a court encircled by a Gothic portico, and above, a fine loggiato with rounded arches carried by columns bearing the Piccolomini seal in the capitals. The ramparts command good views over the surrounding countryside.

The **Museo Marsicana di Arte Sacra** (open summer, daily 09.00–19.00, winter Mon-Sat 09.00–14.00, Sun 09.00–19.00), with examples of the religious art of western Abruzzo, is situated on the recently renovated Gallery Floor. The visit begins in ROOM 2: panels illustrating the history, economy, and art of the region; in the same room, model representing the Marsica area before the draining of Lake Fucino. A computer gives general information about the works displayed, their media, and the techniques used in their restoration. ROOM 3: early medieval sculptural fragments, most from the church of San Pietro at Alba Fucens, where they were found after the earthquake of 1915. Particularly interesting is the little pillar, once part of an iconostasis now lost, inscribed with the names of its patron and makers. Other fragments from the iconostasis include a lion and a capital with acanthus leaves and human and animal figures.

ROOM 4: two sets of wooden doors, one from the church of Santa Maria in Cellis, Carsoli (1132), the other from the church of San Pietro at Albe (late 12C), both formerly displayed in the Museo Nazionale d'Abruzzo. ROOM 5: panel painting from the church of Santa Maria delle Grazie at Colelongo (13C); two sculptures representing the Madonna and Child, from Carsoli and Colli di Monte Bove (13C); panel painting of the Madonna del Latte from Carsoli; some detached frescoes from the church of San Pietro at Albe (14–15C); two panels representing the Virgin and St John, ascribed to Giovanni da Sulmona (15C); and an interesting fragment representing the Virgin, from Cese di Avezzano, recently attributed to Andrea Delitio (1439–42).

ROOM 6: tabernacle with scenes from the life of Christ, from Scurcola Marsicana; small wooden Saint from Magliano dei Marsi; paintings, by an unknown artist, of Christ carrying the Cross, the Assumption of the Virgin, and the Resurrection of Christ from the church of St Angelo, Celano; 15C frescoed Crucifixion from the Palazzo Ducale, Tagliacozzo.

ROOM 7: four wooden sculptures representing St Peter, St Paul, St Benedict, and St Andrew, from the church of Santa Maria at Luco dei Marsi; two 17C paintings, of the Holy Trinity and the Crucifixion. ROOMS 8–9: goldsmiths' art, with precious objects formerly kept at the Museo di Palazzo Venezia in Rome, notably a cross-shaped Byzantine reliquary (13C); a gilded chalice from Celano (14C), the silver Croce degli Orsini with enamels (dated 1334), a small ivory box of the Embriachi school; two silver crucifixes from the church of San Nicola in Albe (15C); and a silver crucifix from Magliano dei Marsi (17C); around the walls are more 15C frescoes from the Palazzo Ducale, Tagliacozzo. ROOMS 10 and 11 contain vestments dating from the 15C to the 19C, notably two silk hempen chasubles from the church of San Cesidio in Trasacco (15–16C).

At the Gole di Celano, just east of the town, a torrent has carved a spectacular canyon in the rock, hundreds of metres deep; the latter can be followed by foot as far as Ovindoli (this is a lonely and at times challenging walk, best done in a group). The station of Celano-Ovindoli is 1.5km south. Our road runs north and ascends in zigzags the flank of Monte La Serra. 10km **Ovindoli** (1379m), a summer–and winter-sports resort, stands at the foot of a rock-girt grassy valley. It is a starting-point for the ascent of Monte Velino (2487m) reached in c 4 hrs via the CAI Sebastiani Refuge (1996m; key at Ovindoli), and of the Colle di Pezza (2070m). The road undulates at a high level between Monte Velino and Monte Sirente (2349m). 9km Rocca di Mezzo

(1329m), in a fine situation overlooking a wide expanse of meadowland, 4km (left) Rocca di Cambio (1433m), is the highest town in Abruzzo. Now follows a descent through magnificent scenery into the valley of L'Aquila, with the snow-capped Gran Sasso always in view. 26km L'Aquila, see Route 13.

The road skirts the north side of Lago Fucino. 13km **Avezzano** (695m), a town of 37,000 inhabitants, was completely destroyed by an earthquake of 13 January 1915, but, in common with the surrounding villages, it has been rebuilt and has the air of a garden city. It suffered further damage in the Second World War, when the Palazzo Torlonia, used by the Germans as a headquarters, was bombed. The Castello degli Orsini dates from 1490. The present building has been largely reconstructed. The Museo Lapidario Marsicano contains tomb inscriptions, and sculptural and architectural fragments from sites in the ancient Marsica (Alba Fucens, Marruvium, Ortona dei Marsi). Temporarily housed in the Palazzo del Comune, it is closed to the public. It is planned to transfer the collection to the castle.

To the east of Avezzano is the Conca del Fucino, the dried-up basin of **Lago Fucino** (669m). The ancient *Lacus Fucinus* was the largest lake in Central Italy (155sq km); it was without visible outlet and was subject to sudden variations, often flooding the countryside. Emperor Claudius first attempted to drain it by digging a tunnel to connect it with the basin of the Liri, 6km south. The tunnel was opened with great rejoicing in AD 52, but without much result; a second attempt met with equal failure, and the tunnel, the most important work of underground engineering until the construction of the Mont Cenis Tunnel, became stopped up.

Frederick II attempted to reopen it in 1240, but it was not until 1852 that the work was seriously taken in hand. A company was then formed which entrusted the plans of a new scheme to Hutton Gregory, an English engineer, and later the operations passed under the control of Alessandro Torlonia, a wealthy Roman, who was aided by Swiss and French engineers. The old route was more or less followed, but the new tunnel is nearly 500m longer than the old one. The work was successfully finished in 1875. The outflow is used by electrical installations at Capistrello, to the south-west. In the spring of 1951 the reclaimed lake area, which formed part of the Torlonia estate, was expropriated. About 14,000 hectares were handed over to 8000 families.

The village of Albe (1010m), 8km north of Avezzano, stands by the ruins of **Alba Fucens** or **Fucentia.** It is reached by a minor road. Alba received from Rome in 304 BC a colony of 6000 citizens and became the chief Roman stronghold in the uplands of central Italy. Its three hilltops, the north-east one of which is occupied by the old village (ruined by the earthquake of 1915), were united by a strong wall of polygonal masonry, constructed in the 3C and 2C BC, part of which was incorporated in the medieval town wall on the west. Another well-preserved stretch, reinforced by an external rampart and by a rectangular platform probably built during the Social War, is visible to the northwest of the modern village.

Excavations conducted jointly by a Belgian mission and by the Soprintendenza Archeologica di Chieti have brought to light a considerable stretch of the ancient Via Valeria, the main street of the town, as well as part of the parallel Via dei Pilastri—so called after the tall shafts (rebuilt) that line the north side of the road—a **forum,** and remains of numerous buildings, including the **basilica,** the **market**, shops and the partially excavated theremae. Opposite the latter is the much-ruined

ALBA FUCENS

S. Pietro

Amphitheatre

key to numbèrs

1 Forum
2 Basilica
3 Market
4 Baths
5 Small 'Temple'
6 Baths
7 'Sanctuary of Hercules?'
8 Theatre

0 metres   100   200

theatre. The recently excavated amphitheatre lies on the east slope of the Collina di San Pietro.

At the top of the hill stands the church of San Pietro, with Corinthian columns and Cosmatesque ornament, which has been expertly restored; on the hill of Pettorino (south-east) are further remains of walls and the houses of the rebuilt village. It is interesting to note that the walls of Alba Fucens had no towers or bastions other than those at the four gates.

From Avezzano to Rieti

Continue at first in the direction of Rome along Via Valeria. At (6km) Cappelle diverge to the right (north). Near the village is the Monumento di Perseo, a ruin of unknown origin. 3km **Magliano de' Marsi** (728m) is noted for the church of Santa Lucia, the 15C façade of which has been rebuilt. A byroad leads to (5km north) **Rosciolo de' Marsi**, with a very fine 15C church, from where Monte Velino (2487m) may be ascended in 5–6hr. About 30min further by bridle-path is the 12C church of *Santa Maria in Vallae Porclaneta, noted for its apse, baldacchino, ambo and iconostasis (key from the custodian, at Rosciolo). Inside the door, on the right, is the tomb of the architect, Maestro Niccolo.

Shortly before (18km) Borgorose (732m) you cross Autostrada A24 and enter the Cicolano, one of the wildest and least known districts of the Apennines. A new (1995) superstrades connects Borgorose with Rieti in 45km, following a more or less level course. The older, scenic road now becomes steep and tortuous. 14km Santa Lucia, turning for Fiamignano, on a parallel byroad (the Strada Alta). Our road descends the valley of the Salto, skirting the shore of the artificial Lago del Salto past (18km) Borgo San Pietro, with its large convent of Poor Clares. 31km Rieti, see *Blue Guide Northern Italy*.

To Tagliacozzo and Rome

Beyond Avezzano the road crosses the Salto, a typical carstic stream that flows partly underground and joins the Velino at Rieti. 6km Cappelle stands at the junction of the Rieti road (see above). 3km **Scurcola Marsicana**, dominated by a castle of the Orsini (1269), preserves in its parish church a fine polychrome wooden Madonna, a relic of the ruined church of Santa Maria della Vittoria built by Charles of Anjou to mark the site of his victory over Conradin, last of the Swabians (12 August 1268; the so-called battle of Tagliacozzo). On the left, further on, is the large convent of Santa Maria d'Oriente.

8km **Tagliacozzo** (823m) is an attractive town (7000 inhab.) built on a slope above the emergence of the Salto.

■ **Information**: AA, Piazza Andrea Argoli, tel. 0863 610318.

The **Palazzo Ducale**, in the imposing piazza, is a fine building of the 14C and 15C. The first floor loggia has 15C frescoes (partially ruined). More frescoes are in the adjoining chapel. **San Francesco** is a 14C convent of Franciscan simplicity, with a Gothic portal and rose window of the mid 15C and a fine frescoed cloister. Within are a 16C wooden crucifix and a 15C Madonna and Child. There are two churches with 13C doorways and many interesting old houses.

The road now follows a winding course, affording fine views and reaching a height of 1210m on the south side of Monte Bove, the flank of which it descends, to enter a narrow valley alongside the railway. 26km **Carsoli** (616m, 5000 inhab.)

stands beneath an ivyed keep. The charming medieval houses in the principal square were completely destroyed in the Second World War, but the 12C church of Santa Maria in Cellis, south-west of the station, escaped injury. 6km Oricola–Pereto station is near the site of *Carseoli*, a station on the ancient Via Valeria from which the town of Carsoli derives its name.

Up the Fioio valley to the south is (6km) **Rocca di Botte**, whose two churches contain 15C and 16C frescoes. In San Pietro are a 13C Cosmatesque pulpit and high altar. The road passes from Abruzzo into Lazio.

5km **Arsoli** (546m), on the Riofreddo, was built, like Carsoli, from the ruins of Carseoli. Above the town rises the **Castello Massimo**, dating from the 11C, but rebuilt in the 16C, with two rooms frescoed by the Zuccari and a chapel with Cosmatesque decoration. Pleasant excursions may be made in the surrounding hills. The river provides water for the Aqua Claudia and Aqua Marcia. Descend a long steep slope into the valley of the Anio and (2km) join the road from Subiaco. The section from here to (58km) Rome is described in *Blue Guide Rome and Environs*.

15 · Termoli to Benevento

There is no easy way across the south-central Italian peninsula from the Adriatic to the Tyrrhenian coast, as the slowness of the rail journey along this route (172km in 3hrs 30min, an average of 49km/hr) amply demonstrates. The route goes as far as **Benevento***, where it links up to Route 17A to Naples. Though not swift (motorists, too, will want to allow at least 2hr 20min), it is certainly scenic, offering an unending series of fine views.* **Larino** *and* **Campobasso** *are interesting for their old town centres, which centuries of emigration have preserved from development, and Larino has some ancient ruins as well; but undoubtedly the finest sight along the route is the excavated Roman town of* **Saepinum***, a miniature Pompeii in a lovely, wild setting far from the package-tour crowds.*

ROAD, 142km. From Termoli, Highways 16 and 87 via (28km) Larino and (49km) Campobasso to (13km) Vinchiaturo; Highway 88 to (52km) Benevento. From Termoli to the intersection of Highways 87 and 88 the road runs parallel to an expressway that is faster but less interesting.

RAILWAY, 172 km in c 3hr 30min, with a change of trains at Campobasso. At certain times of the day service from Termoli to Campobasso is provided by bus, in connection with trains to Benevento. From Benevento to Naples via Caserta, 96km in 1hr 15min–1hr 45min.

RESTAURANT EN ROUTE: Campobasso, *Vecchia Trattoria da Tonino, Corso Vittorio Emanuele 8, tel. 0874 415200.

Inland to Campobasso

Termoli, see Route 11. Follow Highway 16 south to its intersection with Highway 87, pass over Autostrada A14, and after 10km cross the Biferno, the ancient *Tifernus*, to an uninteresting plain.

32km **Larino** (341m, 8000 inhab.; bus from the station in 5min), in charming surroundings, is the ancient *Larinum*, a town of the Frentani, Samnites who lived on the Adriatic coast between the Sagrus (Sangro) on the north and the Frento (Fortore) on the south. The medieval town, damaged by earthquake in 1300, was destroyed by the Saracens shortly thereafter. It was rebuilt in 1316, but in 1656 plague claimed the lives of 9625 of its 10,000 inhabitants. The Sagra di San Pardo, celebrated on 25–27 May, features a torchlight procession of elaborately decorated *plaustri* or pseudo-Roman ox carts.

The **Duomo** (1319), with an attractive façade, has a 16C campanile and a fine Gothic portal by Francesco Petrini, the sculptor of the portal of Santa Maria Maggiore in Lanciano (Route 11). In the lunette, Crucifixion with the Virgin and St John. The large rose window is similar to those that characterise Apulian churches; the mullioned windows on either side open above the level of the aisle roofs. The interior has three tall, narrow aisles separated by pointed arches (six on the south side, five on the north) on cruciform piers with carved capitals. In the south aisle is an Immaculate Conception attributed to Francesco Solimena. The chapter house contains a marble altar built to a design by Andrea Vaccaro and other interesting objects.

The **Palazzo Comunale**, in the cathedral square, contains a monumental staircase of 1818, adorned with Roman architectural fragments and, in the biblioteca, mosaic pavements from Roman villas discovered in the environs of the amphitheatre (see below). Also of interest are a 14C wooden Madonna and numerous ceramic and bronze objects, some dating from the second millennium BC.

The wooded avenue that ascends to the station passes, on the left, the so-called *Ara Frentana*, a cylindrical altar of pre-Roman origin; and other archaeological material (chiefly inscriptions and architectural and sculptural fragments) brought here from nearby excavations. The ruins of *Larinum*, including the conspicuous remains of an amphitheatre of the late 1C or early 2C BC, lie north-east of the station, in and around Piazza San Lorenzo, and in the vicinity of the Torre Sant'Anna and Torre De Gennaro.

From Larino there is an almost continuous ascent to (13km) Casacalenda, where a minor road descends to Guardialfiera, on the Termoli–Campobasso expressway. Beyond the town, after the level-crossing, a road on the left diverges to (500m) the 16C convent of Sant'Onofrio.

Beyond (8km) Taverna Cerrosecco, Morrone del Sannio comes into view, on its hilltop (839m); a road further on mounts to the town. At Taverna Clemente, beyond (14km) Campolieto station, the highest point of the road is reached. The road then descends in broad curves, and crosses the railway several times. On a hill to the right stands the splendid Romanesque church of **Santa Maria della Strada**, reached by a turning further on. 8km the road joins Highway 157 from the Biferno valley.

4km **Campobasso**, with 51,000 inhabitants, is the chief town of the province of the same name, formerly the county of Molise. The local industry of cutlery has dwindled to a handful of artisans who make and engrave scissors and knives, hawked by pedlars. The *Sagra dei Misteri* (Corpus Domini) is celebrated with 18C iron contrivances in which children assume impossible poses (flying angels, etc.) depicting Christian mysteries or miracles of the saints. These human sculptural configurations are borne through the streets on wooden platforms.

■ **Information.** Assessorato al Turismo, Via Mazzini 94; tel. 0874 4291, fax 0874 429523. EPT, Piazza della Vittoria 14, tel. 0874 415662.

■ **Post office.** Via Toscana.

In the old upper town are two churches preserving Romanesque portions: San Bartolomeo, with a fine 14C portal, and San Giorgio, with delicate 12C bas-reliefs. In Via Chiarizia a building (No. 10) is being adapted (1995) to house the Museo Provinciale Sannitico, with Samnite antiquities. Above rises the 15C Castello Monforte, square in plan with six rampart towers. The square before the entrance affords good views over the town and the surrounding countryside.

On the south of the castle hill is the church of Sant'Antonio, with a painting of St Benedict by Fabrizio Santafede. An inscription beneath the portico of the Municipio, in the lower town, records the death, near Campobasso, of Amadeus VI, the Green Count of Savoy (1383). Nearby, in Piazza Vittoria, is a Museo Internazionale del Presepio in Miniatura, containing a fine private collection of Italian and foreign nativity scenes (open by appointment, tel. 0874 63370).

SAEPINUM AND THE WESTERN HIGHLANDS
From Campobasso the road twists, climbing and then descending to (13km) Vinchiaturo, an attractive little town (3000 inhab.) rebuilt after the earthquake of 1805. Beyond the town, join the Isernia–Benevento road and turn left. 6km **Sepino**, on a hill 4km south, is the successor of the Roman ***Saepinum**, the ruins of which lie along the highway on the right. Later named *Atilia*, Saepinum was founded by survivors from the Samnite *Saipins*, destroyed in 293 BC. Its history was not particularly eventful; it was destroyed by the Saracens in the 9C.

The defensive walls, 1250m in circumference, still surround the ancient town. Fortified by 27 bastions, they are pierced by four gates, today known as the Porta di Baiano (north-west), Porta del Tammaro (north-east), Porta di Benevento (south-east) and Porta di Terravecchia (south-west).

Enter by the Porta del Tammaro and cross the site to the Porta di Terravecchia, outside which is an improvised car park surrounded by low walls in *opus reticulatum*. Within (open daily, 09.00–1hr before sunset), the *cardus maximus* leads past modern farmhouses built with the stones of the ancient city. Further on, the road preserves its ancient pavement. The **basilica**, on the left, has a peristyle made up of 20 slender Ionian columns. Turning right, follow the decumanus past the **forum** and a series of public buildings that includes the **curia**, or town hall, and a temple believed to have been dedicated to the Capitoline triad.

Further on, on the left, are the Casa del Frantoio, an olive press (note the brick-lined wells for storing the oil); the Mulino Idraulico or water mill; and the so-called **Casa dell'Impluvio Sannitico**, a house with a graceful fountain, built to the typical Samnite plan around an atrium with impluvium, preceded by shops. Beyond the Porta di Benevento stands a monumental tomb with an inscription describing the civic and military career of the defunct. To the left is a small museum (open Tue–Sun 09.00–13.00) with photographs and texts describing the town and its discovery and a collection of Roman inscriptions.

Returning to the centre of the town, pass behind the basilica to the octagonal market and what appears to be a small temple. Beyond are the remains of private dwellings and, at the end of the street, the imposing **Porta di Baiano**, in *opus tessellatum*, flanked by cylindrical bastions, another of which can be seen along the wall to the north. At the sides of the arch are statues of prisoners on plinths; that on the right is headless. The keystone is carved with a bearded head, possibly of Hercules; the inscription above the arch tells us that the fortification of the town was financed by the future emperor Tiberius and his brother Drusus.

Steps ascend to the top of the gate, from where there is a fine view over the excavations; the rectangular **tomb of the Numisi**, in a field to the north, and the

thermae, the remains of which extend along the town wall between the decumanus and the **theatre**. The latter is reached by a minor gate, an unusual feature suggesting that theatrical performances were combined with fairs held outside the walls. Surrounded by farmhouses, it preserves large portions of the cavea and orchestra.

On the stage, another farm building houses a beautiful collection (open as above) of objects found on the site and in the vicinity, chiefly funerary sculpture from a necropolis brought to light along the extramural portion of the decumanus. Photographs and texts explain the finds. On the first floor are numerous maps and plans describing the territory, the town and its monuments.

Just before (8km) Sassinoro, you cross the boundary between Molise and Campania. To the right are the highlands of the Matese (Route 12), bounded on the south by the Volturno valley. The road goes through a short tunnel to (5km) Morcone (683m) high above its railway station. 3km further on, Highway 87 diverges right to Caserta (Route 5F).

Along this road lie (27km) Telese, a spa near the Samnite town of *Telesia*, of which scanty ruins remain; and (18km) Caiazzo, a pleasant little hillside town with a ruined castle.

Our road winds south through lonely countryside, affording wide views over the hills of east Campania. 30km Benevento, see Route 17A.

16 · The Gargano Peninsula and the Tremiti Islands

*This route offers respite from the hustle and bustle of the Apulian coast, touching on a region that has more in common geologically with the Eastern Adriatic than with the rest of Italy. The **Gargano** and the **Tremiti Islands** in fact form a single geological unit, composed largely of white limestone. Unlike the neighbouring plain, they are densely forested, and the combination of glistening stone, dark forest and azure sea is unforgettable. The forested highlands of the Gargano were declared a national park in 1991, and the unique pine woods of the Tremiti Islands are a specially protected nature reserve. The circuit of the Gargano by road may be made in c 3hr 30min, plus stops.*

The Gargano may be reached by ROAD, Highways 16, 89, 159 and local roads, starting at Foggia. The highway makes a circuit (223km) of the peninsula via 40km Manfredonia—52km Vieste—26km Peschici (to Peschici via Monte Sant Angelo, 59km)—14km Rodi Garganico—53km Foggia.

RAILWAY from Foggia to Manfredonia Città, 36km in c 25 min, with bus connections to Vieste.

The Tremiti Islands are best reached by motorboat or hydrofoil from Ortona (daily Jun–Sep, 1hr 40min),Vasto (daily June–Sep, 2hr 45min), Termoli (daily, 45 min), and Rodi Garganico (daily Jun-Sep, 50min). Ferries daily from Termoli (1hr 40min).

Frequency and times of departure vary from season to season; precise information may be obtained in any of the above-mentioned towns.

HOTELS EN ROUTE: Mattinata, ****Baia delle Zagare, tel. 0884 4115; fax 0884 4884; **Dei Faraglioni, tel. 0884 49584, fax 0884 49651;Vieste, *****Pizzomunno Vieste Palace, tel. 0884 810267, fax 0884 707325; San Domino (Isole Tremiti), ****Kyrie, tel. 0882 663241, fax 0882 663415; ****Gabbiano, tel. 0882 663410, fax 0882 663428; ***San Domino, tel. 0882 663404, fax 0882 663221.

RESTAURANTS EN ROUTE: Foggia, **Il Ventaglio, Via Postiglione 6; tel. 0881 661500.

THE GARGANO

A mountainous peninsula rising in Monte Calvo to 1065m,, the Gargano is still thickly wooded, especially with oak. The Boschi Umbra, Quarto and Spigno are the chief forests. The whole of the promontory is streaked with limestone, and the streams have no outlet except in the fissures where they are swallowed up. There are many unexplored pot-holes and stalactite grottos. The Gargano has the same geological composition as Dalmatia and in the tertiary period was separated from Italy by a strait.

Foggia, Route 11. The highway crosses the Tavoliere, keeping a characteristic straight course through farmland.

San Giovanni Rotondo

Just beyond the Candelaro torrent (29km) a turning on the left winds north to **San Giovanni Rotondo** (18 km, 567m), a small village on a plateau below Monte Calvo (1065m), highest peak of the Gargano. In 1177 it belonged to Joan Plantagenet, wife of William II of Sicily. Interesting are the 14C church of **Sant'Onofrio** and the towers of like date; the **Rotonda di San Giovanni**, a baptistery of uncertain date, is reputedly built on the ruins of a temple of Jupiter. At the west end of the village, the tree-lined Viale dei Cappuccini leads to the 16C convent of **Santa Maria delle Grazie**. The conventual church, consecrated in 1629, contains a much-venerated Madonna delle Grazie. In the crypt of the modern church nearby is buried Padre Pio da Pietralcina (1887–1969), whose reputation for working miracles has made the village a centre of pilgrimage, especially for the sick. The Fiorello La Guardia Hospital, named after a mayor of New York City, is supported largely by American funds.

■ **Information**. AA, Piazza Europa 104; tel. 0882 456240.

Beyond the turning for San Giovanni Rotondo, on the right, are the ruins of an abbey whose 11C church (San Leonardo) has a simple façade with blind arcades, a plain portal and a small rose window. Along the left flank of the church is a richly sculptured **doorway**, in all likelihood of the 13C, in a shallow porch with griffins in the impost blocks and (modern) columns supported by lions.

Beyond (35km) the junction with the road from Cerignola lie the ruins of **Sipontum**, an ancient town abandoned in 1256 probably on account of malaria. Here in 1252 Conrad landed to claim the crown of Sicily. An important Daunian centre, it was conquered by Hannibal and, soon after, by the Romans. By the early

Middle Ages it had become the chief port of northern Apulia and, as such, it attracted the attention of the Lombard princes of Benevento, under whose dominion it remained from the 7–11C. Sipontum was occupied in 1039 by the Normans, under whom its influence extended over most of the Gargano promontory. In the 13C bradyseism caused much of its territory to degenerate into swampland, and the earthquake of 1223 virtually levelled the town. The inhabitants and the diocese were transferred to the new town of Manfredonia.

Little remains of the town proper, other than the scanty ruins visible from the highway. A few metres before the archaeological zone, in a small pine grove, stands ***Santa Maria di Siponto**, the beautiful 12C cathedral, built above an underground church dating probably from the 5C and modified in the 13C and later centuries. The simple but elegant façade, restored in 1975, has a fine **doorway** of local workmanship framed by a shallow porch and flanked by columns borne by lions. At the sides are blind arcades enclosing rhomboid decorative motifs, which are carried around to the south and east walls.

The interior, built to a square plan with a central vault (reconstructed) carried by four rectangular piers and two small apses, has a distinctly Oriental flavour. On three of the four walls are blind arcades with attached shafts, like those of the exterior. On the north wall can be seen mosaic fragments from an early Christian basilica found nearby. The high altar is made from an early Christian sarcophagus; above is a copy of the Madonna and Child in the cathedral of Manfredonia. The circular chapel to the right of the altar is in all probability a later addition.

Steps on the north side of the church descend to the **crypt**, with vaulted ceiling, four squat columns corresponding to the piers above, and 16 small columns, some ancient, with sculptured capitals of Classical and Byzantine design. Remains of a still earlier (4C–7C) church—chiefly bases, capitals and fragments of columns—as well as some Roman and medieval tombs, have been brought to light nearby.

Pass Lido di Siponto, a modern bathing resort, and enter (5km) **Manfredonia**, a town of 59,000 inhabitants on the gulf of the same name, at the foot of the Gargano Promontory. It was founded in 1256 by Manfred (1231–66), King of Sicily and Naples, and peopled by the inhabitants of Sipontum. Much of the town

The old town centre of Manfredonia, at the foot of the Gargano

was destroyed by the Turks in 1620. The first act of Austrian aggression against Italy here was carried out in 1915, with the bombing of the railway station and the sinking of the *Turbine* in the gulf. Now a developing industrial centre, Manfredonia is not a pleasant place; however, it is an excellent starting point for excursions in the Gargano.

■ **Information**: AA, Corso Manfredi 26; tel. 0884 21998, fax 0884 23295 (branch office at Piazza Santa Maria Maggiore, Siponto).

The **Castello Svevo-Angioino**, begun by Manfred in 1256, originally stood outside the town walls. The primitive core, which is still visible today, is a square plan with massive bastions—three cylindrical and one rectangular—at the corners and a tall enceinte surrounding a central court entered by archways in the east and west walls. Charles of Anjou enclosed this earlier fortification within a new set of walls, also built to a rectangular plan with cylindrical towers at the corners. The great spear-head bastion was added in the 16C. The castle houses the **Museo Archeologico Nazionale del Gargano Meridionale** (open daily 08.30–12.30, 15.30–19.30; closed first and last Mon of each month), which has an interesting collection of material from local excavations, notably 6C bronze and ceramic objects of Daunian workmanship and an unusual series of 6C and 5C Daunian grave slabs, carved to represent people and animals. The church of San Domenico (1299, rebuilt in later centuries) has a Gothic doorway and 14C frescoes. The late 17C cattedrale, of little architectural interest, contains a 12C wooden crucifix.

From Manfredonia to Peschici via the Foresta Umbra

Leaving Highway 89 (see below) the road climbs in steep zigzag turns to (16km) **Monte Sant'Angelo**, a town with 16,000 inhabitants situated on a south spur (884m) of Monte Gargano. It owes its origin to the foundation of the **Santuario di San Michele Arcangelo** in a grotto, now in the centre of the town (open Nov–Mar, daily 07.30–12.00, 15.00–17.00; Apr–May 07.30–12.30, 14.30–19.00; Jun–Oct 07.30–12.30, 14.30–19.00). From the portico with two Gothic doorways (that on the right dates from 1395; the other is a modern imitation), flanked by a fine octagonal belfry of 1281, 89 steps descend to the inner vestibule built by Charles I of Anjou, where a bronze door made in Constantinople in 1076 fills the Romanesque portal. From here you enter the church, built of stone (1273), and finally the grotto, consecrated, according to tradition, by the archangel Michael himself, when he revealed it to St Laurence, Bishop of Sipontum, on 8 May 490. The grotto contains a 16C statue of St Michael and a stone bishop's throne of the 11C.

In front of the campanile steps lead down (left) to the ruined church of San Pietro, through which you enter the so-called Tomba di Rotari, probably a baptistery, with a cupola and 12C decorations. To the right is the church of Santa Maria Maggiore (1198). Above the town the massive ruined castle, started by the Normans, affords a wide view. In the lower town, San Francesco contains the supposed tomb of Joan I. Here also is the Museo delle Arti e Tradizioni Popolari del Gargano Giovanni Tancredi (open May–Sep 08.30–20.00, Sun and holidays 10.30–12.30, 15.30–19.00; Oct–Apr, Mon–Fri 08.00–14.00), with an interesting collection of folk art.

From Monte Sant'Angelo follow the Valle Carbonara, leaving to the left a road that runs along the spine of the promontory via San Giovanni Rotondo and San Marco in Lamis to San Severo, then climb over the arid Piano della

Castagna. 29km the Rifugio Foresta Umbra is charmingly situated in the heart of the Foresta Umbra. Descend by (14km) Vico del Gargano, through olive and orange groves, and through the splendid Pineta Marzini to the coast road, turning right to reach (17km) Peschici (see below).

Beyond Manfredonia the road begins to climb round the coast. At (15km) Mattinata (75m, 6000 inhab.), Highway 89 climbs over the east end of the promontory through country alternately rocky and wooded. Bear right and follow the coastline past (26km) the modern resort of Pugnochiuso to (11km) **Vieste**, a small town (14,000 inhab.) with a castle in a fine position on the north-east tip of the Gargano. Here in 1295 Celestin V was arrested by order of Boniface VIII.

■ **Information**: AA, Corso Lorenzo Fazzini 8; tel. 0884 708806, fax 0884 707130 (branch office in Piazza Kennedy)

26km **Peschici** (90m, 4000 inhab.) is a picturesque village perched above a rocky cliff. Beyond, the headland of Monte Pucci commands an admirable view along the coast. 7km our road is joined by Highway 528 from Vico del Gargano and Monte Sant'Angelo (see above). Beyond, San Menaio has a sandy beach that extends to (7km) Rodi Garganico, a fishing village (4000 inhab.) below hills ringed with orange groves and pine woods.

Skirt the Lago di Varano, a shallow lagoon separated from the sea by a strip of sand dominated by (18km) Cagnano Varano. From here a new road flanks the similar Lago di Lesina to Termoli (Route 11). Bear inland to (20km) Sannicandro Garganico; beyond, the last foothills of the Gargano yield to the Tavoliere. 53km Foggia.

THE TREMITI ISLANDS

The **Isole Tremiti**, a group of small limestone islands 22km north of the Gargano Peninsula, are known throughout Italy for their natural beauty, clear waters and mild climate. These are the *Insulae Diomediae*, the place in Classical mythology as being where the companions of Diomedes changed into herons.

Of the three main islands, the largest, **San Domino**, was the scene of the death of Julia, granddaughter of Augustus. In recent years it has undergone a sudden rush of 'green' tourists drawn by its pine forests, marine caves, and other natural assets.

San Nicola, though smaller than San Domino, is the administrative centre of the group and is of greater interest from a historical point of view.

From the Marina at the south-west tip of the island, a narrow, walled road passes through two medieval gates to the town proper and the abbey church of **Santa Maria a Mare**, founded in 1045 and rebuilt in the 15C, 17C and 18C. From its foundation, in the 8C, to the mid 12C, the abbey was governed by the Benedictines of Monte Cassino. In the 12C it passed to the Cistercian Order and was fortified by Charles II of Anjou. In the 14C corsairs, who managed to enter the convent by trickery, laid waste to it and massacred the monks; it was not until 1412 that the Laterans of San Frediano di Lucca, by concession of Gregory XII, took over the complex, embellishing the church and building a new defensive system. Their monastic fortress successfully held off an assault by Süleyman II in 1567.

In 1783, after a period of gradual decline, Ferdinand IV of Naples suppressed the abbey, the possessions of which had once included vast areas of the Gargano, the Terra di Bari, Molise and Abruzzo, establishing in its place a prison, which remained active until 1926. From that year until 1945 it was used for the detention of political prisoners.

The 15C façade of the church incorporates a Renaissance doorway (1473) flanked by double Corinthian columns and surmounted by weather-worn sculptures. The interior has retained its original 11C plan, with a rectangular nave preceded by a double narthex. The painted wooden ceiling dates from the 18C and replaces an earlier dome. The colourful mosaic pavement, of which substantial areas remain, was executed c 1100. The church contains a painted Greco-Byzantine Crucifixion of the 12C and a fine, early 15C Venetian polyptych.

The island of **Capraia** (also called Caprara or Capperara), to the north of San Nicola, is interesting for its many small rock arches or 'archetielli'.

Pianosa, 20km north-east, is not often visited by commercial passenger craft.

17 · Naples to Bari

A.   Via Benevento and Foggia

*The chief attractions on this route are **Benevento**, with its magnificent Roman ruins and museums, and the charming medieval hill towns of **Troia** and **Lucera**. **Foggia**, though largely a modern place and a busy provincial capital, is not unpleasant. The extraordinary cathedrals of the coastal towns between here and Bari are described in Route 11.*

*The rail journey along this route is particularly beautiful. Beyond Caserta the line goes through two tunnels, shortly beyond which it passes under an arch of the **Ponti della Valle**, the colossal bridge by which the Acquedotto Carolino is carried across the valley of Maddaloni. The bridge was designed by Luigi Vanvitelli and has three tiers of arches (96 in all); its height is 65m. Beyond (54km) Frasso Telesino-Dugenta the line approaches the Volturno (left) and shortly after crosses the Calore near its confluence with the Volturno. Hence it follows the Calore and Miscano valleys past (43km) Benevento. Near (38km) Ariano Irpino it tunnels through the mountains, then closely follows the road to Foggia and Bari.*

By car, an alternative start (13km longer) can be made by taking Highway 87 to (28km) Caserta (Route 7G), there joining the Via Appia. You skirt to the south of (8km) Maddaloni, overlooked by three ruined castles, and (8km) Santa Maria a Vico, with an interesting chuch of 1450, to join the above route before Arpaia. Both roads offer exceptionally attractive scenery; travel time is roughly 4hr. Less intersting, but faster, are Autostrada A2/E45 and A16/E842, by which the 98km to Benevento may be covered in 52min.

ROAD 313km. Highways 7b, 162, and 7 (Via Appia), to Benevento; then Highways 90b, 90, and country roads to Foggia and Highway 16 to Bari. 17km Acerra—28km Montesarchio—18km Benevento—24km Buonalbergo—24km Savignano Irpino—33km Troia—17km Lucera—18km Foggia—134km Bari. Keep windows up and doors locked while driving through Bari.

RAILWAY 321km. From Naples Centrale, Piazza Garibaldi, Mergellina and Campi Flegrei to Bari Centrale in 4–5 hr; to Benevento, 97km in c 1hr 30min. This is the main rail line from Rome to Bari. Through trains cover the distance in c 5hr.

HOTELS EN ROUTE: Youth Hostel in Bari, Via Nicola Massaro 33; tel. 080 320282.

RESTAURANTS EN ROUTE: Foggia, **Il Ventaglio, Via Postiglione 6; tel. 0881 ; Barletta, **Antica Cucina, Via Milano 73, tel/fax 0883 68805349; ****Bacco, Via Sipontina 10, tel. 0883 521718; Santo Spirito (Bari), **L'Aragosta, Lungomare Colombo 235, tel. 080 5335427.

East of Naples

Leave Naples by the Porta Capuana (Atlas 5, 7) and, beyond Poggioreale, continue to the north-east. The highway crosses anonymous suburbs, passing turnings for Doganella and Capodichino (left) and San Giovanni a Teduccio (right) before dipping beneath the Aversa–Caserta railway and the Autostrada del Sole; Vesuvius can be seen to the right. At 8km diverge left from Highway 7b, which continues to Avellino (Route 17B).

17km **Acerra** (41,000 inhab.) is one of the larger towns of the Neapolitan hinterland. It takes the place of the ancient *Acerrae*, destroyed by Hannibal and subjected to frequent inundations from the Clanius (now canalised) on which it stood.

8km Cancello is an important railway junction, where two lines to Benevento and one to Torre Annunziata diverge from the old Rome–Naples main line. About 3km west, in the Bosco di Acerra, are the fragmentary ruins of *Suessula*, a town founded by the Ausoni or the Aurunci and destroyed by the Saracens in 879.

Beyond (6km) Arienzo, the road joins the Via Appia, and, climbing, crosses the ravine generally supposed to be the Caudine Forks (*Furculae Caudinae*), where the Romans were trapped by the Samnites in 321 BC. The memory of the disaster is preserved in the names of the hamlet of Forchia, south of the road, where the church of Santa Maria in Iugo marks the supposed site of the battle, and of the Valle Caudina.

6km Arpaia. The road on the left leads in 12km to Sant'Agata dei Goti, a remote village that possessed a castle and some 12C remains in the cathedral and in the church of San Menna, before the earthquake of 1980 left it little more than a pile of rocks. Further along, on the left, is Monte Taburno (1394m), whose streams feed the park of the palace at Caserta (Route 5F), carried there by the Acquedotto Carolino, 48km long.

8km Montesarchio is an agricultural centre picturesquely laid out at the foot of a formidable castle, the 15C stronghold first of the Carafa and subsequently of the D'Avalos. Here the patriot Carlo Poerio, who together with Luigi Settembrini and Silvio Spaventa was one of the leading advocates of Italian unification in the south, was jailed in 1855.

18km **Benevento** (65,000 inhab.), a city of ancient importance, stands on a ridge between the Calore and Sabato rivers in an amphitheatre of mountains. It was badly damaged in the Second World War, the lower town and the cathedral being almost completely destroyed.

History

This is the Oscan or Samnite city of *Malies*. Latinised as *Maleventum*, supposedly because of the bad air of the place, it changed its name to *Beneventum* on its establishment as a Roman colony in 268 BC, soon after the decisive defeat in 275 of Pyrrhus nearby at the hands of Curius Dentatus. An important place under the empire, it stood at the end of the first extension from Capua of the Via Appia, which was later continued as far as Brundisium. It rose again to fame in 571 as the first independent Lombard duchy and preserved its autonomy until 1053, when it passed to the Church. It has been the see of an archbishop since the 10C. On 26 February 1266 Manfred was defeated here by Charles of Anjou and sought a voluntary death in battle after the treacherous defection of his allies. The title of Prince de Bénévent was conferred on Talleyrand by Napoleon. As a consequence of continuous neglect in the postwar years, the present city is one of the less hospitable in Southern Italy.

■ **Railway stations**. Centrale (for all services), 1km north of the centre. Also Benevento Appia, on the light railway via Cancello, 0.5km south-west of the centre; and Porta Rufina, 1km east on the line to Avellino.

■ **Information**. EPT, Via Nicola Sala 31; tel. 0824 310662, fax 0824 312309 (branch office at Via Giustiniani 36).

■ **Post office**. Via Porta Rufina.

■ **Special events**. Opera, classical and modern theatre in the Roman theatre in the summer. *Città Spettacolo*, drama festival (Sep).

The principal artery of the city centre, Corso Garibaldi, crosses the town from east to west. At its east end stands the **Castello** (Rocca dei Rettori), built in 1321 by John XXII; here Attendolo, first of the Sforza, was once imprisoned. The historical section of the Museo del Sannio, housed in the castle, contains material relating to the town's past. The adjoining public garden affords a good view.

In a little piazza on the right of the Corso stands the church of **Santa Sofia**. Built in 760 and rebuilt in 1668, it has a dome borne by antique Corinthian columns and a 12C *cloister with interesting columns, capitals, and carved impost blocks. The decorative scheme is the work of local masters and combines late Roman, Moorish, Byzantine and Lombard motifs in Old and New Testament, mythological, and historical scenes. Adjoining the cloister is the **Museo del Sannio** (open Wed, Thu, Sat, and Sun 09.00–13.00; Tue and Fri 09.00–13.00 and 16.00–19.00), with a collection of Samnite antiquities and sculpture from a Temple of Isis erected by Domitian in AD 88, paintings from the Middle Ages to the contemporary period (chiefly by local artists), and prints and drawings.

Via Arco Traiano leads (right) to the *Arch of Trajan, or Porta Aurea, a single triumphal arch of Parian marble, 15m high. It was erected across the Via Appia in honour of Trajan (114–166) and is one of the finer and better preserved arches of its kind. The bas-reliefs, set between composite columns, depict scenes from the life of Trajan and mythological subjects. The side facing Beneventum and Rome bears a glorification of Trajan's home policy, including, in the attic level, Roman consuls receiving Trajan and Hadrian, and Jupiter offering the emperor his thunderbolt; in the middle level, Trajan conferring benefits on the Roman people; in the lower level, the emperor's triumphal return after the Germanic campaign. The façade facing Brundisium and the overseas provinces celebrates Trajan's provincial policy and benefits, including, in the top registers, river gods welcoming the emperor; in the middle level, Trajan recruiting troops and forming new colonies; and in the lower levels, foreign peoples swearing loyalty or bearing gifts. A continuous frieze in the form of a triumphal procession runs around all four sides of the monument.

Arch of Trajan, erected 114–166

Beneath the arch are personifications of cities and scenes of Trajan inaugurating a new road and distributing funds to the poor.

Continuing along the corso you reach the tiny Piazza Papiniano, with an Egyptian Obelisk of red granite from the Temple of Isis (see above), found nearby in 1872. Beyond this is the **Duomo**, a 13C Romanesque building shattered by bombardment in the Second World War. Its richly sculptured façade, badly damaged, and its campanile of 1279, still standing, incorporate fragments of Roman and Lombard architecture. The famous bronze doors, possibly of Byzantine workmanship, were injured beyond repair, but two-thirds of their plaques were saved and placed in the seminary. The treasury is notable for a **golden rose** and a **bronze coffer** of the 11C or 12C, and the chapter library includes interesting Lombard manuscripts, illuminated choir-books, and the 13C Necrologio di Santo Spirito.

To the north, Corso Vittorio Emanuele descends to the Ponte Vanvitelli, which crosses the Calore. The bridge, built by Luigi Vanvitelli, has been restored several times; remains of a medieval bridge survive 100m upstream. Beyond the river the long Viale Principe di Napoli leads to the Stazione Centrale. Corso Garibaldi continues, changing its name to Corso Dante and then viale San Lorenzo, towards the Madonna delle Grazie, a huge 19C church containing a 6C (?) wooden statue; in front of the church stands a granite bull from the Temple of Isis.

Below the cathedral to the south-west are the pillaged remains of another triumphal arch and the ***Roman theatre**, built in the reign of Hadrian and enlarged by Caracalla to accommodate 20,000 spectators. The first and part of the second of three tiers survive, the remainder having been destroyed to make way for the modern buildings that encroach on its perimeter. Beyond the stage ran a peristyle, possibly intended as a promenade for spectators, which was reached from the exterior by three flights of steps. A lower corridor behind the auditorium remains intact. Notice also the extant fragments of the stage buildings. Further west are the ancient Port'Arsa; the Torre della Catena, part of a Lombard fortress; and, beyond the railway, four arches of the Ponte Leproso, by which the ancient Via Appia crossed the Sabato.

Around Benevento

A pleasant road of 84km winds through cultivated upland country to Volturara on the Foggia–Isernia road, passing (17km) Pesco Sannita, and (19km) San Marco dei Cavoti. Oak forests clothe the hills round (19km) Fioano. Beyond (16km) San Bartolomeo in Galdo, the road commands a fine view of the Abruzzi mountains.

From Benevento to (78km) Campobasso and (86km) Termoli, see Route 15.

Through the hills to Apulia

Leave Benevento by Viale degli Atlantici, passing the park of the Villa Comunale and the Ospedale Civile before turning left in Via Meomartini. The Via Appia diverges right for San Giorgio del Sannio; our road descends to cross the Torrente San Nicola, climbing out with good views back over Benevento and its plain. Each of the small villages visible in the surrounding hills has a castle of some interest. The road descends to the broad Calore valley in a region, the ancient *Irpinia*, rich in the remains of Roman towns; crosses the Calore near a ruined Roman bridge of the Via Traiana; then ascends the gentle slope of Monte Sacro, through olive and oak groves. A turning on the left leads to Paduli (2km, 5000 inhab.), the ancient *Batulum*, on the ridgetop between the Tammaro and Calore rivers. Once the seat of a duchy, it is now an important farming town (olive oil).

24km **Buonalbergo** (570m, 2000 inhab.), in the highlands of Monte San Silvestre, consists of two distinct towns, Terravecchia, to the south, and Terranova, to the north. The latter, with its rectilinear street plan, is thought to be the Roman *Forum Novum*. The town preserves a 7C Lombard fortress known as the Castello di Boemondo; and remains of a bridge from the Via Traiana, the Ponte delle Chianche. The little 17C church of the Madonna della Macchia, just beyond the town, contains a wooden Madonna and Child of the late 12C, supposedly found in the woods (macchia).

Two more hill towns

A road on the right diverges south to (29km) **Ariano Irpino** (780m), a town (24,000 inhab.) on a ridge, with an imposing castle of Norman origin. On the way (9km) is **Montecalvo Irpino**, where the Collegiata dates from the 14C and the Cappella Carafa contains a curious baptismal font consisting of a sarcophagus borne by pillars carved by local craftsmen.

Our road continues through sparsely populated hills, joining Highway 90 from Ariano Irpino and Avellino. 24km Savignano Irpino (698m, 2000 inhab.), above the junction, is reached by a winding road on the right. From here a country road continues via (15km) Monteleone di Puglia and (21km) Sant'Agata di Puglia, two picturesque hilltop villages, to join Route 17B near Candela.

6km A turning on the left ascends to **Montaguto** (6km; 730m, 1000 inhab.), in a wonderful position enjoying broad *views over the highlands of Irpinia, the Monti del Matese and the Tavoliere di Puglia to the Adriatic Sea. You enter Apulia near Stazione Orsara; the valley widens. 20km Quadrivio di Giardinetto. Highway 90 continues across the flat Tavoliere di Puglia to Foggia. Turn left on a country road.

TROIA AND LUCERA

10km **Troia**, a small town (8000 inhab.) founded in 1017 as a Byzantine fortress on the site of the ancient *Aecae*, commands a wide view. The *Cattedrale (1093–1125) is perhaps the most remarkable example of the successful Apulian marriage of Byzantine sculptural ornament of Saracen inspiration to the Pisan Romanesque style. The well-proportioned façade, plain below (with blind arcades and lozenge motifs that continue around the sides and rear of the church) and of singular richness above (note the projecting lion and bull consoles and the beautifully carved moulding of the arch beneath the gable), is pierced by a rose window. The west and south *doors (1119 and 1127), by Oderisius of Benevento, are in bronze; some panels are executed in high relief, others are incised. They show both Eastern and Classical influences, as do the reliefs of the lintel and the capitals above the main door. The apse has double tiers of free-standing columns. The sombre **interior** has three aisles separated by semicircular arches on columns with singularly rich capitals. In the penultimate bay is an ambo of 1169 with curious sculptures, formerly in the nearby domed 11C church of San Basilio (shown by the cathedral sacristan). The rich treasury contains various silver statues and liturgical objects, including a chalice by followers of Cellini (1521).

18km **Lucera**, a town (35,000 inhab.) with a magnificent castle, 219m above the Tavoliere, was until 1806 a provincial capital and preserves many relics of its former greatness.

History

Luceria Augusta, already Roman in 314 BC, became a *colonia* under Augustus. Destroyed by Constans II, Emperor of Byzantium, in 663, it was rebuilt by Frederick II, who repopulated it in 1233 with 20,000 Saracens from Sicily, to whom he granted liberty of worship. It then took on the appearance of an Arab town. It became the stronghold of the Ghibellines in Southern Italy and in 1254 was the refuge of Manfred and, later, of his widow. The city was taken in 1269 by Charles I of Anjou. After the revolt of 1300 Charles II massacred all the Saracens that he could not forcibly convert and repopulated the town with Provenal families.

The **Cattedrale** (Assunta), a curious blend of Romanesque and Gothic, was founded by Charles II of Anjou and built in 1300–17. It is one of the less altered monuments of its age. The simple façade has three Gothic portals, that at the centre incorporating Roman columns and sculptural representations of St Michael and the Madonna and Child. The low campanile is crowned by an octagonal lantern of

The delicately ornamented façade of Troia cathedral

the 16C. The streets at the sides of the church lead round the protruding transepts to the magnificent **apse**, attributed to Pierre d'Agincourt, where massive buttresses and tall lancet windows betray an unmistakably French design.

The **interior** is built to a Latin cross plan, with a tall nave and aisles separated by pointed arches on rectangular piers with attached columnar shafts. The nave and aisle ceilings are in wood, whereas those of the three polygonal apses are vaulted and ribbed. In the south aisle are a Last Supper attributed to Palma Giovane and an elegant pulpit of 1560, obtained by reworking a tomb of the Scassa family. The south apse contains two cenotaphs, one of 14C Neapolitan workmanship; and a 14C wooden crucifix. Above the altar, is a 15C fresco of the Pieta; on the walls, Martyrs, Apostles and Saints frescoed by Belisario Corenzio.

The stone high altar came in part from Castel Fiorentino, the castle (14km north-west; now a ruin) where Frederick II died on 13 December 1250; the choir stalls date from the 17C, the frescoes of the apse from the 18C. In the north apse are a 17C tomb and a heavily repainted,14C wooden statue of the Madonna della Vittoria, commemorating the rise to power of the Angevins. In the north aisle can be seen a Madonna with Saints Nicholas and John the Baptist, by Fabrizio Santafede, a fine baptismal font with Renaissance baldachin and a 15C tabernacle. Below the organ, Madonna delle Stelle, a late 14C sculpture. To the right of the entrance, a relief of God the Father, of the 16C Neapolitan school.

Opposite the cathedral stand the Bishop's Palace and Palazzo Lombardi, both of the 18C. Via de' Nicastri, at the rear of the church, leads to the **Museo Civico Giuseppe Fiorelli** (open Wed, Thu, Sat, Sun 09.00–13.00, Tue and Fri 09.00–13.00, 15.00–18.00), which contains a Roman Venus, a fine mosaic pavement (1C), terracottas (3C BC) and ceramics of the Saracen and Angevin period, as well as 17C paintings and ethnographical exhibits.

About 500m west of the town on an eminence (250m) stands the *Castello, the most magnificent in Apulia, built by Frederick II in 1233 and enlarged by Charles I (1269–83). The enceinte of nearly 1km, with 24 towers, is still complete, and encloses the ruins of the Swabian palace. To the north-east of the town (10 min) are the ruins of a Roman amphitheatre of the Augustan period with two imposing entrance arches (reconstructed).

From Lucera Highway 17 runs straight across the plain to (18km) Foggia. From there to Bari, see Route 11.

B. Via Avellino

This is the fast route to Bari, which is only 261km (c2hr 10min) from Naples by motorway if you exclude the loop, described below, encompassing Melfi, Venosa, and Rionero in Vulture—three medieval towns whose architectural heritage dates back through Frederick II to the Normans. The landscape is extraordinarily beautiful, offering broad, open horizons and dramatic skies in addition to gently rolling hills and, in the Monte Vulture area, vast forests.

ROAD, 352km. Autostrada A16. 28km Nola—31km Avellino—42km Lacedonia—17km junction Highway 655—28km Melfi—6km Rapolla—19km Venosa—20km Rionero in Vulture—39km junction Autostrada A16—45km junction Autosrada A14—77km Bari. Keep windows up and doors locked while driving through Bari.

RAILWAY: The route is followed as far as Baiano (39km in 50–75 min) by a branch of the Circumvesuviana, serving Nola (28km) in 30–35 min. To Avellino by State Railway in c 2hr via Salerno. At Avellino the station lies c 3km east of the town. The line continues to Benevento, Route 17.

HOTELS EN ROUTE: Avellino, ****Hermitage, 5km south-west on Highway 88, tel. 0825 674788, fax 674772. Youth Hostel in Bari, Via Nicola Massaro 33; tel. 080 320282.

THE PLAIN OF NOLA AND THE APENNINE FOOTHILLS

Leave Naples by the Tangenziale and follow the signs to Autostrada A16 for Avellino and Bari. 23km **Nola** (34,000 inhab.), with stations on the Naples–Baiano and Cancello–Avellino railways, lies just beyond the junction with the Rome–Salerno motorway.

History

A town of Oscan origin, it became Etruscan, and later Samnite, under the name of *Novla*. In 313 BC it was taken by the Romans, from whom it received its present name. In ancient times it was famous for its vases of Greek type, which were probably the work of a colony of Chalcidians. Unsuccessfully assaulted by Hannibal on three separate occasions, it fell once more into Samnite hands in 90–80. It was plundered by Spartacus's band, in 73, and by Genseric the Vandal in 455. St Paulinus (353–431), Bishop of Nola, is traditionally said to have invented bells, which from their Campanian origin took the name of campane. His feast is celebrated with a picturesque procession on 22 June. In more recent times, the town was the birthplace of Giovanni da Nola (1488–1558), the sculptor, and of Giordano Bruno (1548–1600), the philosopher.

There is little to see in Nola today. The **Duomo** (San Felice), built in 1395–1402, has a graceful interior redecorated (1878–1909) after a fire. In the crypt, originally a church founded by St Felix on the ruins of a Roman temple, are the saint's relics (moved here from Cimitile) and an 8C paliotto. In the neighbouring Piazza Giordano Bruno are a statue of the great heretic and the Renaissance Palazzo Orsini, both of minor interest. Outside that town, reached by the road on the right of the cathedral and a turning to the left, stands the **Seminario** built by Vanvitelli in 1749. Its courtyard contains Roman inscriptions and the Cippus Abellanus, with Oscan lettering, named after the ruined city of *Abella* (now Avella), 18km north–east. In the suburb of Cimitile (the *coemeterium* of Nola), in 394, St Paulinus founded a monastery over the tomb of St Felix, first Bishop of Nola. Some remains (notably an 8C prothesis) are visible below the church of San Felice in Pineis.

Beyond Nola the motorway climbs amidst wooded hills, which in summer offer welcome respite from the heat and humidity of the plain of Naples.

31km **Avellino** (350m, 56,000 inhab.) lies in a wide basin surrounded by mountains, at the junction of several important roads. The town derives its name from *Abellinum*, an ancient city of the Hirpini, whose site is 4km east. Raised to the status of provincial capital in 1806, it has a spacious modern air, having been many times devastated by earthquakes.

■ **Railway station**. 3km east of the town (trolley-bus from Piazza della Libertà).

■ **Information**. EPT, Via due Principianti 5; tel. 0825 74695, fax 0825 74757 (branch office at Piazza Libertà 50).

■ **Post office**. Via De Sanctis.

In the town are the scanty remains of the Lombard castle, where the antipope Anacletus II recognised Count Roger as King of Sicily in 1130, and the Palazzo della Dogana, rebuilt in 1657 and adorned with antique statues. The **Duomo** has a Romanesque crypt and is adjoined by a museum (open daily 09.00–13.00) containing works of religious art from throughout the province, brought here and restored after the earthquake of 1980. The collections of the **Museo Irpino** are housed in modern quarters in Corso Europa (open daily 08.00–14.00). These include archaeological finds from the Neolithic to the late Roman age, from Mirabella Eclano, Iriano Irpino, Cairano and other sites in the Ofanto valley; a collection of 15–19C paintings; ceramics of Neapolitan and foreign manufacture; a presepio; and a section dedicated to the Risorgimento.

Just below the summit of Monte Partenio, to the north-west, stands the sanctuary of **Montevergine** (1493m; reached by a tortuous road of 18km), celebrated for a greatly venerated picture of the Virgin and visited by pilgrims at Whitsuntide and on 8 September (Nativity of the Virgin). The head of the Virgin,

The Convento di Loreto, winter residence of the abbot of Montevergine, designed in 1735 by Domenico Antonio Vaccaro

in Byzantine style, was rescued in 1265 from Constantinople by Baldwin II and brought here by Catherine of Valois in 1310. It is reputed to have been painted by St Luke. The remainder was executed in 1310 by Montano d'Arezzo. The church in which it is honoured, built by William of Vercelli in 1119–24 on the ruins of a temple of Cybele and rebuilt in the 17C after an earthquake, contains 14C tombs.

Here are buried Catherine of Valois (died 1347) and her son, Louis of Taranto (died 1362), second husband of Joan I. Below the sanctuary is the **Convento di Loreto**, the winter residence of the abbot, designed in 1735 by Domenico Antonio Vaccaro, where 16C Flemish tapestries and the important archives may be seen.

THE HILL TOWNS OF NORTHERN BASILICATA

The motorway turns north into the Sabato valley, then winds gently across the hills, offering a series of fine views over rolling farmland. 19km exit for Benevento, Route 17A. Beyond (42km) Lacedonia, you enter Apulia. 17km our road intersects with State Highway 655, running north to Foggia (36km, Route 11) and south to Potenza (80km, Route 17C). The southern tract crosses the lovely Monte Vulture area, which is well worth a visit.

28km **Melfi** (531m, 16,000 inhab.) was the first capital of the Normans. It is now the capital of Fiat's industrial development scheme in the south. In the **Castello** the investiture of Robert Guiscard was confirmed by Pope Nicholas II in 1059, at the first of four papal councils held at Melfi between that year and 1101. Here the first crusade was proclaimed in 1089, and during his sojourn at Melfi Frederick II set forth his *Constitutiones Augustales*. The **Museo Nazionale del Melfese** (open daily 09.00–19.00), in the castle, contains Bronze and Iron Age finds, Greek and Roman objects, burial treasures from a Daunian necropolis, Byzantine jewellery, and ceramics from the age of Frederick II. The castle itself is under restoration and cannot be visited.

A little further up the hill is the church of **Sant'Antonio di Padova**, with its pleasing rose window. It contains two amusing holy-water stoups, of which that on the left, dating from the 16C, is the more complete.

Via Garibaldi leads on towards the cathedral, passing on the right the 13C portal of the former church of Santa Maria la Nuova (now a cinema) with its dog-tooth carving.

The **Duomo** has a campanile of 1153 with fine decorative brickwork, including the representations of two griffons (emblems of the Norman dynasty in Sicily); the pyramidal top is a modern addition. In the interior can be seen a wooden ceiling and a Baroque high altar and surround. The latter also encloses an elaborate bishop's throne of gilded and painted wood. At the end of the north aisle is a fresco of the Madonna and Child enthroned, a late imitation of a Byzantine model; and in the second chapel on the south side is the much revered Madonna dell'Assunta, protectress of the city. In the adjoining **Bishop's Palace** can be seen a 1C *sarcophagus, on top of which is portrayed the figure of a young girl, and holy objects from the cathedral and other churches in the town.

The district around Melfi contains several painted chapels hollowed in the rock (apply to the Municipio for assistance), of which one of the more easily accessible is to be found on the road to Venosa. About 1km outside Melfi a small lane leads left towards the cemetery and, almost at once, a track leads left again to the **Cappella Santa Margherita**, containing 13C frescoes.

From here it is a short drive to (6km) **Rapolla** (438m, 4000 inhab.), a thermal resort, where the **Cattedrale** dates from the late 13C. Set into the south wall are two bas-reliefs, one representing Original Sin, and the other an Annunciation. Both date from the early 13C and show a marked Byzantine spirit. The church of **Santa Lucia**, a beautiful little building with two cupolas, is built to a Byzantine plan (the key may be obtained from the sacristan of the cathedral).

Turn south on Highway 168. 19km **Venosa** (12,000 inhab.) the ancient *Venusia*, is famous as the birthplace of Horace (Q. Horatius Flaccus, 65–8 BC), whose statue adorns the piazza; and of Manfred (born 1232).

History

The surrounding territory was inhabited in prehistoric times and constitutes one of the more prolific archaeological areas in Basilicata. Traces of Chellean and Acheullean settlements have been found at the borders of the Venosa basin, which at one time probably held a large lake. Some of the objects brought to light by recent excavations may be seen in the modest Briscese collection, described below, although the bulk of the material is distributed among the museums of Potenza, Matera, Rome, Florence and Milan. Venusia, originally an Apulian town, became the largest colony in the Roman world in 290 BC; here Hannibal ambushed and killed the celebrated Roman general Marcellus (208 BC).

In Piazza Umbertoi stands the great 16C **Castello**, to the west of which can be seen the undistinguished remains of the supposed tomb of Marcellus. The **Cattedrale** also dates from the 16C; its walls contain fragments of Roman buildings. The church is entered by a rustic Renaissance portal and contains a painting of the martyrdom of St Felix attributed to Carlo Maratta. In Via Vittorio Emanuele, near the town hall, is the **Museo Briscese** (open 09.00–19.00), containing Palaeolithic finds including Acheulean hand axes and some implements of the so-called Clactonian culture, the third phase of which is named after Venosa.

To the north-east of the town lie the considerable remains of *La Trinita, one of the more impressive monastic complexes in Basilicata. Founded by the Benedictines c 1046, the abbey pre-dates the Norman invasion. It stands on the ruins of an early Christian church, which in turn overlies a Roman temple. The new church (incomplete) dates from 1063. Note the Cluniac form of the building, including a splendid ambulatory; also the beginnings of two campanili and the fine carvings of the capitals. To the south of this part of the group can be seen the remains of an early Christian baptistery. The earlier church dates from the time of the abbey's foundation, but was later enlarged and redecorated. It has a fine façade with, inside the first porch, a beautifully carved second portal with horseshoe arches. Many carved pieces belonging to the buildings are scattered about to the right. The interior contains what is said to be the tomb of Robert Guiscard (died 1085) and of his first wife Alberada, divorced on the grounds of consanguinity. Robert's sarcophagus also contains the remains of his half-brothers, William Bras-de-Fer, first Count of Apulia (died 1046), Drogo (murdered in 1051), and Humphrey (died 1057). Numerous frescoes decorate the walls, including one that is possibly a portrait of Joan I of Naples, under which is a 14C Pietà attributed to Roberto Oderisius. Across the road are remains of a Roman amphitheatre and, further on, Jewish catacombs hewn out of the rock c 50m above the road.

Another ruined abbey

Time permitting, a further excursion can be made from Venosa to the town of **Banzi**, 25km south-east, where the parish church encloses the remains of the ancient **Abbazia di Santa Maria**. These can be seen from the sacristy; a room leading from the end of the north aisle; and in the walls of the adjoining habitations, including one of the entrances (an arch leading from the main street). The church also contains, in the chapel to the left of the high altar, a 12C or 13C wooden polychromed statue of the Madonna and Child and the remains of a triptych attributed to Andrea da Salerno. Over the high altar is a Madonna in the Byzantine manner. High over the west front of the church can be seen a relief of the Madonna and Child.

Leave Venosa from the southwest, via Highway 167. **Rionero in Vulture** (656m, 13,000 inhab.), 11km south of Melfi and 20km east of Venosa, is the starting point for excursions to **Monte Vulture**, an extinct volcano whose summit commands nearly all Apulia. The area to the west, now much frequented by local tourists, is renowned for its natural beauty. Chief among its attractions are the beautiful little Laghi di Monticchio (652m), of which you may make a circuit and from which the ascent of Monte Vulture may be made in a funicular. Near the funicular station stand the ruins of the **Abbazia di Sant'Ippolito**, dating from the 11C and 12C. On the heights above one of the two lakes stands the late 17C Abbazia di San Michele, of small interest. The splendid **Bosco di Monticchio** contains over 970 varieties of flora, some rare.

A small road from Rionero leads (in about 8km) to the village of Ripacandida, in a commanding position at the top of a hill. Just beyond the village stands the **Santuario di San Donato**, where the small church is almost completely covered with 14C frescoes (repainted) depicting scenes from the Old and New Testaments, figures of saints and representations of miracles.

3km **Barile** (620m, 4000 inhab.) is an Albanian colony founded in the 15C; the inhabitants retain their ethnic and linguistic traditions. Weddings and funerals are particularly interesting, as are the ceremonies for religious holidays. In the Scescio and Solagna del Fico areas are a number of curious caves carved in the tufa, formerly inhabited, now used as wine cellars. A troglodytic settlement has been found in the area of San Pietro.

From Barile you may return to Autostrade A16 in c 30 min.

Castel Lagopesole

At Atella, 6km south, the Apulian Aqueduct crosses the valley. The village (4000 inhab.) has a Romanesque-Gothic cathedral of the 14C. 14km further on the same road, stands **Castel Lagopesole** (829m), huddled at the foot of the fortress from which it takes its name, the last of Frederick II's great castles, begun in 1242. Here the emperor spent the last summer of his life. The castle was built as a mountain retreat and a bulwark against the rebellions that became frequent in Basilicata towards the end of Frederick's reign. It was also frequented by Manfred and by Charles of Anjou, who restored it in 1266 and made it the prison of Elena, Manfred's wife.

The reddish tone of the walls is due to the oxidation of iron salts in the rock. The entrance, on the west side, leads to a vaulted hall and then to the imposing court, flanked on the north and west by the royal apartments and containing a series of fine mullioned windows. The chapel, in the south-east corner, is linked by a covered gallery to the emperor's apartments. A double staircase on the south side ascends to a smaller court, at the centre of which stands the massive square **keep**. The entrance, 8m above ground, is marked by corbels that at one time supported an external platform. The roof was carried on the two carved heads visible above, one of which is traditionally said to represent Beatrice, second wife of Emperor Barbarossa, and the other, with ass's ears, to be a likeness of the emperor himself.

Highway 655 continues to (27km) Potenza, offering good views over the city and the Basento valley.

Autostrada A16 runs eastwards across fields planted with grain to join the Adriatic motorway, A14, at Cerignola. From here to Bari, see Route 11.

C.   Via Potenza

*This route proceeds swiftly to **Potenza**, Italy's highest provincial capital, then winds through magnificent open country to **Gravina di Puglia** and **Altamura**, two magnificent ancient centres located in the semi-desertic inland region of Apulia. Gravina stands in a singular position on the edge of the deep, wild ravine (gravina) from which it takes its name, at the centre of an area rich in prehistoric finds; Altamura is the home of one of Apulia's four magnificent palatine cathedrals. Beyond, the road runs straight across the Murge plateau to Bari.*

If you are driving, allow c 4hr travel time.. Avoid driving the country roads around Gravina and Altamura after dark, and keep windows up and doors locked when entering Baril. The alternative road route to Potenza, using Highway 7b to Avellino (Route 17B) and there joining Highway 7, is 35km longer and considerably more mountainous.

ROAD, 299km. Autostrada A3/E45 and E847, and Highways 94 and 92 to Potenza, then Highways 407, 7 (Via Appia), and 96. 55km Salerno—53km Raccordo

Autostradale per Potenza—48km Potenza—88km Gravina di Puglia—12km Altamura—43km Bari.

RAILWAY: 312km in 7–8hr. To Potenza, 166km in c 2hr 30min, with station-to-station bus service substituting for trains from Salerno to Potenza at certain times of day; to Bari, 146km in c 3hr 30min. The latter line, which is privately owned, follows the road closely after Gravina di Puglia.

HOTELS EN ROUTE: Rifreddo (Potenza), ****Giubileo, tel./fax 0971 479910. Youth Hostel in Bari, Via Nicola Massaro 33; tel. 080 320282.

RESTAURANTS EN ROUTE: Muro Lucano, *Delle Colline (with rooms), tel. 0976 2284, fax 0976 2192.

NAPLES TO POTENZA
From Naples to Salerno, see Route 7B. Beyond Salerno the motorway crosses uninteresting countryside dotted with small industries.

29km **Eboli** (35,000 inhab.) stands on a hill to the left of the road. The Collegiata contains an Assumption by Andrea da Salerno, and San Pietro alli Marmi has a plain Romanesque interior (restored). Just beyond the town a road climbs over the mountains to Grottaminarda. The motorway follows the valley, crossing first the Sele, then the Tanagro.

24km Autostrada A3 bends south; a raccordo (link road) bears east towards Potenza, offering a series of fine ***views** back over the Tanagro valley. Vietri di Potenza (405m, 4000 inhab.) comes into sight on its rocky ridge, on the right; followed by **Picerno** (721m, 6000 inhab.), pleasantly situated in verdant farmland, on the left. Picerno is known for its interesting monumental doorways. The 14C chapel of the **Annunziata**, at the centre of the town, has a medieval portal with figures clad in Roman togas.

The old road to Potenza
The traditional route from Naples to Potenza by Highway 7 (Via Appia) passes to the north, beyond Monte Cervialto (1809m). 87km the Ponte Romito on the Calore is 10km north of **Bagnoli Irpino**, where the churches of San Domenico and the Assunta have finely crafted woodwork. Just beyond (18km) Sant'Angelo dei Lombardi is the abbey of **San Guglielmo a Goleto**, founded in 1132 by St William of Vercelli and severely damaged in the earthquake of 1980; its smaller church dates from 1250 and the campanile from 1152.

You cross the Eboli–Grottaminarda road at (25km) the Sella di Conza (697m) near Caposele (21km south-west) where some of the headwaters of the Sele are conducted through a tunnel, 12km long, to the east slope of the Apennines, to form the first stage of the Apulian Aqueduct. Near the town is the Abbey of Materdomini (1748), a pilgrimage centre with a hotel. From here to Potenza, rising in sinuous curves (at two points above 1100m), the road offers magnificent rugged scenery, passing (32km) **Muro Lucano**, with the castle in which Joan I was suffocated (1382), possibly the site of the Battle of Numistrum between Hannibal and Marcellus (210 BC). This route is followed (though not very closely) from Avellino to beyond Sant'Angelo dei Lombardi by a cross-country railway that continues to Rocchetta Sant'Antonio on the Foggia–Potenza line.

48km **Potenza** (68,000 inhab.), the highest provincial capital of the mainland (820m), has suffered much from war and earthquakes, and its architecture is undistinguished. The overall atmosphere of the city is nevertheless quite pleasant.

■ **Information**. Assessorato Regionale al Turismo e Industria Alberghiera, Ufficio Turismo, Via Anzio 44; tel. 0971 332601, fax 0971 332630. APT, Via Cavour 15; tel. 0971 34594, fax 0971 36196 (branch office at Via Alianelli 4).

■ **Railway stations**. Inferiore (FS) on the main Naples–Taranto line, with a branch to Foggia. Stazione Città for Altamura and Bari. Trains on the Avigliano and Laurenzana branch lines serve both stations.

■ **Bus** from the Inferiore station to the centre.

■ **Post office**. Via Sauro.

■ **Special events** Maggio Potentino (May), with artistic, cultural, and sports events, culminating in the Sagra di San Gerardo, with the Sfilata dei Turchi, at the end of the month; also, Sagra di San Rocco (16 Aug), with traditional celebrations.

In Piazza Pagano is the church of **San Francesco** (1274), with a 15C carved door and a good 16C marble tomb. Behind the theatre lies the Romanesque church of San Michele Arcangelo. The Duomo, reconstructed in 1799, stands at the highest point of the town. In Via Lazio is the Museo Archeologico Provinciale Lucano (entrance in Via Cicotto; closed for restoration). The museum contains a fine collection of objects from Metapontum and other Lucanian excavations, notably local antique ceramic ware, archaic bronze statuettes, terracottas, a bronze helmet from Vaglio and a 5C marble tempietto from Metapontum. A short distance to the south of the museum stands the church of **Santa Maria del Sepulcro**, originally of the 13C, altered in the 14C and again in the 17C, and recently restored to its original state. The church contains a fine polyptych attributed to Andrea Solario.

The Cathedral of Acerenza

About 40km north-east of Potenza, with a station (6km) on the Potenza–Bari line (50 min from Potenza), stands **Acerenza**, a small town (3000 inhab.) splendidly situated on a calcareous hill. The Romanesque *cathedral, rebuilt in 1281 (open by appointment; tel. 0971 741112), has an ambulatory with three radiating chapels and a splendid west portal. The crypt contains early 16C frescoes of a rustic charm. Within the church is a small museum with a marble bust said by some to represent Julian the Apostate and, more doubtfully, by others to be a likeness of Frederick II. The curious cylindrical tower is a later addition.

Through the hills to Apulia

Leave Potenza from the east. 14km **Vaglio Basilicata** is the first of the little towns of medieval aspect that crown small hills above the road, which rises and falls along the wooded north slopes of the wide valley of the Basento. At the entrance to the village is a piazza containing two fountains; to the right can be seen a pleasing Renaissance portal, near to which stands an ex-Franciscan monastery, now an orphanage, that encloses the church of **Sant'Antonio** (ring at convent for admittance). The latter contains many excellent examples of Baroque gilded and painted woodwork, including a singular carved and painted wooden pulpit of the 17C. There are also several statues, among the best of which is a terracotta of St Anthony Abbot, in the centre of the screen behind the high altar.

5km Highway 96 leaves the Potenza–Matera road (Highway 7) and diverges north to (11km) **Tolve**, a simple little village (4000 inhab.) where the west portal of the church of San Pietro exhibits a carved architrave containing curious symbolic images. The road continues across an arid, lonely landscape to (34km) **Irsina** (548m, 7000 inhab.) overlooking the valley of the Bradano. The **Cattedrale** has a fine campanile with mullioned openings (some of which are modern replacements) and contains good marble inlaid Baroque altars. The church of **San Francesco**, founded in the 12C, remodelled in the Baroque period and now put back to its Romanesque-Gothic form, was built onto a castle of Frederick II, parts of which, including a good tower, remain. The church contains fine marble inlaid Baroque altars, a 17C crucifix behind the high altar and a crypt with 14C **frescoes** of great interest.

12km cross the railway and enter Apulia, leaving on the right Highway 96b. The road ascends the valley of the Basentella to the Serra di Santa Teresa, with good views ahead to Gravina and Altamura, then follows the railway east, passing on the right a turning for Matera. A few metres further on it ascends sharply past (right) the former convent of San Sebastiano, with an interesting Romanesque cloister.

GRAVINA AND ALTAMURA

12km **Gravina di Puglia** (338m, 40,000 inhab.) is set in a breathtaking position on the edge of a deep ravine. It succeeds the Peucetian centre of *Sidion*, which in Roman times became known as *Silvium*, probably located on the nearby hill of Petramagna, today known as Botromagno. During the Barbarian invasions its inhabitants took refuge in the *gravina* or ravine, and many continued to live in its limestone caves even after the present town began to take shape around the 5C. This town was destroyed in the 10C by Saracen mercenaries and was occupied in the following century by the Normans. In 1420 it passed to the Roman Orsini family, who held it in fee until 1807. The old town is interesting for its winding streets and its ancient houses with balconies carried on corbels.

The centre of the town is Piazza della Republica, flanked by the much-altered Palazzo Orsini. From here Corso Matteotti leads to Piazza Notar Domenico, where the church of the **Purgatorio** (or Santa Maria dei Morti) has a bizarre portal with a *memento mori* of reclining skeletons in the tympanum. The columns carried by bears allude to the Orsini family, who commissioned the building in 1649. Within are a painting of the Madonna and Saints by Francesco Solimena and the tomb of Ferdinando III Orsini (died 1660).

To the left of the church is the Biblioteca Finya, founded by Cardinal Angelo Antonio Finya (1669–1743). From here a narrow street on the left descends to the Rione Fondovico, the oldest quarter of the town, where the church of **San Michele di Grotti** is entirely hewn out of the rock. The interior has five aisles and a flat ceiling borne by monolithic piers; scant remains of frescoes; and in one corner, human bones which tradition attributes to the victims of the Saracen attack of 983. More of these are heaped together in the Grotta di San Marco, above.

In Piazza Benedetto XIII is the **Duomo**, originally of 1092, enlarged in 1420, destroyed by fire in 1447 and rebuilt in 1482. The basilican interior has three aisles separated by semicircular arches on columns with interesting capitals. The gilded wooden ceiling incorporates rather indifferent paintings. Above the fourth altar on the south side is a 16C relief of the Presentation of the Virgin. The wooden choir stalls date from 1561.

Returning to Piazza Notar Domenico, take Via Ambrazzo D'Ales and Via Lelio Orsi to **Palazzo Somarici Santomasi**. Here are collections (open Mon–Sat 09.00–13.00) of archaeological material from Botromagno; coins and medallions; a section devoted to rural life; a reconstruction of the Byzantine crypt of San Vito Vecchio, with 13C frescoes of local workmanship; architectural fragments and ethnographical collections.

Nearby is the small church of **Santa Sofia**, in the presbytery of which can be seen the tomb of Angela Castriata Scanderbeg, wife of Ferdinand I Orsini (died 1518). The Renaissance church of **San Francesco** has a fine rose window and sculptured portals; the Baroque campanile dates from 1766. Also worthy of attention is the church of the **Madonna delle Grazie**, near the station, the unique façade (1602) of which incorporates three crenellated towers in rusticated stone and an enormous eagle with spread wings in low relief.

Proceed through rolling countryside past (left) the ruins of a hunting lodge of Frederick II to (12km) **Altamura** (468m, 58,000 inhab.), a flourishing agricultural and industrial centre built along the top of a ridge.

History

Altamura was a Peucetian centre of considerable importance, the name of which is still unknown. The ancient city was destroyed by the Saracens and the area remained uninhabited until 1230, when Frederick II founded a new town on the site of the former acropolis, with a population of Italians, Greeks and Jews drawn from neighbouring villages by the concession of special privileges.

In the centuries that followed, the town was granted in fee to the Del Balzo and Farnese, among others. In 1799 it was ruthlessly sacked and burned by the Sanfredisti under Cardinal Ruffo for its adherence to the Parthenopean Republic. It became a major intellectual centre in the 18C and possessed its own university from 1748 until the end of the century. Altamura was the seat of the first provisional government of Apulia during the Risorgimento.

You enter the town by Piazza Unità d'Italia. From here Viale Regina Margherita descends to the station, passing the Strada Panoramica, from which considerable remains of the 5C BC Peucetian walls may be seen. Approximately 3700m in circumference, the walls stand in some areas to a height of over 4m, with an average thickness of c 5m.

Return to the piazza and pass through the **Porta di Bari**, medieval in origin but later absorbed by the massive Palazzo Del Balzo. Corso Federico II di Svevia, beyond, leads to the heart of the old town. To the left of the gateway are remains of the 13C walls that give the town its name (Altamura, 'high walls'). Pass, on the left, the little church of **San Niccolo dei Greci**, erected in the 13C by Greek colonists, where the Orthodox rite was celebrated until 1601. The simple but attractive façade has a rose window and an interesting portal decorated with Old and New Testament scenes in bas-relief. Beyond, the corso ends in Piazza Duomo, with its monument to the citizens of Altamura slain in the sack of 1799.

The *Cattedrale (Santa Maria Assunta) is one of the four Palatine basilicas of Apulia (the others being San Nicola di Bari and the cathedrals of Barletta and

Acquaviva delle Fonti). Begun by Frederick II in 1232 and rebuilt after the earthquake of 1316, it was further altered in 1534, when its orientation was inverted and the main portal and rose window were dismantled and reassembled in their present position, on what was formerly the apse.

The façade stands between two 16C campanili to which Baroque pinnacles were added in 1729. In a loggia beneath the pediment can be seen a figure of the Assunta, flanked by Sts Peter and Paul above the arch. Below is the beautiful recessed *rose window, with delicate fretted stonework and multiple bands of ornate carving. The Gothic window of 1232 which originally stood in the apse wall and which was removed to make way for the rose window, is now located in the left portion of the façade, next to three heraldic stems, the largest of which bears the arms of Charles V.

The 14–15C *main portal is one of the more richly decorated doorways of Apulia. It is set beneath a shallow porch with four slender columns and a pointed gable, within which bands of moulding carved with foliate motifs and scenes from the life of Christ establish a formal and visual link between the door posts and the delicately pointed arches above. In the lintel is a relief of the Last Supper. The lunette contains an exquisitely carved Madonna and Child with angels.

Along the unaltered north flank of the church, broad semicircular blind arches enclose slender lancet windows and the elegant Porta Angioina, named for Robert of Anjou whose arms, together with a Gothic inscription commemorating its construction, appear above. Between the tops of the arches and the roof run 12 trefoil windows with intertwining arches. The transept, a 16C addition to the church, incorporates a tall Gothic window from the earlier façade.

The **interior**, a vast, sombre three-aisled basilica, retains its original flavour despite the 19C additions. The nave is divided into three broad bays by semicircular arches on piers alternating with columns with good capitals. Above the nave arcade is a triforium with semicircular arches on slender columns, also bearing interesting capitals. The aisles contain a number of interesting paintings, chiefly by local artists. The inlaid choir stalls, the bishop's throne and the carved marble pulpit all date from the mid 16C

The **Museo Civico** (open Mon–Sat 09.00–14.00; closed Sun and holidays) contains material from local excavations. The collection includes Bronze Age pottery, bronze and ceramic ware from nearby tombs (8–5C BC), locally painted pottery (6–5C), a bronze helmet and Gnathian and Peucetian ware.

Sepulchral monuments and tombs

In the environs of Altamura can be seen numerous 'specchie', free-standing sepulchral monuments of a type quite common in prehistoric Apulia. Interesting excursions may be made to the **Pulo**, 7km north-east of Altamura, a circular dolina 500m in diameter and c 75m deep; and to Casal Sabini, a village 9km east on the Santeramo road, where there are several **rock-cut tombs** of the Bronze Age as well as Peucetian trench-graves dating from the 6–3C BC. The site lies to the right of the highway just beyond the village. Matera (Route 18) lies 17km south on Highway 99.

A series of long, straight tracts bear across rolling country on the highland plain of the Murge, then the road descends through a lonely landscape to (29km) a crossroad leading (left) to Palo del Colle, with its 12C cathedral, and (right) to **Bitetto** (4km), where the **Cattedrale** (San Michele), originally of the 11C, was remodelled in 1335 in Romanesque forms. The handsome façade has a richly decorated central doorway, with reliefs of the Madonna and Child in the lunette, Christ and the Apostles on the architrave, and New Testament scenes on the door-posts. At the north-east corner of the church stands a Romanesque campanile, probably belonging to the original building. The Baroque bell-tower to the left of the façade probably dates from 1764.

The interior has been extensively altered, especially in the 16C, but recent restoration has returned it more or less to its 14C form. It is basilican in plan, with long, narrow aisles, wooden ceilings, slightly pointed arches and a triforium. Behind the main altar is an Assunta by Carlo Rosa (1656).

15km **Modugno** is a large town (38,000 inhab.) with a 17C campanile. The ancient church of San Pietro (or San Felice), 3km south-east on the Bitetto road, is the sole survival of the medieval town of Balsignano.

8km Bari, see Route 11.

18 · Naples to Brindisi

*This route crosses the rocky highlands of the area between **Taranto** and **Gravina in Puglia**, the inhabitants of which (like those of Matera) took refuge in the Middle Ages in caves in the deep, narrow ravines (gravine in Italian) to escape the Saracen massacres. Later, as more conventional settlements grew up on the cliff tops nearby, the caves were frequently made into chapels and decorated with rough frescoes or carved designs. The finest examples of this unusual architectural genre are to be found at **Matera**, which was recently brought under the protection of UNESCO; but there are many others strewn about the region, for instance at **Massafra**. Between the two towns, in the country around **Castellaneta** (which, with its pristine whitewashed houses is well worth a stop) is another fascinating form of local architecture, the masseria fortificata, or fortified farm. Many of these walled agricultural complexes, which usually include a noble residence for the landowner, simple but harmonious peasant homes, and barns and other out-buildings, are now being turned into country inns. Beyond Taranto **Grottaglie** is the best place in Apulia to buy ceramics, **Francavilla Fontana** and **Oria** offer insight into the evolution of Apulian baronial architecture, and the county is dotted with pre-Roman archaeological finds.*

The route entails a long drive (travel time is 5hr 15min), but the scenery throughout is among the most impressive in Southern Europe. At Potenza a bypass skirts south of the city, linking up with Highway 407, which follows the Basento valley east to Metapontum (Route 10). At (252km) Stazione di Ferrandina, Highway 7t branches north to (34km) Matera. This alternative, though faster, is less interesting than the itinerary described below.

ROAD, 402km. Autostrade A3/E45 and E847 and Highways 94 and 92 to Potenza, then Highways 407, 7 (Via Appia), and 96. 55km Salerno—53km Raccordo Autostradale per Potenza—48km Potenza—107km Matera—73km Taranto—66km Brindisi.

RAILWAY: 383km in c 6hr 30min, with a change of trains at Taranto and, often, at Salerno. To Taranto, 313km in c 5hrs; to Potenza, 166km in c 2hr 30min, with station-to-station bus service substituted for trains from Salerno to Potenza at certain times of day; to Ferrandina, 235km in c 3hr 15min, Matera may be reached in c 1hr more. Beyond Potenza the line closely follows the valley of the Basento from near its source to its mouth at Metaponto, continuing to Taranto along the shore, then following the road closely to Brindisi.

HOTELS EN ROUTE: Rifreddo (Potenza), ****Giubileo, tel./fax 0971 479910.

RESTAURANTS EN ROUTE: Ceglie Messapica (16km north of Grottaglie), ***Al Fornello-da Ricci, contrada Montevicoli, tel. 0831 977104, fax 0831 977577.

Naples to Matera

From Naples to Potenza see Route 17C. Beyond Potenza Highway 7 bears east. 6km the Basento valley road (see above) branches off to the right.

14km **Vaglio Basilicata** is the first of the little towns of medieval aspect that crown small hills above the road, which rises and falls along the wooded north slopes of the wide valley of the Basento. At the entrance to the village is a piazza containing two fountains; to the right can be seen a pleasing Renaissance portal, near to which stands an ex-Franciscan monastery, now an orphanage, that encloses the church of **Sant'Antonio** (ring at convent for admittance). The latter contains many excellent examples of Baroque gilded and painted woodwork, including a singular carved and painted wooden pulpit of the 17C. There are also several statues, among the best of which is a terracotta of St Anthony Abbot, in the centre of the screen behind the high altar.

At 5km a lonely road diverges left to Altamura and Bari (see Route 18). Bear right and climb through a magnificent oak forest to the Valico del Cupolicchio, a pass 1028m high, then begin the descent of the east slope of Monte Cupolicchio.

27km **Tricarico** (698m, 7000 inhab.) contains several churches and convents of minor interest, among which may be numbered the monasteries of the **Carmine** and of **Sant'Antonio**, which lie just outside the town. The former contains a cloister with decorative frescoes (much damaged) and, in the church, 17C **frescoes** which display a liveliness both in content and execution, the best being those in the choir and the two figures of saints on the choir arch.

In the town itself is the fine cylindrical tower of the Norman castle. The church of Santa Chiara is entered through a chapel containing a good 17C crucifix; the church has a fine gilded ceiling. The Duomo, erected by Robert Guiscard but many times restored, contains interesting woodwork, exuberant Baroque stucco in the chapel to the right of the high altar and the tomb of Diomedo Carafa (1639).

Several traces of Lucanian settlements are to be found in the environs. These include remains of two concentric wall circuits at (3km) Tempa dell'Altare, traces of habitations and of defensive walls at Piano della Civita, and some tombs of the 4C BC at Cancello (west of Tricarico on Highway 7). Also of interest but less readily accessible is the ruined village of **Calle di Tricarico** (19km north-east), which contains elements dating from Hellenistic times to the High Middle Ages, including a Roman villa with well-preserved baths.

Continue east with broad views over the valley of the Basento. 16km **Grassano** (515m, 6000 inhab.) is reached by a road on the left. In the municipio (a former convent of the Minori) can be seen two 17C frescoes, one of the Last Supper showing affinities with Venetian painting of a century earlier.

13km Grottole stands at the northwest end of the Val di Basento industrial district, which developed in the 1960s following the discovery of an extensive methane gas field. The district extends along the valley floor from the Salandra-Grottole area to Pisticci and draws upon the population and resources of Grottole,

Salandra, Ferrandina, Pomarico, Pisticci and Matera. Methane is piped from here to Matera, Monopoli and Bari.

The road climbs away from the Basento. At (12km) **Miglionico** is the impressive castle where in 1481 Sanseverino and the barons hatched their unsuccessful conspiracy against Ferdinand I of Aragon. The church of **San Francesco** contains a splendid Madonna and Child with Saints by Giovanni Battista Cima (1499). The crucifix over the high altar is flanked on one side by the Madonna and on the other by St Francis. The church of the **Matrice** has a Romanesque campanile, with sculptured figures set into its higher regions (Madonna and Child, Saints, etc). At its east side can be seen a Renaissance-Baroque portal with a Pietà in the lunette. The west portal is also of interest.

Turn north-east and cross the Bradano, which here runs through a deep gorge. On the left is Lago San Giuliano, a lake made by damming the river. From here on you climb through wilder scenery, scarred by ravines carved in the chalk.

MATERA
20km Matera, capital of its province, is beautifully situated (399m) on the edge of a ravine.

History
The environs of Matera appear to have been inhabited since palaeolithic times, and for this reason make up one of the more important archaeological zones of south Italy. Little, however, is known of the city's ancient history. Although Greek tombs have been discovered in the area of the old town or civita, it is generally agreed that the Greek settlement at Matera was of little importance. The town was destroyed by the Saracens in 944 and its inhabitants killed or dispersed. In 1638 it became the capital of Basilicata, a position which it retained until Potenza rose to primacy in 1806. Today Matera is a very pleasant modern city; a few of its 55,000 inhabitants have moved back to the Sassi, ancient cave dwellings, recently renovated.

■ **Information**. EPT, Via De Viti De Marco 9; tel. 0835 331983, fax 0835 333452.

■ **Railway station** (of the Ferrovie Calabro-Lucane) in Piazza Matteotti, with connections for Altamura-Bari and for Ferrandina, on the Potenza–Taranto line of the State Railways.

■ **Post office**. Corso Umberto.

■ **Tours of the Sassi** may be arranged through the EPT and the affiliated Cooperativa Turistica. The young boys who generally offer their services to visitors arriving in Matera are less knowledgeable, but competent (haggling necessary).

■ **Special events**: Sagra della Madonna della Bruna, on 2 July, an annual religious festival commemorating the recovery of a Byzantine Madonna stolen by the Turks and consisting of a colourful triumphal procession ending in the destruction of the papier-mache car on which the image is borne through the streets.

Enter the town by Via Ridola, in which is to be found the former seminary, now called the **Palazzo Lanfranchi**, which houses an interesting collection of paintings, mostly of the Neapolitan school (closed to the public except when the building is open for special events). Further on, on the left, stands the church of Santa Chiara, with 18C woodwork of a certain rustic charm. Next to this, in the former convent, is the **Museo Nazionale Domenico Ridola* (open daily 09.00–19.00), which contains changing displays of material from the local excavations, including Corinthian helmets in bronze of the 5C BC, Roman bronze vases, Greek vases, etc.; and an extraordinary prehistoric collection, ranging from Palaeolithic finds from Matera and its environs, to late Bronze Age material from Timmari. The ambience of the museum is very pleasant, and the exhibits are well displayed and marked. Further on, to the left, stands the church of the **Purgatorio**, with its charming Baroque façade decorated, in part, with strange, somewhat gruesome 18C sculptures.

Now enter **Piazza San Francesco**, with a **church** of that name dating from the 17C, also with a decorative façade. The second south chapel contains an 18C Baroque altar and the 16C tomb of Eustachio Pavlicello. Set into the organ case behind the high altar are panels from a polyptych by Bartolomeo Vivarini. In the fifth chapel on the north is the entrance to the earlier church of Santi Pietro e Paolo, over which the present church stands (closed and difficult of access). In the first north chapel is a polychromed wood statue of St Francis. The holy-water stoup at the entrance rests on a Romanesque capital

The street on the south flank of San Francesco leads into Piazza Vittorio Emanuele. The decorative entrance to the Conservatorio di Musica can be seen on the right. From here The Via del Duomo leads into Piazza del Duomo; along the way, notice the fine palace on the right, opposite which there is a splendid view along the valley of the Sasso Barisano (cf. below). The ***Duomo** dates from the 13C and is in the Apulian Romanesque type. The west end has a large rose window carried by angels; and the central portal, fine basket-work carving and a sculptural group representing the Madonna and Child with Sts Peter and Paul. The south flank has a carved central window. The door to the west (Porta della Piazza) has another good surround and a carved central relief of monks with the word Abraham inscribed above it. That to the east (Porta dei Leoni) has two lions at its base.

The **interior** is built to a Latin cross plan with a tall nave of typically Lombard conception and aisles divided by columns (some from Metapontum, see Route 10) with extraordinary capitals. In the first north chapel is a 13C Madonna and Child of Byzantine taste and the finest inlaid altar in the church. Further on is the **Cappella dell'Annunciata**, a sumptuously decorated 16C edifice containing good sculpture by Altobello Persio a local artist, and helpers. At the end of the north aisle, set into an elaborate carved surround, are other figures by Persio and Sannazaro d'Alessandro, to the left of which is a chapel containing an immense ***Nativity** with a host of sculpted figures, also a work of Altobello Persio and Sannazaro d'Alessandro (1534). The choir contains 15C inlaid stalls by Giovanni Tantino da Ariano Irpino, above which hangs a great painting of the Assumption and Saints, of the early 17C Venetian school. Other paintings of interest are those over the third altar on the south side, Madonna and Child with St Anne, attributed to Sebastiano Majieski (1632); and over the first altar on the same side, Assumption of the Virgin with Saints, by Giovanni Donato Oppido di Matera, both of which are in fine carved frames. Next to the Cappella dell'Annunciata a door leads into a passageway, at the end of which can be seen the portal of the small church of Santa Maria di Constantinopoli, with worn carving and a 13C relief in the lunette showing the carriage procession of the Madonna della Bruna.

The Piazza del Duomo, from which there is another fine view over the Sasso Barisano, and the Via del Duomo split the Sassi into two parts. You can enter both the Sasso Barisano and the Sasso Caveoso from the piazza, as you can from Via Ridola.

Retrace your steps along Via del Duomo, branching off to the right along Via Margherita. This leads into Piazza Vittorio Veneto, which divides the old town from the new. Just off the piazza is **San Domenico**, a 13C church with a rustic façade.The interior contains a repainted statue of the Madonna and Child, of indeterminate date. Above the first altar on the south side hangs a 17C copy of Raphael's Holy Family, near which is the coeval tomb of Orazio Persio. Beyond the church Via San Biagio leads to the church of San Rocco, which contains a brutally realistic crucifix of the early 17C.

Almost opposite stands the early 13C church of **San Giovanni Battista**, with a fine carved portal on the south side (through which you enter the church) with delicate foliate decoration of Byzantine inspiration and a Saracenic arch embedded in the door recess. The interior is of a strangely inarticulate nature, with interesting carved capitals and an extremely high central elevation showing signs of early Northern Gothic inspiration.

From the opposite end of Piazza Vittorio Veneto, Via Lavista leads south-west to a public garden, from which steps ascend to the unfinished Angevin castle. Its builder, the tyrannical Count Tramontano, was killed in a popular revolt on his way out of the cathedral in 1515, in the side street still known as Via del Riscatto, 'street of vengeance'.

In the central Piazza Pascoli are the Pinacoteca d'Errico (temporarily closed) and the **Collezione Carlo Levi** (open Mon–Sat 08.00–13.00), which holds a fine collection of works by the celebrated 20C artist.

THE SASSI

To visit this part of the town it is essential to find some sort of a guide (see above) among the inhabitants of the place, likewise to arrange a price; do not expect to be allowed to enter all the churches and chapels. In this strange valley are to be found habitations, churches and frescoed chapels, some of which are built, but most of which are excavated from the rock itself. The Sassi, which recently came under the protection of UNESCO, are undergoing systematic restoration and rehabilitation; the municipality has begun assigning the renovated homes to newlyweds. The area is divided into 22 work sites, some of which will be closed to the public on any given day.

Among the **rock chapels** may be mentioned those of Santa Maria d'Idris and Santa Lucia, both of which contain 13C wall paintings, the latter having a particularly fine fresco of St Michael and architectural devices carved on the rough stone pillars. Of the **churches** constructed in a more conventional way (identifiable by their campanili) the most interesting are those of San Pietro Caveoso (constructed in the 17C and 18C and San Pietro Barisano (dating from the 12–13C).

Many more chapels are cut into the hillsides elsewhere in the ravine; some of them contain **frescoes** of a surprisingly high quality. A guide is necessary. Of particular interest are **Santa Maria della Valle**, popularly called La Voglia, carved out of the rock near the Altamura road, with an interesting façade of 1280 and 17C frescoes within; the **Cristo alla Gravinella**, a crypt-church of which the façade and frescoes were reworked in the 17C; and **Santa Maria della Colomba** (or Santo Spirito), popularly La Palomba, in a picturesque position overlooking the Gravina di Matera, with a Romanesque façade incorporating a rose window and 15C bas-reliefs.

The well-preserved church of **Santa Barbara**, on the opposite side of the town, is entered through an arched portal flanked by columns and contains 13C frescoes, an iconostasis and, in the ceiling, false domes carved out of the rock.

The territory around Matera is also noted for its **Neolithic trench villages**, curious settlements centring around circular or elliptical trenches, up to 3m in depth, that originally held hut-like habitations and burial chambers and that were excavated with the sole aid of simple stone wedges. The material gathered from these sites, now chiefly at the Museo Ridola, includes incised and painted ceramic ware, the latter of a type peculiar to Matera; and numerous broken or discarded tools. Excavations in the area have also brought to light a burial ground with Villanovan cinerary urns and objects decorated in bronze; a Greek necropolis with Apulo-Peucetian tombs of the 4C and 3C BC containing ceramic ware, bronzes, votive vases and statues; and a sanctuary dedicated to Persephone. Information and guides may be obtained at the Museo Ridola.

Excursion to Montescagliosa

A pleasant excursion may be made from Matera to **Montescagliosa** (20km), a large, mostly whitewashed village, where the Chiesa Maggiore has an imposing Baroque façade and inlaid altars, of which the high altar is particularly fine. Santo Stefano, a tiny church, has an attractive main portal. At the top of the village stands the imposing Abbazia di Sant'Angelo, a foundation dating from the 11C reconstructed by Charles II of Anjou and again partly rebuilt in the late 15C, so that now, from the exterior, it shows a Renaissance face. It contains two interesting cloisters. The territory around the town has yielded traces of Lucanian settlements dating from the 6C BC. Beyond Montescagliosa, you may rejoin the main road (175) leading to Metaponto, Route 10.

Into Apulia

Leave Matera by the Altamura road, turning right onto Highway 7 just outside of the town. 12km enter Apulia and descend gradually to (8km) **Laterza** (340m, 14,000 inhab.), an agricultural town huddled on the brink of a ravine that is lined with cave dwellings and churches carved from the rock. The ancient **Castello**, situated at the north end of the old town, has been extensively rebuilt. The main entrance, on the north side, consists of two double pointed archways preceded by a stone bridge; on the south side a similar doorway gives access to the maze of narrow, winding streets that make up the old town. The Romanesque church of the **Assunta** is the last remaining vestige of the Cistercian monastery of Santa Maria la Grande. Within is an interesting baptismal font with 12C sculptural decoration. The **Chiesa Matrice** (also called San Lorenzo) has a curious Veneto-Dalmatian façade dating from the 15C.

Ginosa, 7km south, is the ancient *Genusia* mentioned by Pliny and the site of important archaeological finds. It is surrounded on three sides by a deep ravine containing cave-churches with frescoes dating from the 12–14C.

Bear eastward through gently rolling country. 12km a road on the left links the Via Appia to Autostrada A14 and Highway 100 (Route 19B); beyond, the descent continues with good views ahead to Castellaneta and the Gulf of Taranto.

3km **Castellaneta** (245m, 16,000 inhab.), dramatically perched on a spur above its ravine, is the birthplace of Rudolph Valentino (Rodolfo Guiglielmi, 1895–1926). The old town is divided into two quarters known locally as Sacco and Muricello, on either side of the **Cattedrale**. Begun in the 13C and rebuilt in the 17C, this has a façade of 1771. The campanile retains blind arcades and mullioned windows belonging to the original Romanesque structure. Via Seminario, on the right of the cathedral, leads to the Bishop's Palace, where there is a fine polyptych depicting the Madonna with Saints, Angels and Apostles, signed by Girolamo da Santacroce and dated 1531. Reached by a dirt track on the south edge of the town is the little church of the **Assunta**, recently restored to its original 14C appearance. The Romanesque façade contains a finely crafted portal and rose window. Within are 14C and 15C frescoes. More fresco fragments can be seen in the ruins adjoining the church.

Highway 7 descends steeply along the west wall of the deep Gravina di Castellaneta, dominated to the north by the lofty railway bridge, then crosses the torrent and climbs out to a small plateau.

7km **Palagianello** (133m, 7000 inhab.) is reached by a turning on the left. The castle, rectangular in plan with sharp corner bastions, dates from the 18C. It stands in a dominant position on the outskirts of the village. To the left of the castle can be seen the gravina, which holds several cave-churches. San Nicola, c 750km south of the village, contains remains of 14C frescoes. San Girolamo, the largest in the area, has a badly damaged fresco of the Madonna dating from the 15C.

Further on, Roman ruins mark the course of the ancient Via Appia. The road descends gently through olive groves. Mottola (Route 19B) is visible on its hill, to the left. Bypassing (4km) Palagiano, cross under the motorway, over the railway, and turn south-east where Highway 7 is joined by Highway 100 from Gioia del Colle (Route 19B).

7km **Massafra** (110m, 30,000 inhab.), situated at the top of a deep ravine, is divided into two distinct parts: the Terra or old town on the west, and the more modern Borgo Santa Caterina on the east. Two lofty bridges—the Viadotto Superiore or Ponte Nuovo, and the Viadotto Inferiore or Ponte Vecchio—span the abyss between the two quarters.

From Piazza Vittorio Emanuele, at the centre of the modern Borgo, Corso Italia bears across the Ponte Vecchio (spectacular view of the ravine with its caves and terraces) to the ancient Terra. Here Via La Terra leads to the imposing **Castello**, built in the mid 15C on the site of a Norman fortification and rebuilt in the late 17C or early 18C by Michele Imperiali, whose eagle emblem can be seen on the entrance wall. Rectangular in plan with cylindrical towers and a massive octagonal bastion at the south–east corner, it incorporates in one rampart the church of San Lorenzo (or Chiesa Matrice), built in the 15C and remodelled in 1533. The terrace below commands a view of the entire coastal plain west of Taranto.

Returning to Piazza Garibaldi at the foot of the bridge, follow Via Vittorio Veneto then Via del Santuario to a terrace on the outskirts of the town, from which a monumental staircase descends to the sanctuary of the **Madonna della Scala**.

Built in 1731, the church contains an unusual 12C or 13C fresco of the Madonna and Child with two kneeling deer from the basilian crypt over which it stands. The latter, believed to date from the 8C or 9C, is reached by steps in the atrium. Several incised crosses can be seen on the walls and piers. The adjacent Cripta della Buona Nuova, partially ruined by the building of the sanctuary, contains a 13C representation of the Madonna della Buona Nuova and a large frescoed Christ Pantokrator.

At the bottom of the valley, c 200m distant, lies the so-called **Farmacia del Mago Greguro**, a complex of adjoining caves, the walls of which contain hundreds of small hollows where, according to tradition, the monks stored their medicinal herbs.

Returning to the town, take Viale Marconi to Via Frappietri (also called Via del Cimitero). Here turn left to (300m, left) the 13C crypt of **San Lorenzo**. The primitive church, only partially intact, contains frescoes of saints, on the arches of the presbytery, and of Christ Enthroned, in the apse. Viale Marconi leads on to the Ponte Nuovo, near which three arches cut in the rock mark the entrance to the recently restored **Cappella-cripta della Candelora**. Located in a private garden, the chapel may be reached from Via dei Canali. 8.5km long and 6m wide, it has three aisles, a low dome, and arched niches in the walls. On the capitals, incised Greek crosses. The walls also bear extensive remains of 13C and 14C frescoes with Greek and Latin inscriptions, including a well-preserved Presentation in the Temple.

In the east wall of the ravine is the unusually well-preserved *Chiesa-cripta di San Marco**, of uncertain date. Access is afforded through a gate at the end of Via Fratelli Bandiera (reached by crossing the bridge to Via Scarano and turning right, then right again; ring for key at the house next door). A stairway carved out of the rock descends to the church. Entry is through a vestibule; on the left is a well, presumably a primitive baptismal font; on the right, a large fresco depicting St Mark. Piers with rough carvings, inscribed in Greek and Latin and surmounted by rounded arches, divide the church into nave and aisles. Steps lead to the raised presbytery and the main apse; another apse, on the right, is closed off by a parapet, possibly used as a pulpit. In the walls are carved niches that may have served as arcosolia. Of the frescoes they once contained, only a 13C representation of Sts Cosma and Damian remains, the others having been destroyed by humidity.

Leave Massafra as you came, from the south. On the outskirts of the town, near the crossroads, stands the 10C Byzantine chapel of **Santa Lucia**. Parts of the original building can still be seen; of particular interest are the distinctive cupolas, pyramidic on the outside but rounded within. The road is straight from here to Taranto. The railway parallels its course across the valley of the Aranceta to a broad plain dominated, on the right, by orchards and fields planted with vegetable crops.

15km you pass through the bleak industrial suburbs of Taranto (Route 19B), bearing north–east on the link road that passes north of the Mare Piccolo before entering the city proper.

Highway 7 is rejoined at (8km) **Grottaglie**, a town (31,000 inhab.) taking its name from the grottoes in its carstic rocks. The **Chiesa Matrice**, at the centre of the town, was erected in the late 11C or early 12C. The façade, which dates from 1379, includes a fine Apulian Romanesque portal with octagonal piers on zoomorphic supports. To the right of the façade can be seen the polychrome tile cupola of the Cappella del Rosario. The church of the **Carmine**, further up the hill, has a beautifully carved **Nativity** of 1530. Behind the massive castello lies the quarter of the celebrated Grottaglie ceramic workers, many of whom still use traditional methods. The countless vases that line the streets and the flat roofs of the houses offer a singular sight.

The Sanctuary of Santa Maria Mutata

6km north-west of Grottaglie on the Martina Franca road lies the 17C sanctuary of **Santa Maria Mutata**, erected on the site of a small basilica built by Basilian hermits and containing a heavily repainted medieval fresco of the Madonna and Child. The image of the Madonna is said to have turned to face Grottaglie during a dispute between the latter city and Martina Franca over the land on which the church stood. The sanctuary also contains a 15C wooden crucifix. In the environs are to be seen the scanty remains of a Messapian settlement, consisting of low walls and tombs, as well as Roman tombs with Latin inscriptions.

Leaving Grottaglie, bear north–east again. At (15km) **Francavilla Fontana** there are several interesting palazzi, of which the most impressive is the **Palazzo Imperiali**, a castle erected in 1450 by Giovanni Antonio del Balzo Orsini, enlarged in the mid 16C and rebuilt in 1730 by Michele Imperiali to plans by Ferdinando Sanfelice. Rectangular in plan with crenellated battlements and imposing corner bastions, the building is adorned with a graceful loggia and balcony surmounted by large windows in richly carved surrounds, all of Baroque workmanship. A wide doorway leads to the cortile, where there are a portico, another loggia, and a 15C or 16C baptismal font.

In the Sala del Consiglio, where the town council now meets, can be seen 16C and 17C paintings and a fireplace bearing the imperial arms. Nearby is the **Duomo**, a sober Baroque edifice with colossal statues of Sts Peter and Paul in the façade and a coloured-tile dome.

A Messapian Mystery

An interesting excursion can be made to the **Specchia Maiano**, 8km north-east. Leave Francavilla by the road for Ceglie Messapica. After c 8km a country road diverges left to the Masseria Bottari, a farm; proceed on foot through the field on the right to (c 500m) the Specchia Maiano, a mysterious dry-work stone edifice of Messapian origin, 20m in diameter and 11m high, made up of six concentric steps of varying heights. Its purpose is unknown.

About 6km south-east of Francavilla Fontana is **Oria** (166m, 15,000 inhab.), on a low ridge in view of the sea on either side. It was the ancient *Hyria*, capital of the Messapians. During the Middle Ages an important Jewish colony lived here, and the quarter of the Giudecca is still distinguishable. The massive **Castello**, built by Frederick II in 1227–33 and enlarged in the 14C, possibly to plans by Pierre d'Agincourt, stands in an indomitable position on top of the ancient acropolis. It is triangular in plan, the tall enceinte surrounding a spacious garden. The south wall, which faces the town, had three towers: one of these, the four-sided bastion at the south-west corner, was the keep of the primitive fortification (see below); the others, built in the Angevin period, are cylindrical in form with rings of corbels that once supported wooden battlements. Inside (open 08.00–12.30, 15.30–18.30) are a

The Baroque cathedral of Oria. The coloured-tile dome a common feature of this area

vaulted hall containing a modest collection of antiquities and the rebuilt Norman keep, a tall room with pointed vaults on heavy piers which was once divided, with two floors, as the remains of a fireplace high up on one wall attest, and now contains a collection of arms and armour. A small stairway mounts to the battlements and the Angevin towers, from the tops of which there is a marvellous view of the town and the Tavoliere di Lecce. The much-restored Palazzo del Castellano extends along the northwest wall. Across the garden (open by special permission only; apply to custodian), among the cypresses at the foot of the south–east tower, steps descend to the **Cripta di Santi Crisante e Daria**, a subterranean chapel dating from the 9C or before. The interior is basilican in form, with three aisles, cruciform piers and four shallow domes (a fifth dome, in the left arm of the transept, was destroyed to make the present entrance).

The Museo Civico (open 09.00–12.00) houses a small collection of Messapian and Graeco-Roman material. The Baroque cathedral, rebuilt after an earthquake of 1743, has a tall, coloured-tile dome of a kind common in the district.

The road follows the final courses of the ancient Via Appia, through olive groves and vineyards.

10km **Latiano** (97m, 16,000 inhab.) has a Palazzo Comunale originally of the 12C, rebuilt in 1526 and 1724. At Muro Tenente (also called Paretone), to the south–east of the town, are the remains of Messapian walls and tombs identified by some with the *Scamnum* mentioned in the Tabula Peutingeriana as lying along the Via Appia between Taranto and Brindisi.

Latiano can be reached directly from Oria by a country road that follows more or less the same course as the railway, passing (3km left) the ruined church of the Madonna di Gallana, which contains, in the apse, a large Byzantine fresco of Christ in Benediction between two angels, in poor repair. From here you may proceed directly to Mesagne (see below) without returning to the State Highway.

11km **Mesagne**, a prosperous market town (31,000 inhab.) is the ancient *Messania*. In the old town is the **Castello**, built by Robert Guiscard in 1062, destroyed (together with the town) by Manfred's Saracens in 1254, rebuilt by Manfred himself in 1256 and enlarged and embellished in the 15C and 17C. Originally a heavily bastioned stronghold against pirates, it was transformed into a lordly residence, as the Renaissance loggia that runs along the north and east façades clearly demonstrates. The Palazzo del Municipio, formerly a Celestine convent, houses the Museo Archeologico U. Granafei (open daily except Sun 10.00–12.00), which contains Messapian ware of the 7–2C BC, Roman inscriptions, and other material of interest. The Baroque Chiesa Madre has a Gothic crypt with a 16C crucifix and numerous paintings by local artists. On the outskirts of the town lies the little 7C church of San Lorenzo, partially rebuilt in the 17C. Recent restoration has brought to light **frescoes** probably dating from the 15C.

Beyond Mesagne the road crosses a featureless plain planted with vines, olives, figs and grain to (14km) Brindisi (Route 19A).

19 · Bari to Lecce

A. Via Brindisi

*Though the coast between Bari and Lecce is flat and monotonous, the beaches are generally quite good. **Monopoli** and **Ostuni** are pleasant places to stay if you are looking for a central base from which to explore Apulia; Monopoli is closer to Bari and the main roads leading north and west, whereas Ostuni, an attractive town with a distinct Oriental air, is nearer Alberobello and the Valle dell'Itri, land of the Trulli (described in Route 19B). **Brindisi**, like Bari, is crowded and busy, and though its museums and monuments repay a visit, you are better off staying elsewhere. South of Brindisi the only place worth a stop is the Romanesque abbey of Santa Maria di Cerrate, near **Squinzano** (which also houses a small ethnographic museum).*

From Monopoli to Brindisi, you may choose to take Highway 16, instead of Highway 379, which follows the coast, bypassing Ostuni and San Vito. An expressway links the two roads, following first the former, then the latter. Travel time by car is c 2hr 10min.

ROAD, 155km. Highway 16 (Adriatica) and local roads. 21km Mola di Bari—13km Polignano a Mare—8km Monopoli—16km Fasano—23km Ostuni—14km San Vito dei Normanni—21km Brindisi—27km Squinzano—14km Lecce.

RAILWAY, 150km in c 1hr 45min. To (111km) Brindisi in c 1hr 15min.

HOTELS EN ROUTE: Monopoli, *****Il Melograno, contrada Torricella 345, tel. 080 690 9030, fax 080 747908; Costa Merlata (Ostuni), ****Grand Hotel Masseria Santa Lucia, tel. 0831 330418, fax 0831 339590; Cisternino, ***Villa Cenci, tel./fax 080 718208; Brindisi, *Il Cantinone, via De Leo 4, tel. 0831 562122.

RESTAURANTS EN ROUTE: Fasano, ***Fagiano, tel. 080 933 1157, fax 080 933 1211; Ceglie Messapica, ***Al Fornello-da Ricci, contrada Montevicoli, tel. 0831 977104, fax 0831 977577.

South-west of Bari

Bari, Route 11. Leave the city by Lungomare Nazario Sauro. Outside the town, the Via Traiano follows the low, rocky coast past the growing resorts of San Giorgio and Torre a Mare.

21km **Mola di Bari** (5m, 27,000 inhab.) was a crusader port. Today it consists of an old town on a headland, and a new quarter that extends inland to the railway. The **Cattedrale**, erected in the mid 16C on the site of an earlier church, combines Romanesque and Dalmatian architectural motifs. The rose window is probably a remnant of the earlier structure. Within is a curious nave arcade, taller at the east end and shorter, with a gallery in the walls above the arches (again a vestige of the old church), at the west. In the south aisle can be seen a baptismal font with dancing putti. Near the head of the promontory rises the **Castello**, built by Pierre d'Agincourt for Charles of Anjou in 1278. Irregular in plan, it has a tall enceinte and polygonal corner bastions with steep scarps.

The highway circles south of Mola, then returns to the coast. At (5km) Cozze, a road on the right leads inland to (9km) Conversano, Route 19B. The Adriatic Highway continues along the coast, paralleled by the railway. To the right rise the east slopes of the Murge. Just before Polignano a Mare a road on the left diverges to the former abbey of **San Vito**, which dates from the 9C but has been repeatedly altered, particularly in the 16C. The abbey church, preceded by a porch, has an unusual nave surmounted by three domes. A medieval watch–tower stands nearby.

8km **Polignano a Mare** (24m, 16,000 inhab.) rises abruptly from the rocks. The Chiesa Matrice, in Piazza Vittorio Emanuele, was consecrated in 1295. The 16C interior contains a contemporary stone presepio by Stefano da Putignano, 17C choir stalls and, in the sacristy, several panels of a polyptych by Bartolomeo Vivarini (1472). Steps descend from the village to two large (25–30m diameter) caves collectively called the Grotta Palazzese; these and the Raccolta Archeologica, in Viale Rimembranza, may be seen on request (open by appointment, 080 740144).

MONOPOLI AND AROUND

The highway bears south across deep ravines, in sight of the coast. After c 3km the trunk road turns inland. Continue straight to (8km) **Monopoli** (9m, 47,000 inhab.), a large, busy town, the livelihood of which derives from fishing, farming and industry. The polygonal **Castello** was built in 1552 and remodelled in 1660. Beyond is the harbour, frequented by merchant and fishing vessels.

The **Cattedrale**, founded in 1107 and rebuilt in 1742–70, is one of the more prominent Baroque buildings in the district. It has a tall façade of grey stone connected, on the right, to a blank wall with statues in niches, a scenographic addition to the piazza. The interior is a Latin cross with nave and aisles faced in coloured marble. It contains paintings by several prominent artists, including (first south altar) Fall of the Rebel Angels by Palma Giovane; (south transept) Last Supper and (in tondi on the walls) Sacrifice of Abraham and Supper at Emmaus, by Francesco de Mura; (further on) Madonna in Glory with Sts Roche and Sebastian, attributed to Palma Giovane, and Circumcision, by Marco da Siena. Steps mount to the presbytery; above the altar is a 13C Byzantine Madonna, possibly by a Campanian painter.

In the sacristy and the adjoining room can be seen architectural fragments from the 12C church, including an architrave with bas-reliefs and a capital bearing a representation of Daniel in the lion's den. The treasury contains an extraordinary 10C or 11C reliquary, possibly from Constantinople, with panels that open to form a triptych representing the Crucifixion and Sts Peter and Paul, a 17C processional cross of Neapolitan workmanship, and other precious objects. In the Vescovado are a Crowning of the Virgin by Palma Giovane, a Madonna and Saints by Paolo Veronese and pupils and other paintings. Behind the church, in the Cala di Porta Vecchia, lies a **medieval cave-church** with Byzantine frescoes.

The church of **San Domenico** is distinguished by an elegant Renaissance façade. Within is Palma Giovane's canvas of the Miracle of Soriano, one of the more noteworthy of the artist's Apulian paintings. The graceful chapel of **Santa Maria Amalfitana**, erected in the 12C by merchants from Amalfi, stands over a Basilian cave-church. The apse and the south flank belong to the original Romanesque structure; later additions were made in the Gothic and Baroque styles. The interior has a nave and two aisles divided by compound piers with good Romanesque capitals. Above, semicircular arches support the nave walls and simple wooden ceiling. From the south aisle, steps descend to the Basilian laura, now the crypt. A doorway at the end of the aisle opens onto a small court, from which may be seen the east end of the church (restored). The largest of the three apses is adorned with slender half-columns, grotesque consoles and a fine window framed between two small columns—motifs which link the chapel to the Lombard Romanesque churches of Northern Italy.

The Liceo Classico, Via Europa Libera, houses a small Museo Archeologico (open by appointment, mornings; phone 080 887 2072). In the suburb of Cozzana, on the Conversano road, the private **Villa Meo-Evoli** has another collection of antiquities (open by appointment; phone 080 803052) from sites in Apulia and Campania.

From Monopoli to Brindisi by the coast road

Leave Monopoli from the south following the railway as far as the turning for Santo Stefano, then bear slightly east for the coast and Torre Cintola. At (12km) Torre Egnazia the road crosses the ruins of **Egnathia** (open daily 08.30–13.00, 14.30–dusk), a Graeco-Messapian town set on the frontier between Messapia and Peucetia, where Horace and his companions were amused at a pretended miracle ('credat Judaeus Apella, non ego'). The Museo Archeologico di Egnathia, at the edge of the archaeological zone (open daily 08.30–13.00, 14.30–18.00; winter 8.30–13.00, 14.30–17.00), houses vases, terracottas and Messapian inscriptions discovered in the course of excavations, late antique and early Christian mosaics and a large Messapian chamber tomb of the 4C or 3C BC. The site is especially important to archaeologists for the so-called **Gnathian ware** (characterised by small coloured designs on a black background, and sometimes ribbed) that was made here in the 4 and 3C BC.

The walled acropolis and the town proper lie respectively on the east and west sides of the highway. The latter contains a Roman forum paved with large blocks of stone and flanked by remains of a colonnaded portico; at the centre of the square are a well, a tribune and other remains. To the north lies the foundation of a basilica, of uncertain date. Further east are remains of what is believed to be the amphitheatre. The south side of the forum is bounded by shops and houses. Beyond lies a well-preserved stretch of the Via Traiana, which crossed the town at this point. Remains of walls and an arch stand to the east; further south, across the Via Traiana, is a ruined early Christian basilica built with materials from pagan edifices. Also visible are numerous rock-cut tombs and an imposing (7m high) section of the town walls.

2km Savelletri is a fishing village and a developing resort. Extensive views over the sea and the Murge are revealed as you continue south.

7km you pass the hamlet of La Forcatella to Torre Canne, a fishing town and spa with good bathing beach. Leaving on the right a turning for the Fasano–Ostuni road, follow the coast east. Near (13km) Villanova, a modest village with a low castle, a road on the right diverges to (6km) Ostuni (see below). Beyond, the coast is marked by modern bathing establishments and tourist villages.

20km, a turning on the right leads inland to Carovigno (see below). From here the road crosses a somewhat monotonous landscape dominated by vineyards to link up with Highway 16 from Fasano and San Vito just before entering (25km) Brindisi.

Highway 16 bears south-east from Monopoli in a straight line through groves of olives and almond trees.

16km **Fasano** (118m, 39,000 inhab.) is a thriving agricultural town with a Palazzo Comunale of 1509. It is developing rapidly as a holiday centre, thanks to a situation between the wooded hills of Selva di Fasano (6km west) and the attractive shore (7km east). It is known principally for its **Zoo-Safari** (open daily 9.30–dusk), a large drive-through zoological park with amusements. A Strada Panoramica, which runs along the north rim of the Murge dei Trulli, connects the town with Castellana Grotte.

■ **Information**: AA, Piazza Ciaia 10; tel. 080 713086 (branch office in Via Potenza, Torre Canne).

From Fasano the road skirts the lower edge of the Murge, past dense olive groves. Beyond Pezze di Greco, roads lead (left) to (6km) Torre Canne and (right) to (9km) Cisternino. Just before (10km) Montalbano, a dirt track leads left to the Masseria Ottava, a farm, near which lies the so-called Dolmen of Cisternino or Tavole Paladine. The straight course of the highway ends as you round the northernmost spur of the Murge. The road begins to climb, with views ahead to Ostuni, its white houses silhouetted against the sky.

OSTUNI AND ENVIRONS
11km **Ostuni** (218m, 32,000 inhab.) is a town of pre-Roman origin built on three hills. Its centre of steep medieval alleys is still circled by ramparts.

■ **Information**: AA, Via Continelli 47; phone 0831 303775 (branch office in Piazza della Libertà).

The focus of town life is the triangular Piazza della Libertà, at one end of which stands the exuberant Guglia di Sant'Oronzo (1771). Slightly set back from the square is the little church of the **Spirito Santo** (1637), with its handsome Renaissance portal bearing reliefs of the Annunciation and of the Crowning and Death of the Virgin. From here Via Vicentini climbs to the old town, passing an 18C Carmelite convent and, next door, the Baroque church of Santa Maria Maddalena, with its cupola of coloured majolica.

The **Cattedrale** stands at the heart of the old quarter. Begun in 1435 and completed some 60 years later, it has an unusual façade of Spanish inspiration, with three rose windows and late Gothic decorative details. The Latin-cross interior was remodelled in the 18C; in the last chapel on the south can be seen a Madonna and Child with Saints by Palma Giovane.

Behind the church stands the Bishop's Palace with its elegant 18C loggia. Further on lie the remains of a castle erected in 1198 by Geoffrey, Count of Lecce, and destroyed in 1559. The church of the Annunziata, in the modern town, contains a Deposition by Paolo Veronese that was stolen in 1975 and recovered in 1977.

From Ostuni the road bears south-east in a straight line to (8km) **Carovigno** (161m, 14,000 inhab.), a large town built on the site of the Messapian *Carbina*. Remains of megalithic walls may be seen to the north and west. The **Castello**, erected in the 14C and 15C as a defence against pirates, was restored in 1906. The almond-shaped bastion at the north-east corner is unusual in Italian military architecture, whereas the triangular ground plan and tall enceinte are typical of late medieval fortifications. Within are rooms with period furniture.

6km **San Vito dei Normanni** (108m, 21,000 inhab.) has a 12C castello transformed into a fortified residence in the 15C. Beyond the town, near its station, lie the **Grotto di San Biagio**, with paintings by Mastro Danieli (1197), and the Grotto di San Giovanni, also with frescoes.

Brindisi and beyond

21km Brindisi, a provincial capital (93,000 inhab.) of modern aspect, has the safest natural harbour on the Adriatic and consequent importance as a trading port with the East.

History

Of Messapian origin, the *Bentesion* of the Greeks and the *Brundisium* of the Latins became a Roman city in the 3C BC and was used as a naval base in the Second Punic War. In 49 BC Caesar tried unsuccessfully to contain Pompey's ships here on his return from Greece. It was the birthplace of Pacuvius (219–129 BC), painter and dramatic poet, and the goal of the journey described by Horace (Satire i, 5). Here Virgil died in 19 BC.

The city flourished under Roman rule, was taken by the Saracens in 836, and rose to prosperity again during the Crusades. It was sacked by Louis of Hungary in 1352 and by Louis of Anjou in 1383. Pestilence and the earthquake of 1456 contributed to its decline, and its modern importance dates only from the opening of the Suez Canal in 1869. An important base in both world wars, Brindisi was occupied by Allied troops on 10 September 1943, and on the same day Badoglio's interim government with King Victor Emmanuel arrived here, having fled before the German advance on Rome.

Today Brindisi derives its wealth largely from agriculture, the processing and packaging of agricultural products, and its chemical industries.

■ **Information**. EPT, Via C. Colombo 88; tel. 0831 222126, fax 0831 562149 (branch office in Lungomare Regina Margherita). AA, c/o EPT, Lungomare Regina Margherita; tel. 0831 521944 (branch office in Via Bastioni Carlo V).

■ **Airport** at Casale, 16km north, with daily service to Rome.

■ **Car ferries** daily to Corfu in 7–8 hr, proceeding to Igoumenitsa and/or Patras, from the **Stazione Marittima**. Timetables and ticketing information from the EPT.

■ **Post office**: Via Tor Pisana.

The city is built on a peninsula between two arms of a land-locked bay, the Seno di Ponente on the north–west and the Seno di Levante on the east, which form the inner harbour and are connected with the outer harbour by the Canale Pigonati (500 metres by 50 wide). The outer harbour is protected by the Pedagne islets and by the large island of Sant'Andrea, on which stands the fortress built in 1481 by Ferdinand I of Aragon after the fall of Otranto to the Turks.

Piazza Vittorio Emanuele opens on the inner harbour. To the right is the Stazione Marittima; to the left the Lungomare Regina Margherita leads to a marble column, with a remarkable capital, and the base of a second column (ruined in 1528 and later removed to Lecce), which are said to mark the end of the Appian Way. On the opposite bank, to the west of the Canale Pigonati, rises the **Monument to the Italian Sailor** (1933), by A. Bartoli and L. Brunati, in the form of a rudder 52m high. This may be reached by ferry and the terrace (lift) commands a fine view of the whole city.

Santa Maria del Casale
About 3km north is Santa Maria del Casale, a beautiful Romanesque church (1322) with a polychrome façade and Byzantine frescoes, of which the most complete and impressive is the immense Last Judgement, on the entrance wall. Note also the Madonna with knights on the south nave wall, an image clearly connected with Brindisi's importance as a Crusader port. The profuse decoration of the apse and transepts is equally fascinating, though less well preserved.

Via Colonne leads away from the harbour and passes beneath the campanile of the cathedral to Piazza del Duomo, the religious centre of the city, with the 18C Duomo and Seminario, the 14C Loggia Balsamo, and the Gothic arches of the so-called Portico dei Cavalieri Templari. In the **Duomo** (begun in the 11C, rebuilt in 1749) Frederick II married his second wife Yolande in 1225. Around the main altar are remains of the original mosaic pavement of 1178, with representations of animals, brought to light in 1957 and 1968. The inland choir stalls date from the late 16C; the silver altar frontal, from the 18C.

On the left of the church stands the **Portico dei Cavalieri Templari**, a 15C construction that gives access to the **Museo Archeologico Provinciale** (open Mon 09.00–13.00, Tue 09.00–13.00 and 15.30–19.00, Wed–Sat 09.00–13.00; closed Sun and holidays). The museum has recently been rearranged to form four itineraries devoted to antiquities and collections from Brindisi and its province, statues and inscriptions, prehistoric civilisations and marine archaeology. PORTICO: **Medieval Sculptural Fragments**, notably four capitals from the 11C Abbey of Sant'Andrea all'Isola, no longer extant.

ROOMS 1, 3 and 4: **Antiquarium**, with archaeological material from excavations in the city and the surrounding territory, notably architectural fragments and capitals; a plaster cast from Trajan's Column in Rome showing the emperor's departure from the harbour at Brindisi during the Dacian campaign; Apulian, proto-Corinthian, Messapian, and Attic ceramics—including Gnathian ware from the excavations at Valesio, and Attic red-figure krater showing a Dionysiac procession and robed figures (5C BC), an Attic bell crater showing Athena with Hercules and Hermes, and an Apulian wine jug with a wedding scene—and several groups of minor sculpture, principally votive statuettes, portrait busts, antefixes, and Gorgon masks.

ROOM 2: **Statues and Inscriptions**. Loricated Roman warrior with a Medusa and a Winged Victory on his cuirass; effigy of Diana, identifiable by her short tunic; lower part of a seated woman, of Greek workmanship; headless female figure probably representing a Victory or a Muse, in the Hellenistic manner. Several of the inscriptions are in Greek or Hebrew.

ROOM 5: **Prehistoric Section**, with finds from the palaeolithic to the Bronze

Age (stone tools, clay vases and so on). ROOM 6: **Marine Archaeology Section**. Here may be seen a variety of material, including a colossal bronze foot from the Secca di Sant'Andrea (4C AD?) and numerous amphorae recovered from Roman shipwrecks, as well as a display tracing the discovery of the Punta del Serrone bronzes. The museum also houses a small Pinacoteca, with late 17C and early 18C paintings.

The Loggia Balsamo, at the entrance to Via Tarantini, was part of an Angevin palace. Via Tarantini and Via San Giovanni (left) lead to **San Giovanni al Sepolcro**, an 11C baptistery of circular plan, erected by the Templars over an early Christian building. The main entrance is decorated with reliefs and fronted by a shallow porch resting on columns (interesting capitals) carried by lions. The interior follows a horseshoe plan. Eight columns (some antique) support the modern roof, which was built to replace the shattered dome. An ambulatory runs round the perimeter of the room; on the walls are 13C and 14C frescoes of Christ, the Madonna and Child, and Saints.

A little south-west is **San Benedetto**, a Romanesque church of 1080, with an elegant cloister. Overlooking the shore, to the northwest, stands the **Castello**, built by Frederick II (1227) and enlarged under Ferdinand I of Aragon and Charles V.

> West of the castle, on the Strada Provinciale San Vito, is the **Fontana Tancredi** (1192), erected by Tancred to celebrate the marriage of his son Roger to Urania of Constantinople; here the Crusaders are said to have watered their horses. To the south-east, along the busy Via Cristoforo Colombo, is the **Porta Mesagne**, a 13C Gothic arch in the city rampart, reinforced in the 16C by Charles V, near which you can see the remains of five tubs, which held mud brought by the Roman aqueduct.

From Piazza Vittorio Emanuele, Corso Garibaldi runs south-west to Piazza del Popolo, the modern centre, from where Corso Umberto leads to the Stazione Centrale. Just south of the piazza is the little church of **Santa Lucia**, preserving traces of its original Romanesque decoration on the right flank. Within are fragmentary **frescoes** from the original building and a fine **crypt** of 1225. The **Chiesa del Cristo** (1230), near the Porta Lecce at the south end of the town, has a polychrome façade and, within, a 13C wooden crucifix and statue of the Madonna.

> In the Cimitero Comunale are 86 graves of officers and men of the British Navy who served with the Adriatic Drifter Fleet (1915–18).

Leave Brindisi from the south. At 3km is the north terminus of the Brindisi–Lecce Expressway. Highway 16 forges straight ahead, across the plain to (15km) San Pietro Vernotico, near which lie the ruins of *Valesio*, a Messapian town, later the Roman *Balentium*. Part of the ramparts and the scanty remains of Roman baths can still be seen.

4km north-east of **Squinzano** is the charming abbey of **Santa Maria di Cerrate**, a Romanesque complex of the early 12C. The simple façade of the abbey church is graced by a richly carved portal and characteristic portico. Within (open Mon–Fri 09.00–13.00, 14.30–19.30; Sun 09.00–13.00), pointed arches spring from columns with interesting sculptured capitals. A ciborium of 1269 and 13–16C frescoes may also be seen. Housed in a former olive press next to the church is the Museo delle Arti e delle Tradizioni Popolari del Salento (open daily except Mon 09.00–13.00, 14.30–19.30), which has an entertaining collection of farm tools and folk objects.

13km Lecce, see Route 20.

B · Via Taranto

*This route goes through the region of the **trulli**. These are curious dwellings, built without mortar of local limestone and usually whitewashed, with conical roofs formed of flat-pitched spiral courses of the same stone, capped with diverse finials. They are found isolated or joined together in groups, and their origin is very remote. It is no doubt related to the rocky character of the soil, and in many cases the same limestone used for the trulli is also adopted in the drywork walls used as boundary markers, which give the agrarian landscape of this area its distinctive appearance.*

*Beyond Taranto the road crosses the Salentine Peninsula through uninteresting countryside, the chief point of interest being the megalithic walls at **Manduria**.*

Travel time from Bari to Lecce is c 3hr 15min. A faster road reaches Taranto via Gioia del Colle (see below). From Taranto to Lecce a road 14km longer and somewhat slower follows the coast to (66km) Porto Cesareo, there turning north-east to Copertino (Route 20) and Lecce, offering good views along the coastline, which is lined with medieval watch-towers.

ROAD 194km. Highway 100 to Capurso, Highway 634 to Putignano, and Highway 172 to Taranto; then Highways 7 and 7ter to Lecce. From Bari, 10km Capurso—9km Rutigliano—11km Conversano—10km Castellana Grotte—5km Putignano—13km Alberobello—9km Locorotondo—6km Martina Franca—36km Taranto—36km Manduria—49km Lecce.

RAILWAY: Bari to Taranto, 112km in c 2hr 15min. The line, which is privately operated, follows the road closely except for brief tracts between Putignano and Alberobello, and between Martina Franca and Taranto. From Taranto to Lecce, 96km in c 2hrs. From Taranto to Francavilla Fontana, on the main Taranto–Brindisi line, 34km in c 1hr. Here change from the State Railway to the privately operated line that runs from Martina Franca to Lecce, rejoining the highway at (14km) Manduria.

RESTAURANTS EN ROUTE: Alberobello, ***Il Poeta Contadino, Via Indipendenza 21, tel./fax 080 721917.

South of Bari

Bari, Route 11. Leave the city by the main Taranto road (see above) and at (10km) Capurso diverge left. Beyond (6km) Noicattero the road bears south to (3km) **Rutigliano** (125m, 17,000 inhab.), which stands on the site of an ancient Apulian town. The church of **Santa Maria della Colonna**, founded by the Normans, was consecrated in 1108. The main portal retains the original carved architrave depicting Christ and the Apostles, and the Annunciation; the Gothic porch dates from the 13C or 14C. Within is a polyptych of 1450 by Alvise Vivarini.

8km pass (right) the conventual church of Santa Maria dell'Isola, built to an unusual plan with two aisles, Gothic arches and vaults and three domes in a row. The church contains the tomb of Giulio Antonio Acquaviva, Duke of Atri, executed in 1482 by Nuzzo Barba di Galatina.

3km **Conversano** (219m, 23,000 inhab.) stands on a hill overlooking the

Adriatic. It appears to have been a Peucetian town, possibly the *Norba* described in the *Tabula Peutingeriana* as lying on the inland route from Bitonto to Egnazia. It was bitterly contested by the Normans and Byzantines during the late Middle Ages. It changed hands several times in the following centuries, ending up among the possessions of the Acquaviva, Counts of Conversano, who retained it until 1806.

From the public gardens of the Villa Garibaldi, at the edge of the town, the view embraces the coastal plain to Bari. Nearby, at the centre of a sloping piazza, stands the **Castello**, originally Norman, transformed over the centuries into a lordly manor with numerous wings and towers. Above the tiled roofs rises the rectangular Norman keep; the low polygonal bastion and the taller cylindrical one respectively located at the north-east and north-west corners date from the 15C; the remaining structures are chiefly 17C. The main entrance, which faces Piazza della Conciliazione, and the elegant gallery in the atrium, were built in 1710 by order of Countess Dorotea Acquaviva. The interior contains private dwellings and the Biblioteca Civica.

Nearby stands the **Duomo**, restored after a fire in 1911. The 14C façade combines Romanesque and Gothic forms, with interesting sculptural decoration above the main portal. At the ends of the transept are two low campanili. The interior, with nave and aisles divided by piers, a trefoil matroneum and triple apse, contains a 13C icon of the Virgin (left aisle), a 14C wooden crucifix, traces of frescoes and a modern pulpit.

From the rear of the cathedral, Via San Benedetto, to the left, leads to the ancient Benedictine monastery founded, according to tradition, by St Mauro or St Placid and documented from the 10C onward. The conventual church, erected in the late 11C and extensively altered in the 16C and 17C, stands beneath a Baroque campanile of 1655. Part of its original decoration can be seen in the rough **mosaic frieze** that runs along the top of the entrance wall. The richly decorated interior has a nave surmounted by three consecutive domes with 17C frescoes. Along the left flank of the church is a pleasing 11C **cloister** with trefoil arches and delicately carved capitals. From here you may enter the crypt, originally a 6–9C Byzantine cenobium. In the apse are some repainted frescoes. The monastery houses the Museo Civico (open Mon–Sat 09.00–12.00, 15.30–19.30), with local art and archaeological finds.

> About 1km north-east of the town stands the unusual little church of **Santa Caterina**, with four semicircular arms arranged in a clover-leaf pattern around a central dome. The edifice is believed to date from the 12C.

From Conversano the road bears south-east through farmland and broken terrain. 5km the Torre del Castiglione, on a hilltop (right), marks the site of an ancient indigenous settlement, later a medieval fortified town abandoned in the 15C.

5km **Castellana Grotte** (290m, 18,000 inhab.) takes its name from the caverns 2km south-west. Possibly the most spectacular series of caverns in all of Italy, the *****Grotte di Castellana** lie along a north-east–south-west axis 1.5km long, at an average depth of c 65m. A series of corridors connects various chambers rich in stalagmites and stalactites in alabaster and other coloured stones. The short guided visit (Apr–Sep 11.00, 13.00, 16.00, 19.00), which terminates at the Grave al Precipizio, takes about an hour; the full tour to the **Grotta Bianca** (considered by some the most beautiful cavern in the world because of its brilliant crystalline formations; hourly Apr–Sep 08.30–12.15, 14.30–18.00; Oct–Mar 09.00–12.00, 14.00–17.00) takes 2 hr. The temperature inside the caverns remains constant around 15°C. The nearby **observation tower** offers good views over the surrounding countryside.

5km Putignano (372m, 27,000 inhab.), a busy market and manufacturing town, is a former fief of the Knights of Malta. The Museo Civico, in Piazza Plebiscito, is closed indefinitely for restoration. More interesting caverns (**Grotta di Putignano**, chiefly in pink alabaster; open 08.00–12.00 and 14.00–dusk) may be seen 1km north-west of the town.

ALBEROBELLO AND THE VALLE D'ITRIA

Here the road turns left, whereas the railway makes a wide loop to the south, through Noci, to (13km) **Alberobello** (438m), a small town (11,000 inhab.) with a quarter wholly composed of trulli flanking narrow streets. The name, Alberobello, derives from *Sylva Arboris Belli*, which refers to the vast oak forest that once covered the area. The town was founded, in all likelihood, by the Acquaviva, Counts of Conversano, in the 15C; but it grew up in the following century around a mill and a tavern established here by Count Gian Girolamo II. The area comprising the Rioni Monti and the Aia Piccola, composed of over 1000 trulli, has been declared a *national monument.

The trulli are usually whitewashed in the lower portions, and religious or folk symbols are traced in white on many of the grey conical roofs. Inside, the rooms are small and usually windowless; the interior walls, like those of the exterior, in most cases receive one or two coats of whitewash each year, which accounts for their immaculate appearance. The Trullo Sovrano, in Piazza Sacramento, has two storeys; and the pretty church of Sant'Antonio derives its inspiration from the trullo style.

The highway continues south-east through rolling countryside planted with vines, olives and almond trees and dotted everywhere by clusters of trulli.

9km **Locorotondo** (410m, 13,000 inhab.) is a strikingly beautiful town of circular plan (hence the name, 'round place') set on a hilltop at the heart of the Murge. From the Villa Comunale at the top of the hill there are splendid views over the Itria valley, with its constellations of trulli, to Martina Franca (see below). The church of **San Marco della Greca**, a late Gothic building erected by Piero Del Balzo, Prince of Taranto, has pilasters and half-columns with interesting capitals and bases. A road to the east connects Locorotondo to Ostuni (Route 19A) via **Cisternino**, a town of almost Greek appearance, made up of white terraced houses with external staircases.

From the crossroads at Locorotondo bear south across the Valle d'Itria, one of the more beautiful and exotic areas of Southern Italy, where the neat trulli, low stone walls, and small, meticulously planted farms combine to create a storybook atmosphere.

6km **Martina Franca** (431m, 46,000 inhab.) is a graceful 18C town known for its strong white wine (used in preparing vermouth and spumanti) and for its many Baroque and Rococo buildings. The town was established in the 10C by refugees from Taranto forced inland by the Saracen invasions, and it was enlarged in the early 14C by Philip of Anjou, who granted it the fiscal immunities from which it derives its appellative, *franca*. In the years that followed it was given defensive walls and no fewer than 24 bastions, to which Raimondello Orsini added a castle in 1388. The town was held in fee by a branch of the Caracciolo family of Naples from 1506 to the extinction of the line in 1827.

Locorotondo, a town of immaculate streets, white houses and beautiful flowering vines

■ **Information.** AA, Piazza Roma 37; phone 080 705702.

The central Piazza XX Settembre is flanked by the Villa Comunale, beyond which stands the 15C Gothic church of **Sant'Antonio**. Across the square rises the Porta Sant'Antonio, an 18C structure surmounted by an equestrian statue of St Martin, patron of the city. In the triangular Piazza Roma, beyond, stands the former **Palazzo Ducale**, now the town hall, attributed to Bernini (1668), with a fine iron-work balcony running the length of its façade. The edifice stands on the site of the Orsini castle. The Palazzo Martucci, across the square, has an elegant, restrained Baroque façade.

The narrow Corso Vittorio Emanuele winds past charming Baroque and Rococo townhouses to the collegiate church of **San Martino** (1747–75), its tall, graceful façade dominated by the sculptural group of St Martin and the beggar above the main door. The Romanesque-Gothic campanile is from a 15C church over which the present edifice was built. The richly adorned interior consists of a single nave with transept. The main altar, in coloured marble, has 18C statues of Charity and Maternity. The paintings above the minor altars are by local artists. The Palazzo della Corte (1763) and the Torre dell'Orologio (1734) stand at the left of the church.

From nearby Piazza Plebiscito, Via Cavour leads past some more 17C and 18C townhouses to Piazza Maria Immacolata. From here, Via Principe Umberto runs past the church of San Domenico and the Conservatorio di Santa Maria della Misericordia, both of the 18C. Further on, in Via Pergolesi outside the town gates, is a terrace offering marvellous views over the Valle d'Itria.

Highway 172 leaves Martina Franca through modern suburbs and proceeds south in a straight line beside the railway, descending the south edge of the Murge to cross a plateau with grain, vines and olives. 12km, crossroads. Roads lead (right) to (6km) Crispiano, near which there are Basilian cave-churches with 13C frescoes, and a small but well-displayed collection of traditional agricultural tools (at the 16C Masserie Lupoli); and (left) to Grottaglie (see below). The Ionian Sea and Taranto, preceded by the Mare Piccolo, stretch out before you as you cross the last low foothills to the coast. 8km a turning (left) bypasses the city centre.

Another way to Taranto

An alternative route to Taranto (87km in c 1hr, by Highways 100, 7, and 7t; closely followed by Autostrada A14) passes via Gioia del Colle. Leave central Bari by Via Amendola. 9km a road leads (right) to the British Military Cemetery, the burial place of 2000 officers and men killed in local fighting.

2km **Capurso** (74m, 14,000 inhab.) has a Renaissance Palazzo Baronale and a venerated icon of the Madonna (reputedly found in a well) in the 18C church of the Madonna del Pozzo.

At 14km Sammichele di Bari (280m, 7000 inhab.), a former Serbian colony, the 17C castle houses a modern museum (open by appointment, phone 080 677297) documenting rural life and peasant culture. From here a secondary road leads west to **Acquaviva delle Fonti** (8km, 21,000 inhab.), whose name reflects the abundant and accessible supply of water that distinguishes this, now a prosperous agricultural district, from neighbouring areas. The elegant **Cattedrale**, a Norman edifice begun under Roger II, was transformed in the 16C in a late Renaissance style. The bipartite façade has a delicate rose window, bold pilasters and a triangular pediment surmounted by statues of the Madonna and Child at the apex, and of saints at the ends. Free-standing columns born by lions, a vestige of the earlier Romanesque building, support the broken pediment above the tall central doorway. In the lunette is St Eustace with the stag, in bas-relief. The municipio, formerly the Palazzo dei Principi, erected in the 17C by the De Mari family, has an open loggia crowned by a decorative course of niches and masks running the length of the façade. The two towers belong to the Norman castle that originally stood on the site.

10km **Gioia del Colle** (360m, 28,000 inhab.) is a busy market town with a massive, austere **Castello** that was begun at the end of the 11C and enlarged by Frederick II, who used it mainly as a hunting lodge. The fortress is built to a rectangular plan with the four walls of the enceinte facing the cardinal points. The walls and towers are heavily rusticated and originally displayed a single, impregnable surface to the outside, the windows being later additions. The interior has been extensively altered; nevertheless, the grace and refinement of the original structure and of the Angevin and Aragonese additions are still visible. According to tradition, the castle was the birthplace of Manfred, son of Frederick and Bianca Lancia, whom the emperor, out of jealousy, imprisoned in the smaller of the two towers.

The rooms now house the Biblioteca Comunale and the small Museo Archeologico Nazionale (open daily 09.00–13.00, 16.00–19.00), displaying material from the nearby excavations at Monte Sannace, where explorations in 1957 and 1961 revealed an unidentified Apulian settlement, believed to be a major Peucetian town. The extensive site includes remains of houses, public buildings, city walls and an acropolis. In some places the street plan can be discerned.

The **defensive walls**, the remains of which include the foundation of a gate, average 4m in thickness and reach 6m in height. The necropolis, in part composed of small tombs beneath the floors of the houses, also extends beyond the city walls. It has yielded much material now in the museums of Gioia, Bari and Taranto.

In the environs of (29km) **Mottola** are numerous cave-churches, some with 12–15C frescoes. 6km join Route 18 from Castellaneta and Matera, passing below (3km) Massafra (Route 18) and across the foothills of the Murge to (14km) Taranto.

TARANTO

6km Taranto, at the north extremity of the gulf that bears its name, is an important commercial port and industrial centre (244,000 inhab.) and the second naval dockyard in Italy after La Spezia.

History

The Spartan colony of *Taras*, founded in 708 BC after successful struggles against the Messapians and Lucanians, rose to be the greatest city in Magna Graecia, famous especially for the purple dye obtained from the murex, a marine mollusec, for the wool of its flocks, which grazed on the banks of the Galaesus, and for its wine, figs, and salt. It was a centre of Pythagorean philosophy. Archytas, the mathematician, president of the town (430–365), who was visited by Plato, and Aristoxenes (4C BC), author of the earliest known treatise on music, were both Tarantines.

Threatened by Rome in the 3C BC, the city summoned Pyrrhus, King of Epirus to its aid, but after a ten years' war lost its independence (272 BC). In 209 BC the city surrendered to Hannibal, for which, after being taken by Fabius Maximus, it was severely punished. Subsequently it was Latinised as *Tarentum*.

Of little importance under the empire, it was destroyed by the Saracens (927), but rebuilt by Nicephorus Phocas, the Byzantine emperor, in 967. It retained its importance under the Normans, Swabians and Angevins, and by the 14C its territory had come to include much of Apulia and Basilicata. Made an independent Signoria under Raimondello Del Balzo Orsini (1393–1406), it was captured by Consalvo di Cordova in 1502. In 1647–48 it was torn by a popular uprising inspired by that of Masaniello in Naples.

The town came under Bourbon rule in 1734 and adhered to the Parthenopean Republic in 1799. Occupied by the French in 1801, it proved to be one of Napoleon's strongest bases against the English and the Russians. With the opening of the Suez Canal, it became one of the newly united Kingdom of Italy's more strategic harbours. During the First World War the port became familiar to British troops proceeding to and from the Eastern

Fronts; in 1940–43 it was attacked repeatedly by Allied aircraft. On 9 September 1943, the Royal Navy entered the harbour and landed troops unopposed.

Taranto was the native town of Giovanni Paisiello (1740–1816), the composer. It gives its name to the tarantula, a species of spider, whose bite was the reputed cause of a peculiar contagious melancholy madness (tarantism), curable only by music and violent dancing. This hysterical mania reached its height in Southern Italy in the 17C and has left its memory in the *tarantella*, the graceful folk dance of that region.

■ **Information**. EPT, Corso Umberto 121; tel. 099 453 2383, fax 099 453 2397.

■ **Airport** at Casale (Brindisi), with daily flights to Rome. **Air terminal**, 49 Corso Umberto, with coach service in conjunction with flights.

■ **Railway station** of the Ferrovie dello Stato and the Ferrovie Sud-Est, in Via Duca d'Aosta.

■ **Post office**. Lungomare Vittorio Emanuele III.

■ **Special events**. Holy Week celebration, with representations of the Passion and Death of Christ and procession through the city streets. Taranto is the site of the annual conference of scholars of Magna Graecia.

The town occupies an unusual site. The industrial Borgo, with the railway station, is on the mainland to the north-west; the Città Vecchia, on an island between the Mare Grande (a bay of the Gulf of Taranto, separated from the open sea by the fortified Isole Cheradi) and the Mare Piccolo (a large lagoon extending some 8km northeast of the town and divided by a peninsula into two bays, of which the first is used as a naval harbour and the second for oyster culture), is the site of the Roman citadel; this is separated from the peninsula to the south–east, on which stands the Città Nuova, by a navigable canal dating from the Middle Ages.

The Città Vecchia, connected with the Borgo by the long Ponte di Porta Napoli, is oblong in plan and crossed by four parallel avenues and many narrow alleys. In the animated Via Duomo is the **Duomo**, dedicated to San Cataldo (St Cathal of Munster), who remained at Taranto after a pilgrimage to the Holy Land in the 7C. Constructed in the 11C over an earlier building, it has been rebuilt several times, most notably in 1596 and 1657. The Baroque façade was added in 1713. Much of the building has recently been restored to its original form. The outside walls of the nave and transept are decorated with charming geometric motifs and blind arcading, as is the cylindrical drum of the Byzantine cupola at the crossing. The campanile, originally of 1413, was completely rebuilt during the recent restoration.

Interior. You enter the church through a 15C vestibule, at the left of which is the baptistery, containing a covered font (1571) incorporating antique columns, and the 17C tomb of Tommaso Caracciolo, Archbishop of Taranto. The interior of the church, a three-aisled basilica, has rounded arches rising from 16 columns of ancient marble (the first on the left is fluted) and marvellous **capitals** of Byzantine and Romanesque craftsmanship; note particularly the figures of bird with foliage, second on the left). On the right of the entrance is a holy-water basin carried by female herms, one of which is missing. The 17C coffered ceiling of the nave bears reliefs of St Cathal and the Virgin. In the floor, scanty remains of the original mosiac pavement. From the aisles, steps mount to the raised transept, which has vaulted ceilings and blind arcading high up on the walls. The cupola, rebuilt in 1657, rises above the crossing.

To the right of the apse, the Baroque Cappella di san Cataldo, with inlaid marble walls, 18C statues and richly frescoed ceiling, is enclosed by ornate bronze- and iron-work gates. The statue of the saint on the altar dates from 1984, replacing an earlier piece stolen. Steps in front of the high altar descend to the Gothic crypt, built on low columns belonging to the first phase of the building. On the walls are frag-

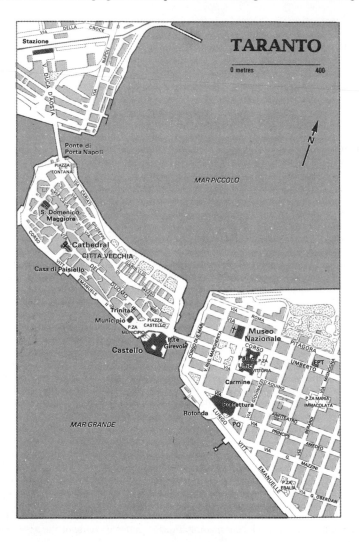

ments of Byzantine frescoes dating from the 12-14C. Also in the room is an early Christian sarcophagus.

Behind the duomo is the church of **San Domenico Maggiore** (also called San Pietro Imperiale), built in the late 11C and remodelled in the Gothic style in 1302. It is preceded by a high Baroque double staircase. The façade has a fine main portal with a baldachin, a graceful rose window and blind arcading. The interior is built to a Latin cross plan with a single nave and a rectangular apse. Along the north wall are 16C chapels with coloured marble decoration; the third of these contains a painting of the Circumcision by Marco Pino.

At the east end of the island, preceded by two antique columns thought to have belonged to a 6C Greek Temple of Neptune, stands the **Castello**, built by Ferdinand of Aragon in 1480, enlarged by the Spaniards in the 16C, and further modified in the 19C. It is now home to the Taranto Naval Command.

The Museo Archeologico Nazionale

A swing bridge crosses the channel to the Città Nuova. Here, in Piazza Archita, its principal square, are the imposing Palazzo degli Uffizi and the ***Museo Archeologico Nazionale** (open Mon–Sat 09.00–14.00, Sunday and holidays 09.00–13.00), containing the largest collection of antiquities in Southern Italy after that of the Museo Archeologico Nazionale in Naples. From the entrance, on the ground floor, steps ascend to the FIRST FLOOR. **Tarentine Collection.** ROOM 1. Greek sculpture. *20923 **archaic kore**; *3885 **head of a female divinity** (Hera or Aphrodite, 5C BC), attributed to a Greek sculptor working at Taras; *6138 **small kore** (c 500 BC); 3881 Apollo (5C BC) by a Greek sculptor working at Taras; 2348, 6142, 52926, 6141, 52925, fragments of small sculptures (4C BC); 3899 Athena (5C); 3883 Athena (5C); no number ***Eros**, attributed to the school of Praxiteles (after 350 BC); *3897 **head of Aphrodite or Artemedes**, attributed to the school of Praxiteles (325 BC); 3905 female head from a tomb sculpture (4C BC), 3893 Aphrodite or kore (400 BC), both by Tarentine artists; 6137 female head (400 BC); 3930 funerary stele of a nude warrior offering a pomegranate to a serpent; no number, Heracles at Rest, male torso, copy after an original by Skopas the Younger (4C BC).

ROOM 2: 3895 Heracles (4C BC) or Boxer Resting (1C BC); 3887 Dionysus, attributed to the school of Praxiteles (after 350 BC); 3918 Dionysus, copy after the school of Praxiteles (4C BC); no number, female head of Tarentine workmanship (3C BC); 10774, 4998, 6139, 20924, 5000, 10137 small heads and fragments (4C BC); 4999 herm (bearded Dionysus? 4C BC); 6143 Athena; no number, Roman mosaic pavement; 3916 headless female figure in the Hellenistic manner (3–2C BC); 3914 late Hellenistic decorative statue (nymph?); 3709–12 ***Hellenistic kline tomb** decorated with caryatids at the corners and reliefs of battle scenes (reconstruction); no number, two Tarantine decorative reliefs of which one representing a chariot race; 119142 female head from a funerary statue.

ROOM 3: **Roman Sculpture**. No number (right of entrance) portrait head of Augustus with veil and (left) of other figures of the Julio-Claudian period; no number (in case on wall) series of folk art portraits from a Roman urn field (1C BC–1C AD); Roman mosaics, including (left and right of entrance) decorative mosaics (2C AD); fragment of mosaic with a deer (4C or 5C); ***mosaic pavement** with representation of a hunting scene, and two tondi from the same pavement (4C or 5C BC); ***mosaic** of a lion and a wild pig fighting (3C AD).

ROOM 4: **architectural and sculptural fragments**. Here are assembled numerous reliefs and sculptures of local workmanship from the 4–2C BC, which decorated the small temples (naiskoi) that stood above the burial chambers of monumental tombs; as well as terracotta architectural ornaments and antefixes, also from the naiskoi, and the painted doors and fronts of burial beds of the chambers below. At the centre of the room is a large architectural sarcophagus with extensive traces of the original painted decoration, containing the remains of an athlete (c 500 BC). Around the sarcophagus were found three Panathenaean amphoras with paintings of games or contests; these are displayed in glass cases. Note also (right of entrance), no number, capital of a funerary column surmounted by a kalathios and decorated with female heads and bucrania; 50777–50783 nikai in flight and architectural elements (late 6C BC).

ROOMS 5–8 contain a beautiful and extensive collection of objects recovered from the necropolis of Taranto, illustrating the development of Greek ceramics from the 8C BC onward. The more interesting items are marked with one to four red stars. A summary description of the collection is given below.

ROOM 5: **Proto-Corinthian and Corinthian Ceramics**. Cases 1–2, Proto-Corinthian vases (8-7C BC), including numerous small unguentaria painted with geometrics and (later) human or animal motifs; Cases 3–4, Palaeo-Corinthian vases (late 7–early 6C BC), notably a fine alabastron with winged panther, aryballos with griffins and more unguentaria; Cases 5–11, Meso-Corinthian (6C BC) and Ionian vases, including a good pyxis with warriors, Meso-Corinthian skyphos with griffins and wild animals, Meso-Corinthian alabastron with sirens, Corinthian and Ionian unguentaria (many in animal forms), late Corinthian skyphos with lion and wild pig, Egyptian statuette, anthropomorphic unguentaria (one of which is from Rhodes), skypos with sirens, Meso-Corinthian amphora by the Dodwell painter and a thymiaterion with Artemis running.

ROOM 6: **Laconic Ceramics (7-6C BC)**. This room contains objects from those tombs in which vases of Corinthian production were mixed with those of other centres (chiefly the Greek islands), as well as some of the earliest Attic pottery. Particularly important are the so-called Laconic vases, after which the room is named, an extremely rare category whose presence at Taras is explained by the continuing trade relations that were maintained between the Spartan colony and its mother city throughout the 7C and 6C BC. Made of highly refined clay, with extremely thin walls and sober decorations, they are among the more elegant products of the archaic period.

Among the finer objects displayed are: Case 13, two Laconic cups with fish and dolphins, by the Painter of the Fish (c 600 BC); Case 15, Laconic ceramics (600–550 BC), late Corinthian hydria, aryballos with lion and wild pig, Meso-Corinthian kylix (600–575 BC). Case 16, Attic kylix with dance scene (579 BC); Case 17, Meso-Corinthian skyphos with dancers and lions, Attic kylix decorated by the Falmouth Painter (c 560 BC); Case 18, Laconic kylix with scenes of votive offering and dance, in the manner of the Arkesilas Painter (540 BC), Laconic kylix with Zeus and the Eagle by the Naukratis Painter (c 575 BC); Case 20, Corinthian, Attic and Ionic vases, including Attic kylix with scenes of battle and Palaeo-Attic oinochoe (580–570 BC).

ROOMS 7–8 are dedicated to Attic black and red figure pottery, of which the more outstanding examples are a large kylix by the Heidelberg Painter (Case 28) and the Lydos Cup, with superimposed colours and fine drawing representing battle scenes on one side and Hercules and Athena on the other. ROOMS 9–10 contain material of local provenance, including Proto-Italiot (430–380 BC) and Apulian vases, Hellenistic and Roman pottery and a very fine collection of Gnathian ware.

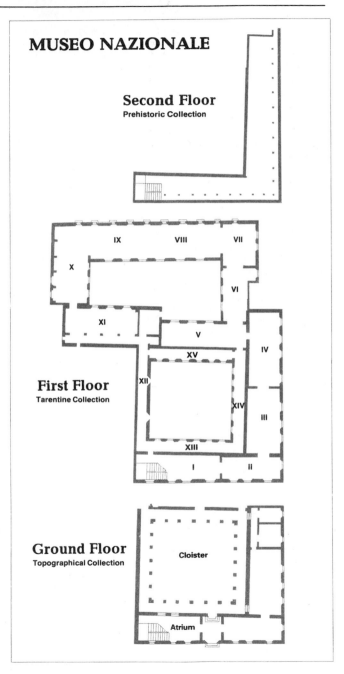

MUSEO NAZIONALE

Second Floor
Prehistoric Collection

First Floor
Tarentine Collection

IX VIII VII

X

VI

XI

V

XV

IV

XII

XIV

III

XIII

I II

Ground Floor
Topographical Collection

Cloister

Atrium

ROOM 11: **Sala degli Ori**. Here are gathered gold and silver ornaments and jewellery from Taranto and other locations throughout Apulia, most of which can be considered of Tarentine workmanship. Among the more striking pieces are several diadems with oak, olive, laurel and rose patterned laminae; many elegant earrings, some with filigrained pendants; a large ring with female head, woven gold necklace and ram's-head bracelet, from Mottola; a shell-shaped jewellery case in gilded silver, flower patterned diadem, laminated tubular sceptre and mirror case, from Canosa. Also in the room are Greek and Roman ivories and bronzes, gilded terracottas (ornaments of burial beds), Byzantine jewellery of the 6C and 7C AD, and (oddly out of place among these minute treasures) an archaic bronze *Poseidon from Ugento. There follow four corridors (ROOMS 12–15) dedicated to terracotta statuary (mainly small votive statues, with some grotesque masks), generally of the Hellenistic age.

The remaining rooms of the museum were closed for rearrangement at the time of writing. The SECOND FLOOR houses the **Regional Prehistoric Collection**, with Palaeolithic and Upper Palaeolithic finds from Terranera di Venosa, the Gargano Peninsula and the Grotta Romanelli (Otranto); Neolithic and Late Neolithic ceramics from the Grotta della Scaloria and Grotta dell'Erba (Avetrana) and the Grotta Sant'Angelo (Ostuni); a substantial collection of (mainly) Bronze Age pottery, and bronze and bone objects from Scoglio del Tonno (Taranto); material from Porto Saturo (Leporano) and Torre Castelluccia (Taranto), including Mycenaean pottery; a cinerary urn of the 10C or 9C BC, from Timmari (Matera) and a collection of protogeometric vases from Taranto, among the oldest examples of indigenous Apulian ceramics. In the Ground Floor Rooms adjoining the entrance to the museum is the **Topographical Collection**, with material (mainly pottery) from various localities in Apulia, Basilicata, and Calabria arranged to reflect the ancient territorial divisions of Messapia (the present provinces of Taranto, Brindisi and Lecce), Peucetia (province of Bari), Daunia (province of Foggia) and Lucania (Basilicata-Calabria).

In nearby Via Roma is the Museo Oceanografico dell'Istituto Talassografico (No. 3; open Mon–Fri 09.00–12.30), with specimens of marine life from the Gulf of Taranto and elsewhere. The geological museum or Museo del Sottosuolo, in the Villa Peripato, is closed for restoration (1995).

Eastward to Lecce

Highway 7 leaves Taranto from the east, skirting the south shore of the Mare Piccolo to (13km) San Giorgio Ionico. From the crossroads north of the town Highway 7t bears south–east for Fragagnano, leaving on the left the road to Grottaglie and Brindisi. After a few metres, a road on the left diverges to Carosino and Francavilla Fontana (Route 18).

3km **Monteparano** (130m, 3000 inhab.) was founded in the 15C by Albanian refugees. The Castello d'Ayala, a fortified residence with merloned walls and a prominent tower, was erected in the 18C and remodelled in the 19C. Beyond Monteparano the road continues to cut a straight path through gently rolling countryside.

6km **Fragagnano** (123m, 6000 inhab.), situated on a hilltop to the left, has a ponderous Baroque castle (16C). The road climbs gently through vineyards and olive groves to (7km) Sava, an important market centre founded at the end of the Middle Ages. Beyond, you resume a straight course through broad, open country planted with vines and grain. On the left, Oria (Route 18) is visible in the distance.

7km **Manduria** (79m, 33,000 inhab.), one of the chief centres of Messapian civilisation, was known even in ancient times for its heroic opposition to the Tarantines, whose mercenary general, Archidamus of Sparta, was killed beneath its walls in a fruitless siege of 338 BC. Now known primarily for its vineyards, it conserves several interesting monuments including Messapian necropoli and a fine stretch of the ancient walls.

The centre of the town is the triangular Piazza Garibaldi, dominated on the left by the **Palazzo Imperiali**, built in 1719 over a bastion of the ancient walls, part of which can still be seen. A balcony with an ironwork balustrade runs the length of the façade; inside are an elegant court and two covered staircases. Across the square, the municipio occupies the 18C convent of the Carmine. On the upper floor is the **Biblioteca Comunale** (open Tue, Wed, and Fri 08.30–13.30; Mon and Thur 08.30–13.30, 16.00–19.00), containing incunabula, manuscripts and an extraordinary collection of first-edition medical texts of the 16C, as well as a small collection of Messapian antiquities.

The **Duomo** (San Gregorio Magno), originally a Romanesque building, was remodelled in Gothic and Renaissance forms. The tripartite façade has a large rose window and three Renaissance portals; the finest, at the centre, incorporates reliefs of the Trinity with Angels and the Annunciation. On the right side stands the Gothic-Renaissance campanile. The apse, with its two orders of columns, dates from the 16C. The interior, restored in 1938, has three aisles with rounded arches in the nave and pointed arches and ribbed cross-vaults in the choir. At the beginning of the south aisle is a 16C baptismal font with figures of Christ and the apostles; the 12 statues of saints in the apse date from the 17C. The two large Baroque chapels, with paintings by local artists, were added in the 18C.

The **medieval ghetto**, beside the cathedral, survives intact in its original form.

The **ancient ruins** are crossed by both the road and the railway, and may be seen in about 1hr. At the heart of the archaeological area, north of the town, is the famous **Well of Pliny**, identified with the lacus recorded in the *Natural Histories* (III, 6), in which the water preserves a constant level however much is drawn from it. To reach the site, leave Manduria by Via Sant'Antonio; just before the modern church of the Cappuccini, a road on the right leads to the cave (visit accompanied by a caretaker) where you can see the celebrated spring.

Just beyond the Cappuccini lies a well-preserved stretch of the ancient **walls**, the remains of which consist of three more or less concentric circuits surrounded by broad, deep ditches. They suggest that Manduria was for several centuries a strategic bastion against Hellenistic penetration of Messapian territory. The three sets of walls, naturally, belong to different phases of the city's history. The innermost circuit, which dates in all likelihood from the 5C BC, is c 2km in circumference and 2m thick. It is made of large, irregular blocks laid lengthwise. The second circuit, attributed to the 4C BC, is made with carefully cut ashlars placed at right angles to one another in a typically Greek way, suggesting that its builders adopted Greek architectural methods—presumably from the enemy at Taras—while they struggled vehemently to maintain their political independence. The third and most impressive circuit is over 5km in circumference and 5.5m thick. The remains stand in some points to a height of 6–7m. The wall has two distinct faces: one, on the inside, composed of irregular blocks and small stones; the other, on the outside, made of regular blocks laid longitudinally; the middle zone having been filled in with rubble and covered over. It appears to have been erected in the 3C BC, perhaps as a defence against Hannibal.

Just north of Pliny's Well is a curious triple gate where converging roads penetrated the outer walls in points a few metres apart, then, coming together in the space between the walls, entered the old wall through a single gate. Other gates have been located in the east wall and near the present Via del Fosso. In addition, three of the underground passages that connected the city with the surrounding countryside and that were used during sieges (to smuggle in supplies, to send out troops or to evacuate the population), have been found near the Cappuccini and in the wall to the south and east.

The Viale Panoramico, which follows the perimeter of the walls, passes numerous rock-cut tombs arranged in groups beside the ancient roads leading out of the town. These tombs, of which over 2000 have been identified, have yielded large quantities of Gnathian and other wares of the 3C BC, now at the Museo Nazionale in Taranto. Those situated along the north wall also have painted decorations.

Leave Manduria from the east and proceed in a straight line across the plain known as the Tavoliere di Lecce; to the left, the railway parallels the highway.

7km a road diverges right to **Avetrana** (8km), where the **Castello**, probably built around the end of the 14C over an earlier fortification, incorporates a tall rectangular keep surrounded by walls, and on the north a cylindrical bastion with a projecting battlement on Renaissance corbels. Adjoining this structure is a feudal residence of somewhat later date; the large rectangular court, with lòggia and portico, is characteristic of the 17C.

3km a road on the left leads to Erchie and (3km) Torre Santa Susanna, (3km more) both with Basilian cave-churches and feudal residences of the 17C and 18C.

Highway 7t continues in a straight line across open countryside to (19km) **San Pancrazio Salentino** (62m, 11,000 inhab.), where the Castello Monaci was a fortified residence in 1221 and has been 'restored' several times since then.

The road crosses an area planted with vines and tobacco to (16km) **Campi Salentina** (12,000 inhab.), a large agricultural centre, where the Palazzo Marchesale was built in 1627 over an earlier castle, of which traces are still visible along the east front. The 15C church of the **Madonna delle Grazie** has a dramatic façade of 1579 and a richly sculpted portal (1658) by Ambrogio Martinelli.

8km Highway 7t joins Highway 16 from Brindisi. Bear right to (6km) Lecce, Route 20.

20 · Lecce and the Salentine Peninsula

*The old town of **Lecce**, with its small squares and winding streets, owes its distinctive charm to the richly decorated Baroque architecture of its churches and houses, which skilfully exploits the properties of local building stone. This pietra leccese, a sandstone of warm golden hue, is easy to work when first quarried, but hardens with the passage of time to form a surface which stands up remarkably well to erosion. The style to which it gave rise flourished from the 16–18C and was applied both to monumental and to private architecture, so that even the most unassuming buildings sometimes present carved window frames, sculptured balconies, and elaborate portals. Of the style's leading exponents, Gabrielo Riccardi and Francesco Antomio Zimbalo were most firmly rooted in Renaissance classicism. Giuseppe Zimbalo (Lo Zingarello) was perhaps the most extravagant. Cesare Penna produced much refined sculpture, whereas Achille Carducci and Giuseppe Cino developed an elegant and (relatively) restrained architectural idiom. However, it is perhaps misleading to concentrate on a few 'masters', since in a profound sense this became a popular style. The 'Barocco Leccese' remained more a decorative phenomenon than an architectural one, for it never really broke away from the spatial models of 16C Rome. Instead, it affirmed itself in the embellishment of traditional architectural forms with imaginative and ingenious sculptural designs.*

*The **Salentine Peninsula**, devoted largely to the cultivation of the vine and the olive, has in addition important tobacco-growing districts. Megalithic remains (dolmen, menhir, etc.) are widespread, though unfortunately somewhat difficult to find; and traces of the Messapian period are visible in cyclopean walls. The following route is proposed as a round trip, but may be broken up into two nearly equal parts around Leuca, which is 96km from Lecce via Otranto (87km via Gallipoli), the return to Lecce being made by Highway 275, which bisects the peninsula, in 67km.*

ROAD: a 184km loop beginning and ending at Lecce. Highways 543 and 611 to (46km) Otranto, then Highway 173 to (51km) Leuca. From Leuca, a secondary road follows the coast to (50km) Gallipoli, from where Highway 101 returns to (37km) Lecce.

HOTELS EN ROUTE: Otranto, ***Rosa Antico, tel. 0836 801563, fax 0836 802106.

RESTAURANTS EN ROUTE: Otranto, ***Il Gambero, at the entrance to the old town, tel. 0836 801107.

LECCE

The chief town (102,000 inhab.) of the Salento, Lecce is clean and spacious, and, because of its 17C and 18C architecture, has been called the Florence of the Baroque. It was the birthplace of Antonio Verrio (c 1639–1707), the painter.

History

A Messapian settlement, afterwards a Greek town and the Roman *Lupiae*, Lecce is the *Licea* of the 10C and the *Litium* of the Swabian epoch. The ancient city reached its greatest prosperity in the Imperial Roman period, at which time its harbour (today San Cataldo), built by Hadrian, was the most important on the Adriatic after Brindisi. Sacked by Totila in 549, Lecce remained under the Eastern Empire for the next 500 years. During this period it was overshadowed by Otranto, which grew to be Byzantine Italy's busiest port; but it regained its primacy following the Norman conquest and from 1053 to 1463 (the date of its inclusion in the Kingdom of Naples) it was ruled as an independent county.

Later it was known as the Apulian Athens because of its scholarship, a tradition that it carried forward, despite the continuous peril of Turkish invasions, from the 15-18C. Today the city hosts one of Apulia's two universities, the other being in Bari.

In 1647–48 Lecce was the scene of a broadly based anti-Spanish and anti-feudal revolt which, although brutally repressed, continued to smoulder until modern times. In 1734 a second uprising won concessions from the Bourbons that the aristocracy failed to implement; violent social struggles again erupted against the wealthy middle class that emerged during the period of French domination, was likewise unsuccessful. The city suffered no damage in the Second World War.

■ **Information**. EPT, Via Monte San Michele 20; tel. 0832 314117, fax 0832 314814 (branch office at Via Rubini 2). AA, Via Zanardelli 66, tel. 0832 316461 (branch office at via Rubini 2).

■ **Airport**. At Casale (Brindisi), with daily flights to Rome. **Air terminal** in Piazza Mazzini, with coach service in connection with flights.

■ **Post office**. Piazza Libertini.

■ **Special events**. National Wine Fair in May–Jun; patron saints of the city, 24–26 Aug, Salentine celebrations, including exhibitions, literary contests/sporting events, etc., in Oct.

The central Piazza Sant'Oronzo, which is mainly modern in appearance, lies roughly midway between the castle and the cathedral. It is dominated by a Roman column (from Brindisi) bearing a statue of St Orontius, tutelary of the city, appointed Bishop of Lecce by St Paul in AD 57 and martyred during Nero's persecution of AD 66 or 68. The square is partly occupied by the **Roman amphitheatre**, built in the 1C BC and excavated in 1938. Only half of the monument is visible. The piers around the outside probably rose in superimposed orders to a height considerably greater than that of the extant fragments; several of their arches are still standing. Only the lower of the two orders of seats remains. The amphitheatre may be entered from the south-west corner. Within, the elliptical passage that provided access to the lower order of seats, partially hewn out of the rock and partially built in *opus reticulatum*, can be followed to the left or right. Many fragments of the bas-reliefs that decorated the high wall that separated the cavea from the arena (depicting wild animals, gladiators, etc.), and a few Roman inscriptions, are still visible. More reliefs, in infinitely better condition, can be seen at the Museo Provinciale (see below). In the environs were found several tombs dating from the 5C BC to Roman times.

Adjoining the amphitheatre on the west are the **Sedile** (1592), formerly the town hall, and the ex-chapel of San Marco. The lion over the doorway recalls the chapel's restoration by Venetian merchants (1543). Opposite is the Baroque church of Santa Maria delle Grazie, behind which lies the 16C **Castello**. The latter, currently a military installation, consists of two concentric trapezoidal structures

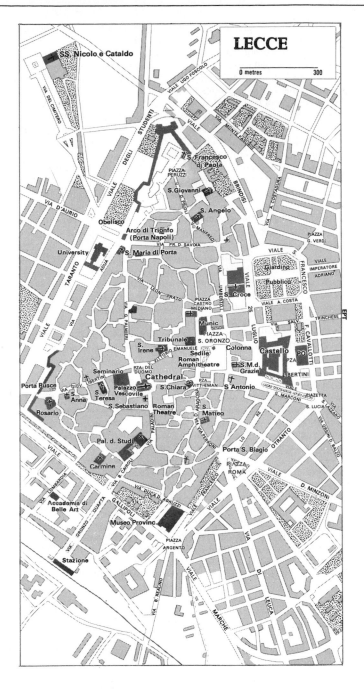

LECCE

0 metres   300

SS. Nicolo e Cataldo

VIA DEL CIMITERO

VIALE UGO FOSCOLO

VIALE

VIA MONTE PASUBIO

VIA DEGLI STUDENTI

S. Francesco di Paola

PIAZZA PERUZZI

S. Giovanni

VIA D'FEDO

S. Angelo

VIA MANFREDI

VIA D'AURIO

Obelisco

Arco di Trionfo (Porta Napoli)

VIA PR. D. SAVOIA

University

S. Maria di Porta

VIA ACQUA

VIA TARANTO

VIA LEON PRATO

VIA G. PALMIERI

PIAZZA CASTRO MEDIANO

S. Croce

VIALE UMBERTO I

VIALE 25 LUGLIO

Giardino

Pubblico

VIALE A. COSTA

PIAZZA G. VERDI

VIALE

VIALE S. FRANCESCO

VIALE IMPERATORE ADRIANO

TRINCHESE

EPT

F. CAVALLOTTI

Munic

PIAZZA S. ORONZO

Tribunale

S. Irene

VIA VITTORIO EMANUELE

Sedile

Colonna

Roman Amphitheatre

Castello

PO

S.M.d. Grazie

PZA. LIBERTINI

LIBERTINI

Seminario

PZA. DEL DUOMO

Cathedral

S. GIOV. LIBERTINI

Palazzo Vescovile

S. Anna

S. Teresa

S. Chiara

S. Sebastiano

Roman Theatre

VIA PALADINI

S. Matteo

VIA VITT-EMAN

VIA PERRONI

S. Antonio

VIALE

G. MARCONI

PIAZZETTA

S. LUCIA LAZARO

VIA ORSINI D. BALZO

VIA

Porta Rusce

Rosario

VIALE

VIA LOMBARDIA

VIA ORONZO QUARTA

Pal. d. Studi

Carmine

VIA B. CAIROLI

Porta S. Blagio

OTRANTO

VIALE D. MINZONI

VIALE

VIA DUCA D. ABRUZZI

GALLIPOLI

Accademia di Belle Art

VIA FRANCESCO

PIAZZA ROMA

VIALE

VIALE

DI

Museo Provinc

PIAZZA ARGENTO

Stazione

VIA B. REALINO

VIALE

MARCHE

LEUCA

BRINDISI

VIA COSTADURA

separated by a courtyard. The outer fortification, nearly 1km in circumference, was built by Charles V; the inner structure dates from the 12C.

A narrow street leads north from Piazza Sant'Oronzo to the impressive church of **Santa Croce, the most celebrated of the town's Baroque monuments. Begun in 1549 by Gabrieli Riccardi, the church was completed in 1679 and bears testimony to the styles of the city's most prominent architects. The façade is built to a general plan by Riccardi, who is directly responsible only for the lower portion, with its columns (note the unusual **capitals**), blind arcading, and elegant frieze. The elaborate main portal and the two lateral doorways were added in 1606 by Francesco Antonio Zimbalo. The upper portion, which rests on a balcony supported by richly carved mensoles, centres around an ornate **rose window** flanked by saints in niches and sculpted columns. It was executed in 1646 by Cesare Penna to a design by Giuseppe Zimbalo (Lo Zingarello). The pediment is also designed by Zimbalo.

The **interior**, begun in 1548 by Riccardi and completed after the artist's death by his followers, embodies a conception of spatial elegance reminiscent of Brunelleschi. Built to a Latin cross plan, it has a nave and aisles separated by columns (note the ornate composite **capitals** with heads of apostles, and at the crossing, symbols of the Evangelists), and 14 lateral chapels. The smaller rectangle of the sanctuary has an elegant apse and sculptured portal. Above the crossing, the luminous cupola (1590) and slightly-pointed arches bear a rich sculptural decoration that is carried over into the vaults of the transept. In the coffered ceiling of the nave is a 19C representation of the Trinity. In the south transept stands the Altare della Croce, by Cesare Penna (1637–39), with a small loggetta for the exhibition of relics. The high altar, of coloured marble, was brought from the church of Santi Nicola e Cataldo (described below). In the chapel on the north side of the sanctuary is the *Altare di San Francesco di Paola with bas-reliefs of the saint's life by Francesco Antonio Zimbalo (1614–15).

Across the public gardens from Santa Croce is the **Museo Missionario Cinese** (Via Imperatore Adriano 79; open Tue, Thu, and Sat, 17.00–19.00 or by appointment, tel. 0832 292580), with a modest collection of Chinese art and crafts.

Adjoining the church is the *Palazzo del Governo (1659–95), initially built as a Celestine convent to a plan attributed to Zingarello. From here turn south-west, past the church of the Gesù or Buon Consiglio (1575–79) and the former Jesuit college adjacent, and cross Via Rubighi. Corsio Vittorio Emanuele diverges west, passing the Theatine church of Sant'Irene (completed 1739). Further on (left) opens *Piazza del Duomo, with its fine Baroque buildings.

The *Duomo, founded in 1114 but rebuilt by Giuseppe Zimbalo in 1569–70, has an unusually tall campanile (68m) terminating in an octagonal aedicule; and two main façades. One, corresponding to the west end of the nave, fronts on the smaller square of the elegant Palazzo Vescovile and incorporates statues by the architect in a sober Classical design. The other, facing the piazza, is a sumptuous composition containing a statue of St Orontius in a monumental triumphal arch.

The **interior** is a rather ponderous Latin cross with nave and aisles divided by compound piers. The coffered ceiling displays scenes from the life of St Orontius and, in the transept, a Last Supper. The first and second south altars were designed by Cesare Penna. Above the altar in the south transept is a painting depicting St Orontius, by Giovanni Andrea Coppola, perhaps the most prominent painter of the Baroque period in Lecce. The crypt, which dates from 1517, was restored in 1956.

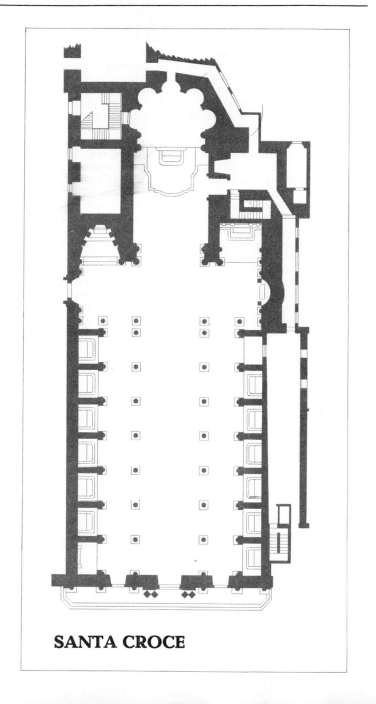

SANTA CROCE

Adjoining the cathedral and somewhat set back from the main square is the
*Palazzo Vescovile, with a fine loggia. Constructed in 1420–38, it was rebuilt in
1632 and restored in the 18C. To the right stands the magnificent *Seminario,
built between 1694 and 1709 to a design by Giuseppe Cino. In the spacious courtyard can be seen a richly decorated **well**, also by Cino.

From Piazza del Duomo Via Libertini continues west past (left) the unfinished
church of Santa Teresa, built, together with the adjacent convent, between 1620
and 1630. Across the street is the little church of the Assunzione (or Santa
Elisabetta), constructed in 1519 but rebuilt in the 19C. The street continues past
the church of Sant'Anna (left) to the **Chiesa del Rosario** (also known as San
Giovanni Battista), Giuseppe Zimbalo's last work, begun 1691 and completed in
1728. The unusual interior follows the plan of a Greek cross developed around a
central, octagonal space. A profusion of sculpture decorates the altars. Across the
street stands the former Ospedale Civile (1548), now occupied by the Tobacco
Administration. Further on is the 18C Porta Rusce (see below).

Returning to Piazza Sant'Oronzo, follow Via Augusto Imperatore south to the
church of Santa Chiara. A street on the right leads to the small (40m diameter) but
well preserved **Roman theatre**, the only known example of its kind in Apulia. The
extensively restored cavea has 12 rows of seats, although in all likelihood there
were initially several more. These are divided into cunei by steps that converged
upon the orchestra, which was separated from the cavea by a parapet, now
replaced by a modern wall. On the performers' side are three rows of broad seats
reserved, as was the custom, for the town notables; access to the orchestra was
provided by lateral passages (paradoi), one of which is still partially intact. The floor
of the orchestra is particularly well preserved. The skene is pierced by numerous
holes: some of these may have served for anchoring scenery, but others belong to a
more recent date. The sculptural decoration of the proskenion and the skene itself
are missing, but excavations of the site have brought to light numerous fragments
(mainly Roman copies of well-known Greek originals), now at the Museo
Provinciale.

Via Augusto Imperatore continues south to the church of **San Matteo**
(1667–1700), the curvilinear façade of which recalls Borromini's San Carlo alle
Quattro Fontane in Rome. The elliptical interior has shallow chapels and 12 statues
of apostles on tall plinths. The high altar, an exemplary expression of local workmanship, dates from 1694. Via Perrone, on the left, leads past former mansions and
through the 18C Porta Biagio to Piazza Roma and the Monumento ai Caduti
(1928).

Follow Viale Francesco lo Re south to the Palazzo Argento and the superbly
appointed quarters of the *Museo Provinciale Sigismondo Castromediano
(open Mon–Fri 09.00–13.30, 14.30–19.30; Sun 09.00–13.30). The
Archaeological Collection, which begins on the First Floor, is reached by a spiral
ramp along which are projecting platforms with texts and illustrations relating to
the Palaeolithic period in Italy; the Neolithic, late Neolithic and Bronze Ages in
Southern Italy; Greek and indigenous pottery; and Greek and Roman coins. Case 1,
Greek and Roman coins. Cases 2–9, Attic black figure vases. Case 10–71, Apulian
ceramics, including a comprehensive collection of Gnathian ware and a fine,
extensive collection of Messapian trozzelle; small bronzes and terracotta statuary
from Egnatia and Ruvo; large vases with reliefs, from Canosa; and a singular large
basin painted in red, yellow, black and white. Cases 78–79, large bronzes, including
hemispherical and conical helmets; bronze belts and belt buckles; cups, bowls, etc.,
chiefly from Rudiae. Case 80, small bronzes, including numerous fibulae, mirrors,

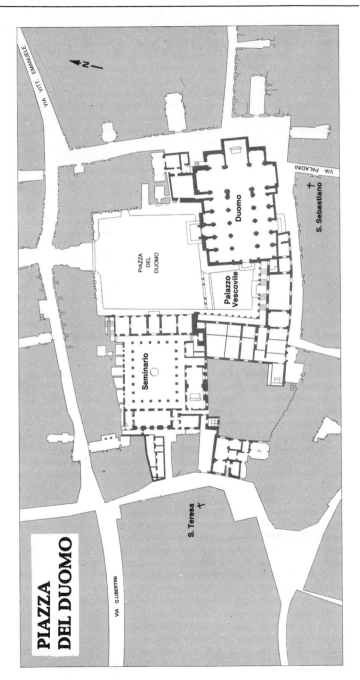

PIAZZA
DEL DUOMO

VIA G. LIBERTINI

S. Teresa

VIA VITT. EMANUELE

N

PIAZZA
DEL
DUOMO

Seminario

Palazzo
Vescovile

Duomo

VIA· PALADINI

S. Sebastiano

statuettes, etc.; Cases 81–82, terracotta statuettes and architectural ornaments. Case 83, terracotta children's toys (*tintinnabula*) from Rudiae. Cases 84–87: fragments of large jugs, oil lamps, fossils, small terracottas, keys, spear heads, etc. in iron. Around the ironwork dividing walls: Roman and Messapian inscriptions dating from the 3C BC–2C AD.

Return to the Ground Floor and follow the corridor around to the left, turning right at the second bank of windows to the **Topographical Collection**, which contains material dating from the Palaeolithic to the late Roman Imperial period, an eloquent testimony to the cultures that continuously inhabited Apulia over the last 20,000 years.

The **Picture Gallery**, on the Third Floor, may be reached by lift. ROOM 1: on the right, 13C gold and enamel psalter cover; 12C architectural fragments of local workmanship; Jacobello di Bonamo, polyptych (c 1380); Jacobello del Fiore, Madonna dell'Umilita; 15C Venetian school polyptych from the church of Santa Caterina at Galatina; Gerolamo da Santacroce, Bishop Saint; 15C and 16C architectural fragments and bas-relief of local workmanship; 18C Byzantine icons and a small reliquary, also of Byzantine craftsmanship; compasses, goods case made from a horn, jewellery box (16C).

Cross the atrium. In cases, on the left, is a collection of coins and medallions ranging from 1220 (Frederick II) to the late 19C. ROOM 2: on the walls, paintings by Southern Italian artists of the 17C and 18C. Cases 1–2, ivories, cameos, Cases 3–4 fans, and local paper and silk compositions (18C); against the pillar, wooden jewellery cabinet with ivory inlay. Case 5 (centre right), Castelli D'Abruzzo ceramics, from the 17C and 18C. Case 6, Venetian glass (also 17C and 18C). Case 7, Salentine ceramics. Against the right wall is a large, gaily painted wardrobe of Neapolitan manufacture (17C).

The **Porta Rusce**, the south-west gate of Lecce, recalls the city of *Rudiae* (3km south-west) where Ennius (239–168 BC) 'ingenio maximus, arte rudis', the father of Latin poetry, was born. The ruins, which may be reached from Via San Pietro in Lama, are of little interest. They include some Roman streets, the scanty remains of public buildings and ramparts, and numerous tombs.

To the north-west, beyond the Porta Napoli (an arch erected in honour of Charles V in 1548) is *****Santi Nicola e Cataldo**, the most important Romanesque church of the Salentine and one of the finer Norman monuments in Italy. Founded in 1180 by Tancred, Count of Lecce, its unique character results from a confluence of Byzantine, Arabian and proto-Gothic influences. The Baroque façade, attributed to Giuseppe Cino, incorporates a richly decorated **portal** (note the heads of women on the architrave and the three orders of freely carved arabesques; the badly damaged fresco in the tympanum dates from the 16C), and the rose window from the original 12C building, together with pilaster strips and statues of saints.

The austere **interior** consists of a tall nave, narrow aisles, and a shallow transept, with Saracenic arches on compound piers that recall the cathedral of Monreale in Sicily. A marked Burgundian feeling is evident in the nave, particularly in its proportions and in the sense of soaring height they produce. Above the crossing the elliptical dome rises from an unusually tall drum. The vaulted roof is also typically northern. Traces of frescoes can be seen along the walls. In the north aisle is an undistinguished statue of St Nicholas by Gabrieli Riccardi; in the south aisle, the 17C tomb of Ascanio Grandi, a native poet. The paintings above the lateral altars are by Giovanni Bernardo Lama.

A door to the right of the façade leads to the monumental 16C **cloister**, at the centre of which stands an elegant Baroque aedicule with spiral columns. To the right is a second, smaller cloister. In the south flank of the church can be seen a fine portal with a fresco of St Nicholas and an inscription regarding the building of the church in the lunette. From the cemetery, on the north side of the building, the blind arcading that runs along the top of the wall, and the singular octagonal cupola, clearly Oriental in derivation, can be seen.

THE SALENTINE PENINSULA

From the public gardens adjoining the castle follow Viale Imperatore Adriano and Via del Mare to the divided highway linking Lecce to the sea. The road turns east and slightly north through verdant farmland to (11km) San Cataldo, a popular bathing beach, just west of which Highway 611 branches right for Otranto.

Near the crossroads are the scanty remains of the **Porto Adriano**, the harbour constructed by Hadrian in 130 AD. Many of the large stones from this site were removed in the 19C to build the breakwater of the modern harbour.

The highway bears south through woods and farmland, parallel to the coast. 3km a road on the right diverges to (6km) **Acaia**, a small village still largely enclosed by walls, with an interesting though somewhat run-down **Castello**. The latter is a typical Renaissance fortification furnished with imposing enceinte and large bastions with steep scarps and projecting battlements (only partially visible). Begun in 1506 by Baron Alfonso dell'Acaja and completed in 1535 by his son Gian Giacomo (known for his contributions to the castle of Lecce, the walls of Crotone and Castel Sant'Elmo in Naples), it is perhaps the purest example in Apulia of Aragonese military architecture. From Acaia, a road to the south returns to the coast via Vanze.

At (12km) San Foca, a road on the right leads inland to (7km) Melendugno, with another fine castle of the 15C and 16C. At (2km) **Rocca Vecchia** a grass-covered mound of rubble and a few metres of low walls are all that remain of the Rocca built by Gualtiero VI de Brienne, Count of Lecce, in the early 14C and destroyed by Charles V in 1544. The ruin stands on a rock ledge overlooking the sea, amid the remains of a Messapian village, which in turn overlays a prehistoric settlement. Here excavations have revealed c 1200m of **megalithic walls** with a gate and two square towers, remains of several buildings and cave dwellings cut into the rock walls of the bay, and numerous graves that have yielded material from the 4C and 3C centuries BC, now at the Museo Provinciale in Lecce.

Continuing south, you pass the popular bathing beach at Torre dell'Orso, flanked on the west by a pine wood. The road goes through the Alimini lakes district, a growing resort area. Further on, it is joined by Highway 16 from Maglie (see below) and enters (29km) **Otranto**, a fishing centre and resort (5000 inhab.) set on the shore of a pleasant bay.

■ **Information**: AA, Ria Rondagli 8; phone 0836 801436.

History

This was *Hydruntum*, a Greek city and a Roman municipium, possibly founded by the Tarentines. It took its name from the stream (the Idro) that runs into the sea here; today, the townspeople still refer to themselves as Idruntini. Located at the mouth of the Adriatic, and separated from the coast of Albania by less than 60 miles of water (now known as the Strait of Otranto), it was one of Republican Rome's leading ports for trade with Greece and Asia Minor, and it is generally thought that the Via Traiana was extended to Otranto to handle this traffic.

Although eclipsed by its rival Brindisi in the Imperial Age, Hydruntum enjoyed renewed activity under the Byzantines, becoming one of the more important centres of the Eastern Empire in Italy and capital of the region still known as the Terra d'Otranto. Together with Taranto and Bari, it was one of the last Byzantine cities to fall to the Normans, surrendering finally in 1070 to Robert Guiscard. At the time of the Crusades it became an embarkation point for the Orient and a leading centre of trade between Venice, Dalmatia and the Levant. In 1480 a Turkish fleet, allied to the Venetians in the latter's struggle against the Kingdom of Naples, ruthlessly attacked the city and slaughtered its inhabitants. The 800 survivors were promised their lives if they renounced their Christian faith, but none did so; they too were killed on the nearby hill of Minerva, together with their executioner, who confessed himself a Christian after witnessing the unwavering faith of his victims.

Alfonso of Aragon recaptured the city in 1481 and provided it with new and more formidable fortifications, including the castle, Horace Walpole's *Castle of Otranto*. But the town shrank in size and population, its port deserted. The surrounding countryside was abandoned and the marshes, only recently improved, bred malaria. Today, Otranto has a modest fishing fleet and is a departure point for the car-ferry to Corfu.

The **Castello**, at the centre of the town, was built under Alfonso of Aragon between 1485 and 1498 and reinforced by the Spanish in the late 16C. It is irregular in plan with cylindrical towers at the corners and a massive spearhead bastion facing the sea. Most of the visible structure (under restoration in 1995) dates from the 16C; nevertheless, the enceinte shows traces of Roman and medieval masonry, as well as of 19C restorations. You enter through the archway on the north side. Within, a narrow entrance hall opens onto the central court; an external staircase climbs to the rooms of the upper floor. Above the main arch are the monumental arms of Charles V.

The road opposite the entrance to the castle descends to the ***Cattedrale** (Santa Maria Annunziata), founded by the Normans in 1080 and reworked in 1481. In the façade are a fine 15C rose window and a Baroque portal of 1764. The basilican interior is divided into a nave and two aisles by 14 marble columns, some antique, from which spring stilted arches. A beautiful ***mosaic pavement** (1163–65) representing the Tree of Life, the Months (with the relevant sign of the Zodiac and agricultural or domestic activity), biblical scenes (Expulsion from the Garden, Cain and Abel, Noah's Ark and the Tower of Babel), scenes of chivalry (Alexander the Great and King Arthur) and mythological episodes, occupies the nave and aisles; recent probes have revealed a Roman mosaic underneath. The roughly made but fascinating Norman work is the largest of its kind. In the south arm of the transept is a rather gruesome chapel with the bones of the inhabitants slain by the Turks.

Steps in the aisles descend to the **crypt**, with five aisles, semicircular apses, and a vaulted ceiling carried by 42 antique, Byzantine and Romanesque columns with sculptured capitals. On the walls, fresco fragments of various ages and relief panels from a dismantled pluteus.

Descend along the north flank of the cathedral to Corso Garibaldi, one block before the sea. To the left lie the two main gates to the old town—the Torre

Alfonsina (1481), with cylindrical bastions; and the Napoleonic Porta di Terra. To the right is a house where the door-jambs incorporate inscriptions dedicated to Marcus Aurelius and Lucius Verus. Further on, Via San Pietro mounts to the little Byzantine church of the same name, built in the form of a Greek cross inscribed in a square. It is said to be the first cathedral of the city. The interior is covered with frescoes of various epochs, some with Greek inscriptions. It has barrel-vaulted ceilings and a cylindrical cupola supported by four squat columns at the crossing. In the walls are indented arches corresponding to the blind arcades of the exterior.

From Otranto to Maglie

Highway 16 bears south-west across the peninsula to (10km) Palmariggi. Just before reaching the town you may turn left and, after a few metres, left again to the Masseria Quattro Macini, a farm, near which you can see a group of seven dolmens and standing stones. 5km further south lies Minervino di Lecce, with a fine Renaissance chiesa parrocchiale; just outside the town, on the road to Uggiano la Chiesa, is the **Dolmen di Scusi*, the largest and best preserved of these primitive structures.

7km **Maglie** is a manufacturing town containing several Baroque buildings, including the church of the Madonna della Grazia; the Chiesa Parrocchiale, the campanile of which recalls that of the duomo of Lecce; and the monumental Palazzo Capece. The latter houses the Museo Comunale di Paleontologia e Paletnologia (open Mon–Wed and Fri 09.00–13.00; Thu, Sat, and Sun 09.00–13.00, 17.00–19.00), which has a collection of fauna of the Pleistocene period and archaeological material from nearby caves.

Leave Otranto by the castle. A road on the left climbs to the hill of Minerva, the name of which may allude to an ancient temple to the goddess. Here a staircase ascends past the spot where the survivors of the attack of 1480 were executed; at the top of the steps is the 16C church of San Francesco di Paola, incorporating the chapel (Santa Maria dei Martiri) erected by Alfonso of Aragon to commemorate the massacre. 2km further south, along the rocky promontory that terminates in the Cape of Otranto, the easternmost point of Italy, lie the ruins (right) of the Basilian abbey of San Nicola di Casole, founded in the late Middle Ages, rebuilt in the 12C and destroyed by the Turks in 1480. In clear weather the **view* spans the Strait of Otranto to Albania and, further south, Corfu.

Beyond the cape the road bears inland and descends, returning to the coast at (11km) Porto Badisco, a small hamlet on a rocky cove. Nearby is the Grotta dei Cervi, a complex of caves, several kilometres long, containing Neolithic paintings of hunting scenes and magic symbols and rich formations of stalactites. The caves are not open to the public; however, numerous objects (ceramic, bone and flint) found on the site as well as colour photographs of the paintings will be housed in an antiquarium, scheduled to be built in the near future. The road climbs and falls along the coast to (5km) **Santa Cesarea Terme**, a bathing resort and spa commanding views to the mountains of Albania. Beyond, you wind past Porto Miggiano, paralleling the sea along a sheer cliff covered with prickly pear.

■ **Information**. AA, Via Roma 209; tel. 0836 944043.

4km a road on the left descends to a largo. Ramps and steps lead down the rock wall to the **Grotta Zinzulusa** (open 10.00–13.00; 14.00–18.00; guide). A long (140m) marine cavern rich in stalagmites and stalactities (*zinzuli* in local dialect), this was occupied in the Upper Palaeolithic period (c 10,000 BC) and in the Copper Age. It is beloved by zoologists for its peculiar species of small crustacea, which seem to have originated in the Eastern Adriatic and suggest that this part of Italy was at one time united to the Balkan Peninsula. Nearby, but somewhat difficult of access, is the **Grotta Romanelli**, discovered in 1879 and also inhabited in the Upper Palaeolithic period. The flint implements found here have given their name to a variant of the so-called Gravettian industry. Figures of animals, stylistically similar to groups in France and Spain, have been found engraved on the walls and on loose blocks of stone. Also discovered here: a stone with schematic drawings in red ochre, considered the oldest painting in Italy. Fossil animal remains in the sediment include warm-climate animals (elephant, hippopotamus and rhinoceros) in the lower levels and cold-climate creatures (goat, northern and steppe birds) in the upper levels. They bear witness to the oscillation of the sea level in the Quarternary period, as a consequence of variations of climate.

Continuing south, you round a headland to (3km) Castro Marina, a fishing village and resort with a small, cliff-bound harbour. Hence a winding road mounts to **Castro** (98m, 2000 inhab.), a fortified town with a Romanesque cathedral, perhaps the ancient *Castrum Minervae* where Aeneas first approached the Italian shore (*Aeneid* III, 521). The **Castello**, erected in 1572 and fortified in the following century, stands on the site of a Roman fortification later used by the Byzantines and the Normans. The former **Cathedral** retains parts of its 12C façade, transept and lateral portals. The north aisle incorporates the remains of a 10C Byzantine church. The town offers magnificent views of the sea and the coastline.

At (6km) Feronzo, a road on the right diverges to (5km) **Andrano**, where the 13C castle was made over into an imposing palazzo by the Caracciolo in the 17C. Further on is Marina d'Andrano, with its medieval tower. 4km Tricase Porto is a fishing village and resort.

4km inland lies **Tricase**, a large (17,000 inhab.) agricultural town with a 14C castello rebuilt and extended in the 16C, and a Chiesa Matrice (1770) containing a Deposition and an Immacolata by Palma Giovane.

From Tricase Porto the road climbs to (4km) Marina Serra and (5km) Marina di Novaglie, then crosses a relatively uninhabited stretch of coastline before reaching (9km) **Capo Santa Maria di Leuca** (60m), a conspicuous cliff of limestone (deriving its name from the Greek 'leucos', white), the *Iapygium* or *Salentinum Promontorium* of the Romans, with a lighthouse. The actual southernmost point of Apulia is the Punta Ristola, somewhat to the west. Marina di Leuca, below the cape, is popular for bathing. The church of Santa Maria Finibus Terrae stands on the site of a temple of Minerva, close to the point where the Apulian Aqueduct ends in an artificial cascade (usually dry).

Around the Cape by boat

Excursions may be made by boat to the several caves on the north-west shore of the cape, beyond Punta Ristola. Among these are the **Grotta del Diavolo**, which has yielded fossil remains of warm-climate animals and Neolithic flint, bone and ceramic objects; the **Grotta della Stalla** and **Grotta Treporte** with their beautiful effects of light and colour, and the **Grotta del Bambino**, also inhabited in prehistoric times. To the east lie the **Grotta Cassafra** and the **Grotta Grande di Ciolo**, both of which present interesting structural and atmospheric effects.

The road rounds Punta Ristola and bears north-west, enjoying good views in all directions.

At (4km) Torre San Gregorio, a turning on the left leads inland to (4km) **Patù** where, opposite the Romanesque church of San Giovanni, you can see the Centopietre, a small (7 x 5.5m) rectangular structure of large ashlars with a pitched roof. Some believe the building to be Messapian in origin, while others hold that it was built during the Middle Ages, using stones belonging to earlier buildings.

Continue along the coast, which is distinguished by rocky bays, many dominated by medieval watch-towers. Beyond (10km) Sant'Antonio, the road is straight and somewhat monotonous, the countryside virtually uninhabited. Near (10km) Marina San Giovanni lie the scanty remains of the Roman harbour of *Usentum*. Just beyond (10km) the 16C Torre Suda (left) a road on the right leads inland to Taviano (8km) and **Casarano** (9km), birthplace of Pope Boniface IX (reigned 1389–1404), where the church of **Casaranello** (or Santa Maria della Croce) contains the only known early Christian mosaics in Apulia. The ancient edifice, initially comprising a single nave, was enlarged during the late Middle Ages and remodelled in the 11C, 13C and 17C. The mosaics occupy the vault of the chancel and the cupola; in the former are geometric designs with animals; in the latter, the Cross set against the night sky. Along the nave walls are 13C frescoes representing the life of St Catherine and New Testament scenes.

The road turns inland, returning to the sea along the shore of a broad bay.

15km enter **Gallipoli** (21,000 inhab.), the *Kallipolis* of the Greeks and the *Anxa* of Pliny, by its modern borgo on the mainland, pass a fountain decorated with antique reliefs, and cross a bridge of 1603. The old city, its narrow streets tightly packed on to a small island, was the last of the Salentine Terre to capitulate to the Normans (1071). Sacked by the Venetians in 1484, it was strong enough to drive off a British naval squadron in 1809. Beyond the bridge is the **Castello**, where in the 13C 34 rebel barons held out for seven months against Charles of Anjou. Rectangular in plan with an imposing enceinte and massive corner bastions, it is fronted by the keyhole-shaped annex built in 1522 to plans by Francesco di Giorgio Martini, who visited the fortification in 1491–92. The original Byzantine fortress has been incorporated into the polygonal bastion at the south-east corner.

Further west, the Baroque **Cattedrale** (1630), with an elaborate façade of 1696, is adorned with many paintings by local artists, including a Madonna and St Orontius by Giovanni Antonio Coppola, the artist's last work. In the nearby Bishop's Palace are an Assunta by Francesco De Mura and other paintings.

The **Museo Civico** (Via De Pace 108; open Tue, Wed, and Fri 08.30–13.30; Mon and Thu 08.30–13.30, 16.00–19.00) houses a collection divided into ten sections encompassing antiquities (largely Messapian sarcophagi and vases), natural history, weapons and clothing, historical and ethnographic relics and curiosities, and prints and paintings of the city. The Baroque church of San Francesco contains wooden carvings of the Two Thieves by Vespasiano Genuino, an outstanding achievement of the realistic school of local sculpture. The church of the **Purità** has a richly stuccoed interior and many paintings; the floor is paved with 18C majolica tiles representing baskets of flowers and fruit.

Beyond Gallipoli the highway bears inland through farmland. 13km **Galatone** is a large town (16,000 inhab.) with several Baroque monuments, and the birthplace of the humanist physician and cosmographer Antonio de Ferrariis (Galateo, 1444–1517). Highway 101 proceeds in a straight line to (24km) Lecce. There are two alternative routes via Galatina (9km north-east), or via Nardo and Copertino (respectively 5km and 11km north-west)—which are considerably more interesting.

Galatina (78m 29,000 inhab.) is one of the more populous cities of the Salentine peninsula and an important wine-producing centre. It hosted an important Greek colony during the Middle Ages, and the Greek dialect and customs were maintained until the dawn of the modern era. Later, it was incorporated into the county of Soleto (see below). The Franciscan church of *Santa Caterina d'Alessandria bears witness to the wealth and influence of the town's feudal lords, the barons Orsini. Begun by Balzo Orsini in 1384 and completed by his son Giovanni in 1460, it has a façade in the late Apulian Romanesque manner, with three gables lined with arched corbel tables. The central portal (1397) is flanked by slender columns on much-worn lions. It has three bands of intricately-carved moulding, of which those nearest the door show a marked Oriental influence. In the lintel are relief figures of Christ and the apostles and, above the rounded arches, a classical pediment, surmounted by a fine rose window. The lateral doorways are placed asymmetrically with respect to the gables above, creating a disturbing sensation of imbalance.

The **interior** (apply for admission at the monastery) is remarkable both for its construction and for its decorative scheme. Massive walls pierced by wide drop arches separate the nave from the double side aisles. The nave, like the aisleless nave of San Francesco in Assisi, is articulated into bays by clusters of columns and pilasters from which spring ribbed cross vaults. On the walls and in the vault, numerous frescoes (badly damaged) illustrate the Old and New Testaments and provide insight into the nature of feudal life in Apulia. Resembling in a superficial way the frescoes of Giotto's school at Assisi, they are attributed to Central Italian artists working in the early 15C. Also of interest are the apocryphal account of the Life of the Virgin depicted in the south aisle and the episodes from the Life of St Catherine of Alexandria in the presbytery. Here, against the north wall, is the tomb of Raimondello del Balzo Orsini, with the deceased depicted supine in a Franciscan habit and again, kneeling, on the sarcophagus. Beyond the sanctuary is the octagonal apsidal chapel constructed by Giovanni Andrea Orsini. The latter's tomb, surmounted by a balcachin with four columns carried by lions, stands against the rear wall.

The **treasury** contains a silver reliquary shrine and other precious objects, possibly of Apulian workmanship, a portable Byzantine mosaic of the Redeemer set on wood and an icon of the Madonna in a silver-gilt frame.

Galatina also has a small Museo Civico (Piazza Umberto), with coins and weapons, and a Museo d'Arte Pietro Cavoti (Piazza Alighieri), both temporarily closed.

4km east of Galatina is **Soleto** (90m, 5000 inhab.), also interesting for its medieval monuments. A Messapian town, it has been identified with the *Soletum* of *Pliny*. Like Galatina, it adhered closely to Eastern cultural and religious traditions throughout the Middle Ages; and the Latin rite was not instituted in its churches until 1598. The parish church of **Santa Maria Assunta**, rebuilt in 1770–83, is flanked by a campanile begun in 1397 by Raimondello Orsini and completed in the early 15C by Giovanni Antonio Orsini. The structure, which is commonly referred to as the Guglia di Raimondello, represents a graceful compromise between Romanesque and Gothic building canons. A similar confluence of styles distinguishes the façade (1347) of the small chapel.

Nardò (45m, 30,000 inhab.) is the third-largest city in the province of Lecce. Founded by the Messapians, it became a Roman municipium under the name of *Neritum*. It retained a decidedly Oriental stamp throughout the Middle Ages, despite repeated efforts to westernise it, and the Greek and Latin rites were practised side-by-side in its churches until the 15C. It was taken by the Turks in 1480. Attacked by the Venetians in 1484, it suddenly surrendered after five days of strenuous resistance, an event which has given rise to much perplexity among historians. It participated in the anti-Spanish revolt that shook Lecce and sent repercussions throughout the peninsula and it adhered enthusiastically to the cause of the Risorgimento.

The centre of the city is the triangular Piazza Antonio Salandra, a theatrical piece of town planning that revolves around the exuberant Guglia dell'Immacolata (1769). The **Palazzo della Prefettura**, rebuilt in 1772, has an open arcade on the ground floor and a vaulted loggia on the floor above, both with trefoil arches. Above the store fronts along the other sides of the piazza are ironwork balconies and elegant loggie, some of which have been wholly or partially walled up. The piazza adjacent takes its name from the church of **San Domenico**, built in the late 16C but restored, in Baroque form, after 1743. The façade hosts a strange colony of grotesque herms and caryatids.

The former **Castello** of the dukes of Conversano, now the town hall, was begun by Giovanni Antonio Acquaviva d'Aragona, who built the central block (distinguished by its crenellated battlements on unadorned arched corbels) and the mandorla-like corner bastions in the early 16C. The other parts are clearly later additions. Adjoining the medieval town walls is a largo containing the curious octagonal aedicule (1603) called the **Osanna**, made up of eight small columns joined by polyfoil arches, surmounted by a segmented stone cupola with eight pinnacles and a sculptured finial.

The **Cattedrale**, founded on the site of a Basilian church by Benedictines in 1090, was partially rebuilt after an earthquake of 1230, enlarged in the following century, and modified several times after that, particularly in 1721 by Ferdinando Sanfelice, when additions were made to the façade and interior. The latter was restored in 1900 to an earlier, though not original, form. Within, the nave and aisles are separated by compound piers with engaged columns. The rounded arches on the south side are those of the original building; the pointed arches on the north are part of the 13C reconstruction. Above the altars are paintings by local artists and a 13C Catalan crucifix which, according to the legend, began to bleed when the Saracens attempted to carry it off. On the walls and piers are frescoes dating from the 13C to the 15C.

In the Bishop's Palace you can see a Madonna with Sts Peter and Paul by Francesco Solimena.

Copertino (34m, 24,000 inhab.) is known for its imposing **Castello**, which stands at the north-west corner of the old town. The fortress is made up of two distinct parts: a Renaissance exterior, rectangular in plan with pointed bastions and a broad moat; and an inner structure of earlier date, which includes the tall Angevin keep and the rooms of the north wing referred to as the Castello Vecchio. The east wall, nearly 120m long, contains an elaborate Renaissance **portal** surmounted by rosettes and medallions with effigies of illustrious figures. Beyond is a vaulted entrance-hall with arrow-loops and offset doorways. The inner court is surrounded by buildings of different epochs; the Renaissance **Cappella di San Marco**, on the right, has a fine portal and a small rose window. Inside you can see frescoes by a local artist and the sarcophagi of Umberto and Stefano Squardiafico (died 1562 and 1568 respectively).

Adjacent to the chapel is a room with a large fireplace. From this room you enter the vaulted corridor that runs round the north, west and south walls. Steps in the south-west corner of the court mount to a terrace from which you enter the monumental apartments of the Castello Vecchio. Go into the Angevin keep through an archway in the south-east corner of the court. The overall design of the castle was drawn up by Evangelista Menga, who is also the architect of the castles of Mola (Route 19A) and Barletta (Route 11).

INDEX

The most important page references are given in **bold**.

Abruzzo 11, 28, 41, 281, 318
Acaia 401
Acciaroli 239
Acerenza 357
Acerra 154, **344**
Acquaviva della Fonti 383
Agerola 170
Agnano Terme 144
Agnone 311
Agropoli 238
Alatri 70, **73**
Alba Fucens 326, **332**
Alberobello 381
Alfedena 311
Alife 309
Altamura 355, **359**
Altomonte 254
Amalfi 15, 27, 94, 154, 155, 156, 158, 169, 170, 171, 173, **175**, 220, 238
Amantea 70, **243**
Amatrice 323
Amiternum 316
Anacapri 227
Anagni 28, 70, 71
Ancona 283
Andrano 404
Andria 294
Anversa degli Abruzzi 314
Aprigliano 263
Apulia 16, 26, 27, 28, 29, 30, 35, 155, 281, 282
L'Aquila 281, 308, 315, **318**, 319, 330
Aquino 74
Arce 74
Arcipelago Ponziano 93
Arco Felice 153
Ariano Irpino 347
Arienzo 344
Arpaia 344
Arsoli 335
Ascoli Piceno 308, 318
Aspromonte 70, 233, 264, **267**

Assergi 315, 318, 324
Atessa 287
Atrani 27, 156, **176**, 177, 178
Atri 283, **284**
Ausonia 91
Avellino 69, 348, **351**
Aversa 78, 155
Avetrana 392
Avezzano 74, 332, 334

Bacoli 151
Badia di San Vincenzo 311
Bagaladi 269
Bagnara Calabra 248, 268
Bagnoli 154
Bagnoli Irpino 356
Baiae 99, 100, 103, 144, **149**
Banzi 354
Bari 28, 29, 30, 283, **299** 343, 371
Barile 354
Barisciano 315
Barletta 24, 30, 283, **292**
Basilicata 29, 220, 240, 281, 282
Bazzano 315, 324
Beffi 330
Belvedere Marittimo 41, 241
Benevento 14, 17, 23, 24, 27, 69, 154, 156, 335, 338, 343, **344**
Bisceglie 296
Bisignano 254
Bitetto 360
Bitonto 18, 28, 29, 30, **298**
Blue Grotto 228
Boiano 309
Bomba 287
Bombile 279
Bominaco 26, **315**
Borgo San Pietro 334
Borgorose 334

Bovalino Superiore 279
Briàttico 244
Brindisi 361, 371, 373, **375**
Buonalbergo 347
Buturo 263

Cagnano Varano 342
Caiazzo 338
Calabria 29, 42, 69, 70, 154, 233
Calanna 268
Calle di Tricarico 362
Calvi 24
Calvi Risorta 77
Campania 11, 26, 27, 28, 69, 99, 220
Campigliatello Silano 259, 260, 261
Campi Salentino 392
Campitello Matese 309, 310
Campli 308, 317
Campobasso 281, 308, 335, **336**
Campochiaro 309
Campo di Giove 329
Cancello 344
Cannae 291
Canosa 27, 30, **290**
Capestrano 315
Capo Miseno 151, 232
Capo Palinuro 233
Capo Santa Maria di Leuca 404
Capo Suvero 243
Capo Vaticano 247
Capraia 343
Capri 12, 95, 99, 169, 174, 179, 195, 220, **223**, 238
Capua 29, 70, **77**, 99, 105, 154, 156
Capurso 383
Caramanico 329
Cariati 274
Carinola 93

Carovigno 375
Carovilli 311
Carpanzano 256
Carpignano 25
Casacalenda 336
Casamari 70, 72
Casamicciola Terme 229,
  231, **232**
Casaranello 23
Casarano 405
Caserta 33, 69, 79, **214**
Caserta Brit. Mil. Cem. 218
Caserta Vecchia 218
Casoli 334
Cassino 74, 158
Cassino Brit. Mil. Cem. 76
Castel Lagopesole 355
Castel del Monte 30, **294**
Castel di Sangro 287, **312**
Le Castella 275
Castellammare di Stabia
  169, 219
Castellana Grotte 380
Castellaneta 361, **367**
Castelvecchio Subequo 330
Castiglione a Casauria 329
Castro 404
Castrovillari 249, **253**
Catanzaro 70, 256, 261,
  275
Caudine Forks 344
Caulonia 277
Celano 326, **330**
Celico 258
Ceprano 74
Cercemaggiore 308
Cerignola 289, 355
Cerro al Volturno 311
Cetaro 242
Chiaromonte 252
Chieti 281, 286, 326, **327**
Cilento, The 233, 238
Cimitile 24
Cisterna di Latina 82
Cisternino 381
Civitella del Tronto 317
Collarmele 330
Conversano 380
Copertino 407
Corato 296
Corfinio 330

Cori 79, **80**
Corigliano Calabro 273
Cosenza 70, 242, 249,
  255, 258
Costiera Amalfitana 169,
  174, 179
Crispiano 383
Cropani 275
Croton 10
Crotone 258, **274**
Cumae 98, 99, 103, 144,
  152

Deserto 174
Diamante 241
Dolmen di Scusi 403

Eboli 41, **356**
Egnathia 373
Ercolano 183

Fago del Soldato 259
Fallascoso 287
Fano Adriano 316
Fasano 374
Ferentino 72
Fiaiano 232
Fioano 347
Fiuggi 73
Fiumefreddo Bruzio 243
Foggia 289, 343
Fondi 88, 158
Fontana 232
Forca Caruso 330
Forio 229, **232**
Formia 74, 89, **90**
Fossa 26
Fossacesia 287
Fossanova, Abbey of 30,
  79, **81**
Fragagnano 391
Francavilla Fontana 361,
  369
Francavilla a Mare 285
Francolise 93
Frosinone 69, **72**, 83
Fuscaldo 242

Gaeta 15, 18, 28, 84, **89**,
  154, 155
Galatina 30, **406**

Gallipoli 405
Gambarie 268, 269
Gargano, The 282, 338,
  339
Gavi 93
Genazzano 72
Gerace 269, **279**
Ginosa 366
Gioia del Colle 383
Gioia Tauro 247
Gioiosa Ionica 277
Giovinazzo 298
Giulianova 284
Gran Sasso d'Italia 308,
  315, 318, **323**, 324
Grassano 362
Gravina di Puglia 355, **358**
Grotta Azzura 228
Grotta di Castellana 380
Grotta di Pertosa 250
Grotta di Smeraldo 175
Grotta Zinzulusa 404
Grottaglie 361, **368**
Grottole 362
Grumento Nova 252
Grumentum 252
Guardiagrele 286
Guardia Piemontese 242

Herculaneum 12, 18, 23,
  44, 94, 99, 100, 103, 106,
  108, **136**

Irsina 358
Ischia 10, 95, 98, 179,
  195, 220, 229, **230**, 231
Isernia 281, **310**
Isola di Capo Rizzuto 275
Isola di Dino 241
Isola del Gran Sasso 326
Itri 74, 88

Lacco Ameno 229, 231,
  232
Lago Ampollino 261, **263**
Lago Arvo 258, **259**, 261,
  263
Lago d'Averno 148
Lago di Campotosto 316
Lago di Cecita 258, 259,
  260

Lago di Fogliano 85
Lago Fucino 332
Lago di Fusaro 152
Lago Lucrino 148
Lagonegro 240, **252**
Lanciano 283, **286**, 287, 313
Larino 335
Laterza 366
Latina 69, 79, **83**
Latiano 370
Lazio 69
Lecce 35, 371, 393
Lempa 318
Letino 309
Licosa 238
Locorotondo 381
Locri 269, **278**
Longobucco 260
Loreto Aprutino 284
Lucera 30, 343, **348**

Macchia d'Iserna 310
Magna Graecia 10, 11, 70, 98
Magliano de'Marsi 334
Maglie 403
Maida, plateau 243
Maiori 178
Manduria 379, **391**
Manfredonia 340, **341**, 342
Maratea 233, 240
Marina di Camerota 240
Marina di Massa 174
Martina Franca 381
Massafra 361, **367**
Massa Lubrense 174
Matera 361, **363**
Matese, The 309, 338, 348
Mattinata 342
Melfi 350, **352**
Melito di Porto Salvo 269, **280**
Mesagne 371
Mesoraca 262
Meta 171
Metaponto 272
Metapontum 269, **270**
Miglionico 363
Minervino Murge 292

Minori 178
Minturnae 91
Minturno 84, **91**
Minturno Brit. Mil. Cem. 92
Minuto 26
Misenum 151
Modugno 361
Mola di Bari 372
Molfetta 30, **297**
Molina Aterno 330
Molise 11, 281
Moliterno 252
Molpa 240
Monopoli 371, **372**, 373
Montaguto 348
Montalto 267, **269**
Monte Bulgheria 238, 240
Monte Cassino, Abbey 25, 26, 27, **74**,
Monte Circeo 83, 85
Monte Epomeo 230, 232
Monte Faito 170
Monte Nuovo 43, 148
Monte Pollino 249
Monte Sacro 238
Monte Sant'Angelo 27, 28, 170, **341**
Monte Vulture 42, **354**
Montecalvo Irpino 347
Montecorvino 181
Monteparano 390
Monteroduni 310
Montescagliosa 366
Montesarchio 344
Montevergine 351
Monti del Matese 309
Montorio al Vomano 310
Morano Calabro 249, **253**
Mormanno 249, **253**
Moscufo 284
Mottola 384
Muro Lucano 356
Muro Tenente 370

Naples 10, 14, 15, 23, 24, 26, 29, 30, 31, 69, **94**, 343, 361
  Accademia di Belle Arte 197
  airport (Capodichino) 95

Naples cont.
  Aquarium 210
  Ascensione a Chiaia 211
  Bibliotecca Nazionale 193
  Borgo Marinaro 194
  Botanic Garden 200
  buses 95
  Calata Trinita Maggiore 160, 162
  Capo di Posillipo 210, 212
  Cappella Palatina 161
  Cappella Sansevero 195, **198**
  Castel Capuano 168, 184
  Castel Nuovo 160, 191, 195
  Castel dell'Ovo 184, 194
  Castel Sant'Elmo 184, 206, **207**
  Catacomba di San Gaudioso 159
  Catacomba di San Gennaro 158, 159
  Cattedrale 102, 158, 159, 160
  Centro Direzionale 220
  Conservatoria di Musica 197
  consulates 97
  Corso Garibaldi 222
  Corso Umberto I 218, 220
  Corso Vittorio Emanuele 196, 206, 211, 213
  Duomo 166
  Fontana dell'Immacolatella 195
  Fontana del Nettuno 220
  funicular 96
  Galleria della Vittoria 195
  Galleria Umberto I 193
  Gesù Nuovo 195, **196**
  Girolamini 195, **199**
  Grotta dei Tuoni 212
  Gugilia dell'Immacolata 195, 196
  Gugilia di San Domenico 195
  harbour 95
  hotels 96
  information 9
  Marechiaro 212

Naples cont.
Maria Egiziaca a
    Pizzofalcone 194
Mergellina 212
Monte della Misericordia
    199
Monteoliveto 31, 32, 160,
    162
Montesanto Funicular
    197, 206
Mostra d'Oltremare 211,
    219
Musei di Antropogia,
    Mineralogia, Zoologia e
    Paleontologia 221
Museo Archeologico
    Nazionale 102, 197
Museo Civico di Castel
    Nuovo 161
Museo Civico Gaetano
    Filangieri 221
Museo di Etnopreistoria
    194
Museo e Gallerie Nazionale
    di Capodimonte 158
Museo Nazionale della
    Ceramica Duca di
    Martina 209
Museo Nazionale di San
    Martino 207
Museo Principe Diego
    Aragona Pignatelli Cortes
    210
Nisida 213
Nunziatella 194
Palazzo d'Angri 197
Palazzo del Balzo 198
Palazzo della Borza 221
Palazzo Caprocotta 194
Palazzo Carafa di Nola
    194
Palazzo Cellamare 194
Palazzo Cuomo 221
Palazzo di Donn'Anna
    212
Palazzo Gravina 162
Palazzo Maddaloni 196
Palazzo Municipale 191
Palazzo Reale 191, 195
Palazzo Reale di
    Capodimonte 18, 26,

Naples cont.
31, 33, 35, 100, 197,
    200
Palazzo Sanfelice 194
Palazzo Serra a Cassano
    194
Parco di Posillipo 213
Parco della Rimembranza
    212
Parco Virgiliano 211
Piazza Amedeo 211
Piazza Bovio 161
Piazza della Carità 195,
    196
Piazza Dante 197
Piazza Garibaldi 200,
    218, 222
Piazza del Gesù Nuovo
    160, 195, 196
Piazza Giovanni Bovio
    220
Piazza dei Martiri 194
Piazza Matteoti 161, 196
Piazza del Municipio 160,
    161, 191, 218
Piazza del Murcato 223
Piazza del Plebiscito 191,
    193, 194, 195
Piazza Reale 193
Piazza San Domenico
    Maggiore 164, 195, 198
Piazza Trieste e Trento
    193, 194, 195, 196
Piazza Vanvitelli 206
Piazza della Vittoria 210
Pizzofalcone 191, **194**
Porta Capuana 160, 168
Porta Nolana 222
Porto Beverello 195
Posillipo 212
post office 97
Quadrivio del Capo 212
Raccolta d'Arte della
    Fondazione Pagliara 210
Rettifilo 218, **220**, 221
railway station 95
Riviera di Chiaia 210,
    219
Rotunda di Posillipo 213
San Domenico Maggiore
    160, **164**

Naples cont.
San Ferdinando 196
San Francesco di Paola
    191, 193
San Gennaro extra Moenia
    158
San Giacomo degli
    Spagnoli 191
San Giorgio Maggiore
    158, 160, 222
San Giovanni Battista 197
San Giovanni a Carbonara
    160
San Giovanni Maggiore
    221
San Gregorio Armeno
    195, **198**
San Lorenzo Maggiore
    101, 160, **165**, 195
San Martino 206, **207**
San Paolo Maggiore 101,
    195, **198**
San Pietro ad Aram 222
San Pietro a Maiella 195,
    197
San Pietro Martire 221
Santa Brigida 196
Santa Caterina 194
Santa Caterina a Formiello
    168
Santa Chiara 160, **162**
Santa Croce al Mercato
    223
Santa Lucia 191, **195**,
    218
Santa Maria degli Angeli
    194
Santa Maria della Carità
    196
Santa Maria del Carmine
    222
Santa Maria Donnaregiona
    160, **167**
Santa Maria Egiziaca 222
Santa Maria Incoronata
    161
Santa Maria di Montesanto
    197
Santa Maria la Nova 161
Santa Maria del Parto 212
Santa Maria di Piedigrotta

Naples cont.
211
Santa Maria di Portosalvo
223
Santa Maria della Sanitá
158
Santa Restituta 167
Santi Severino e Sossio
221
Santissima Annunziata
222
Sant'Agostino alla Zecca
222
Sant'Angelo a Nilo 165
Sant'Eligio 223
Santo Spirito 195, 196
Spaccanapoli 160, **163**,
196
Stazione Centrale 222
Stazione Marittima
Passeggeri 195
taxis 96
Teatro San Carlo 97, **192**
Tomb of Virgil 211
underground 96
University 221
Via dell'Anticaglia
Via Antonio Ranieri 222
Via Benedetto Croce 163,
196
Via Caracciolo 211
Via Chiaia 193, 194
Via Diaz 161
Via del Duomo 102, 158,
159, 160, 199, 221
Via F. Acton 195
Via Medina 160, 161,
219
Via Monte di Dio 194
Via Monteoliveto 160,
162, 219
Via Nazario Sauro 195
Via Nuova della Marina
223
Via Partenope 191, 194,
195
Via Pessina 197
Via Petrarca 213
Via Roma 161, 184, 196,
197
Via San Carlo 192

Naples cont.
Via San Gregorio 199
Via della Sanitá 158, 159
Via Santa Maria la Nova
161
Via Toledo 184, 193, 195,
196, 210
Via dei Tribunali 101,
160, 168, 198, 199
Via Vittorio Emanuele II
191
Vico Donnaregina 168
Villa Communale 210
Villa Floridiana 206, **209**
Vomero 184, 206, 218
youth hostels 96
Zoo 212
Nardò 407
Nardodipace 247
Nicastro 243
Nicotera 247
Ninfa 80
Nocera 24, 154
Nocera Inferiore 182
Nola 154, 190, **350**
Norba 80
Norma 80, 83

Ogliastro Cilento 238
Ogliastro Marina 238
Olevano Romano 73
Oplontis 23, 182
Oria 361, **369**
Ortona 286
Ostuni 371, **374**
Otranto 10, 26, 29, **401**,
403
Ovindoli 331

Padula 250
Paduli 347
Paestum 10, 23, 98, 99,
106, 233, **234**, 270
Basilica 234
Forum 236
Museo Nazionale 237
Porta della Giustizia 234
Porta Marina 236, 238
Porta Sirena 236, 238
Temple of Ceres 234, **236**
Temple of Neptune 234,

Paestum cont.
236
Temple of Peace 236
Tomb of the Diver 236
Theatre 236
Underground Sacellum
236
Via Sacra 234, 236, 237
Walls 238
Paganica 324
Palagianello 367
Paliano 73
Palinuro 240
Palmarola 93, **94**
Palmi 248
Paola 242
Papasidero 241, 253
Parco Nazionale
dell'Abruzzo 311
Parco Nazionale del Circeo
84, **85**
Patu 405
Pazzano 247
Penne 285
Pentedattilo 280
Pescara 281, **285**, 326
Pescasseroli 312
Pesche 310
Peschici 341, **342**
Pescocostanzo 313
Petilia Policastro 262
Phlegraean Fields 42, 43,
94, 98, 100, **144**, 230
Phlegraean Isle 230
Pianella 26, **285**
Pianosa 343
Picerno 356
Piccolo Sant'Angelo 174
Piedimonte Matese 309
Pietrabbondante 311
Pietracamela 316, 325
Pisciarelli 145
Pizzo 243
Policastro 238, 240
Policoro 269, **272**
Polignano a Mare 372
Pompeii 12, 18, 23, 44, 94,
99, 100, 103, 105, **107**,
182
Amphitheatre 122
Basilica 114

Pompeii cont.

Building of Eumachia
115

Casa del Centenario 124

Casa delle Nozze d'Argento
124

Central Thermae 124

College of the Augustali
140

Comitium 115

Cryptoporticus 119

Decumanus Inferior 139

Doric Temple 116

Foro Triangolare 116

Forum 107, **114**

Fullonica Stephani 107,
118

Great Palaestra 123

Hermes Caupona 121

House of the Alcove 139

House of the Bear 124

House of the Beautiful
Courtyard 140

House of the Beautiful
Impluvium 120

House of the Bicentenary
142

House of the Black Hall
140

House of the Bronze Herm
139

House of the Carbonised
Furniture 140

House of the Cithara
Player 117

House of C. Julius Polybius
120

House of the Cloth 143

House of the Corinthian
Atrium 142

House of Cornelius Rufus
123

House of the Deer 143

House of the Ephebus 120

House of Fabius Amandio
120

House of the Faun 107

House of Felix the Fruiterer
120

House of the Fruit Orchard
121

Pompeii cont.

House with the Garden
142

House of the Gem 143

House of the Gladiators
124

House of the Great Portal
143

House of Holconius Rufus
116

House of the Lararium
142

House of L. Ceius Secundus
119

House of Loreius
Tiburtinus 107, **122**

House of the Lovers 120

House of Marcus Lucretius
124

House of Marcus Lucretius
Fronto 124

House of the Marine Venus
122

House of the Menander
107, **119**

House of the Moralist 121

House of the Mosaic
Atrium 138

House of the Neptune
Mosaic 140

House of Opus Craticium
139

House of P. Paquius
Proculus 120

House of Pinarius Cerialis
121

House of Popidius
Montanus 118

House of the Priest
Amandus 120

House of the Relief of
Telephus 143

House of Siricus 123

House of the Skeleton 139

House of Successus 120

House of the Tragic
Poet 107

House of Trebius Valens
121

House of the Wild Boar
116

Pomeii cont.

House of the Wooden
Partition 139

Inn of Sittius 124

Insula Orientalis I 143

Lupanar Africani et
Victoris 124

Marcellum 115

New Excavations 118

Palaestra 142

Palaestra Sannitica 116

Porta Marina 114

Porta di Nola 124

Porta Stabiana 109

Posto di Ristoro 107

Sacrarium of the Lares
115

Samnite House 140

Schola Armaturarum
121

Shoemaker's Shop 124

Shop of Verus the
Blacksmith 119

Tavern of Zosimus 121

Teatro Grande 116

Teatro Piccolo 117

Temple of Apollo 114

Temple of Isi 117

Temple of Jupiter 115

Temple of Venus
Pompeiana 114

Temple of Vespasian 115

Temple of Zeus Meilichios
117

Terme Suburbane 144

theatres 107, 143

thermae 107, 140

Thermae Stabianae 123

Via dell'Abbondanza 123

Via Marina 114

Via di Nola 124

Via Nuceria 121

Via Stabiana 117, 123,
124

Villa of Julia Felix 107,
122

Villa of the Mysteries 107

Villa of the Papyri 144

Weaver's House 140

Workshop of Crescens
120

Pompeii cont.
  Workshop of the Dyers
    118
  Workshop of Verecundus
    118
Pontecagnano 181
Pontecorvo 74
Pontinia 83
Ponza **93**, 94
Popoli 308, 214, **329**
Portici 183
Positano 171, **174**, 220
Potenza 355, **357**
Pozzuoli 44, 100, 103,
  144, **146**, 219
Praia a Mare 70, **241**
Prignano Cilento 238
Priverno 81, 83
Procida 95, 195, 229, **230**
La Provvidenza 316, 325
Punta della Campanella
  174
Punta Licosa 233, 238
Puntone di Scirocco 269
Putignano 381

Raiano 330
Rapolla 353
Ravello 27, 28, 155, 156,
  176, 220
Reggio Calabria 10, 11, 18,
  233, **264**, 268, 269
Rieti 190, 323
Rionero in Vulture 350,
  354
Ripacandida 354
Rivello 241
Rivisondoli 313
Rocca d'Arce 74
Rocca di Botte 335
Rocca di Cambio 332
Rocca di Mezzo 331
Rocca Vecchia 401
Roccacasale 314
Roccaraso 287, 308, **312**,
  313
Roccasecca 74
Roccella Ionica 277
Roccomonfina 42
Rodi Garganico 342
Rogliano 256

Ronzano 26
Rosarno 247
Rosciolo de'Marsi 334
Rossano 24, 26, 29, 260
Rutigliano 379
Ruvo 29, 106, **298**

Sabaudia 83, 85
Saepinum 335, **337**
Sala Consilina 250
Salentine Peninsula 282,
  393
Salerno 27, 28, 69, 94,
  154, 155, 156, 158, 169,
  171, **179**
Sambatello 268
Sammichele di Bari 383
San Clemente in Casauria
  329
San Demitrio Corone 254
San Domino 342
San Felice Circeo 85, **86**
San Fili 242
San Giovanni in Fiore 258,
  259
San Giovanni Rotondo 339
San Giovanni a Teduccio
  169
San Gregorio 309, 315
San Leucio 218
San Marco 238
San Massimo 309
San Menaio 342
San Nicola 342
San Pancrazio Salentino
  392
San Paolo di Civitate 288
San Pietro 262
San Pietro ad Oratorium
  315
San Prisco 79
San Severo 288
San Tommaso 329
San Valentino 329
San Vincenzo al Volturno
  24, 25
San Vito dei Normanni 25,
  375
San Vittorino 315
Sant'Agata sui due Golfi
  174

Sant'Agata dei Goti 344
Sant'Agnello 171
Santa Cesarea Terme 403
Santa Domenica 247
Sant'Eufemia Lamezia 243
Sant'Eufemia a Maiella 329
Santa Maria di Anglona
  253
Santa Maria Capua Vetere
  23, 70, **78**
Santa Maria Mutata 369
Santa Maria in Vallae
  Porclaneta 334
Santa Severina 259
Sant'Angelo 232
Sant'Angelo in Formis 155
Sant'Angelo dei Lombardi
  356
Santo Spirito (abbey of)
  314
Santo Stefano 93, **94**
Santo Stefano in
  Aspromonte 268
Sangro River Brit. Mil. Cem.
  287
Sannicandro 342
Sapri 240
Sassi, The 363, **365**
Sassinoro 338
Savelletri 374
Scala 178
Scalea 241, 253
Scandale 260
Scanno 314
Scauri 91
Schiavi 311
Scilla 248
Scurcola Marsicana 334
Segni 71
Seminara 248
Senise 252
Sermoneta 79, **80**
Serracapriola 288
Serra San Bruno 42, 243,
  245
Sersale 262
Sessa Aurunca 28, 84, 92,
  155, 158
Sezze 79, **81**, 83
Sibari 41
La Sila 42, 70, 258

Sipontum 29, **339**
Soleto 406
Solfatara di Pozzuoli 43,
   145
Sonnino 82
Sorianello 245
Soriano Calabro 245
Sorrentine Peninsula 169
Sorrento 15, 94, 99, 154,
   155, 158, 169, **171**, 195,
   220
Soverato Superiore 276
Sperlonga 84, **89**
Spezzano Albanese 254
Spezzano Piccolo 259
Spezzano della Sila 259
Squillace 30, **276**
Squinzano 371, **378**
Stigliano 252
Stilo 29, 245, 269, **276**
Strongoli 274
Suessula 344
Sulmona 308, **313**, 326
Sybaris 270, **273**

Tagliacozzo 156, 326, **334**
Taranto 10, 26, 269, 270,
   368, 379, 383, **384**
Taverna 261

Teano 77
Teggiano 250
Telese 338
Teramo 281, 308, 315,
   316, 318
Termoli 288, 335
Terracina 83, 84, **86**, 158
Terranova 254
Testaccio 232
Tiriolo 256
Tolve 358
Torre Annunziata 182
Torre Astura 84
Torre Canne 374
Torregaveta 152
Torre del Greco 182
Tovere 175
Trani 29, 30, **295**
Tremiti Islands 338, **342**
Tricario 362
Tricase 404
La Trinita di Cava 182
Troia 27, 29, 30, 343, **348**
Tropea 233, **244**
Tursi 253, 272

Vaglio Basilicata 357, **362**
Valle dei Mulini 175, 178
Vallo della Lucania 238

Vallone di Furore 175
Valvisciolo 81
Vasto 287
Velia 233, **239**
Venafro 310
Venosa 30, 350, **353**
Ventaroli 26
Ventotene 93, **94**
Veroli 73
Vesuvius, Mt 12, 42, 44,
   94, 99, 100, 108, 188
Vettica Minore 175
Vibo Valentia 244, 249,
   257
Vico Equense 170
Vico del Gargano 342
Vieste 342
Vietri 169
Vietri a Mare 179
Villagio Mancuso 261, 263
Villanova 374
Villa Racise 263
Villa San Giovanni 249
Vinchiaturo 308
Vivara 230

Zagarise 262
Zannone 93, **94**

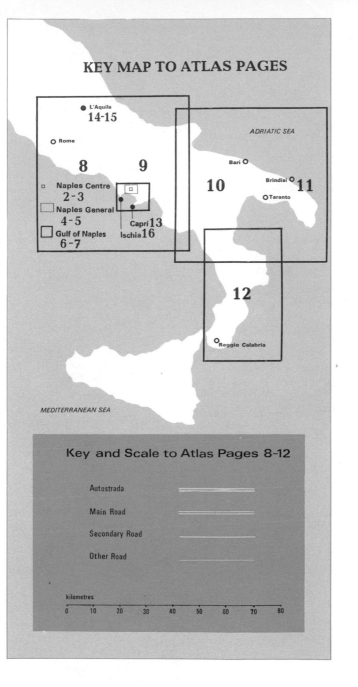

KEY MAP TO ATLAS PAGES

● L'Aquila
14-15

○ Rome

8   **9**

ADRIATIC SEA

Bari ○

Brindisi ○ **11**
10
○ Taranto

□ Naples Centre
2-3

Naples General
4-5

Gulf of Naples
6-7

Capri **13**
Ischia **16**

12

○ Reggio Calabria

MEDITERRANEAN SEA

Key and Scale to Atlas Pages 8-12

Autostrada

Main Road

Secondary Road

Other Road

kilometres

0   10   20   30   40   50   60   70   80

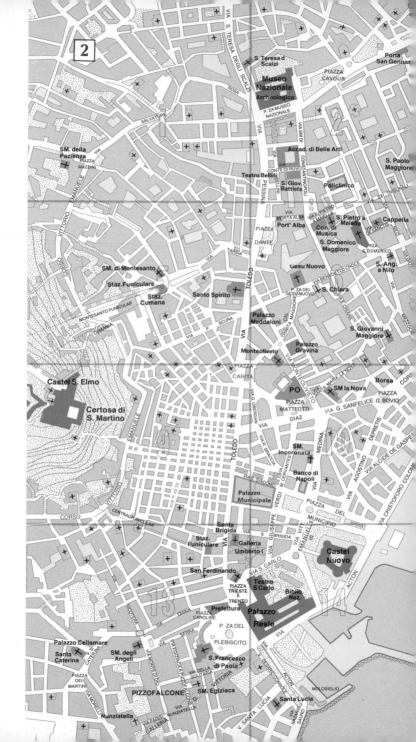

2

S. Teresa d
Scalzi

Porta
San Gennar

S. Teresa degli Scalzi

PIAZZA
CAVOUR

**Museo
Nazionale**
Archeologico

VIA S.M DI CONSTANTINOP

P. ZA MUSEO
NAZIONALE

ROSA

SALVATORE

Accad. di Belle Arti

S. Paolo
Maggiore

**SM. della
Pazienza**

PIAZZA
MAZZINI

VIA
CONTE DI RUVO

Teatro Bellini

S. Giov.
Battista

Policlinico

VIA DEI TRIBUNALI

PESSINA

VIA S.M DI
CONSTANTINOP

VITTORIO

VIA
PORTA ALBA

VIA PIETRO
AMELIO

S. Pietro a
Maiella

Cappella

EMANUELE

Port' Alba

Con. di
Musica

VIA S.SEBASTIANO

VIA NILO

PIAZZA
DANTE

S. Domenico
Maggiore

COSMO

TARSIA

PZA
S. DOMENICO

VIA

SM. di Montesanto

TOLEDO

Gesù Nuovo

S. Ang.
a Nilo

Staz. Funiculare

VIA BENEDETTO CROCE

VIA
CHIAIA

**Staz.
Cumana**

Santo Spirito

P. ZA DEL
GESU'NUOVO

S. Chiara

MONTESANTO FUNICULAR

SCURA

TRINITA MAGGIORE CAL.

VIA S. CHIARA

CUMANA

Palazzo
Maddaloni

S. Giovanni
Maggiore

Monteoliveto

Palazzo
Gravina

VIA MONTEOLIVETO

SANTA MARIA LA NOVA

Castel S. Elmo

PIAZZA
CARITA

PO

Borsa

CORSO

**Certosa di
S. Martino**

EMANUELE

VIA G. SANFELICE

PIAZZA
MATTEOTTI

SM la Nova

PIAZZA
G. BOVIO

VIA OBERDAN

VIA
DIAZ

MEDINA

DEPRETIS

SM.
Incoronata

VIA AGOSTINO

VIA ALCIDE DE GASPE

VIAR. BRACCA

VIA S. GIACOMO

Banco di
Napoli

VITTORIO

VIA M. CERVANTES

VERDI

PIAZZA

VIA CRISTOFORO COLON

Palazzo
Municipale

DEL

CORSO

CENTRAL FUNICULAR

PIAZZA
MUNICIPIO

VIA VITT. EMANUELE

Santa
Brigida

VIA
BRIGIDA

**Castel
Nuovo**

**Staz.
Funiculare**

Galleria
Umberto I

VIA GIUSEPPE

VIA S. CARLO

ACTON

San Ferdinando

VIA S. CARLO

PIAZZA
TRIESTE
E

Teatro
S Carlo

Biblio.
Naz.

NOCTERA

TRENTO

Prefettura

**Palazzo
Reale**

CHIAIA

PIAZZA
CAROLINE

SERRA

P. ZA DEL
PLEBISCITO

VIA

Palazzo Cellamare

SM. degli
Angeli

VIA TOLEDO

S. Francesco
di Paola

**Santa
Caterina**

VIA CATERINA

VIA DELLA
SOLITARIA

VITTORIA

PIAZZA
DEI
MARTIRI

VIAMORELLI

PIZZOFALCONE

SM. Egiziaca

Santa Lucia

MOLOSIGLIO

Nunziatella

GALLERIA NUNZIATELLA

VIA PARISI
VIA NUNZIATELLA

V SANTA LUCIA

VIA SANTA LUCIA

VIA N. SAURO

3

S. Giovanni a Carbonara

S. Monica

VIA CIRILLO

FORIA

VIA GIOVANNI A CARBONARA

CASANOVA

CORSO

VIA NOVARA

S. Caterina a Forniello

P.ZA S. FRAN. VIA DI PAOLA

Porta Capuana

SM. Donnaregina

PIAZZA ENRICO DE NICOLA

VIA

LARGO DONNAREGINA

Tribunale

V. P.S. MANCINI

P. ZA PRINCIPE UMBERTO

Castel Capuano

Cathedral

3

DEL

VIA ALESS

PIAZZA E. DE NICOLA

4

PIAZZA GARIBALDI

Stazione Centrale

EPT

COLLETTA

VIA MADDALENA

V. P.S. MANCINI

CORSO ARNALDO LUCCI

S. Lorenzo Magg.

S. Gregorio Armeno

VIA VICARIA VECCHIA

PIETRO

VIA DEL'ANNUNZIATA

V. CANDIA

CORSO

S. Pietro ad Aram

PIAZZA NOLANA

SS Annunziata

VIA EGIZIACA

UMBERTO

Porta Nolana

Sant' Agrippino

VIA S. BIAGIO AI LIBRAI

DUOMO

S. Giorgio Magg.

S. M. Egiziaca

Pal. Cuomo (Filangieri Mus.)

S. Agostino alla Zecca

Staz. Circumvesuviana

S. Severino

CORSO

P. ZA NICOLA AMORE

VIA DUCA DI S. DONATO

S. Croce al Mercato

VIA DEL CARMINE

PIAZZA G. PEPE

GARIBALDI

VIA

COSENZA

UMBERTO

Sant' Eligio

PIAZZA MERCATO

PIAZZA DEL CARMINE

VIA AMERIGO VESPUCCI

VIA DEL DUOMO

P. ZA MASANIELLO

Porta

SM di Carmine

MALDONIO

University

VIA

NUOVA

MARINA

VIA

MARINELLA

S. Pietro Mart.

Immacolatella Nuova

MOLO DEL CARMINE

SM. di Portosalvo

11

12

MOLO CESARIO CONSOLE

Immacolatella Vecchia

MOLO C. PISACANE

Staz. Marittima

MOLO ANGIOINO

15

16

Porto Beverello

NAPLES
Centre

0 metres   500

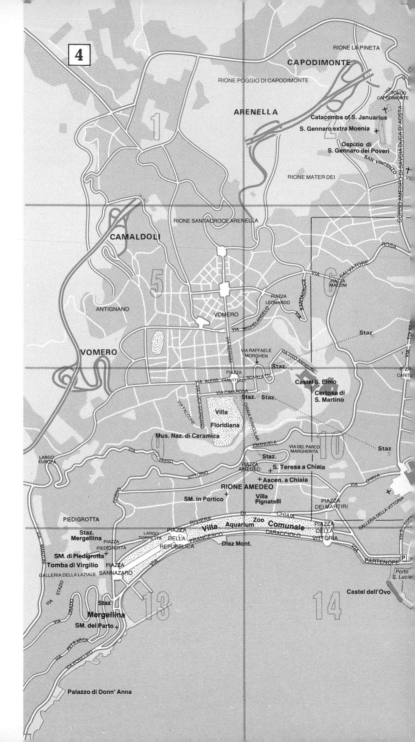

4

RIONE LA PINETA

CAPODIMONTE

RIONE POGGIO DI CAPODIMONTE

ARENELLA

Catacombs of S. Januarius

S. Gennaro extra Moenia

Ospizio di
S. Gennaro dei Poveri

RIONE MATER DEI

RIONE SANTA CROCE ARENELLA

CAMALDOLI

ROSA

ANTIGNANO

PIAZZA
LEONARDO

VOMERO

VIA MICHELANGELO

Staz

VOMERO

VIA RAFFAELE
MORGHEN

Staz.

PIAZZA
MAZZINI

CARIT

Castel S. Elmo

VIA ALESS. VANVITELLI

SCARLATTI

Certosa di
S. Martino

VIA CIMAROSA

Staz.   Staz.

Villa
Floridiana

Mus. Naz. di Ceramica

VIA PALCONE

CHIAIA FUNICULAR

LARGO
EUROPA

EMANUELE

VIA DEL PARCO
MARGHERITA

Staz

TASSO

Staz.

Staz

VIA VITTORIO

PIAZZA
AMEDEO

S. Teresa a Chiaia

Ascen. a Chiaia

RIONE AMEDEO

SM. in Portico

Villa
Pignatelli

PIAZZA
DEI MARTIRI

GALLERIA DELLA VITTORIA

PIEDIGROTTA

Riviera
PIAZZA
DELLA
REPUBBLICA

CHIAIA

Villa   Aquarium   Zoo   **Comunale**

PIAZZA
DELLA
VITTORIA

Staz.
Mergellina

LARGO
TORRETTA

FRANCESCO

CARACCIOLO

PIAZZA
PIEDIGROTTA

SM. di Piedigrotta

Diaz Mont.

Tomba di Virgilio

PIAZZA
SANNAZARO

GALLERIA DELLA LAZIALE

PARTENOPE

P

Porto
S. Lucia

Staz
Mergellina

Castel dell'Ovo

SM. del Parto

Palazzo di Donn' Anna

CAPPODICHINO

RIONE I.N.C.I.S.

Porta
Piccola

apodimonte (Pal. Reale)

Porta Grande

AIRPORT
A1 (ROME) &
A16 (AVELLINO)

NAPLES
EAST

5

DOGANELLA

3

Albergo dei Poveri

4

PIAZZA
CARLO III

ARENACCIA

Orto Botanico

Sant' Antonio
Abate

VIA NUOVA POGGIOREALE

M. della
Sanità

SM. dei
Miracoli

VASTO

Museo
Nazionale

Cathedral

7

P PIAZZA
GARIBALDI

Staz. Centrale

8

POMPEII & HERCULANAEUM
SALERNO & REGGIO CALABRIA

UMBERTO

See large scale plan

VIA NUOVA MARINA

RIONE PRINCIPE DI PIEMONTE

PIAZZA
G. BOVIO

POMPEII

Staz. Marittima

11

12

MOLO ANGIOINO

Castel
Nuovo

Palazzo
Reale

15

16

NAPLES
General

0   metres   1000

Casavatore

Marano
Chiaiano

Quarto

S.Croce

Lido di
Licola

Pianura

Camaldoli

See large
scale plar

Cumae

NAPLES

Arco
Felice
L. Avernus

L. Lucrine

Solfatara
S.Gennaro

Mostra
d'Oltremare

L. Fusaro

Baia

Pozzuoli

POSILLIPO

P. ZA
SAN LUIGI

Bagnoli

CAPO POSILLIPO

Cas di
Baia

Gulf of Pozzuoli

MONTE
DI PROCIDA

Cappella

Marechiaro

Acquamorta

L. Miseno

I. NISIDA

La Gaiola

Miseno

C. MISENO

Procida

PROCIDA

Gulf of Naples

GULF OF NAPLES

0   kilometres

Marina
Grande

Anacapri

CAPRI

Capri

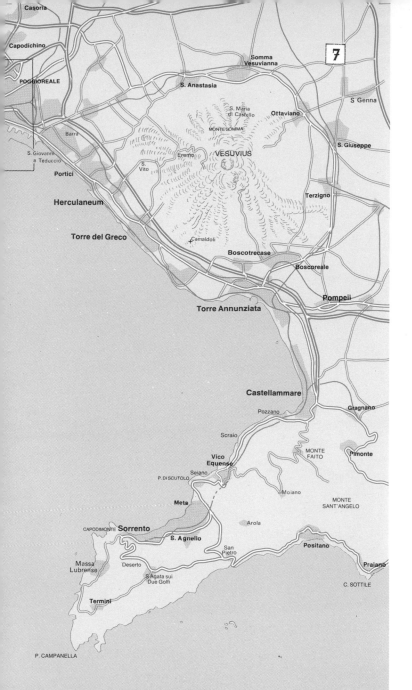

Casoria

Capodichino

POGGIOREALE

S. Giovanni
a Teduccio

Barra

Portici

Herculaneum

Torre del Greco

S. Anastasia

Somma
Vesuvianna

S. Maria
di Castello

Ottaviano

S Genna

MONTE SOMMA

VESUVIUS

S. Giuseppe

Eremo

S.
Vito

Terzigno

Camaldoli

Boscotrecase

Boscoreale

Pompeii

Torre Annunziata

Castellammare

Gragnano

Pozzano

Scraio

MONTE
FAITO

Pimonte

Vico
Equense

Seiano

P. DI SCUTOLO

Moiano

MONTE
SANT'ANGELO

Meta

Arola

CAPODIMONTE Sorrento

S. Agnello

San
Pietro

Positano

Massa
Lubrense

Deserto

S Agata sui
Due Golfi

C. SOTTILE

Praiano

Termini

P. CAMPANELLA

8

See Blue Guide to Northern Italy

Ascoli Piceno

S. Benedetto
del Tronto

Civitella
del T.
Campli
Amatrice
Teramo
Montorio al Vomano
Aringo
Pietracamela
Penne
Montereale
Campotosto
Isola d.
Gr. Sasso
CORNO
GRANDE
GRAN SASSO
D' ITALIA
Pianella
Arischia
Ponte Cermone
Paganica
Antrodoco
Bazzano
Torre de
Passeri
Rieti
Cittaducale
L'Aquila
San
Gregorio
Bariscano
Capestrano
Navelli
Busso
S. Tommaso
Tocco
Fiamignano
Rocca di Cambio
Bominaco
Popoli
Carama
Rocca
di Mezzo
Belfi
Molina
Corfini
Roccacasa
Ovindoli
Castelvecchio
M. VELINO
Subequo
Raiano
Pratola
2487
Peligna
Magliano
Albe
Carsoli
Sulmor
de Marsi
Carsoli
Cappelle
S. Benedetto
Pescina
Tagliacozzo
Avezzano
d. Marsi
Anversa d. Abr
Arsoli
Rocca di Botte
Lago Fucino
Capistrello
Gioia dei Marsi
Scanno
Subiaco
Civitella Roveto
Pescasseroli
Mt. Viglio
Balsorano
Villetta Barrea
Olevano Romano
ROME
Palestrina
Genazzano
Piglio
Guarcino
Sora
Cave
Paliano
Fiuggi
Labico
Valmontone
Anagni
Alatri
See Blue Guide to Rome
Veroli
Isola d.
Atina
Colleferro
Ferentino
Casamari
Liri
Genzano
Segni
Frosinone
Arpino
Velletri
Arce
Ceprano
Roccasecca
Lanuvio
Cori
MONTI LEPINI
Anuno
Cassino
Cisterna di
Doganella
Norma
AUTOSTRADA
DEL S
Latina
Ceccano
Bassiano
S. Giov. Incarico
Pontecorvo
Sezze
Pastena
Pico
Latina
Priverno
Nettuno
Pontinia
Lenola
Anzio
Abb. Fossanova
Sonnino
Fondi
Ausonia
L. di
MONTI
L. di
Minturn
Fogliano
AUSONI
Fondi
Itri
Formia
Lago dei Monaci
Parco Naz.
Terracina
Sperlonga
Scaun
Sabaudia
del Circeo
Porto
Gaeta
L. di Sabaudia
Badino
M. CIRCEO
S. Felice
Circeo
Gulf of Gaeta

Ponza

Ventotene

MEDITERRANEAN SEA

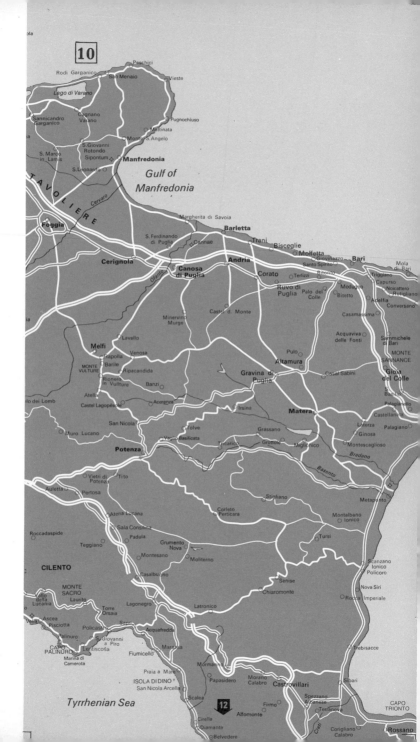

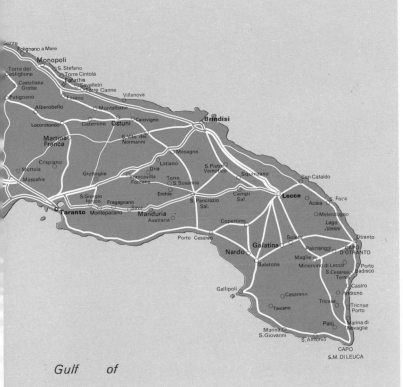

ADRIATIC SEA

Pozze
Folignano a Mare
Monopoli
Torre dei
Castiglione
S. Stefano
Torre Cintola
Castellana
Grotte
Egnathia
Savelletri
Torre Canne
Putignano
Fasano
Villanova
Alberobello
Montalbano
Locorotondo
Cisternino
Ostuni
Carovigno
Brindisi
Martina
Franca
S. Vito dei
Normanni
Mesagne
Crispiano
Latiano
S. Pietro
Vernotico
Mottola
Grottaglie
Oria
Squinzano
San Cataldo
Massafra
Francavilla
Fontana
Torre
S. Susanna
Erchie
S. Giorgio
Ionico
Fragagnano
S. Pancrazio
Sal.
Campi
Sal.
Lecce
S. Foca
Acaia
Taranto
Monteparano
Savo
Manduria
Melendugno
Avetrana
Copertino
Lago
Alimini
Porto Cesareo
Solato
Otranto
Nardo
Galatina
Palmariggi
CAPO
D'OTRANTO
Maglie
Porto
Badisco
Balatone
Minervino di Lecce
S.Cesarea
Terme
Gallipoli
Casarano
Castro
Andrano
Taviano
Tricase
Tricase
Porto
Patù
Marina di
Novaglie
Marina
S.Giovanni
S. Antonio
CAPO
S.M. DI LEUCA

Gulf   of

Taranto

Cariati Marina

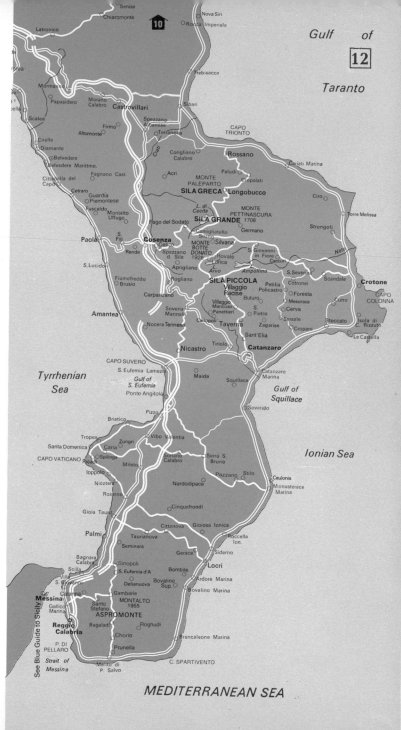

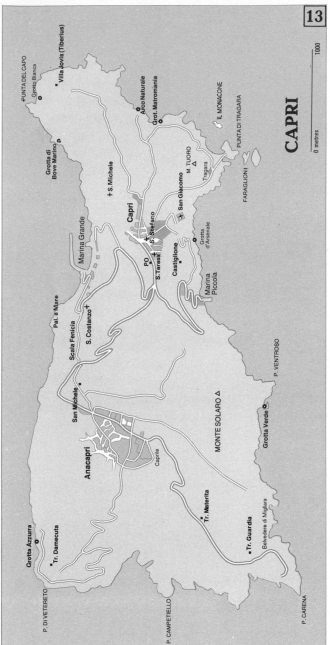

PUNTA DEL CAPO

Grotto Bianca

Villa Jovis (Tiberius)

Arco Naturale

Grot. Matromània

IL MONACONE

Grotta di
Bove Marino

+ S. Michele

+ S. Michele

Capri

San Giacomo

M. TUORO
△

Tragara

PUNTA DI TRAGARA

Marina Grande

S. Stefano

FARAGLIONI

P.O.

S. Teresa

Castiglione

Grotta
d'Arsenale

Pal. a' Mare

Scala Fenicia

S. Costanzo +

Marina
Piccola

San Michele

P. VENTROSO

Grotta Azzurra

Tr. Damecuta

Anacapri

Caprile

MONTE SOLARO △

Grotta Verde

P. DI VETERETO

Tr. Materita

Tr. Guardia

Belvedere di Migliara

P. CAMPETIELLO

P. CARENA

CAPRI

0 metres   1000

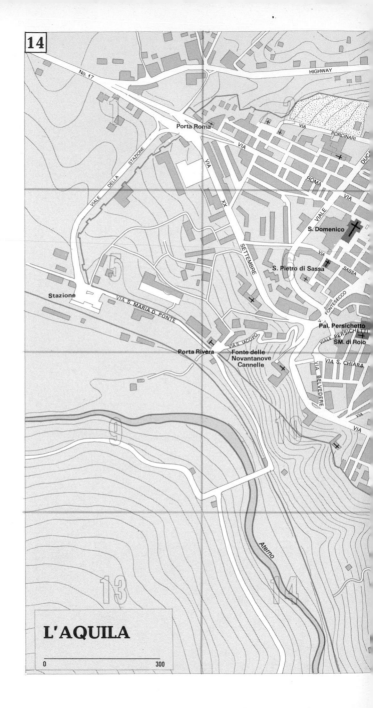

14

HIGHWAY

No. 17

Porta Roma

VIA

VIALE DELLA STAZIONE

VIA

VIA PORCINARI

DUCA

VIA

ROMA

VIALE

VIA

S. Domenico

VIA

XX

SETTEMBRE

S. Pietro di Sassa

SASSA

Stazione

VIA S. MARIA D. PONTE

V. FORTESECCO

Pal. Persichetto

VIALE PERSICHETTI

SM. di Roio

VIA S. JACOPO

Porta Rivera

Fonte delle
Novantanove
Cannelle

VIA S. CHIARA

VIA BELVEDERE

VIA

VIA

9

10

Aterno

13

14

L'AQUILA

0   300

Mad. del Soccorso

NO. 17

BIS

DEGLI

S. Basilio

Pool

Stadium

ABRUZZI

VIA DI PORTA PAGANICA

VIA D. GRAN SASSO D'ITALIA

Castello
(Museo Nazionale)

S. Silvestri

P

VIA

GARIBALDI

TASSONI

Parco d. Castello

P

VIA DEL CORPITO

Pal. Franchi

VIA

VIA

PAGANICA

EPT

VIA DI PORTA

SASSA

ROMA

S. Pietro di Coppito

SM. Paganica

VITTORIO

EMANUELE

VIA CASTELLO

Porta Castello

VIA D. STIRINELLA

SOCCORSO

University

VIA A. BAFILE

Munic.

SM. del Carmine

VIA ANTONELLI

P ZA
PALAZZO

QUATRO
CANTONI

Theatre

San
Bernardino

VIALE

Pal. d. Guistizia

Biblio Prov.
Salvatore
Tommasi

VIA

SALLUSTIO

VIA

SASSA

CORSO

SAN

BERNARDINO

Museo

S. Giuseppe

P

LARGO
BARISCIANELLO

Pal. Rivera

VIA DI ROIO

Cathedral

VIA

Pal. Dragon
de Torres

P ZA DEL
DUOMO

S. Flaviano

VIA FORTEBRACCIO

S. Marciano

V. S. MARCIANO

PO

VIA

Suffragio

CIMINO

BUONE

NOVELLE

S. Marco

FEDERICO

II

S. Agostino

VIA S. FR. DI PAOLA

Pal. Centi

S.
Giusta

Porta Bazzano

Prefettura

CORSO

MICHELE

VIA

XX

SETTEMBRE

CRISPI

P ZA
DELLE
ACACIE

VIA

RENDINA

VIA DI PORTA BAZZANO

Villa

Comunale

VIALE

DI

FRANCESCO

COLLEMAGGIO

P

S.M. di
Collemaggio

VIALE

P. ta Napoli

HIGHWAY

No.17

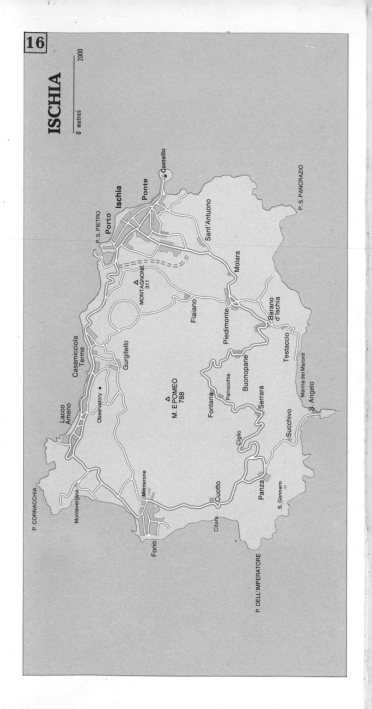

16

ISCHIA

0 metres — 2000

P. CORNACCHIA

Lacco
Ameno

Casamicciola
Terme

Observatory ■

Gurgitello

Montevergine

Monterone

Forio

Citara

Cuotto

Panza

S. Gennaro

P. DELL'IMPERATORE

P.S. PIETRO

Porto

Ischia

Ponte

Castello

Sant'Antuono

△
MONTAGNONE
311

Fiaiano

Molara

Piedimonte

Barano
d'Ischia

Testaccio

△
M. EPOMEO
788

Fontana

Parrocchia

Buonopane

Serrara

Succhivo

Ciglio

Marina dei Maronti

S. Angelo

P.S. PANCRAZIO